OUTSIDE LOOKING IN

McGILL-QUEEN'S NATIVE AND NORTHERN SERIES
BRUCE G. TRIGGER, EDITOR

# Outside Looking In

## Viewing First Nations Peoples in Canadian Dramatic Television Series

MARY JANE MILLER

McGill-Queen's University Press

Montreal & Kingston · London · Ithaca

© McGill-Queen's University Press 2008

ISBN 978-0-7735-3366-0 (cloth)
ISBN 978-0-7735-3367-7 (paper)

Legal deposit second quarter 2008
Bibliothèque nationale du Québec

Printed in Canada on acid-free paper that is 100% ancient forest free
(100% post-consumer recycled), processed chlorine free.

This book has been published with the help of a grant from the Canadian
Federation for the Humanities and Social Sciences, through the Aid to
Scholarly Publications Programme, using funds provided by the Social
Sciences and Humanities Research Council of Canada. Funding has also
been received from Brock University.

McGill-Queen's University Press acknowledges the support of the Canada
Council for the Arts for our publishing program. We also acknowledge the
financial support of the Government of Canada through the Book Publishing
Industry Development Program (BPIDP) for our publishing activities.

---

**Library and Archives Canada Cataloguing in Publication**

Miller, Mary Jane, 1941–
    Outside looking in: viewing First Nations peoples in Canadian dramatic
television series/Mary Jane Miller.

(McGill-Queen's native and northern series; 53)
Includes bibliographical references and index.
ISBN 978-0-7735-3366-0 (bnd)
ISBN 978-0-7735-3367-7 (pbk)

1. Native peoples on television. 2. Television programs – Social
aspects – Canada. 3. Television programs – Canada – History.
4. North of 60 (Television program). I. Title. II. Series.

PN1992.3.C3M54 2008    791.45'652997071    C2008-900120-6

---

This book was typeset by Interscript in 10/13 Palatino.

# Contents

# Acknowledgments

The roots of this book go back a long way – to my mother, Elizabeth Miller, who when I was a teenager introduced me to a little of the arts and cultures of the people then called Indians and Eskimos, and who travelled with me in the 1970s to Alert Bay to see my first Kwakiutl dances and masks. I am sorry she did not live to read this book.

The academic provenance goes back to materials I first saw while archiving CBC drama in the fall of 1979 for what was then the Sound and Moving Images Division of the National Archives, under Sam Kula. By 1990 I was ready to try to discuss the representation of First Nations peoples on television at a conference of the Association for the Study of Canadian Radio and Television/Association des études sur la radio-télévision canadienne (ASCRT/AERTC– now disbanded). The support and feedback on all of my work, from Howard Fink, John Jackson, John Twomey, Ernie Dick, Paul Rutherford, and Sylvie Robitaille in the early years of this research and, most of all, from Renée Legris then and later, were invaluable. I must also thank the two anonymous readers for the Aid to Scholarly Publications Programme (ASPP) and McGill-Queen's University Press, who made many helpful suggestions.

Thirteen consecutive years of support from the Social Sciences and Humanities Research Council of Canada (SSHRC) laid the foundations of this book. When this rather long manuscript was accepted by McGill-Queen's University Press and the successful McGill-Queen's ASPP subvention was received, the publication costs received a top-up thanks to Dean of Humanities Rosemary Hale and the panel at the Humanities Research Institute at Brock University, and thanks as well to Associate Vice-President Research Michael Owen. Throughout the process, Brock University granted me regular sabbaticals and colleagues in the Department of Dramatic Arts provided encouragement.

Leslie Bell, Chris Fraser, Cara Steinberg, and Cole Lewis did useful research for me at various times. I am also grateful to Patty Winter, the author and exemplary website designer for *North of 60*, who provided detailed information in an instantly accessible and searchable form and who encouraged me as I worked on those five chapters, as well as to the fans on the Yahoo *North of 60* discussion list and the "list moms" Kelly Tucker and Nancy Duemling. Thanks, too, to Brenda Carroll at the CBC library for her help in the search for pictures for this book and to Jordy Randall for permission to use Alberta Filmworks pictures of *North of 60*.

Katya Davison proofread and commented on the manuscript at a crucial stage, a difficult and necessary task that only a close friend would undertake. Jonathan Crago provided a lot of help when the book was in the first editing stages (it was even longer then), Judith Turnbull did an exemplary copy edit, and Joan McGilvray shepherded the book through the publication process with tact and skill. Finally and as always, I thank my husband, Jack Miller – critic, proofreader, computer troubleshooter, information manager, always supportive – without whom this book would not have been written.

PART ONE

# Framework

# ONE

# Introduction:
# Establishing the Boundaries of This Exploration

Start with this: White people should not tell First Nations stories. Anishnabe should not tell certain Dene stories. Read, listen to, or watch the particular work of a person who belongs to a family, a clan, a band, a nation – or two or many. The voice is not only individual and rooted in a specific place, time, and tradition; that voice creates an imaginative place that is often strange to those who do not live there. Not just strange in the way a story that catches the essence of Calgary is to a person who grew up in Toronto, but different in other ways difficult to define. Tomson Highway, Lee Maracle, Thomas King, and Drew Hayden Taylor create stories that are not Euro-Canadian or Indo/Southeast Asian/African/ Islamic/Latino/or wherever else–Canadian. The Canadian Broadcasting Corporation (CBC), however, for more than fifty years has been telling the audience that owns it stories *about* the First Nations (many stories), Metis (few), and Inuit (fewer). CTV and Global have contributed a few series, but the CBC is by far the source of most series about or featuring First Nations people.

First Nations peoples, particularly those who do not live in the North and have had no access to the northern broadcasting systems until the Aboriginal People's Television Network (APTN), have not found it easy to use television to tell themselves and each other their own stories, or even to talk directly to the rest of Canada, in either official language. Loretta Todd puts it another way: "If I had asked my grandparents why we tell stories, they would have laughed at me and then told me another story ... Those stories may be all you can leave – you live through your stories ... They may have said storytelling is a way to bring the mythical and real together, a place where they can live together. They may have told me that information just lives in the instant, but the story goes on forever."[1] As an

Alberta Cree/Metis filmmaker who also worked in Northwest Coast culture when she moved to the West Coast,[2] Todd has offered some very cogent criticism about cultural appropriation and the representation of
forms of pan-Indianism. From her perspective and that of many others,
every program described in this book has elements of cultural appropriation. Nevertheless, many viewers from both remote and urban First Nations have enjoyed some characters and episodes in most of these series.
Stories pass on traditions in every culture. Stories acted out, or told and
retold, change with the transmission of culture as understandings change
– or not. Even if the oral culture does not survive and the stories seem to
be lost, objects remain, in attics, basements, museums, and archives, from
enigmatic and ancient T'Simshian stone masks to penny postcards to
forty-year-old television reruns.

The hypothesis of this book is that dramatic representations of First Nations in series television have changed significantly over time, sometimes
ahead of the perceptions of the audience, sometimes reflecting them, and
that the aesthetics of these programs also reflect changing technology and
production conditions. Other premises of the book are that while various
long-standing issues are raised, the ways they are framed change over time;
that the context provided by financing arrangements, by other programs,
and by reviews in magazines and newspapers shapes both the programs
and viewers' perceptions of the programs; that recent scholarship in ethnography and also in popular culture can throw light on both what these series present and what is missing; that the fifty years of programming
covered in this book can create some perspective on the most recent series;
that familiar genres like family adventure, soaps, sitcoms, and cop shows
shape both these series and viewers' expectations as do ever-changing ideas
about Canada's North, where most of them are set; and that new issues appear. The book contains analyses of overall patterns of themes, issues, and
situations within series and between series. It also presents detailed analysis
of specific episodes in chapters on *The Beachcombers*, *Spirit Bay,* and *The Rez.*
At ninety episodes over six years *North of 60* required several chapters. The
book also contains a few hints about what some First Nations people have
said about their perceptions from the inside looking out as well as what regular viewers recorded in e-mails to websites, to fan lists, and to me. Above
all, this book addresses the need for the dominant society that made all of
these programs to know just what in series television it has told itself from
the outside looking in on the First Nations.

Unlike my previous research practice, where I interviewed the makers
of and decision makers in cbc television drama, for this book I have not

sought out the performers or the people behind the cameras (though I have used interviews with them, published in print or on the web or even broadcast because they form part of the intertextual reception of the series). I have not had the resources, the expertise, or the desire to undertake a study of the programs' reception using focus groups or field interviews or to do detailed content analysis. This time out, I wanted to analyse the programs as I found them.

Some of the materials are safely deposited at the Library and Archives of Canada, whose responsibility it is to store the original films and tapes under perfect conditions, transfer them to the next accessible technology, maintain playback equipment to fit every generation of transfer, and continue to do so for the next hundred years. There can be slip-ups at any of those stages, starting with the fact that many television dramas made by independent producers and broadcast on networks other than the CBC, particularly series, are not deposited in the Library and Archives of Canada. Regrettably, even with digitization, it is also possible that the material will outstrip the storage capacity as the originals from the first fifty years deteriorate. Time gnaws away at videotape, kinescopes, and film. Many may be culled. Finally, there may not be money to invest in continual transfers or antiquated playback machines. That is the shadow side of our attempts to keep a record of our stories, and I could be, would like to be, wrong. However, the fact that I have among my off-air study tapes material that does not appear either in the *Guide to CBC Sources at the Public Archives 1936–1986*[3] or on the online catalogue of the Library and Archives of Canada suggests that complete records of even recent programming do not currently exist. Many people, not just specialists, would give a great deal to be transported in time to see a 1601 performance at the Globe or a lavish nineteenth-century production at the Theatre Royal Drury Lane. Only play-scripts, sketches, and reviews survive. For Shakespeare, we have a very few fragments specific to his work; for nineteenth-century productions, there are many. The words on these pages and in other books and articles by a new generation of scholars, along with still photos and newspaper and magazine articles where they exist in libraries, may well be all that the future will retain of the stories that the dominant culture in Canada told itself about its relations with the First Nations, what it saw, what it feared, what it envied. Already memories are short, and much of what I write about has been forgotten or was broadcast too soon for a university student to have seen it or for a young scholar to have taped it for study and analysis.

## OVERVIEW OF CHAPTERS

In chapter 2, I begin by looking at theoretical issues such as ethnicity and the stereotypes of "Indians." In chapter 3, I discuss different definitions of "The North," the imaginative space where every one of these series is located, and consider how, in a country with too much geography, too few people, two languages, and the most popular culture in the world beaming through its porous borders, Canadian broadcasting and the evolving First Nations broadcasting are financed. In chapter 4, I put the 1950s programming in the context of representations of "Indians" for previous generations, using materials from nineteenth-century textbooks, children's alphabets, storybooks, and a 1927 pageant. These are the kinds of materials that could have shaped both the early makers and the adult viewers of those programs. In chapter 5, I look at the precursor to the rest of the programming discussed – the thirty-nine-episode series *Radisson,* broadcast by the CBC/SRC in both languages over two seasons in 1957. *Radisson,* intended primarily for children, was Canada's self-conscious answer to the Davy Crockett craze. In chapter 6, I look at two series that flanked *Radisson,* both filmed in Canada with the CBC's repertory acting company in secondary roles but with no other Canadian content except the setting – *Hudson's Bay* and *Hawkeye and the Last of the Mohicans.* I note the changes brought by the 1960s, a decade in which children as characters became the focus of television series, including those that featured aboriginal characters (until it broadcast *Wojeck* in 1966–68, the CBC made and broadcast very few series for adults). Since these series were filmed and then syndicated, some, such as *The Forest Rangers* (1963–65) and *Adventures in Rainbow Country* (1971), still reappear in reruns. *Adventures in Rainbow Country* appeared just before the nineteen-season run of *The Beachcombers.* I also look briefly at two historical family adventure series – *Matt and Jenny* (1981), set in the 1850s "on the wilderness trail" through eastern Canada, and *The Campbells* (1986–89), set on a pioneer farm in eastern Ontario in the 1830s – both broadcast by the private networks. Given their settings, they inevitably involved Indians in some of their stories. All of these series form the context for chapters 7 and 8.

In chapter 7, I concentrate on *The Beachcombers* (1972–91), the champion for longevity and the one family adventure series that featured several aboriginal characters. The series featured some of the customs of the Coast Salish as well as a few of the aboriginal issues of the 1970s and 1980s – primarily through Jesse, later through his sister Sarah, but also through his wife, Laurel, and stepson, Tommy. As a late teen and then as an adult, Jesse developed strategies for straddling two worlds, creating a new focus in the representation of the First Nations in series television. Chapter 8 is about a short-lived, little-known, but in many ways quite successful series for children, *Spirit Bay* (1985–86, overlapping *The Beachcombers*), whose protagonists were various children in an Anishnabe community. For the first time since *Cariboo Country* (a 1960s anthology for adults), the recurring characters and most of the guest performers were aboriginal. *Spirit Bay*'s attempt to more formally include the contributions of First Nations people and the limitations placed on those attempts provide a valuable contrast to *The Beachcombers*. Chapter 9 continues the examination of television for children and youth with a look at the changes brought about by the late 1990s. *The Rez* (1996–97), a half-hour dramedy intended for a teen and young adult audience, starred young adult actors from First Nation and Metis communities. Although it lasted only two seasons, it was an interesting attempt to portray the life of four young adults living by choice on a reservation that, unlike the much more remote Spirit Bay, is in a resort area only a couple of hours from Toronto. All of them are tempted to leave at various times, and one does, creating an interesting tension in the series. Chapter 10 offers a more detailed consideration of genres, of the fundamental basis of both general viewers' responses, and of specific fan knowledge and fan culture. In the 1990s, technology changed when first the Internet and then the search engines for the web appeared, changing the tools available to fans. *North of 60* (1992–97) appeared the year after *The Beachcombers* ended, and it was overlapped in its last two seasons by *The Rez*. However, this series was primarily for adults. Unlike *The Forest Rangers, Adventures in Rainbow Country,* or *The Rez*, which were set in Northern Ontario, or *The Beachcombers,* located on the accessible Sunshine Coast, *North of 60* was set in a small isolated Dene community in the Northwest Territories. With ninety hour-long episodes, *North of 60* was the longest-running series to concentrate on First Nations characters and issues, and to date it is the only one of all of the series over fifty years that specifically targeted an adult audience. Atypically of the usual afterlife of Canadian series, *North of 60* led to five movies of the week (1999–2005). The series is still on air in reruns and is likely to remain so. To this day, there are many fans of *North of 60* on both sides of the border. With reruns and annual movies of the week, their numbers continue to grow. Such a successful series invites more intense study, which I have tried to supply in chapters 11–15. The conclusion of the book follows.

SITUATING THE CRITIC AND THE READER

I have been thinking about this project since I worked on my first book on television drama in the mid-1980s.[4] I presented my first paper, an overview of the subject (which would look very different now), at the Association for the Study of Canadian Radio and Television at the Learned Societies Congress in Vancouver in 1990. At the same event, Renée Legris, now retired after a distinguished career at the Université du Québec à Montréal, presented a paper that opened my eyes to the differences between the francophone and anglophone cultures made evident through stories about the dominant cultures' history with the First Nations. Since then, I have done extensive research on drama specials and docudramas, as well as television series, featuring First Nations people. I refer to all of these in various places in this book. However, series television is where the viewer is likely to truly engage with characters, narrative arcs, and personal or (more regularly in Canada) political issues. Series television, or long-form television, as it is sometimes called, is what most viewers watch – television that makes a cumulative impact, television that arouses passionate loyalty in some viewers and is long remembered, television that is most likely to be rerun and therefore to be available, for good or ill, years after the series' first run is finished.

Although I try not to look at an early series like *Radisson* solely with the hindsight of fifty years of discourse, I do evaluate all of the programs in terms of aesthetics – what some scholars define as "quality television" – complex designs, interesting camera work, pace appropriate to the narrative, varied and compelling narratives, and the exploration of complex issues, themes, and relationships over time. My working definition of the television aesthetic is influenced by that provided by major television theorist David Thorburn in "Television as an Aesthetic Medium" (1988): "not a valuing of 'aesthetic objects' but a designation of their chief defining feature – their membership in a class of cultural experiences understood to be 'fictional or imaginary,' understood to occur in a symbolic, culturally agreed-upon imaginative space" (49), an approach that offers what he calls a counterpoint to the use of feminist and post-colonial perspectives and questions of social justice that also inform my criticism. Throughout the book I look at questions of stereotype and convention. Television drama series are always based in familiar generic forms, Thorburn's "shared cultural experiences," first described by Horace Newcomb (1974) and redefined ever since by scholars and by makers of television drama – the family adventure, the cop show, the medical show, the lawyers' show, and the sitcom. All of the series in this book are framed by one of those genres, and all are inflected, beginning with series from the1970s that focus on First Peoples (Lorna Roth's useful phrase, 2005) who belong to specific reserves and nations – Coast Salish, Dene, and Anishnabe. That cultural specificity alone creates new subjects, plots, and characters to inflect traditional formats. I also discuss the fact that neither *The Rez* nor *North of 60* conform to their apparent genres, respectively a sitcom with satirical overtones for young adults and a cop show with some conventions and situations that resemble those of soaps. They are hybrids combining conventional expectations imbedded in such forms to create something quite different. As the reader will discover, audience expectations, if shaped by genre, are frustrated by episodes in several of these series.

This is not primarily an ethnography book, but in chapters 2 and 3, I do look at questions that arise from disciplines that use ethnographic methods and I consider issues of reception, reader/response theory, and intertextuality. All of these are interlocked with questions of aesthetics. Intertextuality arises from the many other specials, docudramas, and miniseries that focus on First Peoples and Metis from the 1950s on, from feature articles on makers and actors, and recently from interactive official websites and fans' websites. Unfortunately, many of the websites have vanished; some servers have disappeared; content has been purged (such as for newspapers and the like, although the paper sources may still exist); websites have been taken down (e.g., the sites of seasons 1–5 for *North of 60*). All the sources an academic uses are supposed to be available to the reader to check independently – even if the source is six hundred years old and located in a monastery on a remote island – because that is the only way results and conclusions may be checked or reproduced. But television is still an ephemeral art, and the websites associated with it are more so. In 2006 and 2007 I visited every site referred to in the notes, and I provide the date I did so. I have also identified every site that has disappeared. I do not use websites that have vanished for anything on which a vital argument depends, but only to illustrate a point or to provide less important information. For example, *North of 60*'s well-designed interactive website for season 4 has now gone, but it provided useful facts and opinions. The most obvious methodological problem, particularly with the passage of time, is that episodes from each program analysed in any detail must also be described in enough detail that the reader has some idea of the evidence on which the arguments are based; such descriptions take up the reader's time and make the book longer but they are necessary.

Who am I writing for? As an eclectic critic I address an eclectic audience. I hope that university and college students in native studies, who are trained in many disciplines, will find the results of my research useful. I am filling a gap in our cultural history for communications studies and popular culture studies in Canada. And, of course, I write for scholars in other disciplines, for historians and social scientists, who are unfamiliar with this material but who may find it relevant to their own work. It may be that First Nations, Metis, and Inuit may also find it interesting. Finally, I have tried to make it readable and accessible to those who are simply interested in finding out more about these programs, who want to read a book about them that is not the product of a fan or someone with a vested interest.

Where am I situated as a critic? As the title says, on the "outside looking in." To be more specific, I am a sixty-six-year-old woman, born in the age of radio, who also saw a fair amount of early television as a teenager. A long memory for both the programs and the context has been as useful in this project as my previous work.[5] I am also a sympathetic viewer who has acquired some background in First Nations cultures over twenty-five years of reading and occasionally going to see for myself. Clearly, I am not the typical viewer. For one thing, I was not trained as a film scholar or as a Canadianist or as a dramatic literature scholar (there were no such specializations in the early 1960s). My roots are in English literature. For thirty-eight years of teaching I have concentrated on dramatic literature, from Shakespeare to Tomson Highway, and, since the early 1980s, on television studies (Brock University's curriculum included the first course in Canadian television drama in the country). Publishing papers and books also involved my looking at, thinking about, and researching scholarly comment on television of all types, American, Canadian, and British. Thus, I view episodes, series, and specials with a professionally analytical eye. I have also seen material, now deposited in the Library and Archives of Canada, that is not readily available to scholars dependent on the current limited viewing resources of the archives. In the 1980s and early 1990s I also had access to the CBC archives of kines (8 mm kinescopes copied from the master monitor in the days of live television) and tapes prior to their deposition with the Library and Archives of Canada as well as access to television makers and decision makers at the CBC. This meant that I could select and review material at the archives, having already seen it much earlier and in the context of interviews with the makers, some of whom have passed away.[6] Most of these sources cannot now be accessed by other scholars. If this material is ever available online, those limitations on scholarly access will change. However, the money for this has not yet been allocated, and issues of copyright on drama in particular remain unsolved.7 Another advantage I have had, one I would willingly share with other scholars, is a personal study collection of aging VCR tapes recorded "off-air" from 1984 onward that includes much of the material broadcast on the CBC, with a scattering from other networks. Thus, in this overview of English Canadian television's presentation of aboriginal characters and motifs and related issues, my position as viewer differs substantially from that of many scholars, as well as from that of the more casual viewer, who is looking for adventure stories or a good laugh or good half-hour of television for their children.

With series, it is easy to identify overall narrative patterns. Does the dominant culture persist in seeing the First Nations people as victims? As sources of some unnamed natural wisdom? As problems to be solved? As insoluble problems? As sources of dramatic culture clashes? As excuses for adventure stories? Does the dominant society beat its breast in these series about acts of discrimination that seem to have no resolution? Does it explore the roots of cultural misunderstanding with the clear social agenda of bridging the gaps? Do the programs concentrate on the idea of coexistence, or do they assume that this goal has been achieved? Most (not all) drama specials and docudramas have concentrated on what Euro-Canadians have done to aboriginal peoples and how the latter have survived (or not). Examples are historical dramas like *Dark of Moon* (Big Bear), *Riel* (twice), *Divided Loyalties* (Joseph Brant), *Big Bear*, and *Where the Spirit Lives* (residential schools in the 1930s); some episodes of *Canada: A People's History*; dramas on contemporary subjects such as *Loyalties*, *Trial at Fortitude Bay*, *Medicine River*, and *Spirit Rider* in the 1980s and 1990s and *Cowboys and Indians: The Killing of J.J. Harper, One Dead Indian* (Dudley George), and *Indian Summer: The Oka Crisis* in the 2000s. The opportunities afforded by a series8 meant that *The Beachcombers* and *Spirit Bay* in the 1970s and 1980s and *North of 60* and *The Rez* in the 1990s were able to concentrate on what aboriginal individuals and communities have done for themselves.

My conclusions about all of this material are (*a*) that the same basic obstacles to understanding between the dominant and the aboriginal cultures and the same basic problems bedevilling aboriginal communities and aboriginals in cities have constantly reappeared over nearly fifty years; (*b*) that the CBC in particular has made some balanced, occasionally proactive, television drama about some of the First Nations peoples; (*c*) that series drama has shown us the various cultures in accommodation as well as in conflict; (*d*) that there are odd omissions (e.g., there have been very few dramas about Inuit across the years, which may be a function of distance/weather/costs); (*e*) that the representation of the generic Indian has given way to a reflection of a small part of the diversity of the First Nations in Canada.

Research on aboriginal subjects has advanced a long way since the mid-1980s, when I asked CBC producers about cultural appropriation issues in *Cariboo Country* and *The Beachcombers,* and since the mid-1990s, when I asked then CBC vice-president of television Ivan Fecan about using writers, directors, and producers of aboriginal origin – conversations recorded in *Rewind and Search.* I am an eclectic critic who uses a variety of approaches as they seem to fit the program or answer a particular question. I use content analysis to identify certain basic patterns of character, situation, setting, or recurring motif, and I look for metaphorical and metonymical patterns. I consider contextual and intertextual questions, introducing what viewers themselves may bring to the program on first and subsequent viewings. I have also been a feminist most of my adult life, and that point of view has informed all of my scholarly thinking. And even in these postmodern times, I am something of a nationalist – with all the ambiguity that point of view must evoke in Canada in a new century.

Genre criticism yields insights in series television by identifying the inflection of formulae in episodes as well as the range of a series. When looking at the work, I incorporate the public discourse found in newspapers, periodicals, radio, and television interviews, which are available to the general public, and also, where I can find it, the discourse found in First Nations periodicals. From what position do I look at these materials? Ethnographic? Not really – although close observation of a body of work intended for audiences in the millions can involve some of the ethnographer's skills. As a fan? Not at all, though my admiration for some of the work I analyse will be obvious in certain sections. The ethnographer and the fan can intersect because both seek detailed knowledge. I am not a sociologist either, but some of the tools I use and some of the information I find useful come from branches of that discipline.

The relatively jargon-free semiotics of television criticism opens up new questions about how the codes of television function within the work, how they construct an audience, and how they interact with the experiences of active readers, who are to be found in most audiences. Other codes or systems discussed in this book include setting; lighting; costume and hair; gestural codes (e.g., how actors use their bodies); the development of narratives; the pace and emphasis in an episode established by the director, producer, and editor; and occasionally the structures of meaning created by music and sound effects. As a professor of dramatic literature as well as television, I place a particular emphasis on dialogue. Dialogue is the spine of television drama, especially character-driven drama like *North of 60* and *The Rez*. Subtext, the interplay of some of these codes, conveys what is not said but is understood by the audience. Subtext is vital in drama. Other codes include filmic conventions such as extreme close-ups, slow pans, and voice-overs. As many scholars have noted,[9] the economics of production and even the scheduling and selling of these programs through publicity shape how they are made and also influence how they are perceived. However, most scholars agree that, in a performing or collaborative art like television drama, the analytical emphasis must fall on the *gestalt*, or interaction, of these systems.

Over the years, the dramatic givens, like the issues, have changed. The Indian as victim has been replaced by the First Nations individual or community as survivor and sometimes as winner. Oddly, in the first decade of the twenty-first century, three drama specials present Indians as victims once more: *Cowboys and Indians: The Killing of J.J. Harper* (CBC/APTN 2003), *One Dead Indian* (CTV 2006, Dudley George at Ipperwash), and *Indian Summer: The Oka Crisis* (CBC 2006). Nevertheless, several series, not on the main networks but on specialty channels, are more balanced – and a few are sitcoms: *renegadepress.com, Moose TV, Hank Williams' First Nation,* and *Moccasin Flats* (the latter produced and written, as well as performed, by First Nations men and women). The expectation that authentic aboriginal voices would be heard on the entire Canadian broadcasting system, not just the CBC, was entrenched in the 1991 Broadcasting Act.[10] However, only the Corporation is expected to produce or obtain programs that their managers call "mandate work," expensive programs in drama and in children's programming. Section 3 (o) of the Broadcasting Act states that the CBC specifically will provide "programming that reflects the aboriginal cultures of Canada ... as resources become available for that purpose." Resources for mandate work (i.e., television for the public good) come from the yearly government subsidy that distinguishes the CBC as a crown corporation from a privately owned network. Another factor in the mix is that the rising expectations of the First Nations themselves mean that these viewers expect to see and hear themselves in documentaries, children's programs, and fictions on the universally accessible, mainstream networks, not only on their APTN network or tucked away on the upper tiers of cable specialty channels. At least some viewers also expect not only that stories will be told from the points of view of the Anishnabe, Cree, Dene, or other First Nation/status/non-status/urban/rural/Metis/Inuit, but also stories will be told *by* these peoples. Slowly, those documentaries, children's programs, and dramas are being made, though most are still not broadcast on mainstream television.

## STEREOTYPES OF INDIANS IN MOVING IMAGES

There are viewers who would agree with a white rancher named Smith, who appears repeatedly in *Cariboo Country* and is the protagonist in Phil Keatley's 1966 drama special, written by Paul St Pierre, *How to Break a Quarterhorse*.[11] Talking about Indians, Smith says: "Only two times you get in trouble with them. One is when you try to hurt them. The other is when you try to help them. I mind my own business." Smith doesn't, of course, mind his own business, and neither have the makers of Canadian television drama. Whether that has hurt or helped cannot, I think, ever be definitively answered. But it is generally agreed that both negative and romantically positive stereotypes do harm.

A very good overview of Indian stereotypes in American (and a few Canadian) films appears in the introduction to Jacquelyn Kilpatrick's fine book *Celluloid Indians: Native Americans and Film* (1999). She also identifies the new stereotypes developed at the end of the twentieth century.[12] Unlike the work of Ralph and Natasha Friar and of Michael Hilger cited below, Kilpatrick tries to define the differences between such popular films and "the American Indian aesthetic" using *House of Dawn* (1972, script by N. Scott Momaday), Gerald Vizenor's half-hour film *House of Orange* (1984), *Medicine River* (1994, script by Thomas King; that this is a television movie made for the CBC is not mentioned), and the work of producers/directors George Burdeau, Aaron Carr, and Victor Masayesva, with a coda on Sherman Alexie and Chris Eyre's collaboration on *Smoke Signals* (1998). She also mentions that there are gifted women filmmakers but does not discuss their work. However, the films she does choose demonstrate a broad diversity in technique, point of view, and subject. Certainly, they do not look like, sound like, or present their narratives like mainstream depictions of Indians/Native Americans/First Nations peoples. But add in the work of Shirley Cheechoo, Alanis Obamsawin, Drew Hayden Taylor, Barbara Cranmer, and Loretta Todd and the differences multiply. In my view, it is not possible to try and establish a definitive First Nations film or television aesthetic, although later in this chapter I will try to pin down a few observations drawn from the First Nations films and television materials I have enjoyed.

As early as 1972, Ralph and Natasha Friar, in *The Only Good Indian ... The Hollywood Gospel,* wrote: "No other race or culture depicted on film has been made to assume such a permanent fictional identity ... After all, these other [ethnic and racial minorities] ... are trespassers as well. The fact is that the 'American Indian' is the only legitimate native of this land. Yet he is *racially,* not ethnically, isolated in our minds as *one minority*" (2). Another thorough look at the traditional stereotypes is in the chapter "From Savage to Nobleman: Traditional Images of Native Americans" in Michael Hilger's *From Savage to Nobleman: Images of Native Americans in Film* (1995). He describes dozens of films, from the silent era to the present, under categories like "Native Americans as Victims," "Romances between Native American Men and White Women," "Attacks on Settlers and Other Representatives of Progress," "Vengeance," "Friendship and Loyalty," and "Peace Loving Chiefs."[13] Ted Jojola (Pueblo) takes a further look in "Absurd Reality: Hollywood Goes to the Indian," in *Hollywood's Indian: The Portrayal of Native Americans in Film* (1998).

The elected chief (1989–2001) of the Tsleil-Waututh Nation, actor, storyteller, hereditary chief of the Burrard Inlet band[14] (and youngest son of the late chief Dan George)[15] Leonard George (1991), sums up the effect on those who are "inside looking out": "In hindsight, we can easily say that the native people of North America were oppressed by three major forces. These were government, religion and Hollywood ... This means any kind of media or process, beginning with the early journalists and progressing through film. The media established in people's minds an image of Indians so powerful and controlling that even today it is hard to rise above it" (165, 167). Critics like Hartmut Lutz, Terry Goldie, and Daniel Francis[16] and writers like Monique Mojica (Kuna/Rappahoanuck), in her 1991 play *Princess Pocahontas and the Blue Spots,*[17] remind us that positive stereotypes can do as much damage as negative stereotypes.[18] However, as Scott Ellis (1992),[19] points out, the "phantom Indian" takes many shapes: the Indian as the threatening or promising holder of ritual secrets and lost wisdom; the Rousseauesque figure attempting to escape eighteenth-century racism that constructs the Indian as the innocent child of nature; and the nineteenth- and twentieth-century "noble savage," perceived as warrior, sometimes heroic, more often menacing, often adulterated with contemporary macho values. The equivalent *figurae* for women are the opposite poles of the "Indian princess," for whom Pocahontas is the prototype, and the "Indian squaw" who is stereotyped as sexually voracious and endlessly available. Walt Disney's *Pocahontas,* for example, was the subject of much discussion on NATCHAT[20] when the film opened in

1995. These are among the familiar stereotypes that the CBC has often tried to explain or even deconstruct and, more recently in *North of 60* and especially in *The Rez*, to mock. Other stereotypes depict Indians as alcoholic, violent, abusive and self-abusing, stupid or sullen, and lazy. Note that all these racist characteristics are also applied to English Canada's chosen "others," from the Irish in the 1840s to the West Indians of the 1990s. For the most part, the CBC, while naming these stereotypes, has avoided the most obviously racist, negative versions. At its best, CBC television drama has concentrated on the clash between or the bridging of cultures, with First Nations' values and social systems given equal weight to those of the dominant culture throughout the narrative structures of plot, dialogue, and subtext, characterization, and camera work.

## NOMENCLATURE

Nomenclature is a vexed question. Artist Robert Houle (Ojibway/Saulteaux), in the section "The Right to a Name" in his essay "The Spiritual Legacy of the Ancient Ones,"[21] disputes the right of others to name First Nations at all. In *Windspeaker*, January 2005, Inuk Zebedee Nungak quotes a First Nations elder as saying, "'I've been an Indian all my life! When we were kids, we played cowboys and Indians, not cowboys and First Nations,'" which Nungak revises to "ranch hands and First Nations ... Many First Nation people are sentimentally attached to the name Indian. Many Inuit, myself included, are sentimentally attached to the name Eskimo." Dan David, in "You Can Call Me Al or you Can Call Me ..." in *Windspeaker*, December 2003, had a different point of view: "'First Nations person.' Is there a more clunky, clumsy, or bizarre way for anybody to describe themselves? Call me Mohawk. If you need to, call me an 'aboriginal person.' But, please, don't ever call me a 'First Nations person.'" In this book, I avoid that construction, but "First Nations peoples" does appear – though rarely. Dan David quotes as best usage the guidelines for American journalists that suggest using affiliation. Drew Hayden Taylor (an Ojibway playwright from the Curve Lake Reserve), playwright, essayist, and columnist for *Windspeaker*, had drawn attention to the question some years earlier when he listed the possibilities, tongue-in-cheek, in a column that first appeared in the *Globe and Mail* under the title "An Indian by Any Other Name."[22] He lists "the basics. Status, non-Status, Metis. So far painless. I guess next would come the already mentioned Indian, followed by native, aboriginal, Amerindian, indigenous, First Nations. Pay attention, there's going to be an exam later. From there we can go to on-Reserve, off-Reserve, urban, treaty." He goes on to differentiate among assimilated, enfranchised, reinstated, and traditional, then goes on to the full bloods and the "wannabes" (as in "wannabe Indian") and finishes with "that's why I usually use the term 'Indian.'" As "a blue-eyed Ojibway," he can gently satirize the situation, but as a different kind of writer, and white at that, I need to clarify for the reader the nomenclature used in this book.

Scholars who are not aboriginal struggle with the issue. Media scholar Lorna Roth prefers "First Peoples" because, as she explains in note 5 to her prologue to *Something New in the Air* (2005), the term First Nations "refers only to Amerindians, Metis and mixed blood Amerindians," not to the Inuit and Inuvialuktan. In both Quebec and the rest of Canada, the early name used for the First Nations people was often "sauvage/savage." The use in Quebec of the inaccurate word "Indien" and its clarifier "Amerindien," like "aboriginal/n(N)ative," was considered progress. Quebecois writers have been more likely to designate a specific nation when depicting Amerindiens in their television drama than English scriptwriters.[23] However, more recently, English Canadians have acknowledged the levels of meaning behind the usage of "First Nations" and use it more frequently, although not always excluding the Inuit/Inuvialuktan as they should. "Indian Country" publications like *Windspeaker, Raven's Eye, Birchbark, Aboriginal Voices* (for its too-short run), and the American *Native Peoples: Arts and Lifeways* identify the affiliation of every person from a First Nation. I have tried to do the same for those in front of or behind the camera, using their self-chosen designation when they first enter this book – for example, Graham Greene (Oneida).

Someone who is self-identified as Haida or Saulteaux will use the terms "native," "aboriginal," and "Indian" within a few sentences. My practice is to differentiate between the various terms. I use "Indian" where it is historically in common usage, for example when discussing the 1950s series *Radisson* or where I am quoting its use. I use "aboriginal" to include First Nations, Metis, and Inuit cultures when no distinction among them is intended. I use "native" sparingly because to me it has the historical connotation of a generalized imperial usage, although it is very commonly used. I use "Amerindien" when referring to francophone usage. I try to use "First Peoples" and even more often "First Nations" (yes, there is a political difference between the two) where I can, as a term of respect and of recognition of who was here first and what their claims are on the rest of Canada, but that term can occasionally involve awkward circumlocution.

"White" is also a vexed word in this context, but I am going to use it. It is true that Canada has never been a country of white settlers only (the first black slave was purchased in Quebec in 1606,[24] and there were black United Empire Loyalists in 1783), and it is becoming increasingly multiracial as well as multicultural. But "settler" is a term that is only useful in a discussion of post-colonialism or in a historical context. During decades of referenda, the "rest of Canada" has come to mean, for good or ill, everyone outside of Quebec, which is not a useful distinction to make when discussing a series shot in both languages, such as *Radisson*. Moreover, many of the series in this book were dubbed into French and broadcast by Radio-Canada. "Euro-Canadian" is a term not found in common usage and is, to my ear, an awkward expression. The term "white" is accurate when one is referring to the outsiders who live in *North of 60's* Lynx River, but not when one is describing the culture around Molly's Reach in *The Beachcombers*. Most "Indians" use "white" to refer in general terms to those who are the majority in the dominant culture. "White" is invariably the term used in the dialogue of all of these series. Writing not as a sociologist but as one whose doctorate was in radio drama, where dialogue is the architecture of drama, "white" is the term I will use throughout the book for characters who are in fact white. "White" also accurately describes the majority of makers, decision makers, and critics of these television series, as well as the majority of viewers. The relationship between the anglophone Canadian culture and the resistant, subversive, recovered, or hybrid cultures of the First Nations is still mostly monologic rather than what Russian philosopher Mikhail Bakhtin would call dialogic, and it is almost never polyphonic. Contentions between two – or conversations among several – voices and points of view do not characterize the majority of programs made by whites about Indians. This issue is discussed further in chapter 2, "Who are you calling ethnic?"

### CULTURAL APPROPRIATION

When CBC television began in 1952, the policy of assimilation was still in full force. Potlatches and sun dances had been forbidden for decades. In his definition of a dominant discourse, Karim H. Karim (1993) discusses the representation of aboriginal peoples in television dramas on both the CBC and CTV, the biggest private network: dominant discourse has "the power to comment upon and interpret major issues and events; it maintains its superiority by being dynamic, continually co-opting and transmitting the words, images and symbols of other discursive modes that threaten its propaganda effects" (199). Note, however, that Kassim argues that the goal of post-modern discourses is to make all competing discourses equal, which, he maintains, should lead to "common and non-discriminating citizenship for all." There are those who would see this as a description of assimilation.

The problems of cultural appropriation do not go away and are not easily addressed in television drama made for a wide audience. Here are a few examples of the voices from the inside speaking out to those who tell their stories. Photographer Jolene Rickard defines where this "inside" is in *Partial Recall: With Essays on Photographs on Native North Americans* (Lippard 1992). "My images are not radically chic. I am just one Tuscarora woman who has identified the 'center' as anywhere indigenous people continue to live, knowing that we have the oldest continuously surviving cultures in the world. That has to mean something. Every day I explore that meaning from the inside looking out." Gail Guthrie Valaskakis (Lake Superior Chippewa), an academic with roots in the Lac du Flambeau band in Wisconsin, elaborates:[25] "The conception of resistance as movement – either 'moving forward' or 'moving backward' negates the most important understanding about Indians: First Nations' resistance is cultural persistence; the social memory and lived experience of traditionalism continually negotiated in the discourse and practice of everyday life" (Valaskakis 1993, 293).[26]

Loretta Todd, a Metis film and video maker from Alberta pointed out in 1990[27] that in most native cultures the histories and stories belong to the originators as something to be given and shared only with those chosen to hear or see them: "What is most revealing is that in the appropriation and naming of native as healer, as story teller, as humorist, the appropriators name themselves. We become the object against which the threat of difference is disavowed … we become a style, a fashion, a commodity, a source of script material, of choreographic inspiration, of literary realism." For Loretta Todd and many others, stories about First Peoples told by the dominant culture to the dominant culture are not legitimate, even if told in an effort to understand or to champion the First Peoples' cause.[28] Claiming an aboriginal title over native culture as well as land, she argues that this sometimes well-meaning cultural appropriation denies the rights of individuals and self-determining collectives. She says that there should be no such work until this title is acknowledged in the law. Only then, she says, will coexistence and sharing of history and story be possible.

Ann Brascoupe, in *Windspeaker*, June 2002, explains to her readers: "The cultural and spiritual meaning of songs are not to be commercialized for

mass consumption. Cultural integrity is of paramount concern to ensure
that compositions are not trivialized or misrepresented." She further points
out that much of the intellectual property of First Nations is communal,
made for the benefit of the community, and that there are specific norms
and protocols within the nation, community, and family for its use.

In *Indigena: Contemporary Native Perspectives* (1992), editors Gerald
McMaster (Plains Cree) and Lee-Ann Martin (Mohawk) write: "The stories which we would have liked to tell were largely appropriated and retold by non-aboriginal 'experts' in such fields as anthropology, art and
history and especially in the political realm. Not surprisingly, the appropriated stories distort the realities of our histories, cultures and traditions" (17). Lenore Keeshig-Tobias (Chippewas of Nawash First Nations)
is a storyteller who has passionately attacked the making of the widely
acclaimed and often rerun drama special about residential schools, *Where
the Spirit Lives*. She frames the issue in the story "How to Catch a White
Man (Oops) I Mean a Trickster": "First, find yourself a forest. Any stand
of ancient trees will do; in fact the older the better. Stand in the middle of
it and tell your stories. Soon the white man (I mean Trickster) will come
by carrying a big pack on his back. In that pack he carries the voices of his
women and the voices of other people he has walked over with his long
legs. 'I'm going to tell these stories for you' he'll say. 'You're far too primitive to tell them yourself. I am going to let the world know what you
think. I am going to tell the world how you think when you think and I'm
going to build a golf course here too. These trees are so old, and besides
you're not using them trees" (McMaster and Martin 1992, 108).[29]

Nearly a decade later, Keeshig-Tobias told *Windspeaker* staff writer
Kenneth Williams: "'I think the most important thing for a non-Native
writer to do when they write about Native issues is to have respect – respect means research and talking to the people … One of the reasons I'm
a culture worker is to educate non-Natives about the stereotypes and dis-
information that is put out by non-Aboriginal writers. It's done a great
deal of harm … I get really tired of doing it because we end up doing a lot
of that work and very little of our own work.'"[30] Many First Nations creative people point out that appropriating stories about First Nations also
takes up economic space.

Researcher and museum specialist Deborah Doxtator (Oneida) writes
in *Fluffs and Feathers: An Exhibit on the Symbols of Indianness: A Resource
Guide* (1992): "It has been difficult for industrial Canadian society to accept that non-industrial cultures are still viable … Since the sixteenth century, 'Indians' have been seen as representing earlier, less civilized

versions of Europeans" (12).[31] Delaware poet/playwright Daniel David Moses, after working on *Spirit Bay*, commented on the fact that almost all television drama has been written, directed, designed, produced, and photographed by non-natives: "This goes into the appropriation thing. It's when people from the opposite culture try and tell those stories, they don't know what is going on. They are just going to screw them up. I mean, that's what's got us upset. You say you want the freedom to tell our stories, and then you just screw it up. Freedom of the imagination shouldn't be the freedom to destroy" (Lutz 1991, 166).[32] We will read more of what he has to say in chapter 8.

Diana George and Susan Sanders (1995), quoting Stuart Hall, point out that the representations of the dominant culture in television "were not superficial. They had the power to make us see and experience ourselves as "Other." Every regime of representation is a regime of power framed, as philosopher Michel Foucault reminds us, by the fatal couplet 'power/ knowledge' and this kind of knowledge is internal not external. It is one thing to place some person or set of peoples as the Other of a dominant discourse. It is quite another thing to subject them to that 'knowledge'" (442–3). But not all native writers or performers agree that cultural appropriation is an issue. Actor Graham Greene, who played in Highway's *Dry Lips Ought to Move to Kapuskasing*, had a regular role in *Spirit Bay*, appeared in *North of 60*, starred in the merciless Canadian film *Clearcut* and the American film *Thunderheart*, and will be known to most viewers as Kevin Costner's Lakota mentor in *Dances with Wolves*, has said that he feels free to perform any role he chooses and others should do the same.[33] He was cast as Shylock in the 2007 season of the Stratford Festival.[34]

No television drama wholly written, produced, directed, designed, or shot by any native has as of mid-2007 made it to air on mainstream television. Regrettably, the first CBC effort to rectify that omission, the four half-hours that made up *The Four Directions*, was not a success in terms of giving aboriginal filmmakers experience behind the camera. What it demonstrated are the problems in involved in attempts to avoid cultural appropriation within a huge organization like the CBC. Thomas King (Greek/Cree) was the story editor for the anthology and later wrote a few scripts for *North of 60*. He was also the creator of CBC radio's *Dead Dog Café* and *Dead Dog in the City* as well as an academic at the University of Guelph. In 1993 he told Sid Adilman of the *Toronto Star* that he would be leaving *The Four Directions* because the CBC had reneged on a commitment to pair the experienced producers, directors, and directors of photography with native people to create an infrastructure and because the

CBC had made no formal commitments to film more than three of the twenty scripts in development: "What we wound up with, when I got here, was a producer who is non-native and myself, the only native on it. Loretta Todd, a native, was involved with it earlier on but Todd left ... [He had told an unnamed CBC executive] ... 'I don't want to waste or lose your money ... but at some point you've got to step off the edge.'" *The Four Directions*, the truncated anthology of four half-hours that came from that attempt, was finally presented with very little publicity but has since reappeared repeatedly on Vision, TVOntario (TVO), and other specialty channels. King's comments on developing a series based on W.P. Kinsella's short stories (as *The Rez* later was), rather than continue with *The Four Directions*, are full of ambivalence. He takes the middle road. "I don't mind that Bill writes about natives. I just wish he'd do a better job. I don't mind if the CBC or any other network does work about Indians. I wish they'd do a better job."[35]

In the context of the Trickster Workshops run by Daniel David Moses and Lenore Keeshig-Tobias, Barbara Godard, in "The Politics of Representation: Some Native Canadian Women Writers" (1990), gives the issues of cultural appropriation and the construction of voice a thorough going-over. In discussing the last Trickster Workshop, called "Whose Story Is It Anyway?'" she writes: "As this title announces, questions of property are imbricated in issues of the proper name and propriety, of the tangled concepts of the authorial signature, of *authority,* and of decorum or convention, both social and literary. Who has the right to speak or write? what are the appropriate forms for their utterance to take? These, as Michel Foucault has taught us, are the important questions to ask in order to unravel the knotted interconnectedness of knowledge and power" (185). Television writers, directors, and even producers would be very surprised to find themselves seen as powerful, given their usual estrangement from the managers of the CBC (recall the bitter strike of all of these creative people against the CBC in 2005), and of course the CBC would see itself as the underdog in a contest for money and attention in Parliament or even at the Canadian Radio-television Commission (CRTC). Moreover, given American control over distribution and the sheer quantity of material, the ruling hegemony is found in American television's formats and conventions, which are widely available on CTV and Global, the privately owned Canadian television networks. Yet issues of cultural appropriation continue to arise, both in a general sense – that is, who is making Canadian television series and in what context – and in the specifics of characters and issues, customs and rituals. Who is Andrew Wreggitt that he should write dialogue for Tina Keeper (Cree), who plays the Slavey-speaking Dene RCMP constable and protagonist of *North of 60*? There are many points of view on the matter within and without the aboriginal communities, as will be evident from the interviews quoted in this book's chapters on *Spirit Bay*, *The Rez*, and *North of 60*. The collective identity, the team that makes television drama, is written into the final edit of any episode. Yet as a series continues, this collective identity evolves, as people come and go, as everyone ages, and as ideas about the series develop in new directions.

Series television can erase racial and cultural differences for viewers much of the time. Viewers who watch Sadie or Michelle or Jesse Jim week after week do not think of them as Indian until reminded by a moment of cultural difference. Moreover, things that seem strange to viewers at first come to be accepted as part of the world created by the series. Although conflicts between cultures fuel many plots in *North of 60*, after a while the values of the Dene of Lynx River do not have to be explained. Cultural clashes may continue in the last episodes and in the movies, but they are not in the foreground all of the time.

### POST-COLONIAL HYBRIDITY

The layers of colonization become rather complex when First Nations are represented in Canadian television series. Television fiction in Canada wrestles with two colonizers. We see one in the ubiquity and influence of American television formats for sitcoms, cop shows, soaps, and movies of the week, and the other in the history of television anthology, which includes docudrama, some of it influenced by British television. (An ironic note is that British television anthology had been deeply influenced by Canadian television drama in the 1960s.)[36] The historical context of series that appear from 1957 into the 2000s stretches from the days of Canadian Brownies (every girl a British subject) vowing "to do my duty to God and the King and to help other people every day" in the 1950s' shadow of the Cold War through the creative nationalism of the 1960s and 1970s to the mature artistic, musical, and literary culture of the last twenty-five years.[37]

Canada itself has been a conscious colonizer ever since it became a dominion and started to govern its own settlements. Canada could not blame Britain or the United States for policies of assimilation – the suppression of the potlatch, residential schools, the ignoring of treaties, the denial to First Nations people on reserves of the right to vote, and the institution of passes to control movement. Indians were wall plaques, dolls, toy canoes, salt shakers,[38] or camp songs such as this one, still in use: "Indians are high-minded / Bless my soul they're double jointed / They climb hills and don't mind it / All day long. How!"[39]

By the 1980s the CBC was struggling to clear more space for Canadian drama after a period of drought.[40] One way to do that was to use aboriginal subjects to make Canadian television more distinctive as well as appealing. But there was also in that period a growing sense that the generic Indian was a projection, not a reality. The way had been prepared by *Cariboo Country*, by drama specials like *The Education of Phyllistine* and *How to Break a Quarterhorse*, episodes of *Wojeck* and *Sidestreet*, and early documentaries and docudramas – and by the presence of Jesse Jim and members of his family on *The Beachcombers*. None of these programs had official cultural advisors, although in some instances the actors took on that role.[41] But eventually *North of 60* arrived. The series did use Dene cultural advisors, and as with *Cariboo Country* thirty years before,[42] a different sensibility arose out of that culture.

Only rarely in Canadian television made for a broad adult audience do we see the "message of the week" so often found in 1980s and 1990s American made-for-television movies and in much of their episodic television. This refusal to spell out the moral of the story, characteristic of much of our best television, echoes some common First Nations practices. Listen to Rupert Ross, the assistant crown attorney for the District of Kenora, Ontario, paying tribute in his book *Dancing with a Ghost* (1992) to his partner Charlie Fisher, an elder from the Islington Reserve at White Dog Falls in Northern Ontario: "Loyal to his cultural commandments, Charlie never criticised what I did, nor told me directly how to conduct myself. Instead he told me stories as we flew from place to place. In time I learned how to listen to those stories, how to see beyond their casual appearance. To say that they contained lessons would be wrong; instead, they crystallised various scenarios within which some choices would clearly be wise and others inappropriate. The ultimate choice, however, would always be mine" (xviii–xix). Ross tries to acknowledge and in part explain a little of the "immense gulf between our two cultures" (xvii). So too, at times, have the series under discussion in this book tried to use stories to acknowledge and sometimes bridge that gap. Ross speaks and writes on native justice issues.

More than thirty years ago, in 1972, Margaret Atwood (then relatively unknown) wrote the influential book *Survival: A Thematic Guide to Canadian Literature*, in which she discusses the patterns she sees in Canadian literature and Canadian sensibility up to the 1970s. Basically, she sees both settlers and their heirs who write Canadian literature to that date as colonizers. In chapter 4, "Early People: Indians and Eskimos as Symbols," she extends one of her basic arguments, that our literature from the beginning was obsessed with victims who rarely, and only with great difficulty, moved beyond the position of victim. In fact, in her own challenging book of poetry *The Journals of Susanna Moodie* (1970), the streets of Toronto are haunted by the ghost of settler Susanna Moodie, as she had earlier been haunted by the native people who were there before her. More than a decade later, Gaile McGregor, in *The Wacousta Syndrome: Explorations in the Canadian Langscape* (1985),[43] says that the settler "therefore has the alternatives only of running away (like Moodie) or of transforming *himself* [italics hers]" (43). Atwood notes what has since become a truism, that "[t]he Indians can be idealised only when they're about to vanish." In fact, neither idealized nor vanishing Indians were by the 1970s the commonplace of Canadian television drama,[44] but television drama is not where she is looking. What she does see in Canadian literature is that unlike Americans, who treat natives as either morally good or bad, Canadians "zero in on the relative place of Indians and whites on the aggression-suffering scale" (92). She says that "[w]hat the Indians themselves think is another story, and one that is just beginning to be written" (106). In 1990 Atwood noted with delight what she called in an essay title "A Double-Bladed Knife: Subversive Laughter in Two Stories by Thomas King" (243–53).

Gaile McGregor (1985), in her survey of the Canadian literary landscape, cites books by W.O. Mitchell and Matt Cohen, as well as Margaret Lawrence's Manawaska novels, to demonstrate that Indians are presented as casualties, "victims not of some romantic decline *or* explicit, localized white villainy, but simply of poverty, disease, ignorance, accident, anachronism ... because their victimization, like, indeed, our own, is built into the very nature of things" (218–19). Yet in the same fifteen years between the work of Atwood and that of McGregor, *The Beachcombers* established Jesse Jim as a hard-working, successful man who is proud of his heritage in a series seen all over the world to this day. And by the mid-1980s *Spirit Bay* was showing children a whole raft of kids and their parents, not as victims, but as a community of people who were leading creative and enjoyable lives. Television drama specials are able to come closer to these generalizations because they usually turn on a crisis.

Nevertheless, the problems inherent in attempts by the mainstream media to tell stories about aboriginal peoples are matched by the problems faced by the academic who analyses them. The Chicago Cultural Studies Group (1992) has defined the position of the outsider observer as the impossible one of being caught between the dominant discourse and the alternate discourses struggling to be heard: "The anthropologist or subaltern analyst (or more generally 'the intellectual') finds him or herself in a necessarily tragic position: inserted into a social field of heterogeneous, often contradictory voices, and at the same time representing (or at least addressing) a different field of voices, this individual may be in a position of inescapably bad faith – yet one that is nevertheless indispensable" (541).[45] By analogy, this definition situates both the mainstream broadcaster and the academic critic in the centre of a dilemma, one that must be acknowledged, but I do not accept the designation of "tragic" or even "inescapably bad faith." These series were not made by those who were represented, nor for them alone.

### FILM AND TELEVISION
### MADE BY FIRST NATIONS MAKERS

None of the many programs, mostly documentaries, made by First Nations makers are discussed in this book.[46] I do, however, refer to some of the documentaries made by both native and non-native filmmakers that I have seen on television and that have helped me understand some issues.[47] Clearly, in the 1990s some aboriginal filmmakers learned how to make their voices heard. These films and others form part of the context for some viewers of the 1990s television series discussed in chapters 9–15. As Gloria Cranmer Webster tells viewers in the film *A Strict Law Bids Us Dance*, made for the Kwakiutl of Alert Bay, "aboriginal cultures are engaged in a desperate struggle with Nintendo, Gameboy and satellite television. The few speakers remaining of the dozens of First Nations languages are now old, and their passing threatens the increasing efforts to preserve their heritage, to renew and adapt their traditions of community and Ceremony." Aldona Jonaitis points out in *Chiefly Feasts* (1991)[48] that "today young Kwakiutl children in Alert Bay learn about their heritage by listening to their elders, by practicing songs and dances in the U'Mista Cultural Centre [where confiscated potlatch goods have returned home] and from attending the potlatches that occur on a regular basis in their community. Complementing these more traditional methods of educating young people are means appropriated from white societies, including workbooks in Kwakwakwala" (31).

The following are some of the characteristics of some First Nations films:

- There are gaps where a mainstream narrative would elaborate.
- There is a reticence or refusal to claim credit or special knowledge through usage of expressions like "they say," "apparently," "perhaps."
- The makers often feel responsible to their community and sometimes answer to them directly.
- There is often a taboo about showing a protagonist drinking. When alcohol is presented as a normal part of life, the effect can be strongly transgressive.
- The pace can be leisurely and the narrative discursive and full of apparent non-sequiturs.
- There is a distinctive sense of humour – often very wry, parodic of white stereotypes, on occasion with a lesson attached; sometimes the film contains jokes that are lost on a white viewer.
- There is a strong but unromanticized sense of place.
- There is an emphasis on the differences between bands and between nations.
- There is a refusal to directly represent ceremonies that are sacred and often secret; if represented, some details may be deliberately omitted or presented incorrectly.
- Some films attack "plastic shamans" and other "wannabes" who appropriate and exploit indigenous cultures.
- Many portray ongoing narratives of racist incidents both past and present.
- Most emphasize self-worth and pride in the filmmaker's particular heritage or document the losses to that heritage.
- Some choose to anatomize the causes of a pervasive self-hatred, especially among urban aboriginals.
- Many explore the major disagreements among indigenous communities about how to live with or without the dominant society.

Add to these observations what Marilyn MacGilvray, artistic director of the Awasikan Theatre Company, says: "There has to be a balance with the new world and the old. It's not realistic to be totally traditional and we can't be totally contemporary because we lose our identity as [aboriginal] people."[49] To illustrate just two difficulties – a specific sense of humour and sense of timing – she explains: "Aboriginal humour isn't understood. Nor is silence. Pauses in Awasikan's plays have been criticised for being too long and too frequent. For the aboriginal person silence and stillness are as important as sound and action ... Non-Aboriginal people squirmed during these moments. Aboriginal people listened to the silence."[50] Few of these profound differences are represented in the dominant culture's television fictions about this particular Other.

Most of the North American films on the Native American film festival circuit are made with dialogue in English. It is important to remember that all but one of the television series under discussion were written and performed in English only. *Radisson,* which was shot in English and French in the mid-1950s, is the exception. Most of the episodes in these series use only an occasional phrase or speech in an aboriginal language, if any. Yet each language spoken among the dozens of First Nations in Canada represents a world view substantially different from the others and very different indeed from English. English imposes its own concepts. "Grandmother," describing a mother's or father's mother in English, does not have the complex connotations that "Ehtsu" does in Slavey on *North of 60* or the connotations of the cognate word in many aboriginal languages.

### TELLING THE TALE ON TELEVISION

Television drama does have special and often underestimated strengths. On 10 February 1990 John Haslett Cuff, for many years the television critic of the *Globe and Mail,* made general claims for television that I think are especially relevant to series drama, including those discussed in this book: "The medium's strength lies in its unique intimacy – its ability to bring the moral dilemmas, the terrifying sickness, pain, sorrow, stupidity, bigotry, violence and sheer mundaneness of other lives into the privacy of our homes. Television has the astonishing power of all art to articulate something important about our commonality; but because of its ubiquity and sheer programming volume it rarely exploits this power."

Sixteen years later, his successor in the job for many years, John Doyle, was keynote speaker for Brock University's annual "Two Days of Canada."[51] He began with the "benign influence of the medium"[52] and then identified examples of "cultural assurance" in Canada, such as the depiction of pot growing and smoking and low-grade "habitual criminality" in *Trailer Park Boys,* subjects and attitudes not permitted in the current neo-conservative climate of television regulation in the United States. In the long run of *Da Vinci's Inquest* and then in its follow-up, *Da Vinci's City Hall,* the protagonist, coroner and later Vancouver mayor Dominic Da Vinci argued for moving drug problems and prostitution "out of police jurisdiction and into the realm of a civic problem," creating a distinctly un-American world view that reappeared in 2006 in the equally darkly complex CBC series *Intelligence.*

This point of view may be related to the fact that, as Doyle sees it, Canadians have not moved very far from Atwood's *Survival*. "Canadians like victims," like to sympathize, prefer to find drama specials that leave them "not inspired but heartbroken." Yet they also like many forms of humour, including "sweet, not sugary" series such as *Corner Gas* where nothing happens, but in a very different way from the New York smarts of *Seinfeld*. Doyle also identified and condemned Canadian TV drama that is indistinguishable from American (occasionally called "industrially Canadian" because such shows do qualify for federal and provincial subsidies). Having established that Canadians already enjoy distinctive television, he ended his talk with a call for more "realistic, satiric, complex and truthful series."

Too often Haslett Cuff and Doyle are right. Television rarely exploits its power. But one should never, ever underestimate the power of fiction in its many forms. Viewers will think about a complex issue facing a favourite character when they will not pay attention to a news headline or will reject or ignore arguments raised by an expert. One example comes from Germany. Many First Nations people are aware of the continuing fallout in "wilderness" tourism in North America created by a series of books written early in the last century by Karl May.[53] May wrote about frontier violence, hidden gold, and other melodramatic devices of popular fiction of that period, but most of all about a noble Indian named Winnetou, who is inevitably the faithful friend of a German cowboy named Shatterhand. May wrote seventy-three books, selling over 100 million copies, and his work was translated into thirty languages. Several films in the 1960s and 1970s were based on his books. The result is that First Nations people across Canada are still greeted by visitors from Europe looking for Winnetou.[54] In fact, there was a very funny episode with a serious undercurrent about an encounter between a German academic and Silas and Frank in the "Der Deutscher Indianer" episode on *The Rez*.[55]

Notwithstanding the 1991 Broadcasting Act, the privately owned networks CTV and Global have done little on the subject of First Nations. This is not unexpected, given their reluctance (Global is the worst offender) to spend any money on distinctive Canadian TV drama. Thus, they are scarcely represented in this analysis. However, specialty channels like Vision and public channels like SCN, TVO, and the Knowledge Network (all of which have traditionally done program swaps with each other) have set the pace as outlets for documentaries and, more recently, as co-producers of programs made about and often by aboriginal people. Unfortunately, the plethora of channels and images has also meant that specialty channels offer less acceptable programs; the Family Channel, for example, has recycled 1950s versions of frontiersman Davy Crockett defeating the Indians, and in the 1990s the Youth Channel carried the patriarchal racism of *Bonanza*. The channels specializing in "classic" television carry many of the old programs, and local independent stations have carried the equally racist (by today's standards) series *Cheyenne* and *Gunsmoke*. And yet in 2000 APTN was born, and in 2004 TVO and APTN partnered on *renegadepress.com*, which features an aboriginal youth doing well in high school as one of three leads. More important was the three-season run of *Moccasin Flats* (Showcase and APTN), written, produced, staffed, directed, and partly financed by First Nations makers.

I subscribe to the view that viewers can and do make their own meanings from what makers of television give them, in ways far more complex than even the old sets of class, race, gender, age, nationality, and value preferences indicate – but this is not a work that is based primarily on that kind of analysis. One aboriginal television writer asked my research assistant some years ago, "Who is this person and why does she think she should write about us or the TV drama about us?" She replied that I had done a lot of work on Canadian television drama. That satisfied him and he answered her questions. No doubt my assistant's answer would not please others. It is possible to appropriate the critical voice as well as the creative voice. However, it is worth repeating that even if I were Anishnabe or Mi'kmaq, it would be completely inappropriate to claim to speak for all First Nations people. Asked what Indians thought about these programs, someone from the First Nations would reply with the same bemused or angry expression that a woman gets when asked "What do women want?" Yet, in some places in this book, the reader will hear particular aboriginal people, speaking strictly as themselves to the dominant society, use television drama as their primary reference point. Their comments also help to clarify, though they do not answer, questions such as "What do you perceive that we tell you about you?" "What do you think about what we say?" and "Should we now keep quiet until you have told the stories your way, even if you choose not to tell them at all?"

The potential for intertextual viewers' readings has also grown over the years. Now viewers can see or read the plays of Drew Hayden Taylor and Daniel David Moses, the short stories and novels of Tomson Highway and Thomas King, or the films of Loretta Todd. They can look at documentaries like *Drums* or *the fifth estate* show on residential schools, see documentaries on the election for the chief of the Assembly of First Nations, watch news clips of blockaded logging roads, mainline railway tracks, or streets in Caledonia, or recall images of Mohawk warriors at the barricaded road to an ancestral burying ground at Oka or of MLA Elijah Harper's calm "No" in the

Manitoba legislature. The intertextuality of the television and radio dramas, plays, songs, and dance is only part of an interwoven experience, but it is part of the changing context for the television dramas under discussion.

British critic Richard Collins (1990) claims that Canada is that most modern of nation-states, a country without a mythology. Arguable as that assumption may be (it caused heated debate in academic circles in the mid-1990s when the breakup of Canada seemed imminent), there is no question that the myths of a noble conquest of a hostile and empty land,[56] of nation building and confidence in a Canadian identity that informed our popular culture intermittently until the 1980s, have faded.[57] Ironically, including "Indians" in a television series is one way that Canadian popular culture has claimed authenticity and even tried to distinguish itself from the United States, from *Radisson* to *North of 60*. Yet the specific cultures of many First Nations have survived even the 500-channel universe.

In short, this book tackles this question: *What are the stories that we* (the TV programmers, producers, and directors, who were, it must be noted, until the mid-1980s white, male, middle-class, yet often self-defined resisters to the normative)[58] *tell and show to ourselves* (defined as heterogeneous, male/female/from all classes and increasingly many cultures) *about Indians?* Note that the viewers of these programs are not likely to ask themselves whether radio or television dramas have legitimacy, in the sense of origins and means of production, but rather whether they accurately depict credible characters and situations. Nevertheless, the purpose and some of the implicit assumptions about their audience of the writers, producers, and directors of the series have stayed the same over the years. They usually try to explain to the viewers the different value systems of native peoples, their suffering and their claims to social justice. Both the basic goodwill and the general ignorance of the audience are assumed. Even so, not everything is explained. Finally, the makers of these series seem to operate on the basic premise that, coupled with honest attempts to "get it right" in anthropological or historical terms, the success in telling entertaining stories that also inform the viewer about cultures they are likely not familiar with will justify both the tale and its tellers. They are *not* working on the basic premise of most American television series through the years, which is that audiences don't like complexity or ambiguity. Les Moonves, the chairman of CBS made this clear to Lynn Hirschberg of the *New York Times*, 4 September 2005: "I understand why creative people like dark but American audiences don't like dark. They like story. They do not respond to nervous break-downs and unhappy episodes that lead nowhere ... they like strength, not weakness, a chance to work out any dilemma. This is a country built on optimism." My conclusion in *Turn Up the Contrast* (1987), reinforced through the interviews in *Rewind and Search* (1996) and reasserted in this book on the basis of the evidence drawn from series for children in the 1980s and more so for adults in the 1990s, is that Canadians have a preference for ambiguity, ambivalence, and open endings in some of their own drama. This is a country built on (a sometimes reluctant) realism.

Unlike the early series for children in the early 1970s to mid-1980s, most of them made by independent production companies, the CBC family series, beginning with *The Beachcombers* and continuing with *Spirit Bay* and then the more adult *The Rez* and *North of 60* (where this book ends), did clearly show a few specific First Nations cultures. On occasion, they also focused on issues that were sometimes quite dark. They also reflected the fact that by the 1980s the First Nations were taking control of their education and their health care and were trying to address the chronic lack of jobs on reserves. Even in the downsizing corporate culture of the early 1990s, a combination of First Nations' articulate writers, artists, lawyers, social workers, health professionals, and very visible political leaders tried to create a much clearer sense of the dominant culture's responsibility for the roots of the current problems as well as real hope that downward spirals, where they exist, can be reversed. Those hopes and fears are reflected in English Canadian television fiction series.

Television drama is often the first place to detect basic changes in the thinking of viewers. For example, writers and producers of drama specials regularly assume that a sympathetic white sharing the function of protagonist is a necessary narrative strategy to avoid alienating the audience through an implication of their own responsibility for issues raised. Over a sustained period of time, the strategy of surrogate white not only keeps the audience in a sympathetic frame of mind, but also works to familiarize the audience with some basic beliefs and values of the particular band. *Spirit Bay* and *The Rez* have no white characters who appear in every episode as bridges to the outsider audience. *North of 60* began by using this strategy but grew out of it.

This book focuses primarily on what these programs say and how they say it. What the dominant culture has not yet addressed is what Jeanette Armstrong (1993) thought the dominant culture should concentrate on: "Imagine interpreting for us [indigenous people] writing in honesty, free of the romantic bias about the courageous 'pioneering spirit' of colonialist practice and imperialist process. Imagine interpreting for us your own people's thinking towards us, instead of interpreting for us our thinking, our lives and our stories" (143–4). Perhaps that will be the focus of a future television drama series for adults on the CBC or other main networks. One can hope so.

# TWO

# "Who are you calling ethnic?"

"When asked by an anthropologist what the Indian called America before the white man came, an Indian simply said 'Ours.'"

Attributed to Vine Deloria Jr[1]

In the opening chapter of *Television Criticism: Approaches and Applications* (1991), Leah R Van de Berg and Lawrence A. Wenner have this to say about discourse analysis: "In cultural studies, discourse is defined … as a socially produced and conventionalized representation system which conveys a set of power relationships." They quote John Fiske, who writes that the analysis of any discourse must include "'its topic area, its social origin and its ideological work'" (29). But, as they also point out, "[W]hen writing criticism, in practice few essays rely on a pristine use of a single critical approach" (30). Their book then goes on to provide essays on auteur, dialogic, discourse, ethnographic, gender ideology, hermeneutic, historical, mythic, reader response, rhetorical, sociological, structural, and genre criticism. Some of these approaches appear in this book; others do not. This chapter concentrates primarily on the contributions of sociology, ethnography, anthropology, gender studies, and reader/response to the study of television in relation to issues raised in this book.

The problematics of ethnicity and its stepsister race are particularly relevant to this study. Ethnicity is a vexed term. "Ethnic" often connotes "recent immigrant." It can also signify race, even generations later. In then premier of Quebec Jacques Parizeau's mouth, it was coupled with money, as in "money and the ethnic vote," to describe an alliance that he thought prevented *pur laine* Quebecers from winning the 1995 referendum. His remark was perceived as a racist slur in anglophone Canada – and among some in francophone Canada as well.[2] "Ethnic" always connotes "not from here," wherever "here" is. It must be stressed that "Indians" do not see themselves as ethnic. They were here already. And yet the discourse about them is often framed in questions of ethnic identity.

## AUTHENTICITY AND ETHNOGRAPHY

I am not an ethnographer. I don't even play one in this book. But when questions of the authentic or inauthentic representation of First Nations peoples are raised, ethnography and its cousin anthropology are bound to appear. Claims of authenticity are made about almost all of the series discussed in this book. Ironically, both broadcasters and critics claim authority on questions of authenticity. Television producers and public relations people claim that their series is authentic on several bases: factual content like the shape of a canoe; the use of "real Indians" as actors or (much later) writers; relevant issues taken from recent headlines in the news as plot lines; modes of speech; and historical references. In the case of *North of 60* (1992–97), instead of the common practice of using the actors, extras, or members of the community where the series is shot as unpaid sources of advice, the series employed Dene cultural advisors for every episode. However, for most of the series in this book, the research done by producers, writers, and story editors depended on earlier research by ethnographers and anthropologists, even though what researchers for the series found and used would often be adapted to the dramatic requirements of the episode or the series.

Many viewers do not read the credits. When asked about whether a seventeenth-century canoe is correctly built, they may well reply, "Who cares?" They just want the narrative arc, dialogue, and characters to be credible – which, as Aristotle pointed out, usually means plausible, not accurate. Note, however, that there is in the word "credible" the potential for falling back on stereotypes. There is also the "authenticity" of performance, which depends not on the actors' specific aboriginal heritage but primarily on their approach to the characters as conceived. Casting may also depend on how 'Indian' the actor appears to be. In *North of 60,* where all of the major characters are Dene, Tina Keeper as Michelle Kenidi is actually Northern Plains Cree; Tom Jackson as her brother Peter, the band chief, is Metis (Cree/English), born on a reserve near Batoche and raised in Winnipeg; and Gordon Tootoosis, as Albert Golo, the series antagonist, is Cree/Stoney. In *Screening Culture: Constructing Image and Identity* (2003), Heather Norris Nicholson comments that her own research at the Glenbow Museum in Calgary in 1993–94 "coincided with visits by members of the [*North of 60*] cast involved in aspects of research related to production work [that] drew my attention to the personal search for culturally specific information prompted by the series" (18).[3]

In the 1990s academic researchers who had provided some of that information were rethinking their processes and their conclusions, as Julie

Cruikshank demonstrates in "Changing Traditions in Northern Ethnography" (1995).[4] Jean-Guy A. Goulet, in *Ways of Knowing: Experience, Knowledge and Power among the Dene Tha* (1998), says that for the ethnographer "the problem is that investigators who hold to research methods that clearly separate observer and observed stand to lose, because, in the eyes of the Dene, they are too far removed from the authoritative source of knowledge" (xxxi). Goulet defends his willingness to experience some of the vision knowledge that the Dene value, as well as his desire to observe people who know how to do things and to hear stories that teach. He had to learn when a question had been answered, even if the answer came months later; he also had to learn that some information was not to be written down at all; that two equally credible explanations could be presented about spiritual matters, leaving him free to choose the one he considered most appropriate (192). This strategy was used in *North of 60*, for example, in the episode of the Bushman, who may exist or may be imaginary, according to the choice of the viewer, a narrative strategy also used in some *Beachcombers* episodes.

## WATCHING HIGH-QUALITY TELEVISION

Authenticity can also be discussed in a much more general way, as an experience of the viewer when he/she sees television of high quality. John Caughie values critiques of specific programs based on aesthetics as well as on conditions of production and reception, and in *Television Drama: Realism, Modernism and British Culture* (2000), he provides useful insights into how television series can be evaluated (the post-modernist refusal to evaluate works is rejected in my work): "In the absence of an adequate sociology, such 'ethnography' [focusing on the consumption of the product] comes dangerously close to confusing itself with aesthetics, confusing description with evaluation … It gives criticism, and critical theory no way of knowing what it is for: no way, that is, of arguing for one kind of production against another, or of valuing some forms over others" (232). Caughie's description of what constitutes high-quality television is instructive:

> The centrality of character demands an organization of time and space which will allow all of the materiality and complexity of characters to emerge in all their idiosyncrasy. The camera gives sufficient time and space to characters to allow them to reveal their eccentric particularity because, while these eccentricities may pull the narrative "off-centre," they also demonstrate its reality. Its truth claims are based on the

particularity of visible detail rather than on the generality and [its] natu-
ralized invisibility of convention. It is this which makes acting so important in understanding how television drama works, because if narrative
time and space are organized around character, the visual elaboration of
· this "chronotope" [Bakhtin's word for the specific organization of time,
which he uses to distinguish between genres in novels] is organized
around a performance ... It is a continuing characteristic of television
drama that it is cut to the measure of character, but always of character
as revealed in performance."(132)

Series television provides the space for this, even though, as Caughie
notes, the flow of television narrative is constantly being interrupted by
commercials and station breaks. (His critique of Lacanian film theory as
applied to television seems very apt in an examination of series television.) He also makes a more debatable point that the multiplicity of plot
lines compensates for televisions interruptions: "For television, interrupt-
ibility and the possibility of resumption structures [the viewer's] activity
and identification quite differently, occupying a different structure of in-
terruptible time every day, [thus creating a different relationship to fantasy that is] motivated much less by desire, loss, and lack" (139).

Caughie's version of Bakhtin is particularly applicable to *North of 60*, as
well as to some episodes of *The Beachcombers*, *Spirit Bay*, and *The Rez*,
when he emphasizes the dialogic "between the 'serious' and 'light,' 'authentic culture' and 'entertainment' each working on the other, each qualifying and transforming the other, sometimes in unpredictable ways"
(230). He goes on: "Television, in its regularity and its availability, [is]
seen as regulated by repetition and modulated by acceptable difference ...
a difference which is not 'indifferent' but in which something is at stake"
(231). One of the things at stake, for good or ill, from the 1950s into this
century is the complexity, accuracy, and credibility (Caughie's drama of
the "real") of the representations of Canada's First Nations in our television drama.

Robin Nelson, in *TV Drama in Transition: Forms, Values and Cultural
Changes* (1997),[5] provides another more political set of criteria for distinguishing high-quality, authentic television when he quotes John Mepham:
"High quality television is television which is excellent as measured by
its faithfulness to these principles – the rule of diversity, the cultural
purpose of providing usable stories and the ethic of truth-telling."
Nelson then defines "diverse" "as pursuing a means to sustain a diverse
output such that varied social – as well as individual – needs are

served" (7). That the series looked at in this book fulfil social needs cannot be demonstrated other than anecdotally within the limits of this study. As Nelson says, "Usable stories are those told according to the conventions the audience understands but which – in order to pursue the ethic of truth telling – avoid mere conventionalism" (7). Truth-telling, he makes clear later on, does not rest on the assumption of "the absolutism of objectivity," but on "situated practices" that "afford connections to be made between human behavior and the social, historical and political conditions of life which inform it" (120). How well each of these series succeeds in doing that is part of the problematics of this book. The CBC did repeatedly claim authenticity to historical detail (as early as *Radisson*), to the geographical place depicted (the Sunshine Coast of *Spirit Bay*, the near north of Ontario in *The Rez*, and most clearly the series set north of 60), and to the kind of lives lived by the First Nations there and then. In the service of such claims, the CBC cited in publicity releases, interviews with producers and writers, and on websites quotes from the aboriginal actors, viewers (their letters and later their emails and chat room comments), and even the people depicted.

Critics often decry some forms of viewing pleasure, even while acknowledging, as Nelson (1997) does, that "pleasure or unpleasure is by no means a simple matter of political correctness. Moreover, people get pleasure from processes in which they know they are consenting to forms of domination. Sentiment, regret, nostalgia, desire, ambition and identification play a significant role in the economy of pleasure" (171). Throughout his book Nelson struggles with post-modern critical theory and post-modern television culture that privilege the short term (cf. the brief immersion in reality shows in the last few years) and a "diverse range of microcultures [that] conveniently corresponds with the postmodern market's need for diversity and flexibility" (212–13) and is now apparently more diverse through the growth of digital channels and increased access to satellite dishes. He points out, quite rightly, that an expensive form like television drama is not where large audiences are likely encouraged to contest what constitutes cultural value. Moreover, fluidity in identity and subject position does not mean that people, while viewing, are incapable of making "distinctions of worth all the time, about all aspects of life" (218), a point well worth remembering. Nelson is correct when he says that "the important contribution of audience ethnography has been to show that situated people do not passively consume all they are offered. Indeed, it may be easier to resist attempted imposition if the message is closed and unambiguous rather than open and polysemic" (247). I argue that the characteristic tolerance – even preference – for open, ambiguous, ambivalent, and polysemic dialogue, situations, and characters among many Canadian viewers is exactly what prevents simple-minded messages from being imposed on them.

## LANGUAGE

Basil Johnston's title "One Generation from Extinction" (1990), his contribution to a special issue of *Canadian Literature,* shows how passionate he is about what happens to First Nations' identities when their own languages are lost: "No longer will they think or feel Indian" (12). He goes on to say that not knowing the language has meant that tellers of Indian legends, such as creation stories, lose their ability to convey the subtle meanings in the narratives that helped people know how to live.[6] He discusses physical beatings and verbal dismissals of the languages as being not good for abstract thought, difficult to say, useless for getting ahead: "To instill respect for language the old counselled youth, 'don't talk too much' … [which] also meant 'Don't talk too often … don't talk too long. Don't talk about those matters that you know nothing about' … So precious did the tribe regard language and speech that it held those who abused language and speech and truth in contempt and ridicule and withheld from them their trust and confidence" (12).

Ethnographic scholar James Clifford (1988) addresses questions about ethnographic authority arising from Bakhtin's ideas about heteroglossia that also relate to the viewing of a television series like *North of 60,* which offers a complex portrait over ninety episodes and six years about a culture unlike that of the majority of viewers. "Heteroglossia" is defined as languages in uses that do not exclude each other; that is, they do not drown each other out or fade into one dominant system of language. According to Clifford, "What is said of languages applies equally to 'cultures' and 'sub-cultures'" (23), but also to the complex codes offered by a way of life interacting with a different way of life. When these languages intersect in many different ways without privileging one over the other, the result is heteroglossia – a process can also result in good television drama. Clifford comments that "[t]his ambiguous, multivocal world makes it increasingly hard to conceive of human diversity as inscribed as bounded independent cultures" (23). The major narratives of *North of 60* and to some degree of *The Beachcombers, Spirit Bay,* and *The Rez* contain just such discourses – for example, about specific cultural understandings of what constitutes work; of how and whether a person should try to exert influence over another; and of how to make individual and communal decisions. In some episodes, the dominant discourses appear to win; in others, there is no resolution to the conflicts of concept and language; and in a few, the languages intersect. Clifford writes: "For Bakhtin ... there are no integrated worlds or languages. All attempts to posit such abstract unities are constructs of monological power. A 'culture' is, concretely, an open-ended, creative dialogue of subcultures, of insiders and outsiders, of diverse factions" (46). In the 1980s *Spirit Bay* explored the values of contemporary Anishnabe life in Northern Ontario. In the 1990s *The Rez*, set a little farther south, emphasized the loss of culture in the community's younger generations. Because *North of 60* ran for ninety episodes, the Dene culture presented the writers with many opportunities for heteroglossia.

One of the most interesting comments on verbal and gestural language in *North of 60* came from one of the two series creators, Barbara Samuels. In 1993, at the end of the first season, she was quoted in the *Vancouver Sun*: "'We chose specifically to write about people, both white and non-white, who either choose not to speak or are just not too articulate. So you end up writing the way one would always hope one would write, which is mostly in subtext ... that means relying on body language and expressions ... to convey what you would normally say with dialogue ... You'd just learn to do TV slightly differently ... We're doing a show about two cultures in a conflict.'"[7] Also in 1993 Jordan Wheeler, then a *North of 60* story editor, travelled into the Dene territory known as the Deh Cho to Trout Lake, population 70, lending credibility to the producers' claims about *North of 60*'s authenticity in his article about the trip in the *Runner* (1994). He writes: "'Welcome to Lynx River' said ... Chief Ralph Sanguez and I laughed and shook his hand ... A drum group from Fort Simpson said (the fictitious) Lynx River is a pretty good match for the land around the (NWT) Liard River and Nahanni Butte regions; but the work place Lynx River has less mosquitoes." When he talks about the reception of the series in the North, he says that those viewers "see parts of the show that reflect their lives. They also see parts that are television fantasy; but it's their show." He points to the flood of calls from the NWT when the Anik satellite went down: "'How are we gonna see our show?' the people in the North asked" (13–15).

A world away, James Clifford (1988) repeatedly asks scholarly questions about constructed identities and cultures, about a world where it is "increasingly difficult to attach human identity and meaning to a coherent 'culture' or 'language'" (95). Television fiction, however, constructs identities in every frame and tries to construct meaning from the choices writers, producers, designers, directors, and actors make when they bring to life the complex narrative arcs. A series is always influenced by the *zeitgeist* of the time. Although in reruns it occupies a different time and space, many of its stories continue to mean something (multiple some-things) to viewers years later.[8]

Clifford (1988) writes further about heteroglossia, describing it as part of the interplay of distinctive identities: "A 'language' is the interplay and struggle of regional dialects, professional jargons, generic commonplaces, the speech of different age groups, individuals and so forth" (46). One of the things my radio-trained ear detects is that when Elsie, Joe, Michelle, Peter, Albert, or Betty in *North of 60*, or Ma or Mad Etta in *The Rez*, or Jesse Jim or Laurel in *The Beachcombers'* speak, each actor has, to a larger or smaller degree, a way of speaking English that is not quite "standard" English. Standard Canadian English with little regional inflection is spoken on *North of 60* by the white characters Harris, Gerry, Sarah, Eric, and Fletcher, which makes the differences more audible. I am not referring to grammar or vocabulary, although those are perceptibly different among the older generation, but to pronunciation and inflection. I suspect that some of those in Indian Country would hear the specific inflections and pronunciations that characterize variations of Cree, Mohawk, or the languages spoken in wherever the actors grew up. Agnes Grant (1995), in her contribution to *Contemporary Issues in Canadian Drama*, quotes Chief Dan George speaking about the dialogue in George Ryga's 1967 play, *The Ecstasy of Rita Joe*: "My main difficulty was to combine the memory of the lines with the necessary voice tone. This means so much to an Indian. Your people speak with inflection, but our emphasis is quite different and much more subtle, for the range is limited" (106). As a well-known stage, television, and movie actor, Chief Dan George bridged that gap. Viewers of *North of 60* would hear passages of seemingly uninflected dialogue from some of the actors in the series; they would then learn to listen more closely to the words and perhaps to hear how vocal nuances were presented differently. The need for this process does not necessarily present a problem to a viewer. It just adds another hint of difference, a ground line to the polyphony. Wilf Tootoosis, in an interview recorded in *In the Words of the Elders: Aboriginal Cultures in Transition* (Kulchyski et al. 1999), says that some of these distinctive aboriginal speech patterns in English arose because "[t]he nuns spoke French. We spoke Cree. The only time they spoke English was when they spoke to us. I can hear it from anybody that comes in here and they say a few words in English. I'll know he's been in a residential school from

Catholic or the Anglican, two different accents in English. The ones that went to Catholic, they all have accents in French" (313–14). In *North of 60* Joe Gomba (played by Jimmy Herman, the only Dene actor in the series), elder and master hunter, tends to use short phrases and is sparing of language. Elsie, also an elder, seems to have the speech pattern described by Hugh Brody in *Living Arctic: Hunters of the Canadian North* (1987) as "slow, exploratory, often somewhat discursive and almost completely lacking the equivalent of English [phatic sounds] *ers* and *ums*" (159). Michelle Kenidi, a protagonist of *North of 60* who fought residential school and tried to retain her Dene language, seldom wastes words. Brody states that Athapaskans have borrowed the phrase *marsai* from the French *merci* for "thank you" (153). This is contentious. Michelle and the Dene cultural website say that *marsai* is an indigenous phrase. See the section "Sisters of Mercy" in chapter 13 where it is an important plot point: when the sister tells her daughter that the word comes from the French, there is the implication that the Dene did not have the concept for giving thanks to other humans. Michelle's brother, Peter, MBA and now chief, and Teevee, the young rebel, both use more southern idioms and rhythms in English. Peter tries to use his own language with his young son. Albert, who does speak his own language and is a traditionalist in his own way, seldom minces words. He does not directly answer Sarah's question about whether he killed a man. He answers with what seem like anecdotes. In his Dene culture, he has answered her.

The threat of or the actual loss of native languages is a fundamental issue in *Spirit Bay* as well as in *North of 60*. It is not an issue in *The Rez*, because it would appear that the local variant of Anishnabe has already virtually disappeared. However, on *Spirit Bay* and *North of 60*, it is clearly established that elders like Teawash, Elsie, and Joe can speak their own language. The point is made as early as the third episode in *North of 60* that classes in Slavey are offered for the children.[9]

## SOCIOLOGY'S CONTRIBUTION

In his introduction to *Questions of Cultural Identity*, Stuart Hall (1996), an influential thinker about questions of cultural identity, starts with a word of caution: "The discursive approach sees identification – a process never completed – always 'in process.' It is not determined in the sense that it can always be 'won' or 'lost,' sustained or abandoned. Though not without its determinate conditions of existence, including the material and symbolic resources required to sustain it, identification is in the end a conditional lodged in contingency. Once secured, it does not obliterate difference. The total merging it suggests is, in fact, a fantasy of incorporation" (2). He also observes that "[i]dentities ... relate to the invention of tradition as much as to tradition itself ... they arise from the narrativization of the self" (4). In matters of "performativity" – that is, the performing of identity – Hall cites Judith Butler, a key theorist in this area who argues that the normative or regulative rules understood to form a given identity are continuously negotiated, resisted, or accommodated, a process we see repeatedly articulated or demonstrated in *Spirit Bay, The Beachcombers, The Rez,* and *North of 60* not only among the young people but among the adults as well. We also see in practice Butler's idea that "'[a] performative is that discursive practice that enacts or produces that which it names.'"[10] Her work emphasizes the construction of gender identity, but her observations can apply to other constructions of identity, such as "Indian" or "OjiCree" or "Mountie" or "single mother in a small town."

Television "performs" identities for viewers, offering some of them versions of identities to perform for themselves. According to Laura Edles (2002), "the media's 'true' lies become especially important when we *have* no first-hand experience of 'the other'" (100). The Lynx River staple of moose stew is not a familiar dish on most viewers' tables; sentencing circles in *The Rez* and *North of 60* are not part of most viewers' experience of the law and the courts. It would also be easy to distort the truth of moose stew, sentencing circles, and other aspects of lives lived in a First Nations community without a viewer detecting it. But viewers can measure the credibility of the representations of bored teenagers like Teevee or Frank Fencepost, or worry about teenaged parties whether in the bush or at an unsupervised house, or wonder if a job will last, or if a man is faithful when he works many miles away. It is the blend of the familiar and the different that exerts a strong hold on viewers.

Edles (2002) uses narrative analysis as a general term that refers to the study of narratives defined as "structured stories with a *plot* (or 'message'), *setting* and *characters* as found in texts, discourse or events" (199). A little later she contextualizes these three elements within genre theory, pointing out that the organization imposed by generic conventions drives the text forward, which is one reason why a lot of time is spent on characters, plots, settings, and genre in the coming chapters. Another element broken out from plot in my study is a set of themes based on systems of values and meanings. Edles points out that the events in a narrative (often referred to among television writers as the "story arc") have a causal relationship within a clear chronology. Even so, invariably in series television the story arc is accompanied by a "back story" derived from both previous episodes and off-screen information that may or may not be revealed to the audience but that informs the understanding of the actors as well as the designers, the producers, and, most vital of all, the writing team. The series bible, which contains the back story, is vital to a long-running series, as is shown in this book's chapter on *The Beachcombers* (chapter 7).

Edles's usage is "heroes" and "anti-heroes" – a matter of debate because of the values connoted in both terms. I prefer the dramatic literature nomenclature taken from fifth-century BCE Athens – "protagonist" and "antagonist," which connote importance in the narrative, the relationship of character to character, and the significance of the characters' roles in the plot. I do not, as some analysts do, distinguish between "story" denoting the plot in the text and "narrative" denoting the patterns I detect. In my view "story" needs to retain its overtones of larger narrative, larger context; the term is more useful when the fudge factor is left in.

## TELEVISION IS A PROCESS AS WELL AS A PRODUCT

Sociologist Pierre Bourdieu is correct in theorizing that watching at least some forms of television, particularly for a fan, can bring the viewer cultural capital. But television can also be the great leveller. Virtually everyone has access to it and an opinion about some aspect of it. Some television is intended for viewers of a specific class. Advertisers certainly look for viewers of a particular age, sex, education, and class. But some popular television series cut across class, age, sex, and education.

Television producers often refer to the programs they make as "product," an industrial term that masks the creativity, the ad hoc decisions, the serendipity that accompanies the process of making television on location. The fact is that it does not matter what the planners want, what the Broadcasting Act dictates, or what the audience is primed for. One can say with certainty that nothing will be produced unless writers want to write about it, producers want to produce it, and specific actors agree to appear in it – and unless enough of them remain committed to the series for the length of time finances can be found and a network will broadcast it.[11] Television still starts with the artists. The result may well inflect or even resist the hegemonic discourse. Foucault's emphasis on the fluidity and contradiction in what is present in the frame of an artifact and what is absent is one way to detect better–than–average television drama. Good television drama frames problems, issues, ideas, characters, and actions in a complex interplay both within the confines of the screen and between the viewers and what they see. Good television directors frame scripts in what they choose to record on film or tape. Then the program is reframed by the editor and the director/producer's cut – and occasionally by interventions from high in the broadcast hierarchy. Since discussions accompany all of these decisions, the framing is already interactive long before the results are broadcast. The average viewer at this point does not engage actively with most programs or their producers, but viewer feedback through focus groups, letters, email, and websites may influence elements like story arcs or how frequently specific characters appear. Metis producer/writer/director Bob Rock told me in 2004 that independent small producers such as he are being told to prepare rich websites for any program they make.[12] This kind of expertise was not expected to be part of the professional's tool kit in the 1990s, but the producers of *North of 60*, a little ahead of their time, did solicit viewer feedback on their website.

I find Bakhtin a more useful theorist for television analysis than Foucault. He and those he influenced acknowledge the potential dynamic interplay of the spoken word and the role of a self-identified subject in dialogue with another – the most basic definition of the theatrical act. Monologic speech is common in the theatre – where one person's words exclude the others' words rather than acknowledging them; characters who do not listen to one another are common. Both are also common in television drama because monologic speech creates dramatic conflict. But dialogic speech opens up possibilities because the words are given more than one voice. Although occasionally there is direct communication between the powerful and those with less power, monologic speech is more common in those exchanges. But there are times when that dialogue will be hybrid, when the powerful are influenced by those without power, when one voice inflects the speech of another.

## ETHNICITY AND SOMETIMES RACE

White is the colour of the network executives, producers, and initial creators of all of the series discussed in this book. Eva Mackey, in *The House of Difference: Cultural Politics and National Identity in Canada* (1999), writes: "Ruth Frankenberg[13] suggests that 'whiteness' has three interlinked dimensions ... whiteness is a location of 'structural' advantage, of race privilege. [It is also] a standpoint[, a place from which we can] look at ourselves, at others, and at society Finally, whiteness refers to a 'set of cultural practices that are usually unmarked and unnamed.'" Mackey argues that a model of normal Canadianness "is defined not by any particular characteristics, but by its difference from (and often its ability to tolerate) other marked Canadian identities such as multicultural-Canadian, Native-Canadian or French-Canadian" (21). Looking at the history of the process of "making the Indians 'ethnic'" (60), she points to the centennial celebrations of 1967, where they were both identified as special and yet subsumed into the evolving idea of "Canadian."

Seth Feldman (2002), in his foreword to *North of Everything: English-Canadian Cinema*, points out that films made by First Nations filmmakers now make up a coherent body of work but also that "First Nations are for most Anglophone Canadians the vicarious thrill of a deserving nationalism. They are the non-threatening distinct society, a people linked to the land whose singular case we can all affirm with some guilt but minimal real cost" (xiii). This may partly explain why *North of 60* and *The Rez* attracted so many non-indigenous viewers. Feldman continues: "Whether or not First Nations people see themselves this way is irrelevant to this particular corner of the national project (having seen some of the Native films … I think they are far less somber about their identity than we are)" (xiv).

The federal government has actually looked at the issues of race and representation on television in the last few years. In response to the August 2001 CRTC call on the Canadian Association of Broadcasters (CAB, all private) to "develop an industry action plan addressing the reflection and portrayal of Canada's cultural diversity on television," CAB commissioned a report on cultural diversity on television that concentrates on both networks and specialty channels.[14] It appeared in December 2003 and was posted on the web in July 2004. The report presents statistics for times when a "[c]haracter's race or ethnicity is part of plot, is personally involved in Racial/Ethnic Conflict"(155). CAB defines a dramatic protagonist as a figure who is shown "on balance, in a positive light" and an antagonist as "on balance, in a negative light." The coders rated characters using adjectives like intelligent, successful, respected, ethical, caring, or threatening (154).

The report's findings are based on 756 speaking roles from forty-five hours of drama (41). The sample ranged from *Trailer Park Boys* to *Road to Avonlea* (42). In the latter case among others, the inclusion of earlier material not commissioned by the private broadcasters complicates the picture. Also included are stats for the representation of all visible minorities in English-language drama. Visible minorities make up 13.5 per cent of all characters, but only 10.3 per cent of primary characters (13). They are slightly more likely to be criminal or threatening or to be police or emergency personnel (14).

They may be portrayed as younger (20–39), may speak with accents, and may be shown at work and in urban environments (48–9). Visible minorities are more likely to be shown in a generally negative light and somewhat less likely to be shown as intelligent or successful, and it is somewhat more likely that their race/ethnicity is part of the plot (43). Their characters are likely to be involved personally in racial or ethnic conflict in only (an astonishing) 2 per cent of the time (55). Aboriginal peoples appear in less than 1 per cent of the series (17), although in Saskatchewan and Manitoba they comprise 14 per cent of the population.[15] This snapshot provides a picture of the private networks and their specialty channels fifteen years after the CRTC compelled them to carry more Canadian drama. In "Star Wars: Canadian TV Drama,"[16] Catherine Murray, Roger De la Garde, and Claude Martin (2000) found that in the 1999–2000 fall and winter season "Canadian English Drama appears to be reaching for apparent gender equity; female and male protagonists were virtually equal in number and many group or ensemble casts reach a fairly even balance … Ethno-cultural diversity is not as prevalent" (23).

But it should be emphasized that viewers do not necessarily register the racial identity of characters in series television unless it is in some way relevant to themselves or to the character or the story. John Caughie (2000) talks about how television itself is perceived: "One of the key determinations of television is its repetition – week in, week out, same time, same channel … to ease the program into a familiarity – a repetition which absorbs a difference with astonishing rapidity … difference rapidly becomes acceptable … as a system whose repetition and availability seem constantly to normalize, drawing difference into acceptable limits" (130). Caughie is speaking of formal innovations in television, but his observation is equally relevant to whether Dene becomes racially normative in *North of 60* and even more so to the Anishnabe in *Spirit Bay*, where no white characters appear weekly. Homi K. Bhabi, in "Cultures In-between" (1996), discusses the problems of "*thinking* culture": "The Discourse of minorities, spoken for and against in the multicultural wars, proposes a social subject constituted through cultural hybridization, the over determination of communal or group differences, the articulation of baffling alikeness and banal divergence" (53–4). He claims: "The multicultural has itself become a 'flaunting signifier' which is made to serve postcolonial critique, gay and lesbian studies, minority discourse" (55). He does not agree with Charles Taylor that the dilemmas of representation can be addressed and solved by mutual respect and the attribution of "equal cultural worth" (56), because he dismisses what he sees as partial cultures. Indeed, Bhabi prefers a minority culture that is both inside and outside the dominant culture.

Stuart Hall (1990) quotes Ernesto Laclau on the polarity of terms, which, as Jacques Derrida shows, always excludes something, as in man/woman or white/native, reducing the second term to the "function of an accident opposed to the essentiality of the first." By extension "native" or "Indian" are marked terms "in contrast to the unmarked terms of 'white'" (5). bell hooks (1990) quotes Coco Fusco: "'Racial identities are not only Black, Latino, Asian, Native American and so on: they are also white. To ignore white ethnicity is to redouble its hegemony by naturalising it. Without specifically addressing white ethnicity, there can be no evaluation of the construction of the other" (171).

When Edles (2002) sketches the history of race and representation, she points out that defining race and ethnicity is no longer easy. Ethnically similar people can be seen as racially different, nowhere more obviously than in Drew Hayden Taylor's self-identification as a blonde, blue-eyed Ojibway. Yet, as she says, "[n]ext to gender, 'race' and 'ethnicity' are fundamental ways we *order* our experience, and organize meaning." Moreover, people define 'race' as a *social* – rather than a physiological – *fact* ... which [quoting Moon Kie Jung] she says 'provides people with a deep sense of belonging to an imagined and limited community" (100). She also notes that the "others" who manage to achieve successful middle-class working and living situations are seen as sellouts by those "others" who are less successful. To what extent one should conform to the dominant society's goals and expectations is an ongoing theme, as are the problems of those apparently left behind. Early on in *The Beachcombers* Jesse's uncle fears that he will end up on skid row if he leaves the Seahost band; in *Spirit Bay* a father tries to conceal his illiteracy and his fears that if his daughter wins a writing contest, it will take her to high school in southern Canada; in *The Rez* Silas is reluctant to submit his writing to outside eyes; and in *North of 60* Peter Kenidi agonizes over having to leave Lynx River if he succeeds in his bid for a seat in the NWT legislature. In each case, the decision to move beyond the boundaries set by older authority figures or by the characters themselves is the right one, but the costs to themselves and their families are also explored. Nevertheless, the programs also clearly assert that none of these characters will be assimilated as a result of their decision.

Ethnocentric questions are the focus of Ian Angus's study *A Border Within: National Identity, Cultural Plurality, and Wilderness* (1997). As a Canadian, he asks why and how the nationalist project of English Canada has used representations of First Nations. He sees negotiations of anglophone Canada, Quebec, and the First Nations as essential to "what the country will be" (112). But he also says that "it is a mistake to describe Canada's sense of self as including the otherness of Quebec" and by implication the First Nations: "English Canada is certainly in origin a settler society predicated on the importation of European culture and the marginalisation of aboriginal cultures by immigration. But ... there is now a plurality of settler cultures. English Canada is no longer simply English or even European and this fact requires that we think through what a multicultural society may mean in a much more radical fashion than was necessary previously" (130). Angus's theory implies that from the mid-1960s to the present, a period that overlaps most of the television series discussed, Canadians of all derivations have been implicated in the marginalization of aboriginal cultures as well as in the project of continuously defining the term "Canadian." In contrast to Angus, Richard Day, in *Multiculturalism and the History of Canadian Diversity* (2000), condemns a "fantasy of fullness and harmony" that must give way to "those aspects of history which have been most vigorously excluded and repressed" (223). He imagines a space of "free play ... out of which almost anything might emerge ... so that the problem of Canadian diversity can be *dissolved*" (225–6).

Quebec has always had its own culturally specific take on aboriginal subjects. Benedict Anderson, quoted by E. Price Monroe (1995), suggests one of the reasons why that may be. His "imagined political community" involves a specific strategy that can be used by marginalized or conquered people: "To survive the vicissitudes of political and geographical disarray [such as the British conquest of New France] it is precisely the remembered idea of the nation that is important, that can provide the prospect of a future of regained glory. A nation, in this sense, must transcend space and time and rest largely in the imagination"(47–8). Renée Legris (2000) wrote an article about the five different ways of characterizing "les Amerindiens" that she could identify in television dramas and teleromans from 1952 to 2000. Because the article appeared in Portuguese (a language I have not mastered), I have used her manuscript, which is in French.[17] The first way of characterizing Indians is tied to a definition of Quebec's "myth of origins," which valorizes the knowledge and skills of the Amerindien – skills that are later transferred in fiction to the explorer/fur trader. In its strictly defined form, there is no equivalent to this *typos* in English Canadian television drama. The second characterization uses the ostracized Amerindien who functions as an individual rather than as part of a community. The third stresses the marginalization of Amerindiens by portraying their retreat to or forced enclosure by reserves. The fourth concentrates on acculturation and the Amerindien individual's quest for a new identity, social or religious. These three types appear in English television, though the details are very different. The fifth is the configuration of the Metis or half-breed as a halfway stage on the path to acculturation and Western assimilation. Most English television series and drama specials do not portray the Metis as a halfway stage, but rather, almost always, as a variation of "Indian." Some of the francophone dramas using these five approaches also have a distinctly anticlerical thread that may well reflect the many years of the fusion of church and state in Quebec. Identifiable anticlericalism does not appear in English Canadian drama, even in programs about residential schools, although *North of 60* episodes do contain a sadistic nun, an old and tired Oblate priest responsible for a vast territory, and, in the last movie, *A Distant Drummer*, a repentant priest who wishes to be forgiven for what he did in a residential school.

Just who can claim to be an aboriginal/Amerindien is contested by both status and non-status Indians when freedom from taxation, the right to education, and the right to live on a reserve are in question. Until the 1980s, First Nations women who married men of other races lost their Indian status and their homes on reserves. They were eventually given the same right of status as men, and many returned to the reserves where they had grown up. Now there are controversies about their children and grandchildren, with "blood quanta" becoming an issue in Canada as it has been for decades in the United States. Drew Hayden Taylor, who wrote a book called *Funny You don't look Like One: Observations from a Blue-Eyed Ojibway*, puts it wryly in a January 2003 article for *Windspeaker*, the only aboriginal periodical that covers all of Canada. He had been told he did not look Indian enough to appear in a political documentary: "We have been colonized right down to the genetic level. You don't just owe us land claim compensation, you owe us child support.[18]" After four hundred years of contact, not looking like an Indian is no sure indicator of status or lack of status.[19]

To speak sympathetically about racial problems is not in itself to avoid racist assumptions, the most dangerous being a claim to understand how it feels, or worse, how it should feel, to be represented in a particular way – and that *caveat* includes works of fiction like television drama. But in *North of 60* there are at least two additional complications to that paradigm. Over ninety hours, television characters become like friends to regular viewers.

Indeed, viewers know more about most running characters in a character-driven TV drama over six years than they do about many of their neighbours or family members. Michelle's struggle to come to terms with her history as a child locked up in a distant residential school is not an experience shared by the majority of viewers south of 60. Yet she may be perceived by a viewer as no more "different" than a white character who is raised in foster care – like Harris, the band manager. Even so, there is a profound difference, since all the Dene children the authorities could find, not just those from abusive homes, were apprehended by federal government order and sent to residential schools. By eliding such difference, television drama can do harm. On the other hand, *North of 60* demonstrates repeatedly that all of the white characters in the series are outsiders. Each experiences estrangement from the communal problems of Lynx River. They have no vote, no claim on the outcome of band decisions, although those decisions may affect them directly. Each of them is allowed to live in Lynx River only as long as the band agrees that he or she may.

Trinh Minh-ha, in her influential *Woman, Native, Other: Writing Postcoloniality and Feminism* (1989), writes: "Terming us the 'natives' focuses on our innate qualities and our belonging to a particular place by birth; terming them the 'natives' on *their being born inferior and 'non-Europeans'* ... Don't be us ... Just be 'like' and bear the chameleon's fate, never infecting *us* but only yourself" (52). What is different is often defined not only as "other" but also as "problem." Paradoxically, exploration of an "other" culture that results in acculturation is also seen as a problem. Many episodes that turn on the relationship between the Lynx River band and Yellowknife or Ottawa demonstrate what Minh-ha calls "[o]ne truth at home and another abroad. The same logic compels the native to endure the enculturation process and resist acculturation" (58).

Some of the series specifically raise questions of identity; for example, in the first appearance of Jesse Jim in *The Beachcombers,* Jesse at age seventeen or eighteen is finding his way both as a young adult and as a member of the Seahost band of the Coast Salish in an off-reservation world. Here the CBC opens up issues raised about the construction of identity for the modern Indian. The children in *Spirit Bay* are younger than Jesse, roughly the same age as his sister, but they, too, think about whether to exercise their spiritual or artistic gifts in the traditional way. The teens in *The Rez* are a little older, and the boys are more ambivalent about their culture. Teevee in *North of 60*, like Jesse Jim twenty-five years before him, grows from troubled late adolescence into manhood, responsibilities, and eventually, in the later movies, marriage. As time passes, pride replaces the sense of inferiority rooted in his being Indian, and capability replaces a sense of rage and helplessness. Echoing the confidence Teevee achieves, Brian Maracle, in "One More Whining Indian Tilting at Windmills" (1996) points out, that he does not find any substantive difference between anglophone and francophone coverage of issues like Oka and "Indian tobacco trade" and that "[t]he way that the [Onkewehonwe] see it, there are two kinds of people on Great Turtle Island – there are Indians and there are immigrants" (17).

Ella Shohat and Robert Stam, in *Unthinking Eurocentrism: Multiculturalism and the Media* (1994), argue that "racism is positional, relational which means that diverse groups have occupied the functional slot of the oppressed ... Racism thus 'trickles down' and circulates laterally; oppressed people can perpetuate the hegemonic system by scape-goating one another 'sideways'" (19), a process visible in several of these series as characters battle self-hatred. They further note that "[r]acism differs from *ethnocentrism*. Any group of people can be ethnocentric, in that it sees the world through the lenses provided by its own culture ... what is racist is the stigmatising of difference in order to justify unfair advantage or the abuse of power, economic, political, cultural, or psychological" (22). Racism in this definition seems to be not what you think or feel but what you do.

In his introduction to *All My Relations: An Anthology of Contemporary Canadian Native Fiction*, Thomas King (1990) raises the basic point that defining native literature in racial terms is oversimplifying the reality of "full-bloods who live in cities, half-bloods raised on farms, quarter-bloods raised on reservations, Indians adopted and raised by white families, Indians who speak their tribal language, Indians who speak only English, traditionally educated Indians, university-trained Indians, Indians with little education ... the sheer number of cultural groups in North America, the variety of Native languages and the varied conditions of the various tribes" (x–xi).[20] The next year he commented to Hartmut Lutz (1991), "I think of myself as a Native writer and a Canadian writer. I doubt if I could call myself a Canadian Native writer, just because I'm not from one of the tribes up here." Nevertheless, all of his writing is "Canadian material" (107). He also told Lutz, "I'm tired of negative descriptions of Indians and I'm tired of romantic images too! So, I would like to see some very calm, very ordinary images, Indians doing ordinary things" (114).

Eva Mackey (1999) points out that one of the most common notions about First Nations people, one that some of them also subscribe to, is that they are the original and best keepers of "the land," a point made in most of the series and as recently as *North of 60's* third and fourth made-for-TV movies, *Dream Storm* (2001) and *Another Country* (2003). Mackey observes tartly that "[t]he process of 'giving to the land' … is presented as if settlers and aboriginal people were really, after all, involved in the same sort of transformative, yet ecologically sound endeavor … as if ab-originals were 'helpmates to the settlers'" (80). She argues that in Canada caring for the land has been equated with nation building. By the 1990s the nation had been formulated as "a collective hybridity engaged in a shared and progress oriented project" (82): "All the individual ethnic identities, which if left to their own devices, are unstable, ambiguous and 'in-between' (in fact so unstable that they create chaos and destruction), are presented as if they need the project of nation-building (defined as caring for the land) to give them an anchor and a goal, a goal that in turn creates the heterogeneous (hybrid) yet unified nation … not Homi Bhaba's politically liberatory hybridity … but *the nation itself* as a 'Third Space' of hybridity' … [where] the modern project of progress is still the key to nation-building" (82–3). The Lynx River band's land claim is not settled during the series or in the first movies. Its members do not think of themselves as partners with Ottawa or Yellowknife in their care of the land. From the early days of the series, the band makes decisions about land use with its own interests in mind, thus challenging the ideology of an untroubled partnership with white interests. The idea of building a na-tion called Canada never comes up.

## AND CRIME

Criminality is one of the stereotypes that beset the Indian male. The cop show is one of television's most successful genres, and a protagonist who is an RCMP constable (*North of 60*) would seem to promise stories about crime. Jim Frideres, in "Native Canadian Deviance and the Social Control of Race" (1996), summarizes an argument advanced by Breton in *The Governance of Ethnic Communities* (1991) that holds that "social cleav-ages and opposition, instead of being indicators of destruction of a com-munity, can be viewed as essential ingredients of a viable community" – a point repeatedly made in *The Beachcombers, Spirit Bay, North of 60, The Rez,* and even *Radisson*. Frideres continues: "Nevertheless, those individ-uals who transgress the social boundaries of the community are defined as deviant and are dealt with in some fashion. In order to deal with these transgressions the community develops cohesiveness and solidarity to confront the deviant individual(s)" (288–9), processes that can be seen in all of the series. These communities eject the con artist, the exploiter, the criminal outsider, but there is still some dysfunctionality, defined by Frideres as "the structural level, e.g., inability to establish economic activities, lack of jobs, lack of community" (289), which is the crux of many plot lines in both *The Rez* and *North of 60*. The statistics offered by Frideres on non-native versus native jail time identify a formidable problem. The threat of time in Hay River is used more than once against Teevee on *North of 60*, and two of Albert's sons do eventually go to prison. (It is clear that they are not smart enough to stay out. However, Albert, the bootlegger, blackmailer, and entrepreneur, and his young protégé, William, spend very little time in jail.) The intrinsic racism in the justice and prison systems is explored at length in the movie *Another Country* when Teevee, by now a chief, is picked up because he is driving an expensive car (rented), then framed for murder. Prison time is a norm for some of the fathers and older brothers in the series, although it is not emphasized. In *North of 60* many people spend time in the local lock-up for drinking, often sleeping it off, but the community tries to keep most of its people out of prison, often refusing to testify, sometimes using a sentencing circle or community service, or on a few notable occasions resorting to more informal means of justice. To reintegrate or in worst cases to exclude someone who is a danger to the community is still the time-honoured custom in this Dene community.[21]

Frideres (1996) acknowledges the history of First Nations being regarded as "infidels or simply part of the animal world," so that the social and legal rules of Euro-Canadians were not thought to apply to them – "attitudes that were commonplace and widely accepted just a few years ago"(297). Note that First Nations peoples on reserves did not obtain the federal vote until 1960, the provincial vote in Alberta until 1965, and the provincial vote in Quebec until 1969. Moreover, they could not serve on juries or school boards until 1972. However, as might be expected, the rates of deviance go down if a person graduates, marries, finds a job, or goes on to post-secondary education (305). These goals are also identified as desirable in Lynx River, Spirit Bay, Gibson's Landing, and on "the Rez." Nevertheless, in those communities, other more traditional values coexist and occasionally trump the new expectations. In a special issue of *Canadian Literature*, editor W.H. New (1990) writes: "Margins have a way of speaking back from the edges of power ... If they are not recognized for the creativity of the differences they bring to bear on cultural perception, margins also have a way of making the centre irrelevant, and of speaking on their own" (8).

## AND THEN THERE IS GENDER

Early in the new century, David Hogarth (2001) quoted CBC supervisor Dodi Robb: "[O]nly daytime magazines treated women as 'intelligent, lively and curious people who like to think and learn and know' (*CBC Times*, 1965)."[22] The 1970s saw a change as women put down the coffee pots, walked away from the Gestetners, and refused to fetch and carry any longer in the protest movements, rooted in the 1960s, for which they had made significant sacrifices. The only social revolution in history where the members routinely became more militant with age was underway. One phase culminated in the early 1980s in a remarkable mobilization of women across Canada that forced the politicians to put women's rights into the Constitution. The contributors (Belenky et al. 1986) to *Women's Ways of Knowing: The Development of Self, Mind and Voice* use several findings of Carol Gilligan's seminal 1982 book, *In a Different Voice: Psychological theory and Women's Development*, as well as their own experimental work and thinking to explore the different ways that women "know" the world and their place in it and how differently they can interact with and react to the same event experienced by a man. The insights of Gilligan, although taken further and sometimes in different directions, are basic to many subsequent books and articles on women's ways of knowing.[23]

The double issue of *Camera Obscura*, nos 20 and 21 (1989–90), is a very personal, though thoroughly theorized, dialogue/overview of television and film scholarship and where these might go in the 1990s, providing various feminist perspectives on the analysis of television and film artifacts. Some of the leading scholars in the field identify the limitations of what they perceive to be male paradigms, including Lacanian notions of who and how the "other" is arrived at. The issue also includes an overview essay (the only one with a title), "The Female Spectator: Contexts and Directions" by Janet Bergstrom and Mary Anne Doane, on issues of contextualization and historical specificity. Mary Anne Doane, very helpfully in the context of the discussions in this book, reminds the reader that "racial difference and sexual difference are not parallel modes of differentiation" (146). As Annette Kuhn points out in her contribution, "Television asks us to be many things, not only at different times but simultaneously: female is only one of them. It is pointless ... to talk as if a specific female audience can be assumed already constituted for television – or even a female spectator constructed by it" (215). Finally, Patricia Mellancamp notes the inherent "deep bias in film theory, dependent on the dominance of vision linked to power and knowledge where 'to see' means 'to understand'" (237). It has since been widely observed that viewers of television often listen more than look at what is on while they knit, wash the dog, even read.

Seven years later, *Feminist Television Criticism: A Reader* (Brunsdon et al. 1997) presented a useful summary of the history of feminist television criticism, from the 1970s to the 1990s,[24] citing the valuable work of Seiter, Mellancamp, Modleski, Ang, Allen, Flitterman-Lewis, Liebes, and Katz, particularly on situation comedies and soaps. All of the contributors but Robert C. Allen were women. Sitcoms and soaps were often identified as women's genres in that period – and still are in some quarters – as distinct from cop shows, which were seen as men's genres. Note that *North of 60* is, among other things, a hybrid of a soap and a cop show. In the 1980s and early 1990s scholars such as those named above made the discourse on feminist issues in television series, particularly soaps and early sitcoms, respectable. Even so, feminist criticism took a while to become part of an everyday critical vocabulary. On the complex, ongoing question of "otherness," Charlotte Brunsdon in her chapter in *Feminist Television Criticism* suggests that feminist typology falls into three categories: "a) transparent – no others; b) hegemonic – non-feminist women others; c) fragmented – everyone an other." In this context, feminist critics often defined the "other" as "the ordinary woman, the non-feminist woman, the housewife, the television viewer ... I am suggesting that the feminist critical discourse itself constructs and produces, rather than simply analyses, a series of positions for 'women'" (117).

In "Melodramatic Identifications: Television Fiction and Women's Fantasy" in the same volume, Ien Ang makes the helpful argument that elements of melodrama are pleasurable as well as common in television fiction. Women characters can be symbolic realizations of feminine and subject positions with which viewers can identify in fantasy. She points out that psychoanalytical theory argues that fantasy is a reality in itself "which creates pleasure and fulfils conscious or unconscious wishes," a pleasure that "lies in its offering the subject an opportunity to take up positions which she could not do in real life: ... [to] explore other situations, other identities, other lives. It is totally unimportant here whether these are realistic or not" (162). Ang elaborates further: "Fantasy and fiction can play a distinctive role. They offer a private and unconstrained space in which socially unacceptable subject positions, or those which are in some way too dangerous or too risky to be acted out in real life, can be adopted." Balancing that argument, she also argues that "sentimental and melancholic feelings of masochism and powerlessness ... are the core of melodramatic imagination" (164), reflecting the common recognition that no one is in full control of every aspect of their life. There are certainly elements of fantasy in all of these series: for children, speeding through British Columbia's coastal waters, flying in a bush plane, rescuing a busload of children in a blizzard, being visited by vivid dreams from spirits that mark you as special; and for young adults, subverting the adult world, having handsome lovers, being a singer or writer. *North of 60*, the series specifically for adults, also provides many fantasies for its viewers: hunting caribou, fishing in a clear cold stream that flows by your door, teaching your kids to live off the land, being a Mountie or a band chief or even an uncatchable outlaw who still has a place in the community, living where doors are unlocked and everyone knows everyone else, being on the run, being kidnapped/held hostage and being rescued, or being romanced by Tom Jackson or Michael Horse, Sarah Birkett, or Tina Keeper. Every successful television series provides food for fantasy even if it appears to reflect the daily life of the individual viewer.

Although, as bell hooks points out in *Feminist Theory: From Margin to Center* (2000), "white" is the default colour when the "other" is identified, women's relationships, class and race, culture and history complicate matters (50). "[Women] cannot afford to see themselves as 'victims' because their survival depends on continued exercise of whatever personal powers they possess ... They bond with other women on the basis of shared strengths and resources" (46). In *North of 60* Sarah, the white nurse, refuses to see those complications on several occasions; Michelle, the Dene Mountie, does see them. Yet the two women remain good friends. Although they come from what hooks (and Canadians as well) would see as different classes, Sarah (parents upper-middle class) and Michelle (parents subsistence trappers) are both "professionals." Sarah is a nurse, a traditional occupation but a pattern she has reworked by coming to an isolated post in the far north and then staying there. But Michelle is that rarity in the early 1990s, a female RCMP constable. She represents order and white law but occasionally interprets that law in the light of her own cultural traditions. She also defends her culture to the outside world. These women occupy powerful but contingent roles in the community. It is also worth noting that Rosie, the waitress in the coffee shop, and Michelle both move up the ladder, Rosie to owning half of the motel/store/coffee shop, Michelle to a promotion as corporal. All three women basically find satisfaction in their work – and their responsibilities at work. All three are shown to be creative and essential to their community as hooks would define it (103).

On issues of power, hooks (2000) is refreshing. She points out that the title of "life-affirming nurturer" is often a sentimentalized way for society to deflect women's demands for real power (91). There is no role model of a successful male parent in Lynx River except for Leon after he stops drinking. Peter is too driven to parent his children successfully, Albert has his own demons, Nathan is unreliable, and Teevee is too immature. hooks points out that in the United States single mothers are pathologized (xvi), but this is certainly not the case in Lynx River, where single mothers, including Michelle, appear to be the norm. On the other hand, hooks's rejection of victimhood finds a clear analogy in both series. None of the Dene characters in Lynx River are perpetually sorry for themselves for being born Dene, with the exception of Teevee, who eventually grows out of it. They are proud of it, as the abusive nun from the residential school discovers in the first season. The characters on *The Rez* do not see themselves as victims either. Sadie actively works to change things on the reserve, while Silas becomes the keeper of traditional stories as well as the recorder of its contemporary life.

## THE IMPORTANCE OF STORIES

The following words, by Larry Hill (Seneca), were quoted on a banner in the Museum of Civilization in the "First People's Hall," in August 2003: "Our stories were us, what we knew, where we came from and where we were going. They were told to remind us of our responsibility, to instruct and to entertain. There were stories of the Creation, our travels, our laws. There were legends of hard-fought battles, funny anecdotes – some from the smokehouse, some from the trickster – and there were scary stories to remind us of danger, spiritual and otherwise. Stories were our life and they still are."[25]

There is an apparent disconnect between the oral culture of the First Nations and stories told on television. In 1975 seminal cultural theorist Raymond Williams identified television as the storyteller in the corner that through the flow of action, representation, and performance had made drama a habitual experience that elevated looking at nightly stories to the level of basic need. Television series are connected stories with running characters, a structure that has its roots in oral cultures worldwide. They have also been vital to the economic health of television since its inception. In fact, a web of stories, on a frame of a few genres, has supported television (and radio before it) since broadcasting was invented. For the most part in North America, series television has sold cars and ideologies, but it has also helped to shape the social agenda and bring the news to life while regularly providing the comforts of closure. Usually, not always, series have also presented a commonly held set of values.

First Nations stories and songs are traditional, yet they are inevitably altered in transmission over many generations.[26] New stories and songs are gradually added to the cultural store. In some cultures, such as the Kwakiutl, possession of the right to sing certain traditional songs signifies an individual's standing in the First Nation. These songs and dances are possessed/danced/sung only by those who have inherited, earned, or bought a right to them. In others cultures, stories are more widely known and circulated. They are retold in relationship to the circumstances of their telling, and those who listen are expected to remember and use them or retell them when their meanings will help or guide the listener. This may well be in different circumstances, often years later when the listener's understanding has changed – an analogy to what professors of dramatic literature expect will happen to their students when they recall *King Lear* or *The Oresteia* thirty years after having read it. Stories told in families around the world are reshaped and retold to match different circumstances and understandings. Whether within families or more formal institutions of learning, it is a human activity to pack the bags of the young for their lifetimes, not just for the next month or the next exam.

Julie Cruikshank's influential book *The Social Life of Stories: Narrative and Knowledge in the Yukon Territory* (1998) is, among other things, about how stories work in the lives of her informants and others: "If postmodern analyses attribute fragmentation to late twentieth-century uncertainties, Yukon storytellers have long experienced such fragmentation as springing from the structure of colonial practices that took root more than a century ago ... [This book shows] ways that narrative storytelling can construct meaningful bridges in disruptive situations. When potential for division emerges, successful resolution often involves demonstrating how a story can reframe issues by providing a larger context" (3–4). She goes on to show how her questions as an anthropologist were continually answered indirectly by stories, not facts, sometimes retold until the teller thought she understood them. She shows how such stories relate to land claims; to moiety, family, clan, and nation; to the history and sense of the future; to the seamless relationship of each natural element to the other; to relationships to the outside world. The wording is important. In the tradition she studies, accuracy matters more than translation. She then points out that knowing how to *use* the stories is part of what makes people recognize a person as an elder (13, 17).

The introduction to *In the Words of the Elders: Aboriginal Cultures in Transition*[27] (Kulchyski et al. 1999) points out that teachings are usually earned. They do not come pre-packaged for students or anthropologists, but in specific contexts of ceremonies, events, or "time spent with an individual at a particular time in his or her development … often very personal and intuitive in addition to ideas that address the intellect … Humour is usually central to the teaching style of the elder" (xv).[28] Episodes in *Spirit Bay, North of 60,* and *The Rez* all raise questions about the proper use of stories.[29]

Cruikshank (1998) cites two papers by Scott Rushforth in the *American Ethnologist*[30] to support her conclusion that "Dene hunters [like other] indigenous people repeatedly assert the authority of their own local knowledge and reject the validity of those expert systems, which they see as derived from second-hand information rather than from direct experience" (136). Cruikshank also discusses the many different levels of understanding in some audiences and the multiple ways facts can be framed by the narratives that the elders create. The context of a storytelling festival in Whitehorse guarantees diversity: members of the audience who are unfamiliar with the story may simply be entertained; others may be provoked into thought; members of the elders' own communities will know the stories and be sensitive to nuance or get the humour that the audience at large may miss (144, 158). These different modes of reception are reflected to some degree in APTN television audiences. Even a "product" of a mainstream broadcasting system like *North of 60* can produce a meta-narrative. As Cruikshank repeatedly points out, literal interpretations of stories are too narrow. For both teller and listener, they are "stor[ies] that they can think with, if they chose to do so" (39). Learn what the story says and then what the story can do (41).

Stories are also embodied in objects, not only masks and ceremonial objects but also spoons, dishes, knives. Spirit power, sometimes manifest in dreams, can come from any part of the Dene world, from a rock to a rainbow. An implied back story about Albert's hunting knife appears in the made-for-television *Dream Storm* (2001). Although the subtext suggests that Elsie knows the story, she does not tell it. When the children in Lynx River fall sick, Michelle and Teevee have fragmented waking visions. The story and the meaning they seek to understand are first presented to each of them in cascades of images and sounds. In two different ways Michelle and Teevee seek the story's direction for what they or the community need to do. They do not piece together a conventional narrative, but rather achieve an experience that both of them eventually share, mingling with their ancestors of centuries ago as they go about their work while the children play. From this but particularly from Michelle's encounters with Albert's spirit, which acts as her guide and is not part of Teevee's experience (he uses a sweat lodge to enter the spirit world), they bring back the knowledge of why the children are sick – and the children start to recover. The use of Albert, Michelle's antagonist for the whole series, adds a rich dimension to the story, one that is understood only by Michelle and the viewers.

In *Playing Indian*, Philip J. Deloria (1998) provides a wide-ranging history of Indianness being performed as an identity – from the men who dressed like Indians in the Boston Tea Party during the American Revolution to the contemporary New Age wannabes. (Deloria's father, Vine Deloria, wrote *Custer Died for Your Sins*. His grandfather was Yankton Dakota.) In his introduction, Deloria writes: "It would be folly to imagine that white Americans blissfully used Indianness to tangle with their ideological dilemmas while native people stood idly by, exerting no influence over the resulting Indian images. Throughout a long history of Indian play, native people have been present at the margins, insinuating their way into Euro-American discourse, often attempting to nudge notions of Indianness in directions they found useful ... assisting, confirming, co-opting, challenging and legitimating the performative tradition of aboriginal American identity" (8). In many interviews over the years, the actors in *North of 60* have talked about their influence on the producers and the scripts and about their own interpretations of the characters they play. Deloria concludes his book with this paradox: "The self-defining pairing of American truth with American freedom rests on the ability to wield power against Indians ... while simultaneously drawing power from them ... And so while Indian people have lived out a collection of historical nightmares in the material world, they have also haunted a long night of American dreams. As many native people have observed, to be American is to be unfinished, and although that state is powerful and creative, it carries with it nightmares all its own" (191). As audiences, Canadians have consumed that American dream, only to find out that Canada is not Deloria's United States. Canada's search for a national identity is quite different. Its relationships with its First Nations and Metis are also different, as is the broadcasting system. Thus it is reasonable to expect that the representation of these peoples will also differ significantly. Michael Ames raises an interesting question in *Cannibal Tours and Glass Boxes: The Anthropology of Museums* (1992): "We adopt the Indians as our ancestors. Now that they are reclaiming their history, where will that leave us?" (87).[31] According to Trinh Minh-ha (1989), the cloak of fiction, which must also give shape to some kind of emotional if not 'factual' truth if the drama is to work, is even more selective about what is presented to the viewer than any anthropology paper on identity construction – and most of the audience understand that they are watching fiction doing its selective work, seeking coherence as it presents something new or deepens or alters existing understanding. The "North" of television fiction is not anyone's "real north" often signified by an Indian somewhere in the story, but it does reveal aspects of the "norths" where Canadians live and work and something about the First Nations peoples who live there.

I close this chapter with a cautionary note about stories from someone who has written books, articles, and plays from the left for forty years, Rick Salutin (2006): "One wants to politicize the genuinely political, insist on it, where that quality has been concealed. But that doesn't mean everything is political. It means lots of things are … The notion that everything is political … is reductive and formulaic."[32] And a reading of the programs discussed in this book that was primarily political – looking only for gender, identity, nationality – would be one that oversimplified the many narratives, characters, and personalities behind and on he screen, and among those who watch.

# THREE

# "The North is where?"

As the last chapter demonstrated, however politically fraught the quest or contingent the result, the search for identity goes on within and among ethnicity, gender, race, class, and level of education, all the familiar demographic subsets and many others. But one of the important contributors to identity for most people is place. "Where are you from?" is the usual question when strangers meet abroad. The replies range from – "No kidding! I live down the road," to "No, I don't know your aunt in Calgary. Winnipeg is not that close and both are big cities."

Cities are where the majority of Canadians come from, not small towns or rural areas or the boreal forests. Despite or perhaps because of this, most of us feel an ancient and compelling longing for a golden age or green world. This longing first appears in European culture in the "pastoral" forms of sixth-century BCE Greek literature, later in Sydney's Arcadia and the transformative "green world" of Arden in *As You Like It*, and now in some forms of the Hollywood and television Western. The Quebecois variant is found in the freedom of the wilderness represented by the coureurs de bois – hence *Radisson* and other series. Anglophone Canada is much less sanguine about its early history, preferring the nostalgic pastoral settings of the later nineteenth century like the settled farms and villages in *A Gift to Last* and *Road to Avonlea*. In episodes of every series in this book, set in someone's idea of the North, the viewers can find an escape from their own place. The secret coves and rugged shoreline of the northwest coast of *The Beachcombers* or the rocks and lakes of the Canadian Shield in *Spirit Bay* and *The Rez* pull the audience into a greener, more adventurous, slightly exotic landscape. Although the viewers may never have fished the coastal waters of the Pacific or experienced the sudden storms of Lake Nipigon or the icy waters of Lynx River, they can claim them as places in Canada, even as places to visit. *The Rez* is set around a marina, a place tourists regularly visit, and tourists turn up in the locations of both *The Beachcombers* and *Spirit Bay*.

The urban audience sees these places both as accessible escapes, portraying parts of Canada they can visit in safety for a little while, and as places that offer a compelling glimpse of very different lives, where when a boat springs a leak in a remote inlet or a school bus goes off the road in a blizzard, the land itself is hostile. In an early episode of *The Beachcombers*, "The Sea Is Our Friend," Nick, who believes the truth of the title, is trapped under a log in a rising tide, about to drown. Young Hughie devises a way for him to breathe, and the sea lifts the log, a very neat analogy to the paradoxes presented by the wilderness in these series. It is a Canadian cliché that even the majority huddling along our southern borders treasure the endless space to the north at our backs, not just as people trapped in Frye's fortress – that too, of course – but as people metaphorically at least free to travel north until we hit the Arctic Ocean or Hudson Bay. I would argue that we do not – cannot – see these series the way the Europeans, Asians, Africans, and even Australians later saw them, because the near or far north, belongs to us.

## NORTH OF WHAT? NORTH OF WHOM?

Where is "North"? North of what? North of whom? Every one of these series is set in the North, but they each inhabit a very different geographical space. Definitions of the North, are usually created by people who are not native to the North. Louis-Edmond Hamelin, in "An Attempt to Regionalize the Canadian North" (2003), writes that one can conceive the North as a continuation of the South for exploitation purposes or think of the hundreds of scattered hamlets out of touch by rail or road as "forming as many miniscule independent regions" (8). His map of the North is divided into (*a*) the southern base, which includes Vancouver and the Sunshine Coast (*The Beachcombers*, but also *The Rez*); (*b*) the Near North (*Spirit Bay*); (*c*) the Middle North, where *North of 60* is located and which has no regular communications running east/west; (*d*) the High North, which includes most of the inhabited Arctic; and (*e*) the Far North as defined by Greenland and Ellesmere Island.

In her introduction to *Un/covering the North: News, Media and Aboriginal People*, Valerie Alia (1999) writes: "I often call the North a huge small town. Despite the enormous distances, people know each other" (3). (Soaps and sitcoms, genres that provide elements in several of the series under discussion, depend on the fact that people know each other's background, relationships, job, health, happenings – and the place where they live.) Her map of "nordicity zones" (5) differentiates between the Near North, the Middle North, and the Extreme North well above Baffin Island. All of Southern Ontario and the Sunshine Coast of British Columbia are excluded from Alia's map. But in Canadian usage, "up north" is an all-purpose phrase defined by context. "Up north" is where our cottage is – two hundred kilometres from St Catharines, a city in Canada's "banana belt," south of almost everywhere in Canada, but colder than Vancouver, which is much farther north in latitude. Moreover, any Canadian who travels beyond city streets in winter with a candle, thermal blanket, shovel, and chocolate in the car acknowledges a fact of life in this country – winter whiteouts happen everywhere and they can kill you.

W.L. Morton, in "The North in Canadian History" (2003), argues convincingly that Canada is not a "United States that failed to come off ... [It is] a northern country, with a northern economy, a northern way of life and a northern destiny" (158), where Scots and Icelanders have also played an important part. Renée Hulan, writing on the "northern imaginary" in *Northern Experience and the Myths of Canadian Culture* (2002), quotes Rob Shields, who describes the "representation of the north as a constant tension of 'imaginary North' and 'ideological North'" (5).[1] The imaginary North is a blank slate or the last frontier, and the ideological North is connected to Canadianness and difference from urban life. The Canadian wilderness can demonstrably kill you: you can die by storm at sea or by getting lost in the coastal rainforest (*The Beachcombers*), by sudden storms on the lake (*Spirit Bay*), by exile to a deserted island on the Shield in late fall (*The Rez*), or by getting lost "out on the land," especially in the longer, more severe winters of Lynx River. Jesse Jim in *The Beachcombers* is at ease in boats, swims like a fish, and lives off the land, making use of logs that have broken loose from log booms. The adults who live in Spirit Bay are comfortable with the wilderness, and like them, some of the children also know how to build a snow cave to survive in a blizzard. On the other hand, the young adults on the Rez never really connect to their land, even as landscape. The roads out are good, the boats simply a means of transportation. They do not hunt or willingly camp out. In the episode "Windigo," the bush is portrayed as actively hostile. Silas does not enjoy sleeping out on an island with his exiled father, or in a lean-to with Frank, while the German tourists sleep in their large and comfortable, if misplaced, Plains Indian–style wigwam. Unlike the alienated teenager Teevee in *North of 60,* these young adults never come to terms with the place where they live. In *North of 60,* time out on the land is essential for Michelle, Teevee survives in a snow house, Joe nearly dies of an injury in the bush – only his considerable skills save him – and two years alone in the bush drives the white Mountie Brian Fletcher crazy.

The blizzard of '77 blew four inches of snow off the entire length of flash-frozen Lake Erie and on to the southern and eastern parts of the Niagara Peninsula. Winds of hurricane force kept everyone inside for three days. Snow buried cars and houses, villages and parts of cities, in some places up to the top of the telephone poles.[2] In Quebec it was an ice storm that knocked out electrical power for weeks. Such events are assumed to be once-in-a-century storms, but the threat of our inevitable cold weather is real for every Canadian. The lore of the cold and our pride in toughing it out permeate our popular culture. Of course, everywhere in Canada, even Point Pelee, is perceived to be the North to most other people in this hemisphere. Canadians reinforce the impression every time we sing "true north, strong and free" at sports events south of the border. And to other viewers in other countries, it is that hint of danger sensed in the northern wilderness – not only its beauty – that helps to sell these television series abroad.

Unlike the other series in this discussion, *North of 60* is set in the remote hinterland. It is abundant with wildlife who give themselves to First Nations people, making up part of the staple diet, and most of the residents can hunt and fish successfully. The northern lights, seen during the credits at the top of every show, are commonplace in winter. The title of episode 79 is simply "Cold." Other than a few hunters, the tourists who visit the locations for *The Rez* and *Spirit Bay* do not visit this far north. Yet this version of the North is the one that people both inside the country and abroad are most likely to imagine as "the true north." Even so, at least some Canadians do not conflate the Arctic, the tundra, and the boreal forest any more than they confuse the Inuit with their neighbours (and historically their enemies), the Dene, or the Northern Cree. In some ways, over the decades Canadian series television has reprised what Amelia Kalant, in *National Identity and the Conflict at Oka* (2004), notes as a cultural trend: "Moving 'the north' northward has continued throughout the 20th century, as writers and others go on a quest to find the 'real' Canada" (75).

Renée Hulan (2002) also points out that, in literature, protagonists go north "to escape, to prove something, to learn something and usually to leave again" (15). But in *North of 60* the major characters from the South,

Sarah the nurse and Harris the band manager, who came for all those reasons, to their own surprise choose not to leave. The series also makes an ironic point in that Harper, the urban Indian RCMP constable who partners Michelle in the last two seasons, cannot wait to get back to southern Canada. There is a hierarchy, of course, as she points out: "experience as" a northerner (the majority in this category belong to the First Nations) is more useful and more respected than "experience in" the North (mostly associated with whites), which in turn is more credible than passing through the North as a hunter, tourist, government employee, and such (15). All of the series that are set in modern times demonstrate that hierarchy.

However, Hulan (2002) argues that spatializing the difference in the distinction between the "inside" and "outside," or north and south, is to suggest that the boundary between them can be crossed: "Because the geographical boundaries can be crossed whereas the boundaries between cultures and identities are not so well defined, reimagining difference in terms of geography may even be nostalgia for the separate stable cultures of the ethnographic past." She concludes that "the idea of Canada as a northern nation is one of these representations [created in the interest of maintaining power], a myth that seems to transcend local and individual identities and unify Canadians" (187), even as they constrain or erase differences between other groups defined by geography or ethnicity. But in a country whose television drama habitually demythologizes not only its history but also its contemporary stories, the North does not really work as a myth to unify Canada. *Radisson*, made in the mid-1950s, was the only series that was a self-consciously nationalist project – with mixed results.

In her introduction to *Staging the North: Twelve Canadian Plays* (1999), Sherrill Grace agrees with Hulan.[3] After listing beer ads, Inuit sculpture, and books, poems, and paintings, she argues that "these icons of cultural identity, using powerful images of a deeply felt nordicity, contribute directly to the construction of what it means to be Canadian. They function as patriotic reminders to Canadians who have been here for generations and they train newer Canadians to recognise where they are ... What is sometimes forgotten is that they are *representations* of North and they do crucial ideological work" (xi). She goes on: "For many southern Canadians, North has come to signify a place of adventure, and of physical and moral challenge" (xi).

In her full-length study of "nordicity," *Canada and the Idea of North* (2001), Grace presents the North of the historiographers, geographers, and sociologists, acknowledging – as W.L. Morton had forty years before in *The Canadian Identity* (1961) – that the North also connotes freezing emptiness, arctic void, silent space – "the very palpable signs of northern difference waiting to be invoked, storied, told, heard, and *listened to* by all Canadians" (63). Although she analyses plays, documentaries, and fictional films made in Canada, her sole reference to television is in a paragraph that first mentions Nell Shipman's early Canadian film, *Back to God's Country* (1919), then other films, then the CBC television series *RCMP*, and finally what she calls "a highly successful run on CBC television of *North of 60*" (142). Grace considers these stories valuable primarily for what they can tell "southern Euro-Canadians" about how they are perceived through other eyes (229). But she also points out that the Dene can tell people south of 60 how in the Deh Cho "Yamoria brought law and order to Denendah ages before the RCMP arrived in the North West Territories" (230).

The television series considered in this study do raise some of Grace's (2001) questions: "[I]s it [the North] hostile or friendly, barren or fruitful, an Eldorado or a deadly trap? Is it *here*, all around us, or in North of 60, north of the tree-line and the permafrost? … is it the quintessential place of unspoiled wilderness adventure or is it home? Well, it depends. North is both/and, not either/or" (75). And later she says that the North has symbolized "future hopes for purity, freedom, adventure, wealth, fame, and regional and national identity" (267). In recent television series, the hunt for those values through representations of the North has been subverted: for example, in *The Rez* Lucy sees southern Canada as the home of freedom, wealth, and fame and imagines that there she might be a pop singer. In one of many ironies in *North of 60*, the Vancouver Coast Salish street kid, Nevada, comes north seeking purity, escape, healing (at least for his spirit – he has AIDS), but as a stranger cannot find it. He is asked to leave by one of the elders.

## THE BROADCASTING CONTEXT IN THE NORTH

In "First People's Television in Canada's North: A Case Study of the Aboriginal Peoples Television Network" (2002, 295–310), Lorna Roth gives a short coherent account of the complicated evolution of broadcasting in the North. TVNC (Television Northern Canada) began to evolve into APTN almost immediately, first through discussions of its board and then with the CRTC, which granted it mandatory coverage on basic cable. Cable operators resisted both the order to carry it and the fifteen cents a month to be collected from subscribers, then tried to bury it in the upper reaches of the dial. Nevertheless, APTN was launched on 1 September 1999. Since then, as a specialty channel, it has struggled for ad revenue, for promotion, and for attention. Yet, as the *Globe and Mail* said in an editorial quoted by Roth, "Just to be seen on TV makes people genuine ... this is the psychological underpinning for the CRTC's recent decision ... [First Peoples'] relationship to other Canadians isn't tangential, it is inevitable," what she calls an "opportunity to share imagery and histories" (307). In *Something New in the Air: The Story of First Peoples Television Broadcasting in Canada* (2005),[4] based in part on longitudinal and reception studies she did for APTN, Roth elaborates throughout on many of the myths of nordicity and gives a more detailed account of the history as well as an analysis of what needs to be done to further strengthen northern broadcasting.[5]

APTN's arrival in 2000 changed the picture. Speaking from the inside, Kenneth Deer (1999) discusses some of the issues raised by the decision to license APTN. In "The Aboriginal Peoples Television Network: Pro and Contra," an article in the native newspaper the *Eastern Door*,[6] he writes:

My concern is, if we have our own cable channel, will there be less energy in the mainstream media to produce movies or a television series about us? Are the producers and media moguls going to decide that a good script about native people should be sent to the Aboriginal Network where "they" can do their own thing? Is it the end of shows like *North of 60* in the mainstream media? This is a real danger. The audience for *North of 60* is much larger and more varied than that of any series on APTN. If we are to educate the general public about ourselves, we have to do it in the mainstream media. APTN will attract its viewers mostly from native people. There is nothing wrong with that except that our message will be to the converted and not the ignorant. We still need good movies and television shows about us in the mainstream; we can't allow the creation of APTN to be used as an excuse for other networks not to produce good shows about native people. Another danger is the loss of native people who are already in the mainstream media to be diverted to APTN. There are not enough native people in mainstream media as it is ...

This is not an attack on APTN. APTN is a positive development and an exciting opportunity for our people. This newspaper will support it any way we can. We are just advising caution about the negative impact it could have. The solution, of course, is up to ourselves. The media is a new field for most of us. Our people who are looking for a career should take a hard look at the opportunities in this area. If enough of us get involved, then we can have enough personnel to stock APTN and the mainstream media as well.

There is no direct evidence of the effects, good or bad, of APTN – it is far too soon.

Doris Baltruschat, in "Television and Canada's Aboriginal Communities" (2004),[7] cites her 2003 interview with Barbara Cranmer (Kwakiutl): "'I see myself as a messenger of stories people entrust me with'" (53). Cranmer expresses concern about the potential "'exoticization' of First Nations life in mainstream media. This may even arise from young First Nations filmmakers who seek to adapt and popularize indigenous histories and cultural values for sensationalist mainstream consumption" (53). Baltruschat comments on the emphasis APTN puts on the youth audience as both the growing demographic and the target audience, suggesting that this may explain why the first co-production efforts that use expensive mainstream dramatic forms have been the 2004–05 young teens series *renegade.com*, about an e'zine edited by an aboriginal boy and a Euro-Canadian girl (2004–present), and the 2003–05 series *Moccasin Flats*, a very gritty look at life lived by older teens in Winnipeg's North End, written and produced by Big Soul Productions, which is owned by two First Nations women. Both series concentrate on characters who live off-reserve. From my outsider's perspective, neither one makes the problems and rewards of urban aboriginal life seem exotic or the subject of fantasy. In the case of *Moccasin Flats*, the fragmented MTV shooting style does create what Baltruschat, using the spatial metaphor often used in this kind of discourse, calls "a hybrid experience where *globalization* and *localization* are negotiated for new territories of cultural expression" (57).

Baltruschat (2004) also gives a good summary of the history of APTN and its predecessors[7] and points to Telefilm annual reports that document an increasing number of First Nations producers of documentaries and television programs (48–51). Her figures for APTN up to 2004 show that 70 per cent of its programs originated in Canada: English-language shows make up is 60 per cent, French 15 percent, and aboriginal languages 25 per cent. As in the examples above, she discusses the trends towards interprovincial and international co-productions. She quotes Jim Compton, a senior executive at APTN, as being unsure how many First Nations people are watching because of "lack of access to broadcasting signals in First Nations communities" and lack of information about how many own television sets and how many actually watch (55). She says that APTN has been good for aboriginal producers, although even this is controversial because some southern and Metis producers have felt excluded. Although APTN has only been on air for seven years, it has already gone through one major financial crisis, in 2004. But it is fair to say, as Baltruschat does, that "APTN is a unique network that combines alternative programming and mainstream broadcasting styles in a blend that does not exist anywhere else" (57).[8]

On 31 August 2005, APTN's licence was renewed by the CRTC.[9] The network was also given an increase in subscribers' rates, giving it $10–$12 million in additional revenue. In return, it is improving access by doing an Eastern and Western feed (the station is homed in Winnipeg), giving both halves of the country a chance to see its programs in prime time. A condition of its license was a change in its governance such that the board – and therefore the programming at APTN – would not be dominated by representatives from Inuktitut-language programmers and other northern organizations.

## NORTH (AND SOUTH) TELEVISION DRAMA MATTERS

Amid the welter of reports and learned articles and books, it is easy to lose track of the vital importance of dramatic programming itself. Trina McQueen, formerly a vice-president in the CBC and executive vice-president at CTV, was commissioned by the CRTC and Telefilm in May 2003 to undertake a study of Canadian English-language drama. In her introduction to the resulting report, *Dramatic Choices*,[10] she reminds the regulators, financiers, policy makers, and members of government who will read her report of television drama's history and importance:

Drama has never had a golden age, an easy time, a rosy past. Since production started in 1952, there has been only one weather report for drama: continuing cloudy, threats of a storm, some sunny breaks. This report must focus on the clouds and the threats of a storm: threats that are particularly ominous today. Our drama has filled every role that can be asked of a nation's story telling. It has created memorable characters … It has imagined our history with care … It has taken us to the heart of our country's darkness … It has inspired us, saddened us and delighted us with stories of our own heroes and villains … It has invented communities where all human passions played for us each week … There is an honorable tradition of success in drama, although it rests on very many fewer works than in most other countries. There is a clear voice, though it speaks more softly and not as often as in most other countries. There is no failure in our drama that relates to some inherent national inability. But we have asked of our artists that they overcome, not only the immense difficulties of their own profession, but also all the accidents of geography, technology and economics that stand between them and their audiences.

There has been no perceptible response to this report or to the others commissioned around the same time. And yet another was commissioned in the late fall of 2005.

Without intending to, I often find myself writing articles and books about Canadian television during the storms, not the sunny breaks. In 2005–07 it has happened again. In general, production of Canadian television drama is down significantly. Mainstream dramas featuring First Nations people, and even more so indigenous TV drama, is in dire straights in Canada, with little relief in sight. We may live in a multi-layered North, all of it north of our great neighbour to the south, much of it exotic wilderness to the rest of the world, but very little of the series television in prime time on our major networks, CBC, CTV, and Global, reflects our complexities, and none in the last ten years have shown the adult audiences in the rest of anglophone Canada the urban First Nations, the reserves, or the northern First Nations. Yet the reliable audience numbers of North of 60 (1992–97) and the audiences that stayed with those characters through five television movies (1999–2005) suggest that there is a deep interest in First Nations subjects and characters. It is over due time for another sunny break.

PART TWO

# Series for Children, Families, and Youth

# FOUR

# Background: From Pageant to Prime Time

Twenty-five years before television's 1952 debut in Canada, during the early days of radio and silent movies, people still organized all kinds of fundraisers – elaborate garden parties with singers and a highland fling or two, school concerts, minstrel shows, and one-act plays – for local charities, churches, and more general causes, to entertain themselves and their neighbours. On a few very special occasions, such as the sixtieth anniversary of Confederation, a town committee would hire someone to write and direct a pageant. The Canadian makers of *Radisson, Hudson's Bay, Forest Rangers,* and *Adventures in Rainbow Country* (1957–71) would have seen such representations and could well have read some of the material discussed below in school or at home, as would the adults in their audiences. Not only Hollywood stereotypes but also school readers, popular novels, and children's stories would have shaped their ideas about who and what Indians were.[1] What follows is a snapshot from the 1920s, an account of one such effort that reflected the assumptions of its makers and it audience about Canada, about Indians, and about their own place as the descendants of settlers in the story of the country. This account is based on a few pictures in an album, a conversation with an elderly friend, and a program.

According to the founding story of the town of Durham, Ontario, the first settler, Archibald Hunter, crossed the Saugeen River with two others and found "a deserted Indian wigwam near where the Anglican church now stands. Here they passed the night."[2] "CONFEDERATION: An Indian Pipe Dream" is the allegorical and rather arch title of a pageant staged in Durham in 1927. "Mrs. (Dr.) Farewell, Compiler and Directress" staged it "in the skating rink [indoor arena] for Canada's Diamond Jubilee Wedding:

commemorating the 60th anniversary of [Canada's] marriage to 'Prosperity,' Tuesday, June 28, 1927." As young teens, my mother Elizabeth, her sister Jean, and their friends, as well as most of my grandparents' friends and acquaintances, took part. The cast numbered over seventy-five, not counting the massed schools who sang between each scene.

The synopsis of the scenes presented below and the quotations from various authors that serve as epigraphs in the program, as well as other details, were selected and directly transcribed from the program.

PROLOGUE

"Thank God for pluck unknown to slaves / The self ne'er of itself bereft / Who, when the right arm's shattered, waves/ The good flag with the left – Ethelwyn Wetherald

Dame Canada holding sceptre of power. Gen. Wolfe and Marquis du Montcalm with crossed swords upholding the flags of their two then contending races, England and France. Canada's two Gracchi,[3] Lord Durham and Lord Elgin. Hope and Faith holding the door of entrance into "The land that flows with milk and honey" – admits emigrants [sic] of all nations.

The land where the U.E. Loyalists found peace and plenty under the "Grand Old Flag."

Canada, holding the "Lamp of Remembrance" lighted by her "Gracchi," passing on that light of Hope and Faith to her newfound children.

"Lord God of hosts be with us yet /Lest we forget / lest we forget." – Rudyard Kipling

FIRST SCENE – "DAWN"

"Rise lovely goddess of the Dawn / And open the gate with rosy fingers." – Homer

Canada as a little child dancing with the "Mound Builders,"[4] ending with Childland's "battle of the roses." The Esquimaux, the Red Man and his almost extermination. Triumphal entry of Provinces into the Dominion, led there by the Fathers of Confederation.

The child Canada taken from the Red Man [represented by an "Indian Pipe dreamer," an "Indian Princess,"· an "Indian Chief," "Ojistoh" [female], eight "Indian boys," four "Esquimaux" and eleven female "mound builders" [of various ages] by the Provinces [all women] and the Fathers of Confederation, offering her the bounty of the land and decking her in womanhood's attire: [she] is enthroned "Dominion of Canada," while winged messengers, Boy Scouts and Sailors lay at her feet the fruit of the people's brains – Railways, Airplanes, Ships of the Air, Ships of the Ocean, Telephone, Radio, Telegraph, Hydro Electric etc. Canada now receives the "great Charter" ratified by Queen Victoria, "the good" [who is also on stage with a "hindu attendant"].

[The scene ends in the program, and probably on the stage as well, with a verse:] "We first saw light in Canada, the Land beloved of God, / We are the pulse of Canada, its marrow and its blood" – Pauline Johnston [a quote from the famous "Mohawk Princess" and poet that wholly subsumes her into the triumphalist narrative].

THE SECOND SCENE – RIDEAU HALL, OTTAWA

[This scene reimagines the state reception for celebrities at Rideau Hall.]

THIRD SCENE – RURAL CANADA

[The pageant ends with a sentimentalized representation of the pioneer days, which some in that audience could still clearly remember, including songs and recitations by Canadian authors, e.g., "The Old Oaken Bucket." The Grand Finale began with an "old time dance" that was followed by a verse by William Henry Drummond, writing in faux Quebec dialect. The title of the "Final Tableau" asserted Canada's place in the British Empire – "Canada the Gem in the Crown." The program tells its audience that in the finale the "(e)ntire cast (is) showered with maple leaves." The pageant ends with a "grand march of all of the Schools of South East Grey" and a round of "Land of Hope and Glory," presumably sung by the cast and the audience.][5]

Written by a woman educated in the Victorian era, this remarkable pastiche of the Roman and British empires, nationalism and imperialism, celebration and commemoration, was staged on one occasion only, for the town, by the town, using handmade costumes of cotton, muslin, cheese

cloth, cotton batten, and paper.[6] Thus, the town, from the leading nota-
bles to the smallest children, reproduced for itself widely shared nationalist myths about the formation and maturation of Canada. Although in
1927 there were still Saugeen Indians selling baskets and twig furniture to
the townspeople of Durham, in the pageant, Indians were acknowledged,
romanticized, superseded, subsumed, and then they vanished – and it is
unlikely that anyone on that stage or in the audience saw the inherent
contradictions.[7]

Two other comments. There have been many occasions – right up to the
present – when Canadian television producers and writers and directors,
as well as makers of TV commercials, have stereotyped or subsumed aboriginal people. However, it is also true that, like my family in later years,
like other Canadians, some of the tellers of those stories on television
learned to do better. Secondly, Gary Farmer, the well-known Mohawk ac-
tor/writer/filmmaker, during a talk at Brock University referred ironically
to the decades-old tradition of an outdoor presentation of a Six Nations
pageant at his home, the Six Nations Grand River (Ohswekan) reserve in
southwestern Ontario. As he saw it, two hundred years after they settled
on that land as United Empire Loyalists, his people still have to put on a
"public face" to signify "that all is well."[8]

## "HISTORY" IN CHILDREN'S FICTION
## AND SCHOOL TEXTS, 1868–1952

What books were available into the 1950s to the early makers of CBC TV
drama and their audiences? Before writing this chapter, I took a look
around my own house to find the books that an average, middle-class, non-
academic household might have owned in this period. In this accumulation
of the books of four households over five generations can be traced the evolution of the representation of First Nations peoples in books for children,
school texts, and popular novels for adults. A contemporary child visiting
us could still read them, of course, but now she would have access to all
kinds of films, videos, and books with a more modern point of view to balance the pictures written and painted in these older materials. The collection ranges from *The Fifth Reader* in the Canadian Series of School Books
authorized by the Council of Public Instruction for Ontario (according to its
embossed cover, 1868)[9] to popular novels like *Glengarry Schooldays: Early
Days in Glengarry* (1902) and *Corporal Cameron of the North West Mounted
Police* (1912) by the Canadian novelist and Presbyterian minister Charles

Gordon (pen name Ralph Connor).[10] There is also Laura Lee Hope's *The Bobbsey Twins in the Great West* (1920), written for children. It is interesting that materials like these were reprinted even after the CBC's 1960s children's series *The Forest Rangers*, briefly discussed in chapter 6, was broadcast. In fact, some accounts of "Indians" written in the early 1930s found their way back into print in 1967, when early Canadian books were reprinted in inexpensive editions. The reprint of *The Queen's Bush: A Tale of the Early Days of Bruce County* (1932)[11] is a durable hard-bound book.

The following dialogue from the unrevised version of Laura Lee Hope's *The Bobbsey Twins in the Great West* (1920) gives a flavour of the ambiguities and outright racism of some materials; it had its copyright renewed in 1948 (a few years before *Radisson* was planned).[12]

> "And can I get an Indian Doll?" asked Nan.
> "Well, there are a few Indians around here," the foreman said slowly. "They come to the ranch now and then to get something to eat, or trade a pony. I don't know that I've ever seen any of 'em with a doll, though maybe they do have some."
> "Will any Indians come soon?" Nan wanted to know.
> "I hope they do – real wild ones!" cried Bert [her twin].
> "We don't have that here," said the foreman. "All the Indians around here are tame. And I can't say when they will come." (195)

Later, the foreman says that Indians have taken some steers: "'The [Indians] are not the wild kind. Only now and again they run off a bunch of cattle from some herd that is far off the main ranch.'" When Mrs Bobbsey speculates that "'maybe the poor Indians were hungry,'" he replies that "'they have money and can buy what they want. I wouldn't mind giving them a beef or two, but when it comes to taking part of a herd, it must be stopped.' ... 'But let the Indians have a steer or two for food, if they need it,' begged Mrs. Bobbsey who had a kind heart even toward an Indian cattle thief or 'rustler' as they are called" (222–4). Eventually, Nan gets her Indian doll. An adult reader in the twenty-first century would note the longing of the children to see real and therefore "wild" Indians, the characterization of the Indian as a thief, the magnanimity of the white family and even the ranch foreman, as well as the commodification and infantilization of the Indian, represented as playthings for children. A child from the dominant culture reading the book in 1957, when *Radisson* was broadcast, would see none of that.

A child attending school in 1915 might have acted in a play from *Christmas Candles: Plays for Boys and Girls* by Elsie Hobart Carter, which was still in use in a one-room school in the 1930s. In "A Puritan Christmas," Patience and Prudence fear the Indians who, inevitably, talk like this: "'No hungry. Braves go hunt. [*Draws his bow*] Kill much, much, much deer. [*Spreads out his arms*] No hungry; cold. [*Folds his arms and shivers*]'" (128). The pilgrim mother replies "'Does thee think, lad, that savage as thou art, I would drive thee out into the bitter night?'"(132). Eaglefeather, in gratitude, not only defends the family and their Christmas tree from Puritan fanatics who hate Christmas, but also tells them that their kindness to him has averted a massacre. For many years, teachers on both sides of the border, responsible for the well-loved Christmas concerts in their one-room schoolhouses, found this kind of book a godsend.[13] They might also have had to teach the 1899 "abridged for the use of schools" version of Longfellow's (1899) *Hiawatha*.[14]

Three generations later, in *A Garden of Stories for Grade Two* (1939),[15] Indians make their sole appearance in Annette Wynne's "Indian Children," a poem that belongs in the all-too-common genre of eulogy to a "dying race": "Where we walk to school each day / Indian children used to play ... and the trees were very tall / And there were no streets at all / Not a church and not a steeple / Only woods and Indian people / Only wigwams on the ground / And at night bears prowling around. / What a different place today / Where we live and work and play" (209).

In 1940 Jean Harding[16] was given, as a Christmas present from another teacher, a book called *Tale of the Nativity*[17] "as told by the Indian children of Inkameep, British Columbia to Anthony Walsh, the teacher on the Inkameep Indian Reserve." Inkameep is described in the foreword as a place where "a contented band of Indians, possessed of a large number of horses, estimated at 200, and many times that number of cattle," live (5). The book was illustrated by "an older lad (Sis-hu-lk)," whose art, after being exhibited by the Royal Drawing Society in 1938, had been shown to the king and queen. The illustrations are striking. The shepherds do have a lamb, but a big-horned mountain sheep and a chipmunk look on while the family dog watches over the baby, who is tucked in a cradleboard (11). The three wise men are chiefs. The text tells us that the one from the West Coast has brought a tiny canoe that had taken a year to make, that the other two kings have brought gifts from "the people from the Pinyon Brush country [who] sent sweet smelling gum that would scent the lodge for the baby. While people from the dry south were Darkies [*sic*], and they sent a cloak from palm leaves to protect Him from the weather." The "darkie" chief rides a camel.[18] The story has real energy, thoughtful detail, and a prominent place for Joseph in the story. The last picture is of Joseph fishing in a stream that flows through pine woods, with his son, the two-year-old Jesus, clinging to the dog. There are also depictions of flowers, birds, butterflies, a birchbark basket, and the fish for supper. This nineteen-page book is miles ahead of the Bobbsey Twins, and it is the earliest in my informal sample to show direct First Nations input.

Ten years after the publication of the retold nativity story, a child in the early 1950s could read Catherine Anthony Clark's *The Golden Pine Cone* (1950) and then her *The Sun Horse* (1952), winner of the Canadian Library Association Book of the Year for Children,[19] and learn that Indians were to be respected. In Clark's books the First Peoples have their own culture and customs, heroes, villains, medicine men, warriors, excellent sewers, and brewers of medicinal plants (who still prosper in the mountains and back country of British Columbia). Such people also live in a world of magic, of spirits of ice, snow, wind, and flowers, with a cruel Thunderbird, but also a ruling spirit, the lovely and wise Tekontha. The children in the two unconnected books have a half-wolf/half-dog, a "Head Goose" (the leader of the flock), and a bat as companions – not cute little Disney creatures but carefully observed animals with their own busy lives. The books make Indians exotic yet familiar, both respected and feared. Clark drew elements from several different First Nations for her portrayal but did not perpetuate the familiar stereotypes. Both books break gender stereotypes in the actions of the boy and girl (in *The Golden Pine Cone*, a brother and sister; in *The Sun Horse*, two friends), who are equally partners and protagonists. In each book, the children are on quests that change their lives. *The Golden Pine Cone* was reprinted in the 1990s and appears on a 2000 National Library site among eight select books of fantasy for children and young adults.[20]

Two excerpts from schoolbooks also show a marked change in the depiction of First Peoples. *The Story of Canada* (published in 1927 but used for how long?) tells the student that "[w]hen the White men discovered Canada, it was the home of the Indians. But they were not the first people who lived there. Traces have been found of another race, called mound builders ... The mound builders were an intelligent and skilful race" (27). The implication, of course, is that if they were an intelligent and skilful race, they could not have been Indians.[21] There is a plate, in glorious

colour with lots of blood, titled "Daulac Strikes His Last Blow [against attacking Iroquois]" (53). The author also tells a few legends, as well as the
story of Hiawatha. In the last chapter, "The Canada of Today," the children learn that "[e]xcept in the Far North, the few that are left live on land
set apart by the Government." No pass laws are mentioned,[22] and it is
clearly assumed that Indians will disappear some day. "Some of them
farm in a small way. There are schools in the settlements and the children
are taught very much as white children are … There are churches, too,
and missionaries to preach in them. Many of the Indians belong to the
white man's church, though some still cling to their own religion." Marsh
tells the students that residential schools "in the far north" teach children
to garden so that they can feed themselves when game is scarce (256–7).
For younger readers, there was *A First Book of Canadian History* by W.
Stewart Wallace (1928),[23] which includes some of C.W. Jefferys's very well
known illustrations of Canadian history. When mound builders appear,
again the implication is that ancestors of the twentieth-century Indians –
that is, those influenced by the Hopewell and Adena cultures – could not
have built such complex earth monuments.

By 1954, there are changes in attitude in the history textbook *Canada
Then and Now*[24] by Aileen Garland (1954, reprinted with some revisions
in 1955, a year before production began on *Radisson*). It is more comprehensive, with more points of view and the sense that historians are still
making discoveries. The triumphalism is less pronounced, and the notion that the assimilation of the Indian is necessary and inevitable is less
evident. It presents a map of where various First Nations live and notes
that scholars are examining legends and sites to put together a history of
these peoples. Garland is clearly trying to offset stereotypes when she
writes: "Indian women spend their money wisely on food and clothing
for their children," using a "small amount of money from the government" (11–12). The book includes a few paragraphs on tools, weapons,
housing, and transportation, a paragraph on the "Eskimo," and, a
marked change, references to what the white men has learned from the
Indians and Eskimo. It ends with an explanation of reserves, discussions
about people off-reserve, and a note about brave native soldiers in
World War II, including a brigadier in the army and a member of the
Legislative Assembly.

Eventually, in the early 1970s (the last years of a period often carelessly
labelled "the 60s"), young teenagers who might have been watching *The
Beachcombers* were presented with a very different picture of Indians in

the textbook *Listen! Songs and Poems of Canada,* edited by Homer Hogan (1972).[25] It contains Gordon Lightfoot's *Railroad Trilogy,* which portrays pre-contact Canada this way, "Long before the white man and long before the wheel / When the green dark forest was too silent to be real" (3), as well as Charles Mair's *Tecumseh* (not identified as written as a nineteenth-century closet drama, except in the small print), which talks about "the sun burnt savage free" (6). But the anthology also contains translations of a Haida song, a Wabanaki song, "a traditional Eskimo song," songs by Willie Dunn (Mi'kmaq and Scottish), poems by Sarain Stump and Jim Dumont, Chief Dan George's "A Lament for Confederation," a poem of longing (which is not identified as written by a girl in a residential school, except in the small print of the biography), and two searching poems by high school students, "Pride" and "Of Pride and Race – Written in Anger." The editor of this collection and his high school classes are a long way from the students of *The Fifth Reader.* By the 1970s, Canada was telling its students something quite different about the indigenous aboriginal peoples who live here – and so was *The Beachcombers,* which began that year and showed them a competent and likeable Coast Salish teenager called Jesse Jim.

Change on a personal level does happen, often preceding societal change. Rewind the tape to 1957, while the second season of *Radisson* is on. In the corner of the living room of a house in a new suburb, on top of the television set, is something rarely seen in that neighbourhood – an Eskimo soapstone sculpture, a representation of a woman in a parka, feet planted squarely over a small hole in the ice through which the alert head of a seal peeks. Her skirt moves slightly in the arctic wind. Her owner, Elizabeth Miller, one of the former mound builders in the 1927 pageant, now a teacher and housewife, is forty-three. Although she became a little interested in Indians of the Southwest after a trip through Arizona in the 1950s and will become more so after a stop at Alert Bay to see the social dances of the Kwakiutl in the early 1970s, she will never travel to the Arctic. In the 1950s organized tours to the Arctic, a part of the country where most people still live off the land and spend their winters in snow houses, are inconceivable. She occasionally polishes the sculpture with vegetable oil and often strokes it. She does not articulate why she loves it and, like most Canadians then, knows very little about the culture it comes from. But she knows that part of the sculpture's life can be known only in the sense of touch. She teaches her teenaged daughter to feel its curves, as well as to look at it. Her daughter will develop an interest in many North American First Nations, in the mid-1990s will visit tiny Bathurst Inlet in the Arctic, and eventually will write this book. As generations of television makers and audiences have come and gone and as new ones have appeared, so have the representations of First Nations people evolved from pageant to contemporary prime time.

# FIVE

# *Radisson:* The Baseline Set in the 1950s

This is the only chapter that does not deal with programs I could view and then analyse. All of the anglophone episodes of *Radisson* have disappeared, and while the francophone versions may survive somewhere, I haven't found them. Neither the French nor the English episodes are in the National Archives Sound and Moving Image Collection (now the Library and Archives of Canada). Nevertheless, as the first series featuring First Nations characters, this series deserves attention. *Radisson* was a major effort, made only four years after the CBC began television broadcasts, and framed by reams of publicity.[1] *Radisson* was broadcast over two television seasons, the first from 9 February to 4 May 1957 and the second from 2 November 1957 to 25 January 1958. The reasons for the making of the series, the way it was made, and the cultural tensions it embodied are also relevant to this study. From the surviving paper sources and a website that gives an episode guide,[2] it is clear that the series not only valorized a pre-Conquest figure but also depicted the tensions between settlers, traders, and First Nations. Yet it is also clear that, at times, it elided or erased those tensions, a further reason for looking at it. Finally, *Radisson* was intended to be a family adventure series primarily for children, and its importance as a template for the representation of First Nations peoples in the early years of television earns it a place in this book. (I did see *Radisson* on air when I was fifteen, which is not helpful except to have provided an impression.)

In his chapter "History TV and Popular Memory" in *Television Histories: Shaping Collective Memory in the Media Age* (2001), Steve Anderson explores the various debates about the representation of history on television: Is television a part of "an epidemic of cultural amnesia" (19)? Does television makes history banal? Are television histories, like others, "over-determined" by the needs of the present, the desires of the historians, and the ideological contexts of historical research" (20)? And "among other things [do] these narratives obscure [quoting Hayden White] the 'discontinuity, disruption and chaos' of the past and enable the construction of histories which may be filtered, politicised, or influenced by their relation to systems of authority"? (25).

Add to these questions and strictures the fact that *Radisson* was produced for the only Canadian television network then broadcasting, CBC / SRC; was shot in English and French by an independent film company, partly on location on the St Lawrence River; was written by an expatriate from Britain; was made specifically for children as an action/adventure series; claimed historical authenticity in its designs of props and costumes; and came in with cost overruns that became the subject of parliamentary debate. The series was intended to strike a blow against the overwhelming popularity of the new American film and television icon, Davy Crockett. In these post-modern times, most of these facts leave the series open to any or all of the charges above. Moreover, although *Radisson* raises these questions, fifty years later little remains to help us judge how it was received, apart from the very limited audience research done by the CBC (cited below) and the clippings in the CBC library on the making of the series and its reception by a few television journalists. Although it is now so thoroughly forgotten that whatever impact it may have had on children and adults in the 1950s then or since is impossible to say, I will consider some of the issues raised by Anderson and others. The major focus of this analysis, however, is how *Radisson* works as a children's action/adventure show and how it came to be made. It also provides a very useful baseline from which the evolution of television's representations of First Nations peoples can be traced. In the early years of television, representations of First Nations peoples often appear in family adventure series like this one, rather than in television shows intended specifically for adults.

Paul Rutherford, in *Primetime Canada: When Television Was Young* (1990), is the only English Canadian scholar to discuss the series. He calls it a "historical adventure otherwise known as 'Radishes' in the trade ... Much later, Hugh Gauntlett, an assistant program director, noted that the Corporation had been reluctant to get into the film business because that meant competing with private film companies ... Presumably the CBC also thought it wiser to rely on the experience of outsiders in this new field of telefilms" (375). At that time the CBC/SRC had no drama film unit.

Pierre Radisson was a forerunner of the coureurs de bois, on whom the fur trade depended. In *Multiculturalism and the History of Canadian Diversity* (2000), Richard J.F. Day discusses "hybrid identities" such as those of the coureurs de bois, "half-breeds" and Metis who were "deeply feared and repressed by both the British and the French state organisations and continue to be marginalised today ... a negative other-ascription" (74). For many, these adventurers were ambiguous figures with a touch of the outlaw. Although they embodied all of the strengths and many of the specialized skills of the indigenous peoples, they were safely white (at least white enough). Thus, by the displacement of specific characteristics – endurance, special knowledge of the wilderness, survival skills – they subsume the Indian into white heroics. Day outlines state policy in New France, backed by the church, which insisted that the settlers stay put on their land, not go off fur trading: "Those who chose instead to live a semi-nomadic life and take on the ways of the Native peoples posed an ongoing problem to the Jesuits, proper French visitors and above all the colonial administration. Themes of wanton alcoholism, interracial sex and idleness were central" (86). He describes the coureurs de bois as being a "nomadic – that is, emergent, local, decentralised and non-authoritarian – mode of organisation ... the first repressed *semi-internal* Other in the history of Canadian diversity" (87). He points out that their descendants, one branch of the Metis, still occupy a liminal position as a nation and that they had no formal place in Canada until the Charter of Rights and Freedoms. He goes on to note that "[t]he British, of course, learned everything they needed to know about working with Indians from Radisson and Groseilliers [Radisson's brother-in-law], two notorious *coureurs du bois* ... The British fur traders assimilated New World Practices evolved by the French and Native peoples" (95).[3]

Amelia Kalant, in *National Identity and the Conflict at Oka* (2004), suggests another connotation of the choice of Radisson for a television series when she points out that the coureurs de bois who followed in his footsteps evoked the "hope of a fusion between indigenous and settler to form a 'new people' through a mingling of blood just as [they portended] the opposite claim: degeneration of the master race ... de-civilizing and nativizing French Canadians at the same time" (102–3). Radisson the historical figure can be a hero who prefigures the best of the bravery, skills, and deeds of exploration and adventure of the coureurs de bois but is comfortable in courts and marries a French woman – or he can embody much that governments feared and settlers envied.

## THE HOLLYWOOD FILM CONTEXT

*The Only Good Indian ... The Hollywood Gospel,* by Ralph E. Friar and Natasha A. Friar (1972), is an imaginatively written polemic and an invaluable source of details about the history of Indians in American films.[4] Of the historical figures in American lore, Davy Crockett appeared in only three films between 1916 and 1949 and then in two more, so he is not the legendary figure that Buffalo Bill (27 films) or Custer (23) is. Fennimore Cooper's Deerslayer/Hawkeye character had lasting fame (22 movies from 1911 to 1957), but the First Nations associated with him (Six Nations, Mohican, Huron) did not have nearly the popular appeal that the Sioux and Apache did (I presume that this was partly because Hawkeye's Indians did not ride horses through miles of wonderful scenery). The Ojibway appear in only two films (1911 and 1912). Titles and plots included "Indian princesses" (20 +) and a fair number of "squaws" – as well as many "maids and maidens" – up to 1956, when *Radisson* was being made.

On television, the small-screen version of the Western was moving from *Hopalong Cassidy* (dozens of movies, radio and television, 1952–54), *Roy Rogers* (many movies, radio and television, 1951–57), and *The Lone Ranger* to more adult fare like *Broken Arrow,* but the form did not yet dominate prime time as it would from the late 1950s well into the 1960s. Smart innovative series like *Have Gun Will Travel* and the more traditional and much longer lived series *Gunsmoke* (with its roots in a successful radio series), as well as *Bonanza,* with its emphasis on family and property, were still on the horizon. Nevertheless, on television, running simultaneously, were *Zane Grey Theater, Cheyenne, Wyatt Earp, Broken Arrow, The Lone Ranger, Sgt. Preston of the Yukon,* and *Jim Bowie.*[5]

### EPISODE ANALYSIS

*Radisson* began as a serial but then seems to have become more a series of self-contained episodes, in other words a series. Since in this unique instance I could not view any of the episodes, I have had to depend on the incomplete accounts of the weekly episodes in the CBC *Times* and on outlines of the many episodes in the American as well as Canadian sources used by Des Martin, who compiled the *Radisson* website, housed on the Classic TV Archive, which classifies the series as a "Canadian TV Western."[6] The site also gives American broadcast dates for fourteen episodes of the series, renamed *Tomahawk* for the syndication market, as well as information about it being broadcast in the United Kingdom on ABC North Midlands in 1959

Jacques Godin as Radisson, "Lord of the Wilderness." *CBC Times.*

and apparently on Tyne Tees in 1961. Martin has broadcast dates for a scattering of these and for episodes 15–18. Although Boyce Hart consulted the *CBC Times*, there are no details for the second season, only the titles for episodes 16–19 and one-sentence synopses for 20–26. The site also cautions that the correct order for continuity of the first twenty-six episodes has yet to be verified. As noted, at least once the episodes were broadcast in the wrong order, making nonsense of the serial. In fact, piecing the narrative together from these short entries can even suggest a different running order for later more self-contained episodes.

Episode 1, "Capture," shows an angry Radisson going after the Iroquois for killing two friends; it establishes who the hostile Indians are as well as the hero's resourcefulness and courage under torture after he is captured. He is ransomed at Fort Orange in episode 2, "Escape from the Indians." There is an unnumbered episode called the "Old and New," which would suggest that the episode fits between 2 and 3, since the UK synopsis mentions that Radisson meets Des Groseilliers after a trip to France, where he is "horrified to discover that the French attitude to New France (Canada) is that it is merely a source of revenue." In episode 3, "Feast of Gluttons," Radisson accompanies a missionary into Iroquois country only to discover that the Huron converts have been massacred. (Missionary work was one of the justifications of the young French colony.) The cast list suggests that this episode also introduced his family. In episode 4, "The (Three) Gentlemen of New France" (a rather arch allusion to Shakespeare's *Two Gentlemen of Verona* but replaced by "Cat and Mouse" for export), he accompanies three French nobles, shown in CBC promotional pictures as effete and needing protection, all the way to Lake Winnipeg while being followed by Iroquois. In episode 5, "The Adventurers," en route to Lake Winnipeg Radisson comes to the aid of the Huron. In episode 6, "The Iroquois Blockade," the synopsis reads: "[H]aving subdued [?] the Hurons, [they] continue on their journey through Iroquois territory. Meanwhile, the Iroquois have attacked a French settlement and massacred the inhabitants. Radisson and his party are bypassed by the main body of Iroquois but a small party led by an old enemy, Nahala, discovers them." The description sounds like the Dollard massacre of 1660, and an unnumbered episode for American viewers is called "The Adam Dollard Massacre." In episode 7, "Fear and Fireworks," they decide to find the sea to the north, but the "[t]he governor of Three Rivers will not allow them to leave, however, unless they agree to share the furs they collect during the trip." In episode 8, "Feast and Famine," they continue to search for Hudson Bay. Highlighting how difficult it is to put this puzzle together, episode 9, according to the *CBC Times* description, seems to be much like episode 7. In episode 10, "Race against Time," Radisson and his party are still on their way to the northern sea and they are trapped by winter. According to a conflation of the American and the *CBC Times'* (27 April 1957) descriptions, Radisson is worried about how the food will hold out, but unspecified Indian "companions" do not worry. Inevitably he turns out to be right, for in episode 11, "The Famine" (US title), Radisson, Des Groseilliers, and the Hurons are on strict rations when they are approached by starving "Ottowa" (Odawa) "begging for food" – the phrase used in all of the sources. Presumably, because this was a children's show, there was enough food to go around in the end, although one hopes that the Odawa were not portrayed so uncharacteristically as "begging." One band would expect another to share food in an emergency unless they were actively enemies or if the band that had the food was also close to starving. On the other hand, these scripts are supposed to be based on Radisson's journals, and thus, "begging" may be the word he used.

In episode 12, "The Sea to the North," Radisson and the Huron reach Hudson Bay, but the Huron do not want to spend the winter there. Episode 13, "The Mighty Hunter," raises more interesting questions. The Huron chief, who does not think much of Radisson's fur-trapping skill, goes off to trap his own beaver and prove his skill. The cbc *Times* of 4 May 1957 adds the detail that they "rescue the chief of the Huron's band from a hungry wolf pack," again fulfilling the conventional expectations about television heroes in the 1950s. In episode 14 the series falls back on the movie cliché of the hero being offered an Indian bride (that plot line will reappear in *Hudson Bay* and two decades later in *The Campbells*). Since heroes of adventures must stay unmarried, Radisson somehow extricates himself. Episode 15, "Caesars of the Wilderness," unlike 13, suggests that Radisson is not always cast in a heroic light. Confined by a blizzard to a cabin for three weeks, Radisson nearly goes mad. But the American synopsis suggests another plot line, where Des Groseilliers is hit by a Cree arrow and both men are taken prisoner. I suspect that this episode should go before 14, but perhaps the attack was the result of Radisson refusing the Cree wife. Episode 16 has a title – "The Fight with Lerca" – but there is no synopsis in any source. The website provides no information for episodes 17 and 18, but my notes based on the cbc *Times* listing suggest that in 17, "The Fur Traders," Radisson, Des Groseilliers, and the Hurons head for a cabin where they have left their furs with the Odawa. Episode 19 also has no title, but the synopsis describes how the two men "discover a band of warlike Iroquois heading toward the camp of the Ottawas." In episode 20 they arc cheated by the French, and in 21 "Quebec officials force Radisson and Des Groseilliers to seek financial aid from the British in order to continue their fur trading." itv Tyne Tees in the United Kingdom calls episode 22 "The Mutiny": "Radisson and Médard [Des Groseilliers], after many refusals for a ship, finally are talked into hiring an old vessel by two schemers – a captain and his first mate." The us sources suggest that the two partners face a mutiny on board their ship where they are caught between the captain and the crew. The cbc *Times* of 22 December 1957 elaborates, saying that they are sailing on the *Maid of Derby* in northern waters, dealing with treacherous officers, fending off mutinies over food, avoiding icebergs. That half-hour certainly seems to have been packed with plot lines. Nahala (Radisson's enemy), Onenga (his "blood brother"), Mojida (the Huron chief), and an Iroquois chieftain all appear in this episode. It is hard to imagine how they would fit in with a search for a ship.

In episode 23 Radisson and Des Groseilliers are diverted to Boston. In the 24th, they "run into trouble when they visit a tiny fishing village gripped by strange tensions." Clearly, these last few episodes change both the tone and the setting of the series, leaving behind the endless battles with Indians, the greedy French officials, and the rigours of winter. In episode 25 they are "branded traitors in New France because they attempted to reach Hudson Bay in an English ship." The second and last season ends quite oddly. In episode 26, "Radisson and Des Groseilliers are taken into protective custody by the British when authorities of French Canada issue a warrant for their arrest," a plot line that created some controversy in Quebec because Radisson was portrayed as a traitor to Quebec's French forefathers, even though historically he did join the English at that point. Scriptwriter John Lucarotti had to defend Radisson's actions by highlighting the corruption of both French and English governments and recasting Radisson's concerns as being the defence of the real interests of the colony. Stray titles on Des Martin's website are "The Thief," "The Long Night," "The Decision," "A Fair Bargain," "The Betrayal," "The Defeat," and "The Personal Grudge" – all of them generic enough to suit more than one – or none – of the previous list. Two of them might be the missing titles for episodes 16 and 17.

A set of four descriptions of unnumbered episodes in a CBC press release dated October 1957 (i.e. before the second season) includes one about the chief of a Cree village who wants Radisson to summer as his guest, another about an invitation that it "could be fatal" to refuse, and a third about a fight to the death over a "beautiful Indian girl" (at least she is not called a maiden) with a Cree warrior who fears she is "in love with the white trapper." These may provide clues about where the producers thought the series would go next. In an article for the *Star Weekly* a year earlier, 20 October 1956, Harold Hilliard refers to future plots that would include Radisson's participation in French expeditions to West Africa and the West Indies. He also said that the producers planned episodes that would show that Radisson spied on the Hudson's Bay Company on behalf of the French. These ideas were not used because the series ended after two seasons.

In Rutherford's (1990) view, the series was a failure because it could not match "the polish of the Hollywood product" (376). I disagree. The series had been given enough money and talent to ensure that the production values were high. But one of the problems was the apparent repetitiveness of the plot lines. The American series *Hawkeye and the Last of the Mohicans* (produced in Canada a year later – discussed briefly in chapter 6) gives some idea of how the writers and producers solved this problem: introduce famous characters; deal with white captives and Indians captured by whites; have the hero encounter shamans and war chiefs; and, most importantly, explore the different tensions created by the hero having a Mohican for a friend rather than another Frenchman.

## THE MAKING OF *RADISSON*

To date, there has been only one book published on children's television in Canada. F.B. Rainsberry (1988), supervisor of the CBC Children's Television Department for many years, wrote *History of Children's Television in English Canada 1952–1986.*[7] The book supplies many details derived from his own first-hand knowledge and found in no other place. Rainsberry puts *Radisson* in the context of early "attempts to provide Canadian serialized dramas for children. The first abortive attempt was a joint project between the English Network and Radio Canada … [M]ost of the budget was used up after six or seven shows had been completed." The head of children's TV at Radio-Canada took over, "revising the budget and predictably, scaling down the size and extent of the enterprise." Rainsberry also acknowledges the careful research that went into the co-production, as well as the involvement of Omega Productions of Montreal, which had the expertise in filming drama (128) that the studio-bound director/producers at the CBC did not. Clearly, from the start there were difficulties with the ambitious project.

It seems self-evident why the CBC/SRC would choose Radisson as their first protagonist for a filmed series shot in both languages. Radisson was an explorer and fur trader, a man who worked for the French and the English – perfect for a young television service that was trying to broadcast in two languages to two cultures. *The Plouffe Family /La Famille Plouffe,* which preceded it (1954–57 in English),[8] was a gentle, very popular comedy performed live on simple sets, once in English and once in French. But those modest episodes had been televised live from a studio, using familiar techniques, with experienced, mostly bilingual actors. *Radisson* was very different. It was shot on film, on location as well as in the studio, and it also had to be shot twice, in English and French. Not only was film expensive and rarely used in Canadian television drama until the mid-1960s, but with its higher resolution and its enabling filmmakers to see rushes, reshoot, and then edit, it was very different from live television and its successor, live-to-videotape, which had a lower resolution and was very difficult to edit.

### NOT *DAVY CROCKETT*

Like CBC's *Cariboo Country*, begun two years after *Radisson* had finished, *Radisson* was consciously conceived to differ substantially from the immensely popular television adult Westerns of the time and was a reaction to, rather than an imitation of, a hugely popular American artifact – Disney's *Davy Crockett*.[9] The Davy Crockett craze began in 1954–55 with just five episodes – in colour – of the *Disneyland* television program. The first was titled "Davy Crockett Indian Fighter" and was aired on 12 December 1954. The four that followed had him going to Congress, fighting river pirates, having a "keelboat race," and, on 14 December 1955, being killed at the Alamo. Alex McNeil, in *Total Television* (1980), claims that these five separated hours formed the first television miniseries.[10] They were then edited into two movies that were shown in theatres in 1955 and 1956.[11] But by 1956 the fad had faded, although television followed up a decade later with *Daniel Boone* (1964–70),[12] which some viewers have conflated in memory with *Davy Crockett*, also starring Fess Parker, to produce the widespread impression that *Davy Crockett* was a long and successful series. Meanwhile, the five originals, backed by Disney's marketing skills, spawned a continent-wide fad that even produced a song on the Hit Parade ("killed him a b'ar when he was only three / … Davy, Davy Crockett, / King of the Wild Frontier"). Everywhere you looked in 1955, on the heads of thousands and thousands of English Canadian kids, there were Davy Crockett "coonskin" caps, tail and all – with one relevant exception. The craze apparently did not catch on in Quebec.[13] Looking for an anglophone Canadian antidote, preferably one who could speak to both linguistic cultures, Monica Clare,[14] CBC head of children's programs, thought of the French explorer turned English, turned French, turned English again, Pierre-Esprit Radisson, and his partner Médard Chouart Des Groseilliers – known to generations of anglophone children learning about the explorers of North America by their nicknames in the seventeenth-century English court, "Radishes and Gooseberries."[15] Francophone kids might not know Davy Crockett, but they had heard of Radisson in school.

According to Barbara Moon, whose feature article in *Maclean's*, 19 January 1957, "How They're Making a Hero of Pierre Radisson," provides much of the surviving information about the series, Clare had no television budget, so approached the head of src's children's programs in Montreal. Moon writes: "Radisson was chosen chiefly because he lent himself to bilingual treatment." She summarizes the explorer's career using the demythologizing tone that often characterizes much of the discourse about heroes in Canada. Radisson was "captured by the Iroquois in his teens, stumbled on a land route to Hudson Bay in his twenties, sold his secret to the English in his thirties (hereby prompting the formation of the Hudson's Bay Company), spied on the English for the French in his forties and died broke in London in his seventies." Needless to say, the series presented a rather different version. Renée Legris, in a paper delivered to ASCRT / AERTC at the Learneds in 1990, says that coureurs de bois were the figures in the (pre-conquest) golden age of New France who embodied the best of the wilderness – freedom, hardiness, adventure, mysterious skills – but who were safely white and French speaking – that is, specifically not the "other," the Amerindiens. English Canada has no such mythology of a golden age.[16] Nevertheless, there may well have been a longing for this kind of romance in all parts of Canada, stuck as it was in the depths of the Cold War during the prosperous but conformist 1950s.

It should be emphasized that in the 1950s there were only four or five channels available to most Canadian households (cbc and/or src, cbs, nbc, and abc). But in much of Canada, away from the borders, there was only one channel available, cbc or src (bilingual Montrealers could watch both). ctv had not begun operations. In any case, *Radisson* was the sort of enterprise that only a crown corporation like the cbc/src would or could undertake at that time – or even today – given that all of the episodes were shot twice, once in English, once in French on film.

*Radisson* had a huge cast. The ability to swim was one of the prerequisites for being cast, since the canoes were often swamped by the wake of ships in the St Lawrence. Design and construction costs were enormous, since they built 'to scale' a replica of Fort Orange and two Indian villages. Having to build sets on location and shoot outdoors on the St Lawrence River added to the difficulties and the expense. The heading of a press release of 1 October 1956 was probably typical: "Bad weather delays 'Radisson' production." Weather set back the planned broadcast of the series for several months.

John Lucarotti, the scriptwriter for the series, was a thirty-year-old Englishman with little television experience, although he had worked on

CBC radio[17] (and would go on to write episodes of two British television cult classics, *The Avengers* and *Dr. Who*). He wrote every script, in English, and then Renée Normand translated them into French. The SRC provided the executive producer, Pierre Gauvreau[18] (Pierre Desroches is also mentioned in one report),[19] and the supervising producer, Jean-Yves Bigras. Jean Duprez, the director of photography, came from Omega Productions, the production partner most experienced in film.[20] "Film" suggests to the contemporary reader that what the viewer saw were crisp bright images. Certainly, a film image was much better than the kinescopes that recorded the image from a studio monitor during a live performance, which is what much of the country saw before there was cross-country feed.[21] Nevertheless, whatever the quality of the originating image, the image received by television sets of the period was small, black and white, variable, and often "snowy." Moreover, when reels of film were involved, glitches could occur. According to the *Daily Star* of 20 April 1957, one episode ended with Radisson about to blow up Fort Orange. In the episode shown the following week, he was shooting at a duck. The CBC technicians had mixed up the cans of film. The missing episode had to be re-edited on the fly so that it could be shown out of sequence one week late. Barbara Moon writes: "When Radisson is tortured by the Iroquois, only his contorted face is to be shown. But [producer] Gauvreau insisted on a piece of raw pork tied to the actor's waist so that, when a red-hot poker was touched to it, there would be a suitable sizzle and curl of smoke." "Savagery" was definitely on the menu for the first episode. Since this was a serial, the episode ended in approved cliff-hanger fashion, with Radisson's survival in doubt.

The serial starred Jacques Godin, whose love of the outdoors and athleticism are emphasized in several articles about the series.[22] René Caron played Des Groseilliers. Caron began as a young radio comedian "particularly well-known … as both an actor and M.C." to francophones,[23] which would have given him a start as a familiar and lively figure. According to the Internet Movie Database (IMDb),[24] the cast also included Raymond Royer as Onenga (Radisson's Indian blood brother), Percy Rodriguez (a bilingual black actor)[25] as an Iroquois chieftain, and Julien Bessette as Nahala (Radisson's Indian enemy). There was to be "tasteful" tie-in merchandise, including Radisson fur caps (converted Crockett raccoon fur caps without the tails and with an upright white feather added), a doll modelled on actor Jacques Godin, "a rifle, a knife, a belt, a music box, suit of buckskins, a T-shirt … and a game … with tiny canoes for counters, setbacks like 'fighting Iroquois' and alternative routes from Three Rivers to Hudson Bay." It is

Médard Des Groseilliers (René Caron) and Pierre Radisson are stalking – game? hostile "Indians"? *cbc Times.*

not clear whether any of these items actually made it into the stores, and a Google/eBay search in May 2007 turned up no evidence. The cbc/src answer to the ubiquitous *Davy Crockett* theme song was the *Radisson* theme song, which reinforced the idea that Radisson was the conqueror of the wilderness, lord of all he "discovered," once more reflecting the triumphalism of the 1940s and 1950s Hollywood and television Westerns.

Peter Kentner's breezy, fairly comprehensive book *tv North: everything you wanted to know about canadian television* (2001)[26] is not always accurate in every detail and is as opinionated as Geoff Pevere and Greg Dymond's *Mondo Canuck* (1996), but it does have lots of illustrations, including pictures of this series. Kentner even quotes a verse of the theme song: "'Radisson, Radisson / Canada's courageous pioneer! / Radisson, Radisson, Lord of the Wilderness, / The man who knew no fear ... '" (143).

## CLAIMS OF AUTHENTICITY

Over the last fifty years, the cbc (and occasionally ctv) has often been anxious to claim authentic representation when it comes to historical or regional content. The CBC *Times* of 3–9 February 1956 featured an article that uses a shot of Godin, with large bold type RADISSON, and a subheading "The Authentic Chronicles of a Canadian Adventurer Filmed in Canada for TV with an All-Canadian Cast." The word "chronicles" signifies both sobriety and an account close to the event as well as solid research. The stress on the claim of Radisson as a Canadian hero, which is everywhere in the publicity and in the reporting, suggests that there was a time two generations ago when both cultures claimed the pre-Conquest history as "Canadian" and as a common heritage without apparent problems, a claim reasserted after two Quebec referenda on separation from Canada by the documentary series (with dramatized sections) *Canada: A People's History* (2000–01), also shot in both languages.

Location shooting and historical authenticity is always costly. According to *Canadian High News* (19 January 1957), a newspaper for teenagers in secondary schools, there were "[n]o pre-cooked sirloins, rubber-tipped arrows, machined canoes, stuffed ducks or preserved trout here, but the real stuff wherever possible." The designers found out that only leather for buckskins looks and wears like leather. They used real birchbark canoes. The claim is reiterated in CBC *Times* on 27 October 1957 for the series' return when the designers had to plan for and build a three-masted schooner. In the CBC *Times* of 2 November 1957, costume designer Janine Carson and set designer Leo Jacques both said that a large part of their time was spent on research. Harold Hilliard in the *Star Weekly* of 20 October 1956 had reported that "[p]rops, in some cases, are authentic hand-me downs of 300 years ago," but he also praised the hard-working props department. He had been told that the "Indian and early Canadian period dress is based on the famous series of Canadian historical sketches by C.W. Jefferys," which appeared in the 1928–38 *A First Book of Canadian History,* already cited. It is likely that these illustrations, which were reproduced in school books and on classroom walls, had a major influence on the way Canadians imagined their history at that time, particularly the interaction of white explorers and settlers and the First Nations people they encountered.[27]

Clearly, the CBC did try to be authentic in *Radisson*, but with this notable exception: white actors played all but one of the Indians. In a 1956 issue of *Weekend Magazine*, Fran Lowe comments: "For the children there is one discouraging note in the Radisson story. There is a not a single Indian in the drama. All Indian roles are filled by white actors."[28] Producer Jean-Yves Bigras had "sadly explained" to her that "'Iroquois braves today make more money as high steel workers than they could as actors. So we could get no Indians.'" Bigras's comment suggests that only nearby Akwesasne and Kahnewake had been canvassed. Yet Jay Silverheels from the Six Nations reserve near Brantford, Ontario, was appearing as Tonto in both the films and the television series *The Lone Ranger* (1949–57), and other First Nations actors performed in Hollywood films. Other reporters also raised questions. In her article (1957), Moon refers to exactly one "real Indian" on the set playing an unspecified role. A caption under a picture of a sweatered man lighting a fire reads: "Four Indian braves watch impassively while paleface Jean lights a signal fire for them." (Casting white actors as Indians appears to have been the norm at the CBC at that time. On 17 October 1956, in the drama *Dark of Moon*, presented by the prestigious TV anthology *First Performance*, a white actor played a very highly stereotyped Big Bear, with other white actors playing assorted "braves.") Moon comments that the francophone actors in *Radisson*, whose English was problematic at best, "had codified their assorted redskin roles into seven primary facial expressions." She is not more specific, but we can assume that her reader would fill in stolidity, ferocity, nobility, et al.[29] However, if no Indian actors could be found in the East, producers in the West found or developed many First Nations performers. In 1960, after a false start in the first two episodes of the anthology *Cariboo Country*, CBC producer/directors Frank Goodship and Philip Keatley found Chief Dan George to play the key role of Ol' Antoine in the rest of the series and never again cast a white actor in a native role.

### RADISSON: THE PROBLEMATIC PROTAGONIST

A claim of authenticity is reiterated in several CBC press releases, particularly as it relates to their choice of Radisson as a focus for a series. In the *CBC Times* of 9–15 September 1956, scriptwriter John Lucarotti talks about his vision that "pioneering Canada was a titanic undertaking – a saga to stir the blood of every Canadian." The issue of 3 February 1957 tells its readers that Lucarotti "based his scripts on Radisson's own journal as well as historic accounts of his life. 'I'm not creating a cardboard hero … It's a full dimensional portrayal of an ordinary man'" who presumably did not kill a bear when he was only three, even in jokey legend, but "'whose life was literally packed with exciting incident.'"

In fact, there was potential for considerable complexity in the choice of Radisson as a protagonist. Germaine Warkentin discusses Radisson's journals in "Discovering Radisson: A Renaissance Adventurer between Two Worlds" (1996) and finds in them a man who identified both with his

Provençal[30] roots and with some of the customs of his aboriginal allies, including the Feast of the Dead and the torture of prisoners. She traces a man who lived between two worlds all of his life, who was a publicist of his own interests in the fur trade and of himself, multilingual, able to persuade the monied class to finance his expeditions by using the metaphors common to the political life of the court, and immensely self-confident. In her view, whatever he said at the time, he believed. In other words, she describes a survivor who is something of a rascal – not the usual television hero for children in the 1950s. Unlike Davy Crockett, he was one of the first television protagonists in a series drawn from what Canadian historians now call the "middle ground." Warkentin describes the middle ground as "[t]he social space of that broad and shifting border territory between the increasingly European settled east and the distant and still unknown west, where, for a brief period between 1650 and 1815, French and Native Americans established a common cultural language and shared way of life typical of neither the settlement or the 'wilderness'" (48). Warkentin's Radisson seems to bear little resemblance to the television Radisson. One wishes that this complex, challenging character could have appeared in a drama special or miniseries for adult viewers in the intervening fifty years – but that has not happened.

André Laurendeau gave a radio talk about the series that was adapted for and published in *Canadian High News*, 19 January 1957.[31] It ran under a picture captioned "Sneaking up on a hostile Indian encampment, Pierre Radisson is ready for adventure." Laurendeau sketches Radisson's life story for his student readers and argues that Radisson was at home in several cultures: "He married an English woman, as if he foresaw the future of New France ... [F]inally, born French, he ended up English, which might become a symbol of Canadian unity ... Saved by his adoptive [Mohawk] family, he became an Indian again ... [then] he escaped for good. Years later ... he discovered the Great North West. He slipped through the Iroquois territory and had made friends with the Cree and the Sioux. He bought their furs and persuaded 500 Cree (think of that – 500!) to accompany him to Quebec. His party arrived in time to save the finances of the colony ... The next year ... with a small party of Indians he managed to make his way to the west."

When controversy erupted over what kind of hero for children a "turn-coat makes," John Lucarotti again explains his point of view in the *CBC Times* (no date but best guess is 2 November 1957, just before the second season opened). He picks up on the idea that Radisson represented the bilingual/bicultural nature of Canada – ten years before the Royal

Commission on Bilingualism and Biculturalism. In the maze of Radisson's political manoeuvring, one nationalistic idea remains clear: as Lucarotti claims, "Radisson was prepared to serve any man who would serve Canada well ... it was this land – all of it – which concerned him ... He succeeded and he failed. His success – the discovery of the all-important overland route to Hudson Bay. His failure – to stop men thinking selfishly. How strange it is that the one man who really deserves to be known as 'the first Canadian' is called by so many 'a traitor.'" The CBC brochure intended for teachers and students (no date) merely says that he was "born in St. Malo ... Although he took sides alternately with the French and the English, Radisson's loyalty was primarily to himself, and to the wild rugged outdoors in which he moved and carried on the hunt for furs, the 'gold' of the New World."

As the first season went to air, Lucarotti, in the CBC *Times* of 3 February 1957, repeats what he had said earlier and again emphasizes another theme that appears regularly in the presentation of historical docudrama on the CBC: "The pioneering of this country was a titanic undertaking – a saga to stir the blood of every Canadian. Radisson is but one exciting chapter. If it succeeds, as I think it will, it will be a great thing, for it will open the door to others." Opening the door to more costly historical dramas has been a dream of many Canadian television executives, too seldom realized. Although the series was intended for children, who would not be interested in the complexities of the English/French/First Nations politics of the period, the choice of Radisson as a protagonist suggests that this series served as a precursor for more complex characteristics. These, as is typical of the Canadian sensibility,[32] tended to demystify their protagonists – Riel, Brant, and Big Bear among Metis and First Nations protagonists; Sir John A. MacDonald, D'Arcy McGee, Sam Hughes, Samuel Lount, and Banting among the white historical figures – who were given complex motives and, for the most part, rounded characters in docudramas over the years.

The many roles played by Radisson are summarized by some of the captions of the pictures accompanying Barbara Moon's article: "The Diplomat," "The Expert Canoeist," "The Pioneer," "The Indian Fighter." Yet the text's construction of the heroic figure is self-consciously undercut by other pictures and captions: a canoe on the floor of the studio; a frogman with electric cable; details about the mosquitoes that plague the actors. There is an unlabelled shot of a scalp-locked "Iroquois" huddled under a blanket reading the comics section of a newspaper. "The Indian Fighter" is superimposed on a shot of a bare-chested, war-painted, breech-clouted

Indian, with necklaces and knife. Radisson, of course, is fully clad, complete with hat and perky feather – and knife. The caption, emphasizing the merchandising of this hero reads: "Buck-skin clad Radisson fights hand-to-hand with Iroquois brave. The feathered hat is being produced for the kids." The emphasis on the marketing of this series may come from the sheer novelty of selling merchandise related to Canadian television. The issue of casting also kept nagging away. On the next page are more behind-the-scenes shots. In a casual aside, a caption to a shot of an actor with a cage of ducks (used "for hunting scenes") tells the reader that it is "actor Paul Germain, playing an Indian. [He] is the only real Indian in the Radisson cast."

How far this children's series tried to represent the cultural clashes of the French, English, and various First Nations is hard to say at this distance. Was there any attempt to differentiate between the various customs and dress of the nations portrayed? The PR emphasizes the research done, but no First Nations consultants were used. And because there were no Indian actors, no informal and unpaid consultants were on set, and there is no record of research into what little there was in print from an aboriginal perspective. After all, the Iroquois, Odawa, and Cree would have a very different view from the Huron and Neutral nations of this man and this period. The paper trail suggests that Indians in this series may have been basically divided into enemies and friends.

### RESCHEDULING FOR A BROADER AUDIENCE

According to Barbara Moon, the CBC did not seek a sponsor for the show before production started, in case a sponsor "might possibly impair something the CBC called 'the series integrity.'" However, there were commercials in the broadcast. When the network, on 12 December 1956, finally announced the launch of the *Radisson* series for 1 February 1957 on Radio-Canada and 8 February for the CBC, it was advertised as a children's serial of fifteen chapters, to be broadcast at the children's supper hour, 5:00–5:30 p.m., on Fridays. But the series was rapidly moved before the English airdate to Saturdays at 7:00–7:30 p.m., "to allow more convenient family viewing."[33] This rescheduling redefined the audience for *Radisson* from children who watched before supper to the broader demographic of a family settling down to watch television on a Saturday night. The show ended only a half-hour before the hockey game started. The serial was then to return in the fall of 1957 for the remaining episodes. It did make an impression. My husband, then seventeen, remembers seeing it in the common room of the YMCA in Montreal. My family, with only one child (me – age fifteen), sampled it. My brother-in-law, who was in the targeted demographic, remembers it. A middle-aged man I encountered by chance remembered it vividly, from when he was six. With all of the publicity surrounding it and few choices available, thousands of adults with or without children watched it, an audience sponsors were happy to entertain.

### THE REVIEWS

Although Paul Rutherford gives his readers the impression that the response to *Radisson* both by professional critics and by children was negative, the reviews from both were mixed. Ordinary viewers wrote to the papers about the design and costumes, especially the heavy, black, braided "Indian" wigs. One Montreal woman said the Indians looked like white men "who have dunked their heads in a bucket of multicoloured paint, then donned ill-fitting and badly decorated bathing caps." On 12 February 1957, the *Globe and Mail* reviewer, who liked the show, commented that the Iroquois "makeup has the odd effect, occasionally, of making it seem as if they were wearing helmets, instead of having shaven heads."[34] There were other viewer complaints: swimmers did the crawl, a stroke invented in the twentieth century; the paddles were factory made; the paddlers did not use the stroke that Indians had used. Canadians, then as now, took their history seriously. Did American viewers write to the papers about this kind of detail in *Hawkeye*? Some viewers complained that the episodes were all action and no dialogue, others that the early episodes were too slow. One thought that Godin was too old to credibly appear as age seventeen in the first episode. Others thought that he was a believable athlete and fighter. Finally, there were complaints that the first season's final episode ended in mid-paddle stroke without any explanation. This was a bad habit of the CBC, right into the 1970s, when they finally began to tell viewers that a series would return in the fall. Cliff-hangers at the end of a season would not be the norm until 1980, when *Dallas* (basically a nighttime soap) in its second season pioneered what became a television cliché with its "Who Shot J.R." episode.

Some professional reviewers quite liked *Radisson*. The reviewer at the *Daily Star* (Toronto), 11 February 1957, reported: "[It] had a simple story line [with] almost constant movement … an essential in that sort of series … and the acting, while broad, was more restrained than I had expected." He then commented on the French accent of the French and the unaccented English of the Indians. He liked the athletic Godin, but wanted him to smile once in a while. In fact several reviewers thought the series could use some comic relief. The *Telegram* (Toronto), 12 February 1957, complained that adults would notice too many errors, that the series covered too much ground too quickly, and that the Iroquois skullcaps were wrinkled. This newspaper, whose owners wanted to start a private network, was usually hostile to public broadcasting. Yet even the "Tely" reviewer was sure that children would like it. He also liked the camera work and the "lean and muscled" Godin. Ron Poulton, in the *Telegram*, 12 March 1957, while admitting Radisson was a far more wholesome hero for Canadian children than Davy Crockett, complained that there was still "entirely too much time occupied with too little action in each chapter" and thus the series "could have been wrapped up in less time at less cost to the taxpayer" – a reiterated theme over the last fifty years of newspaper criticism. John Haslett-Cuff made the same complaints about *North of 60* in 1992.

By 3 April, J.E. Belliveau of the *Daily Star* wrote that "we now admit that the criticism of grown-ups was not necessarily well-founded. The series is for kids and the youngsters are getting a bang out of it. They don't care about the Indians, as Pierre is heroic enough for them and the music is incidental. We know they have been impressed because we have been ducking flying arrows, jumping in fright at sudden war whoops, and watching small boys leaping from bed to bed in semi-nude Indian state. Just missed being scalped last night. When a seven year old knows and can pronounce Des Groseilliers, that's proof enough for us that the series has 'taken.'" If this was so, then it also appears that *Radisson* reinforced some Hollywood stereotypes for some children. In the 1940s and 1950s, boys and the occasional girl were given toy guns so they could play Cowboys and Indians. Most chose to be cowboys or even cowgirls. The Indians were, in more than one sense, usually imaginary. But not all fans were under ten. When the series began the second season, the CBC *Times*, a not unbiased source, reported on 2 November 1957 that "[y]oungsters kept an all-day vigil in front of the hotel [in Magog] where the actors were staying … They have recognised [Jacques Godin] wherever he goes and many have made the trip to his home in Verdun for an autograph."

Typically, the most serious complaints were about the costs of the production. English-speaking actors are reported to have protested that too much money was spent on a cast that was 80 per cent francophone. Originally each episode was budgeted at $3,500 from Radio-Canada, the usual price for a half-hour filmed show in the United States at that time. Then the CBC added $3,500 for a single airplay on its new microwave network, including a broadcast on any station added to its network in the next three years. In a very unusual step, all other rights were given to the writer, John Lucarotti (Moon [1957] calls him an "ardent naturalised Canadian").[35] He was apparently paid $300 per script, not a princely sum even in 1950s dollars. The budget soon and predictably rose to $15,000 an episode, adding up to $600,000 for the whole series, an unheard-of investment in one program for the CBC in those days. Eventually the cost rose to $25,000 an episode or "$800,000 to a million,"[36] and the final overall cost was pegged at $821,600 without factoring in the costs of CBC's own facilities and staff. Supervising producer Jean-Yves Bigras, as reported in the *Montreal Gazette*, 25 August 1957, claimed, however, that simultaneous filming in two languages cost 30 per cent less than two separate film series of this kind. He also said, quite rightly, that up until 1955–56 it would not have been possible for the CBC to undertake anything on this scale. After all, the series involved a hundred actors, a crew of forty-five, and a process of shooting five episodes at once. He did not mention that syndication, made possible by filming the series, could recoup some of the costs.

Under the heading "Last Laugh" (and widely reported elsewhere), *Variety* on 4 September 1957 proudly proclaimed that the series had been sold to the United States under the title *Tomahawk – The Adventures of Pierre Radisson*, as well as to ITV Tyne Tees and Australia. *Radisson* is still remembered by some Canadians who lived close to the border as *Tomahawk*. On 5 January 1958 *Variety* reported on the Nielsen ratings: "Tomahawk has pulled a neat surprise in the New York market, ranking first of all syndicated product [i.e., scheduled out of primetime] in its time period, Sundays at 6:30 p.m."[37] The American series *Hawkeye: The Last of the Mohicans* was next in the ratings. Then, as now, success in the United States was highly valued. However, catching a trend, American production companies with bigger resources than the CBC/SRC were making adventure series like *Hawkeye* in Canada in the late 1950s so that by meeting favourable quota stipulations they could access Commonwealth markets.[38]

### WHAT DID THE TARGET AUDIENCE THINK?

Because the people who made *Radisson* believed in its value as children's programming, the CBC commissioned a study called "Survey of Children's Reactions to the English Radisson Series and Radisson Audience Size Trends." In a press release in October 1957 (before the second season began) the CBC noted: "A survey of the French-speaking audience, conducted by the CBC in Montreal, shows that the findings are markedly similar to those in Ottawa." A short thirteen-page summary of the report, dated September 1957, survives.[39] It was based on a survey of students in grades 5–8 in two schools, one in Ottawa and one in Montreal – not, it was acknowledged, a very representative sample. Methods of sampling ratings, both quantitative and in this case qualitative, were relatively unsophisticated in the 1950s.[40] Grades 5 and 6 liked it most. Boys were the more loyal viewers. Predictably, they liked the suspense, adventure, and excitement, but they also enjoyed seeing the way people lived in the early days. Older students criticized the show's lack of polish, the pace, and the acting, and found the Indians' costumes and makeup unrealistic. According to the summary, "Many felt that Radisson emerged as an exaggerated and implausible figure."[41] More younger students than those in grades 7 and 8 saw him as a hero. Interestingly, the survey found that in both the French and English markets 57 per cent of the audience (that is, the majority) were adults. The summary says that many of the same observations held for the francophone audience as well, except that the French-speaking children were less critical of the production values (perhaps because they watched very little American television at that time) and the accents of the Indians. Many children called particular attention to the scene where Radisson is tortured by the Indians but did not say that they disliked the scene. The summary also notes that "10% spontaneously wanted more historical drama about explorers."

Many praised the scenery. Reruns of American TV Westerns, all shot on sound stages, now appear to viewers as painfully set-bound. I wonder if a similar group of American children during the Cold War would have made the following complaint (from a nine-year-old boy) about Davy Crockett: "I don't like it because he always wins," or (from a twelve-year-old girl) "There is one thing I don't like about many other programs on TV as well as *Radisson* and that is that they hardly ever get hurt … why couldn't Radisson get scurvy and just barely pull through" (11). Canada's taste for more realistic docudrama appears to have started early. Others remarked, "When a fort of a hundred is about to be attacked, you only see about six Indians getting ready to attack," suggesting that the production values of 1950s Hollywood Westerns, not the early television Westerns, shaped the expectations of some young viewers. The last comment in the report brings these children of fifty years ago very close: "I would like to suggest that it be earlier on Saturday evenings. My younger brother and I have a bath … I usually have mine last … so I miss most of *Radisson*" (13).

Nearly fifty years later, Dr Barry Worthington, who had watched *Radisson/Tomahawk* as a boy in Britain in 1961, remembered the show with affection:

As a child, this television series fascinated me. It was, in essence, a western, but it was unlike any other example of the genre on television at the time. It was not so much that it was set in Canada in the eighteenth century (when it was a French colony), though that was interesting. For it was the approach to the story lines that made it stand out – a drama documentary approach that employed, from time to time, a narrator. (Of course, the episodes were based on real events, and the principal characters were historical personages.) The majority of episodes were about incidents in exploration, and relations with the Indian tribes. Interestingly enough, the details of everyday life were sometimes dealt with at length, including the construction of a winter shelter, hunting beaver, and the navigation of the great rivers by canoe. Indeed, the series had some superb outdoor photography. It all seemed to be more realistic than offerings like "Gunsmoke," which seemed very much rooted in the studio (where the characters seemed to spend most of their time in the marshal's office or the town saloon).[42]

## AND SO TO BED

What are we to make of all these contradictions? As indisputably Canadian children's television entertainment made in the mid-1950s, *Radisson* was certainly not *Davy Crockett*. It stressed its historical roots, although authentic details and glitches appeared in the same frame. It introduced children and their families to a little-known, but fascinating, character. The goal of shooting television drama in both languages for both cultures has always been worthwhile, even though, as the decades pass, it has been more and more difficult to achieve.[43] Many years later, in 2000, Tony Atherton, one of the few television critics with a long memory for nearly five decades of CBC television programming (the only other that I am aware of is Jim Bawden), writes about *Radisson* as part of the historical context of the first season of *Canada: A People's History*: "The CBC has gone down this road before ... In February of 1957, CBC slipped a birch-bark canoe into the stream of pop history and paddled furiously against a torrent of Hollywood myth making. Radisson, a family adventure series loosely based on the journals of 17th-century coureur de bois, Pierre Radisson, was the network's first venture into filmed drama. But it wasn't merely entertainment; it was meant to reclaim cultural turf ... The success of Radisson, it was assumed, would inspire a flood of other pop-culture paeans to Canada's past."[44]

Then Atherton repeats what has become the myth that has dogged *Radisson* since 1957, perhaps because, when it comes to the history of

Canadian television, only myths of disaster seem to remain in the popular imagination: "Alas, the expected Radisson craze never materialized ... The finished product had nothing like the energy and polish of an American series. The acting was stilted, the writing turgid, and the locations were constrained. Young viewers, the show's primary target, were its most unforgiving critics ... Radisson lasted one season [sic] and lost almost all of its $1-million investment [although it was resold as Tomahawk]. Needless to say, the predicted boom in Canadian pop-history TV never materialised." Which is true. He continues: "Instead, for the next four decades, the CBC proceeded on a cautious [not always – see the 1961 two-part docudrama Riel] and erratic course when it came to popularising Canada's heritage, recording some remarkable triumphs – like the documentary series The National Dream in 1976, the feature-length drama Riel in 1979,[45] and the Gemini-winning Banting and Best miniseries, Glory Enough For All in 1988 – as well as many disappointing failures of will and imagination."[46] In the end, Canada: A People's History was a major success for a broad audience and as a resource for schools.

From the fragmentary print evidence that survives, plot summaries indicate that Radisson focused on the relationship between the French and the Iroquois, which was hostile at that time, and then on contacts with the more remote nations in the Northwest and around Hudson Bay. Radisson was certainly somewhat racist in its treatment of Indians. An Indian "blood brother" who seldom appears in the plot summaries and clearly does not accompany Radisson on his voyages does not balance the equation. The series to some degree seems to have reflected the Hollywood film treatment of Indians. Although named as different First Nations, all appear to be have been treated as exotic but dangerous cultures, as obstacles to trade, as noble redmen, as savages, and above all as useful tools to procure more furs. Most of these pan-Indian stereotypes were identities performed by white actors because "no real Indians were available." Clearly, none were consulted.

In Radisson, we see the transference of the best qualities of aboriginal life, as recognized and defined by the settler society, from the First Nations who already flourished in Canada to Radisson as white precursor of the coureurs de bois. The series was not just about finding a hero to counteract Disney's Davy Crockett, but also represented, in some fashion, the adult impulse to return to a long-lost pastoral age of innocence, to recreate the sense of a continent new and unexplored, to escape from the conformist 1950s and its Cold War threats. Crockett, the "King of the Wild Frontier," and Radisson, the "Lord of the Wilderness," satisfied the same urban longing for a New World version of a "green world." The series valorized Radisson's exploits instead of recognizing the complex truths of ongoing contact between the two societies and the eventual conquest of one by the other. According to Renée Legris, the choice of the coureurs de bois as the way to erase of that history and to represent a mythical golden age is a specifically Quebec phenomenon that endures.[47] She points out in her review of French television drama for the *Canadian Encyclopedia* that Radio-Canada and some of the private networks have continued to broadcast historical dramas whose subjects date from the founding of Quebec City to the continuing settlement of the province's northern frontiers in the early twentieth century. The early years of New France, the French-Indian Wars, the Seven Years' War, the War of 1812, and the rebellions of 1837–38 seldom appear in our English popular culture. If we were to look for Indians in English television drama series for children after *Radisson,* we would only find them as secondary figures – as in *The Forest Rangers* and *Adventures in Rainbow Country* – or as largely absent, except for single guest appearances – as in *Matt and Jenny* and *The Campbells*. These four programs are the subject of the next chapter.

# SIX

# Other Early Children's Series: The Context of the 1960s to 1980s

"My first students are now in their forties. Many are First Nations, Metis, Inuits, Dene, Nishnawbe, Cree. And when I was living up north and certainly teaching out west and acting as a school counsellor in three different provinces, Ontario, Alberta and British Columbia, I was distressed, as were other non-native teachers that there were not [aboriginal] role models."

Ms Samantha McIntyre, teacher

Why do the early series for families and children matter? I think that Ms McIntyre spoke for many on 16 March 1999 when she took the trouble to intervene at the Canadian Radio-television and Telecommunications Commission's public consultation on the CBC/SRC. Her remarks are edited from the transcript of proceedings:[1]

And when there were such shows on television, on CBC, "[Adventures in] Rainbow Country" was one of the first TV shows that I saw that had First Nations actors not white guys painted to look native like Victor Mature, but First Nations actors. "The Beachcombers" was the next one, "Spirit Bay" was my introduction to the great and wonderful Tom Jackson … the mini series "Four Directions," of course "North of 60." For younger people, "The Rez" was fun … "Life and Times," "Man Alive," "Nature of Things," "Witness," also have had shows dealing with First Nations issues. On other specials such as the broadcast of … Canadian films, such as "Loyalties," "Big Bear," "The Diviners," allowed my First Nations students to see people like Tom Jackson, Tantoo Cardinal, Gordon Tootoosis along with the entire cast of "North of 60," all of whom I thought were wonderful. [Note that her list covers thirty years of broadcasting.] I will be very upset if anything worse happens to the CBC. I am mad as hell at our government for cutting the funding, I am furious that that has happened. Because I know that it will affect young people growing up in this country and I know that it affects me. And so I would ask for people in the CRTC to do the right thing, even if our various government and elected officials will not, not cannot, will not. The CRTC has the power to influence and, you know, we are counting on the CRTC at this point to make it so.

Regrettably, the CRTC does not have the power to stabilize the CBC's finances. That is the responsibility of Parliament. The steadily eroding financial support the CBC has received in the last fifteen years may account for the fact that, during the several years after this hearing, there have been no replacements for the kinds of dramas Ms McIntyre mentions, those that represent First Nations and Metis peoples to a wider audience. In fact, there are fewer dramatic series, miniseries, and specials produced today than at any time since the early 1970s, partly because the CRTC redefined "Canadian content" in entertainment to include cheap reality shows. During a seven-week lockout in 2005, politicians, even ministers and then prime minister Paul Martin, stoutly supported the necessity of having a public broadcaster, but they did not support it with dollars or permit long-term planning with stable funding. More recently, Stephen Harper's Conservatives are on the record as wanting to privatize all of broadcasting. The outlook for citizens like Ms McIntyre, who value the mandate work of the CBC, is grim.

Piecing together the history of the series discussed in this chapter – *Hawkeye and the Last of the Mohicans, Hudson's Bay, R.C.M.P., The Forest Rangers, Adventures in Rainbow Country, The Campbells,* and *Matt And Jenny* (the least well documented) – has been a challenge. Without the recent appearance of detailed, lovingly constructed fan sites and IMDb-based information to supplement the fragmentary information in CBC press releases and other material in the always cooperative CBC library, it would have been difficult to get even a sense of what happened. Adding to the difficulties, for shows not made by the CBC, there is no accessible paper trail.

## HAWKEYE AND HUDSON'S BAY

Two American series, shot in Canada and set in the eighteenth century, appeared around the same time as *Radisson. Hawkeye and the Last of the Mohicans* was broadcast in 1957–58 and *Hudson's Bay* in 1959–60. Both were syndicated series featuring romantic heroes and their Indian or Metis companions. Neither is mentioned in Rutherford's *When Television Was Young* (1990), *The Encyclopedia of Television,* or the online *Queen's University Directory of* CBC *Television Series.* They were not financed in Canada and did not have Canadians in the leading roles, yet they are both classified as Canadian productions on IMDb and in McNeil's *Total Television* (1980). If place and period establish national content, then *Hudson's Bay* qualifies, as it was set mostly in nineteenth-century Canada; *Hawkeye* takes place before the boundaries of the English and French colonies were established.

*Halliwell's Television Companion* (1982) calls *Hawkeye* a "modest schoolboy adventure" and is the only reference work to mention *Hudson's Bay*. Both appear as "Canadian adventure series" on the episode guides posted on the Classic TV Archive website (www.angelfire.com/retro/cta/can/, in its Canadian TV Western series subsection, which claims that *Hawkeye* was made with the cooperation of the CBC. Whether that meant that there was actually CBC input cannot be gleaned from the fragmentary materials available, but given that it must have been filmed during or just after *Radisson*, it may be that there was a swap of props or costumes or even sets. Both *Hawkeye*[2] and *Hudson's Bay*[3] were probably meant to cash in on the Davy Crockett craze. As with the Davy Crockett episodes, a few of Hawkeye's thirty-nine episodes were repackaged into four movies.

*Hawkeye* was first broadcast in the United States in April 1957, as the first season of *Radisson* was underway. *Hudson's Bay* followed. Tuscaroras, Ojibways, Shawnees, and Oneidas all appear by name in the three series, which suggests that these series did not always present a generic Indian, however inaccurate the practices shown might have been. All three inevitably featured many episodes with plots revolving around Indians, none of whom were likely to have been played by Indians. The Hurons are the good guys in *Radisson*, but in *Hawkeye*, set a century later and with a focus on English colonists, they are the bad guys.

There are a few surprises in *Hawkeye*. Ben Franklin and Ethan Allen appear, for example, and in episode 4, "The Wild One," Hawkeye and Chingachgook "come to the aid of a young Indian doctor who attempts to practice in an intolerant town," a plot that would have addressed the issue of racism in some fashion. In episode 5, "The Delaware Hoax," the Delawares are being "framed by white men for looting, pillaging and murder," a plot motif that appears several times and seems to be a counter-narrative to the standard 1950s Hollywood movie that depicted First Nations as looting, pillaging savages. In episode 9, "The Medicine Man," an aged Conestogo medicine man has been driven out by "Shenahbe an ambitious young brave" and then is presumably restored to his band. In episode 11, "The Search," an old white woman who has been enslaved by Indians since her husband was killed is presumably restored to her people. But in episode 12,

"Snake Tattoo," reversing stereotyped captive narratives, Hawkeye and Chingachgook help "a young Indian boy raised by the white man" (predictably the son of a Cree chief) return to his people. Heritage and family trump "civilization" here, an unusual plot twist in 1950s television. In episode 32, "Revenge," a young lieutenant swears revenge against all Shawnee because his parents were murdered by the war chief. This may or may not be linked to 39 (the last episode), "Circle of Hate," where a young lieutenant "has developed a fanatical hatred of the Red Man … killing or injuring any Indian he meets." Hawkeye and Chingachgook try to keep the peace in both episodes. The fearless pair also rescue settlers, uncover villains both white and native, make peace between settlers and various First Nations, are inevitably captured by hostiles, and save the life and honour of a chief threatened by "a fierce, degenerate brave." Like Radisson, they are threatened with starvation in a harsh winter. They even defend the sacredness of a Dakota burial ground in episode 28, "La Salle's Treasure."[4]

It is hard at this distance to tell exactly what role Chingachgook played in the series. In Fenimore Cooper's novels, for all of their limitations, he is no Tonto and neither is his son, Uncas. The white men – trappers, voyageurs, scouts, and soldiers – all depend on Indians to teach them their skills, to guide them, and sometimes to keep them safe. In this series, fanatics and renegades are white as well as native, and the actions of the two protagonists, who are presented as bridges between both worlds in Cooper's novels, seem to be even-handed, helping Indians, soldiers, and settlers. But television convention also demands that they be the weekly problem solvers who seldom, if ever, need the help of others, white or Indian.

The thirty-nine episodes of Hudson's Bay[5] were filmed in Canada, as already noted, but like Hawkeye the series was a completely American enterprise, made by Northstar productions, an MGM–Pathe Communications company, and released by United Artists. Its basic premise was to portray the "[a]dventures of a trapper in the Canadian Northlands," and it starred serviceable Hollywood actor Barry Nelson as John Banner. Character actor George Tobias, who, according to the IMDb site, "specialized in none-too-bright pals of the lead," played Pierre Falcone.[6] It was created and directed by Sidney Furie, a Canadian who became the well-known director of films like The Ipcress File, The Boys in Company C, and Superman IV, which, along with being shot in Canada, may account for the large number of Canadian actors I recognize from having seen them in demanding roles in productions broadcast during what came to be known as the Golden Age of CBC anthology. Most episodes were written by Lawrence Menkin, who also wrote scripts for several US television Westerns. The sites noted in notes 5 and 6 (above) and *Halliwell's Television Companion* (1982) describe *Hudson's Bay* as a Canadian Western adventure series. If the series were to be produced now, scholars would call it "industrially Canadian" even though it reflected our history in some fashion. Since there is no scheduling information, it is not possible to guess the demographic of the target audience. Was it made for adults or, more probably, for family viewing? The problem is that there are no short descriptions of the episodes available that amplify on the provocative titles, and there is no fan site for this forgotten series where that information might appear. Again, Indians do not seem to have played Indians, although there was lots of interaction between the Hudson's Bay Company (HBC) trapper and the Indians; for example, Eric Clavering (who would reappear as Shing Wauk in *The Forest Rangers*) appears as Sequoia/Fly Fly four times, according to the IMDb. Episodes whose titles suggest an Indian focus are 18, "Blue Eyed Squaw" (another captive narrative?); 29, "The Crees" [*sic*]; 36, "The Northern Cheyenne"; 38, "Chippewah Banner"; and 39, the last, "Blackfoot Barrier." Canadian history may have been drawn on in episode 12, "The Prophet," but Tecumseh's brother, the well-known "prophet," lived in the eighteenth century and episodes 14 ("Rebels of Red River") and 15 ("Red River Outpost") appear to define the period as the 1870s. Regrettably, while other fictional series or miniseries with a Hudson's Bay theme have been announced in the last (nearly) fifty years, so far the subject has only appeared wearing documentary dress.

### R . C . M . P .

*R.C.M.P.* was the only adult contemporary series in the late 1950s and for many years thereafter to feature Indian subjects. Scheduled from 8:00 to 8:30 and then from 8:30 to 9:00 p.m. on Wednesday, it was not, unlike *Radisson*, specifically for children. (However, in 1964 it was rerun in a children's slot, 4:00–4:30 p.m.) The thirty-nine episodes were broadcast for one season, 1959–60, and then either rerun the following year or split between two seasons, as happened with *Radisson*. *The Queen's University Directory of CBC Television Series 1952–1982* online[7] is not clear about the exact broadcast dates, probably because the paper records are also not clear. Unlike *Radisson* or *Hudson's Bay*, this series was rerun many times, right into the 1990s. It was not an in-house CBC production but a co-production of the CBC, BBC television, and Crawley-McConnell Films, shot on location in Ontario, Quebec, and Saskatchewan. According to James Forrester's article about F.R. "Budge" Crawley in *Take One* (summer 1998),[8] Crawley was the executive producer. *R.C.M.P.* was sold to Australia and syndicated in the

United States as well as being broadcast by the BBC. Since the BBC's Vincent Tilsey was script editor for the series, the BBC had very direct input into what went to air. On the Classic TV Archive site the compilers used both the Canadian TV and American TV synopses.

R.C.M.P.'s cast list for episode 7 includes Inuit names, and the cast for episode 16, "Johnny Wolf," includes Charles Smith and Peter Buckshot as first and second Indians and Alan Crowfoot as Joe.[9] However, Johnny Wolf was played by Larry Zahab (later known as Lawrence Dane).[10] The plot summary of this episode raises an interesting question, one that reappears in *Spirit Bay* and *North of 60*: What is First Nations art? There was little serious attention paid to such art in 1960, but this episode points to the existence of such work, not as craft but as art: "Johnny Wolf's father walked among the white men – an artist and a hero. Johnny tries to do the same, only to find he has only the ambition not the ability." The episode was well ahead of its time. In episode 20, "Moonshine," Angeline Maheux plays Mother Smoke, and Bobbie Buckshot and Joe Jocko play Peter and Matthew Smoke.

Peter Kentner (2001) had this to say about *R.C.M.P.*: "A great forgotten Canadian program, *R.C.M.P.* should be required viewing for fans of good police drama, grim story lines, cool music and retro scenery" (155–6). See also *The Queen's University Directory of CBC Television Series*.

### OTHER CANADIAN HISTORICAL AND CONTEMPORARY SERIES

With the short-lived exception of *R.C.M.P* in the 1960s, from the 1950s through the 1980s Indians only appeared in series for children. They seem to have signified both the "North" and authentic wilderness experiences. Between *Radisson* and *Spirit Bay*, there were several contemporary and period children's series set in what to Canadians would be the near north but to most Americans and other viewers abroad would simply be the North. In *The Campbells* (1986–89), the North is defined as the wilderness in southeastern Ontario in the 1830s. *Matt and Jenny* (1981, set in the 1850s), subtitled *On the Wilderness Trail*, begins in Halifax and works its way, it seems, to Upper Canada before the end. Both of these historical series for families were preceded in the mid-1960s and early 1970s by the contemporary characters and settings of *The Forest Rangers* (1963–65) and *Adventures in Rainbow Country* (1971), both set in the well-explored near north of Ontario.[11] *The Beachcombers* (1972–90), a series for families set in British Columbia's Sunshine Coast, spanned nineteen seasons, a time of substantial change for

family structures and values and a time of major changes for the First Nations. The quite different children's series *Spirit Bay*, aired in the mid-1980s,
made those changes very plain with its all-aboriginal cast and stories centred entirely on the reserve. When one examines the sensibilities of both the
makers and the audiences, there is almost a greater gulf between *Radisson*
and *Spirit Bay* than there is between the 1927 pageant described in chapter 4
and today's prime-time representations.

In all cases, the signifiers of "North" were lots of trees, water (preferably dangerous rivers, rapids, or swamps), rough or dangerous characters
who were also struggling to survive, wild animals like bears and wolves,
harsh winters, and encounters with Indians or Metis who could be dangerous or helpful. *The Campbells*, like *The Beachcombers*, was a family adventure series that focused on both children and adults. *The Forest
Rangers, Adventures in Rainbow Country,* and *Matt and Jenny* featured primarily the children and young teens. In contrast, *Radisson,* although originally intended for children, had few children in the narratives, while
*Hudson's Bay,* it would appear, concentrated on the adult trappers and
coureurs de bois as well as on their allies and adversaries.

## THE FOREST RANGERS

Six years after *Radisson, The Forest Rangers* (1963–65, dubbed in French as *Les
cadets de la Forêt*)[12] went to air. Kentner (2001) points out that the series began
as six-minute segments on the daily children's program *Razzle Dazzle*
(though it soon expanded to fill a half-hour on its own) and that the shows
were mostly about children's adventures not about their personal lives.
Sandy Stewart created *Razzle Dazzle* with producer/writer Bill Davidson,
and in his book *Here's Looking at Us: A Personal History of Television in Canada*
(1986), he traces Davidson's career in children's programming from there
to *The Forest Rangers* to *Adventures in Rainbow Country* to *Matt and Jenny*
(246). *The Forest Rangers* was set near a Metis community and had a recurring character called Joe Two Rivers, a Metis guide, played by white actor
Michael Zenon. Fred Rainsberry (1988) offers a brief description of the series: "The stories ranged from scenes of actual forest fire fighting to gold
prospecting to slapstick comedy" (128). The *Queen's University Directory* entry for *The Forest Rangers* characterizes it as

a highly successful adventure series for children, [which] was developed by executive producer Maxine Samuels as an independent venture, with the cooperation of the CBC. By the time the show aired in

Young forest rangers learn from Joe Two Rivers, played by Michael Zenon. The rangers are (*left to right*) Susan Conway as Kathy, Ronald Cohoon as Zeke, Peter Tully as Mike Forbes, Ralph Endersby as Chub Stanley, and George Allan as Ted Keeley. *Associated Screen Productions in association with the* CBC.

Canada, it had already been sold to networks in England, France, West Germany, and Australia, and by 1966, over forty countries could watch the adventures of a gang of resourceful Canadian young people who lived in northern Ontario ... The real focus of the story was an abandoned fort where they set up their ham radio, and helped keep watch for forest fires and other conservational offences. They ran up against not only poachers, but a succession of thieves, escaped criminals, spies, and other wrongdoers ... Although the program's stories were principally adventures, they sometimes had an educational slant ...

The leader of the Junior Rangers was Peter Keeley ... Ralph Endersby ... [was] a city boy who moves to Indian River to live with foster parents, and is welcomed into the Junior Rangers [which would help city children identify with the situation and characters, a strategy also used in *Spirit Bay*]. The other rangers included Mike Forbes ... and Kathy[13] [her predecessor was Gaby LaRoche] ... Other adult characters included Uncle Raoul

LaRoche ... Indian [sic] Joe Two Rivers, and R.C.M.P. Sergeant Brian Scott ... The dog was named Spike and the bear was Carol.

Kentner characterizes Joe Two Rivers, as a "smooth talkin' Metis fur trapper who occasionally helped the kids" and summarizes the plots as being about the young heroes humbling juvenile delinquents, fighting forest fires (to the dismay of the real Junior Rangers, who would never let a kid fight a forest fire) and Windigo, and catching beaver poachers. The newspaper critics that Kentner quotes emphasize the improbability of some of the plots but also the conservation message (56–7). The show's enduring popularity is clear. In 2007 eighteen hours of season 1 appeared in two DVD boxed sets.[14] No other series in this book has that distinction.

In *The Forest Rangers,* Indians are primarily represented by Shing Wauk, an old medicine man, played by a white actor, Eric Clavering, who appeared in episodes 5, 33, 57, 75, 84, and 103. The real Shingwauk, a highly respected chief who had requested an education for his Anishnabe people in 1871, would have been astonished at episode 84, "The Great Hypnotist," where another character, during a celebration of "The old Indian warrior days of early Canadian history," hypnotises him into believing that "he is his great grandfather ... and he goes crazy and starts letting arrows fly at his head."[15] A picture on Clayton Self's very helpful fan website, discussed in chapter 10 and used with permission, shows this Anishnabe chief shooting arrows from the back of a horse and wearing a huge Plains war bonnet.[16] More respectably, Shing Wauk cures a sick horse in episode 5. In 57 he has a vision of a plane crashing. It is not clear to me how in the second to last episode, 103, "The Lost Tribe," Shing Wauk could be involved with finding a lost tribe of Mi'kmaq, who are located in the Maritimes, Newfoundland, and the Gaspé Peninsula, not in the series' setting of Ontario's near north.[17] However, the episode raises an raised important issue when Shing Wauk tries to prevent a professor from looting an ancient burial site – an act that had occurred in *Hawkeye,* recurs in one of the best episodes of *Spirit Bay,* and is alluded to in the first season of *North of 60.* Shing Wauk is the healer, the mystic, and a figure of fun, all roles that television Indians were called upon to play in the Hollywood mould.

In later episodes, a recurring Indian character would be used to signify authenticity. In *The Forest Rangers,* the producers chose Joe Two Rivers for this character, a Metis from Ontario, not the West (i.e., the "other Metis"),[18] who, from the sketchy details in the episode guide, seems not only to have spoken Ojibway but also to have carried many of the plots that had

Michael Zenon as Joe Two Rivers, the modern Metis
with fringed buckskin jacket and paddle subsumed in
practice into a generic "Indian." The image promises
all kinds of special knowledge of the forest and adventures in canoes. *Associated Screen Productions in
association with the* CBC.

Indian themes, which may explain why he is often incorrectly referred to
as an Indian in various published accounts. This character talks to the
animals. In episode 19, "The Bear Story," "three bears are tamed by Joe
Two Rivers when he talks in his Ojibway tongue." Again, in episode 32,
"The Hero," he talks to a bear "in his native tongue – Ojibway Indian,"
and in a neat twist he saves the life of a panicked Western action hero. In
episode 33, "The Wolverine," he calls a wolverine that is killing farmer's
stock by its Ojibway (and other nations') name – "'carcajou' ... a name
meant to strike fear into all those that know of this evil little killer."
Joe Two Rivers is a mystical healer in episode 11, "The Rattlesnake," and

as expected of Indian heroes, he is the tallest, strongest, fastest character. In episode 64, "The River," he has to run dangerous rapids "to clear the name of an Indian Reserve friend accused of murder," then "swim in the icy autumn waters." Later, in episode 77, "The Gunshot," he climbs a fire tower to catch a killer. In episode 99, "The Invaders," he reluctantly takes on "three punks from the city" and "single-handedly" drives them off. Metis Joe Two Rivers, so often remembered and referred to as an Indian, can be perceived either as a halfway point to the recognition of Indians as valuable people or as an uneasy displacement of a set of stereotyped virtues. The producers may have thought he would be a character who bridged white and Indian worlds. Instead, reflecting what often happened in the real world, his young audience and the critics seem to have seen him as Indian.

There are other Indian elements in the series. "The Wendigo" of episode 47 is an evil spirit who is also discussed on *Spirit Bay*, appears on *The Rez*, and is seen again as variant called a "Bushman" in *North of 60*. In this version a little girl is chased by Wendigo but "fights off the spirit with a ceremonial mask." (Oddly, in episode 53, the series also features – a leprechaun.) Episode 38, "A Christmas Story," has two descriptions – "An Indian cares for a watch for Macleod" and "Macleod desperate for a pocket watch takes the watch. When Amik is accused of the crime, Macleod fesses [*sic*] up." Len Birman, who played the Indian in George Ryga's half-hour television play *Q for Quest*, plays Amik, then reappears in episode 98 as a "famous Indian movie star who once killed a child by accident. The child's father tries to avenge his son's death at a staged pow-wow event involving great suspense." The cast list for this episode includes Chief Richard Pine as a drummer, Chief Wilmer Naditwan as Old Bear, and "the Thunderbird Dancers." This episode would have required the active cooperation of whatever Anishnabe band supplied the drum and the dancers. In episode 72, "Merry Christmas" "Old Macleod helps out an Indian woman who is in need of hospitalization and her newborn baby back in the bush." In episode 73, "The Choice," Lawrence Dane (again) plays an Indian called John Madamin "who saves George [but] must deal with his criminal past in order to help his fellow Indians"– a synopsis that offers many possibilities. Late in the series, in episode 88, "Jimmy Twenty," an "Indian teen wants to stay but must return a stolen wallet." Episode 94, "The Bulldozer," reverses the stereotype of Indians losing land when "an Indian chief uses a treaty with a mine company from the distant past [and] saves the kid's fort from being bulldozed." In this episode, however, the chief, Little Eagle, is played by Pietro Mauro, not by a native actor. Italian often seemed to be the default for Indian for the casting directors in those years. The title of the final episode, 104, "The Ojibway Beat," refers to a song written by Ralph Endersby (Chub) and William Davidson. It wasn't Indian-made rock and roll, yet "Ojibway" appears in the title. Indians and wild animals do appear in this version of the North, but just as the Ontario town of Kleinberg substitutes for wilderness in all of these series but R.C.M.P., substitutes often stand in for the real thing.

The IMDb site[19] has messages from one fan who remembers lessons on native life from Joe Two Rivers, and one from someone who, after watching *The Forest Rangers* again as an adult, found that the stories were rather simplistic but thought that their message remains valid. According to Clayton Self's detailed fan website, the series was airing on a digital and satellite channel called "TV Land" in 2004. On the UK site of CultTV, the entry by John Hutchinson (no date, but from internal evidence probably 2003–04)[20] sets the scene of a British child watching at tea-time on the co-producer's channel, ATV. He also remembers Joe Two Rivers fondly as "a nearby woodsman whose deep knowledge of Indian Folklore and the outdoor life was often called upon … [C]ourage, knowledge of the outdoors and good-natured humour … are perhaps the elements which have ensured that the series remains so fondly in the memories of viewers the world over." CultTV also refers to Self's website as "widely admired by fans and former cast and production members alike." Self's guest book and quotations from answers from the cast to questions he posed would seem to authenticate the latter claim, and Self is also a named source on the Classic TV Archive site, which provides a link to his.

Greg Dymond and Geoff Pevere (1996) remember watching *The Forest Rangers* when they were kids: "[T]o kick back after an invigorating game of road hockey by watching *The Forest Rangers* while eating packaged butter tarts off the back of the first Guess Who LP cover was to just know that you were up to something culturally distinctive … We knew that *The Forest Rangers*, an 'adventure' show with a polite emphasis on collective problem-solving, was different from *Lost in Space* [an industrially Canadian production]."[21] According to Pevere and Dymond, *The Forest Rangers* was sold to over fifty countries (156), a real success for the mid-1960s. At 104 episodes it was easy to syndicate and is still running (as of June 2007) in the Toronto market on SUN TV.[22] Some, not all, of the episodes were rerun on APTN in 2002–03. In 2000–01 APTN broadcast both *The Forest Rangers* and *Adventures in Rainbow Country*. In an interview on the *4 to 6* show on CBC Toronto, 1 May 2000, Jim Compton explained that the Aboriginal People's Television Network had selected only 52 of the 104 episodes of *The Forest Rangers* (and may have shown the series primarily because the CRTC had required APTN to broadcast some drama as a condition of licensing). Compton also pointed out that in *The Forest Rangers* Joe Two Rivers was played by an actor of Ukrainian background and that the role model was not necessarily positive, but he did not elaborate on how it was less than positive for First Nations viewers. He also made clear that although both *The Forest Rangers* and *Adventures in Rainbow Country* had a strong environmental focus and were ahead of their time in that respect, they did not reflect the worlds of the First Nations. Even so, for good or ill, the 104-episode run of *The Forest Rangers* has had staying power.

### ADVENTURES IN RAINBOW COUNTRY

Five years after *The Forest Rangers* had its debut, *Adventures in Rainbow Country* (1970–71) featured a major character called Pete Gawa, a somewhat older Ojibway teenager than Billy, the fourteen-year-old, fair-haired lead. Played by Buckley Petawabano and appearing in every episode, he is often placed in the background of a shot, but he is present and sometimes essential to the plot. Pete is a modern, quite competent young man who earns his living as a fishing guide. I think it is arguable that this shows significant progress in the representation of First Nations characters, since it precedes Jesse Jim on *The Beachcombers* by a year.

Kentner (2001) calls *Adventures in Rainbow Country* "*The Forest Rangers* in bell bottoms" and says that it was a Canadian/Australian/British co-production. He also reports that it was cancelled despite good ratings and large numbers of viewers. The undated but damning reviews he quotes from the *Globe and Mail* and the Toronto *Telegram* criticize the writing, the acting, and the character motivations. However, it too is still in reruns, and adults with long memories enjoyed a reunion in August 2006.[23] The executive producer was Ralph Ellis, and the creator/producer was William Davidson, who had been the producer of the last season of *The Forest Rangers*. Leslie Millin's review in the *Globe and Mail*, no date, is quoted by Dymond and Pevere (1996): "[Billy] leads the life of the true North strong and free in that he goes fishing for brook trout, puts down his sister and accepts his buddy as damn nearly an equal" (156).[24] Pevere and Dymond claim that the series had 4 million viewers. Kentner (2001) cites a Nielsen rating that listed the program as having 4.6 million viewers. I have not seen the Nielsen report, but the number seems doubtful, even for the early 1970s, when audiences were not fragmented as they are now.[25] However, on the Classic TV Archive website, William Davidson, identified as creator/producer, disputes as a myth the "disappointment" in the series. Listing the difficulties he faced, he says that the producers

Buckley Petawabano as the modern older teenager
Pete Gawa in *Adventures in Rainbow Country. Manitou
Productions, in association with the* CBC, ABC *Films Ltd
of Britain, and the Australian Broadcasting Commission.*

had to work with three different program directors in CBC English network television. In fact, the early 1970s were a difficult time for any kind
of drama at the CBC (see Miller 1987 *passim*). Davidson says that "[t]he CBC
involvement during production was limited to one excellent liaison person George Desmond, the only CBC person to spend any time up north,
on location, and a friend of the production." He points out that the Manitou independent production company made the series (with participation
from British and Australian television), not the CBC (which did in fact provide financial support), and reiterates that "four million people watched
it every week" and that it "played for years on USA cable channels." Fred
Rainsberry (1988) lists the writers as Martin Lager, William Davidson,
John Craig, and Lindsay Galloway (135).[26]

According to the *Queen's University Directory*, *Adventures in Rainbow
Country* was repeated multiple times after its first airing. It is described in

the directory as follows: "A filmed drama series ... starring Lois Maxwell as Nancy Williams, Stephen Cottier as her son Billy ... and Susan Conway [once a forest ranger] as her daughter Hannah. Other performers included Buckley Petawabano as Pete Gawa, Wally Koster as the bush pilot Dennis Mogubgub, Albert Millaire as Roger Lemieux [the obligatory francophone character] and Alan Mills as Dougal MacGregor. The drama concentrated on the adventures of the teenager Billy (whose sister occasionally appeared) and his Ojibway friend Pete in the bushland of northern Ontario. The series was ... also an international co-production." The *Queen's* entry reiterates that "the series met with critical disappointment."[27] According to the Classic TV Archive website, the CBC ran the twenty-six episodes six more times until 1977.[28] I have not been able to find anything in the CBC library on the series.

The series was "shot on the White River First Nation ... Birch Island Ontario," according to Chief Frank Paibmosai. Davidson says that "Buckley Petawabano just walked into our office one day and introduced himself. He was Cree and from the Lac St. John region in Quebec. His marvellous smile and personality made up for a slight awkwardness in speech, but he was a real human being and a tremendous asset to the series, both off and on screen. A classy gentleman, about 20 at the time, and a role model for younger native boys in the Manitoulin district. He was the most loved member of our cast and crew."[29] Clay Self's website supplies these quotes as well as photos provided by the producer and makeup artist.[30] He also posts what appears to be a public relations release for prospective buyers by an American distributor that describes the show this way: "Every foot of film has been shot on location in one of the wildest, richest, most picturesque regions of Canada ... In the audience-holding tradition of 'Lassie' (?!) it combines exciting stories with natural settings. However, this series takes family adventure several steps beyond anything that's been done for television ... Viewers of all ages will be fascinated as Billy Williams and his friends shoot the rapids, follow the trails of early explorers, go skydiving, get lost in the bush, discover the legends and lore of the Ojibway Indian people, search for wrecks beneath the waters of the Great Lakes."

The IMDb site provides a running order of the list of episodes that differs from the one on Classic TV Archives.[31] Some interest in aboriginal issues is shown in a few of the twenty-six episodes. The first episode, "La Chute" (which I saw), was clearly intended to set a tone of adventure for subsequent episodes, with "pretend voyageurs," imitating Étienne Brûlé, getting trapped in the gorge and needing to be rescued. But adding a different note

Stephen Cottier as Billy (*left, standing*) and Buckley Petawabano as Pete (*right, standing*) – unknown episode. *Manitou Productions, in association with the CBC, ABC Films Ltd of Britain, and the Australian Broadcasting Commission.*

to the episode, Pete's rescue of them also validates his people's oral history, which says that they had to rescue Brûlé, even though he did not mention this in his journal. (In episode 6, "Panic in the Bush," Pete has to rescue Billy.) In episode 7, "Long Tough Race," guest star Duke Redbird plays a runner. Davidson on the Classic TV Archive site points out that Redbird was a respected painter and poet in the 1960s.[32] I also saw episode 16, "Wall of Silence," an improbable tale about a secret military box that the two central characters retrieve from a downed plane, a box that "contains valuable information which is vital to the safety of the free world," according to the plot summary. Pete returns it to the colonel with this comment, the last line in the episode: "Lucky it fell into my hands. My people have a treaty with your people." Of course, as in most children's television, this episode ends in laughter, even though Petawabano delivers his line with a clear shot of wry. Episode 17, "Where the Rice Grows," features the centuries-old custom of harvesting wild rice. The last episode, "Dreamer's Rock," touches on a sensitive topic. Located on Birch Island, Dreamer's Rock is associated with vision quests undertaken by members of the Whitefish River band. As Drew

Hayden Taylor (1990), Ojibway playwright and columnist from the Curve Lake First Nation, puts it, "Dreamer's Rock is a real place with real power. It's located beside a highway on Birch Island Reserve, and many people still go there for guidance. Care should be taken in the depiction of such a sacred place" (10).[33] The synopsis suggests that a mining company wants to mine around and under it, thus destroying it, but the Indian band objects. Wilmer Nadjiwon, born on Cape Croker Reserve and chief of the Chippewas of Nawash,[34] played the Indian chief.[35] Given that he agreed to act in the series, there was considerable potential for self-reflexivity, but only for those in the audience who knew of his life.

Dymond and Pevere have a post-Oka take on what they call "The Great Outdoor Adventure Show," which they say usually includes "a wise and occasionally wise-cracking Native character whose presence reaffirms the comforting myth of Canada as a country not beset by race problems" (155).[36] Drew Hayden Taylor, when looking back on the children's and family adventure series that included aboriginal characters, did not share their sunny view of these shows. Writing in *Cinema Canada*, May 1987, in a sidebar to an article titled "Adapting Native Scripts" that focused on *Spirit Bay*, he provides an overview of the representation of First Nations adults and children to that date. He points out that native writers are not used on shows with "Native Themes ... adventure shows ... like *Adventures in Rainbow Country*, *Matt and Jenny*, *The Beachcombers* and to a much lesser extent *Danger Bay*." He quotes *The Beachcombers* story editor for the sixteenth season, Karen Petersen: "'As far as I can remember we have used virtually no native writers on the show though we average at least one Native flavoured show a season. We rely on a lot of input from the actors as well as accuracy from the writers.'" After four seasons of *Danger Bay*, another family adventure series co-produced with Germany, Taylor points out that "*Danger Bay* has never used a [native] writer," and he quotes the publicist, who says, "'We've only done one that was concerned with Native issues and that was in the first year,'" probably the episode that used the ancient and memorable T'simshian twin stone masks in a completely unmemorable way, unlike *Due South*, which used them to raise questions about the repatriation of native artifacts. Taylor also quotes Ralph Ellis, executive producer of *Adventures in Rainbow Country*: "[W]e did go out of our way to make sure that everything was correct. We'd go to pains to authenticate everything ... Indian legends made it intensely popular overseas. Because of Buckley's involvement [playing Pete], a part of every episode was Native. Good writers are scarce and good Native writers are even more scarce" – that was in the early 1970s. Taylor's comments on *Spirit Bay,* aired sixteen years later, are discussed in the chapter on *Spirit Bay. Adventures in Rainbow Country* ran on the digital rerun *Dejaview* in 2004–05.

## *MATT AND JENNY*

Ten years later, Ralph Ellis returned to the family adventure genre to produce *Matt and Jenny,* sometimes called *Matt and Jenny on the Wilderness Trail 1850.*[37] It was first broadcast on 7 January 1981 and was an anglophone/francophone co-production. The SRC (Radio-Canada) and the Global TV network were the production partners, while money for dubbing came from TF1 (TV Française 1), Antenna 2, Channel J, RTBF (Radio télévision belges francophones), TMC (Telemontecarlo), and SRC, opening up the francophone market. There were twenty-six 26-minute episodes. Young Megan Follows (later Anne of Green Gables) played Jenny, and Derrick Jones played Matt. There is not much to be found about this series, except for a full episode guide on the Classic TV Archive website.[38] It is not deposited in the National Archives of Canada (NAC), and there is nothing about it in the CBC's English library. I managed to tape only three episodes during the reruns in the mid-1980s. A website for TFI in 2005, now gone, suggested that the show was in reruns at that time. A fan site for Duncan Regehr, one of the actors, tells us that "[t]his series has also been re-run on Nickelodeon."[39] On a Quebec site, now missing from the web, the full title was changed to (in English) "On the Road of Friendship." This site reported that "Matt and Jenny debark from a boat from England. Their mother died during the crossing. The authorities want to return them to England but the two orphans do not want to return and flee. They have only one plan, to join their uncle Bill somewhere in Canada." In France the show debuted on TF1 almost simultaneously with the Global broadcast in January 1981.[40] Some German sites list a first broadcast in 1981 on ARD as well.

An IMDb site has a translation of an entry from one person who only partially remembers *Matt and Jenny.*[41] Apparently, when it was aired in Germany, the viewer found the series spooky because the children were left alone a lot. According to a website for a children's program on the French channel TF1 that included pictures of the series, "for them the route is long and they must deal with hunger, cold, fatigue, and despair. Happily, they encounter on their route people ready to come to their aid like Kit or Adam Cardston. The series, often very sad, had only twenty-six episodes [and] was made in 1980 and 1981" (my translation).[42]

A description of the first episode in Rainsberry's (1988) history supplies some detail about the series' background. The tone of the quotation suggests that Rainsberry had access to the pitch to the network or other potential partners: "A colourful and exciting, early prime time, outdoor action–adventure series set in Canada and the bordering United States … Matt and Jenny Tanner, brother and sister, aged about fourteen, [are] working class, street-wise children from Bristol, England, who emigrate to Canada with their mother in 1850, about a year after their father's death. They are leaving the world of Charles Dickens for the World of Mark Twain, Fenimore Cooper, Hawthorne and Thoreau translated into Canadian experience" – an interesting way to suggest culture shock as a major motif. The children are supposed to join their uncle in Halifax. Their mother dies of typhoid on board ship, and they elude the authorities to find their uncle. Falsely accused of theft, they are helped by another passenger. According to Rainsberry, this passenger, "Adam Cardston, a tall, mysterious man in his forties" and a world traveller, is returning to the "Canadian West" (the home of many First Nations and the Metis at that time). Using a rough map sent them by their uncle Bill, Matt and Jenny set out for his farm with Adam. They have a "wild ride on a runaway raft" and then meet "Kit, another unique wilderness character … twenty-five, a young Daniel Boone. knowledgable about life in the bush, expert with animals, strong and agile." When they reach their uncle's farm, "[a]n old Indian woman" tells them that the family left for the West by wagon three months earlier (130–1). We can see the appeal to various regions and age groups and the possibility of stories centring around the quest to find their uncle or around Cardston, the mysterious stranger, or Kit, the handsome young man, their companions and protectors "on the wilderness trail" in a period of major immigration to Canada. The series must have included encounters with Indians as the children moved across the country. Drew Hayden Taylor quotes Ellis as saying that, given the period and the wilderness setting, "'they couldn't help but include many Native stories'" and that they did "'a lot of research on a particular Iroquois ceremony.'" But the evidence from the episode list is fragmentary

Of the three episodes that I recorded off-air during reruns on Global and watched years later, only two are centred on an Indian story. Episode 13, "Wolf Howl at Kennebec Cliff," by William Davidson, features a family camped in a covered wagon. The settler is shooting at wolves and deer, convinced that he is hunting a werewolf. Going mad in the bush is a motif used in Canadian historical and contemporary television series that are set in the wilderness. It turns out that the werewolf is a "wolf child," a "wild child" raised by wolves. The boy never speaks and runs when the settler tries to kill him, but then (predictably) he saves the settler's life when the settler is about to be attacked by a wolf. Kit tells the settler that the moral of that story is "Live and let live." While deconstructing the idea of a werewolf, this episode presents as fact what Rudyard Kipling presents as fiction, a boy raised by wolves. However, unlike Mowgli in *The Jungle Book*, this child is without speech and, therefore, says Jenny, "primitive." In fact, he represents what settlers fear about the First Nations people who lived on the land. He is at one with dangerous animals, speaks no language they understand, is apparently hostile at first, and dresses in skins. Matt and Jenny leave him in the wilderness with his wolves and continue their trek.

The other episode that featured Indians was the twenty-sixth, the last in the series, "The Ghost of Pocomoonshine Swamp." It was written by William Davidson, who wrote several others, and directed by the very experienced René Bonnière. It featured Johnny Yesno.[43] The episode begins by showing the many animals who live in the swamp and how Matt and Jenny are drawn further into it by their delight in the new creatures they find. Then they hear an unearthly roar, and Jenny, startled, falls and hurts her arm. Suddenly a menacing figure in a breechclout with a bow and arrows (in the East in 1850?) appears and talks to them. At least he uses English, not "Tonto speak." He tells them his name is Joe, then gets some medicine plants from the swamp for her arm. He also tells them about the ghost of Jean Big Canoe, who was murdered there and now haunts the swamp. They return to their camp. Kit says: "Indians don't like folks leaving a mess. It spoils the scenery." With time in hand, they return to the swamp and inevitably get lost. As night comes on, their rescuer Joe reappears, tells them the swamp is a place for lost souls, and takes them to Jean Big Canoe's cabin. The two children bed down, but they hear footsteps on the roof accompanied by the unearthly roar. When they emerge with billets of wood in their hands to fight off the menace, they see nothing, but they decide that Matt should take first watch. Joe rejoins him by the fire. Time passes and then Matt sees a figure in a canoe on the misty moonlit water. He wakens Joe, but there is no one there. Later, after Joe shows Matt how to paint his face with mud to repel mosquitoes, Jenny teases him: "Some kind of war paint?"

Once Joe sets them on the right trail, they are joined by Kit, Adam Cardston, and "Red Bird," an older Indian in braids, a hat, shirt, and trousers who is to be their guide. Suddenly there is the same roar off-camera, and into the clearing between the children and Kit steps a cougar. Unsurprised, Kit raises his rifle, but Jenny calls to him to stop – and he does. Joe grins. He and Red Bird, with their tales of a ghost in the swamp, have been protecting the cougar from the settlers who would hunt and kill it, because the "place is sacred. All life is sacred." Joe goes on to explain that it had been the cougar on the roof in the night, but he had been nearby to make sure it did not hurt Matt or Jenny. There was indeed a murdered man called Jean Big Canoe but there is no ghost. However, the camera had shown the canoe and its paddler in the mist independently of Matt's point of view. Among the young viewers, both the rationalists and those who prefer ghostly explanations are satisfied. Aside from the intrusion of bits of perky disco music, the tale is competently written and told and the two youngsters are appealing.

Here, as in some other episodes outlined in the episode guide, the wilderness is more colourful than dangerous and so are the many Indians – played by First Nations actors for the most part – the two young protagonists meet. Even so, in episode 4, "The Long Return," Michael Ansara (Syrian in origin)[44] plays a chief whose adopted white son, found and raised by Indians, must choose which parents to live with. This echoes other captive narratives (including one on *Hawkeye*). Episode 8 of *Matt and Jenny*, "The Devil's Gorge," mentions that "a strangely masked figure with a golden eagle perched on its arm" appears. In episode 14, "Ceremony at Whispering Pines," Iron Eyes Cody portrays a shaman performing a healing ceremony on a young boy while Adam, Kit, Matt, and Jenny surreptitiously watch; Adam, who has had some medical training, also wants to help the boy. There is no indication of whether, by the end of the episode, white medicine is seen to be superior or whether the boy is cured by traditional means. Gordon Tootoosis plays the chief. In episode 17, "Skiba the Bear," Oquaga, an elder played by Chief Dan George, shows Matt and Kit a "magical bow." Oquaga's grandson is on a spirit quest (the episode description calls it "a journey into the 'Big Empty' to test his manhood"), and Matt takes the bow into the forest where the Spirit Bear Skiba lives. If the concept of a vision quest is taken seriously, Matt will not encounter the Spirit Bear because he is not spiritually prepared to meet any spirit helper. However, narrative conventions of children's adventure series, with their usually happy endings, suggest that Matt probably does meet Skiba, a dangerous encounter for an unprepared white boy with a "magical" bow he doesn't know how to use. It is also probable that the grandson extricates him from the situation.

There is clearly some effort to stay within period in the series, but it is difficult to say whether there was any effort to convey the problems experienced by European settlers having to adapt to settlement in the backwoods of Nova Scotia, Quebec, and Ontario. The subjects of many of the episodes – a wild child, a spirit quest, a white foundling adopted by Indians, Indians as keepers of the ecology – emphasize mysterious ways and hidden secrets; they start with familiar stereotypes that are reinforced by the historical setting, although the execution of the two I saw did not produce egregious mistakes in speech or emphasize inappropriately "native" costumes. It must be added that, with a short twenty-six-episode run, the children never do find their relatives or reach the West.

## THE CAMPBELLS

In contrast to *Matt and Jenny*, this series (1986–89), which overlapped *The Beachcombers* and *Spirit Bay*, made it comfortably into syndication, with a hundred half-hour episodes listed in an episode guide on TV.com[45] and on a "companion home page" constructed by a fan of the series who is not named on his/her site.[46] (The Classic TV Archive site does not have an episode guide, but TVArchive.ca has a brief entry for *The Campbells*.)[47] The series was nominated for several Gemini awards. It was made by Settler Films and broadcast on CTV and the Family Channel (US) in 1986–89; on ITV (UK) in 1986; and on several other European channels.[48] In the list of thirty-seven writers on tv.com, no one writer seems to have dominated the series. Among the twenty-four directors were stalwarts of series television. One producer kept it all together, John Delmage.

I saw and took notes on five episodes of this series when it was broadcast but could find no reruns while writing this book. Again, an analysis of the TV.com episode guide shows that the series used the familiar improbables of children's television: lots of robberies, a homicidal hermit, imposters, kidnapping. But this one, like *Hawkeye*, also used historical figures: Colt, the inventor of the revolver; William Lyon Mackenzie; the Irish-American Fenians; a run-away slave; and a character who appears to be based on Anna Jameson, who toured Upper Canada in 1838.[49] There are also echoes of the War of 1812. As with most family adventure series, there are both comic episodes and episodes full of suspense, with occasional stories that involve romance and very often ones that present a lesson in growing up for Emma, who is just entering puberty; for John, her younger brother; or for Neil (the obligatory teenager), her older brother. The series has episodes featuring a guest character with Down's syndrome, an indentured servant, and problems with large landholders who exploit pioneers who are promised land if they clear and plant it (a prime cause in Upper Canada of the 1837 Rebellion). Reflecting some 1980s feminist issues, Emma hates the drudgery of women's work in a pioneer household. Eventually, as she grows up, she finds an outlet as a published writer (with perhaps an allusion to Susanna Moodie and Catharine Parr Traill). Women in the 1830s marry only with permission, find it difficult to take charge of an inn, get in trouble when dressed like a man, are charged with witchcraft but actually serve as healers – all useful historical lessons for young girls growing up in the second twentieth-century wave of feminism.

If details from history were to be one sign of authenticity, then a series set around the period of 1836 would require contact with First Nations peoples. In episode 6, "The Visitors," Monique Mojica appears as an Iroquois woman who heals Emma of a snakebite, even though John has unintentionally desecrated a "native religious tribute." In episodes 15 and 16, the two-part "Autumn and Smoke," Graham Greene, Gordon Tootoosis, and René Highway play Iroquois. The father, James, gets involved in a "blood feud" when he is unwittingly given stolen goods. When his son John is captured, James must substitute himself for his son. Greene appears again as an unnamed Iroquois man in episode 31, "Star Light, Star Bright," about an attempt by Captain Sims, the gruff antagonist in the series who was a captain in the war of 1812, to raise a militia.

In episode 47, "The Siege," Tom Jackson plays Black Cloud. James helps a wounded Iroquois man who has been punished by the band. The man is inspired when James bravely gives himself up for the unspecified offence – but to whom? No further details, but I can't help but wonder if the First Nations' custom was presented accurately or was judged barbaric or what the man had done or how it all came out. Jackson reappears in episode 55, "Gateway to the World," as an Iroquois visitor. In episode 77, "Mirrors of the Soul," James is somehow rescued from drowning by the Ojibway, but this time no First Nations actors playing the characters are named in this complicated plot about a three-way love triangle that involves a white trader who loves an Ojibway girl. The band does not approve and offers her to James. The girl's wishes do not appear in the plot summary, which seems to rest on customs that may or may not be accurate (offering a daughter in thanks for the healing of a son). The summary does make the point that the Ojibway read the trader's character accurately. The online descriptions for season 4 are much less detailed and nothing in the guest lists or descriptions suggests that anyone from the First Nations was foregrounded.[50]

It is clear that both generic Indians and specific First Nations appeared in television for children and families consistently in the thirty years from 1958 to 1989, but their representation did not reflect much of the complex identities of these First Nations peoples. *Hawkeye* had presented a wide variety of situations involving Indians, some reinforcing stereotypes, others not, but it had no informed input from consultants or even real Indians in the cast. *Hudson's Bay* does not appear to have been an improvement. Neither *Hawkeye* nor *Hudson's Bay* seem to have appeared in reruns in the last few decades.[51] The young characters of *The Forest Rangers*, their adventures, the wilderness setting, and perhaps what was then called the "conservation message" made the series unique in its day and ensured a long life in syndication sales, but in the context of this study, the series did not do justice to its Metis and Ojibway characters. Joe Two Rivers was intended to portray a Metis but was read as an Indian hero figure by the young viewers and, as noted earlier, as problematic by the programmers at APTN. The old chief in *The Forest Rangers*, Shing Wauk, did not fare so well, being presented as stereotypical in several instances and shown, not as drunk (never on a children's program of that period), but as hypnotized, acting in a way easily seen as metonymical for drunkenness, both foolishly and dangerously. Neither character was played by a First Nations actor. Buckley Petawabano's Pete Gawa was a step forward, ever present as the older and wiser friend. However, in most television series of that time, the protagonist dominated every episode – and there were no First Nations protagonists.

In *Matt and Jenny*, Kit, a frontiersman and a white, teenaged heart-throb, displaces the role of an Indian, subsuming many of the characteristics such as possession of wilderness lore and sharp-shooting. In the later frontier stories of *The Campbells*, which is set in an earlier period, there are a few stereotypical narratives (Ojibway rescuers, traditional healers, the custom of offering a young woman as a wife), but there are no First Nations writers or even formal consultants for the series. Graham Greene, Tom Jackson, Gordon Tootoosis, René Highway, and Monique Mojica may have offered suggestions but had little clout at that time as performers. There is, however, a movement away from non-Indians playing Indians trapped in occasionally absurdly insulting plot lines towards First Nations actors (now well known) who appear in series that are more in tune with the realities of the period or culture they represent.

The audience for *Adventures in Rainbow Country* (broadcast on CBC), *Matt and Jenny*, and *The Campbells* (broadcast on Global – that is, commissioned by a private network) had to turn to *The Beachcombers* (a family adventure series made by the CBC) to find a First Nations character who was well established in the first few episodes, sometimes took the lead, and grew up, matured, and changed over the nineteen years of the series – Jesse Jim. He and his sister Sara, a younger recurring character who also took the lead in some episodes, along with Jesse's wife and stepson, presented a complex, non-melodramatic, non-stereotypical portrait of the contemporary life of the Coast Salish/Nootka people living off-reserve. They deserve a chapter to themselves, which follows.

# SEVEN

# The Beachcombers:
# Jesse Jim Matures as a Family Role Model

Nick: "Is it a deal, Indian?"
Jesse: "It's a deal, Greek."

*The Beachcombers* appears in my book *Turn Up the Contrast: CBC Television Drama Since 1952* (1987) at some length,[1] and another of my books, *Rewind and Search* (1996), contains interviews with Philip Keatley, the first executive producer, who gave the series many of its basic elements, and Don S. Williams, one of the subsequent executive producers. Both men had worked with sensitive aboriginal material before working on *The Beachcombers*. When the show was cancelled, after its run from 1972 to 1990, the CBC did a retrospective of the series. According to a CBC broadcast in 2002, it had appeared in seventy countries, and in 2004 it was selected as a Masterwork by the Audiovisual Trust.[2]

*The Beachcombers* starred Bruno Gerussi as Nick Adonidas, Robert Clothier as Relic, and until 1985 Rae Brown as Molly, grandmother and owner of Molly's Reach. The early years of the series, which many prefer, featured Bob Park as grandson Hugh (1972–82) and Nancy Chapple (1972–75) and then Juliet Randall (1975–81) as his younger sister, Margaret Carmody. In the second season Reg Romero joined the cast as McLoskey (1973–85), and a year later Jackson Davies began his long run as Constable John (1974–90). Charlene Aleck played Jesse's sister Sara (1976–90), and Marianne Jones (1982–90) played his wife Laurel.[3]

Jackson Davies was the executive producer of two movies of the week made over a decade after the show was cancelled. Both include one native character, Colin Reid (played by Graham Greene), an eco-activist and newspaper columnist. This character is reasonably well written and very modern, but he belongs to no identifiable First Nation – a backward step. Both movies centre around a con man and his once-estranged daughter who reopen and then maintain the "Reach." The first, titled *The New Beachcombers* and broadcast 25 November 2002, introduces a romantic interest

The original cast of *The Beachcombers* on Nick's salvage boat, the *Persephone:* Bruno Gerussi as Nick Adonidas, Rae Brown as Molly Carmody, Nancy Chapple as Margaret, Bob Park as Hugh, and Pat Johns as Jesse Jim. CBC.

for the daughter. Jesse and Sara appear in this movie for five minutes. The second, *A Beachcomber Christmas*, broadcast 6 December 2004, is a comedy with lots of slapstick and confusion around a charity hockey game.[4] The con-man father, played by Dave Thomas, seems designed to blend the wily amorality of Relic and the insouciance of Nick. He is an amiable-enough character, but the first movie, which was really a pilot for a hoped-for resurrection of some of the elements and a few characters from the old series, did not take off as hoped. Neither movie provided much of interest regarding the representation of First Nations people.

My point in returning to the original series in this study after writing about it extensively many years ago is to take a fresh look at Jesse, concentrating on the first thirteen seasons of the run when his character evolved. *The Beachcombers* depended for its success on two key elements – interpersonal conflict and the relationship of humans to the beautiful and dangerous natural environment of Canada's northwest coast. Jesse was included in the very first episode as a major character because of Philip Keatley's long-standing interest in the relationship between white and Indian – see his three specials on

*Festival*, two of which came out of his 1960s anthology *Cariboo Country*, which concentrated on the Shushwap up in the Chilcotin but included two Coast Salish individuals as well. Jesse is Coast Salish, a member of the Seahost band. At the very beginning, when he and Nick agree that he will come to work on the *Persephone* as a beachcomber, this exchange occurs: "Is it a deal, Indian?" "It's a deal, Greek." They spit on their palms and shake hands.[5]

## THE WORLD OF THE COAST SALISH IN *THE BEACHCOMBERS*

First, it must be emphasized that the character of Jesse does not signify "Indian" all of the time. He wears his culture lightly, and the family adventure series format means that the writers do not include specifically Coast Salish elements in every episode. Critic bell hooks and others to the contrary, in a series that becomes part of the viewer's life and routine, a character's race can disappear and then reappear intermittently, just as it does in a classroom or workplace or among a group of friends. I will concentrate on the episodes where Jesse's heritage is foregrounded as the focus and on others where the fact that he is Coast Salish is relevant but not the only focus of his storyline. And there are literally hundreds of episodes where, for the viewer, it is not relevant at all.

In *The Beachcombers*, two apparently different worlds regularly appear. The first is the world of boats and planes, logging and fishing, restaurants and marinas, where there are analogies to everyday experiences around the world. The second is the world of belief, where the natural world is an intrinsic part of the spirit world. In an early episode, "Evil Eye," 14 January 1973, the subject is not treated in a complex way. Nick is Greek, emotional, impulsive, a daring skipper, and a lady's man. Relic, his antagonist, is as scruffy as his unnamed boat, devious, a schemer, grouchy, unethical, fond of sardonic comments. The audience eventually learns that he emigrated from Wales, leaving behind a hard life in the mines. Both men have a strong sense of the supernatural. Nick firmly believes in the evil eye of the Greeks and thinks that Relic has it. Jesse confirms this and is both angry and firm with Hughie, who doubts it. Hugh is a kid who loves to read and figure things out. His younger sister, Margaret, who is unhappy with Jesse's entry into her surrogate family, tries out the evil eye on Jesse because neither he nor Hugh will take her to a concert. Jesse has a near car accident and then, without explanation (which is a credible touch), goes off to see if he can live off the land for a few days. Hugh, thinking it is his fault that Jesse has left because he had

Hughie, Nick, and Jesse. *CBC*.

mocked the evil eye, performs a garbled version of a purification ritual – from a book – to bring him home. Margaret also thinks it is all her fault. Relic tells her to cut a toad in half and do an old Welsh spell. Nick decides his blue stone is more powerful than Relic's magic. In any case, Jesse, having finished his time away, returns.

In episode 80, one of the best, the well-loved, oft-repeated (eight times) "Hexman" (by Arthur Mayse), Jesse and Nick meet the "hexman" (Gordon Pinsent) and his silent companion, who is shrouded in oilskins. The encounter takes place in a cove marked with a petroglyph – which defines them all (except Jesse) as intruders. The hexman explains, through the verses of a ballad that interweaves into the narrative, that he is the ghost of an East Coast maritime fisherman who had been hanged (with his voiceless companion) for murder. Nick tries to ward off his hex – which has been placed on a particularly valuable log – with his Greek amulet for the evil eye, but his charm doesn't hold. Finally, Jesse, holding his own argillite raven amulet like a microphone, calls his shaman/great-grandfather to help. After he promises supplies to the old man, who is never clearly seen (the expectation of repayment is cultural), the two supernatural powers engage in a struggle for Nick's boat. Great-grandfather wins,

Hughie (*left, in shadow*), Nick, and Jesse. The sea and its riches is a major theme in *The Beachcombers,* established both by plot and by location shooting at Gibson's Landing and along the coast. *CBC.*

the hex is broken, and the hexman and his companion row off into the mists.[6] The horror and the humour are nicely balanced in this. More importantly, as is so often the case in this series, the European and native belief systems are treated as equally valuable. Here the indigenous belief is more useful, and again as often happens in the series, the outcome is never explained by something more scientific. The episode not only is comedic, but also mingles pragmatism with the supernatural, functions as a good ghost story, and presents the clashes of four cultures: Greek, Canadian, Coast Salish, and that of nineteenth-century Newfoundland.

The Canadian TVArchive.ca website has a link to a site on *The Beachcombers* that is being constructed by Patrick Allec but is already useful.[7]

Jesse and his little sister Sara (Charlene Aleck). *CBC.*

However, I have a copy of the CBC guide for the first 221 episodes. This list gives some hints about other elements of Coast Salish life and belief. In an early episode, Nick and Jesse prevent someone from removing an old totem pole that was disintegrating in the undergrowth and setting it up in front of a motel. In another, Jesse gives a potlatch and "has to capture a bear to start the party," with comic confusion ensuing. In the second season, reversing stereotype, all but "Jesse, the amused skeptic," go chasing the sasquatch (the rarely glimpsed Big Foot, who is part of the world view of many First Nations). Eventually they discover that Relic and Jesse have exploited the tourist potential of the sighting by having Jesse play the sasquatch. It would be hard to know how First Nations viewers might see this episode – funny? sacrilegious? dangerous?

Sara (Charlene Aleck) plays Jesse's six-year-old sister. She enters the series in episode 97, unceremoniously presented at the Reach by Grandpa

Jim (Clarence Joe) and Uncle Louie (Bob George). Troubles follow as the family attempts to adjust to the new youngest child, while Sara tries to solve her problems on her own, making a pal out of Ol' Relic in the process. Sara is the first character to develop a real, if often strained, rapport with Relic. Somehow she disarms his malice, which provides the series with a new perspective on a favourite character. Meanwhile, Margaret has her first crush, with Jesse as the unwitting target. Episode 107, "Hail to the Chief," includes three generations of the George family – Chief Dan George, his sons Bob and Lenny, and his granddaughter Charlene Aleck – playing four related characters in a story about "self-styled 'progressive' elements in Jesse's former home on the Seahost Reserve [who] are making trouble for the wise [*sic*] old chief.[8] The old man, with an assist from Nick, conspires to teach the troublemakers a gentle lesson by nominating Jesse as Acting Chief." Judging from the rest of the description, slapstick follows.

Episode 98, "Steelhead" by Marc Strange, takes a more serious look at Jesse's heritage. When Jesse returns on horseback to the mountains in search of something, Nick comes along to look for steelhead fish, using Jesse's secret bait, "goat cheese." Jesse feels he has been in the city too much, driving a car, eating restaurant food most nights. He has lost his sense of self. Nick, uncomprehending, says, "You know who you are. You are a beachcomber, my partner." But Jesse refuses Nick's feast (of three kinds of sausages) and chooses water. He then tells Nick it sometimes takes four days, sometimes longer, to find a vision. He describes how "[l]ong ago in the old days, before he called himself a man, he went on a quest." Nick, who is a rootless immigrant with a self-chosen family, speaks for many viewers when he replies, "You invented yourself." As a self-made man, he has no idea of how a collective identity might work. Jesse retorts, "Don't hassle me," and Nick apologizes. Eventually Jesse leaves the camp and goes out onto a mountainside that has been clear-cut. The bleached bones of the trees surround him. Long camera shots emphasize his helplessness. Ravens call. He drinks from a canteen, walks, sits, clearly doesn't know how to chant, and self-consciously tries dance steps. Then he waits. The crane shot of Jesse on the mountain surrounded by grey slash as far as the eye can see is its own metonym for the deprivations of a vision quest overlaid with the irretrievable losses suffered by aboriginal peoples. But Jesse's presence also signifies the endurance of the culture that remains.[9]

Meanwhile, a bear has scared the horses off, leaving them truly stranded and with no food. While Nick fishes ineptly and provides other comic distractions, Jesse, still on his own, sees carvings in the tree stumps,

Sara with her grandfather (Chief Dan George), who is the
chief of Jesse's Seahost band. CBC.

then sits quietly wrapped in a blanket. The sun on the water flashes into
his eyes as five black crows flap by. He hears Nick stumbling around and
calling him. He continues to sit quietly, listening to the waves, until finally, dizzy and now weak from hunger, he returns to Nick, saying, "I
made it Nick. Where's my fish?" What Jesse sees is not explained,[10] a narrative strategy that is consciously adopted by producer Philip Keatley
here, as in *Cariboo Country*. No final vision is shown to the audience either. Instead Jesse tells tell Nick that his vision told him to go home. He
then calls the steelhead by its proper Coast Salish name and both begin to
fish. Nick makes a hash of it, but Jesse jumps into the river to get the fish
on his line. As both whoop with joy, Jesse says, "That fish is part of us
now. He gave his strength so we could live." Nick: "Did you find out
what you wanted to know?" Jesse: "I thought I heard a gull. Gull said

'what are you doing on a mountaintop. Your people are from the sea. Go home.'" Again we see Jesse's dry humour and direct honesty. The script suggests how and where a vision quest may be pursued, yet shows that even if the seeker doesn't get the ritual quite right, he or she can still find what is sought. And Jesse now knows that he is "on the right path." Only then are he and Nick rescued.

In episode 114, "The Great Shaman of the North," "Sara is so feverish that she confuses Santa Claus with 'the Great Shaman' who appears like an angel of death driving a sled and dog team. Hilarious complications ensue when Nick masquerades as the Shaman ... to prove to the stricken Sara that he's not coming to carry her away." This plot line might have seemed both implausible and offensive, but the child's confusion with two belief systems does strike a chord. In episode 125, "Wolf Song," "[a] half-forgotten war canoe is repaired and made to race again for Jesse's little Seahost band and their old chief (played by Chief Dan George). When the tiny band can't muster a full crew, Nick is 'captured' as a slave and set to work with a paddle," which seems to me a very strange take on the centuries-old history of slaving up and down the Northwest Coast and the high status that slaves brought to their captors. Episode 132, "Talking Stick," is based on the story of the "Golden Tree" (the actual sacred tree that was wantonly cut down in the 1990s) and is described this way: "Old Moses Charlie knows more than he tells when he delegates Jesse to search for the rare golden hemlock needles deep in the forest near the legendary Valley of Headless Men." According to notes I took during a single off-air viewing, this episode did not have a happy ending. Three or four times a season in these years, the series would present an open, ambivalent, or even sad ending – rarities in the family adventure genre. In episode 175, "Voice of the People," "Nick and Jesse find ancient Indian artifacts ... The band chief refuses, despite pressure from Nick, to dig them up for the band but orders them to be reburied." Again we have the motif of returning artifacts and bones to their resting places in the earth where they belong, whether this is done immediately or whether they are repatriated decades later from museums and collectors.

Episode 184, "Soul Snatcher" by Arthur and Win Mayse, pits Coast Salish traditional healing against the methods of a doctor in a hospital. It begins with Sara playing in her granny's old shed and coming across a box full of regalia. She puts on the ermine headdress and button blanket, handles a (beautifully lit) rattle, then catches sight of herself in a mirror. Discovering her, her grandfather (George Clutesi [Nootka], Nuu chah' Nulth) explains that the regalia is "kind of special" because it belonged to the shaman of the

Seahost people and has powers. When Sara rejects the idea, her grandfather tells her that the lightly carved hollow tube she has found is used to drain the soul from the body to cleanse it and that his father also had power in his hands to heal. Reflecting on the losses over the 150 years of contact, her grandfather then says, "I have it but I don't know how to use it. Father died too soon." When Relic steals the smoked salmon her granny gave her, Sara takes the soul catcher out of the box and puts it on the sleeping Relic's chest. When he wakes with a start, she realizes that she really does have his soul. He staggers into the hold, knocks ketchup on the floor, scattering gouts of bright red everywhere, tries to scoop it up, and collapses, unconscious. Coming round, he says to her, "You made me sick. [To Jesse:] She grabbed my soul." Jesse takes this seriously, but also wonders if Relic scared himself sick. He asks his grandfather about this modern psychoanalytical explanation, only to be told, "Play acting? This isn't a game!" When Jesse reasons that the best way to tell if you have the power is to use it, he is forcefully reminded that any fool can pull a trigger. Meanwhile, Relic is taken to hospital. The grandfather tries to remedy the harm Sara has caused, telling the viewers (while pulling his sacred objects from his old black doctor's bag) that he uses, not charcoal and bear grease as the original shaman would have, but what he has on hand – graphite and Vaseline, plus bush tea to make Relic sweat. The nurse looks in and backs out, but the hospital doctor is furious because his diagnosis is measles: "Get out of here you witch doctor, you charlatan!" Grandfather replies fiercely, "I'm healing, that's what – it's more than you can do!" And he sings him right out of the room. Finally, he gets Sara to help him with the transfer of the soul back into the body.[11] The two of them put their hands on the box under Relic's blanket. Relic's eyes snap open as he says, "You put my soul back." The elder replies, with a touch of humour, "I could feel it snuggling down in there."

In the second episode of a new season, 206, "Courtship," Jesse starts to court and eventually proposes to Laurel, his friend's widow. In the next, "Marriage," Laurel's son Tommy's feelings are explored. From the episode guide, it seems that Jesse is not the focus for some time thereafter. The copy of the list of plot outlines I have ends in the middle of the thirteenth season (1985). I also ended my off-air sampling/note taking at that time. The list for that period shows that Jesse was featured in fifty-one episodes and that specific cultural concerns appeared as the primary narrative in twelve episodes in the first two years (which had forty-nine episodes) and then in ten scattered episodes up to 1985. Fewer episodes dealt with these issues thereafter. Episodes made after 1985 are given as titles only because no numbers are available. In "Legacy," Laurel's father comes to stay, "determined to educate Tommy ... in the ways of his people," while Jesse and Laurel are just as determined to make sure he has a "white man's education." The next year, in "Tongues of Stone," Tommy's grandfather looks for stolen petroglyphs with the help of Nick and Constable John, and later, in "Raven," his grandson, assisted by the "Spirit of the Raven," helps to foil an attempt to put up a nuclear reactor.

By the time I interviewed executive producer Don S. Williams in 1985 and certainly after he left to do other things, the series had more or less abandoned its focus on Coast Salish beliefs and traditions, even though this had given the series a distinctive flavour. In the circumstances, it may have been the right decision, yet leaving touches of a Coast Salish world view out of the equation seemed to me to oversimplify the way the First Nations characters were portrayed from then on.

In the context of the series' final (one-hour) episode, John Haslett Cuff, the television critic for the *Globe and Mail* who would be so hard on *North of 60* from 1992 on, made some perceptive comments (12 December 1990): "Canadian television owes more than it may even acknowledge to the success of the *Beachcombers* ... It has functioned as the prototype for all the family action/adventure series produced in this country since 1971 and made Canada – particularly the West Coast – known to viewers around the world ... [It] made every subsequent export of a domestic television show a bit easier." He also pointed out, quite rightly, that the series had a code that upheld "the values of tolerance and the sanctity of the family (modern, single parent, extended and traditional variety)."

### JESSE JIM GROWS INTO HIS COMPLEX ROLE

For many years, Jesse Jim was the nearest thing we had ever had to a consistent First Nations role model on television for children and young adults.[12] The early thinking on this character was that Jesse would represent both the Coast Salish as one of the aboriginal peoples who live on the Sunshine coast and also be a teenager to attract teen viewers. Children are essential on family adventure series. Hugh and Margaret were both too young to fill the role of teenager. Jesse, however, rapidly grew into an adult on the series. The two children also grew up, overlapped with Sara, and eventually left. Later Jesse's stepson Tommy (Cory Douglas) was added to the mix.

Jesse is on the original list of characters and was therefore part of the original concept.[13] At that time, he was described as a "16 year old West

Coast Indian boy. He has taken off for the summer to see something of the coast and to try and learn something about himself and how he fits into the world. He is unsure whether he wants to go back to school and needs to think about things"– like many teenagers. "He is self-sufficient and self-contained. He swims like a fish" (unlike Nick, who cannot swim). Note that nothing in this description is culture specific. As is often the case in television, by the time the series was underway, many changes had occurred. Jesse's character seems older than sixteen, and several episodes in the first few years refer very specifically to his heritage, beginning with the first, in which he appears. In the 1970s, a show about cultural conflict, Northwest Coast First Nation's culture, and a late adolescent growing into an adult would have appealed to adult viewers watching with their kids.

In looking at Jesse's character as it developed, I have an advantage that viewers at home did not have, access to a tape of a pilot never broadcast, called "Jesse's Car." Jesse is concentrating on getting a Model A car (with a 1939 licence plate) fixed up so he can "drive clear across Canada."[14] Nick: "Why?" Jesse: "To see the land we once had." The series nails its colours to the mast with that phrase. Nick's offer to Jesse of a partnership in the same episode is clearly tied to Nick's interest in having access to the car itself. The lines about a potential partnership between them are basically an afterthought. In the first episode broadcast, on 8 October 1972, Jesse is already aboard a rich salvage when he meets Nick. The idea of his becoming an apprentice beachcomber is now more important, and the car has almost disappeared from the plot. Jesse's uncle Louie (who does not like cars) comes to Gibson's Landing to find "a boy who ran away from home." It is an appropriate touch that "uncle" replaces "grandfather" in the script because uncles often have more to do with raising a son than the parents in many First Nations cultures. Nick, remembering his own arguments with his father and liking the independence and initiative shown by Jesse, asks Jesse if he would like to work as his apprentice beachcomber/partner. Uncle Louie agrees to the arrangement, although he does mention his fears that Jesse might end up on Vancouver's skid row. There is no contract. Nick and Jesse shake hands, establishing that both share a sense of honour. The episode also plays a little with the stereotype of the laconic Indian by having Jesse ignore the florid speech Nick had prepared for him to use in persuading his uncle. He says it his own way over a cup of coffee, in one sentence: "I love you Uncle Louie, but I have to do things my way. Pass the cream."

All series provide potential scriptwriters with a "bible" that outlines characters, suggests relationships, indicates how these may develop, and traces potential story arcs. The writer's bible for the third season, written by the story editor Suzanne Finlay (who was story editor/script consultant from 1971 to 1979), tells new scriptwriters that Jesse drifted into Gibson's landing and, "though he's still in his teens, proved himself enough of a man for Nick to offer him a partnership ... Jesse generally drives the boat and is responsible for her mechanical maintenance." Note the deconstruction of the stereotypes that follows. Unlike Nick, "he is practical, efficient, adventurous but not foolhardy, agile, strong and fast. He expects to get up in the morning and go to work salvaging logs, and is constantly being surprised by the number of diversions to this workaday pattern Nick's agile curiosity can provide" – in other words, Jesse is the anchor figure and straight man. In fact, as the series develops, he is often shown as the more practical half of the partnership. At first he is working for money to drive his car and for day-to-day expenses. At one point, when actor Pat Johns left the series, Jesse's absence was explained by his love of travel and the need to be out on his own. Eventually, with Johns's return, Jesse comes back to the business, and about halfway into the series' long life, he creates a family with Laurel and her son. Jesse is chunky, athletic, and has ordinary but reasonable looks – he is a young man who is attractive to young women. He usually dresses in jeans, shirt, and work boots. Early in the series, he learns to be a good beachcomber. The *Persephone* is not a war canoe, but she is a good boat that Jesse's mechanical skills keep running. Later he acquires professional diving skills. Unlike Nick or Relic, he loves being in the water. His point of view is often realistic, and he takes a wait-and-see approach to problems, unlike Nick, who tends to be impulsive. Jesse is not laconic, but he is not particularly talkative. He uses the latest slang without an accent or idiom from a dialect. He does use specific nouns and verbs in his own language, but they are used in context, so that the viewer can figure out roughly what they mean. After the early episodes, his wariness and guarded body language give way to a wide range of openly expressed emotions, belying the stereotype of Indian stolidity. He has a wide grin and a ready laugh.

With two families, the one at the Reach and his own on the reserve, Jesse is part of two worlds. One mediating signifier is the sea. He seems to come from the Coast Salish tradition of both taking what the sea brings to shore and using a boat to go out and harvest what the sea will give. He is also an older brother to the younger Hugh and Margaret in the early years, then to his "real" sister, Sara, and finally he becomes a "real" father to his stepson Tommy.

Nick and Jesse struggle with equipment on the *Persephone*. CBC.

The scriptwriter's guide of 1978–80, prepared by executive producer Hugh Beard, identifies the elements that the producers thought made the series popular – its "comedy, action-adventure and melodrama," and also, interestingly, its "optimism." Beard writes: "Jesse was mostly running away – from the reserve. From his parents' untimely deaths, from a lot of his Indian heritage about which he still has mixed feelings. It's a source of pride and also a source of pain. But he is coming to realize that he is what he is and to be proud of it; he's Bear clan, a leader, responsible not merely for himself but for other members of the little Seahost band to which he belongs. The influence of his Chief, Moses Charlie, has been much present lately in Jesse's life." Beard then slips in a few notes about anger and impulsiveness: "Slow to anger, he is nonetheless capable of rage. Content with his life at Gibson's, he could take off without a word of warning." Odd. Jesse may leave for a while, but "without a word of warning" is improbable and seems to play into the stereotype of unreliability. The sketch concludes: "A strong man and tough as a beach boulder, he keeps much of himself buried far below his calm detached surface" – in contrast to the volatile Nick – and "He views human failings as inevitable and for the most part, wryly funny." I do not know anything about Pat Johns as a person, but given what usually happens in a long-running series to continuing characters, it is likely that by 1978 aspects of his own personality had been imprinted on the character.

Five years later, during Don S. Williams's time as executive producer, the 1984 scriptwriter's guide (no author) informs writers that Jesse is now "26, Native Indian, Coast Salish, the son and grandson of hereditary chiefs … who doesn't allow himself to become a 'Tonto' to Nick's 'Lone Ranger.' [Note that the language used in the bible has now become more self-conscious.] This is not to say that working with Nick doesn't have its frustrations. He succeeds in the white man's world, but often counts on his heritage and upbringing to give him a perspective on life. At times his native mind [whatever that means] finds the white man's ways don't seem to make any sense." The guide goes on to describe the growth of Jesse's feeling for Laurel, her son Tommy, their marriage, and their life on a houseboat. But it also emphasizes that Jesse is "very much a part of the 'family' at the Reach." Laurel is described as "late 20s, Native Indian (Nootka tribe) – resilient, strong-willed, proud of her Indian heritage." As a Nootka, she has a significantly different heritage from Jesse's, but it is not clear whether that difference as such ever became a plot point. She works in a bank. Her son is seven and "has a strong connection with his grandfather, George Douglas, who imparts his heritage and Native learning to the young boy." George Douglas, who appears occasionally, is in his "late 60s, Nootka tribe … a man of great integrity and strength. He frequently finds himself in conflict between the Indian culture and the 'white man's ways.'" In the mid-1980s this culture clash was still seen as a potential storyline, but as noted previously, this theme had disappeared by the last few years of the series.

By this point, the mid-1980s, Jesse has been allowed to grow and change in ways that the protagonist Nick and antagonist Relic never do. The past reappears to haunt Nick and Relic in several episodes, and it is clear that they had immigrated to leave it (in Nick's case war ravaged Greece and in Relic's the mines of Wales and his abusive father) behind them. Both are first-generation immigrants who, as time goes on, become more set in their ways. In contrast, Jesse lives continuously with his past and his present. He and his people, the Seahost band, are rooted in the land and sea of the

Perpetual antagonist Relic (Robert Clothier) from Wales, protagonist Nick from Greece, and Jesse, whose people have been here all along. *CBC.*

Sunshine Coast. Although he is often the voice of reason and pragmatism, it is evident throughout the series that he has a growing, but quite private, trust in the value of the old beliefs. He exhibits sexist behaviour towards Laurel, but Laurel names and then usually succeeds in resisting his sexism. When, despite his protests, she wants to take an auto mechanics course, she does. On the whole, unlike Nick, Jesse respects the freedom of others to be left alone. He also has a sense of irony that includes himself, derived both from his own temperament and his position as an outsider, in some ways, to the culture he lives in. He also has a sense of humour and loves practical jokes. He laughs easily. He has a broad tolerance of different ways, including both the old ways and passing fads. At times he is very sensitive to other people's feelings and unsure how to react. That he is in his own territory is made very explicit in "A Fine Line," an episode about land claims. The regular characters are stunned by the notion that Molly's Reach stands on native land and is leased. Jesse has to resolve the conflict between his band's rights and fact that his friends are threatened with eviction. Of course, a resolution is found, but from its early days, the series reminds the viewers that the First Nations were here first.

Jesse's function in the narrative arcs of the series is usually that of the faithful friend, a very ancient dramatic role but here with a very different perspective, based on both his temperament and his culture. He usually follows Nick's schemes but sometimes initiates actions on his own. In critic Claude Levi Strauss's classic formulation of archetypal narratives, Jesse functions as a "third term"[15] that links two opposites yet denies fundamental elements in them. Jesse sometimes mediates between the narrative functions of protagonist Nick and antagonist Relic and sometimes he transcends them – most specifically when, unlike them, he takes on the responsibilities inherent in marrying a widow and being father to her son. He is not as deeply involved with some of the other characters as Nick is, and he is not a loner like Relic. He is neither feckless nor obsessed with money, neither flamboyantly nor drably dressed, neither habitually passionate and optimistic nor paranoid and pessimistic. He is wary but nevertheless interested in experiences of all kinds. Nick said in one episode that if he had stayed in Greece, he would be herding goats or tourists. If Relic had stayed in Wales, he would have been down in the mines. Jesse has also made a decision – to stay home and yet adapt to the changing times. On *The Beachcombers* Jesse is the one most at home.

In a key 1987–88 season episode, "Sign of the Times," written by Marc Strange and produced by Don S. Williams, Jesse and Nick have a serious quarrel because Nick is treating Jesse "like a hired hand." Nick rages at Jesse for the shambles he himself had created in the office, then expects Jesse to do all the painting and plastering. Then Nick buys a $4,000 computer system (this is the 1980s) without consulting his partner, compounding the offence by not giving Jesse any time with the instructor so that he can learn how to use it. Laurel tells Nick, "Sometimes you can be a bit of a nerd," but he doesn't hear the warning. In fact, what he does in personal terms (quite in character, since he tends to run roughshod over most people) is to recreate, at this late stage, the Tonto relationship of hundreds of Westerns. Relic, sensing the potential for mischief, stirs the pot by mocking Jesse's protest that he is an "equal partner." As he points out, for the last fourteen years (in both real and series time) the business's hanging sign has read "Nick's Salvage," with "Nick Adonidas prop." in the corner. Since Nick has now made Jesse feel that he is very much a second-class partner, Jesse tells him, "I want it [the sign] changed or I want out." But Nick, ever oblivious, argues that it represents "a corporate identity." Jesse's response is this: "I don't get respect from you, period!"

Complications, of course, ensue. Nick can't buy out Jesse's $25,000 share immediately. Meanwhile, Jesse goes beachcombing with Relic, only to discover that Relic is interested in scavenging bottles or any other detritus that will bring in a few bucks, not the huge logs that have been Jesse's prizes as

Nick's partner. Jesse is also rightly suspicious of Relic's offer of partnership. Meanwhile, Nick is distressed that Jesse would even be seen with Relic. He doggedly transfers all the office files to the computer and burns the "mountain of paper" that started it all, only to find that a lightning strike has hit his computer and eaten his data. Laurel, thoroughly exasperated with Nick, finally tells him very directly that Jesse loves him, that Nick is the one man in the world he completely trusts, but that he doesn't like to be treated like a hired hand. She also mentions that Jesse remembers every financial detail – always has. Note that it takes a woman to articulate the subtext in the two men's long-standing relationship. So Jesse, not unwilling to show another of his talents, sits down to re-enter all the data from memory. Laurel had already shown him how to operate the computer one afternoon at the bank. Nick returns with a new sign – "Adonidas and Jim." "[A]lphabetical order," he replies when Jesse teases him about who is first, and the show ends with the two of them embracing. *The Beachcombers* thus deconstructs once more the old stereotypes, but in this case also consciously constructs a new partnership, one based on both public and private tokens of respect and on using responsibly the resources of the West Coast – a hopeful ending with a clear message for both children and adult viewers. Things are less easily resolved when, in a later episode, "Redemption," Laurel is offered the job of band manager on her old reserve. Not only a different job but also old loyalties – and her relationship with Jesse – come into play.

By the time the series ended four years later, Pat Johns had played Jesse all his adult life. Les Wiseman, in the 8 December 1990 issue of *TV Guide*, reported that, according to Johns, "[a]mong his favourite memories is playing with his hero Chief Dan George." When Wiseman asked Johns whether he could keep a career going as a native actor, he replied that acting was in his blood but that he had had no other acting job. He was also thirty-seven, and in the last two years he had been one of twelve regular characters in the series. In the 2002 CBC retrospective, Johns said that Bruno Gerussi had stood up for him when his drinking threatened his place in the show and had stepped in to help him several times. (Partying is common after a "wrap" on many sets.) In 2002 I learned anecdotally from a conversation with a television critic that Johns was said to have a real beachcomber's licence and was making a living at it. He does not appear on any websites of actors' resumés or native actors' resumés that I have located.[16]

*The Beachcombers* was sold around the world, including to the American public network, PBS, and to Germany, where it was known as "Strandpiratem" (sounds more exciting than "Beachcombers"), and was dubbed

Marianne Jones as Laurel, Jesse's wife; Cory Douglas as Tommy, Jesse's stepson (*front*); and Pat Johns as Jesse. *CBC.*

into twenty languages.[17] From November 1972 to October 1983, it had followed *The Wonderful World of Disney* on Sunday nights at 7:00 p.m., a prime slot for family viewing. In 1983 it was rescheduled to Sundays at 7:30–8:00 p.m., where it remained until 1989. However, for the last two seasons, when new leads were introduced and many of the scripts were less than satisfactory, the program was shifted to Wednesdays at 7:00–7:30. The last season consisted of six new episodes plus five that had been held back from the previous season. After 324 episodes and nineteen seasons, the series ended on 12 December 1990 with a one-hour special that insulted the series with gratuitous violence and improbable plot lines. Bruno Gerussi died in 1995, Robert Clothier in 1999. In the *Toronto Sun*, 22 November 1995, Jim Slotek, writing about the death of Gerussi, said that he was "the ringleader of a coterie of earthy characters – Relic, Jesse, Molly et al. ... More than a million Canadians adopted [them] as friends." Since the series was sold widely abroad, those characters also had friends around the world.[18]

The series sank for many reasons: many fewer episodes on the water (they were expensive); less focus on Nick; a shift in the broadcast schedule from family-friendly Sunday to Wednesday to make room for *Road to*

*Avonlea*; and frequent pre-emptions in its last seasons. Worst of all, the series did not have good scripts and it tried to include too many regular characters. Robert Clothier (Relic) said quite accurately that the series had been gentle, funny, adventurous, silly at times, and romantic, but had had a gentle sense of humour. The last episode, authored by Marc Strange (who co-created the series and wrote many scripts in the series), was presumably written to the producers' specifications. It was an Americanized finale, with shootings, deadly violence, and malicious people, and as Haslett Cuff says in the article already cited, it showed little of the life and complexity that had characterized the series. It even showed characters "turning on each other as if the past 20 years of friendship never happened."

In that hour-long finale, Jesse is now a fisherman, not a beachcomber, and has little to do with Nick on a daily basis.[19] As he tells Nick, "It's not like the old days." Violence and crime have invaded the Sunshine Coast, and Nick is now the last honest beachcomber and is losing his way of life. Relic tells him contemptuously, "You're too old, Adonidas." And Jesse agrees: "The logging business is all over … Things get bad enough, they'll get smart and start putting things back. Maybe it should die … before the land dies." In the last scene between them, Nick and Jesse are tossing stones into the water. Through the dialogue the actors express their own unspoken thoughts for viewers who have either been with the series for a long time or have returned for the final episode.

> Jesse: "That's it. It's all over."
> Nick: "I never thought it would last this long."
> Jesse: "You'll get bored."
> Nick: "See you later."
> Jesse: "See you."

As far as the characters are concerned, for Nick, the ending is more bitter than sweet; for Jesse, life goes on. The last shot that includes Jesse is of the backs of his Nootkah/Salish family, Tommy, Laurel, Sara, and Jesse himself, as they walk away from the camera.[20] The sea and its riches, the future itself, belong to them.

That optimistic shot, which also signified Jesse's full maturity, fits who the character has become over the nineteen years of the series. Jesse's Coast Salish culture was crucial to making *The Beachcombers* a distinctive series. The issues of cultural appropriation and representation that the series' makers consciously addressed, with variable results, in the 1970s to

Shooting *The Beachcombers*, date unknown. CBC.

mid-1980s anticipated the renaissance of Northwest Coast cultures and the increasing recognition of the complexity of the relations between Northwest Coast First Nations and the white majority – and between each other. As a bridge to television series that would concentrate primarily on First Nations characters and issues – *Spirit Bay, North of 60,* and *The Rez* – *The Beachcombers* was an honourable and durable attempt by the CBC through the 1970s and 1980s to move past victims, past sentimentality, past stereotypes.

# EIGHT

# *Spirit Bay:* An "All Indian" Series for Children

"Students ... are as interested as are adults in other people, other races ... They are more interested in the hunter than the bows and arrows, more in the grandmother than the shirts she is sewing."

Basil Johnston (Ojibway)[1]

## *SPIRIT BAY:* SOMETHING QUITE NEW

*The Beachcombers* and *Spirit Bay* overlapped, but *Spirit Bay* was a very different series, with seven weekly episodes from 26 April 1986 to 7 June 1986 and then six weekly episodes from 7 December 1986 to 11 January 1987.[2] It was probably sold abroad. Like *The Forest Rangers* and *Adventures in Rainbow Country,* it was made specifically for children and young teens. All thirteen episodes were about children who lived on the fictional Ojibway reserve of Spirit Bay.

Up to that time, there had never been a series for adults or children that had an almost all aboriginal cast (one cast member, a child who played a recurring character called Rabbit, an urban Indian sent from a foster home to the reserve, was not aboriginal). Here are the titles of the thirteen 28-minute episodes: "A Time to Be Brave," "Rabbit Goes Fishing," "A Real Kid," "The Blueberry Bicycle," "Words on a Page," "Circle of Life," "Hack's Choice," "Rabbit Pulls His Weight," "Hot News," "Big Save," "Dancing Feathers," "The Pride of Spirit Bay," and "Water Magic." The use of an ensemble of inexperienced actors who could draw on their own experience may have been influenced by the way Linda Schuyler worked when she made the earlier (and more didactic) series *Kids of Degrassi,* broadcast in 1982.[3] That there were no more than thirteen episodes may be a reflection of low ratings or perhaps the decision to support the new series, *Degrassi Junior High,* which targeted early to mid-teens. These factors were compounded by the fact that serious cutbacks on CBC financing had begun by the mid-1980s.

The basic plot line in *Spirit Bay* concerns Rabbit, a kid from the city who has been in many foster homes, and the things he learns after coming to live on a northern reserve. He provides the young viewers who do not live on an Anishnabe reserve with a bridge into the community; he is a character who does not know, as they do not know, what to expect. He is not the focus of every story because this series is a hybrid of anthology and series. Tafia (Cynthia Debassige), Hack (Lance Migwans), Elton (Mark Bruder), and Rabbit (Trevor Smith) are friends. Along with the slightly older Mavis (Diane Debassige) and Lenore (Liz Haldane) and teenager Minnow (Eugene Thompson), they form the ensemble, but other characters, like Rose, appear for an episode or two.

### EPISODES

Although clearly meant for children and constrained by the half-hour format, the series offers pleasure for the adults watching as well as for the younger viewers. Many stereotypes are deconstructed, and as in *The Beachcombers,* the settings are spectacular. The huge lake with its many islands and steep cliffs offsets a reserve that is full of basically well-kept houses on dirt roads. The interiors are plain but comfortable. There are berry bogs and a beautiful waterfall where the kids play. The details of the settings are convincing. In one example, we see a beaten-up cabin with "Blackie's snick [*sic*] stand" painted on it. One of the elders – a woman named Teawash – has the only place that's surrounded by junk and looks as though it will fall down, but this is not a stereotype of poverty on a reserve. She is a recycler – scrounging junk from the dump and roadsides for resale. Along with Old Bernard, she is also a respected elder in the community. Old Bernard sits out of doors in early morning, reading the sports pages and joking about the fact that the Blue Jays won't pay his way south so he can tell them how to fix their losing streak, but he also appears in many episodes as an elder to whom the children bring dreams they have had. In different episodes, Rabbit, Tafia, and Lenore consult with him about their discoveries of bones and artifacts. He explains to Hack that the contents of an old chest are very sacred objects belonging to Hack's dead father. In another episode, in a dream that is more than a dream, he shows budding artist Tafia the pictographs of her heritage. The kids and adults wear ordinary clothing, although in one scene Teawash wears a more traditional print dress trimmed with ribbon.

Based on the running order of the CBC press release of 12 March 1985, "Circle of Life," written by Linda Zwicki, is the first episode. Lenore and Ruth get caught up in a classic haunted house scenario. For a joke, after teasing Minnow, Lenore's older brother, about asking a girl he likes to go

"Blueberry Bicycle." Elton (Mark Bruder) exchanges blueberries for a bicycle put together by Teawash (Gladys Taylor). His little brother and his friend Rabbit (Trevor Smith) look on. *Spirit Bay Productions in association with cbc Television/ Radio, Canada; TVOntario; and Telefilm Canada.*

with him "to look at the bears at the dump," they take the boat that belongs to Lenore and Minnow's father, Pete, who earns a good living by fishing, hunting, and trapping. However, they run out of gas, land on an island as a storm comes up, seek refuge in a cottage that is (improbably) furnished with everything they need (even though it has been deserted for forty years), and find a diary that identifies the owners as anthropologists on the trail of an old Anishnabe burial. Meanwhile, Pete finds Lenore's pack drifting on the lake and fears the worst. The girls make use of their basic fire-lighting skills, find some canned food, and make themselves comfortable, though they don't like the lightning storm that adds to the spooky atmosphere for them and the young viewers. The next day – late in this short episode – just before they are rescued, they come across a skeleton while searching for berries, and the whole scenario turns into something quite different. The police, who have helped Pete find the girls, accept his claim that the position and condition of the bones do not suggest homicide. However, they insist on bundling them up into a black plastic garbage bag and taking them away.

The bones are then delivered to a museum in Thunder Bay and left in the hands of an unctuous administrator and a pleasant young grad student. After a month has passed, it becomes clear to Pete and the children that the museum doesn't plan to give the 500-year-old (carbon-dated) skeleton back. When Pete says that the bones are those of a warrior, the museum administrator predictably replies, "Well, we don't know that." Pete: "Well, *we* know that ... It's the way my people have been buried for thousands of years." When the administrator says, "Let's not be precipitous here," Pete spells out the issue for the young audience very straightforwardly: "Your cemeteries are protected by law. Ours are robbed. That's not right." The administrator, again predictably, says that the museum is the best place for the skeleton and that the bones are now museum property. Lenore, however, sees it differently. With understated eloquence she says, "In a way, the bones don't belong to anyone. They belong to the earth. My dad says we are guardians of the earth ... the earth gave him life. The bones should go back to her." The administrator retorts that museums preserve things and "that's not what you people want." Provoked, Pete responds: "That's exactly what we want, to preserve them in the culture in which they were found." They walk out, but as Pete says, "[T]here is more than one way to debone a fish." On the way out, he bluffs the secretary into producing the bones, but at the last minute she checks with the administrator's grad student. After a very brief pause and direct eye contact with Pete, the student tells the secretary that the return has been cleared. This act of complicity with a different world view suggests that the new generation of scholars will do things and see things differently. A specific cultural point is made in the last scene. The camera observes the recommittal of the young warrior to the earth from a distance. Some participants speak passionately and others are persuasive by their silence. The prayers are in Anishnabe but we also hear English words: "This is a good day ... the circle of life is complete."

"The Pride of Spirit Bay," written by Keith Leckie, raises these questions: What can be defined as real (First Nations) art? What is craft? What is junk? Tafia's Aunt Lily (Colleen Loucks) paints superbly. Viewers may have recognized the painting attributed to Lily as in the style of Daphne Odjig. The camera also shows the viewers that Lily has a Norval Morrisseau (Ojibway) spirit painting on her wall.[4] The episode begins with guest star Tom Jackson playing Will, wearing a rakish hat with a feather and a choker. Will owns an art gallery. When he tries to get a white bar owner in town to sell him the Morrisseau paintings on the walls of the bar, the owner refuses, first because Morrisseau had painted them in return for room and board when he needed money, and also because, he says, Norval comes back to see them sometimes "to remember what he was." This scene establishes that whites can treat both native art and native artists with respect. Hearing about Lily's talent, Will goes in search of her. Swiftly (this is, after all, a half-hour episode), long looks between Will and Lily establish an attraction. Nevertheless, when Will picks up one of Lily's works-in-progress and spouts the kind of jargon used by many art critics, saying that it is "primitive but precise," she sends him up in Anishnabe – with no subtitles. Her intonation and his laughing response establish that she has mocked his pretensions. He promises to come back when the painting is finished. Back at his car, he shows Tafia and her friends his trunkful of local, well-made crafts, which, he explains, he displays to get tourists into his gallery and which he sells to them if that is all they can afford.

Tafia and her friends hurriedly scratch off some "native" stuff – "primitive but precise," echoes Tafia. After one kid makes a picture of an elephant, Tafia scolds, "It's not authentic!" The kids set up a table by the roadside, advertising their offerings as "real native art for the tourists." A couple of white tourists do stop, and one of the kids volunteers to do a spirit drawing on birchbark to their specifications, which would be questionable on several levels, but when they find out they are charging thirty-five dollars for a sketch, they leave. It is clear that even tourists see their efforts as junk. The gentle satire cuts both ways, at the white buyers and at the exploitive children, while at the same time establishing that there are knowledgeable sellers and serious buyers. Out of the corner of her eye Tafia sees Old Bernard looking disapprovingly at her work. The next day, the rest of the kids are bored and go swimming, leaving Tafia and her older sister, Mavis, to sell their wares. When Aunt Lily sees the work, she is disappointed, pointing out to Tafia that she is just making a bad copy of someone else's work. Then she turns to a painting of a wolf that Tafia had worked very hard on, that her mother has put on the wall and thinks highly of. Will, returning to get Lily's painting, also stops at their table to look and says, "I'd be lying if I told you this was good." The people who do the work he buys "all work very hard and carefully and they take pride in what they do." Mavis, disappointed, dismisses the "big shot" – "Who does he think he is?" – but Tafia recognizes that when she does her own work her way, she gets a special feeling, as though "there is something inside of me showing me how."

She leaves the table and sits on the beach nearby to look at the water and reflect on what has happened. The sun on the waves leads her into a

dream where Old Bernard and she are paddling in a canoe over calm water (shot with a golden filter, edges out of focus). There is a nice slow pace
to this scene as Old Bernard helps her to gradually see, hear, feel, smell,
and taste where she is. Her senses come alive. "Spirits," he says. As he
sings softly, a rainbow appears. Her face appears to be superimposed on
various parts of the shoreline. At the end of the sequence, he shows her
pictographs that are only visible when he splashes water on them. He
tells her he thinks they were not made, as some others think, by the "little
people" but by their own ancestors. Tafia: "It feels very strong." Old
Bernard: "It has power. You will see. Do you dream? The paintings will
make your dreams more powerful." She asks him how she will know if
her dream, and her painting of it, is the right one. He laughs: "If the pictures come from you, they'll be right." Tafia wakes and tells Mavis, "We
got to get rid of that junk." When she asks her aunt if her experience was
just a dream, Lily's answer points to a fundamental difference between
her culture and the dominant culture: "Does it matter?" Tafia: "No."
Only then does Lily tell her that Old Bernard had once taken her to see
the pictographs, leaving a clear inference that Tafia may also be an artist
one day.

"Hack's Choice," from the second season, originated in a story treatment by Michael Doxtater (Mohawk)[5] that Keith Leckie turned into a
script. It starts with Hack, whose father is dead, consulting Old Bernard
about a dream in which he is trying to fly like an eagle but is not able to
leave the earth. He is told that when he is an adult, he will "leave the
earth like the eagle" because the eagle is a spirit special to his father and
grandfather. Hack's uncle Cole arrives in a blue convertible pulling an
old house-trailer and receives a less than warm welcome from Hack's
mother, Gloria. Bitterly, she reminds him that he had not visited his
brother before he died. When he asks about his brother's medicine bundle, she says that she has hidden it for Hack for when he has grown up.
Cole mocks her, calling the medicine bundle "crazy superstition." Note
that in this culture, as in that of many First Nations, uncles have a specific
role in the education of their nephews, although that irony is left as subtext. The view on life that Cole shares with Hack is basic: "You want
something, you gotta go out and take it." Yet because he had been a professional hockey player in the WHA (World Hockey Association), Cole is
a hero to the kids, even though the boys are too young to know about that
short-lived (1972–79) rival to the NHL (National Hockey League).

Cole takes Hack and Rabbit to town in his convertible to shoot pool.
First he buys Hack a very expensive cue, then successfully hustles money

by playing pool against the white locals, who have made the mistake of thinking he is an easy mark. Just as things start to turn ugly, Cheemo (Gary Farmer) appears at the door and quells the menacing locals with a look. When they get back to the reserve, Rabbit, who as a city kid is less impressed with Cole, listens in on Cole's attempt to hustle Hack into giving him the medicine bundle. Later Rabbit learns that Cole intends to sell it to a museum or auction it off. Once again the series raises the issue of where cultural objects belong, this time in the context of a rising movement to repatriate ceremonial objects back to the First Nations from whom they were often stolen or confiscated. In "Circle of Life," the white museum curator wanted the bones for study. Here the issue of the sale of something sacred is complicated by Cole, an adult Anishnabe who has rejected his own people. Hack is one of a new generation that may make different choices.

In the middle of the night, Hack takes the box containing the medicine bundle from the back of a shelf where his mother has hidden it as an eagle screams (off-camera), but he does not bring it to his uncle. He brings it to Old Bernard. The camera looks at the contents, including a pipe – would this be a violation of something defined as clearly sacred? – while Old Bernard explains that Hack's father and grandfather made good medicine, gave good counsel, and saw the future. He explains that the pipe bearer must go through "years of patient instruction, before [he] light[s] the pipe." After making a prayer for a new day, addressing the sun, earth, water, and air, Old Bernard offers the troubled Hack an opportunity to look into a birchbark bowl of water. Hack (with the viewers) sees in the water a close-up of a crow. Old Bernard: "Beware of him. His coat is shiny but he is a trickster and a thief." Then he drinks the water to finish the ritual and covers the bowl. Again, I do not know whether it is appropriate to show the ceremony, but in this case the plot depends on it. Confronted by Cole, who demands the bundle before he leaves, Hack who is carrying the box, gives him back the pool cue and tells him that "the medicine belongs with our family." Cole snatches the box from him but finds it empty. Hack says, "[M]y friend [unnamed – he has learned a lot] is keeping it for me." As the crow caws, Cole rants about the real world and how the only value the contents of the bundle have is the money they could bring. As Cole drives away, Hack says he feels sorry for him. The values of heritage, of community, and of making good decisions are reaffirmed.

Daniel David Moses (Delaware), a major Canadian playwright, supplied the story treatment for "Words on a Page," the most complex episode of the ones discussed here.[6] David Anderson and Lenore Keeshig-Tobias are given credits as story consultants for this episode, which turns in part on a dream. Lenore has dreamed repeatedly of a raven hovering over her head. She knows it has something to say to her, but it never lands or speaks. The episode's dramatic conflict centres on a story she has written, which her teacher wants entered in a contest in Thunder Bay. If Lenore wins, she could study at a special high school in Sudbury and perhaps be given a scholarship to attend university. She is anxious to submit her story in the contest, but her father, Pete (whom she calls Baba), refuses to let her enter. Father and daughter are obviously close, a fact made clear subtextually from the beginning, and so she tells him her dream. Pete says it sounds like a good dream – making the point to those in the audience who don't know it that not all dreams are good. He then tells Lenore a funny cautionary story about Nanabouzo (the Ojibway/Cree trickster figure, often called Nanabush in English) as they canoe on the lake. As all such tales are, this is a teaching story, ironically juxtaposed with her desire to turn back because she has school learning to do – homework. Pete, disappointed, says, "Isn't it enough that they have you in that school all day?" That he is a loving father who makes a good living fishing and is knowledgeable about his culture has been established in other episodes, and this one reinforces it. She does not argue with him at the dinner table when, after she has asked him for permission, he forbids her to enter her story. However, she does talk to her mother. "He wants to trap me!" she says, and her mother replies, "He believes he is protecting you." Then her mother tells her a different story, perhaps learned in school (another irony), the old European fable about how the gentle warm sun bested the gusting wind because her warmth, not the cold wind, made a man take his coat off.

When the time comes to prepare Pete's trapline for winter, Lenore again tries to coax him to her point of view. He expresses disappointment when she tells him that she isn't allowed to leave school to go out with him for a week on his trapline. The subtext clearly suggests that she has a greater need to learn from him than from the school – a tension played out on many reserves whenever the need to learn traditional ways at the right time in the right place comes up against the set times of the school year. Trying to find out why he won't let her enter the contest, she asks if he would rather have a son. He replies, "Someday. I wouldn't trade you for ten sons." But even after their talk he still won't meet with the teacher to discuss giving Lenore his permission to submit her story. Lenore dreams again – there are more ravens circling overhead and now there is snow beneath her feet. Cut to Nipigon Junior High, where the parents are assembled for a program. There

"Words on a Page." Lenore (Liz Haldane) learns Anishnabe skills from her father, Pete (Graham Greene). *Spirit Bay Productions in association with CBC Television/Radio, Canada; TVOntario; and Telefilm Canada.*

is suspense as Lenore waits to go up and read her story, because, despite everything, she is expecting that Pete will come in time to hear her. But only her mother arrives. Lenore leaves the room without reading her story and, in the hall, dumps it at her teacher's feet. Her mother, caught in the middle, tries to explain: "Baba doesn't believe in being cooped up." Yet she wants this opportunity for her daughter.

In another indirect effort to persuade Pete, the mother asks the teacher to come for dinner. Dinner is uncomfortable for everyone. "Pass the moose" is the only dialogue to break the uneasy silence. Finally, the teacher tells the family that even in Sudbury Lenore will be able to study the Ojibway language and customs. Pete interrupts sardonically, "[L]ike one of them dead civilizations?" He makes it very clear that to him the writing contest is "a one-way ticket out of here!" Lenore's talent and imagination, the fact that she is top of the class, are not important values in the world he is maintaining for her. He fears she will be an outsider in the South and then be persuaded to forget who she is. These fears must have resonated with parents watching the show who lived in a small, remote community and who also faced loss when their children had to leave for further education. Historically, many of the children from reserves who went away to high school dropped out and came home. But others, whether they graduated or not, never returned to the reserve except to visit. Nevertheless the younger audience would have empathized with Lenore's uncharacteristic outburst: "You don't know who I am. Neither of you. No one cares about what I want!"[7]

The next scene is the key to the episode. Pete and Lenore are sitting on the dock, their profiles outlined against the distant cliffs. The hints dropped in the earlier scenes about Pete's secret may have been more visible to adults than to the younger viewers. For example, when a crucial component for his boat is not delivered because Pete had not written it on an order form, he blusters at the delivery man who shows him the form, then takes it, crumples it, and tosses it away. Now, sitting on the dock, Lenore asks her father very directly why he won't read her story. He tells her, without looking at her, "I can't read ... When I went to school, there was this teacher. When I couldn't learn my lesson or spoke Indian, he beat me with a switch. Never been in a school since." As they walk back home, he says once again that he is afraid she will "become a stranger to us." She replies, quietly, "I'll always be Nishnawbe."[8] Cut to a long shot of the reserve as she tells him of her latest dream. There are "more birds, hundreds of them on a wide-open field of snow, black against the snow, like letters on a page, words, my words." Pete: "Sounds like you were meant to be a writer." Lenore: "I need your help. I need you to be there." In the final scene, in a half-filled classroom at Lakehead University, in front of a panel of three white judges, Lenore, wearing beautiful earrings and a choker, finishes reading her story. Her father stands up and claps. The other parents and friends are embarrassed. Not caring, perhaps not noticing, he continues to clap with a big smile. He is then joined by his family and finally by the rest. Freeze frame. End of episode.

## THE POLITICS OF REPRESENTATION

*Spirit Bay* was the first series to put aboriginal people behind the camera and then draw information and ideas from them, not just from the actors in front of the camera or the extras in the background. Daniel David Moses, for "Words on a Page," and Michael Doxtater, for "Hack's Choice," both received the credit "story by," but neither wrote the resulting script. Lenore Keeshig-Tobias was story consultant on "Words on a Page," and four of the production assistants have recognizably Anishnabe names. According to Drew Hayden Taylor, there were several other First Nations participants at a workshop that preceded the development of the scripts, but he does not name them and none of the names in the credits are familiar to me. Buffy Ste Marie wrote the title song, which is both stirring and fun. Laura Fasick reported in the *Globe and Mail's Broadcast Week*, 20 April 1986, that Tomson Highway supplied some of the music as well and Shirley Cheechoo some of the "art direction." *Spirit Bay* featured an ensemble cast drawn from among Metis and several First Nations. The adults included Graham Greene,[9] who had a major role as Pete; Tantoo Cardinal as Rabbit's foster mother on the reserve; Gary Farmer as Cheemo, another protective father and Hack's uncle; Monique Mojica as Gloria (Hack's widowed mother); Shirley Cheechoo (whose art was also given a credit in one episode) as an understanding but firm mother to Tafia and Mavis; George Clutesi (Nootka) as Old Bernard; and Gladys Taylor as Teawash – the latter two both elders and the children's advisors. Margot Kane guested as a teacher.

Drew Hayden Taylor, in his early twenties, worked for the series for over a year as a casting assistant, a production assistant, and a consultant. Then he went on to write the last episode of the seventeenth season of *The Beachcombers* as well as episodes in other television series. In an article in *Cinema Canada*, May 1987, on the dearth of aboriginal writers, Taylor discusses *Spirit Bay*. After calling television series producers all over Canada, he concludes, "[I]t becomes apparent that little has really changed over the years. Native people are used basically as performers. They have very little influence in production. *Spirit Bay* is the first show I am aware of that used them as sources of information."[10] As he points out, *The Beachcombers* never had a writer, producer, or director of native origin. He characterizes Joe Two Rivers of *The Forest Rangers* and Peter Gawa in *Adventures in Rainbow Country* as second bananas. He says that "*Spirit Bay* has prided itself on its use of Native people in the cast, crew and as storytellers … I wrote the series 'bible' to be used by Native and non-Native writers. [This would be under the direction of the series producers.] During my time there, it became apparent that the production company took a lot more care and time soliciting story outlines from the Native community and developing the stories … [but only] as far as the treatment stage" (16). In other words, the writers from various First Nations were asked to write the story with more detail than just a one-page outline, but never an actual script.

However, in his article, Taylor goes on to outline the real problem in having First Nations writers write for a half-hour children's television show, a format that usually calls for conflict and arguments. As he points out, "to verbally admonish someone or create an incident that draws attention is not part of the [in the case of *Spirit Bay* Anishnabe] culture." He reports that the series' director and producer Paul Stephens, who had "handled story outlines from approximately fifteen Native writers since the show's inception," warned that "care must be taken because one is 'translating a fairly non-aggressive, non-verbal, non-confrontational approach to a medium that is very confrontational, that is very aggressive.'" Taylor agrees: "[T]he standard formula (setup, confrontation, resolution) doesn't work very well for Native writers." But he also observes that "the average viewer ... could find soft, introspective Native stories unacceptable. Basically a story adapter walks a tightrope between being faithful to the culture and being faithful to the medium" – an argument also made by people working on *North of 60* six years later. The point is well taken. There is no doubt about the fact that, with any non-native writer, no matter how much research he or she does, "there are certain subtleties and nuances that will be missed" (17). Taylor quotes Lenore Keeshig-Tobias: "'I believe it's Native people themselves who know best what is going on in the hearts and minds of Native people'"(17). Ironically, Keeshig-Tobias would confront Keith Leckie, one of *Spirit Bay*'s chief writers, a few years later about appropriation of cultural voice in *Where the Spirit Lives*, the drama special about residential schools. He wrote the script, and his wife (who worked on *Spirit Bay*) co-produced the special.[11] Taylor provides an excellent example of this conflict. His own story about the cultural difference between the kids from Spirit Bay and the kids from another reserve was rejected as too subtle, not likely to cause a confrontation. Yet he acknowledges the need to communicate with the predominantly white society from which most of the viewers are drawn. His comment "If they don't get it, what's the point?" is a succinct summary of the balance to be sought between communicating effectively with the dominant society, which is outside looking in, and connecting effectively with the culture(s) that are being represented. He says that many of the stories in film and television about native people perpetuate the stereotypes or "could just as well be made about Ukrainians or Estonians," and he sums up the probable result of trying to reconcile conflicting goals of natives and non-natives working on television drama this way: "[I]f the producer opts for a proven, non-native screenwriter who relies on research, the result could be a well-written but culturally dubious program"(17). Taylor later wrote an episode for the first season of *North of 60*, but he is said to have been troubled by it because it was substantially altered. Then he appears to have given up writing television drama.

Barbara Godard (1990) discusses the workshops that preceded the filming of *Spirit Bay*. Those who joined included people who had already been part of a series of workshops "in Native cultural production organised by the Committee to Re-establish the Trickster" (this committee also published the journal *The Trickster*). She quotes from the posters and application forms circulated at the time. In one workshop, under the guidance of David Maclean, "story telling for 'television' explored 'the creation of new conventions.'" Lenore Keeshig-Tobias, Daniel David Moses, and Tomson Highway also offered workshops. Godard's view is complex: "In this challenge, however, the Native writer is situating herself or himself not just as the Other, an author of radically different texts from an entirely different mode of production. Those following *The Trickster* constitute a contestatory discourse that positions itself as a literature of resistance within the conventions, though marginally so, of the dominant discourse" (184).

Daniel David Moses (Delaware) put it rather differently in an informal conversation on 22 March 2003, nearly twenty years after the fact. Some of the writers who participated in the process became or already were quite close friends at that time. The effort to get aboriginal television scripts for *Spirit Bay* from people who had not written for television began with this three-to-four-day workshop. Moses's impression was that the connections between the producers and the First Nations writers lasted until the government grant for the workshops and presumably for First Nations writers to work on the production ran out. The writers did provide *Spirit Bay* with story ideas. Moses, for example, sold his award-winning story idea ("Words on a Page") and so got "a bit of money out of it" in royalties, but it gradually became clear that the native writers were never going to be allowed to write actual scripts. When Moses brought three or four other story ideas/scripts to the producers, they said they were "too strong," which he translated as meaning that the producers desired more clearly defined emotions for an audience of children. After a year, discouraged, Moses severed his connection to the series. Like Taylor years before, Moses thought that the major tension plaguing *Spirit Bay* lay in the demand for dramatic conflict within the limits of a family- or child-oriented television series and the very different aboriginal ways of storytelling.

Sandy Greer, also an aboriginal writer, amplifies the theme. He begins an article in *Starweek*, 6 December 1986, by pointing out that *Spirit Bay* "raises more questions than it answers on how accurately the cultural life of contemporary native people can be dramatized on television" – a question that underlies much of this book. He points out that the dilemmas in each episode are those that any child can relate to and that the value of the series also lies in "its portrayal of contemporary native people in a positive yet realistic mode, rather than in a woeful, romantic or militant way. This achievement is light-years away from Hollywood movie and news media tendencies." But Greer continues: "*Spirit Bay* fails to convey consistently the native cultural approach to problem-solving and how to resolve other moral dilemmas because of the preoccupation of the scripts with plot and conflicts. The conflict between two worlds, native and non-native, however, is a genuine reality to address in the lives of native people." He quotes George Clutesi, who plays Old Bernard, the elder and healer on the series, on the "respectful treatment of the children. 'That's what makes it so holy. It's sincere and real'" – high praise indeed. On the other hand, Clutesi was not happy that Hack and Rabbit "'visit a sacred place to give an offering to appease the spirits that live in the crevices of rocks. Little boys do not perform that way until they grow up ... In our way of philosophy, children listen to an elder instead of giving an offering. Personally I don't think they should do that [on TV].'"

In the *Starweek* article, Greer mentions that four episodes in the first season won honourable mention at film festivals and also makes an interesting comment about the "Words on a Page" episode: "Heated verbal exchanges ... plus the aggressive adult intrusion concerning a child's future are not typical native approaches to resolve the situations depicted. However, such exchanges push the right emotional buttons for a TV viewer primed for an exciting dramatic half hour ... The question remains: Can the stories of native people based on the wealth of native cultural philosophy, be told on television."[12] The raising of such questions before the second season of the series was underway, coupled with Don S. Williams's increasing hesitancy to use aboriginal stories in *The Beachcombers* at about the same time, makes it clear that, in the mid-1980s, cultural appropriation was already in the discourse about Canadian television; specific cultural characteristics of First Nations were recognized and written about; and cultural authenticity was an issue. These questions continued to arise both in the making of *North of 60* and *The Rez* and in their reception. Bill Prentice, writing in *Broadcast Week* in the *Globe and Mail*, 6 December 1986, quoted Clutesi: "'We (native people) should somehow find the means to do films, short films to start with ... written by an Indian, directed by an Indian and maybe filmed by Indian photographers.'" Some of the people who worked on *Spirit Bay*, actors Shirley Cheechoo and Gary Farmer included, went on to do just that. Yet Herbie Barnes, when playing Joseph in *The Rez*, made an almost identical comment a decade later. Clearly, access to the means of production and distribution continued to be a problem.

MAKING, SCHEDULING, AND FRAMING *SPIRIT BAY*·

The CBC contracted the independent production company the Film Works to make *Spirit Bay*. The Film Works was started by Paul Stephens and Eric Jordan in the late 1970s and had begun with low-budget documentaries. After moving on to *Spirit Bay* (produced by Stephens with Jordan), it also produced *Where the Spirit Lives*.[13] TVOntario, Ontario's educational network, joined the CBC and Telefilm to finance the first season of *Spirit Bay*. In terms of investment and shelf life, successful shows for children that are not too dated have resale value because as the target audience grows up, it is continuously being replaced. A Quebec website supplied a list of the programs broadcast in Quebec at that time but is no longer online. However, it does not list this series as dubbed into French, and no web or CBC library search has turned up anything about the series being distributed in any other languages or about foreign sales.

The CBC originally programmed *Spirit Bay* as after-school specials, Fridays at 4:30, beginning 26 April 1985. In its usual fashion, the network had done a dress rehearsal, this one called "A Time to Be Brave" (in which Tafia, who is very afraid of trains, flags one down because she needs to find help for her injured father), which it folded into the first season. The season must have been successful, because an undated CBC release for the second season calls *Spirit Bay* a "unique series of contemporary dramas" and reveals that it would be scheduled to Sundays at 5:00 p.m., that is, as a lead-in to *The Wonderful World of Disney* at 6:00 p.m., a very favourable spot. The episodes in both seasons usually began and sometimes closed with the narrated voice-over of one of the children.

In an earlier press release, 12 March 1985, the CBC framed the first season as "a new seven part series of family dramas." Producer Paul Stephens was quoted: "We are tired of negative films about Canada's native people ... We wanted to make a sensitive and positive film ['A Time to Be Brave'] about life in the north. Spirit Bay grew from the film and we believe it is a realistic portrait of native community life." The episodes were in order of broadcast: "A Time to Be Brave," "Circle of Life," "Dancing Feathers," "Rabbit Goes Fishing," "The Blueberry Bicycle," and "The Pride of Spirit Bay." The producers of *Spirit Bay* checked its accuracy with the members of the Rocky Bay reserve in McDiarmid Bay, where the series was shot. But this series is the antithesis of *Kids of Degrassi* in that its setting was in a remote settlement, not in an inner city. The issues the children faced occurred in a very different context, although they were often related to the experience of any child – looking after a little brother, trying to get money to buy a bike, facing the fears of a thunderstorm, being teased for being different. Perhaps because these producers were interested in documentaries the scripts were less didactic than the earlier *Kids of Degrassi*.

On 6 May 1986, the CBC announced six more episodes of *Spirit Bay* for a short season with a December air-date, but no running order (i.e., the order in which each would be broadcast). The press release said that the residents of Spirit Bay had "adapted to white society while retaining traditional links to the land through trapping, fishing and hunting. Episodes focus on the spiritual kinship between Spirit Bay families, nature and modern life on the reserve from a child's point of view." This season was produced by Eric Jordan and Paul Stephens. The first two "winter" episodes were "Big Save," written by *Degrassi* scriptwriter Yan Moore, and "Break In" by Keith Leckie. "Big Save" is described inaccurately in a CBC press release. A guest, Rose (a young girl from the bush), saves the broomball team from freezing in a blizzard; she is the focus, not Rabbit.[14] Like *Spirit Bay*'s first season, its second usually featured an ensemble, not one character. In "Break In," Rabbit finds out that his foster mother on the reserve, Annie (Tantoo Cardinal), is pregnant; fearing that he will be ignored when her new baby arrives, he considers running away. From an undated CBC press release, "Life in the small Indian community of SPIRIT BAY is told through the children, who share with us the complexities of love and loyalty, friendship and family, contemporary and traditional influences." This press release also contains an error, describing the boy Hack as the "elderly medicine man." CBC press releases and entries in *TV Guide* are not always reliable.

After its run on CBC, the series later appeared on TVO, one of the production partners. TVO reran it again in the 1990s (it may have been shown on other provincial educational television stations in the 1980s). More recently it was shown on Vision, Showcase, and (with many repeats) APTN in 2002–03. Given that the first season of only seven episodes and the second of only six were broadcast nearly eighteen months apart, it is no wonder that this series did not succeed in finding a big enough audience to be renewed. In the article "All-Native Cast Is Also an All-Star Cast," *Ottawa Citizen*, 26 September 1993, Tony Atherton uses *Spirit Bay* as a reference point for an article on the made-for-TV-movie *Spirit Rider*: the series "was scattered so wildly about CBC's daytime schedule from 1982 [oops] to 1986" that few Canadians ever saw it. Atherton is correct when he says, "With a miniscule budget and a social conscience somewhere between *Beachcombers* and *Degrassi Junior High*, *Spirit Bay* was not an earth-shaking dramatic achievement. But it gave something like steady employment to a number of Canadian actors in

"Big Save." The broomball team, stranded in a blizzard, seek warmth in a shelter made of snow that they built thanks to the know-how of "bush baby" Rose. *Spirit Bay Productions in association with CBC Television/Radio, Canada; TVOntario; and Telefilm Canada.*

roles that made them seem like people, not symbols ... But more than that *Spirit Bay* signaled a growing interest in Canada's native culture as a dramatic vehicle." Citing productions from Anne Wheeler's *Loyalties* in the 1980s to *North of 60* in the 1990s, he concludes that the drama special *Spirit Rider* "shows how far natives have come in a few short years," but like Taylor eight years earlier, he also notes that the filmmakers are not native, which "points to the ground still left to cover" in 1993.[15]

Although connected by paved road, Thunder Bay is a long way south from Spirit Bay. "The cast and crew of Spirit Bay ... aren't just filming scenes of culture shock – very often they are living them," writes Laura Fasick about the second season in her article "Turning Culture Shock into TV Drama" (*Globe and Mail, Broadcast Week,* 20 April 1986). She continues: "Many of the extras are Rocky Bay inhabitants ... A Spirit Bay committee, with representatives from native organizations, helps ensure fidelity to life." Actor Graham Greene is quoted in Fasick's piece: "'The community is the heart and soul of the project.'" In the same article Paul Stephens seems to be unaware of both the 1970s and 1980s drama specials and the anthology *Cariboo Country* and also seems to be dismissing *The Beachcombers* when he claims that there are no films on native lives (or television representations of native lives, by implication) other than portrayals of "noble savages or social documentaries on tough times." Stephens continues: "We've dealt with (social issues) on a community level, without making them news-style 'problems.'"

Bill Prentice reports in *Broadcast Week*, 6 December 1986, that producer Eric Jordan said that *Spirit Bay* had been well received by both urban and rural audiences, which suggests that the series had wide appeal and had reached a slice of the desirable urban demographic. He also says that "the response from native kids has been fantastic ... Indians watch a lot of television. When they're on it, when they can see themselves, they really enjoy it."

### THE LEARNING CURVE

Although in "Traditional Knowledge and Children's Right" (2001), authors Philip Cook and William White/Xelimuxw are dealing primarily with Northwest Coast cultures, they assert that "[t]ribal peoples throughout the Indigenous world consistently reinforce the importance of children learning how to watch, to listen and keep quiet" (337). They continue: "Traditionally Aboriginal learning is accomplished by observing adult role modes. This style of learning is sometimes referred to as 'field dependent' as opposed to the abstract or rote learning of Euro-American schooling which is more 'field independent' ... With repetition the child learns the many and varied ways [in which] the old people listen to new information, ways in which inquiries – if any – are made, ways in which new information is discussed with their contemporaries, and finally, learning the ways in which solutions are brought forward" (338). This process is also partly visible in band meetings and community meetings in Lynx River. Jesse of *The Beachcombers*, the children in *Spirit Bay*, and Joey in *North of 60* go to or have gone to school, but they also learn by watching and doing in the traditional way.

In the earlier *Spirit Bay*, Hack consults an elder when asked to sell a medicine bundle, and the episode suggests that he will train to use the bundle properly when he is older. Rabbit fails in his early efforts to learn set a trap on a trapline because he talks too much. Tafia discovers that, to be an artist, she must learn, not only to draw and paint (partly by observing her aunt at work, as is the custom), but also to be spiritually aware under the direction of an elder. Learning by observing versus learning in school is especially relevant to Lenore when her father wants time to teach her how to set traps and hunt but her schoolwork interferes, and when he sees her scholarships to high school and university as depriving her of what he and the community can teach her directly.

As in all children's television of this kind, there is a lesson to be learned every week by the children of Spirit Bay and the young viewers are expected to learn it as well. The lessons are often culture-specific yet also applicable to a wider audience, an interesting challenge for the writers. In this mid-1980s series, both boys and girls take initiatives and have adventures. Hack learns not to trust his smooth-talking uncle. When the school bus breaks down, Rabbit learns that Rose, a broomball goalie who has grown up in the bush, a girl no less, knows survival skills he doesn't. Mavis learns that worthwhile art takes time and patience as well as talent. Lenore and Ruth learn that the bones of their ancestors should be returned to the earth, not be studied in a museum. Elton learns that his bicycle, repaired by the elder Teawash from used bits she had scrounged and that he had paid for by picking blueberries, works just fine despite its strange appearance. He also learns to be more responsible for Tonka, his younger brother. Rabbit learns that he can pull his weight, literally, when he helps to rescue an injured pilot from a downed plane. Lenore and her father, Pete, both learn a lesson: she learns to persevere and to trust her own talent, and Pete, in revealing his painful secret to his daughter, learns to let her become the excellent student and imaginative writer she is meant to be, even if it means she will leave Spirit Bay.

*Spirit Bay* played an important role in the development of Canadian children's television because it introduced children who lived outside the First Nations cultures to children and their families who lived on a reserve. It both pointed out the differences in their lives and beliefs and bridged the space between by finding elements common to most kids – school and homework; role models; parents who protect, guide, or interfere; the fun of riding bicycles, playing broomball, swimming. Few of the details in the stories make them appear dated, not even the music. The series also provided early behind-the-cameras training for First Nations people. It was clearly made from the outside looking in, but it did celebrate the values of the community as the writers and producers understood them. It presented a kind of pervasive belief system that was sometimes, but not always, foregrounded and was treated with some respect, without too much melodrama and mystery. Overall, the series served as a corrective to the idea that all reserves are places plagued by poverty, hopelessness, and substance abuse. One can even argue that it was a bridge to its more grownup cousin, *The Rez*, which was broadcast from 1996 to 1997. But as will become evident in the next chapter, the territory would change in the intervening ten years.

*Discussions of three other episodes – "Blueberry Bicycle," Big Save," and "Rabbit Pulls His Weight" – are posted on the Brock Humanities Research Institute website: www.brocku.ca/hri/associates/miller/outside_looking_in.pdf.*

# NINE

# *The Rez:* A Sitcom/Dramedy for 1990s Youth

*The Rez* is a very different series from *Spirit Bay*. Made in the later 1990s for late-teen and young adult viewers, it is a "dramedy" offering few obvious lessons and defining Anishnabe values largely by inference. It has no honoured elders – "Mad· Etta" is a highly ambivalent figure – few visible parents, and a much more adult range of topics. It is also one of a kind to date for prime time on a major network.

Brian Maracle of the Onkewhone (Mohawk) comes from the Six Nations Grand River Territory, one of the oldest reserves in the country. In *Back on the Rez: Finding the Way Home* (1996),[1] published about the time *The Rez* went to air, he lists all of the stereotypes that he thinks "most Canadians" have about Indian reserves: "[H]opeless puddles of poverty … Men drink and beat their wives. The wives play bingo and neglect their kids. The boys sniff gasoline and the girls have babies. Everyone has a frightening disease … the band council is always broke – it can't balance its chequebook let alone run a government. All the kids are dirty and have runny noses; they can barely read, if they go to school at all. Worst of all, they just sit and complain about how much the government owes them." They also have "weird customs" and "superstitious rituals." An urban man who returned to his roots, Maracle continues: "Luckily not all Canadians think that way. What's more … people have jobs. They go to work. They have nice homes. They're sober … their children graduate from schools"(1). As was done by *Spirit Bay* with less attention and publicity in the mid-1980s, this set of stereotypes was deconstructed by two overlapping television series in the 1990s, *North of 60* (1992–97) and *The Rez* (1996–97).

On 14 February 1996 an email correspondent, Kristine Donahue, sent me the CBC web description of the six episodes of the first season of *The Rez*. The site is no longer available, but I have used it for the plot synopses

The four friends in the marina: (*left to right*) Lucy (Tamara Podemski), Silas (Ryan Black), Sadie (Jennifer Podemski), and Frank (Darrell Dennis). *A Yorktown and Shadow Shows presentation of a production by Rez Productions Ltd in association with the CBC.*

of episodes not discussed elsewhere. After a reference to *Dance Me Outside*, the series synopsis reads: "The Rez continues our romp though the lives of Silas, Frank and Sadie, three smart and lippy First Nations teenagers. The Rez is neither a sitcom, although offbeat and funny, nor a political tract, although often provoking. The half-hour prime time series is a swift, sweet sequence of tales the 19-year-old Silas Crow tells of his life, his friends, his family, and the world of the Kidiabanasee Reserve." The press release suggests that the series is not like its more serious predecessors. The adjectives suggest something light, fast-moving, funny with an edge, already building on a proven success (the film), and intended primarily for teenagers and young adults.

Peter Kentner, who is not fond of the series, seems to reinforce Maracle's comments on stereotypes. In his *TV North* (2001), he calls *The Rez* a comedy/drama, claiming that "[s]ome audience members were challenged by the show's depiction of racism (Sadie supported an avowed anti-white candidate for chief, then backed out when her candidate secretly admitted he actually thought whites were probably OK) [Are young First Nations adults not allowed to display incipient racism, even though several episodes explore examples of white racism?] and the not altogether sympathetic male leads who cussed, drank beer, smoked cigarettes and engaged in some questionable behavior." His judgmental tone is strange. Why the behaviour of Silas and Frank, two young adults who smoke and drink and very mildly swear, is not acceptable in the context of a "rez" is unclear, unless normal young men on a rez behaving pretty normally is somehow threatening. Kentner seems to be looking for one-dimensional characters such as he might have found on the contemporary American night soaps for teens, such as *Beverley Hills 90210* (1990–2000). However, Laura Lind seems to have understood the series. Writing in the Toronto alternative newspaper *eye weekly*, 18 September 1997, about the second season, she shows the irony in her self-identifying as a "white housewife" when she admits that she identifies more with *The Rez* than with the CBC twice-weekly soap *Riverdale*:[2] "It's got a good beat; you can laugh to it ... No doubt there are problems with the show. The politics seem a little bit pat. Is the big issue on reserves the establishment of day-care centres? And the sub-plot from the first episode is reintroduced as the main plot of the second. But otherwise the stories are denser than last year. The community of actors playing the denizens of the reserve has expanded and that has resulted in more depth of character for everyone. This is particularly true of the post-menopausal [white] bar owner who's given a chance to do something other than drink and seduce youths."

Unlike its practice with *The Beachcombers* or *North of 60*, the CBC only commissioned nineteen episodes of *The Rez*, six for a try-out season in 1996 and thirteen, after a hiatus, in 1997. When the series did not get the ratings the CBC was looking for, it was cancelled. Yet *The Rez* was unique in its attempt to portray a group of young adults living on a reserve whose lives are both distinctive culturally and yet instantly recognizable to its target viewers. Like *M\*A\*S\*H\** or *Buffy the Vampire Slayer*, this series was rather loosely based on a film, in this case *Dance Me Outside*, but as in the other examples many of the elements were significantly transformed. Unlike most television series that evolve out of movies, *The Rez* retained as executive producer the film's director, Bruce McDonald, who had shared the duties for the film and subsequently for the television series with Canada's most successful Hollywood filmmaker, Norman Jewison. The producer of *The Rez*, John Frizell, had co-written the screenplay with Don McKellar. This alone should have ensured that the series was different from the simple format of sitcom, sub-genre "friends hang out together." The credit for series "creator" reads W.P. Kinsella, whose book of short stories *Dance Me Outside* (1977) was adapted for McDonald's film.[3] The film was broadcast on the CBC at least twice, giving it a much bigger audience than its release in movie houses could generate.

## ANTECEDENTS TO *THE REZ:*
## *DANCE ME OUTSIDE*, THE BOOK AND THE FILM

Kinsella's book is written in a highly problematic dialect. Set on the Hobbema reserve in Alberta, the stories are narrated by Silas Crow, with his friend Frank Fencepost appearing in many of them. The film script is based on the short story "Dance Me Outside," but elements from other stories are added. Kinsella is not an aboriginal writer, and his stories have been sharply criticized as appropriation of voice. Lenore Keeshig-Tobias cited Kinsella in her attack on *Where the Spirit Lives* well before the release of *Dance Me Outside,* the film.[4] However, Thomas King (academic, novelist, radio writer/performer, and television scriptwriter for *North of 60*), as quoted in "Tribal Tribulations,"[5] in *Maclean's,* 19 February 1990, took a different tack: "'I think some of his stories are good, but too many descend into the horribly burlesque. Too often he goes for the cheap laugh.' In replying to his critics, Kinsella bluntly told Maclean's that Indians 'Don't have the skill or experience to tell their stories well.'"[6] Six years later, Drew Hayden Taylor gave the issue a more gentle ribbing, saying that Kinsella's stories about the Hobbema reserve are not nearly as good as his baseball stories: "The man can write, but it's his choice and treatment of subject matter that I would question ... [S]o contrary to rumors you may have heard, I have not put out a contract on him or an ancient Ojibway curse on him. I figure anybody who looks and dresses like George Armstrong Custer ... is a marked man anyway."[7] In the *Windspeaker* article "Cultural Appropriation and Aboriginal Literature," Kenneth Williams records this ironic comment by Beth Cut Hand [Cree]: "We actually have Kinsella to thank for an increased awareness and sensitivity to a First Nation voice.'"[8]

After reading the stories in *Dance Me Outside,* I agree with King, Cut Hand, and Taylor. I wish Kinsella had done better. I particularly dislike the *faux naïveté* of his narrator Silas Ermineskin and the strange dialect that he uses. From "Feathers": "'You ever do any experiments in that there political science?' my friend Frank Fencepost ask him one time. 'Like make up stuff to smell like rotten eggs the way we do sometimes down to the Technical School.' 'No,' Chief Tom say to Frank and look down on him like maybe he a pile of cow chips" (121). However, the film, which draws on many plot details but changes the characters substantially, is very different from Kinsella's stories – the television series even more so. Both abandon that kind of dialect. In the series, one reason may well have been that Metis Jordan Wheeler, who had served as story editor on *North of 60*, was the story editor as well as one of the writers for *The Rez*. But the issue of cultural appropriation in film and television cannot be so easily resolved, since both are controlled by and largely created by teams of people from the dominant white culture.

The 1994 film *Dance Me Outside* was financed by CBC and Telefilm. The CBC chose to rerun it a week before the debut of *The Rez*. Well-known critic of Canadian films Gerald Pratley, in his entry on the film in *A Century of Canadian Cinema: Gerald Pratley's Feature Film Guide, 1900 to the Present* (2003), makes the acute observation that, "with genuinely funny moments, the film's weakness is in the script." He, too, notes that "[t]he writers failed to develop the female character who goes through most profound change ... so the climax falls flat."[9] The climax of the first half of the film occurs when Frank (Adam Beach) and his friend Silas (Ryan Black) find a young girl's body. The white murderer, however, is given a ludicrously light sentence of one year, and he then returns to the area. The second half of the movie focuses on what to do about the murderer. Director Bruce McDonald likes to play with genres, as he does in this blackly comic drama.[10] Nevertheless, his ending, which mixed absurd horror and humour, is unsatisfactory. Sadie, Silas's girlfriend, leads the other girls to impose their own form of justice while the comically inept guys are getting up their nerve and making stupid mistakes. Yet there is no real characterization of the young women who actually do kill the murderer, not even of Sadie. In *The Rez*, Sadie is one of the leads, not the secondary character she is in the film until its last scenes. Interestingly, neither the murder nor the young women's revenge is ever alluded to in the series. *Dance Me Outside* is all over the map – part "good old boys" comedy and part examination of loss, drift, and despair in unjust circumstances. A combination of comedy, irony, and tragedy can work in drama (Chekov, Pinter, George Walker, Tomson Highway, and Thomas King come to mind), but it does not work very well here, primarily because the characters are not fleshed out, even Silas and Frank, but also because the film's structure is very episodic.[11]

Even the use of dance as a metaphor is loaded with inappropriate overtones in this film. Dancing a victim outside so he can be killed is the antithesis of how dance is used by First Nations peoples. From the great dance dramas of the Kwakiutl to the small powwows that dot the summer landscape all over the country, dance is sacred as well as secular.

In "Dance Me Inside: Pow Wow and Being Indian," in *Fuse,* summer 1993, Gail Guthrie Valaskasis traces some of the scholarship on powwows that emphasizes the commercial, the pan-Indian elements, the politics, and the historical roots without ever, as she sees it, coming to terms with the affective element, what she calls "a circle of socialization ... a mixture of fragmented feelings of community and spirituality ... My memories of growing up Indian on the Lac du Flambeau reserve in Wisconsin and your memories of Indians growing up wherever you did, are rooted in images of pow wow" (39).

When the film was rebroadcast, John Doyle, in *Broadcast Week* (*Globe and Mail,* 26 August 2000) said he liked the film but he was negative about the series because of "the CBC's traditional, heavy-handed, righteous treatment of the material" (he also disliked *North of 60;* see chapter 15). Given the comic tone that prevails in much of the series, from the first scene of the first episode, the comment "heavy-handed, righteous treatment" is simply very odd.[12]

## CHARACTERS AND SITUATION

As he did in *Dance Me Outside*, Ryan Black played Silas Crow in the series, the young writer who eventually becomes the bearer of his people's stories; Darrell Dennis played Frank Fencepost, the mechanical whiz, jokester, impractical dreamer, and the far less mature of the two; Jennifer Podemski reprised Sadie Maracle, who is smart, ambitious, and has already been admitted to the University of Toronto; and Tamara Podemski played Lucy, Frank's girlfriend, who has dreams of being a singer or a model or an actress.[13] All four have been friends since childhood. Patricia Collins obviously relished her role as the hard-drinking, oversexed owner of the Loose Moose Marina, Eleanor Nanibush; in the second season Kari Matchett convincingly played her daughter, the voluptuous but vulnerable Tanya, who has a baby and so is forced to find a home with the mother she never knew. Shirley Cheechoo played Silas's mother ("Ma"),[14] and Herbie Barnes played Silas's mentally and physically challenged brother, Joseph. Gary Farmer played the golf-playing, corrupt, nepotistic but adept politico Chief Tom, and in the second season Adam Beach played Chief Tom's son, Charlie, who has gone to Ryerson and is much more sophisticated and a shade older than Silas and Frank. In a strange bit of casting, the producers replaced the compelling Monique Mojica,[15] who had played Mad Etta in the first season, with the less expressive, though confident Elaine Miles (Marilyn Whirlwind of *Northern Exposure*).

One thing missing in the series is an extended family for Silas, Frank, or Sadie.[16] Its predecessors differed in this respect. In *The Beachcombers*, Nick and Jesse formed part of an extended, though self-chosen, family – Mollie, Constable John, Hugh, Margaret, and even Relic. Jesse's wife, Laurel, his sister, Sarah, and his stepson, Tommy, were added in later years, and both Jesse's and Laurel's grandfathers appeared on a few occasions. The adults of *Spirit Bay* form a tightly knit, interrelated community. However, the oldest generation is not a constant presence in *The Rez* as it is in those series or in *North of 60*, and the fictional reserve does not appear to be a cohesive unit. Of the four young adults in the series, only Silas seems to have a mother who is a presence in his life. Despite its setting, the series is almost urban in its feel, with characters dropping in and out of what often seems like a neighbourhood. In television series for teens and young adults like *Degrassi High* or *Beverley Hills 90210*, parents are often invisible, making only irregular appearances, but this is a reserve, not Toronto or Los Angeles. A large cast means a larger payroll, but the lack of a sense of a complex community on a small reserve seems very marked to me. Although many in the community look out for Silas's disabled brother, not everyone bothers with him and some are afraid of him. Nepotism is also obvious – for example, Chief Tom's wheeler-dealer son Charlie automatically gets a job in the band office.

Toronto is the polar opposite to the reserve. Frank's girlfriend, Lucy, dreams of making her fortune there as a singer or an actress. Sadie passes up a University of Toronto entrance scholarship to remain with Silas for another year and also to work for political and social change in the band office. Silas needs the city's publishing community to become a real writer. Frank is less interested in the city, which he sees as alluring but also dangerous. When Lucy has been in Toronto for a while, Frank (because of what happened to his sister in the city), with Silas, mounts a needless rescue of her, fearing she has been kidnapped into prostitution – she is actually appearing in an amateur movie made by a film student at Ryerson. Overall, the series suggests that Silas will need to remain close to the Rez for material for his writing and that Frank will stay because he is at home there, working part-time and enjoying life. Sadie is likely to leave eventually, at least to get her degree, and Lucy will make more attempts to find work as a performer in the city.

People often make flippant use of the word *trickster* to describe any character who is funny or tricky. This shows how poorly they understand the very complex concepts behind this word, which is often associated with Nanabush. Eleanor Nanibush, the white widow of the Anishnabe owner of the marina, represents through her behaviour the worst stereotypes of Indian women – the sexually insatiable, sexually available "squaw." She scares the boys on the Rez silly with her come-ons and even seduces Mad Etta's boyfriend, which is very unwise since it leads to Mad Etta mysteriously making Eleanor's waterbed collapse. Even though Eleanor is a single mother and grandmother, as a character she remains the completely self-involved seductress. That the writers gave Eleanor the last name of Nanibush (so spelled) is troubling. Tomson Highway's Nanabush in *The Rez Sisters* and *Dry Lips Oughta Move to Kapuskasing* is one prototype of the trickster archetype – both man and woman, the life-giver full of overt bawdy sexuality whose stories show that sometimes s/he learns lessons after getting into trouble and sometimes s/he does not. Always, s/he brings lessons to those whose lives s/he touches or who hear stories about her/him. Nanabush is a liminal figure in *The Rez Sisters*, appearing as an MC of the Biggest Bingo in the World, a seagull, and a spirit guide to a peaceful death, visible only to the dying Marie-Adele and the mentally deficient Zha, whose pain he dances. This rich complexity is simply absent in the character of Eleanor Nanibush, who leers and preens, drinks and exploits, and is utterly contemptuous of much of reserve life. She improves a bit as a credible character in the second season, but I wonder if her name was insulting to those in the audience who were Anishnabe and Woodland Cree.[17] If Frank is partly Nanabush in his misplaced ambitions, devious ways of avoiding work, cleverness with engines, and general air of a bumbler, then Silas, with his surname Crow (this part of Ontario, not very far north, has no ravens), may also allude to Nanabush elements in the stories he tells, which include the ones in the series.

Looking at the episodes in season 1 and comparing them to those in the longer season 2, a viewer can see the characters taking firmer, more complex shape. Silas's sister, Illiana, and Robert, the white lawyer she married, are gone. Mad Etta has been recast. The story arcs are a little longer.

### SEASON 1

### *"Dressed like a Fish"*

Episode 1, "Dressed like a Fish," like all opening episodes of a series, set up this one. John Frizzell served as both writer and supervising producer for the episode. It begins with a little banter, and then the owner of the marina, who employs the boys in the summer, drops dead. Frank is shocked, tries to utter a chant over the body, and, hearing a roll of thunder, takes it as a

At the marina window: Silas Crow (Ryan Black), the series' narrator; Eleanor Nanibush (Patricia Collins), merry widow and marina owner; and Frank Fencepost (Darrell Dennis). *A Yorktown and Shadow Shows presentation of a production by Rez Productions Ltd in association with the* CBC.

supernatural response, saying, "Cool." The scene establishes Frank's light-hearted, often self-centred attitude to most things, including death, and signals the basic tone of the episode. Frank then thinks it would also be cool to stage his own funeral, and he appears lying in his "coffin" with everyone good-naturedly joining in on the play-acting and funeral "feast" while Silas sends up the custom of a eulogy. There is also a distant echo of a suicide on the reserve a month ago in the dialogue. The rest of the plot is about who will take over the marina, which is not on reserve land. Robert, Illianna, Mad Etta (who claims she uses "JoJo's Psychic Alliance" – a topical joke, as well as a nice send-up of stereotype), Joseph, and Ma are introduced, and Silas is established as the narrator/writer of the series. Eleanor, the widow of the marina owner turns up in an outrageous outfit, fires the boys, then struggles to do the work herself as they kibitz – without malice but audibly. But Sadie sounds a warning note when she tells Silas she is going to the University of Toronto because "life here is making me too sad, Silas." However, the series does not really elaborate on that undertone in the first season. Sadie eventually agrees to give Silas a year of her life so that they can get ready for what life holds for them both. The episode ends with a party, food, fire, rock music. It's an energetic and often funny beginning.

## "The Long House"

Episode 4, "The Long House," written by John Frizzell, crosses the line between comedy and questionable material. Lucy wants to leave for Toronto. Frank is frantic because, as we find out much later, his sister had gone to the city, had become a hooker, and had come home with a baby. Clearly, he is also insecure and emotionally unable to let her go. He seeks a "spell" from Mad Etta (in this season played by Monique Mojica), who points out that she is "a healer not a witch." Frank's ideas about medicine women seem to be based on white fairy tales and cartoons. Yet a hint of Mad Etta's real powers is established from the beginning. She radiates quiet confidence and amusement at their request. One of the boys asks, "Don't you think our kids should stay here?" – a recurring question in this series, a focus in two episodes of *Spirit Bay,* and a major motif in *North of 60.* Mad Etta, however, goes to the heart of the problem in one line: "Not without jobs or money." She tells Frank about the "African tradition" of making a person about to make a mistake sit in a longhouse, "a sacred place of contemplation," and think about what they are about to do before they act. When (not *if,* in her account) the person has reconsidered, there is a big party. Frank ignores the word *African* (i.e., it's not in his own culture) and seizes on the idea.

Meanwhile, as the boys work on a boat in the marina, they wonder why Eleanor hasn't been seen for days and conclude she is depressed or frightened. Later Sadie makes a gesture of friendship and knocks on her door, hoping to get her out of her depression. Eleanor, in black underwear, opens the door and tells an embarrassed Sadie, "This is the world, this is where Whitey comes to rot, but I sure wasn't doing it alone." Mad Etta's former lover joins her at the door, literally sweeps Eleanor off her feet, and closes the door. There are other funny bits that would appeal to a young audience; for example, as Sadie stuffs envelopes, Silas says, with a look, "I'd like to see you lick something in black and white." Sadie: "That lets you out, red man."

The boys then lock Lucy up, with her reluctant consent, in an old log cabin without a bathroom "to think." Later she discovers that no one is around to let her out. Despite the comedy, this is where the show goes over the line. That she agrees to be locked in is improbable, a transparent attempt to change the victim into a willing accomplice. And a girl being held against her will – for whatever reason – by a stronger, bigger male is not funny. Lucy is not the only one who will react with rage to that plot twist. The tone of this narrative is all over the map, skating far too close to a portrait of an abusive and obsessive man rather than to one of a "loveable lug," which is what Frank is supposed to be. Eventually, Silas recognizes his complicity in holding Lucy against her will and lets her out. Silas and Lucy sit together in the dawn light, talking about her dream to sing in musical theatre. When she sings "Aquarius" from *Hair* not badly, not spectacularly well, Silas is surprised and impressed. Frank returns to find Silas sleeping on a rock. Lucy is gone. Frank is unrepentant – an open ending that at least refuses to include an unlikely moment of enlightenment. Silas replies to his "What am I gonna do without her?" with silence. The last shot of the episode is of Lucy singing to herself as she hitchhikes out of the Rez down the road.

### *"Dirty Girls, Kill! Kill!"*

Written by John Frizzell, episode 6, "Dirty Girls, Kill! Kill!," has a thread about the outside intruding into the safe world of the Rez, bringing unwanted change. Sadie has sent Silas's story to *Quarry* magazine without his knowledge. To her surprise, he is very angry and hurt that she took the initiative. (The subtext is that she exposed him to a critical eye before he felt he was ready.) Meanwhile, Frank has arranged a fundraiser at the marina that involves hiring women described as "dirty girls, wearing little, getting down in big vats of tapioca pudding." Sadie is outraged at the sexist scheme and tired of always feeling like the grown-up among the three friends. She acknowledges that she is "a tight ass," fights tears, and then lets go in fury at "big-busted wrestlers wearing butt floss! … Men wear emotional diapers forever!" This silences Silas and sends Frank to hide in a telephone booth. Yet, when Sadie goes out and finds Frank, they both recall that he protected her like a big brother when they were in school. One of the better elements in the series is the reiterated motif of the kids on the Rez growing up together and dealing with changes in their friendships as they mature.

In the end, no one shows up at the charity event because the women on the reserve won't let their men come – except for one teenager who has bought all the tickets with the money he earned working in the bush. A series of two-handed encounters follows – Sadie to Silas, Illianna to Robert, Frank to Ma, Etta to Eleanor – as formal a structure as you would find in a late seventeenth-century comedy. Meanwhile, Joseph, briefly ignored, has been sitting in the vat in thigh-deep tapioca playing with his action figures. When the others remember to look, there is no sign of him. Frank wades into the tapioca, feels around, and gets covered in the stuff, only to find that Joseph is now playing behind a counter. Enter the wrestlers – anticlimactically. The episode ends. Much of the physical comedy is funny, as are some of the one-liners. The narrative is very loosely structured until the four encounters, which do not really resolve anything. Again the tone is all over the map. Unexpectedly, Eleanor's hunger for sex and Frank's big dreams are both given a touch of pathos, but Joseph's disappearance borders on the grotesque, allowing the viewers' imagination to briefly take over. As the last of six episodes, this one offers hints of ongoing narratives, but like the others, it is basically self-contained.

### SEASON 2

In the second season of thirteen episodes, the themes were more complex and the techniques used to combine serious issues and humour were much more sure-footed. The episodes discussed below are (I believe) in roughly chronological order, as suggested by internal evidence rather than an episode guide, which I have been unable to find in the CBC library or (as yet) online. Despite the longer narrative arcs promised by the producers in interviews, *The Rez* could still be enjoyed whenever a viewer dropped in.

### *"Strange Bedfellows"*

"Strange Bedfellows," by Peter Mitchell, is about band politics. George (played by Raoul Trujillo), new to the reserve, is running for chief against Chief Tom. The satire is pretty mild, although some of it does cut both ways. Frank calls George "that Apple" (out of his hearing). When George sees Frank and Silas having a cigarette and a beer in the bar, he says he hates to see two young men drinking the day away, which alienates the viewers, who know better. Some of the jokes are broad. Silas is drawn to a huge car and ignores Sadie, who asks what she has to do to get his attention. His reply: "Get bigger hubcaps." Sadie retorts, "Get a bigger hose." George's law degree, column in the *Globe and Mail,* and connections to an activist organization put him streets ahead of Chief Tom, who makes a lacklustre speech at the still-unfinished band centre, ending with a dispirited "[W]hatever he promises, I promise too." George promises a daycare centre to enthusiastic applause. He then asks why a white woman owns the most valuable piece of property on the reserve and says that, although they should not hate, they should not get screwed any more. (A few viewers might wonder why he is bothering to run as chief of such a small band, but that is never explained.)

The three leading characters: Silas, Frank, and Sadie. Note the marina's sign for gas on sale. *A Yorktown and Shadow Shows presentation of a production by Rez Productions Ltd in association with the CBC.*

The plot is complicated by Sadie's admiration for George, who gets her to work on his campaign even though it costs her her job as Chief Tom's aide. Sadie will make sacrifices for her ideals, but she is so obsessed she even talks politics with Silas in bed, destroying the mood. Charlie, the chief's son, infuriates his father with his purple fingernails and extravagant car, but Chief Tom contains his anger until he can get Charlie to do a computer search for dirt on his rival. Chief Tom and Charlie tell Eleanor about George's plan to get rid of her and recruit her with the promise of no taxes. Cut to George in his T-shirt in a very basic cabin with a gas stove and oil lamp. Eleanor knocks on the door with bottle and cleavage both displayed. The kettle whistles. Of course, Charlie arranges for pictures –

slow pan on a sheaf of them. George: "You set me up." Chief Tom: "Seems you have a reputation for this kind of thing. What's Eleanor? Number 15?" George: "They'll still vote for me." Chief Tom: "These folks know who I am. I may not be a great champion of Native Causes but I don't cheat on my wife with every piece of white meat I can get my hands on." Charlie caps the exchange: "I thought you said we didn't need to get screwed by white people." George says, "Touché," and withdraws from the race. That exchange would touch a nerve in some First Nations communities because several prominent leaders had white wives. The episode's take on First Nations politicians is that too many are corrupt, inept, hypocritical, or inexperienced. Yet at least one website saw the episode as anti-white. When both sides feel targeted by satire, there is the clear suggestion that the satire has found its mark.

### *"Lust"*

"Lust," written by Peter Mitchell, raises some troubling questions. It plays off the unrecognized tension between Silas's sexual experiments with Sadie (who has picked up some ideas from Tanya, Eleanor's daughter) and Joseph's mental and physical disabilities, which frustrate his normal teen-aged longings for sexual contact. When Sadie coaxes Silas to visit her while her parents are away, Silas leaves Joseph with a younger girl who has a crush on Silas. Joseph "attacks" her by grabbing her breasts. When the girl, genuinely traumatized, tells Sadie and Lucy, they reply that he has done that to them too but stopped when told to and never did it again. However, the girl's brother, just out of prison, threatens to beat up Silas, backing off only when Frank, thinking fast, points out that as an ex-con he will forfeit his parole. First Ma and then Silas and Sadie tell Joseph not to touch girls that way, but Joseph can't see why Silas should have all the girls; so it is explained to him that both people must want to do that kind of touching for it to happen. Joseph rounds on Silas and says, with the truth that comes out of the mouth of a holy fool, "[N]o girl for me, I'm mental." Joseph's dilemma gets Silas thinking about whether they can or should keep Joseph at home. The context and contrast for Joseph's behaviour are both the transparent crush the younger girl has on Silas and the explicitly sexual but loving fun Sadie and Silas have. Joseph's loneliness and his unresolved needs are underlined at the end, when the credits run over a long shot of Joseph, alone, watching on a fuzzy television screen the ads for phone sex. A difficult problem is handled with care as well as humour in this episode. Better still, there is no easy sitcom resolution.

*"Like Father, Like Son"*

"Like Father, Like Son," by Peter Mitchell, takes on another loaded subject – absent fathers. When Silas's father, Ron, shows up for the first time in years, he is promptly arrested. Silas angrily presses his mother to explain why she has welcomed him: "He abandoned you!" But Ma simply explains that she felt no anger at Ron – they were both "real young and it didn't stick!" Silas makes it clear that he wishes Ron were Joseph's father, not his.

The subplot is an unconnected but comic take on cultural appropriation. Frank discovers an unopened carton on the road containing "Indian" souvenirs for tourists "made by our relations the Taiwan." Indian dolls, ugly Indian masks, and snow globes create a chance for him to follow his dream of becoming an entrepreneur. He negotiates with Eleanor for 40 per cent of the profit of sales at the marina. Sadie, outraged at what she rightly calls "cultural appropriation," is doubly outraged when Chief Tom won't intervene. Apparently Eleanor can sell anything that is legal, since the marina is not on land belonging to the band. Frank, without admitting he found the goods and is Eleanor's partner, points out to Sadie that the tourists never leave the marina to see the real reserve anyway, because "the reserve scares them."

Sadie's politics are put to much more effective use when she persuades Chief Tom to get the courts to accept a sentencing circle for Ron. As the chief says in exasperation later, when she persists on the issue of the Indian junk on sale at the marina, "I got the sentencing circle. I culturally appropriated his ass right back here." Cut to a long shot of the sentencing circle. The stone used to designate who is speaking is passed to Silas, who says nothing as Ma, with Joseph leaning on her shoulder, watches. Etta, the next speaker, then defends Ron. Ron makes a self-serving speech, saying that while he does "drink a bit" and "did abandon [his] family," he came back "to turn [his] life around." His words are not particularly credible, but Etta prevails and he is "exiled" for three months to one of the many distant islands in the lake. Etta also arranges for Silas to drop his father off at the island, but Silas, still alienated, plays loud rock and roll all the way there. Once ashore, Ron tries to talk to him. Silas says abruptly, "Stay warm," and roars back.

Eventually, persuaded by Etta, Silas goes back to the island to see his father, who clearly has had no problem surviving with the scant supplies he has. He has built a lean-to and collected firewood, skills his son does not have because no one taught them to him. Ron is not the sentimental type. His greeting to Silas is "How the hell are you?" Beside the fire in the evening after a meal, Ron claims that he always kept track of his son by phoning Silas's mother, who told him that Silas is the smartest kid on the reserve. Silas shrugs, saying his girlfriend is the smartest, and without irony but making a point, he tells Ron that Ma did a good job. Finally, he asks the question that haunts such kids, why did his father leave? Ron evades – "We all have to leave" – then tries to set up a specious identification with the inevitable restlessness a young man like Silas would feel. Silas rejects the argument. His father, unlike him, had a wife and kid. Ron, perhaps more honestly, then replies, "That's why I left. To make our lives better … Think how it would feel to come back a failure." Silas can only respond to the subtext: "Hey, I'm here, even though I'm breaking the rules."

The next scene opens with a close-up of a dead fire, cigarette butts on the ground, a frying pan crusted with food – not a sentimental father-and-son camping scene in the wilderness – then the camera pans to Silas asleep on the ground. Finding the boat gone when he wakens, Silas, livid, shouts over the water, "Looks like you were wrong, Etta!" When he hears about it, Chief Tom is angry because the police will be upset. Ma says Ron always took the easy way out. Etta defends Silas for following his heart and going out to see his father. Ron's voice off-camera nonchalantly interrupts to ask if they have seen the movie *Independence Day* – a bad joke that angers Silas even more. Ron says, with only a touch of defensiveness, "Hey, I came back. I did the right thing." And then the writer regrettably makes the emotional subtext improbably explicit. Ron: "Maybe I came back so I'd be a man you could respect." Note that no one blames time spent in residential schools or poverty or even alcohol for Ron's irresponsibility and disinterest in parenting. Ron is responsible for who he is. When Silas returns his father to the island, he says to him as Ron steps ashore, "Watch out for the black flies." Ron, drawing attention to his knowledge of the old ways, jokes that he will slather on the bear grease and roll around in the dirt. This series, however, often tries to show that much of what was traditional doesn't work anymore, and the episode leaves it very much up to the viewer to decide whether the traditional way of restoring someone to his or her place in the circle of the community will work. Silas: "See you in three months." Ron never reappears in the series.

### "Poster Girl"

The issue of cultural appropriation reappears in "Poster Girl" by Metis story editor Jordan Wheeler. Most of the young women on the reserve hope to be chosen as the cover girl for a new line of clothing (the ironically named "Savoy jeans") in which the Kidiabanasee reserve is a major investor. The advertising firm is set to shoot a campaign on the reserve under the supervision of Charlie as band liaison and all-around fixer. Predictably, the Toronto creative types are clueless about the culture they hope to represent. What's more, they are vegetarian and can't even find anything to eat. Sadie thinks the whole advertising shoot is exploitive, and when the ad agency sets up a cattle call to find its model, she refuses to audition. She even blasts Lucy for competing, ignoring the fact that Lucy wants to be an actress and is looking for any entrée. Lucy retaliates, telling Sadie, "I don't want to be another loser on the Rez." Sadie, with shocked surprise: "What, like me?" Lucy, stubbornly refusing to take it back: "You said it." However, when the admen accidentally catch Sadie on film during the auditions, it turns out that she has the face and body they want. To everyone's surprise and chagrin, especially Lucy's, Sadie takes the job. Viewers can see that when she puts on the new clothing, she finds a new hip identity that she obviously enjoys.

The story turns on what constitutes identity on the Rez, on what exploits a "native" look and identity, and on how Lucy and Sadie define their identity as young women and as aboriginal women. Sadie wants it all. In fact, a young audience might well have found her initial rejection of such a chance unlikely. In any case, although she chooses to work with the appropriators of her culture, she refuses to wear what, to this viewer, looks like a Six Nations headdress because it does not belong to her own culture (still unidentified by name). If the reserve is Anishnabe, she is right. Sadie, the politicized one among the four friends, manipulates the cultural appropriation intrinsic in the shoot to get what she wants on her terms. The compromises she makes are mitigated by the arguments she wins during the shoot and, of course, by the money she earns.

### "Der Deutscher Indianer"

Themes of identity and representation reappear in "Der Deutscher Indianer," one of the funniest episodes. It was written by Penny Gray and directed by Metis film director Gil Cardinal, who like Jordan Wheeler had previously worked on *North of 60*. The subplot focuses on Lucy's restlessness. This time she is encouraged by Sadie, who gives her a loan but does not tell Frank. The main plot is about three German tourists who want to live authentically on an island for two days,[18] but in a plot twist, it turns out that the "wannabes" include a professor of native studies who has his own tipi, bakes bannock for Frank and Silas, and already gives lectures to his classes on what he calls, in verbal italics, *"the stories."* His daughter and her boyfriend, who accompany him on a trip, are also very fit, much more so than their two guides. In 2004, Adam Gilders would present a detailed account of such a phenomenon in his article "Ich Bin Ein Indianer" in the first issue of the *Walrus*.[19] He explores the "reality of *Indianthusiasmus*" (75), where thousands of people, fuelled by Karl May's old stories, choose to be Indians. According to Murray Small Legs, a Blackfoot, some Germans "have an 'Indian' feeling. They believe that on the outside they are German but on the inside they are Indian" (77). After sketching the long history of this love affair, including the chilling fact that Hitler ordered the officers on the Russian front to carry a copy of May's books on how to fight Indians, Gilders proposes that this long-standing fascination with playing Indian still satisfies the impulse to racial and cultural purity. He quotes Lindbergh Namingha, founder of the Native American Association of Germany, who says, "I find [thinking about these cultures as 'living museums'] very offensive, especially when they refuse to let true American Indians participate in their events. They say we're too modern and believe we have lost our Native American-ness" (80). Moreover, as Trina Mather tells Gilders (Mather-Simard is president of the Turtle Island Tourism Company), whether in Germany or in North America, some aspects of First Nations cultures, political and spiritual, should not be shared with tourists. Yet these "Deutsche Indian-ers" can equate a very distant history of Teutonic tribes with the life the Plains Indians no longer live and so seek a "homecoming."

This episode of *The Rez*, aired years before Gilders's article, touches lightly but succinctly on the ironies inherent in a German professor, a specialist in Native Americans, seeking an authentic experience from two young men who have little idea of the stories or lifeways of their ancestors. Frank packs Cheezies and other processed food, then immediately unpacks them when his visitor points out that he expects "native" food. Silas stumbles over the stories he is expected to tell the tourists, because he cannot remember the ones Etta told him when he was a child. First he tries to catch up by reading a children's book of Indian legends, but Sadie enjoyably distracts him from his preparation. Finally he goes to see Etta. Etta refuses to tell him the stories again because, in their shared tradition, he should not tell them for money – an apt and accurate reaction that places the tales in a sacred context not understood by the German professor or by Silas. Back on the island, under pressure from the professor, Silas does remember the beginning of one story, but then he draws a blank. Meanwhile, Frank gets some frozen moose meat, tries ineptly to cook it with a blowtorch, and burns down the professor's tipi. Neither of them can find the promised petroglyphs. Eventually, the equally comic self-delusion of the Germans gives way to outrage.

By the time they all return to the marina, the professor is threatening to sue. But Etta appears unexpectedly and volunteers to show him the petroglyphs, which appropriately appear in long shot only. She also tells them "the story," which the viewer hears only as it ends. In fact, Silas finishes it. Etta then explains that he is still in the early stages of learning the stories from her. She tells Silas directly, in front of the strangers, that he has been chosen to tell the stories to the next generation. "An apprentice, ja?" says the professor, satisfied. After the tourists have left, having paid in full, Silas asks Etta if she meant what she said. Yes, if he wants it, is her answer.

As often happens in this series, the satire cuts two ways, directed both at Frank and Silas for ineptly faking "authentic" Indian experiences for a big fee and at the Germans for searching for "authentic" experiences and expecting to find a place and people frozen in the nineteenth century on a modern rez. The professor with his tape recorder is an observer and a collector, not, as he fantasizes, a participant. Moreover, he expects to have the authentic experience within two days. He is eager and, in the initial stages, easy to gull with a fake chant. Although he has studied a lot and now teaches, he is not very different from the tourists who buy Frank's trinkets from Taiwan. Frank has no qualms about this kind of tourist. But here we see Silas developing a new respect for his culture, a respect that might bloom into a vocation. Meanwhile, Sadie, who wants to live and work on the Rez, helps Lucy leave it. The modern rez presents complexities invisible to the tourists. Overall this is one of the most successful episodes in the short run of the series.

### "No Way to Treat a Lady"

The equally successful and complex episode "No Way to Treat a Lady" takes on another loaded topic (especially in a First Nations context) – alcohol. Penny Gay's script is good. Collins's broad performance of Eleanor is played off against the understated performance of Shirley Cheechoo as Ma. Frank, ever the awkward adolescent male, makes a move on Tanya and asks her to Silas's party. She asks, with heavy irony, if white girls are allowed to go to the party. More than once in this series the audience is introduced to the idea that there can be reverse racism. When she asks if Charlie is invited, Frank replies, "Just us plain folks," which suggests not only envy but also class differentiation. Tanya and Charlie go anyway. Even when he is in the bar, Charlie does not drink because he wants to be in control, saying that soft drinks are all that he drank at Ryerson. The regular viewer will admire his determination, yet also knows from previous episodes that he relishes manipulation and control. Later it is obvious that Tanya, with her soft drink at the party, is much older in spirit than the kids partying (after all, she supports a baby) and the subtext makes it clear that Charlie understands her situation yet enjoys her company.

The other plot concentrates on Simone (Ma), who finally gets to hear her adult name used rather than being designated only by her role as mother. Such a split focus with an adult story is unusual in television made primarily for youth. Simone has gone to the city overnight, one line only suggesting that she is looking into a residence for Joseph. She divides the expenses with Eleanor, who wants a taste of city life again and gets a ride in Simone's truck. The rest of the episode intercuts party scenes with Eleanor and Simone's night in the city.

Simone decides to enjoy a quiet night of room service and television, while Eleanor goes out on the town to a bar she knows and picks up three white guys – a man in his mid-forties, a follower, and a younger lad – who buy her drinks. They are stereotypes and the audience never hears their names. That she does not anticipate their intentions seems improbable, particularly since she has been emphatically defined as a sexually experienced woman who welcomes all comers on her own terms. However, the plot demands an ironic turn of events, having her get into something she can't handle because she has been drinking and therefore needs to be rescued by Simone. When she finds out what part of town Eleanor has gone to, Simone gives up the rare pleasure of being alone and a little pampered, puts her street clothes back on, and goes out to find her. But when she does, Eleanor refuses to leave, and Simone agrees to have a drink so that she can stay and keep an eye on her. Clearly she can drink with discretion.

Before long the three men try to force Eleanor into the back of a car (with lots of unnecessarily ominous music). Simone, thinking quickly, goes along but offers them videos and more beer if they go to her place. The older guy in the car tips his hand (for those few viewers who haven't figured out where this is going): "Don't spend another nickel on them boys, they're ready." When they arrive, Simone quickly gets out of the car to ring the door bell. A very big, quite friendly man, backlit in the doorway, makes her welcome, while expressing a little surprise because he hasn't seen her for a while. The belligerent older man lurches out of the car, spits out epithets, and shows a knife in a sheath. But Simone's friend walks up to him and quietly shows him a holstered gun at his belt.

The next morning Simone drives home with the hungover, haggard, but grateful Eleanor. Simone says, with more than a touch of irony, perhaps conscious of the inversion of stereotype: "I was sober, that's all. Jimmy was an old squeeze from way back, when I was living life." Now Ma again, she goes inside and sees the remaining litter: "Had a party, eh?" Silas: "'Course not." Sadie, with more confidence, kids the two older women: "Behave yourself?" Eleanor, ruefully: "She did." Simone goes into the back of the house. We hear a cry, off-camera, followed by a close-up of Ma's look of absolute disgust. She has discovered Tanya and Charlie in her bed.

This episode would appeal to teens and young adults because they would recognize how it feels to have someone of higher status like Charlie (and more maturity) walk in and take your girl, and because one of the adults behaves as stupidly as, and even more dangerously then, one of the young people. However, raising the issue of alcohol is touching on a complex matter. This is not a dry reserve, as the marina is licensed. Simone drank at one time – Joseph may be the result – yet she speaks of that time as "when I had a life." Nevertheless, she obviously stopped drinking too much some time ago. Charlie chooses to have a soft drink because he doesn't like to lose control, and Tanya joins him. Frank sulks and then becomes a belligerent drunk when he can't have the girl he wants. But it is the older white adult, Eleanor, who gets drunk out of loneliness and bravado, then gets into trouble she can't handle. Basically, unlike *North of 60*, where drinking in Lynx River presents all kinds of political and sociological issues, here the issue is cut free from race, rez, and gender. Simone can have one drink and stop. The young people are either responsible or safely drunk within walking distance of home and not in the wintertime. Alcoholism is not a problem for First Nations peoples in this series. Some of the male youth and men have gone to jail, but this is simply taken for granted.

No reference in the episodes I saw is made to the effects of education or acculturation in Simone's generation, and atypically Sadie, Silas, Frank, and Lucy have graduated from high school. Defeats, losses, absent fathers and brothers, and unemployment are kept to the periphery.

## THE BROADCAST CONTEXT

Originally the CBC may have intended *The Rez* as a replacement for the cancelled "dramedy" *Liberty Street* (1994–95),[20] by Linda Schuyler, which targeted young adults out or soon to be out in the working world. It tried to cover several of the issues surrounding the representation of aboriginal people on television by casting Billy Merasty (Cree) as Nathan, a character who is both aboriginal and gay (Schuyler got two minorities for one) and an older and wiser brother figure to some of the other characters. Pamela Cuthbert writes in "Behind the Scenes," *Playback*, 19 June 1995:[21] "The concept for The Rez was initiated in the summer of 1993, at the same time CBC stepped in to pre-buy the feature, which was then in the last stages of prep." The development deal for six episodes was signed in March 1994, "with plans to have it open up from there," says Darrell Dennis. Allison Vale and Teressa Iezzi reported in *Playback*,[22] 12 February 1996: "Next season's CBC all-Canadian primetime will be without the Canadian drama entries of the last two seasons. Liberty Street and Side Effects hit the skids this month and Straight Up and The Rez are moving in to fill the void ... [*The Rez*] focuses on young people but is family-oriented too and may keep a healthy share of the Air Farce audience, which is regularly averaging 1.5 million viewers."

Scheduled for 8 p.m., *The Rez* was clearly intended for Canadians in their late teens and the young adults who had grown up in the 1980s with the *Degrassi Classic* trilogy, which looked with honesty at the dilemmas facing urban teens. Several other Canadian 1990s series also formed the context for *The Rez*. *Northwood* (1991–94), for example, preceded *The Rez*, and *Madison* (1993–97) on Global overlapped it.[23] *The Rez* may have been cancelled after two short seasons, but it did break new ground, winning the "Canada award from the Department of Canadian Heritage for excellence in mainstream television programming which reflects the racial and cultural diversity of Canada."[24]

## THE MAKERS AND CRITICS GRAPPLE WITH ISSUES OF CULTURAL APPROPRIATION AND A HYBRID FORM

*The Rez* was shot in and around the Shawanaga First Nation reserve in May and then in the fall, since the place was very busy with tourists in the summer months. According to a page on Telefilm's website on the first six episodes: "Kidiabanasee's residents know that life is a swift sequence of events whose meaning is not always crystal clear. Neither a sitcom – although funny and offbeat – nor a political tract – although often provocative – The Rez is a splendidly entertaining, well-told drama about the absurdities and joys of ordinary life."[25] In a press release (14 April 1997), *The Rez* productions publicist with the CBC described the series as an "irreverent look at the lives of Silas, Frank and Sadie – three young Native Canadians experimenting with adulthood and sex, always with a quirky sense of humour." Sid Adilman reported in the *Toronto Star*, 19 November 1995, before the series went to air, that Frizzell told him "that the Indian's trickery of well-meaning whites, which ran through Kinsella's book and the movie, is gone. 'This community is integrated and interdependent; white people are popular here ... There is a lot of conning going on, but the natives do the grift, mostly on each other.'" However, the role of white people is much more ambiguous. Eleanor and Tanya become complex characters; other whites are exploitive or racist.[26] Frizzell pointed out to him that *The Rez* is "'not Molly's Reach [*The Beachcombers*], not a family show ... It's for 8:30 p.m. or 9 p.m. We were told by CBC, "Don't come up with a 7:30 show."'" (Note that later APTN, simulcasting to all regions, scheduled it for 7:30 Eastern, which would be 6:30 Central.) According to Adilman, Frizzell said that the native community didn't dislike Kinsella's stories. Since some well-known writers in the community, like Taylor, King, and Keeshig-Tobias, certainly did dislike them (which may have been the unrecorded context for his point), what he says is debatable.

John McKay, in a CP story in the *St Catharines Standard*, 3 February 1996, writes:

[T]he series parts ways with the movie in several respects. For one thing, the "reverse racism," while hilarious in the film, has been toned down. And Frizzell says the halting monotone used by many aboriginals in other dramas [if he was quoted accurately, clearly Frizzell had not seen any of the programs already discussed in this book or most of the drama specials in the 1970s, 1980s and 1990s] has been avoided. He says this "kind of a Tonto construct" is also a notion left over from Kinsella's writing that is no longer relevant.[27] "These kids are as articulate, as well-educated as any kid," he says. "Why would we have them speaking this kind of foreign gobbledegook? What does it serve?" Indeed, the dialogue suggests a Rez 90210 atmosphere as Silas, Frankie and other younger-generation characters deliver their lines in typical teen valley-speak. First Nations issues, from suicide to land claims, also float on the periphery of the story lines, but don't occupy centre stage, unlike the serious tone set by that other CBC show about aboriginals, North of 60.

A year later John McKay, again for CP but in the *Toronto Star*, 23 September 1997, writes that "the cast agrees that the series should continue with its light-hearted approach to aboriginal life," despite the complaints of some community leaders who "objected to what they saw as a waste of a potential platform to drive home a cultural or political message. But the majority agree with the existing style."[28]

In "Native Life Hits a Funny Bone in the cbc Comedy *The Rez*," in the *Sunday Sun*, 5 November 1995, Claire Bickley once more raises by inference the issue of authenticity that First Nations subjects inevitably seem to create:

> The episodes are scripted by Jordan Wheeler who is native and John Frizzell, who is not but who worked on the film. Every script draft is passed around to "fine tune the sensibility" says Frizzell who is also the show's supervising producer ... Darrell Dennis [Frank Fencepost] ... the only one of the three leads who was raised on a reserve, specifically Alkali Lake in the B.C. interior [which was then known to be a very troubled place], recalls, "If somebody's in trouble another person's there to help him. And I don't think that's something that gets portrayed a lot in films and television. A lot of times what they see is the dark side of it, where everyone's in pain and tortured. What I remember most is how much everybody laughed. That came maybe from the feeling of hopelessness or poverty. What you do is you laugh to counteract that."

Bickley reports that Herbie Barnes and Shirley Cheechoo were "director observers on the set." Frizzell told Bickley that if the series were renewed, he hoped that it "'would eventually be native produced'" and spoke of "'a planned obsolescence about our role.'" (This did not happen in the second reincarnation of the series of thirteen episodes.) Herb Barnes was more cautious: "'I think we're looking quite a ways down the road ... I think a lot of us feel we don't want to produce bad work for the sake of doing all-native work. Not to say that a native cast and crew would create bad work, but it's a new field for us.'"[29] Louise Leger, who found the series quite funny and concluded that it would appeal to any viewer looking for a good laugh, told her readers in the *Globe and Mail*, *Broadcast Week* (17 February 1996), that Frizzell said, "'As an urban white guy, it behooves me to work with the native people. I'm working with the actors to tell the stories they want to tell, so in many ways I'm a facilitator more than a writer ... ' [Darrell] Dennis likes the fact that actors get to see the scripts early. 'There are slang expressions that are common on reserves that we might add ... or we may have a problem with where a character is going and we can discuss it ... I think the fact that we are not political or issue-oriented is a message in itself.'" Comparing season 1 to season 2 in the 30 August 1997 issue of *Broadcast Week,* Leger writes: "The stories are much denser ... As before, Canadian references abound ... On issues of cultural appropriation Brian Dennis explains that '[o]ur executive story editor is Jordan Wheeler,[30] a native with experience on *North of 60.* He is an integral part of the team, who makes solid contributions to the stories' and that the cast also tells them if something isn't right.'"

### THE NEWSPAPER CRITICS' EVALUATION

*Toronto Star* critic Henry Mietkeiwicz (23 February 1996) liked what he saw as much as he had liked *Dance Me Outside*: the first six episodes fuse "so many diverse elements into an integrated, wide-angle view of tragedy and joy on an Indian reserve ... It barely seemed possible to duplicate this approach [of the film] but *The Rez* has pulled it off with confidence and panache." Mietkeiwicz sees the dark side of "Long House," the episode about the imprisonment of Lucy until she agrees to stay on the reserve, but justifies it on the (to me sexist) grounds of the "untold anguish" she causes Frank by simply wanting to leave. He finds her dream of being a Broadway musical star strange. It is ironic, perhaps, but not strange unless the Rez is perceived as a place sealed off from the contemporary world. Yet Mietkeiwicz does say that these teens have "much the same hopes, fears, ambitions and insecurities as practically any Canadian" – also debatable. He picks a nice moment from the first episode to end the column. Frank wants a twenty-one-gun salute for his mock funeral along with some beer. "Silas' jaw drops. 'Booze and guns together?' he asks in genuine surprise and alarm. Frank shrugs and the idea is dropped. That moment says it all." Another reporter picks a different moment (in a CP story of 1 February 1996 in the *St Catharines Standard,* headlined "New TV Series Portrays Native Humour on The Rez"): "Frankie Fencepost leans over the old man's dead body, uncertain what to do. The aboriginal teenager hesitates, then begins a rhythmic authentic-sounding chant. Suddenly the skies rumble ominously. 'Cool!' an impressed Fencepost declares with a grin, looking skyward." In her article "No One Spared from Rez's Irreverence" (in the *Calgary Sun,* 24 September 1997), Lyn Cockburn writes:

> Sly, slippery and irreverent, The Rez dares to go where no other series about Native life has gone. Into the quicksand of humour. Now in its second season with 13 new episodes, it spares no one – whites, Natives,

young and old. And politicians ... Patricia Collins as the somewhat ripe, white barkeep Eleanor Nanibush is fall-down-funny in her role of female lech. In episode 1 [of the second season] amidst fast ball repartee ... the fun and the teasing, serious issues get raised – like health care, drinking, community activities, employment and nepotism. "How about not hiring all your relatives for the band office?" Sadie asks Chief Tom. To which he replies in horror: "My wife would kill me, if I didn't." Where the acclaimed North of 60 is issue oriented, The Rez slips the real-life issues in amidst the humour, leaving the viewer howling. And thinking.[31]

Leger (*Globe and Mail, Broadcast Week*, 30 August 1997) quoted Brian Dennis: "The Native press was critical. One thing was, reserves can go from looking like Scarborough to some pretty awful-looking places. We chose a representation somewhere in the middle, so we got letters saying 'you make reserve life look so crappy' and others that said 'you make the reserve look so good – you're trivializing the plight of our people.'" Whether the show was welcomed by First Nations people or not is actually raised in these media reports. It was not an issue in the PR or the reviews of the early seasons of *North of 60*, which suggests that by 1997 consciousness has been raised, at least among reporters. Jim Bawden, in *Starweek* (11 October 1997) writes: "Will Canada's native community take offence? Or will it embrace this as a long-overdue look at the lighter side of aboriginal life? John Frizzell, supervising producer and chief writer of the six episodes filmed so far, hopes aboriginals like the show. And he says he did something new with these scripts ... He vetted them with the native actors on the show for anything potentially offensive. 'I actually thought, OK, if we get some flak, you guys defend it,' he says. 'You're the ones who said you believe in it, now it's as much yours as it is mine.'" Frizzell seems to me to be disingenuous. Of course, using the actors as unpaid consultants in television series is not new. It goes back at least to *The Beachcombers*. Producers and directors of films and of some television dramas will ask native actors if something is authentic – or the actors may protest when it is not. But it would be unfair for readers (and for Frizzell) to expect the young actors to take responsibility for the tone and detail of the series. Note that the addition to the cast of Adam Beach in the second season got major attention because he was then one of the better-known First Nations actors.

As with all of the series discussed in this book, how the series was framed by the producers and by the CBC may have affected some viewers' expectations of the show and thus their readings of the episodes. The advertisements for the series and the series itself demonstrated that it was specifically aimed at the prized 1990s demographic of eighteen- to twenty-four-year-olds who had lots of discretionary cash to spend. That was the theory of television executives then. It still is.

FURTHER THOUGHTS

*The Rez* seems intended to move away from the serious dilemmas and on-going difficult issues of the more adult *North of 60* towards the comically flavoured issues of a kind of hybrid dramedy, and away from the earlier audience of children targeted by *Spirit Bay* or the families with children and young teens targeted by *The Beachcombers* towards an older, more dif-ficult-to-please but demographically more desirable audience, the eigh-teen- to twenty-four-year-olds. The Liberal government of the day was pleased with the series. A 1998 *Equity Newsletter* reported that "CBC TV's dramatic series about life on an Indian reserve, was awarded this year's Canada Award by the Department of Canadian Heritage for excellence in mainstream television programming which best reflects the racial and cultural diversity of Canada."[32]

Like every other series looked at in this book, *The Rez* is not about urban aboriginal characters. And like *Spirit Bay* ten years before, it is racially ho-mogeneous. Problems are treated as either systemic, and thus largely ig-nored, or as obstacles that are relatively easily overcome. Questions of identity do arise, as they are bound to in this age group, but they are rarely framed as being specific to a young adult from a reserve. The dialogue is shot through with quick comic references to racial stereotypes. Sadie re-fuses to dress up for the ad agency in a headdress that is not worn by her people; yet there are few role models for any of them. Sentencing circles, Windigos, and even petroglyphs are found in *The Beachcombers, Spirit Bay,* and *North of 60,* and each of those series also presents some characteristics of the cultural setting unique to, respectively, the Coast Salish, the Anishnabe, and the Slavey-speaking Dene. Lynx River is on traditional unceded lands, but this reserve, unlike Spirit Bay, seems out of touch with its own roots. Mad Etta, the only elder in the series, is both distrusted and respected, at least by Silas, but her name makes her position in the community uncer-tain. Is she the subject of mockery? Is she dismissed? Often the basic values and beliefs she represents seem to hover around the edges of the episodes rather than being a thread through the daily lives of the protagonists. Three accessible sources that introduce the many profound differences between the presumably Anishnabe people living on the Rez and the white culture that penetrates it so deeply were published before the scripts were written: *Dancing with a Ghost: Exploring Indian Reality* (1992) by Rupert Ross, with a foreword by Ojibway Basil Johnston;[33] Basil Johnston's *Ojibway Heritage: The Ceremonies, Rituals, Songs, Dances, Prayers and Legends of the Ojibway* (1973, reprinted 1990); and Paulette Jiles's poetic and personal *North Spirit: Travels among the Cree and the Ojibway Nations and Their Star Maps* (1995).[34] The lack of specific details about the life and culture of this admittedly fictional reserve substantially weakens the impact of the series, making it a little bland, a little superficial. There are also some problems in tone, as well as several improbable plot twists, and there are superficial characterizations of some of the guests. The series is, however, well crafted in its presentation of the uncertain, compelling delights and desires of young sexuality. It also has a deft comic touch on a wide range of topics, including sex, that was refreshing after the angst of night soaps and the prurience of many sitcoms.

The series also reflects more general changes in young women's self-perception over the years. Laurel, an independent mother who works in a bank, was a late addition to *The Beachcombers*, but Sara, Jesse's young sister who came into the show in the late 1970s, also shows independent thinking and often acts on her own. The girls are just as independent as the boys in *Spirit Bay* and regularly carry the storylines. Michele, Rosie, and Sarah in *North of 60* in the early 1990s are working mothers, as are some of the other women. All of them perform the hard tasks inherent in living in a small settlement in the North. In fact, many of the women in these series are subverters, not just survivors. By the 1990s they were usually portrayed in credible but equal terms. Sadie, with a healthy sexual appetite, escapes the stereotype of the pure little princess and its shadow, the insatiable "squaw." (I note that safe sex seems to be assumed on *The Rez*. Tanya, not any of the First Nations' characters, is the unmarried mother with the baby.) Yet Sadie says in one episode that she is tired of being the mature woman to the adolescent antics of Frank and Silas. She is often seen to be smarter than they are, which can portray its own kind of sexism. It could be construed that to be a woman who is a leader, you have to be better than the rest. In *The Rez*, Silas, who narrates, and Frank are the focus of almost all the episodes, but Sadie and Lucy are more than their equals in their desire to shape their own lives.

In a very useful book that explores the subtleties and complexities of what Allan Ryan calls *The Trickster Shift: Humour and Irony in Contemporary Native Art* (1999), Ryan quotes the artists and critics Gerald Vizenor and Carl Beam, who define the work of comedy and irony in an aboriginal context as "serious play, the ultimate goal of which is a radical shift in viewer perspective and even political positioning by imagining and imaging alternative viewpoints" (5). That is a tall order for *The Rez,* a nineteen-episode half-hour television series made by the dominant culture. *The Trickster Shift,* a book full of colour plates, reproduces the painting *Dance Me on Sovereignty, Dance Me outside Anywhere I Want* by Lawrence Paul Yuxweluptun (Coast Salish).[35] A footnote nearby (page 212) draws attention to the play on both the title of Kinsella's novel and the television series. The painting shows a dancing male figure, with a large hole in his chest, whose features Yuxweluptun depicted using the form lines of traditional Northwest Coast art. The figure dances on what the accompanying text calls "government files." The hole in his chest is identified as signifying an incomplete identity (but it could be read in other ways). At the edge of the dark red and gold utterly stylized landscape, a rainbow reaches to touch the puffy clouds of a pale blue sky. The figure conveys a sense of an unknown future, of an ancient ritual with a modern twist, of lightness of being, of humour; it is missing essential parts but dances anyway. There is the sense that the figure is both trapped by a place and rooted in it – as the young adults on *The Rez* often feel. I suspect that the series would have improved even more if it had been given a longer run.

Like its direct progenitor, the film *Dance Me Outside, The Rez* is basically a comic turn on reserve life that takes some risks and struggles to find a balance. Given that television series like *The Rez* and *North of 60* are subsidized by the state through the cbc, Telefilm, and other agencies, they would be rightly suspect to First Nations writers, directors, actors, and most important of all audiences. Yet to *laugh with* is not to *laugh at* a people. The issue is not political correctness, the term so often used to mask an inadequate response to a real question, but rather a long history of misrepresentation and scurrilous, mocking denigration. Thomas King and Jordan Wheeler both wrote comic scenes in their scripts for *North of 60,* and Wheeler also did for *The Rez.* Nevertheless, this is not to forget that the point of view of every series examined in this book, no matter who advised or who edited the scripts, and despite there having been some Metis and First Nations writers, is still primarily from the outside looking in. The producers and the money come from outside.

A white viewer who has also listened to Thomas King's *The Dead Dog Cafe* on cbc radio, where King exerts artistic control, or who has seen Drew Hayden Taylor's plays or Tomson Highway's, or who watches comedians like Lorne Cardinal and Don Burnt Stick on aptn's *Buffalo Tracks* will recognize a certain flavour of comedy that, while very difficult to pin down, is related to a confident, focused address to a particular audience. This is missing from *The Rez*. How not? Each of the examples just named is quite different from the other, but each is comfortable in turning the searchlight of comedy on the Rez, the urban scene, the quirks of individual First Nations, and the "other," white world in part because each one speaks from within specifically to listeners and viewers who live within the aboriginal cultures. The rest of us can look or listen in if we want to. *The Rez* with its white producer and all of the decision-making apparatus behind him targets a broad audience. *Me Funny* (2005), compiled and edited by Drew Hayden Taylor, is complete with a pipe-smoking war-bonneted Indian on the cover who, we are told, is not Taylor. The book's mock subtitle, also on the cover, reads: "*A far-reaching* exploration of the **HUMOUR**, wittiness and repartee **DOMINANT** among the *First Nations people* of North America, as witnessed, *experienced* and **CREATED DIRECTLY** by themselves and with the **INCLUSION** of outside *but reputable* sources, necessarily *familiar* with the **INDIGENOUS** sense of humour as **SEEN** from an *objective perspective*." Perhaps some day such humour, produced by First Nations production companies and made by aboriginal writers and directors, will appear on the bigger, more established networks on a regular basis on prime time.

For a non-native audience, *The Rez* opened up some questions, threw some fresh light on racism and occasionally refused to provide a sitcom's pat comic ending. The episodes were entertaining, even for viewers outside its target demographic, no mean feat. That the series was given only two seasons is a pity, because it did appeal to a different audience than *North of 60* and did remind viewers that laughter is often used as a way to deal with the world on the Rez. For two brief years there were actually two series that focused on First Nations peoples on (where else?) the CBC. Since 1998, there have been none. *The Rez* was usually worth watching. I am sorry that we did not get to see Silas, Sadie, and Frank become more full-fledged adults, that we did not get to know more young people, and perhaps a few more parents, on their home reserve, that we did not have the chance to see them at the University of Toronto or Ryerson and thus to see a huge multicultural city, Toronto, through their eyes. Only one episode, the one where Frank (afraid that Lucy might become a streetwalker) and Silas hunt for Lucy at Ryerson, gave us a taste of what that might have been like. I would have liked Sadie to meet Teevee from *North of 60* at a training conference for young First Nations leaders. With only nineteen episodes, the series was just finding its feet.

*Summaries of three episodes from season 1 – "Golf and Politics," "A Little Revealing," and "The Lark" – are posted on the Brock Humanities Research Institute website: www.brocku.ca/hri/associates/miller/outside_looking_in.pdf. These were derived from the CBC's own website, from which they have disappeared. Discussions of four episodes (three by Metis story editor and writer Jordan Wheeler) from the second season are also found on this site: "Windigo" (the boys must fight and defeat the dreaded Windigo), "They Call Me Tanya" (Eleanor's daughter, Tanya, is introduced), "Too Many Chiefs" (Sadie takes over from Chief Tom); and "A Rock and a Hard Place" (a growing relationship between Charlie and Tanya and a racist boss at a construction site both challenge stereotypes).*

# TEN

# Fans and Genres and How They Intersect

Why do fans and genres belong together in one chapter? Because no one knows the rules of any particular genre format as well as an adult fan does, and any major inflection of the formula must persuade viewers who love the usual format that value has been added to the program. Such innovations often occur when a series is already established, more rarely early in its lifetime. Examples would include the episode of *M\*A\*S\*H* that was shot from a mute wounded soldier's point of view and the less successful "it was all a dream" framing of a whole season of *Dallas* and later of *Roseanne*. The overwhelming majority of television drama series in the last fifty-plus years have belonged to recognizable genres – some long gone, such as variety shows, or inflected like the "amateur hour," now *American/Canadian Idol* and cognates; some coming back in recurring cycles, such as Westerns; and some having endured for more than fifty years, such as medical shows, cop shows, mysteries, family adventure shows, soaps, sitcoms, and domestic comedies.

## FANS

Fans are not typical viewers. They take their enjoyment of a series well beyond the usual "I watch the show regularly" to "I must see every episode, buy the DVDs, and collect memorabilia if available, make or find websites devoted to the program, join a discussion list or chat room of other people who love the show, and find other shows the actors are in." Not all of the series discussed so far have a fan website, although nostalgic websites are proliferating. The Canadian TV Archive,[1] which is not TVArchive.ca, has the most complete listings for early Canadian television programming now available, with useful cast lists and production details. Episode guides for more modern material, however, are in short supply. After nineteen seasons and 342 episodes engendering many scattered references on the web, *The Beachcombers* surprisingly did not have a fully useful site until 2007, when it appeared on TVArchive.ca.[2] Yet it was given the designation of a masterwork in 2004 by the Audio-Visual Trust.[3] An appeal by a member of the legislature in 2002 that it be revived appears in Hansard for the legislature of British Columbia.[4] It has yet to appear on DVD. Not surprisingly given its short and scattered run, *Spirit Bay,* despite its quality, is invisible on the web except for Canadian TV Archive's short entry. *The Rez* has no fan site or episode guide, perhaps because it had only two seasons of six and then thirteen episodes or because it is too soon for nostalgia. Both *Spirit Bay* and *The Rez* have had a second life rerun on APTN. *The Rez* was also rerun on Showcase. As we shall see, on the web *North of 60* is by far the best served.

The earliest series, *Radisson* (American title *Tomahawk*) and its non-Canadian cousins *Hawkeye and the Last of the Mohicans* and *Hudson's Bay,* do appear on the very detailed Classic TV Archive pages[5] thanks to webmaster Des Martin, who saw episodes of *Radisson* out of order in the early years of Britain's independent network ITV. The people who do the primary work on such a website are willing to do the basic research and then share it with other fans, creating sites that are very useful for providing complete episode guides, basic background on the productions, links to related shows, and feedback. The problems of broadcast order and varying titles are highlighted on Martin's website, not always on others. Some contributors simply state that their information comes directly from watching an episode, which is of course the most reliable source of information for nostalgic fans and others. Des Martin asks for comments, corrections, information from old videos and TV guides, and information on other TV series; he also asks visitors to let him know if "a certain episode of a particular series coincided with a key moment in your life or in world events – and has left a memory of when it was shown." He welcomes suggestions for any other guides. The site is careful to document its sources: *TV Guide*, the Library of Congress, the Internet Movie Database (IMDb), which is not error free, and the UCLA Film and Television Archive. Martin's Canadian site on Classic TV Archive does include *Forest Rangers*, but also credits Clay Self's flourishing, lovingly maintained, and detailed fan site for *Forest Rangers*, discussed below. Less detailed fan sites can provide useful tidbits as well; one such example is a short article on *Forest Rangers* on Cult TV by a nostalgic BBC viewer: "Down to the woods we go but no need to fear this 1960s classic."[6] *Matt and Jenny* is a new addition to the site.[7] *The Campbells* has an episode guide with variable degrees of detail on tv.com.[8] Fans who have made transcripts from off-air materials or have had access to a collection of *TV Guides* can correct or augment others' memories. However, not all are set up for additions and corrections, or function as places where fans discuss specific shows. Many are fragmentary at best, and some violate copyright. A look at the comments on the discussion list or those posted on fan sites for *Forest Rangers*, a program with a long life in reruns but made for a generation who were children in the early 1960s, reveals that its pleasures are now chiefly nostalgic.

Before the web had really become part of our lives, John Fiske, in "The Cultural Economy of Fandom" (1992), argues that "industrially produced texts," like television series, "with their contradictions, inadequacies and superficialities … make the text open and provocative rather than completed and satisfying" (47), which suggests to me that they encourage speculation, discussion, and even redaction among some viewers, particularly fans. Lawrence Grossberg, in "The Affective Sensibility of Fandom" (1992), reminds us that fans of popular culture formats value authenticity of meaning, pleasure, and identity, defined in specific ways that are determined by the medium, the genre, and the program itself. A decade later, Matt Hills's definition of a fan in *Fan Cultures* (2002) includes someone who is obsessed.

Patty Winter's "North of 60" web page is an excellent example of how fans interact with programs and each other.[9] It is focused on *North of 60*, which was made for adults in the 1990s, and is geared to ongoing enjoyment of the series and related movies. Constructed and maintained by an American (the irony is obvious – but the series did attract an international fan base), the website is splendidly detailed and well-run, and it is complemented by a *North of 60* fan list on Yahoo, discussed below. I have read roughly 25 per cent of the 12,000 posts on the *North of 60* Yahoo Group Archives[10] since its inception on 28 July 1999 (the date is from an email still in the "N of 60" archive), and I have read all of them since the summer of 2004. Most of the people on this list do not appear to be obsessed by the program. However, they love the program enough to have found the list as well as Winter's website, and most of them want a complete run of episodes and all the movies on tape or DVD. They also fit Hills's description of people "who can produce reams of information" and are often highly articulate (ix). He warns scholars that ethnographic analysis does not deal with the passionate, inarticulate level of attachment of a fan (66).[11] Ethnography can deal, however, with the specialized knowledge of fans who "interpret [the programs] ... in a variety of ... ways" and "who participate in communal activities" (ix), although the fact is that fan lists are both communal activities and as solitary as writing and reading. He also argues that fandom is performative; it entails performing "cultural work" within a space that allows for both the types of knowledge valued by other fans and a shared attachment to the program (xi). Citing D.W. Winnicott and Theodor Adorno, he adds the useful comment that "individual and subjective moments of fan attachment interact with communal constructions and justifications without either moment over-writing or surmounting the other" (xiii). Part of the value of Hills's book is that he tries to reconcile academic practices with the understanding that many academics are also fans. Some, like many of those writing in *Growing Up Degrassi*, grew up with the series.

One of the interesting paradoxes of the *North of 60* fans is that so many value what is perceived as the show's realism, that is, the credibility of its characters and stories. They see the setting in the wilderness and the Dene lifestyle as more "real." One person even said that watching *North of 60* is almost like watching a reality show, and many say it is easy to forget that it is a drama with a script. Although people like the different world found north of the sixtieth latitude, specifically aspects of Dene culture such as the healing and visions, they also see the show as more universal, as "very human," showing the complex motives and inner lives of the characters, who are flawed but show compassion and love. They see the characters as looking and behaving normally, and appreciate both the longer narrative arcs and the small anecdotal touches. There is a preference for the movies that are set in Lynx River and include more of the cast from the series.

The term "cult fan" does not apply to most of the *North of 60* Yahoo Group members, even though Hills defines the cult fan as someone attached to programs long after their cancellation (28). Many remain attached partly because there were movies of the week up to 30 January 2005. There had been merchandise available early on "for promotional purposes," T-shirts and a CD.[12] However, no other merchandising related to the series had been available, no VHS/DVDs, for example, except for a version of the movie *Dream Storm* made for the hearing impaired.[13] The soundtrack CD was available for several years, then was no longer available. One was sold on eBay in 2007 for well over a hundred dollars. There are no books, mugs, sweatshirts, or other modest gear on sale. But the *North of 60* fans continue to be much more angry that Alliance Atlantis, the distributor, has not put the ninety episodes or even the movies on

DVD. To protect copyright, the rules of the *North of 60* list,[14] as with all Yahoo groups, now preclude tape trading on the list. (Private exchanges are, of course, impossible to regulate.) Fans have also put pressure on various specialty channels to carry the series (in August 2004, they wrote to TNT in the United States) and are currently (2006–07) writing to CBC programming executives to back a sixth movie of the week.

During its run, the series had a website for each season, five provided by Alberta Filmworks and the sixth apparently by the CBC. All but the sixth disappeared when the series went off the air. Information about these sites in this study comes from printouts made at the time. The movies have had increasingly complex web pages.[15] Fans certainly corresponded with the producers while the *North of 60* websites were live, voicing opinions on the story arcs and characters, and there is evidence that the producers listened. But there are perils in responding to those wishes. As Hills points out, what fans want is not necessarily what the broader audience wants and not always the most creative way to go. He insists on the individual critic's/fan's awareness of an inner self "lived and experienced even by sociologists wanting to argue that this is an ideological/constructed self of social structures … While maintaining this awareness, fans are able to play with (and across) the boundaries between 'fantasy' and 'reality'"(106). Hills is correct: all of us in adult life use cultural artifacts as "transitional objects" between external and internal reality. He goes on to distinguish primary and secondary transitional objects and argues that the latter form a site of struggle between intersubjective cultural experience and personal experience, "which helps to explain fans' seemingly irrational claims of 'ownership' over texts and icons" (109).

The rise of detailed websites for series old and new is a major asset to scholarly research if they prove to be reliable. Clay Self's website for *Forest Rangers*[16] has a guest book that contains comments by stars of the show, young people who caught it late at night, parents who loved the show as children and watch the reruns as adults, and grown men who had a big crush on the only girl on the show. He also constructed a website for *Adventures in Rainbow Country*[17] that is more modest but provides copies of faded colour production and backstage photos. Self has provided an accurate and complete episode synopsis of both shows, which is enormously helpful to a researcher, and for *Forest Rangers* new photos, facts, filming locations, production details, the musical theme, and updates on reruns and on where the actors are now. In his case, Self is returning to a show that was part of his childhood, and nostalgia is a major factor in his account of the show and its feedback.

*North of 60* is a much more recent show for adults, and Patty Winter's very professionally designed fan site reflects this. Her site also exemplifies many of the complex relationships fans have with a series. Visitors have access to additional information, including very good interviews that she initiated and carried out with writers, producers, and actors over several years during her visits to the set. They reveal both the thinking and the emotions of the interviewees and show the process of the making of the series and the movies. The subjects also answer questions about the story arcs and characters themselves. Anyone visiting that site can travel between intertextual sightings of the *North of 60* actors in other series; find three lists of episodes, one of which includes accurate short descriptions of each episode as well as writer, director, and selected acting credits; pictures of the sets; and a tongue-in-cheek touch of real life north of 60 with a continuous update on the weather in the hamlet of Fort Liard, Northwest Territories, which self-identifies as the model for the fictional Lynx River. The site gives the visitor a multiplicity of shifts between the fictional and real worlds, a way for a fan to locate any single episode within the whole series, glimpses into the maker's world, a way to keep track of the appearances of favourite actors on television and elsewhere since the last movie (although the list is where people find out if a favourite is on that very evening), and links to the actual world of the Dene and the Northwest Territories.

The list was not started until February/March 1999, well after the show had ended its run in Canada. After a year or two, the originator (Anna from Vancouver, no last name ever supplied) handed it over to three Americans who became "list moms": Lonnie Cruise, Patty Winter, and Nancy Duemling. Lonnie later resigned and was replaced by Kelly Tucker, a Canadian. Kelly has since chosen to become a backup moderator, with Nancy and Patty handling the day-to-day duties. List moms basically nurture the list, establishing a few rules, having a word with someone if there is a flameout, welcoming newcomers, and occasionally introducing new topics. They moderate all new members for a while. As the list's interface with the server – Yahoo in this case – they also do "housekeeping," to check whether overfull mailboxes are bouncing the posts. The three original list moms also decided that there would be no "fanfic," that is, fiction written by fans using the characters in the series on the list. Someone else could start a separate *North of 60* fanfic list, of course, but no one appears to have done so.[18] The first run of the series ended in Canada in 1997. The American run on TRIO[19] ended a few years later. At this writing (2006–07), in Canada only, the series still appears in daily reruns on CBC Country Canada, Showcase, and Showcase Diva, and will reappear on APTN. Meanwhile, on the *North of 60* list on Yahoo, over half of the participants are American and therefore cut off from the series. Yet it keeps going, fed in part by Patty Winter's website, also started in 1999. Other reasons for the list to continue? Perhaps people wanted to talk about the show with others, having lost the chance to see new episodes. Or maybe it is more interesting to talk about a finished series.

Having been a member of the Yahoo Group for three years, I have noticed a set of ripples in the discussions concerning the more recent movies and the first run of the series years ago. I extrapolated the priorities of the people who still actively post and then checked the list with Winter, who agreed with my analysis. In order of importance:

- The characters, plots, details of costume and sets, and dialogue of *North of 60* – these have been the nexus of discussion. However, there are also periods of time when no one actually discusses the series itself.
- Programs similar to *North of 60*. Many of the fans also liked *Northern Exposure* and *Due South*, both quirky shows, both involving northern or distinctly Canadian elements, and both having distinctly comic as well as ironic overtones. (*Mocassin Flats*, set in the inner city and intended primarily for teens and young adults, got a mixed reception, as did the more comic *Hank Snow's First Nations* of 2006–07.)
- Other programs, films, live appearances, or even ads featuring actors from the show, including actors who were only in four or five episodes
- The exchange of news and anecdotes about being in the North
- More rarely, anecdotes that identify the poster's own First Nations perspective – for example, the person who made a good argument about why Canada Day is not observed on her reserve, but shared details about what the community does together on National First Nations Day
- In-jokes about, say, moose stew or Eric's tight jeans; rounds of Q and A and trivia contests with small prizes, such as (tongue firmly in cheek) an RCMP Christmas ornament
- Occasionally news about themselves
- Autobiographies. Most "newbies" begin by posting a short biography about themselves and how they came to find and then love *North of 60*.

It takes a little nerve to join a bunch of strangers and reveal how enthusiastic you are about a television show. A sampling of the *North of 60* list shows that some of the old hands have always welcomed newcomers.

Fandom takes many forms. Related merchandise accompanies some American or British series, one of the oldest being the "newspaper" published in "Ambridge" (the fictional setting of the bbc Home Service/Radio 4 radio series *The Archers* [1951–present]) and sold by the corner newsagent all over Britain for years. Fan magazines (fanzines) that follow the series or the lives of actors in the series often include fanfic, where fans write stories, poems, art work, or short films or animations using some of the characters of the series – and occasionally bring down the wrath of the corporations that own the programs and see not products of individuals' imagination but copyright violation and troublesome variations on their own products.[20] Clips posted by fans on Youtube have just complicated the picture further. These fan projects can elaborate on an existing narrative arc, propose and explore alternate endings, introduce new characters, or invent new story arcs. There are also clubs where people can meet face to face and talk or view/exchange off-air tapes or dvds. Canadian fans of *Coronation Street* meet for a pint and a chat as if they were at the Rover's Arms. For "Corrie" fans and a few others, there are enormous conventions and sponsored appearances for actors in shopping malls.

According to Robert Abelman, in *Reaching a Critical Mass* (1998), in 1995 ex-cbs ceo William Paley suggested that "'the most important and virtually unfailing indication of a good program – over and above basic good writing, direction, casting, costumes, and sets is likable, intriguing characters who capture the imagination, interest, or concern of the audience" (101). Abelman argues that even when there is an ensemble cast some viewers tune in "for the individual performances of a particular actor rather than that of a character" (102), an observation that any fan list will also demonstrate. A minority will also form attachments to minor characters. There is evidence that various *North of 60* viewers were hooked on the individual performances, perhaps even on the actors' own personae, specifically that of Tom Jackson and Gordon Tootoosis. Tina Keeper certainly attracted her own fans as Michelle, and Joe, Teevee, Elsie, Rosie, Sarah, and even Gerry also had their fans; but in those cases I would speculate that, as with Pat Johns playing Jesse Jim, the characters rather than the performances were the main point of connection.[21] Note that *North of 60* fans remember with pleasure jokes on the show, despite the general critics' opinion that the show lacked humour. Some fans have even supplied Patty with translations of some of the Slavey words in the opening credits of the *North of 60* movie *Trial by Fire*.[22]

Winter estimates that currently 90 per cent of the posters to the Yahoo Group are women, although there may be many men who do not post but do listen in. A few men do participate.

*Where From?*

The Fan Map on Patty's website shows people in Alaska, Yukon, the Northwest Territories, Nunavut, and Baffin Island, with concentrations in Ontario, Manitoba, and British Columbia, and in most states (except in the Midwest), including Florida with 4, Texas with 10, and California with 10. Michigan has the most at 32 (many cable TV systems in Michigan, Washington State, and other border states carry CBC); Ontario has 41; British Columbia has 29; Manitoba has 14; and the Northwest Territories, Saskatchewan, and Quebec have 7. All told, as of 2005 when the map was last updated, there are 136 Canadians and around 190 Americans. Roughly 330 people were interested enough to supply this information. Of course, not all of them post to the list.[23]

*A Sampler of Comments on the List*

See chapter 11 for an introduction to the characters and cast of the *North of 60* series.

- Anna the founder had been hooked on the series by daily CBC reruns. She begins by saying that her favourite character is James Harper, Michelle's third partner, introduced late in season 5. Oddly, Harper is not overall a fan favourite.
- Several say that they see the series as pulling them into Lynx River with characters who seem to be part of their extended families.
- A few also note that the problems and solutions presented in the show reflect their experience as social workers or workers in various health fields.
- One says that it takes time to warm to Michelle because her character keeps people at arm's length. However, others reply that this is because she is a recovering alcoholic, or that the RCMP demand it, or that she is walking a line between the values of the white world and those of her own culture.
- One fan, noting that the teenaged Teevee moons the new Mountie, Eric, in the very first episode and in the fifth season shows his butt with no fanfare in an intimate scene with a girl, takes both incidents as a sign that this series was made in Canada, not the United States. (Teevee is also shown naked with another man as part of a survival strategy when caught in a blizzard. They are both blue and shivering. The effect is the antithesis of the erotic.)
- Eric's tight jeans and the moments when he is shirtless get a lot of favourable, even raunchy but good-humoured, comment.

- Some get fed up with all the male infidelity in Lynx River. Others point to Sarah's four partners and two pregnancies and Lois's affair with Ben Montour.
- Although several like the fact that some characters are attractive, many praise the fact that on the whole the cast members have average looks and lead recognizable lives.
- There is lots of discussion about what is seen as accurate glimpses into aboriginal life.
- The list members also discuss the off-screen domestic troubles between Tina Keeper (Michelle) and John Oliver (Eric – they parted company) and speculate on how she could have been pregnant without it becoming a storyline. (Heavy winter parkas help.) Many enjoy the playful yet heated sex between Eric and Sarah.
- There is much speculation and argument about characters' motives – for example, about whether Albert loved Sarah or not.
- Most fans love the trilogy of episodes about Hannah's death but also argue about why the writers felt the need to write out her character in that definitive way.
- This leads to some discussion about grieving and how it is handled on the show. Some share aboriginal customs for grieving. A few find that the trilogy reminds them of their own losses, and other people express sympathy.
- One reiterated theme is that the series is full of subtle touches. A corollary is that people often disagree on exactly what happened or what it meant.
- Many agree on a "worst" episode (episode 18, "Ciao Baby"), even though it begins one major story arc and ends another, which suggests that plot is definitely not enough for members of this list, and then propose many different "bests."
- Some found the movies too political; others enjoyed the more detailed context for issues that they provide.
- There is a sustained discussion on how Albert died and Joe's role in his death, down to the level of the kind of rifle, whether there would be a spent round for anyone to find, and how Joe, with his bad knees, could bury him in the bush. Others just reach for the Kleenex, but feel that part of the last episode is very satisfying – a tribute to the writers who did not find an easy ending to that six-season-long story arc.
- One person uses freeze frame to trace Albert's shot at Sarah and Nathan's shot defending her, comparing the kind of gun with the damage it can or cannot do.
- The apparent suicide of the rogue Mountie, Fletcher, provoked a lot of discussion about motives and even about what actually happened,

discussion that continues when Fletcher reappeared in the movie *In the Blue Ground*. Another detailed discussion follows the narrative arc about Nevada, the rent boy with AIDS who takes refuge in Lynx River and is eventually told to leave.

- Many enjoyed the transformation of Teevee from punk to responsible adult, even though his body language and behaviour tested their patience.
- One fan eloquently defends the series as appropriate viewing for older children because it shows people on welfare as respected citizens, a community looking after the kids, sex that is not exploitive, realistic dialogue, and honest emotions.
- People recount episodes in their own life or family history that are analogous to the residential school episode, which for them really explains Michelle's rigidity. One viewer's native grandmother had been sold as a child to a white family.
- They wonder about the number of children who appear in the series then vanish. Patty Winter raises the question with Tom Dent Cox; the answer is posted on her website.
- They admire and want a copy of Ben Montour's raven sculpture.
- One person watches the series twice a day, the rerun in the afternoon and then the tape she has made with her husband in the evening.
- Two policemen compare Eric's domestic troubles with those of other police and discuss their preoccupation with their jobs.
- A discussion by the list members about who caught their eye first ranges over almost every character, including guests, suggesting the show's broad appeal.
- A flood of wishes and prayers on 9/11 went to Americans on the list from other Americans and Canadians. The list was one place Canadians could immediately express their shock and sympathy, comfort and support to people they "knew" who were affected – and their American friends expressed gratitude in return.
- People on the list include a teacher on a Paiute reserve who identifies with the young people; someone "from a Navajo rez"; an Osage/Cherokee; at least one person who closes with "Na'hanee miigwetch" (Take care); someone who lives near Bragg Creek, where the show was made, who is the mother of Teevee's on-screen baby; the wife of a Saskatchewan Cree; a twenty-six-year-old single guy in Vancouver; and a trucker from Winnipeg. One fan identifies with Lynx River politics, having served on the school board of her small Michigan town. Others are from Australia, Iran, and Germany, where the show was called "Die Mounties von Lynx River."[24]

This cross-section of fans may give an indication of the interests and values of the people who have found and stayed with this particular fan list and perhaps of the wider audience as well.

## GENRE

When we leave the land of Baudrillard and Bourdieu for the more prosaic land of television formulae and format, genres rule much of series television drama. Soaps concentrate on domestic complications that are rarely permanently resolved. Cop shows deliver both crimes and punishment. Comedies make you smile, even laugh, usually at domestic mishaps, sometimes at misunderstandings and glitches in the lives of a working family. News shows discuss mostly what news organizations think are the headlines of the day. Sports shows concentrate on recognizable sports, either using highlights from or broadcasting whole games or events. Quiz shows feature contestants who must answer questions for prizes. Reality shows dip into a little of each of these genres but include clear rules for the contest, even though the alliances, enmities, humiliations, and heavily edited situations and dialogue pretend to be non-scripted. If Michelle Kenidi started taking pratfalls or winning immunity challenges or analysing the prime minister's visit to the G 8 summit, viewers would know that the rules of "their" show had been broken in an improbable way for no apparent reason.

Genre is one of the hooks that catch viewers who like a particular, familiar kind of program. Most of the series discussed so far have belonged to the family adventure genre; yet a single episode of *The Beachcombers* could vary widely in tone. In fact, the series ranged over several genres: broad slapstick comedy; adventures with boats and planes; characters in peril from the elements, the sea, or wild animals; mysteries to solve; depictions of Coast Salish traditions; conservation of resources; and, occasionally, quite serious examinations of or shifts in the characters' interrelationships. As Tony Atherton said in the *Ottawa Citizen,* 27 November 2002, "[from 1972] it would remain one of the CBC's highest rated shows for another 15 years, occasionally reaching as many as three million viewers a week. Regular viewers came to love the cast, and even to accept that the show was never quite one thing or another. It was a comic drama with hints of social commentary and even fantasy."[25]

If the response to the colonization of culture is a post-colonial hybridity of forms that originate with the colonizer, in this case family adventure series (*The Beachcombers, Spirit Bay*), cop shows, mysteries, and soaps (*North of 60*), sitcoms, and the later hybrid dramedies (*The Rez*), then it is not unexpected that some of episodes of each of these series are clearly hybrid. The ongoing colonization of genres in Canada by the ubiquitous American television culture and Canadian television's inflection or resistance to that influence are found in those series. One formulaic element that is inflected is the inscription of white as "other" and the substitution of First Nations issues or ways of life as the norms. The assumptions about the content of a familiar television genre can be upended when the majority of leading cast members and most of the other characters are completely native. Nevertheless, it would be well to remember once again that these series are in English and not made by First Nations peoples. As Emma Laroque points out in her preface to *Writing the Circle* (1990), "Perhaps the height of cheekiness in a colonizer is to steal your language, withhold his from you as long as he can, then turn around and demand that you speak or write better than he does. And when you do, he accuses you of 'uppityness' or inauthenticity" (xxi). But she continues: "English is the new Native language. Literally and politically … the common language of Aboriginal peoples" (xxci).

One of Baudrillard's now standard post-modern cultural notions is "that we are witnessing a proliferation of media genres and techniques that intentionally and explicitly fuse 'fact' and 'fiction'" (81).[26] None of these series claim to be fact. Yet *North of 60*, explicitly through topical references in the plots and even the characterization, and especially through the on-air credits to Dene advisors in every episode and movie, connects to the factual world. Baudrillard's axiom – that all such programming is mediated – is, of course, true. Series television is based on treatments turned into scripts, drafts of which are then heavily mediated by designers, cameramen, directors of photography, directors, producers, editors, and actors. Perhaps most important in that process for the viewer are the scripts and the actors who embody the continuing characters. In all long-running series, adult actors play a significant role in the development of their character over the years. But the world this mediation creates also creates its own rules over time; for example, it cannot be invaded by some kinds of digitally manipulated elements, such as a high-rise on the streets of Lynx River, because the viewers have rapidly come to know a lot about the settings. Intertextually they know that although Albert Golo the character is dead, the actor, Gordon Tootoosis, who plays him is not. They could have seen him in the Senate chamber delivering a monologue during the installation of Governor General Michaëlle Jean. Thus they accept a significant variation on the mystery/cop show format in the television movie *Dream Storm: A North of 60 Mystery* when Albert's ghost appears and interacts decisively with Michelle. Most viewers, admittedly not all, also know that Michelle Kenidi, Silas Crow, and Jesse Jim are not real people they might meet in a corner store, although in the TV special *Dream Makers*, on 17 December 2006 (Bravo/APTN, directed by Susan Cardinal), Gordon Tootoosis said that television series need villains. "I created Albert Golo [this juxtaposed to a clip where he cuts a young henchman's face to terrorize him]. I've gotten a lot of 'compliments' ... old people wanted to slap me," he said, clearly not distinguishing between himself and the character.

As Laura Edles points out in *Cultural Sociology in Practice* (2002),[27] the difficulty of the post-modern ethnographer who rejects the distinction between literature and the social sciences, fiction and non-fiction, is the fact that the relatively conventional storytelling in television series creates a largely consistent world with formulaic narratives and roles, rules and expectations, that viewers can understand (151) and will accept. Inflecting formulae is what keeps genres fresh. Creating hybrid forms is a greater challenge, as the hybrid makes more demands on the viewers and sometimes gives them much more for the hour they spend watching the show. As is already apparent, episodes of *The Beachcombers* and *Spirit Bay* did both. However, the most contemporary examples of genre and its inflection discussed in this book are the series *North of 60* and *The Rez*.

### North of 60

Many *North of 60* fans praise their show because it is real to them (*real* is a recurring word in the archives of the *North of 60* list as well as in the answer to a question I posed to its current members), because they recognize the characters as credible and many of their dilemmas as close to their own experience. Robert Abelman, when writing about cop shows and other hour-long series going back to *Dragnet* and *Gunsmoke* (one could add the very popular and long running original *CSI*) in *Reaching a Critical Mass* (1998), describes the American television hero as having "a long and rich history in the stories embraced by Americans. [He] has always possessed qualities in line with American ideals, values, and the pioneering characteristics that represent the paragon of what made this country strong ... Heroes are independent, emotionally and intellectually balanced, dedicated, morally incorruptible, just, and always dependable. Although often tempted by evil, heroes do not often yield to temptation (or if they do, it is transitory). They are not infallible, but they get it right most of the time, are quick to right a wrong, and always end up on top by the end of the program" (406–7). Over many years of watching Canadian television drama, I have never seen a television hero of either sex who resembled this portrait of the American hero. Not unexpectedly there are none on *North of 60*.

In *Re-Viewing Reception: Television, Gender and Postmodern Culture* (1996), Lynne Joyrich, who like Abelman is writing when *North of 60* was in production, calls television "The Melodramatic Screen" (47) on which play the conventions of composition, dress and hair coding, and settings either in homes or "at the intersection of public and private spaces that are central to personal concerns." In a needs-and-uses sense, Joyrich also argues that postmodern life is "lacking a sense of tradition, place and meaning" (65). Yet *North of 60* is rich in all three. Joyrich identifies interesting parallels between soaps and cop shows. Soaps, which since their inception in the 1930s have been serials, not series, are characterized as being full of repetitions of both plot and character traits. The term "soap" is often used pejoratively to connote the genre's improbable characters and plots, the endless grief of carefully coiffed or ruggedly handsome (and usually well-off) characters, and intricate and usually very long storylines. But as Carol Traynor Williams points out in *"It's Time for My Story"* (1992), soaps are complex discourses that require from the viewers a lot of attention to storylines and sophisticated knowledge of the conventions of the genre. In fact, soaps aren't primarily about "what happened" or even "to whom." Rather they are about the different reactions of each character to what happened. Suspense is only part of the attraction. When writers ignore the details of past narratives and make mistakes about how a given character might react, soap viewers protest loudly to the producers or head writer. Drew Hayden Taylor, in *Funny You Don't Look Like One* (1996), complained about *North of 60*: "[E]ach episode became a tour de force for dysfunctionalism" (79). Dysfunctional is one way to describe the families in most soaps. Moreover, the CBC reran the *North of 60* daily in the afternoons in 2000–01, and some email correspondents perceived it to be a superior soap.

Series television demands that, in the case of cop shows, the protagonists continually identify crimes and chase perpetrators, "trapping them," as Taylor wrote back in 1996, "within a restricted world of victimization and thereby lessening the gap between these dramas and the soap operas where perpetual suffering is the rule" (48). *North of 60* has been classified as a cop show by its makers in their publicity. The gestural codes of soaps are expressive and intimate, made very visible in the default shot of the close-up. The action scenes of cop shows require long shots, tracking shots, and jump cuts. *North of 60* uses both. As for the acting codes, some cop shows emphasize the stoicism of the police, a code that appears in some *North of 60* episodes, particularly those that involve Michelle's partner, Brian Fletcher, while others permit the characters to react to each other, if not to the violence surrounding them, which is the norm on this series. The gestural language and facial expressions of other characters in *North of 60* range from impassivity, which blocks the gaze of both viewers and the characters who are outsiders, to warmly expressive. The teenaged Teevee often wears a sullen mask of anger and contempt. Until he matures, his range of facial expression is much more limited than his body language. The motherly Rosie is very expressive, unless she requires a poker face. Michelle, in the middle years of the series, often appears to exert hard control over her expressions and body language, both in professional contexts, where she functions as an RCMP constable, and in more personal situations, such as when she is under pressure at home. However, actress Tina Keeper also conveys some of the most difficult subtext in the series, using her body and her vocal pitch and inflection. Tom Jackson as her brother Peter, the band chief, is an expert at conveying depths of emotion economically. Michelle's chief antagonist Albert is the epitome of carefully controlled voice, body language and facial expression. Control is the key to his character. The white characters are also protective of their feelings. Yet Eric slowly opens up to the community. After Sarah has a mental breakdown she becomes a licensed fool/truth-teller to the community.

*North of 60* is a conventional cop show in one key element – it often focuses on what Joyrich (1996) calls "the affective center that sustains viewer interest ... the struggles and dynamics that exist between members of the investigative unit or police 'family' itself" (103). Each of Michelle's partners over the six seasons sets up a different dynamic in a show where a crime can be defined as a stolen axe or a drunken punch and murder is very rare. Eric is the traditional senior male partner who outranks Michelle but rapidly discovers that she knows the community as he does not and sometimes cannot; for example, what appears as theft of an axe to him is basic custom in the Dene culture. Fletcher is also her senior, but he is married. His domestic problems form individual story arcs separate from most of the others, and his corruption makes him an antagonist to Michelle by the fourth season. Late in the fifth and through the sixth season, "urban Indian" James Harper is her junior, with important political connections that mean nothing in Lynx River. Atypically with a cop show, the viewers get to know most of the criminals over several weeks, and in the cases of Albert, Nathan, and William over several years. A few other criminals come in from outside, but their chase and capture has less flavour than the six-year pursuit of Albert, which, breaking formula, no one really wins. In this series "the familial and the feminine" do not "become subsumed within this masculine sphere" (Joyrich 1996, 103). Although women are foregrounded in the series, *North of 60* is not a typical night soap (such as *Dallas*, *Dynasty*, and *The OC*). The stories move more quickly, and some are resolved within an episode. Moreover, while what happens in the real world rarely intrudes on night soaps, in *North of 60* and its movies, major real world issues appear. Some of them are unresolved. The show's hybridity will be discussed further in chapter 11.

## The Rez

Abelman's view is that "[t]he humor of a sitcom is derived from the often outlandish situations in which the characters find themselves. In some sitcoms, the outlandish situation is built into the program in what has been called the ingroup-outgroup scheme where one character or group of characters who are outsiders are inserted into the 'norm'" (1998, 316). In some *Beachcomber* episodes, Jesse functions as that outsider, an ironic commentator on the norms of Molly's Reach. Tanya, the white barmaid in the second season of *The Rez*, would also qualify. According to Abelman, "*Outlandish situations are typically singular (1 per episode) and highly predictable ...* complicated kernel story lines, multiple satellite story lines, and the coexisting situations are not welcome in sitcoms. These elements breed complexity, and complexity has little to do with situational comedy" (316). None of the series discussed in this book use the old (but still in use) sitcom formula of three jokes per page peppering repetitive, highly predictable plots and outcomes, although some of the physical comedy and a few of Frank's scams in *The Rez* come close. Nor is there usually "one or more hapless protagonists," although Frank and Silas do function in that way at times. Their girlfriends, Sadie and Lucy, who are socially more adept, are not simply foils whose normality makes the boys seem funny. In fact, *The Rez* is more accurately defined as what Abelman calls a "domcom" – domestic comedy – that depends on "humour which is inherent in the characters." He argues that "the depth and warmth of character interaction, the establishment of love of family and the focus on domestic issues is the basis for domestic comedy. As such, the humor tends to be more realistic than that presented in a sitcom ... It depends not on situations but the people ... The action often revolves around more than one story-line per episode ... The humour revolves around multiple, mimetic protagonists ... Roles [can be] interchangeable across the population of characters ... characters experience personal growth from their adventures; they learn from their mistakes and devolve over the course of the program … the domcom can address serious subject matter" (326–7). *The Rez* demonstrated all of these characteristics.

William Douglas supplies another perspective on the content of generic television in his *Television Families: Is Something Wrong in Suburbia?* (2003), a good summary of the sociology and ethnography of the viewing of television in families, its casual uses, its now infrequent use as a family activity, its interruptions and distractions, its often hotly debated effects on social cognition.[28] He also outlines the kinds of families portrayed and their roles in series television, as well as the socialization of values for each member of the family, first by radio and then by postwar television. Citing a content analysis of American television in 2001, he reiterates that even in the new century, for Americans at least (and probably for Canadians), "to a large extent, the television world remains White, male and middle-class" (105), a world where the middle-class family is usually portrayed as benign (106). In American television families, married couples are still the norm and families rarely have "routine or extensive interaction between family members and their neighbors and friends" (105). Most television families live in suburbia and have the suburban values that privilege "white Americans over minorities, young over old, parenthood over childlessness and affluence over poverty" (105–6).

The history of the treatment of the family in series television in Canada differs from that in the United States.[29] *The Beachcombers, Spirit Bay, North of 60,* and *The Rez* are quite unlike the norms of American television identified by Douglas. They feature single mothers and marginal characters, value old people, show many narrative arcs where the whole community is involved, and portray routine neighbourly interaction. *The Beachcombers* is embedded in a surrogate family with Jesse functioning as both the insider and outsider. Douglas says that in American soaps "acts of sexual intimacy have become more common over time, and sexual intimacy between partners not married to each other is especially common" (109) as demonstrated as long ago as 1996 in a study that he cites (110) and that is contemporaneous with *North of 60*'s fourth season. But in *North of 60* there are no handsome, rugged, powerful, businessmen/patriarchs, no clinging females, no queen bitches with six or seven husbands. Adultery is not the food of love in *North of 60*. There is little titillating sex, babies are part of life, children are both loved and a burden. The series also regularly displays tensions between whites and Dene and embeds the "cop stories" in all of these other concerns.

Douglas cites a 2001 study showing that "characters over 65 comprised only 2 per cent of the television population," a statistic that is attributed to the negative stereotypes about older people held by American viewers (150–1). Jesse Jim's elders and chiefs are treated with respect and affection and are given some comic quirks. The elders on *Spirit Bay*, Teawash and Old Bernard, are also respected, and they clearly perform important functions in the community and in the narrative arcs. Characters over sixty-five are missing in *The Rez*, but on *North of 60* the older characters – Elsie, Joe, and Willie – are fully developed characters with habits and quirks. Elsie and Joe appear in most episodes, have major influence on some narratives, ground the other characters, help when they can, hinder when they think they should. They continue to age. Joe is diabetic, then becomes lame and has other health problems. In *Dream Storm*, an aging Elsie starts to forget her traditional knowledge. The younger women – Sarah, Michelle, and Rosie – also age as the series and movies progress. As inflections or hybrids of popular genres, most of the series made by or for the CBC are substantially different from those most Canadian viewers could watch from the United States. Clearly, Canadian viewers accept series that do not necessarily reflect the generic conventions or other norms common to North American television.

In its early seasons, *North of 60* defied the viewers' expectations of a mystery, cop show, or a soap and then continued to evolve over the rest of the ninety episodes and five made-for-television movies. More important for this study, this body of work represented for the larger audience a group of South Slavey–speaking Dene characters. By using Dene advisors for every script, a Metis story editor, and a Metis director, by using a few (too few) scripts by First Nations writers, and by referring frequently to the specifics of the culture represented, *North of 60* – despite its limitations – changed the history of the representation of First Nations peoples in Canada. This is why the following five chapters concentrate on this series.

PART THREE

# A Long-Form Series for Adults:
## *North of 60* (1992–1997)

# ELEVEN

# Set-up, or How *North of 60* Was Framed

*"North of 60* treats Indians as people, not people as Indians."
Tina Keeper (Michelle Kenidi), quoting her father

Patty Winter, list mom and maker of a superb *North of 60* website, wrote to me in a private email, 20 March 2002 (quoted with permission), about what she thought the appeal of the series was: "I think its primary appeal is to people who prefer character-driven rather than plot-driven series. Every character in the show was so realistic that a compelling storyline could easily be developed around any of them at any time. And there were always cultural conflicts between the Native and white residents (or visitors) that could be explored. As well, I suspect that the mystique of getting a glimpse into a small Native town in the Northwest Territories was very interesting to a lot of people." After reading four thousand fan mail postings on the *North of 60* fan site archive, and as a result of online discussions in the last few years,[1] I can agree that she sums it up very well.

I have focused on *North of 60* in several chapters of this book because, at six seasons (3 December 1992–18 December 1997), it is the longest-running show on Canadian television that takes a searching look at the daily life of a First Nations community. Set in the Deh Cho[2] and concerned with very particular characters whose personalities and storylines continued to develop over the years, the series gave life and immediacy to many of the issues that affect the present and future of the First Nations peoples. This chapter sets up the series by looking at financing, sales abroad, and how the CBC framed the series (giving glimpses of the process). It also provides a brief outline of the cast and the characters, considers the series as a hybrid genre, explores issues of authenticity, and examines the narrative strategies. Chapter 12 looks at the design elements of the series and the key characters. Chapter 13 discusses a selection of episodes, including those written by First Nations writers, and takes a brief look at the five movies of the week.

Sarah Birkett (Tracey Cook), Peter Kenidi (Tom Jackson), Constable Michelle
Kenidi (Tina Keeper), and Corporal Eric Olssen (John Oliver). *Alberta Filmworks,
in association with the* CBC, *distributed by Alliance Atlantis.*

Chapter 14 identifies themes and examines how specific issues are
addressed. Chapter 15 concludes the section with a discussion of the
critical and general audience reception of the series.

In 2001–02 the Aboriginal People's Television Network acquired the
broadcast rights to *North of 60*. The show had already appeared in daily
afternoon reruns on the CBC as well as on Showtime, and had been
widely sold to other countries, including the TRIO network in the United
States. This popularity does not imply that Canada's aboriginal people
approved of the series. In the first seasons of APTN, if First Nations or
Metis were presented as leading or major supporting characters in series
and films, the network had shown it all – the good, the bad, and the indifferent – as long as the depictions were not too offensive. Drama is the
most expensive programming on air, and APTN in its early years could
not afford to produce drama programming on its own that would have
the production values of mainstream series and TV movies.[3] When it acquired *North of 60*, APTN chose to run the show at 8 p.m. EST, juxtaposing

the *North of 60* characters, who are very specifically South Slavey-speaking Dene, with the generic Indians in the otherwise quirky and entertaining American cult hit *Northern Exposure,* scheduled for 9:00 p.m. Anecdotal evidence (that is, conversations with First Nations people) suggests that some First Nations viewers enjoyed both shows in different ways. *Northern Exposure* was basically comedic in sensibility and distinctively American. *North of 60* was fundamentally serious in tone and wholly Canadian in its approach to storytelling. Yet in 1992, mainstream television critics regularly compared *North of 60* to this very distant American cousin, just as Canadian critics in the 1980s had inappropriately compared *L. A. Law,* with its corporate mentality and LA lifestyle, to the CBC's very different – and successful – *Street Legal,* with its storefront law practice and topical issues. More recently, according to its posted schedule in April/May 2005, APTN ran the *North of 60* episodes out of sequence, a few from one season, then a few from another (APTN was running the series weekly, not daily). This sort of confusion in syndicated daily or even weekly scheduling is not uncommon and always to be deplored, because the mistake would make nonsense of any continuing story arcs and, quite simply, shows disrespect for the people who made the series with such care.

North of 60* originated with writers/producers Barbara Samuels and Wayne Grigsby, who had earlier been the executive story editors for CTV's late-1980s successful series about a local television newsroom, *E.N.G.* Nada Harcourt was the creative head of drama series when the CBC initially decided to support the series. The people behind the cameras in the beginning included executive producer Robert Lantos, co-producers Tom Dent-Cox and Doug Macleod, and supervising producers Steven Denure and Stephane Reichel. Producer David Barlow (who produced all of the episodes of the 1980s CBC hit *Seeing Things*) served as a very experienced story editor in the first season. Regular series writer Peter Lauterman functioned in later years as executive producer after Samuels and Grigsby had moved on to another series. Samuels and Grigsby continued as consulting producers, however, until the *North of 60* ended. Bob Blakey of the *Calgary Herald* reported (9 February 1993) that *North of 60* was shot on 16 mm film and then transferred to video for easy editing. Six years later, its last season was shot on Digital Betacam, according to the Telefilm website. Thus, *North of 60* spanned a major technological shift.[4] The production companies were Alliance (Alliance Atlantis has been the distributor of the series and, to the distress of its fans, refused to release it in DVD or video) and Alberta Filmworks, which remained the primary production house of the movies. Both the series and the movies were produced in association with the CBC, which provided the crucial first window of broadcast necessary to obtain the financial subsidies needed by all distinctive Canadian television programming.

## NORTH OF 60 FINANCING

Financing depends above all on the producers' ability to find a network willing to commit prime time on its schedule to the project. There was a natural fit between the CBC as a crown corporation with specific responsibilities under the Broadcasting Act of 1991 and this unusual series. Telefilm was the major source of funding; this agency uses public money to provide a substantial share of funding for expensive dramatic television series and specials shown on both private and public networks.[5] *North of 60* also received funding from the Alberta Motion Picture Development Corporation and Rogers Telefund. The problem with this game of cobbling together financing is that if one piece disappears, the whole deal may collapse.[6] Such constraints also mean that, unlike American television programs, Canadian series are not cancelled after a few episodes. If a made-for-TV movie or a six pack of six episodes gets an acceptable audience, as *The Rez* did with its first short season, Telefilm is likely to support the series – and that will usually mean at least thirteen episodes slotted firmly into the schedule of the host broadcaster the following year. This gives an audience time to find the program and to develop some loyalty to it. Our system does not permit the luxury of pilots, as such. Instead, a half-hour tryout may appear in another series, or perhaps a movie will be made that can spin off into a series if the ratings are good and the focus groups like it. Even if a series is a dud, all of its episodes will appear at some time on the network, which cannot afford to waste resources or its "Canadian content" by throwing out failures.

Telefilm policy at that time was that after a period of five years its subsidy would end, despite the fact that no distinctively Canadian drama could be made without it, then or now, a decade later. By early 1997, *North of 60* had run its course after five years and seventy-seven episodes. In its last, "sixth" season, however, the producers scrambled to get one more season, partly because syndication sales usually depend on there being ninety to one hundred episodes available. They successfully applied for money from the Canada Television and Cable Production Fund's (CTCPF's) Equity Investment Program and Licence Fee Program and the Government of Canada's Tax Credit Program. Equally important was a fudge factor for funding from Telefilm. The producers called the new episodes an extension of the fifth season, although they were shown in the sixth, that is, in the fall of 1997, which creates a confusing variable in the paper sources. (Just to make it more complicated, a broadcast season is September to September, so that a program can have two seasons in one calendar year.)[7] Seasons one to four each had sixteen episodes; seasons five and six had thirteen. In its last broadcast season, *North of 60* was drawing, according to the *Toronto Star*, 20 January 1997, an audience of "well over 900,000 viewers a week," a very respectable number by that time, as audience fragmentation accelerated. Although the made-for-TV movies are very much rooted in the series, particularly the third, *Dream Storm*, they had to stand alone in order to be sold abroad as independent productions. Lynn Carlson, in the *Toronto Star* (31 August 1997), quotes producer Doug MacLeod: "'[P]art of the problem with a production that is so strongly indigenous, [is that] such strongly identifiable content becomes the property of its region ... and therefore less appealing to markets outside of Canada.'" At that time he was thinking about a storyline for the first TV movie that would take the characters into an urban setting. Clearly, he thought better of it. *In the Blue Ground*, which aired 28 March 1999, stays in Lynx River. The fact is that viewers in foreign markets are not as interested in cities like Calgary or Toronto as they are in unfamiliar settings and less familiar characters.

## NORTH OF 60 WALKS ABROAD

*North of 60* represents Canada all over the world, just as *The Beachcombers* did. According to the CBC, by the start of its sixth season, it was broadcast in sixty countries and territories and dubbed in more than ten languages.[8] Note that, unlike Canadians and Americans, viewers in most countries have no difficulty with subtitles on television. In Mexico, where it was subtitled in Spanish, it was called *Paralelo Norte, La Ultima Frontera*. From Mexico, anything north of the sixtieth parallel must have felt like the ultimate frontier. Alliance Atlantis, through Dianne King at Alberta Filmworks, kindly supplied me with sales figures in international markets for the series and its first four movies of the week. In total, 122 countries and territories bought the series, including various cable channels in the United States but not, however, Great Britain. But even more countries, 130, bought the first movie, *In the Blue Ground*, ranging from Thailand and Barbados to Denmark. The number dropped to 77 for the second, *Trial by Fire* (but North Korea now appears on the list) and dropped again to 61 for the third, *Dream Storm*, which had a strong focus on Dene spirituality. However, 85 countries bought the fourth, *Another Country*, which was set in Calgary as well as in Lynx River and focused on both police corruption and racism.

Because the series was dubbed in French in Quebec,[9] many francophone countries in Europe and Africa bought the series: Congo, Burkina Faso, Benin, Mauritania, and Mauritius, as well as Luxembourg, Belgium, and France. Fees charged to broadcasters for the rights to television series are on a sliding scale. Belgium, for example, pays considerably more than Lesotho.

*North of 60* did present issues from a uniquely northern perspective – the impact of the weather, the impact of the anti-fur lobbies, the traditional First Nations governance by consensus, questions about the impact on a remote community of developing its natural resources. Still, there were always storylines about situations familiar to most viewers around the world: culture clashes, differences between generations, romantic entanglements. Viewers in Muslim countries (Algeria, Bahrain, Egypt, Ethiopia, Iran, Iraq, Saudi Arabia, Libya, Jordan, Indonesia) might well have read the ongoing struggles of some characters with alcoholism differently from Western viewers, but some of them, such as viewers in the United Arab Emirates, could empathize with the issues raised by the impact of oil revenues and how they might be shared with a population that had been nomadic, at least part of the year, within living memory.

In any case, the series *North of 60* was successfully sold to 122 countries and territories. How was it viewed in cultures as diverse as those of Portugal, Romania, Mexico, Kenya, Indonesia, and Iceland? I have no idea. The basic storylines would resonate in many cultures, but the readings around the world must have been variable indeed. I am not even sure how the series would be perceived in Quebec, but the struggle of a minority to hang on to its own culture and language against all kinds of outside pressure may have resonated there in a different way than it did in anglophone Canada. The face of Canada in countries all around the world continues to be the face of *The Beachcombers* and *North of 60*. To be very Canadian about it – we could do worse.

HOW THE CBC FRAMED THE SERIES

The way in which the CBC framed *North of 60* in the beginning suggests how it was first perceived within the corporation, how it was presented to the public through press releases and ads, and how a series can change and mature over the years. A good series almost never sticks to the original "bible," that is, the outline of the imagined history of the characters and plots that tells a new writer where the show is expected to go.[10] In this case, the most obvious change in the series was the foregrounding of Michelle and her brother Peter, the band chief.

A CP report with no byline appeared 11 October 1992 sounding like a virtually untouched CBC press release, although there is no copy in the CBC files:

> The newest town in the Northwest Territories has an airstrip, its own postal code, a community owned satellite dish, a couple of rusty over-turned trucks and more dogs than the local pound. It's located in the south west corner of the territories near the Liard and Mackenzie rivers but you won't find it on any map. [Producer] Tom Dent-Cox says "For many southern Canadians and many people in the world [it is] an exotic location … [with] characters not normally seen on TV. They are wonder-ful characters with their own sensibilities and unique sense of humour." Filmed just inside Kananaskis Provincial Park it is a typical [northern set-tlement] with quonset huts and log houses … Its Slavey name, Noda Deh appears on signs in the general store and band council offices.

A CBC press release of 25 November 1992 begins: "Welcome to Lynx River, a community of 150 people, 33 dogs, a great looking nurse, and a lousy motel … two worlds coming together to form an intriguing portrait of a part of Canada that's largely unknown. Lynx River is a ramshackle lit-tle community [it wasn't] built on a river bank [it was] … [In Lynx River] traditions abound and Slavey is spoken. The drinking problem became so severe that the town is now officially 'dry.' Despite its isolation, Lynx River is very much a part of the 90's and the residents' lives are complex and challenging." About Eric Olssen, the white RCMP corporal, it says, "The new officer must make an enormous effort to win over the town. That means coming to terms with some of the traditions of the North that are very alien to him." Teevee, who becomes a major character, is described as "a teenage troublemaker [who] provides an instant challenge for Olssen"; Leon, as a man "who has a weakness for drink"; Rosie, as a "recovered al-coholic, now coffee shop server"; Harris, as a "drifter who doesn't have much use for authority figures"; and Albert, simply as "the ex chief who bootlegs across the river." Compound the clichés of the mysterious North with mysterious Indians and a cop show that promises mysteries to solve and the result could have been murky indeed. Fortunately, the series is bet-ter than the official prose that was used to describe it.

The next season's press release (22 September 1993) reflects the evolution of the series, giving the "predominantly native ensemble" more emphasis:

"The new season continues as an emotional whirlwind. The white cop from the South is drawn further into the mysteries of the North while the Northern cop is torn between her professional allegiance to white law and her identity as a Dene woman. The nurse, who thought she could hide from her past, learns otherwise, and the ambitious band chief takes political gambles that may cost him his career, and Lynx River its future."

Three years later, a CBC press release of 3 October 1996 continues that theme: "Season five begins with the realisation that the North is rapidly developing. Diamond mines, oil and gas exploration, and logging are creeping into the Deh Cho. The people of Lynx River are being forced to deal with the notion of progress, both personal and communal. It's a clash of the old and new worlds. Lines are drawn between tradition and progress, isolation and community, law and lawlessness, but the outcome is never predictable. This season the inhabitants of Lynx River must decide on their own future or risk having one imposed upon them."

A press release for the sixth season (9 September 1997) asks in a rather overwrought tone: "What price progress? That's the main question faced by the residents of Lynx River. The fifth season left us anxiously awaiting new developments, with the discovery of a gas pool. This season they'll find Lynx River faced with road crews, drillers, financial crises and all the hope and horror that follows in the wake of prosperity. In the words of band chief Peter Kenidi, the only certainty is that 'the news will never be the same again.'"

## INTRODUCING THE CHARACTERS AND THE CAST

Although most were discussed briefly earlier, a refresher on the characters may help the reader navigate the next chapters. The leading actors in the series for its duration were Tina Keeper as Michelle Kenidi,[11] a mother and an RCMP constable, who became the central character; Tom Jackson as Peter Kenidi,[12] Michelle's brother, the band chief, and eventually a member of the NWT Legislative Assembly; and Gordon Tootoosis as Michelle's most important antagonist, Albert Golo, the bootlegger and occasionally the band chief.[13] Both Tootoosis and Jackson disappeared from the series for stretches of time. Keeper, the protagonist of the series, was also absent for a few episodes later in the run. Nevertheless, these three made up the emotional centre of the series. The tough teenager Teevee Tenia (played by Dakota House)[14] often shared the focus; eventually he became an entrepreneur and, with much more difficulty, a responsible father. Less central to many of the issues but a major source of plot and character interplay was the nurse Sarah Birkett, played by Tracey Cook.[15] Sarah is vitally important as the liminal figure between the white and Dene worlds who evolved from a somewhat stereotypical white nurse into a more complex character, the mother of two children, one each by Albert and Nathan Golo, and a friend of Michelle. The first of the two RCMP officers, both white, who partnered Michelle was Corporal Eric Olssen (the series' other protagonist for the first two seasons), played by John Oliver.[16] He was followed for two seasons by Corporal Brian Fletcher (played by Robert Bockstael),[17] who became a major antagonist. Both of them were killed off, although Fletcher came back from the dead (having survived an apparent suicide) as a sadistic kidnapper/wild hermit in the first movie. Towards the end of the fifth season, Michelle's first native partner, this time her junior in rank, appeared – Constable James Harper, a self-described urban Indian (played by Peter Kelly Gaudreault). Harper was later a character in some of the TV movies.[18]

The actors in *North of 60* came from a dozen different First Nations – many from Saskatchewan but ranging east and west. Renae Morriseau gave a solid performance as Ellen Kenidi, a strong foil to husband Peter, but was eventually written out.[19] Selina Hanuse (Hannah, Michelle's daughter) was also written out after supplying the traditional mother and teenaged daughter conflict. Erroll Kinistino played Leon De'ela, one of two parts originally offered to Tom Jackson, so one that was likely originally intended to be a continuing focus.[20] He made many welcome appearances but the character was not central – another example of how organically and unexpectedly the shape of a television show can develop over time. Tina Louise Bomberry, as Rosie De'ela, was a continuing character who worked at the coffee shop, looked after three kids, and was occasionally the pivot of an episode.[21] Willene Tootoosis, however, had less to do as Lois Tenia, Teevee's mother and Elsie's insecure and self-abusive daughter, although she too was the focus of some episodes. Lori Lea Okemaw played Bertha Kizha, the mother of Teevee's child. In the final seasons and in the movies, she came into her own as both a character and an actress. Wilma Pelly played one of the viewers' favourite characters, elder Elsie Tsa Che, Teevee's grandmother.[22] She appeared in most episodes and was regularly featured. Jimmy Herman (interestingly enough the only Dene [Chipewyan branch] in the series) played another elder, a master hunter, trapper, and source of dry wit throughout the series.[23]

Mervin Good Eagle played Joey Smallboat, Teevee's friend and rival. He was not formally written out, but the actor's tragic suicide, recognized without elaboration by a note at the end of an episode, was never

Corporal Brian Fletcher (Robert Bockstael), Michelle (*front and centre*), Peter, and Sarah. *Alberta Filmworks, in association with the* CBC, *distributed by Alliance Atlantis.*

mentioned within the show. From discussions in the media at the time and later, it is clear that the creative team could not find a way to deal with it on-screen. Michael P. Obey played Nathan, Albert's feckless, inarticulate youngest son.[24] Michael Horse came into the series later as Andrew One Sky, giving a charismatic and honest performance as a counsellor, bush pilot, and Michelle's lover.[25] Simon Baker played Charlie Muskrat, the child of an alcoholic mother who became Michelle's adopted son. Nathaniel Arcand played William MacNeil, who replaced Teevee as a slick, more dangerous bad boy/antagonist.[26] Two other major characters are Gerry Kisilenko, the begrudging, solitary motel/store keeper (played by Lubomir Mykytiuk),[27] and Harris

Miller (played by Timothy Webber),[28] the band manager who serves at the pleasure of the band council and remains an outsider even though he marries Lois Tenia. Both Mykytiuk and Webber were experienced actors whose characters became more nuanced as the series progressed.

First Nations and Metis guest stars who appeared over several episodes in the series included Tantoo Cardinal as Betty Moses, a hardhitting alcohol abuse counsellor; August Schellenberg as hell-raising artist Ben Montour; and Adam Beach as Nevada, the "rent" boy with AIDS on the run from Vancouver.[29] As Miles Morriseau writes in "Out of the Darkness" (1997), they "make up the brownest cast in Canadian television history" (22).

### NORTH OF 60 AS A HYBRID GENRE

*North of 60* has elements of a nighttime soap,[30] where the characters, plot lines, and problems are derived from daytime soaps but the pace is much faster because the show appears only once a week. It was advertised as a cop show or mystery show (the difference between them being that cop shows emphasize procedure, while mystery shows often feature amateur or unofficial sleuthing and emphasize the why). But like much of Canadian television drama over several decades, it has overtones of docudrama, other examples of this genre stretching from the late 1960s *Wojeck* to the late 1990s *Da Vinci's Inquest*. With its emphasis on the Dene in the Northwest Territories, the series adds a dash of the exotic. For all of these reasons, *North of 60* is a hybrid. Its emphasis is less on the traditional fodder of soaps, such as romances, betrayals, pregnancies, and illnesses (although all of those recur), and more on work, family relationships, and friendships. For one thing, all of the characters in *North of 60* are struggling to survive in much more literal terms than do the city lawyers or doctors or ruthless businessmen, the scheming trophy wives and mistresses, and the innocent dupes in American soaps. The small size and the isolation of Lynx River force people to deal with one another on a daily basis. Small communities also provide long oral histories to the conflicts and loyalties that continued to unfold in the made-for-TV movies. As a Dene community, Lynx River also provides everyone with a history of coping with the historical pressures of forced assimilation and dislocation that continue to reverberate in their lives. Nevertheless, Native American Andrew One Sky articulates how different the conditions and attitudes to a native heritage can be in Canada from those in the United States, a statement that can be read as a self-reflexive moment, since the existence of the series itself is one demonstration of that difference. Although it has open endings to some narrative arcs and a few long involved storylines each season, *North of 60* is not, strictly speaking, a serial, téléroman, or télénovella. Radio-Canada's Quebecois téléromans are serials that can go on for years but do have a clear ending in view, unlike soaps. They also foreground complicated back stories and accommodate many shifts in tone, from the playful to the ironic. Yet there are a few elements of the téléroman in *North of 60*, including long story arcs that are eventually and permanently resolved and a concluding wrap-up episode that ties up the many threads.

*North of 60* is not a family-friendly adventure story either. The problems in Lynx River are chronic and serious. The dangers in this series are human beings, not the landscape and weather. Although there are certainly elements of adventure in the series – people get lost in the bush, learn to hunt, find out new things about each other around a camp fire, survive blizzards – there are also problems familiar to young people – the influence of television, foolish dares, crushes on indifferent girls, problems with child care, competition at school, tattling. But in this series, which was made for adults not children, people freeze to death in the snow when they are drunk, push drugs, sell booze, deal with the pain of absent fathers and husbands who have deserted their families or have had to leave Lynx River to find work hundreds of miles away. People are shunned, have nervous breakdowns, have fatal accidents, get ill and die. Marriages break up. Reflected in the opening shots of every episode, under the credits, is the setting of *North of 60*, the northern lights and the boreal forests of the "true" North. Gaile McGregor, in *The Wacousta Syndrome* (1985) writes: "A northern frontier ... denotes the *limits of endurance* [her italics]. It is ... an intangible but ineradicable line between the 'self' and the 'other,' between what is and what is not humanly possible. While the western frontier is simply a culturally defined interface, the northern frontier is an existential one" (59). It becomes not only a testing ground for everyone who lives in a place like Lynx River or out on the land, but also a continuous, defining pressure on the characters.

### INSIDE *NORTH OF 60* AND ISSUES OF AUTHENTIC REPRESENTATION

The actors had a lot to say about how they saw the series and their own place in it as both actors and characters. They made their comments on radio and television as well as in print. From off-air notes comes the following excerpt from a CBC *Midday* interview, on 2 March 1995, in which Tina Keeper says that Lynx River is quite close to real life, both in its

strengths and in its flaws. Talking about the bridge the series built between aboriginal and non-aboriginal Canadians, she quotes her father,
who said that *North of 60* presents "Indians as people, not people as Indians." In her view, the issues raised in the series are less important than
the depiction of how people coped with them. When asked if she was a
role model, she says she had tried to be. She did and still does visit
schools, but now as a re-elected Liberal member of a minority Parliament.

In a later interview (10 March 1997) on *Morningside* with Peter Gzowski,
at a time when, much to her surprise, they were shooting a sixth season, she
talked about the changes in Michelle, her character: "Over the years
Michelle tried to be so controlled but in the last season she has let go a bit. If
everything falls apart, it does. Michelle is very serious and very tough ... I
understand her commitment to family and community ... She's an ex-
drinker and single mother ... But I am very definitely 'an urban Indian'
from Winnipeg." Tina Keeper's parents grew up in the bush; her mother
was an ordained Anglican priest, and her father was given the Order of
Canada for his work on native causes. Her Cree language skills are still very
basic, although her parents spoke the language. Like Michelle, Keeper had
stopped drinking ten years before the series started, with the help of friends
and family. She said that as an actress she took inspiration from all kinds of
people, especially traditional people, even though, at that point, she had
never actually travelled north of 60. Like other less-experienced actors on
the series, she found her fame "bizarre" and "didn't know how to cope with
it at all," but Tom Jackson and Gordon Tootoosis had helped her[31] – "You
watch them ... they're very gracious."[32] Actors Graham Greene and Tantoo
Cardinal were also role models for her. Like others before her, she found
that "the actor and the character can get fused in people's minds." "Strangers ask you questions, thinking you are Michelle." But it was Tina Keeper,
not Michelle who was elected as a member of Parliament in 2006.

As time went on, the people who produced and wrote the series
learned more about Lynx River, Dene life, and the North, just as viewers
did. After a year with the show, producer Tom Dent-Cox told Ken Eisner
in *Playback*, 1 March 1993, that "there was no intent on the part of the
writers to be forcing native stories. That was just the nature of the scripts.
And it's evolved nicely." Original creator and producer Barbara Samuels,
speaking for herself and co-creator/producer Wayne Grigsby, told Eisner:
"[W]e wanted to do a story that hadn't been done on a TV before. Let's
face it, most are about white people in big cities, talking about their problems. We were looking for a new physical terrain and emotional landscape, with people we haven't seen before."

As with many long-running series, life and art interpenetrate for the actors and, perhaps, for some members of the audience. Bob Blakey, in the *Calgary Herald*, 31 August 1994, writes that the exit of both John Oliver and his character Eric Olssen was the result of a domestic violence charge laid by Tina Keeper, who lived with Oliver. The charge was stayed. However, Mary Jane Kletke writes in the *Calgary Sun*, 31 August 1994, that "Keeper said that her character will miss Eric because he is the only white person Michelle trusted." The writers gave Eric a heroic exit. While on leave in Vancouver, he tries to prevent a fight and is knifed. Headlined "Northern Fights," Rick Overall's article in the *Ottawa Sun*, 6 October 1994, comments on other problems off-screen. Dakota House (Teevee), then twenty, had pleaded guilty to beating his seventeen-year-old girlfriend and was given a suspended sentence, six months' probation, and fifty hours of community work. He separated from his partner. (Now, ten years after the series ended, House has a successful career as an actor but is also working with media and youth.) These extratextual details are relevant because, since these facts were widely reported at the time, they may have affected how some viewers reacted to the characters of Eric, Michelle, and Teevee. In the last season, well after the events reported, Teevee hit Bertha, the mother of his baby, while she was pregnant with a second. Immediately she left him, taking the child and giving him no forwarding address. How he cleanses himself of the anger and genuinely asks for her forgiveness is one of the threads in the very last episode.

Greg Quill, in the *Toronto Star* of 10 November 1994, first misidentifies Keeper as Northern Innu and then goes on to quote her: "'There's a rhythm in native Canadian storytelling ... that is slow and powerful. It's not like television, where the pace is quick, a cut here, a cut there. And outsiders listening to our stories might wonder where the punctuation is ... But the rhythm itself is compelling if you abandon yourself to it. Often ... the rhythm is the point.' It is that rhythm that Keeper and the other cast members of the dramatic series hope sets the show apart." Although Quill thought that too many bad things had happened to the characters, he reports that *North of 60* "rings true to most Indians and has a huge following in small regional communities." He then asks Keeper about the loaded issue of cultural appropriation. She replies: "I don't feel [producers Samuels and Grigsby] are trying to appropriate our culture. They just make good stories about native people, about things that happen to all people. It may be an idealised version of life in a Northern Native community, but every script has input from native advisers and consultants. It works for me ... Until recently this country was not willing to deal with the realities of native life. The stereotypes were so hard to shake. And the issues that come with being an Indian can override our humanity, particularly on television. That's why the characters in North of 60 are so important: people can identify with them at last." Quill then continues: "*North of 60* is a character piece, a study of the emotions and psychology played upon by differing perspectives. The actors, mostly unknown, many of whom have little or no experience, are … wisely cast and are capable of strong performances." Unlike the *Globe and Mail*'s John Haslett-Cuff, who sees the series through Toronto-tinted glasses, Greg Quill identifies one of the crucial factors that makes the series work: "But the most influential character is not in the credits. It's that sense of a place and the culture that is unique and refreshingly under-exposed."

Bob Blakey writes in the *Calgary Herald*, 31 August 1994: "[S]o far North of 60 has [both] loyal viewers and detractors. The former send a steady stream of praise. The letters are usually hand-written, typically articulate … Peter Lauterman, first as head writer and now as producer, wants to hold on to that audience – about 1.5 million Canadians – while easing this show in the direction of a bit more levity. He keeps in touch with native Indians in the north, and the especially fervent group of fans, who have noted the mood. 'They actually say "you should lighten it up a little, eh." We'll try to but we don't want to slip on a banana peel.'" I will include many more comments from the audience and the critics in chapter 15.

Greg Quill asks in the *Toronto Star*, 8 November 1995, "Is TV's hit North of 60 real or a white fantasy?"

"That it's a success among white and Indian viewers, says a lot" says Tom Jackson. "At the end of last season, we knew the show had hit its mark. Now … we recognise that the show's popularity stretches way beyond the communities it represents. It's a hit in Toronto and Montreal. It manages on occasion to challenge the American Blockbuster *E.R.* in the same time slot. Is [this] series about life on the Northwest Territories reserve, a series about unresolved conflict between officials, white law and aboriginal mores? between materialism and spiritualism? A series that looks hard at problems and issues identified in Canada's media as particularly Indian – drug and alcohol abuse, teen suicide, marital breakdowns, sexual violence, criminal activity, neglect? A series that highlights the talents of dozens of North America's almost forgotten native actors? This is a hit on Canadian TV." "So it's not quirky and commercial" said Michael Horse [his character Andrew One Sky had just been added]. "It's not Northern Exposure. It's about people who happen to be natives …

Native communities in the US with access to satellite TV loved the show. In America, native subject matter is not treated as well, the drama is not as well written. It tends to be patronising and the acting suffers because of that. I'd work on the show as long as they have me. It has a spiritual centre all human beings can relate to, that part of who we are as a species. Sure these problems are typical on ... reserves in North America but they are to be found in any community."

To Claire Bickley in the *Toronto Sun*, 8 November 1995, Michael Horse says: "'I showed this show to a couple of Hopi elders that were staying at my house this weekend and they loved it ... What's interesting about this show is it doesn't play the cheap shot. A lot of the things that are written in the States have to do with the medicine man and the vision quest. This isn't. You can see these people ... have a centre, a balance.'" Three years after the series ended, Dianne Meili, in the aboriginal newspaper *Windspeaker*, June 2000, reports that Michael Horse asked the crowd at the Miss Indian World Pageant in Albuquerque, New Mexico, if they had ever heard of *North of 60*. "[After] loud hoots and hollers. 'Great show isn't it? I love Canada. But their frybread ... Where I come from we'd call that doughnut holes!' Later he said 'I really enjoyed being directed by [Metis] Gil Cardinal. He's Indian. I didn't have to keep stopping and explaining things.'"

In an 8 November 1995 *Toronto Star* article, Greg Quill reports:

Keeper, a tough and proud actor and a vigorous campaigner for Indian rights and defender of her culture, bristled at the suggestion that North of 60 was white television's view of her life and people. "There's room for argument on the show, it really is a team effort. Though they no longer write the show, Wayne and Barbara look at every sentence in every script. Our senior script editor is an aboriginal [Jordan Wheeler]. And as native actors, we all have a say when it comes to lines and set ups. I remember one script, where we were all supposed to be dancing around a fire, and I objected because it felt like something out of *Dances with Wolves*. Other times I'll lose the argument, but only after I'm convinced that the dialogue and action are honest ... We're always talking about how to avoid stereotypes. Many native people don't see themselves as victims." ... She [also] insisted, "there's a lot of very subtle humour in the show."

The *Toronto Star* paired this article by Quill with Drew Hayden Taylor's attack on the series, which will be discussed in chapter 15.

It is a fact that the location and the backup production facilities for the series were a few miles from Calgary. The two co-creators (Grigsby and Samuels), all of the other producers, all but one of the directors, all but two of the story editors, and all but three of the many writers were not from the First Nations. None had lived in the North. In some cases they had not even travelled north of the sixtieth parallel. Jordan Wheeler, the Metis story editor, did go up to the Acho Dene Koe (in the Deh Cho) to Trout Lake (population 70) in 1993, a visit that resulted in an article headlined "Lynx River Has Trout: An Inside Look at CBC's Popular TV Series *North of 60*" for the aboriginal magazine *The Runner* (spring 1994). The series could be said to be made from "the outside looking in" in two ways. First and most obviously, the dominant culture was representing aspects of the life of the South Slavey–speaking Dene. Second, the south was looking north. However, unlike all the other series discussed in this book, this one had Dene cultural advisors working on it every season. One of them, Nick Sibbeston, a senator in the Northwest Territories, was consistently involved with the series as well as with the made-for-TV movies, and there were several other Dene over the years. Even so, in a lunchtime conversation at a 1994 conference, an aboriginal academic and artist dismissed the series altogether. If the series was not made by First Nations people, then it was irrelevant and anything I, as a white academic, had to say about it was also irrelevant. When he later pointed out to the conference that his people planned ahead for seven generations and their history spanned millennia, his perspective threw the ephemeral nature of television into high relief. Professor Frances Abele reminded the same conference that in Saskatchewan and in the Territories there would be an aboriginal majority in twenty to thirty years. As she pointed out, in instances where First People internalize the *other*ness of the dominant society, speaking English is a politically charged act and can be emotionally painful.[33]

In 1996 producer Tom Dent-Cox commented on the fourth season of the series on the series website:[34] "We don't get mail. We get recipes, songs, prayers and advice to the characters." Producer Doug MacLeod told site visitors, "[S]ome band meetings and community events are rescheduled … so that no one misses an episode." This was a very interactive website (no longer on the internet), with a "Viewer Band Council" through which viewers contributed reactions, suggestions, and answers to questions set by the producers or the webmaster such as "Do you think Lois will stick with the Catholic Church?" Although the site was maintained by the production company that made the show, some of the support was verified in several press interviews with the actors. The site also claimed that the RCMP were pleased with the way they were represented. Of course, *North of 60* could never have survived on ratings from First Nations, Metis, and RCMP audiences alone.[35] Like every other program discussed in this book, it had to work for the average, non-native viewer.[36]

### A TALE TOLD BY ...

Given the outside-looking-in perspective and that it was made by the dominant society, the series raises post-colonialist questions. During *North of 60*'s fifth season, Miles Morriseau (1997) writes in the First Nations publication (edited by well-known actor Gary Farmer) *Aboriginal Voices* about performing in a show written by non-natives: "[It] shows lives of contemporary natives in a realistic setting ... It has been in the last three seasons when Tina Keeper's character Michelle Kenidi has taken centre stage that the show has hit its stride. In its current incarnation, the non-Native characters play the supporting roles ... [Tina Keeper][37] appreciates the attempts made by the creators and producers ... to be respectful of Aboriginal people; but that doesn't change the fact that real creative control does not lie in Aboriginal hands. It's a fact that isn't lost on Peter Lauterman, 'North of 60 is an interim step between the old stereotypes and the next phase when Native directors, Native producers and Native actors will be in control'" (25). (Drew Hayden Taylor [1996] reports, in an otherwise highly critical article on the series, that "the show has a fine reputation for training Native people in story editing and other television jobs" [79].). A decade later *Moccasin Flats* (2004–present), a hard-hitting half-hour series set in the inner city, may not be what Lauterman imagined, but it is made by First Nations actors, writers, and producers.

Claims and questions of authenticity were raised throughout the media coverage of the series, not just white/Indian questions but also issues about the generic Indian versus a specific culture. Story editor Jordan Wheeler, writing for the *Runner* (spring 1994) says: "I'm not Dene, and we want the show to be rooted in reality within the limits of television drama. So we depend heavily on resource people in the North beginning with Eleanor Bran, Bertha Norwegian, Leo Norwegian and Nick Sibbeston who keep us culturally accurate ... Many an idea or story has been shaped by their telling words." Admittedly, he is writing from inside the show, but in this article he is also writing for aboriginal readers who are especially mindful of the fact that a Cree person is not interchangeable with a Dene and cannot know the cultural details that will make the show work for the Dene. Wheeler does not list all of the cultural advisors but does list people like Robin Melting Tallow, Eva Macgregor, Roland Bellrose, and Carol Grey Eyes (15). Like him, they went on to careers in film, television, and other media. After the series ended, an article by Liz Crompton in the *Globe and Mail,* 13 January 2000, covering a *North of 60* movie, further pursued a more general issue of authenticity in the made-for-TV movies. She writes: "Nick Sibbeston, who has been an adviser on the culture and language of the South Slavey culture and language from the start says 'It's always a challenge. It's little things that southerners don't understand.' [Producer] Dent-Cox says that Northern viewers have always been vocal: 'They're quick to tell us when we stray from reality, and quick to tell us when we got it right ... without fear, favour or affection.'"

In the documentary *Dream Makers*, aired 17 December 2006,[38] Tom Jackson says that the series spoke for itself: "Anybody who embraced North of 60, embraced it because it was a window into a new world." Lorne Cardinal (Daniel De'ela) says that people loved the characters, that the plots were "soap operaish," but the shows were full of good talented people whose characters were permitted to go beyond stereotypes. Dakota House says that Teevee was "going through a lot of things I was going through in real life ... He was a rebel without a clue," but the show offered "great developments for the character." Indeed, he felt as if the writers were looking over his shoulder but also that the show did what the arts in general can do, help young people focus their energy in a positive way.

Nearly a decade earlier, in the last season, Tina Keeper told Miles Morriseau (1997) that "'[i]n the beginning, there was a really strong feeling aside from being an actor, but as an Indian person, to work with the writers and the producers to say this is getting out of hand or there is too much stereotypical imagery here ... I felt a sense of being on guard.'" This would eventually be compounded by the fact that, as she says, "'Indian people have a sense of ownership about the show because there hasn't been anything like it'" (24). That puts a lot of weight on any television series. It is no surprise that there has not been, and perhaps will not be for who knows how long, another made-for-adults television series that focuses on First Nations. Everyone involved knew that there was more riding on the series and the movies than is usual in television. At the Imagining Indians: A Native American Film and Video Conference, held in Scottsdale, Arizona, in 1994, Gary Farmer and Tantoo Cardinal talked about trying to make sure that the plots as well as the characters they performed in film and television were truthful to aboriginal experience. They also spoke of their sense that they had to live as people who were in the public eye, both because some members of their audience confused the characters with the actors, and because their own accomplishments made them legitimately a focus of attention. Somehow they had to try to ensure some authenticity on the screen and live as examples in real life. In 2000 at a conference at Brock University, Gary Farmer reiterated this point of view. I cannot think of anywhere else in television where such expectations exist, where such burdens are assumed by the actors whose faces and bodies bring to life the stories of others.

It is a long way from *Radisson* to *North of 60*. The film technology of the earlier show was radically different. The financing was much more complicated for *North of 60*. Unlike the white producers of *Radisson*, the white producers of *North of 60* used native (Dene) consultants for every episode and obtained the services of some, though not enough, aboriginal writers. The actors playing the Dene may have been Stoney Cree, Salteaux, Metis, or Huron, but all were First Nations or Metis. Some had years of experience and the rest were given the chance to develop as actors in a contemporary series that deconstructed stereotypes, took on topical issues, was intended for adults, and won very good ratings at home. *North of 60* has been broadcast all over the world and is still in reruns. The series and the made-for-TV movies of *North of 60* that followed contributed to and perhaps reflected viewers' changing expectations over the five decades since *Radisson* about First Nations peoples – and about how their stories should be told.

# TWELVE

# Looking at Setting and Character in *North of 60*

Michelle (to Eric): "Most everyone in this town is healing. One more is OK."

## ROLES BEHIND THE CAMERA

Television has always been a collective art, even though it is produced by a hierarchy of people, both on set and off. Series television uses an even wider collective of people to work on a particular show over the years. The producers and executive producers look after logistics, cast the main roles, keep track of the series, and have the final say in the sound mix and the edit. The story editors, head writers, and writing team discuss with the producers, before, during, and after the season, where the basic narrative arcs are going. A bible for new and old writers helps keep them on track.[1] The directors, with the directors of photography, determine what is actually caught on film, from the angle of the camera to what should be in-frame. The director also works with the actors and is responsible, with them, for their performances. The designers try to fit costumes, props, sets, and locations to characters and situations, and thus provide an ambience visible to the audience but usually not obtrusive. The makeup artist for *North of 60* created unobtrusive makeup for the women to go with their parkas and jeans, but also created special effects like wounds.

But television is also a black art, not a science. All of these decisions by all these people either can make a good episode and, overall, a successful series, or can inexplicably (though often the reasons are obvious) cause an episode or even a series to fail miserably. Failure is defined as "no one is watching," neither the desired demographic nor, often, anyone else.

For series and movies, the producers provide the logistics and do the hiring; the scripts provide the spine; the actors, the flesh and blood; and the directors, the skill in capturing the gestalt. Editors give it more coherence. To the editor's cut, music and sound effects are added. Nevertheless, paradoxically for a visual medium, the dialogue is often the key both to my analysis and to the reader's understanding of a scene. Since I do not wish to distract the reader with endless endnotes for small patches of dialogue, phrases, or incidents, I have listed in one place, in the endnote following this sentence, all of the writers of this series by season.[2] Some have written major films for the CBC or contributed extensively to other series. Others are less well known. All of the directors are also listed. An asterisk represents several contributions to the series.

## DESIGN: SETTINGS

In a series specifically called *North of 60*, the settings are crucial to the sense of place. North of 60 is unfamiliar territory. (The various understandings of "north" are discussed in chapter 3, "The North is where?") The set of Lynx River has to do a lot of work over ninety episodes. The following details relating to the set play into the mythology and also, to some degree, deconstruct it. The opening credits always begin with a shot of the northern lights in the limitless sky. Then, through a blue filter, the viewer sees an aerial shot of the endless miles of trees, a snow goose, a small plane. Each is metonymous for a northern journey. This is followed by shots of the fire-lit faces of the leading characters contained within one half of a split screen and paired with blue-filtered scenes from the show in the other half. Thus, from the top of the show, the clips full of action are set off by these portraits of reflection. The sequence ends with Willy, in sunglasses, beating on a hand drum, another blend of the traditional and the modern, and finally in medium shot, the clear, shallow, flowing "Lynx" river. The credits promise the viewer that this series will not present the familiar southern or urban Canada, nor perhaps merely the clichés of northernness.

## WILDERNESS AS EXTERIOR

The wilderness is the exterior for many scenes in the series. There is not a lot of colour in the episodes set in the fall, since the bush consists mostly of evergreens, broken up with yellow alders and a bit of birch. There is lots of crunchy snow and cold wind in winter and a sense of green everywhere in the spring and summer.[3] Real (Alberta) weather created production problems but contributed to the visual richness. One anonymous participant in the online nativecelebs discussion list says: "One thing I like about this show is the attention to detail. For instance, if two characters are inside a building, talking, you still hear things going on outside, as if it is a real town, things like planes taking off, snowmobiles, chain saws, etc."[4] Nevertheless, the settlement is, by definition, small and could be claustrophobic for viewers.

There is one unpaved street in Lynx River, a school, a church (interiors we rarely see), the band offices, a meeting hall, the RCMP post, and the nursing station, the latter two with living quarters attached. In the grave-yard, the individual graves are surrounded by small white picket fences. Some have birchbark tubes hanging on them for small gifts. Outside of town is the airstrip. The one road out leads to Wolverine Lake, a few miles away. The only other way out is by the shallow though fast-moving river. For the first five seasons there is no road to the larger world. In Lynx River, as a change from life in the small community, people regularly go out on the traplines – sometimes to seek solitude – or they may go to the hunting camps, practices that are often defined as essential ways of get-ting in touch with the land and the roots of the culture. Although only a very few people still make their living from the land, hunting and guid-ing, most still hunt and fish for food for themselves and others. From the beginning of the series, Teevee and many others of his generation do not feel this need to be out on the land for rejuvenation. A motif in the series is the alienation of the young as they measure Lynx River by what they see on satellite television from the South. Even the road that breaches that isolation late in the series does not really cure it. Isolation in the bush also takes its toll. When Albert's son Nathan is sent into exile by a sentencing circle as a substitute for jail time, this traditional punishment causes him to hallucinate. As the community, trying to be just but also trying to retain traditional forms of justice, learns to its dismay, this modern young man cannot endure the silence and isolation of a cabin in the bush as his father and grandfather could.

The series does not reinforce stereotypes of what is natural for First Na-tions people. The wilderness is both home and dangerously unforgiving. Some people get lost very easily, while others make their living as guides. In one early episode, a hunter's bones are found years after he had gone missing and are given ritual burial. Characters who do not go out on the land, like Fletcher, Harper, and even Peter Kenidi, find themselves run-ning in panic through the bush. Yet Teevee, who has refused to learn the traditional skills, surprises his family when he survives a blizzard by making a snow cave and keeping himself and his companion alive. In the last episode of the series, Teevee again surprises himself and others by taking his first moose. But in that same season James Harper, Michelle's last partner, who is a senator's son and an urban Indian, deconstructs an-other stereotype when he demonstrates that he has no instinctive feeling for the wilderness.

In Lynx River itself, there is little sign of boarded-up windows, peeling paint, wrecked snowmobiles, or even much junk. It seems rather pristine

for a community so isolated, although Corporal Fletcher's wife, Rosemary, does not endear herself to the town when she starts busily picking
up litter. There are not many disintegrating cars, partly because Willy can
fix things and partly because cars are largely irrelevant. However, trucks
for hauling all kinds of things are vital. Gasoline is stored in drums. In the
back ways between the houses, propane tanks appear, as well as stacks of
lumber, a large tipi without a covering (for smoking meat?), snowmobiles, but no food garbage. Some aboriginal viewers noted that there were
few dogs. There is evidence of porcupines but no visible rabbits, caribou,
or bear. Moose, a staple in the diet, do turn up. We hear lots of birdcalls
but rarely see any birds, not even the friendly chickadees or whisky-jacks.
Ravens are a presence in some episodes, rarely with overt significance.
And no one looks meaningfully up, up to an eagle soaring. This series is
mercifully free of a romanticized view of the natural world. The river itself, though, deserves special mention. It reappears over and over as a
place where people go when they are in distress or need to think and, if a
boat is at hand, as a way to get across to Albert's cabin. It is therefore a
boundary between outlaw/outsider and the settlement. It is both barrier
and highway, where the characters go to be alone, to talk together, to
travel. The river is also a source of food and of companionship when people fish together. One of its huge driftwood logs speaks to an artist and in
the end is carved as a huge raven that turns into a tribute to a lad with
AIDS (who is driven out of town). Like the bush, the river is many things
to many people.

Lynx River shares some of the characteristics typical of a community,
as defined by Clara Thomas (quoted in McGregor 1985):[5] "'any formally
self-defined aggregate small enough for face-to-face communication but
large enough to make social norms rather than emotions the standard basis for interpersonal relation ... [A small town is] where everyone had his
place – even the slot called 'outsider' is better than no place at all [for
Harris, Gerry, Sarah] – and where nobody's child could be lost'" (431).
Even so, a few teens on *North of 60* seem to be without parental or community support. McGregor goes on to point out that isolated settlements
and small towns loom large in the imaginative landscapes of Canada.
Where Lynx River leaves the Canadian typology is in its relationship to
the wilderness surrounding it. Where southerners would see borders between civilization and bush, the Dene do not. As Rinaldo Walcott reports
in *Fuse Magazine*, the "Gei ni gy gwe dage (Four People Together) ...
wrote in their statement [about an installation at the Art Gallery of On-
tario] that the First Nations have no word for landscape. Landscape is

part of the interior life of the people" (20). In the last season, the sense of the bush surrounding Lynx River recedes as the numbers of visitors from outside increase and the road arrives, only to be foregrounded as life-threatening in the first movie, *In the Blue Ground,* and as literally and spiritually life-saving in the third movie, *Dream Storm.*

## PUBLIC AND PRIVATE SPACES: INTERIORS

One of the major themes of *North of 60* is how public responsibilities and private lives intersect for Michelle, Peter, Eric, Fletcher, Harris, Sarah, and Teevee. The RCMP's private quarters are fairly Spartan. When Brian's wife, Rosemary, is in residence, the rooms are not really individualized. The apartment in the nursing station is modern and rather soulless, despite the fact that Sarah has already lived there for four years when the series opens. Both apartments join private to public spaces. The RCMP detachment itself has two desks and two jail cells behind a door that is rarely closed. This means that prisoners, nearly always well known to the community, are perpetually present, whether they are being disruptive or just conversational. The walls are whitewashed wooden logs, decorated with unobtrusive framed pictures of red-coated Mounted Police and a few up-to-date posters. The detachment is furnished with a mix of computers, filing cabinets, a stove, and a coffee pot – all fairly impersonal. The nursing station is modern, with a clinic, a bed, and posters on health concerns, a place where medical crises happen and accident victims come to be fixed up. It is backed up by radio-telephone access to a medevac.[6]

The band offices and meeting rooms include an office that the chief occupies, another for Harris, the band manager, and a large open meeting space for full band meetings as well as bingos. There is a large sign in the Slavey language in the big hall, which doubles as an after-school play area. One good storyline, in an early season, centred around the kids' determination to build themselves an ice rink after the band council had turned them down. Sometimes the street has many children underfoot, playing and kidding around – often not. Gerry's general store/coffee shop/motel is where people shop for everything, including junk food and videos, and it's the program's real meeting place. It's here that people work out their antagonisms, check the news, plan and scheme, and watch and wait over cups of coffee. And lonely people take refuge in the motel. Gerry is the only person in the village who has ready cash. The viewers find out how characters are doing by seeing whether he gives them credit. He is treated as an outsider, partly because with his control over credit he exercises petty tyranny over the community.

People walk in and out of each other's houses quite freely, but their homes are also their only truly private spaces. Peter Kenidi, the chief of Lynx River for three of the first four seasons, has an MBA and contacts in Yellowknife and Ottawa, but remains in Lynx River because of his loyalty to the town. His house is a little larger than, but not unlike, the other band houses. It has a log interior and a fully-equipped modern kitchen, with various pieces of native art on the walls. Peter also has a computer (this is the early 1990s) and bookshelves, which are not evident in any other house. Michelle's house is also quite modern inside, finished with separate bedrooms, open living room/kitchen (like most of the others), and an enclosed loft upstairs. Hannah's room is typical of teenagers anywhere. Of course, both Kenidis earn reasonable salaries. For others, money can be tight. Rosie and Leon De'ela both work but at low wages, until she becomes Gerry's partner. Their home has a loft and an open downstairs with a decent kitchen. It looks sturdy, not elaborate, and was hand-finished by Leon, who is a carpenter. The Tenias' is somewhat like it – smaller but with a loft and an open plan for the rest. The television is usually on. Elsie has a modern iron, stove, and fridge, as well as a curtained room of her own off the kitchen, because, as she says in one episode loudly and firmly to Teevee, "It's MY house." Neither Lois, her daughter, nor Teevee, her grandson, has steady work in the early years, though Lois, like Elsie, does make crafts to sell.[7] Elsie's old age cheque is the only steady money. For most people, outhouses are the norm. Conversations in the early years, one person inside and one outside, happen without fuss. When Joe moves his, it pollutes Gerry's water, prompting many toilet jokes. Albert attempts to bribe the community into letting him drill in the centre of town by promising indoor plumbing for every household – a tempting offer. Badly worn trailers also reflect the chronic shortage of money, and therefore housing, for band members. Gerry's trailer is moved onto muskeg, begins to list, then leaks, and finally, when he botches fixing it, blows up. Bertha is supposed to take her baby, Kyla, to Elsie's home, since Teevee is the father. Instead she chooses to live in a shack belonging to her aunt that, with great effort, Bertha and Joey, not Teevee, make liveable. A few bare hunting cabins are scattered in the bush; they save lives occasionally and once in a while serve as "booze cans" or, in one case, house a failed marijuana grow-op. The standard house is of peeled-log construction, but for cabins in the bush, bits of siding, logs, plastic, and plywood are all used.

The two equally matched alpha males, Joe and Albert, have very distinctive places to live. Joe, a traditionalist, the best hunter, and an elder, is the person most at home where he lives. His cabin is liminal – at the edge of the bush outside of town – but accessible to those who need to talk to him. We rarely see inside his cabin, which is very small. He cooks on an open fire. It is a basic camp, as close as the series gets to modelling how life was lived in the old days, but it is also connected to the modern world. Joe loves Dad's chocolate chip cookies. He lives in voluntary exile at the edge of town because he was disrespectful to a caribou he had killed, causing the caribou to avoid the band's hunting grounds for several years. Eventually, his health being not what it once was, he takes over looking after the air strip from Willy. But the strip too is liminal, the leaving/arriving place that connects the town to the outside world.

Albert's cabin, like Joe's, reflects his relationship with the town. It looks precarious, braced over the edge of the riverbank, looking down on the village, but it is quite sturdy. He shares it with his three grown sons. It is larger than most of the others, plain but durable and warm, a shelter for Sarah in her breakdown, a place where they seem to act as man and wife. When it becomes the site of a violent confrontation with Sarah and his son Nathan, shots are exchanged, a lamp full of oil is spilled, and the cabin burns down. At first glance, the interior is puzzling. It is clear that Albert has money – he has been chief and has worked many schemes quite successfully. Yet, by choice, he has no generator, no pumped or running water. The walls are unfinished, there are no pictures, and the cabin looks unkempt. After Sarah moves in, he provides a curtained-off place for their double bed. Curtains on the windows, a few other "woman's" touches appear, but Sarah has to teach the boys how to do the laundry in a bucket. In many ways, it looks like a camp, inside as well as out. The reason for its Spartan nature, like many mysteries about Albert, is never explained. Albert has a vegetable garden, but it is in the bush surrounding his property that he can hide his booze operation and there that he can use all of his survival skills to disappear. Wherever anyone goes in the community, the bush is a step away.

## COSTUMES

Inventive costumes, together with good sets, props, and locations such as those just described, engage a viewer, but opportunities for creative costuming in this series are limited. As the other older women do, Elsie always wears a head scarf outdoors, usually with a housedress and sweater. Her winter coat is the traditional one of flower-printed cloth lined with warm fur. When Elsie beads something for granddaughter Kyla, it is in a traditional design, "so she'll know she's Slavey." She can recognize which woman did the beadwork on a fifty-year-old knife sheathe. The younger women wear slacks or jeans, shirts or blouses, and modern parkas. Most have long hair that is braided or tied back, except for Michelle, whose hair varies from shoulder-length and loose to tightly braided, in part reflecting her mood. Viewers often see her out of uniform or wearing an RCMP shirt with jeans. Whether she is on or off duty is signified by whether she is wearing any part of her uniform. Rosie's more ample form appears in colours, and her hair is a little more flyaway. Lois is slender and lovely, her wonderful long black hair generally braided but often left loose in a traditional fashion. When Lois gets married, she turns down a standard wedding dress to wear a beautiful white doe-skin dress with complex embroidery. Ellen, Peter's wife, usually looks "put together." No one wears visible makeup. All wear earrings. Sarah evolves from a competent and smart-looking nurse in practical bush gear to (during her breakdown) a woman with blowsy hair, unkempt jeans, and a man's shirt and, finally, to an expectant mother who wears practical bush wear (though less expensive than before) and baggy denim overalls that suit her condition. The younger girls' clothes are indistinguishable from those of kids anywhere. The teens wear eyeshadow and purple nail polish or whatever else has been fashionable in the past year that they can afford. Michelle's daughter, back from Calgary, tries to impress the others with a nose ring, but it turns out to be fake. (Nose-piercing is not available in Lynx River.)

The boys wear jeans, shirts, boots, caps. The men wear shirts and denims, with jackets or parkas in very cold weather. The white RCMP officer from Vancouver, Eric Olssen, soon learns to wear jeans – which still elicits bawdy comments from fans. Teevee starts out in a black leather jacket with studs but later wears various work outfits. In episode 73, his clothing is a plot point. He has had a confrontation with Bertha because he has bought a new jacket instead of saving money for her classes in nursing. But when he speaks to the band about a serious decision they must make, he is wearing a superbly beaded buckskin jacket presumably made by Elsie. William, Albert's young henchman, wears newer, more expensive up-to-date clothes. We seldom see Eric's replacement, Brian Fletcher, out of uniform, which emphasizes how out of place he is in the town. Harris wears a peaked cap, indoors and out, and what look like bush jackets and vests out of a catalogue. However, he is given a finely beaded leather vest to wear at his wedding. Gerry wears slightly less casual shirts and pants, often donning an apron in the store and making no concession to the fur, leather, and beadwork the others wear – until one of the women makes him a beaded leather jacket because he had (reluctantly) donated a valuable prize for the kids' art contest. However, in a much later episode, at the wedding of Harris and Lois, he appears in beautifully embroidered Ukrainian shirt and pants, proclaiming his own heritage as well as honouring the newlyweds.

For most part, the white men have short hair and are close-shaven. For the first few seasons, Joe Gomba is the only man who wears his hair loose, shoulder-length, and around his face. Most of the other middle-aged men, like Willy, wear theirs shorter. Peter wears his in a tight braid to his shoulder blades, with hair trimmed in a contemporary way around his face – a double message. The Native American counsellor from Calgary, Andrew One Sky, wears his hair shoulder-length and loose. Albert's sons wear theirs longer and carelessly tied back. Albert's own iron-grey hair is, like so many other things about the character, a paradox. For most of the series it is nearly waist-length, always clean and carefully combed, always tied back. It is almost defiantly, and in the context unexpectedly, traditional and yet completely different from Joe's or anyone else's. Albert's refusal to cut his hair sends a very interesting signal to any viewer who is aware that hair of that length signifies someone rooted in tradition who values his difference and has had a long commitment to his or her culture, having lived for many years without having it cut. He wears it this way until he disappears after being shot by his son. When he returns, he wears it short, which could signify many things. Cutting hair can signify mourning – or does it signal a new start?

### CHARACTERS

#### *Michelle Kenidi*

Michelle Kenidi (Tina Keeper) is the pivotal character in the series. The producers created an ensemble that survived her absence (at Tina Keeper's request) for several episodes, but without her the program is basically not *North of 60*.[8] She is also central to all five of the movies. Michelle is one of the most private of the characters, having a quality that creates barriers for the audience as well as for the other characters but also leads to surprises. In episode 12, "Sisters of Mercy"(explored in chapter 13), viewers find out in some detail about her experiences in a residential school, where she was severely and publicly humiliated and beaten for her rebellious behaviour. As the series continues, they find out just what kind of impact those years had on her; after a long period of drinking, she decided to live clean and search for a job with clear rules and a clear role. All of this is back story, revealed as the series progresses. When Rosemary Fletcher, in season 4, asks, horrified, "Were you in one of those residential schools?" Michelle visibly shuts down as she replies, "I don't want to talk about it." Michelle distrusts people she doesn't know and yet feels a counter-impulse, not only to serve and protect, but also to look after everyone and solve their problems, even the problems of those who are hostile to her, like the drunk and disorderly rakehell and gifted artist Ben Montour. As Sarah says to her in exasperation at one point, "You don't have to fix everything!" Predictably, Michelle is tough on her daughter, Hannah, a normally rebellious teen who also resents being the child of the town cop. Michelle's oblique sense of humour does occasionally soften her often sober demeanour. It becomes apparent that, as a Kenidi, she is a member of a family that has had leadership roles in the band for generations. The Golos are ancient rivals of the Kenidis, and she hunts Albert with passion but often without perspective. Early on, the town is so fed up with the bickering between Albert and Peter that they asked Michelle to stand for chief. After thinking it over, she refuses – after all, Peter is her brother. However, although both sexes serve on the band council, which includes Elsie as a respected elder and Rosie as a vocal member, no other reference is made to the possibility of a woman as chief. After Hannah's death, Michelle adopts a son. She has many sides. She is a mother, a sister, a friend who includes Sarah in her circle, an unpaid social worker, and counsellor. She gets involved in a romance with a white archaeologist and finds a true love in Andrew One Sky, a professional counsellor to troubled teenaged youth in Calgary. She is an RCMP constable, later a corporal, a vocation that is very important to her. (In Canada, the RCMP are the police in every province and territory except Ontario and Quebec.)[9] The mixed history of the RCMP – ranging from the suppression of whisky traders, to attacks on Riel's First Nations' allies, to historical friendships with several First Nations leaders, and finally to its current, often troubled relations with some First Nations peoples – provides a key both to the security she feels in being an RCMP officer and to the mixed emotions that the Lynx River community has about the essentially colonial laws and institutions she has to enforce. Perhaps inevitably the issue of aboriginal policing replacing the RCMP detachment is part of the focus of the last made-for-TV movie, *Distant Drumming.*

*Peter Kenidi*

Tom Jackson's performance through the six years of the series is nuanced and layered with subtext once his character moves beyond the obvious anger and suspicion of the first few episodes. Because he had been a professional singer/actor in the early years (and still is), his acting experience was a vital contribution to the series. In the CBC *Life and Times* portrait of him,[10] he talks of the rubbing together of two cultures that is at the heart of *North of 60*, though by no means always its central focus: "I believe that [the program] changes opinions … I'm a halfbreed. I'm locked right in the middle of that. I don't want to say 'I'm not my father's son. I'm not my mother's son … '[Yet] others say 'He's Indian like us.'"

When the series opens, Peter Kenidi is the Lynx River band chief, but eventually he is voted out in favour of Albert Golo, the patriarch of the Golo clan. Peter is deeply hurt, refuses to advise or help, and instead sets about gathering an oral history of the town. Even after he is re-elected chief, on at least one occasion the apparently generations-old conflict between the Golos and their allies and the Kenedis and their friends leads to open brawls on the street. As for the rivalry between Peter and Albert for the job of chief, Hugh Brody, in *The Living Arctic* (1987), quotes *Denendeh: A Dene Celebration*[11] (1984): "'[A]lthough our leaders are very important to us: they are meant to guide us and not to have power over us'" (112), a statement that is at odds with the power both men have over jobs for their supporters, which they exercise in everything from selecting firefighting crews to choosing who will build the rehab centre. Brody also writes: "In the 1970s … Dene leaders set up decision making bodies that relied on the consent of everyone in all communities" (131), a system that reflected their traditional lack of formal hierarchy. Like Michelle, Peter has his demons, but they are well hidden under his charm and apparent confidence. He says at one point: "I had to be good for so long. I was the youngest M.B.A., band chief and had 12 happy years of marriage." His marriage survives a brief fling with Sylvie LeBret, but workaholism eventually costs him his wife and son. When Michelle asks him when he was last out on the land, not counting weekends, he replies that it was when he was ten, with his uncle. They ate boiled moose nose, "a delicacy," as he says wryly. In contrast, despite her years away, Michelle has reintegrated into her community, learning from Joe Gomba how to go back out on the land. Joe tells Eric, "You want to go hunting, you take Michelle. If [Peter] had to feed his family, they would starve." Except when talking to the elders, Peter does not show the Dene cultural stance of modesty about his accomplishments or status (Brody 1987, 69).

One of Peter's strengths is that he knows the system. He can work comfortably with bureaucrats in Yellow Knife or Ottawa. He can work the system so that he is not disadvantaged as a Dene chief of a small band. Politically, in fact, he is sometimes ahead of the game. When helping Teevee with his application for training as a band manager, he tells him that he should do well because "You're smart, you're Native, you're Northern, you have all your working parts." He can play hardball with Harry Dobbs and the oil interests to get the best deal for the town, then walk away from it because the band council is clearly not yet ready. Peter is also a liminal figure – comfortable in both worlds. He is also a rarity. He has worked hard to get an education and experience, but then, unlike most young aboriginal men who succeed, he comes back home to the North – and thus fulfils a dream of so many viewers in small or remote communities, north or south of 60. The first time he is tempted by an important job in Ottawa, after some deep-rooted conflict within himself, he turns it down. When he does leave Lynx River, it is part-time as a member of the Legislative Assembly. Peter has considerable intelligence, works very hard, and is widely liked. He is also wilful, takes indefensible risks with the band's future, and is sometimes secretive and impatient with the band's tradition of consensual government. Over the years, he learns patience in the face of the conflicting, often contradictory, voices of his community. His heroes are evident when he tries to decide upon a name for his new baby, having narrowed it down to Elijah, Ovide, and Peter Jr – thinking presumably of Elijah Harper[12] and Ovide Mercredi.[13] He chooses Elijah.

Peter's relationship with Michelle, who is five years younger than he is, is perhaps the most complex relationship in the series and a rarity for adult characters in television drama. The way sisters and brothers relate is not usually central to mainstream television, where work families, husbands, wives, children, and even friends take the focus. Peter is haunted by what he sees as his failure (in fact, his inability as a child) to protect his sister when they were both hauled off to residential school. As he says, "We were all each other had. They tore us from the bush, everything we loved." He is predictably angry and jealous about her brief affair with David, the white archaeologist. He can be dangerously overprotective, such as when he has a bitter battle with Betty, a substance abuse counsellor and Michelle's close friend, who arrives in Lynx River to try to help Michelle confront her deep grief for her daughter, Hannah. In season 5, "Bushman," episode 66, he confronts a more serious threat to their closeness. Andrew One Sky has applied for a job as counsellor at the addiction treatment centre in Lynx River so that he can court Michelle. Although Peter has reluctantly facilitated the application to keep the centre open, he is hostile to Andrew thereafter. In their final confrontation, Andrew deliberately taunts him: "You want to sleep with her. Just get it over with!" Peter decks him, which is probably not the kind of showdown Andrew had intended to provoke. However, Michelle knows her own mind, intervenes in the brawl, and then, in her own good time, partners with Andrew. Eventually, under pressure from Inspector Cormier in relation to her promotion, she marries him. In a later scene in this episode, Peter reminds Michelle that she was afraid of the Bushman when she was three and he was eight. She doesn't remember how he "comforted her ... just before the nuns took us away to school." Michelle replies very simply: "Now we have to let each other go." He nods and leaves.

Peter and Michelle also differ in the way they relate to tradition and ceremony. Until Hannah's death, visions apparently had not been a major part of Michelle's life, and even after her daughter's death, only briefly. The world of "fact" is too important to her, although she fully accepts that the spirit world exists around her and she respects the beliefs of Joe, Elsie, and others. Peter is the one who has visions of himself as a boy on his way to residential school, visions that teach him to embrace that boy's fear and pain. But in a late episode, number 83, "Peter and the Wolf," the spirit of their mother identifies Michelle to Peter as his mentor in things spiritual. In *Dream Storm*, Michelle's role develops further as she follows a vision quest that helps her heal the community.

Peter and Michelle are created as two opposites. Peter is the brother who made good, got a post-graduate education, learned the system, and excelled. Michelle is the rebel who refused to assimilate, who internalized the lessons of self-hatred, and who learned to think of her mother as "Bush" and to be ashamed of her. Unlike Peter, Michelle has learned to articulate rather than ignore some (not all) of her hurts and she has rejected a leadership role. She even finds being a corporal, in charge of training Constable James Harper, very difficult. Peter, however, is a natural mentor, a man who charms his opposition, who loves politics and the power and influence that accompanies it. They are alike in one key aspect: although Michelle chose the RCMP because of its clearly defined command structure and rules, like Peter, she regularly uses her own judgment and sometimes bends the rules.

*Teevee*

Teevee (Dakota House) becomes a major character in the series but begins as a high-school dropout whose ideas about the south, places like Vancouver and Edmonton, have been formed almost entirely by watching television.[14] When he runs away, a brief encounter with skid row in Vancouver does not substantially change him, and Teevee continues to yearn for an apparently exciting and certainly materially richer life. He often spars with Eric, who tries to reach out to him. But it is Peter who gives him opportunities, first helping him get a job as a counsellor in an after-school program, later helping him with applications for training as a band manager. Teevee then gets a grant to help finance his partnership with Gerry in a small logging business, and eventually, in the last season, he manages the paperwork as a chief with a little help from Peter's knowledge about how Yellowknife and the Department of Indian Affairs work. In episode 57, "Revolving Door," by Stacy Kaser, Teevee drops in on Bertha and assumes the right to take his daughter, Kyla, out whenever he chooses, even when he does not provide reliable financial and emotional support. The issue here is a father's responsibilities and his rights to access. Bertha suggests that he take Kyla every other day. But the next time that Bertha comes to pick her up at Elsie's, Elsie tells Bertha that Teevee has taken her to Wolverine Lake, perhaps overnight. Angrily Bertha protests. Elsie: "Teevee is her father." Bertha: "So where is his father? Where is everybody's father?" Elsie, imperturbably: "Teevee is here." When he gets into trouble and lands in jail, Elsie brings his daughter to him because, as she says with a touch of irony, he now has time for her. His character is a nexus for a variety of issues. He suffers from having had a mother who has been abused and from the lack of job opportunities; he is tempted to make easy money selling booze; he gets into fights and commits petty crimes; and he feels pressure from the various factions in the band.

How the next generation will find work is a major concern in the series. The character of Teevee provides variations on this motif. He makes obvious mistakes, due both to his circumstances and inexperience and to his own impatient, often self-centred temperament. Early on, he does run booze but finds the courage to testify against his accomplices and does not flee to a "nothing" job elsewhere. When he works in a mine, he makes good money but ends up as a supervisor, pulling a scam on the striking workers. He is an attractive young male, yet so

Teevee Tenia (Dakota House) is not such a tough guy with his grandmother (*ehtsu*), Elsie Tsa Che (Wilma Pelly), who is an excellent craftswoman and a healer. *Alberta Filmworks, in association with the CBC, distributed by Alliance Atlantis.*

irresponsible that Bertha, after living with him, decides she no longer loves him. In the last season, he hits her and she leaves Lynx River with the baby, refusing to speak to him on the telephone, even when he gets into a confrontation on a barricade that involves guns and is rapidly getting out of hand. Yet he observes the devious tactics of both Albert and Peter and learns how the world of politics – tribal and national – works. Eventually, on his own initiative but with help, he creates a new opportunity for himself with a portable sawmill. With the exception of one jealous outburst, which lands him in jail, things go well and he starts to straighten out. Clearly regular work and responsibility make a difference. Around him are role models to choose from: Joe Gomba, the hunter/elder; Peter, a chief with an MBA; Michelle, a woman Mountie and a recovering alcoholic who is constantly on his case; his traditional grandmother, Elsie; and Albert, the sometime chief whose tactics would shame Machiavelli. Over six seasons and in the television movies, it is apparent that Teevee learns from all of them.

*Albert Golo*

Albert (Gordon Tootoosis) is the series' chief antagonist. Michelle, in episode 44 ("Bargains"), talks about how Albert leans on many people: "What kills me about Albert is not what he does. It's what he makes you do to yourself" – a nice irony in view of the later movie *Dream Storm*, where the spirit of Albert compels Michelle to find and heal herself and her community. Tootoosis is an actor who can take focus if he wishes by simply standing still. He is perhaps the most charismatic actor in the series, and he is further assisted by the directors, who enhance his impact. Even within an individual episode, he tends to appear suddenly in a shot, which makes him even more mysterious. He is associated with the wolverine in the dialogue several times. Wolverine has magical powers to travel "because he folds the land and takes one step for your hundred" (Blondin 1997, 107), which may be the context for Albert's sudden appearances and disappearances and for his survival in the bush despite being shot by his son.

Albert reverses the usual sexual stereotype by using white/native sex as a trap for others. A neglected fifteen-year-old Dene girl, Brenda Shore, is set up by Albert's young confederate, William, to seduce Corporal Brian Fletcher so that Albert can blackmail him. It works. Fletcher's eager response to Brenda's seduction (she is drunk at the time) makes him vulnerable to Albert's plots. More to the point, Brenda is underage and both men ruthlessly exploit of her. Fletcher's sex with her is adulterous, impulsive, unprofessional, and illegal. And it touches on a raw nerve, historically, since it demonstrates that a Dene woman can still be a mere "squaw" to an RCMP corporal, severely damaging Brenda's sense of worth. Then Albert forces Brenda to leave town. (Even after she returns from a rehab centre, she still does not fit into the community – she is another of Albert's casualties.) Albert is ruthless, seeing lives that were ruined as a consequence of his bootlegging as actually the fault of others. He tries to make sure that a boy with AIDS who sought refuge in Lynx River is forced to leave because, as he tells Sarah, he is a sick and therefore weak person. Albert has an odd friendship with a rebellious and hard-drinking artist. He is contemptuous of his three inept sons, yet will fight for them. He is tender with his small daughter. His most dangerous enemy is Joe Gomba. In season 1, as the best shot in Lynx River, Joe carefully shoots Albert in the shoulder to complete the town's sentence of exile. (Exile, in this case for illegally selling alcohol to a man who then froze to death, is again acceptable within the legal system in the North, while

A watchful Albert Golo (Gordon Tootoosis), Michele's ongoing antagonist, temporarily works with her in a few episodes when their interests coincide. *Alberta Filmworks, in association with the CBC, distributed by Alliance Atlantis.*

shooting a person is not.) Only Joe could be sure that the shot would not permanently disable Albert, but he is never charged with the "crime." By the same ancient code, it follows that Albert would later have no compunction about leaving Joe to die in the bush when he comes across him with a broken leg. Their rivalry is not resolved until the final episode.

To Albert, no white laws are legitimate, and so he enjoys breaking or circumventing them. He is devious, astute, acidly mocking when the town turns against him, and he believes in the old necessary virtues on which a hunter's strength and skill depend. As early as episode 4, "Fair Trade," he defends Dene tradition by taking hostage the bones of a long-dead white hunter the children have found, because "I was looking through that glass at the bodies of my grandparents ... their cycle of life is not complete." But he can also joke with Michelle, who is searching for the bones: "I hear you have an osteological problem." And when she looks a trifle stunned, he says with a grin, "Reader's Digest Word Power." In the end, the hunter's bones are returned and buried by the band at the widow's request. Not unexpectedly, Albert shows great courage on several occasions, when first Charlie (Michelle's young adopted son), then Rosie (an excellent shot), and finally Joe confront him when he is unarmed. He values some of the same things Michelle does. As he says in the last episode, she is more like him than she will admit. That link is demonstrated very powerfully when, after his death, he chooses to visit her in *Dream Storm* to help her discover that the source of the illness of the children of Lynx River lies in the erosion of the Dene traditions – an erosion symbolized very practically by a neglected dump left behind by the Americans who passed through during the war on Dene land (which Teevee and Bertha clean up as the credits roll) and also by the temptation offered by foreign interests to trade the band's water rights for money just to keep the profligate South from thirst (an offer ultimately rejected by the community).

## Sarah Birkett

Tracey Cook, who played Sarah, made her character's evolution credible in sometimes difficult circumstances. *Northern Nurses: True Nursing Adventures from Canada's North* (Scott 2002) is a collection of anecdotes about nursing in remote locations across Canada. It reminds us that, along with the bush pilot and the Mountie, there is the Canadian archetype of the caring outpost nurse who improvises on diagnoses and treatment in emergencies when doctors are far away. This stereotype of the selfless heroine, who sacrifices comfort and even safety to serve the tiny communities on reserves and in the Arctic, satisfies the longing of girls and women in the south for heroic women to read about. Such women do exist, although the stereotype is also part of the larger twentieth-century narrative of whites providing help to the helpless among the First Nations and Inuit. Like all stereotypes, there is a kernel of lived experience within the situation and character, as this book demonstrates. The character of Sarah Birkett consciously breaks the stereotype of northern nurse. She does have to cope with emergencies when the medevac is unavailable, and she does try to teach modern health practices. But she lives in some comfort at the nursing station, and when she learns that Elsie is a good midwife, she respects her as a healer of a different sort. Sarah has an affair with Eric and has two children by two different Dene fathers (contrast this with the nurse of popular novels – Cherry Ames comes to mind, dressed in white and definitely virginal),[15] and she has a nervous breakdown (nurses are supposed to be reliable, fountains of sturdy common sense). She manages to create a strong, though sometimes strained, friendship with Michelle. Language barriers often prevented such friendships in earlier times, and cultural barriers remain. Sarah had begun the series as

Sarah and Albert. Albert's cabin is in the background, on a hill across the river. *Alberta Filmworks, in association with the* CBC, *distributed by Alliance Atlantis.*

the emotionally brittle professional who is not really connected to the community, but she soon becomes Eric's lover, invoking a different stereotype from Harlequin romances. Yet, even as he seeks in her a permanent replacement for his divorced wife, she withdraws, afraid of commitment. Eventually they part. Then she makes a serious medical mistake and has a breakdown. Ironically, after spending time in a hospital, she discovers that she is only able to complete her recovery in Lynx River, even though it is clear that the culture clash and her subsequent sense of isolation were partly to blame for her mental distress.

For a long while Sarah refuses categorically to practise nursing again. The responsibility of being the only person who can treat sickness has overwhelmed her. When she does start to take an interest in the rehab centre, she is rejected as a counsellor because she is white. Nevertheless, when she manages to make friends with a particularly difficult client, Betty Moses grudgingly accepts her. She is effective as a counsellor at the treatment centre partly because she has hit rock bottom and partly because, like the clients, she is still not altogether "sane" and so functions as a truth teller to the clients as well as to the community. By this time the remaining traces of her upper-middle-class background have largely vanished.

Much more complex is her relationship with Albert Golo. Drew Hayden Taylor's unnamed academic (in *Funny You Don't Look Like One* [1996]) called her "a defective icon" (80) and found the scripts in which she was "given" to Albert highly problematic, a reading I find somewhat sexist given the complexities of the relationship. During her nervous breakdown and her wanderings, Albert, the older alpha male, takes care of her and lets her move in with him. Theirs is a love-hate relationship in which he expects to control her and she comes to distrust and rebel against him. Unexpectedly, he shows real tenderness towards her. She returns his love but requires emotional support in more ways than Albert, or perhaps the traditional ways of his culture, can provide. For no clear reason, he refuses to be present when she has her baby, although to the last moment she expects him to be there. Yet he is worried when she acquires some financial independence.

In episode 45, "Breakdance," Sarah finds Albert's cache of booze and confronts him. Albert says, "I found you, took care of you. If you wanted 'nice,' you should have had a curly headed white boy." On whether she will stay or go, he says to another character, "She should stay here for reasons of her own ... then I'll know." But later, after they reconcile, he says, "I don't care about much, but I care about you." Yet they continually test one another. Finally, when the community suspects him of having murdered Rosie's father twenty years before, Sarah, too, believes he is capable of it – which he clearly is. At the end of the episode, she asks him if he did commit the murder, refusing to trust him unless he denies it, which he refuses to do. He leaves her and their child again, this time for good, and starts a campaign to get control of their baby, Elizabeth. Still, he continues to send her money orders for the baby, thus making Sarah what she wryly calls "a kept woman." However, in a climactic episode, 76, "Hunting in the Dark," Albert, in a rage, returns to their cabin intending to shoot her as well as the baby, but his son Nathan's shot reaches him first. As he falls back, Sarah and Nathan flee. The cabin burns down, but no body is found. Inevitably, Albert turns up again later.

Albert and Sarah, now lovers; Michelle in full uniform;
and Peter, on the porch of the Lynx River Community Hall.
*Alberta Filmworks, in association with the* CBC, *distributed by*
*Alliance Atlantis.*

Sarah's sense of humour in later seasons makes her far more attractive as a
character. Nevertheless, she never quite belongs. In episode 54, "Revolving
Door," she discovers that her job at the treatment centre is to be sacrificed so
that there will be money for a well-qualified Arapaho therapist, Andrew One
Sky. In the end she functions as the community nurse, although she refuses to
live in the clinic. Albert in later episodes makes only occasional appearances
in her life, often with little explanation. However, in the last season and in the
first movie, Sarah finds a new partner in Martin, a white foreman in an oil
rig. By the end of the series, Sarah has learned not only to stand up to Albert,
but also to acknowledge her affection for him, look after him in her role as
nurse when he comes into the clinic, and keep his last secret.

*Elsie Tse Cha*

Elsie Tse Cha, played by Wilma Pelly, is Teevee's grandmother and a
shrewd old lady. She tries to get her own way, usually by indirect means,

and often succeeds. Very occasionally she sends Teevee on expeditions – without explanation – that turn out to be life changing. Elsie never went to residential school because when they came for her, she was out fishing with her father. When Peter tries to get a teaching job for Sylvie LeBret (with whom he had a brief affair),[16] Elsie opposes this because she hopes that he will be reunited with his wife, Ellen. Her ostensible reason is that Sylvie does not speak Slavey (this is because Sylvie's mother, conditioned by residential school, had been beaten whenever she tried to use the language), which is a reasonable objection. By threatening to leave town, Peter gets his way, however.

Elsie is an elder who is resistant to change. She has a picture of the pope and a statue of the Virgin Mary in her house,[17] she gathers plants in the bush for medicines, she knows and participates in the ceremonies and customs of her people, and she is a midwife. Yet she eventually welcomes Harris as a son-in-law, because he is good to Lois and has a steady job. She knows how things should be done and freely points out to others when they do wrong. When she is worried about Harris and Lois leaving her on her own, she makes jam in the middle of the night. When Harris reassures her that they will stay, however, she sets the rules – Harris must be a good Catholic, live in her house as extended family, and think about having babies. Babies, to her, are a panacea for many things; for example, she thinks having Sarah and her new baby live with her will help Michelle get over her grief about Hannah's death, a solution Michelle rejects out of hand. Elsie is the only one who with a word can make the young and angry Teevee stop and think. When this happens, he often calls her "Ehtsu,"[18] a term of respect. She opposes many innovations, fearing that change will mean that the young people will go away and the old ways will vanish altogether. She also fears that when any young person leaves town, "they will get lost" to drugs, drink, and other hazards of larger, alien towns and cities. Wilma Pelly began by playing her as fairly impassive, though with a twinkle, and almost always slow spoken and deliberate in what she said. As time passed, Pelly became more animated. She did excellent work in *Dream Storm* when Elsie if forced to recognize that in old her age her memory is going; she has forgotten how to help the sick children. Yet in the end she teaches Teevee how to build a sweat lodge so that he can rediscover the visions she has not been granted. Teevee meets Michelle with her spirit guide Albert, and together they learn what must be learned. Given the reticence of Dene tradition, it is not clear that Elsie ever knows what happened. Yet she is comforted by the fact that her grandson has come back with new wisdom.

Elsie (Wilma Pelly) sits by the river and prays to the creator. *Alberta Filmworks, in association with the CBC, distributed by Alliance Atlantis.*

## Joe Gomba

George Blondin (1997) points to at least two attributes of Joe Gomba. Not only is he the best hunter, he is also an elder with his own power. People with caribou power say that "the herd meets with their leader ... checking on the attitudes human beings have toward them in the areas they are going to pass through. Sometimes they avoid areas where people who failed to show them proper respect are living" (123). In pre-contact times, every part of the caribou supplied all of the needs of the Dene. Caribou remain central to the people's sense of themselves. Michelle tells Eric that Joe put his foot on the head of a caribou he had killed instead of thanking the animal for giving itself to him. For many years no one in Lynx River has been able to find one – Joe's error has hurt the whole community. Yet

Joe's wisdom and his unspecified medicine powers are respected and sought out. Joe recognizes Leon's struggle to stay sober, for example, and tells him to start making a drum with the wood Joe has given him because the process will make him better. With the passage of time, he makes friends with outsiders like Eric and Sarah, helping Eric to understand Dene ways and protecting Sarah from Albert (without ever saying so) by letting her live near him. Although his health deteriorates as he ages (bad knees, bad leg, diabetes), he stubbornly lives on his own and refuses a diabetic diet. His sense of humour is very dry, and he leaves much unspoken. He is perhaps the only completely confident human being in the series.

### Michelle's Three RCMP Partners

Television series often reflect basic changes in societal attitudes, for they supply a safe space where various viewpoints can contend. By the 1990s, First Nations were higher on the political agenda than they had been previously. By the second season of *North of 60*, Eric Olssen has learned that he cannot keep the peace without the help of Michelle, who understands the ways of Lynx River. Every episode in the first two seasons explores one more cultural dissonance, one more lesson Eric learns. Over a sustained period of time, then, the strategy of using a surrogate white character not only kept the audience in a sympathetic frame of mind, it also worked to familiarize the audience with some of the basic beliefs and values of this particular band. Eric's successor, Brian Fletcher, had more experience in the North to start with but refuses to learn what the North could teach him. The third, James Harper, the "urban Indian," is almost as ill at ease as Eric, because he does not want to be in the remote bush of Lynx River. Slowly, he does learn about policing a small Dene community in the North, but he never truly integrates into the community.

### Eric Olssen

Eric Olssen, played by John Oliver (now using the professional name John Bean), gives the role a solid, straightforward interpretation. He is a favourite of the fans on the fan list, who see him as both ruggedly handsome and sensitive. Eric is a tough but decent guy, unexpectedly open to discoveries about the North and Lynx River. A veteran undercover narcotics agent in Vancouver who insisted on a transfer in order to get away from his alienated wife and children and his lost sense of self, he actually

Michelle mourns Eric's death. His ex-wife has claimed his body but his memorial cross is set on the hill overlooking Lynx River. *Alberta Filmworks, in association with the CBC, distributed by Alliance Atlantis.*

wants to be in Lynx River. Early on, he tries to apply a big-city solution to the conflicts among the male teens, setting up a boxing match, which means individualistic hand-to-hand fighting. Michelle tells him, acidly, that this is not a part of Dene culture. In fact, her initial reaction to Eric and to those who preceded him is dismissive: "You guys always leave." But after a rocky start, Eric learns to compromise. In episode 32, "The Getting of Wisdom," by Grigsby and Samuels (the last episode of the 1993–94 season and Oliver's last appearance on the show), he confronts Andy's now blatant racism. Andy, a reluctant visitor, spouts ideas that he has picked up from his mother and his stepfather. He insists on using the sheets he has brought, telling Michelle, "[M]y mother says that Indians have lice," and later, when his younger sister has been happily playing with the local kids, he tells her, "[Y]ou know, they give you stuff, they get drunk, they do drugs and they smell" – attitudes picked up from "you, Bill, Mom, everybody." Confronting that truth, Eric tells Andy that what he thought back in Vancouver was wrong. The narrative strategy is interesting. A pre-pubescent boy names many of the classic stereotypes, but only after the two preceding seasons have fully disarmed the viewers.

At the end of the second season, Eric says he is thinking about requesting a transfer so that he can be closer to his children – this could be seen as an acceptable way to write him out of the series but one that could allow his return. However, at the beginning of the third season, the writers seem to have changed their minds. The viewers are told that Eric was killed in Vancouver while on leave and out of uniform when he tried to stop a knife fight. This account makes it impossible for the actor to return to the series but also gives the character a hero's death. In episode 34, "The Long Good-bye," Michelle and Sarah both mourn him, Teevee reacts with anger to cover his sense of loss, and Leon makes a wooden cross for him. Trying to decide on an epitaph, he settles on one that expresses an insider's judgment of someone who could never belong but who has tried: "He was better than most." Most cops? Most white men? The ambiguity fits. Eric was forever the outsider but he is missed, a wry but honest balance for writer Hart Hanson and the producers to strike. Then the community kills a moose and has a feast in his honour. After prayers, a plate is set aside for his spirit. The last scene of this episode is rather contrived. Sarah and Michelle both look at Leon's cross, which Michelle had planted on the hillside (not in the cemetery) even though Eric's wife has decided he will not be buried in Lynx River. Sarah's "He's here with us" simply sounds too pat. The previous wordless scene was much more effective, a metonym for Eric's place in the community. Eric had often brought chocolate chip cookies to Joe's camp when he visited. Joe, alone, pours two cups of coffee and puts one on the stump where Eric used to sit; he picks up the bag of cookies, pauses, puts one cookie on the fire as a silent offering, dips the other in the coffee, and eats it.

### Brian Fletcher

Fletcher is Michelle's second partner. He appears in part of the third season, all of the fourth, and most of the fifth, that is, in episodes 38–74. Robert Bockstael played Brian Fletcher's complexity and contradictions with considerable intensity. He often infused what could have been a rather one-dimensional, heavy-handed role with some subtextual vulnerability. Unlike Olssen, Fletcher has had experience in the North, yet from the very beginning, he is something of a bully, particularly around the younger men. When his wife, Rosemary, joins him, despite their efforts his relationship with her very quickly becomes strained. He is not interested in the values and customs of Lynx River, treating Michelle first with condescension and eventually with open hostility. He is often

A desperate and paranoid Brian Fletcher is on the hunt for Albert, who has been blackmailing him. *Alberta Filmworks, in association with the CBC, distributed by Alliance Atlantis.*

abrupt, and he is very aware of being an outsider; he was probably born an outsider and a loner. In episode 66, "Bushman," Brenda has sex with him, and immediately afterwards, even before he has finished dressing, he is already writing a script for her to explain where she has been. He tries frantically to cover up traces of her presence in his vehicle, then lies unconvincingly to Michelle. When Brenda attempts to persuade him that he "did it" because he liked her, he tries to convince her that her memory is actually a delusion, a flashback from dropping acid. In that scene, typically, he both kisses and threatens her. When he muses, "If I was single and 20 years younger," she is instinctively repelled. Others have committed adultery on the show but his is an act of lust.

Fletcher serves chiefly as a foil for Michelle, who has now clearly become the show's the protagonist. After Brenda leaves Lynx River, Michelle begins to gather evidence against him because he is clearly failing to prosecute either Albert or his allies. Although he manages to steal the notebook in which she keeps evidence of his growing corruption, he is still paranoid. Michelle's growing distrust and dislike of him add to his disintegration. His paranoia, anger, and fear make it obvious that he had begun to unravel into insanity well before his "suicide" (apparently by drowning, although no body is found). Michelle takes more than her share of responsibility and guilt for this outcome, specifically over her inability to help him. However, in the first TV movie, *In the Blue Ground*, Fletcher reappears as a sort of mad trapper/vengeful sadist who kidnaps Sarah but is really seeking revenge on Michelle. The plot is overly melodramatic, but the psychological portraits remain reasonably convincing. At the end of the movie, he forces Michelle to shoot him, a form of revenge that ensures that she will live with his death for a long time.

*James Harper*

Harper, played by Peter Kelly Gaudreault (Huron/francophone/Miskika/Spanish), enters the series in the last episode of season 5. As the privileged and sophisticated son of a Cree senator, he thinks he should have been promoted to corporal by now. He cannot deal with Michelle as his superior – she is a woman and a "bush Indian" (not that he ever admits to such a sexist/racist attitude). Handsome, graceful, and very earnest, he is nevertheless disrespectful to the elders and impatient. He is good with computers, as his detection of Albert's tax fraud demonstrates in the last episode of the series. Like many characters in *North of 60*, he carries a burden of guilt, in one instance for not covering Michelle when she is shot and then panicking. In the movie *In the Blue Ground*, having fallen into a hunter's noose, he is late on the scene for Fletcher's capture. Fletcher then tricks him into coming too close, so that Fletcher can get his weapon, get free, and force a last confrontation with Michelle. Harper learns to back her up in the movie *Trial by Fire*, in which they become a little closer. But he is completely shut out of what really happens in *Dream Storm*, baffled that he could not find Michelle after having searched "six times" the place where she is found sound asleep on the ground. He cannot penetrate Joe's opaque answer to his question "[D]id you kill him [Albert]?" "I buried him," Joe replies. He does not understand what Michelle means when she tells Peter, without elaboration, that she was "visiting" – in this case her ancestors of a hundred years ago –

although Peter understands quite well. Like Sarah, he never knows that the children's sickness was spiritual. He may or may not take lessons learned at Lynx River into his later career, but he clearly belongs back in the city.

## Rosie, Gerry, and Harris

Rosie De'ela (played by Teena Bomberry) is another major recurring character, an important foil for Michelle and her loyal friend. She never left Lynx River after returning from residential school. Like Michelle, she has basically conquered a drinking problem, although she lapses once or twice. Bigger than the stocky little Leon, the father of her three children (whom she agrees to marry at the end of the first season because he has stayed dry for some months), Rosie is a motherly, humorous, outspoken, feisty woman (she heaves rocks at the boy with AIDS, who seems to her to threaten her children). Later, with the band's help, she seizes the chance to force Gerry to take her on as a partner in the coffee shop/store, and she does a very good job. She is an excellent shot and is sorely tempted to shoot an unarmed Albert because she thinks he murdered her father years before. She is faithful to the long-absent Leon and desperately hurt when he strays. She sometimes lets Gerry act as a father to her children but is not tempted by his evident longing for her – and her family. She is a band council member and is eventually appointed by the band to the board of the oil company.

Gerry Kisilenko (played by Lubomir Mykytiuk) never really fits into Lynx River. As owner of the only store, he has economic power, but he is regularly in open conflict with Peter and other band members. Rosie's application for a government loan to become his partner changes his relationship with her and to a lesser degree with the town. His bachelor pal Harris marries Lois Tenia. Finally, when in Leon's absence Gerry starts to act as a father to Rosie's children, he slowly falls in love with her. Rosie does not acknowledge his love but finds a way to remain kind. As the permanent outsider, he gives the series a touch of bitters with his comments. The viewer is not given his back story until the last episode.[19]

Harris (played by Timothy Webber) is an ambivalent character, good at his job as band manager, manipulative of the band and counsel within limits, an excellent fly fisherman, seldom seen outside of town. He is loving with Lois but afraid of taking on responsibility. He is at odds with Teevee until shortly before his marriage to Lois. He often makes tartly sardonic and sometimes funny comments about the band's politics, the relationships among the Dene, Sarah's expectations, Teevee's machinations, Albert as chief, and Peter as chief. As the series progresses, he is

Rosie De'ela (Tina Louise Bomberry), Michelle's independent, feisty, loyal friend. *Alberta Filmworks, in association with the CBC, distributed by Alliance Atlantis.*

less out for the main chance, less manipulative. As with Sarah, he can never be part of the Dene community but his child will be.

### Others

Nathan Golo (played by Michael P. Obey) is Albert Golo's son. Although he has a recurring role in every season and appears in the first two movies, he never becomes a well-rounded character. He is characterized as immature, not very bright, terrified of his father, violent when frightened, sometimes a bully. With his brothers, he even manages to screw up a marijuana "farm" by turning up the growing lights to the point where the plants shrivel. In "Limbo," episode 52, he is banished to a cabin for a year because he has committed crimes against the community. Michelle wants to see him in jail but agrees not to oppose the community's sentencing circle, which chooses exile instead, a sentence that is also Albert's preference. Although Nathan is expected to live without human contact, various people in the town bring him supplies. Nevertheless, the isolation of the wilderness slowly drives him mad. Eventually, braving Nathan's wild words about his being a wolverine and his threat to shoot his father, Albert climbs the roof and coaxes him down. Nathan is accepted back into the community. Sarah will not, however, let him father the child they conceive, since she knows, as does everyone else, that he is not ready to be a husband or father – and she has never loved him. In the movies he is drunk and unemployed, or absent. Obey was constrained by the limitations of the role and was not the most expressive actor on set, but he managed a key scene between Nathan and his father in the last episode of the series with real grace.

William (played by Nathaniel Arcand) is Albert's protégé and likely successor – smart, ruthless, inventive, and defiant. He finds weak spots very easily, as Albert does. At one point he manages to provoke Michelle into beating him unconscious. At times he seems to have feelings for Brenda but never stands up for her to Albert. Once, he tries to take on Albert, who pulls him back into line very quickly. His storyline ends with the series, but the viewer will assume that he will take over Albert's bootlegging and other scams after Albert's death.

Of the guest characters, Betty Moses (Tantoo Cardinal) is the most memorable. She is the antithesis of Elsie, a politicized, experienced, driven counsellor of alcoholics who had to quell her own demons first. Michelle is one of her early successes, and they have a close bond that is tested to the limit when Michelle loses Hannah. Betty is matter-of-fact, abrasive, sometimes ruthless, a heavy smoker, sardonic, and utterly convinced of her cause – in other words, a powerful yet oddly rootless woman. Her Indians are every Indian in the Northwest Territories, on- and off-reserve, and in her role as director of rehabilitation clinics in the territory, she shows a sense of the culture that seems to be pan-Indian as well. She blows into town, gets the rehab centre going, leaves, but reappears every once in while.

The success of *North of 60* came primarily from the range of characters in the series and their development over six years. Good writing was the spine of the series, together with skilled story editing. Good performances gave the characters flesh. Directors, ranging from workmanlike to excellent, along with the editors, gave the episodes their shape. Imaginative art

direction anchored the series in a believable reality while adding information about the characters and their world. After taking a closer look at some
of the episodes in chapter 13, we shall see in chapter 14 that the other crucial element in the success of the series was its exploration not only of the
issues facing the Dene and other First Nations in the 1990s, but also of more
universal themes more familiar to the audience. The blend ensured the
longer than usual run of this unusual series.

*An interview with Glenn Warren, a Mountie who has lived in the Northwest Ter-
ritories and the Arctic much of his life, is posted at www.brocku.ca/hri/associates/
miller/outside_looking_in.pdf. His is a unique take on* North of 60. *Other northerners also express an opinion on the site.*

# THIRTEEN

# Focusing on a Selection of *North of 60* Episodes

Peter (to Michelle, on whether Eric is allowed to remain in Lynx River): "You do the work. You've always done the work."
Michelle: "I've heard this speech."

As we have seen, various kinds of stories are a vital element of First Nation cultures. Although Lynx River is portrayed as a village with strong traditional roots, storytelling and allusions to stories are a rather thin thread in the weave of life there – compared to *Spirit Bay*, for example. Storytelling does appear in Thomas King's episodes and occasionally in Jordan Wheeler's but rarely elsewhere. A television series cannot provide the texture of stories told by mothers to children, hunters to young men, elders to the community. But television tells its own stories. The episodes below were chosen because they were important to the development of the characters, because they illustrated an issue particularly well, or because I thought they were particularly good. That does not mean that every one of them outshines all the others – there are many more good episodes than bad in the series, far more than I have room for here. The makers of the series identified the trilogy of episodes that focus on Hannah's death as a key turning point, and so I have included them. I have also looked at all the episodes by Thomas King (Cherokee/Greek) and a selection of those by Jordan Wheeler (Metis). Because Drew Hayden Taylor (Ojibway) thought his single episode was heavily rewritten and thus doesn't really consider it his own, I did not include it here. Since the ones written by King and Wheeler are the only episodes that were written from the "inside" and that therefore arguably have a claim to a kind of authenticity the others cannot have, I begin with them.

## TRAPPED

Thomas King wrote episode 29, "Trapped," directed by Stacy Stewart Curtis, towards the end of the second season, well before the two others he wrote for the series (episode 42, "The Ties That Bind," and episode 71, "Simple Sufferings"). The focus of "Trapped" is the anti-fur protest. An organization called Animals First has found out about a proposed tannery that will prepare the trappers' furs for the Italian fashion industry and thus provide jobs for several people. The issue is still a sensitive one in the North, where prices for fur and therefore livelihoods crashed in the cumulative backlash of 1970s publicity about the clubbing of baby seals. It is an ongoing battle.[1] Two activists, Tim and Kate, have flown in to persuade the people of Lynx River of their misguided ways (and to gather evidence of cruel practices), suggesting ecotourism as a substitute. Peter responds: "So we can be guides for nice white tourists." On the whole, the script is balanced between the economic ramifications of falling fur prices as a result of such campaigns and the cold facts about what happens when animals are trapped for their fur. Some of the resistance is comic. Since Gerry owns 25 per cent of the tannery (and is seen reading the aboriginal monthly newspaper *Windspeaker* – a nice touch), he won't give Tim and Kate a room. Rosie gives them a choice of chops, liver, or bacon, throws out the peas, and refuses them salad. Sarah walks in wearing her old racoon coat. Teevee's anger over the campaign strikes Joey Smallboat as funny, since Teevee has never trapped in his life, but Teevee retorts: "It doesn't bother you that some woman comes up here from the south and tells us what to do?" The rest of the community greet the two outsiders in the coffee shop with dead quiet. Peter, though, is unhappy with the tactics; savvy in the ways of the media, he realizes that to make the activists truly uncomfortable is to give them a story. Meanwhile Kate, who is the more experienced activist as well as the more fanatical, has been talking with unconscious condescension about the fact that "this old guy with this incredible face [Joe Gomba] actually agreed with me." Nevertheless, although she calls the fur industry the "vanity trade,"[2] she at least acknowledges that the issue for Lynx River is jobs. Someone says, slamming the door in her face, "I know you. I have been watching you come and go for 300 years." The series has reiterated, and will continue to do so through the final season, that the Dene believe that animals, in return for respect, give their lives so that the hunter can live. In this context, Joe Gomba's point of view that he is better off since he left the trapline is unexpected. Elsie, however, points out that not everyone can live in a camp with a few necessities. In another scene, Joe explains (for the benefit of southern viewers) the problems presented by the new, more-humane quick-kill traps: they are a pain to set and hard to clean, and sometimes the animal freezes, so the trapper has to bring both the trap and the animal back to camp. Nevertheless, near the end of the episode, it is established that the furs tanned and sold to Milan will not be from leg-hold traps, a major compromise.

Tim, the other half of Animals First, retaliates against the hostility he meets by putting a tape not intended for children in the kids' VCR in the recreation centre that vividly portrays animals suffering in traps. Over Tim's apologies, Michelle orders the two activists out of the building. Teevee, supposedly helping Tim and Kate gather evidence, leads them to a leg-hold trap with a dead marten in it. He laughs, "Gross, eh?" He then springs an empty trap. When Tim steps into a third, well-hidden trap, Teevee laughs again and shrugs: "Is that traditional enough for you?" But the viewer sees in close-up that Tim's foot is cut and swollen. The tactic works. Tim just wants to go home to Vancouver. Later, Michelle explains traditional fur-trapping practices to her daughter, Hannah, this way: "We live off the land. The land provides animals, like when Joe brings us a moose." She also points out that getting money for fur is no different from raising cows and selling the leather, but she explains that, in the North, the people have a many-faceted relationship with the animals. Even so, Hannah silences Michelle by telling her that she has seen the tape of a lynx caught and strangled in a noose. The argument remains – trapping for food and a livelihood versus fur for fun and fashion. In the end, Kate gives Michelle the tape the two activists had made on the trapline. Peter, later, to Michelle: "Why?" Michelle: "I don't know." And in fact it does seem like a rather pat ending to a plot that otherwise explores a very difficult subject quite well.

## "THE TIES THAT BIND"

"The Ties That Bind," episode 42, by Thomas King, introduces Ben Montour (August Schellenberg, Mohawk), a visiting Mohawk artist from Toronto. In this episode, one of the best in the series, King shows his characteristic sense of humour. There are two major plot elements, one focused on Ben the artist, who is on the run from the police and from himself,[3] and the other on Peter's troubled visions of a lost little boy. The intensity of this episode, with its focus on Peter's spiritual crisis, could be undercut by the interpolation of the secondary Albert-and-Ben plot, but instead it strengthens, by contrast, the themes of responsibility and identity in the primary plot. This episode sets up a recurring character whose story over several episodes raises questions about the role of First Nations artists within their own communities and in the wider world. Ben has a government grant to teach, as well as support, the arts and crafts made in Lynx River, money that is intended to last him until Christmas. His character is a deft twist on the Romantic era's notions of an artist and his demons, and in fact he embodies an idea expressed by Gerald McMaster in "Borderzones" (1995), that artists, particularly aboriginal artists, live as initiates, liminally, "where the experience is one of separation or detachment from the social structure, the cultural conditions or both ... [Citing bell hooks, the space occupied] is a created space"[4] within the culture of domination. Ben Montour is a tragicomic figure. Early on, the viewer is surprised to discover that he is also an old friend of Albert's, Lynx River's current chief. Perhaps unexpectedly, Albert acts as a friend to Ben, refusing to get him any booze or to tell him where to get some. Albert also makes it clear that Ben is welcome to stay in town despite the fact that there are what he sees as "Mickey Mouse" warrants out for his arrest. Ben, in turn, kids Albert about his election: "What did you promise them? Why did they elect you? Free snowmobiles? Self-rule?" Yet when Michelle eventually confronts Ben, Albert withdraws, saying: "You do what you want. I can't protect you. You work it out with the cop." Ben does manage to get liquor from Teevee – at $140 a bottle – and he asks Teevee how "a guy gets laid around here." But his pain has roots in more than booze and loneliness. Later he reveals that his famous brother, also an artist, committed suicide, even though his artwork had become well known and appears on a stamp – an echo perhaps of what happened to Ojibway artist Benjamin Chee Chee.[5] Ben concludes, sardonically, that "the world loves a good suicide," turning the camera's eye back out on the audience.

In another scene, Ben is unable to pay his bill at the store because all his credit cards have been cancelled. He scrawls a drawing of Michelle on a napkin, saying to Gerry, "You know ... it doesn't matter what I make or do. All that matters is my signature." Then (the script echoes here a period in Norval Morriseau's life) he tells Rosie that she can get two hundred bucks for the napkin.[6] Being an artist is not a saving grace but a curse to this man, but his visit touches on a larger question – What is "art" when it is seen by some as the only way for people in remote First Nations and Inuit communities to make money? Montour is cynical about the value of his art and about his own value as a human being. He plays the artist as doomed hell-raiser yet also feels compelled to make art that is rooted in his own Mohawk experience. The scene showing the reception the town gives Ben combines low comedy with humiliation. Snowshoes, note cards, carvings, and beadwork are displayed beneath a homemade banner reading, WELCOME. Ben, clearly drunk, calls some of the items works of genius and trashes others, apparently at random, alienating the town and reneging on the promise he made to the granting agency to upgrade the arts in the community. The stereotype of the tormented artist as buffoon is leavened by the biting humour – and the pratfalls. Ben runs away from both the reception and Michelle, who had threatened to arrest him, straight into a lamppost. His excuse to her for his behaviour is "self-defence." "Lock up your daughters. The Indian artist is on the loose," he proclaims and proves it by charming Teevee's mother, Lois Tenia, into his bed. Yet on another occasion, staggering drunk, he says, "People love to watch the bear dance," an ambivalent phrase with its European connotation of the captive dancing bear and the potential connotation of a ceremonial dance honouring the bear. Both work. Only one implies self-hatred. At other times Ben is fiercely proud as well as ironic. As he says, truthfully, "I'm an agent of chaos." Although it is not wise to go looking for tricksters in every corner, Ben partly functions as one. Lynx River, in the end, learns several valuable lessons from his mistakes, his anarchic and individualistic morality, and his wisdom; the narrative arc culminates in the episode "Life Is a Memory," written by Rob Forsyth, discussed below. If the comments on the two episodes are read together, the reader will see first-hand how two very different writers can together develop a complex character who seems to the viewers a seamless creation.

Elsie, one of the best craftswomen in Lynx River, links the two narrative arcs in "The Ties That Bind." Peter has decided (he thinks) to take a job in Ottawa, but he is not sleeping. Elsie gives him a packet of her bush tea for his insomnia, commenting offhandedly, "Sometimes it works." There is a comic moment when Elsie recaps what is happening on her soap opera at that moment: "The man just found out that his wife was a man, but he'd been his best friend." She goes on to say, "If you leave, Teevee will stay angry. It will make me angry." In another scene Teevee bursts out at Peter: "You and your big job in Ottawa ... going to help all the poor Indians of the North!" Meanwhile, conflict mounts with Ellen, Peter's wife. She confesses to Sarah that after working at the rehab centre she cannot go back to being a chief's wife, "nice, good, patient and solid," never mind to an uncertain job market in Ottawa, away from her community.

The episode had opened with Willy Tsa Che (in the same family as Elsie) seeing, through the muddy window of his truck, a young boy carrying a suitcase on the sunlit road. Then Joe sees the boy, also in daylight (which makes the boy's appearance a waking vision shared by two of the elders). In both cases, and when Peter sees him, the boy's back is turned.

But Peter sees him at four in the morning on a cold and empty road. To the credit of the producers, at no point in this episode is the music obviously eerie or supernatural; nor does it telegraph or pump up emotions. Director Brad Turner uses no special camera work to distinguish the vision from the ordinary world, in marked contrast to the much later and less successful episode 83, "Peter and the Wolf." Peter describes the boy in detail, as nine, maybe ten, a strong kid and big, with a jacket that his mother probably made, a suitcase, and shining shoes. Very distressed that the boy is alone, Peter insists that a search be made: "He's a lost child and he's scared to death!" The viewer soon learns that no one else knows anything about the boy and that because Peter has been going without sleep for a long time, he may be in an altered state of consciousness – a rational explanation for the fact that he has seen the boy, if a viewer wants one. However, when Michelle asks Joe what is going on, Joe replies obliquely, "Remember when our brother died? He didn't leave for a while." In an apparent non-sequitur, Joe then gives Peter a new, adult-size slingshot. Peter recalls that Joe had made him a slingshot when he was a boy, and he asks Joe why he needs one now. Joe points out that he had made the first slingshot for him because Peter had been afraid. Peter, asking no more questions, takes obvious pleasure in aiming and shooting the small weapon.

Thematically, the two plots are linked by Peter's unrecognized crisis over leaving Lynx River and Ben's inability, as he says, to "live in a dry town with no road out." Nevertheless, Ben is seeking a refuge from the outside world, while Peter is weighing what he thinks is the greater good, an important job in Ottawa that will allow him to help the Dene all through the North as well as give him greater responsibility, provide a bigger salary, and increase his reputation. The alternative, as he sees it, is to stay as a band counsellor who is without influence in a town controlled by his enemy, Albert Golo. Eventually, Peter goes to Joe to ask if he has seen the little boy with the suitcase. Joe replies, truthfully, but as so often, ambiguously, "Nobody I haven't seen before," a remark that Peter understands a little better when he asks the right question, "What does he want?" Joe does not directly tell him. Throughout this exchange, there is no eye contact between them, perhaps in this context a sign of Peter's respect.

Later, Ellen wakes in the night to find that Peter has not been to bed. She rouses Michelle, who with Joe mounts a fruitless search. Finally Joe offers Michelle coffee and a cookie, and they wait together. Peter, walking in the early daylight, again sees the boy, who turns and faces him, then runs away. Peter crashes through the bush after him. Their meeting is the

"The Ties That Bind." Peter hunts for and eventually finds himself as a young boy (Mitchell Hourie). *Alberta Filmworks, in association with the CBC, distributed by Alliance Atlantis.*

climax of the episode. As Peter approaches, the boy opens his suitcase, paws through it, and gets out his slingshot. When Peter comes nearer, the boy aims and shoots, cutting Peter badly on the forehead. He grabs the boy, speaking to him in Slavey, the language the boy is using as he struggles to escape. Then Peter blurts out in English, "I am not the Indian Agent. I'm not going to take you away," and his hold turns into an embrace to comfort the terrified boy as he repeats, "I will not take you away." Language, here as elsewhere, is found at the heart of the matter.[7]

Cut to Willy and Michelle waiting in front of Joe's cabin. Peter appears with a slingshot in his hand and a bloody cut on his forehead. Michelle touches it as he eats a cookie. With his mouth full, he says, "I'm okay, I'm okay now. When they came for us I ran into the bush." Between laughter and tears, around another mouthful of cookie, he continues: "I had my slingshot from Joe but ..." Michelle: "... they took it away." Peter: "When we got to the residential school, they burned my slingshot." Peter goes into the cabin. Michelle to Joe: "Now what?" Joe: "Let him sleep." The Dad's chocolate chip cookie made far in the south is real. The wound is real. Therefore, so is the boy. But the meaning of the experience is left to the audience to assess and to Peter to act on. Later, Peter comes out of the cabin to find Ellen sitting there quietly. She touches his face. He says, "I can't go," and they embrace.

In the last scene, Michelle walks straight into Peter's place (no one locks their door in Lynx River). Peter, the elder brother, says to Michelle: "You're the strong one – those speeches they made us do? You always did yours in Dene." Michelle: "They beat me for it." Peter: "I was so angry they let us go." Michelle: "Mom and Dad?" Peter: "Them, the town ..." Michelle points out that they couldn't do anything about it. Peter: "And so I put the town behind me, did my speech in English, [gestures around himself] became this. I don't think, if I left this time, I would ever come back." Ellen touches him while Michelle, in a reaction shot, smiles. Then the camera pulls back to reveal that Peter is carrying two slingshots, one man-sized and one child-sized, as real as the wound on his forehead. He puts them both on his desk. As his son calls, "Daddy," Peter walks out of the frame, replying in Slavey. Thomas King's script and Brad Turner's direction show how complex issues of spirituality and identity can be handled with discretion, as well as with a matter-of-fact kind of humour that makes the story and the sensibility it conveys very persuasive.

## "SIMPLE SUFFERINGS"

Episode 71, "Simple Sufferings" is the third script by Thomas King. As in "The Ties That Bind," King is tackling Dene spirituality, this time as an issue complicated by lapsed Catholicism. Unlike his first script for *North of 60*, this one has a few comic touches. Lois is finding that learning to be a lay minister in the Catholic Church is not so easy. Harris is willing to attend her ordination, but won't promise that he will attend services every Sunday. Under Father Smuts's influence, Lois has also stopped practising birth control, to Harris's dismay. He may finally be married, but he dreads more responsibility. Meanwhile Elsie appears to be talking to herself and is overheard saying, "There's danger here." What the camera sees from Harris's point of view is Elsie nodding to empty space. What the viewer sees is an indistinct spirit figure, brightly backlit, who nods. This is a different camera convention for the depiction of a new element in the traditional belief system. When Elsie tells Lois that "Teevee needs to be careful ... Listen to me," Lois replies that she will ask God for guidance. Elsie replies, forcefully, that Teevee is her son, she should try and help him, and ends her admonition in Slavey before turning back to the house. In another scene Elsie, as she works on something made of birchbark, tells the other women that Lois was never very strong – a fact made evident over the years by both her physical frailty and her self-hatred, which had led to her involvement with a string of abusive men. Elsie warns Teevee, who is trying to figure out how to run his portable sawmill, but he doesn't listen. Yet when Lois asks about her continuing encounters with the spirit figure, Elsie eventually retorts, "No one else is here. You must be crazy. I was praying. You go around town saying I'm crazy. Maybe, you want to get rid of me." It is rare in this series to show real conflict between the church and the traditional beliefs.

Michelle takes a turn trying to find out what is worrying Elsie so deeply. Elsie responds: "Last time they took my son Francis –" Michelle cuts in: "Francis went to Winnipeg –" Elsie presses on: "– and he never came back." Michelle, who has her own conversations with the spirits of the dead, says, "That's who you've been talking to." Elsie very uncharacteristically puts her hand on Michelle's shoulder, pleading with her: "I don't know what to do." Finally Elsie builds a fire by the river, offers tobacco, and once more sees the spirit, who now resembles Teevee. (The viewer wonders if Francis had been Teevee's father.) Elsie and Father Smuts have an unexpectedly amiable encounter around her fire. When she says, "She told you I'm crazy," he replies in a comradely way, "All old people are crazy. We've seen too much."

Despite the spirit's warnings, when Teevee is threatened by William (Albert's not-all-that-tame thug), he insists on delivering the wood he had cut to the man who had signed a contract for it. He is beaten, a cheque is thrown at him, and his wood is taken, vindicating Elsie's vision. But Teevee is not as easily intimidated as he was when he was a kid. Typically, his assertion of self-confidence takes the form of driving Albert's huge Caterpillar tractor right through the wall of William's cabin while William is in it. A satisfying crash is followed by the cabin's near collapse. As the service of ordination for Lois is about to start, Elsie insists that they wait for Teevee. He arrives late and sits down beside her, replacing the fading "spirit Teevee," who had been sitting there. Elsie uncharacteristically caresses his cheek. In the final scene, Teevee remembers that when he had been in bed with strep throat as a child, the star people had talked to him for three days. Elsie explains that they don't always come to take people away: "Sometimes they come to guide and protect us." Teevee replies that he feels they are still watching over him.

### "SPIN DRY"

Jordan Wheeler's episode 39, "Spin Dry," directed by Metis Gil Cardinal (who went on to direct and co-write the 1999 miniseries *Big Bear*), sensitively explores Michelle's attempt to reconnect with Dene traditions, broken by years in residential school. Michelle cherishes the memory of how, when she was thirteen, she and her mother had gone out on the land – the air had smelled of pine – and her mother had given her a very special necklace. She is determined to give the same necklace to Hannah in the same way. Hannah, a teenager, is not keen to go, but she agrees to after her uncle Peter decides to come along. By the end of the episode, Peter has gently forced Michelle to separate the buried facts from her wish/dream. He reminds her that, after the age of ten, she had never returned to Lynx River from residential school, that her Mother had died when she was fifteen, and that he himself had been the one to send the necklace to her at the school. The reality is agonizing for Michelle, but the truth in the end is more important than the comforting illusion that had helped her survive the loss and death of her mother. She then tells Hannah the truth. When she hears about one more way that residential school had scarred her mother, Hannah grows closer to her. While the three of them sit around a campfire, with the air smelling of pine, Hannah receives the gift and the story that has come down through the years – that the necklace was a gift given to her great-great-great-grandmother from the famous explorer Alexander Mackenzie.[8] With this gift given to Hannah out on the land as it should have been given to Michelle, Michelle recovers and adds to the unbroken tradition of generations of her Dene ancestors. Hannah will now remember the gift, the smell of the fire and the pine. She also retells the story to her mother. The oral culture demands that the hearer listen, remember, and at the right time retell the story.[9]

### "A SHOT RANG OUT"

Episode 56, "A Shot Rang Out," also written by Jordan Wheeler and directed by Gil Cardinal, is one of the most ambivalent yet tightly structured episodes in the series. Superficially, it seems to be a murder mystery in the cop show "cold case" mould, but in fact, it uncovers new back stories to the current relationships in Lynx River and proves to be a turning point for Sarah and Albert. Michelle, at a healing lodge to grieve for her daughter, does not appear until late in the episode, and then, for once, she refuses to get involved.[10] Sarah, who believes Albert would have been capable of murdering Rosie's father, Jimmy, twenty-seven years before, as alleged by the dying Freddy Smallboat, asks him if he did commit the murder. She says that she won't be able to trust him unless he denies having done it, which he refuses to do. Albert does supply another version of the events, one that is plausible, but then, apparently sadistically, he tells Rosie that her

"Spin Dry." Michelle gives her daughter Hannah (Selina Hanuse) "a very special necklace." *Alberta Filmworks, in association with the* CBC, *distributed by Alliance Atlantis.*

father had reason to try to kill him all those years ago because Albert had been her mother's lover. In the climax of the episode, Rosie confronts Albert, gun in hand. The repercussions of Albert's demand that Sarah trust him absolutely, despite conflicting evidence, as well as his refusal to flatly deny having committed the murder and her inability to accept that, are felt throughout subsequent episodes.

This episode shows the tangled history of any small town, complicated by family relationships, the values (and opportunities for violence) afforded by a hunting community, and the power of oral history, long memories, and past grudges. It underlines how difficult it can be for Brian Fletcher, the outsider, to do his job. When, inevitably, Rosie hears about Smallboat's allegations, she wants Albert arrested. Brian confronts Albert – there are many reaction shots in close-up of Sarah with the baby as Albert refuses to elaborate on the statement he gave the RCMP at the time. After Brian leaves, Sarah demands an explanation. Albert tells her that Freddy's allegation was the result of a grudge, that he and Freddy had never gotten along. When Sarah, appalled at his dismissal of the accusation, points out that the charge was murder, Albert, laughing fully and openly with admiration, says that Freddy "got the last shot in" and then says no more.

There are other humanizing glimpses of Albert in the episode. He sends his inept sons (but not Nathan) out of the area in case the community's resentment boils over into violence. He recalls that "Freddy and me used to do [the journey on foot] in two days, three if we stopped for a beer." Later, when Sarah complains about the noise he and the boys make, he replies, "The baby should hear laughter and know it's safe." All are attractive glimpses into his character. Given the past seasons' evidence, the viewer knows that Albert is capable of having killed Jimmy but is persuaded, mostly by the subtext of dialogue and performance, that he is unlikely to have done it.

In one of the episode's best scenes, Rosie sits down to tell her children about her father. The scene begins with a close-up of a rifle that she lays carefully on the table. She tells them that there was no better man, especially in a tight spot, than their grandfather. When she was a girl, there had been a grizzly bear that ate a lot of dogs. One day, when Jimmy was teaching Rosie to shoot (Brian comes in at this point), they heard a yelp from a wounded husky who had tangled with the bear. "Dad went to it … I turned, the grizzly was charging toward me, I couldn't move, I couldn't yell, Dad had one shot – in the eye. He did it." Rosie concludes quietly, "He was a good man. He gave the meat away [as a good hunter was expected to do] but he kept the teeth and claws" – and then she shows them the bear-claw necklace that was made from them. When Brian tells her an autopsy on Jimmy has been ordered, she is deeply distressed, since it goes against every Dene cultural norm. Brian, oblivious, tells her, "Let the bones prove it."

The next scene begins with the Tenias recalling that Albert had forced Teevee out of town after he had testified against Nathan and that, as chief, he had forced Leon, who had voted for Peter, to look for work far away. Brian tries to find out what happened from Joe Gomba, who had found the body all those years ago, but Joe points out that the Mounties had decided it was an accident and, further, that a lot of things can kill a man in the bush – a nicely ambiguous answer. In the coffee shop Elsie's contribution to the discussion is observe that "[s]ometimes the dead don't bother to tell us. Have to use our own eyes." With the implication that she thinks Albert may be innocent, she says, "[Albert] may have gone on the trip to get Jimmy but Fred, he got to him first." If Freddy Smallboat is the killer, what happened long ago is even more complicated. Eventually, as the issue continues to simmer, Peter comes to see Albert. Albert: [referring to the hostility between them] "So, you happy?" Peter: "I could be happier. I'm worried for Sarah … I'm not here to fight … You can go anywhere you want, until this is over." Albert, imperturbably: "The cop says stay, the chief says go." Cut to the cemetery. Jimmy's body lies in a shallow grave, the bones are very visible, including the skull. Rosie is clearly devastated, but even here band politics intrude when there is an objection about who is the observer for the band. As the police official describes abrasions, makes other clinical observations, and then bags the bones, Rosie, infuriated, tackles Nathan Golo. There is a fight, broken up by others in the community. With this episode, *North of 60* again presents the dynamics of an isolated community with a history of conflict spanning centuries, a potentially dangerous wilderness environment, and men, women, and teenagers who own guns. Or seen an another way, Lynx River is a community whose members have always hunted and been at home in a wilderness that supplies all their needs, but it is also a place where accidents can happen. Both depictions are true and there lies the mystery – not your average cop show.

In a later scene, Albert reaches for Sarah to comfort her, telling her that he will not tell her the whole story of what happened because he told it twenty-seven years ago and that's enough. Then, typically, he makes the issue a test of loyalty: "You're worried that I did it." Sarah shakes her head: "That they'll send you to prison." When Brian Fletcher asks Elsie about Rosie's mother's affair with Albert, she will only say that Jimmy had thought there was an affair. Brian, frustrated again, resents the fact that Peter has not told him everything, but Peter had been trying to protect Rosie from the rumours of the long-ago affair. In the end, Peter tries to mediate, arranging for Rosie to meet Albert at the band office. Albert: "We need no provocation on either side." Rosie to Peter, refusing to address Albert: "He killed people with booze ... threatened them, drove them out of town. My father was a good man." Albert gets up, crosses the floor to her, and quietly puts in the knife: "If he was so good, why did Mavis [her mother] keep showing up at my door. It wasn't my idea – but I have no regrets." With a grin, he leaves. Later, trying again to get to the truth, Brian goes to Albert's cabin, where Sarah and Albert are playing cribbage by lantern light. He sketches a scenario where there are four men on a hunting party (Frankie, Freddy, Jimmy, and Albert) and asks, "Does Jimmy go for Albert?" Albert replies, "Or the other way around?" By this point, either seems plausible to the audience. Brian leaves, no further ahead. As Albert washes himself in a basin, Sarah, rocking in a rocking chair, tries to get the truth. The juxtaposition of small domestic details with the seriousness of the charge grounds this and the other scenes between them in an emotional truth that works with the theme of the ebb and flow of trust and mistrust.

More complicating facts emerge. Joe tells Brian that Albert had forced the accuser, Freddy, out of business. The autopsy, moreover, is inconclusive. When Brian tells Rosie and Leon that it is possible that Albert is innocent within the law, they storm out of the detachment. Cut to a crowd scene. Rosie De'ela, the Tenias, the Kenidis, and their allies all confront the Golo clan. When Peter tries but fails to stop the confrontation, Albert laughs, this time contemptuously. Punches get thrown, and Brian stops the melee with a shot in the air. Cut to a close-up of Michelle as she gets out of a plane and takes a deep breath. Smiling at Peter, who hugs her, she remarks, with a nice bit of dramatic irony, "The town's so quiet." Later, Albert, who is now in protective custody, and Brian talk about the past. Albert says that he and Freddy Smallboat started a small trucking business in Fort Simpson. Time went on and Freddy was impatient. Albert finally "paid him 300 bucks and he walked. I kept going." Five years later Albert sold the business for $125,000 – "Pissed Freddy off." This account makes Freddy's dying accusation less credible, of course, since he could have nursed a grudge over the years about the money. Albert never tells Sarah about this important detail.

Brian asks Michelle to talk to Rosie, saying, "You know these people better than I do," but Michelle refuses, unable to take up the burden of being the cop, mediator, and mother to the town that she had been before Hannah's death. A medium shot of Albert heading for the river. The sound of a rifle being cocked, off-screen. The shot widens to reveal Rosie pointing the rifle directly at Albert as she says quietly, "Man, it's so easy." In close-up, Albert tenses, swallows, but stands his ground. Cut to a reaction shot of Rosie, very determined but not yet pressing the trigger. Albert says to her, very simply, "Think about it." Rosie, without a word, nearly pulls the trigger, but conflict shows on her face. After what seems like an age, she says, "You're not worth the meat," and turns away. A close-up of Albert taking a big breath. His hands come into view as they unclench. It is a fine performance of the subtext from both actors.

Cut to Sarah playing solitaire. Albert: "It's over." She is very relieved but nevertheless presses him: "Did you do it?" Albert: "It doesn't matter." Sarah, like Albert, turns it into a test: "Your not telling me matters, because I've got to trust you." "You mean you don't?" "Just tell me." "I shouldn't have to," and without another word he moves away from her to pack his clothes. When she asks him when he will be back, he gives her no answer. The scene ends with a close-up of Sarah grieving as he continues to pack. In the last scene, we see Leon putting the finishing touches on the new wooden cross inside the newly fenced grave. Rosie is sobbing: "He deserved better and Albert got away with it." Michelle replies, "We'll never know," and hugs her. She then cautions Rosie, drawing from her own experience, that unresolved grief will make her sick: "Let it go." Rosie continues to sob. A long shot from the hill overlooking the cemetery shows Michelle withdrawing as the family huddles together. The audience, too, will never know the truth. Occasional open and ambiguous endings are one of the major strengths of *North of 60* as a complex television series.

### THE TRILOGY

In mid-series the writers and producers went into deeper waters with a trilogy of episodes ("The Visit," "Take Me Home," and "The Weight"), making more demands on Tina Keeper as an actress and introducing Michael Horse as Andrew One Sky. For many fans this trilogy was the centrepiece of *North of 60*, and certainly it involves one of the most difficult stories to tell effectively. Episode 54 centres on Michelle's hunt for Hannah, who has disappeared from her father's house in Calgary; episode 55, on Michelle's continued hunt and eventual discovery that Hannah is dead; and episode 56, on the aftermath back in Lynx River. Although each episode was by a different writer (respectively, Andrew Wreggitt, Hart Hanson, and veteran Peter Lauterman), the producers and the writing team, with Wreggitt as the story editor for the two that followed his own script, worked the sequence into a seamless narrative.

As a character, Michelle shows new vulnerabilities and is profoundly changed by the loss of her daughter, becoming at first more isolated and eventually, with the shift in her perspective, more open and relaxed, finding a new man in her life. It is very rare to kill a recurring character, especially a child on a series such as this. Interviewed by Patty Winter, Wreggitt tells the fans who visit her website why the production team did this:[11]

AW: It all came out of what to do with Michelle, because the original Michelle had been so brittle. We'd created a character who was so tied up in knots that, in order for the show to really spread out, we had to find a way to shake her loose somehow.

PW: … Tina Keeper mentioned that people came up to her in the street afterwards and told her about their own experiences with losing a child.

## THE TRILOGY (#1): "THE VISIT"

Episode 54, "The Visit" by Andrew Wreggitt, sets the scene. It begins with Michelle, hair soft, face lively with anticipation, on a short leave to see Hannah, who is attending high school and living with her father, Louis (Byron Chief Moon), in Calgary. Teevee kids Michelle as she boards the plane: "Watch out for those cowboys and that, they don't like Indians."

There are also subplots involving Sarah finally having her baby and Teevee arriving back in Lynx River with a lot of money and a long-legged and gorgeous new girlfriend, Anne Marie George (Tara Anderson). It turns out that Teevee, despite being shop steward, has accepted money from the mining company during a strike and agreed to leave town for the duration. But the company forces the union to decertify, and the job it promised him disappears. At home in Lynx River, his girlfriend gets bored when his money runs out and eventually leaves (her airfare is paid by Elsie). He is left with a completely alienated Bertha and no job. Harris makes a sardonic comment: "Confucius say: 'play both ends against the middle, get squished.'" The connection between Hannah's disappearance and Teevee's return is a variation on a motif, the difficulty of trying to fit into a large community or city and then return to Lynx River.

When Michelle arrives in Calgary, Louis, her ex-husband, admits when pressed that he has no idea where Hannah is and that he hasn't been able to find her. As Michelle starts to pursue the fact that her daughter is missing with the Calgary RCMP, it becomes clear that, even though she is also a cop, they will treat her daughter as a runaway, another missing Indian kid. Desperately afraid, she breaks in on Andrew One Sky, a counsellor at an inner-city friendship centre. He is initially sceptical about the missing girl and then offended by Michelle's insistence that he help her find her daughter immediately. But he is moved by her desperation and reluctantly agrees to help her in her search. His first act, to take Michelle to the bars in the prostitutes' side of town, complicates the viewers' judgment about racism among the Calgary police. However, Michelle, uncharacteristically out of control, scares Andrew's young contact into running away. Trying to find out more about Hannah, Andrew gets Michelle to tell him about herself. There had been some heavy drinking years ago (defined as ten years ago in the first season, which means that it would have been when Hannah was very young), "but we both quit. [Louis] doesn't drink anymore." Probing further, Andrew wonders if Michelle's visit to Calgary somehow triggered in Hannah bad memories of her parents' earlier drinking bouts: "And that is why Hannah has disappeared."

Michelle turns on him. "Do you have any kids?" "No." "If you had any," she says, through her teeth, "you'd know that that's bullshit." She leaves, but eventually her anxiety forces her to return and Andrew gives her better advice: "Don't try to be a cop and a mother."

Michelle, using Andrew's contacts, gives an interview to a newspaper about Hannah's disappearance. The story appears the next morning on the back page, folded into a short item about the body of another teenager, known to be a prostitute. The clear inference is racism in the media. In the climactic scene, Andrew takes Michelle to a "squat" lit by candles – filth, dark corners, graffiti scrawled everywhere. Michelle: "It stinks." Their search turns up no reliable information. The scene and the episode end with Michelle sobbing to Andrew, "I can't stand this." Andrew quietly attempts to reassure her: "She wasn't there. That's a good thing. We're not giving up."

## THE TRILOGY (#2): "TAKE ME HOME"

In "Take Me Home" by Hart Hanson, directed by Stacey Curtis, Sarah delivers her long-awaited baby and Michelle finds out what happened to Hannah. Usually, in television, a long-awaited birth is the climax of an episode. Here it collides with the even more important climax of finding Hannah – a risky but in this case a successful narrative strategy. Sarah is in a panic about having her baby in Lynx River without Albert, whose absence is unexplained. Eventually Elsie invites her to stay with her family. This works better than the Teevee subplot because it changes the setting, tone, and narrative line, but not the level of tension. The strategy also makes the basic and in some ways ironic connection between of the loss of the much-loved Hannah, born to a mother who has a job and a place in her community, and the birth of Elizabeth, whose mother is essentially homeless and whose father has vanished. In this episode, Michelle begins to find out more about Andrew. His house is modern, full of light, with good contemporary aboriginal art on the walls. He tells her he has a couple of ex-wives and is Arapaho. "Not much sign of us, anymore. Not like here. Here you go to Buffalo Jump and it all comes alive." He has a clinical practice in downtown Calgary but spends most of his time volunteering at the Friendship Centre.

This episode foregrounds Dene spirituality but, as usual, without elaborate explanation. A long shot of a large campfire in Lynx River shows the central characters walking towards it in a quiet, informal manner. The audience is told that the fire is for Hannah – a communal form of waiting

"The Trilogy." Michelle hunts for Hannah on the streets of Calgary, helped by so-cial worker Andrew One Sky (Michael Horse). *Alberta Filmworks, in association with the CBC, distributed by Alliance Atlantis.*

and hoping and praying. The close-up on Elsie tells the viewer nothing more. Michelle, in Calgary, does confess on the telephone to Peter, in Lynx River: "It's like I have no instincts on this. It's like I'm in a foreign country." When she starts to have visions of Hannah, another connota-tion is added to what is meant by a foreign country.

Michelle seeks out a riverside park, where she sits on an empty park bench and relaxes. As she watches the river, her eyes close. She opens them to see Hannah sitting beside her. Her first line is very teenage mat-ter-of-fact: "Mom, you look awful." Michelle grins and replies, "I look tired. I can't sleep here." Hannah: "Neither could I at first. Now I can. It's nice here by the river." Michelle: "Like home." Michelle opens her eyes with a peaceful expression. Hannah is gone. She calls her daughter's name, staring around at the park. After a telephone conversation with Joe, who cannot tell her whether or not it was a vision or what it means, she follows his advice and goes to a nearby (nation unspecified but per-haps Blackfoot) reserve to find someone who can help her. The implica-tion is that elders known to have spiritual wisdom can nevertheless help people who are not from their nation or who have a substantially differ-ent belief system. Michelle, driving on a country road, turns at a mailbox with the name Whitney on it. She walks up to the porch, where a man is sleeping, hat over his eyes and earphones plugged into a Walkman, a nice subversion of the stereotype of a wise medicine man. She wakes him and gives him a small gift to express a respectful "thank you" for the help she is requesting. "Could I talk to you?" she asks. He replies, gently teasing her, but also interrogating her, "Didn't know Mounties had visions." Michelle asks him, very bluntly: "Is she dead?" No answer. Cut to a long shot of the two of them walking in a field. In an apparently featureless place, he says to her, "Here is a good place to rest." But he also tells her "to go where you were and take an offering. A good thought may come to you. Then you'll know what to do." He leaves her sitting in the grass in the sunshine.

Michelle again crosses the river, finds the bench, sits down. The director chooses to shoot in long shot in both directions, front and back, as if the camera seeks to examine her yet is reluctant to intrude. Then, in close-up, we see her place some tobacco as an offering beside her on the bench. There is a shot of Michelle from behind, with the children on the river-bank and the river. Suddenly, in extreme close-up, we see her face crumpling into tears, but this time the viewer does not see what she sees. The privacy of the character is protected by the writer and director, while the actor tells us wordlessly the only thing we need to know. Hannah is dead.

Apparently bowing to the dictates of television suspense formulae, the episode now cuts to Sarah, who, with great difficulty, is having her baby with the help of Elsie and Bertha. Bertha, in a burst of none too subtly linked metaphoric language, urges her to "think of the river. That's what I did. Clear and cold." Sarah, however, between contractions keeps saying, "Damn you, damn you, damn you." Damn who? Albert? the baby? her midwives? In those circumstances, likely all three. This sequence is intercut with Michelle's visit with Hannah's boyfriend, Michael Thunder Child. Keeper makes it clear without a word of dialogue that in Michelle's heart of hearts she now knows Hannah is dead. Back to Sarah's labour. "Something's wrong," Elsie says firmly to Sarah. "Albert's not coming. This is your baby. Stop waiting for Albert. Let the baby come." Sarah pushes and the baby is born. Elsie: "It's a strong baby like her mother." The scene may strike some viewers as a rather contrived contrast to the unrelenting tragedy of the main plot. Others will be delighted.

Michael Thunder Child arrives at Mr Whitney's to tell his story, but as teenagers will, he refuses to say exactly what happened at the party on the night Hannah was last seen. However, a glance from the elder sends him out to the car after Michelle with the full account. He tells her that it was not much of a party because Hannah doesn't drink and he doesn't drink when he's with her. He had asked her to spend the night, but she had said no because she wanted to meet her mother at the airport. They had had a fight. She had started to walk back to the city along the river. He had offered to drive her but she had refused. When he followed her, she threw stones at him. He kept waiting for her to call but she never did. "She's so stubborn," he says. After she hears his story, Michelle asks Calgary police and firemen to drag the river. On the banks of the Bow, firemen come up the bank with a body in a body bag on a stretcher, which Louis identifies with a nod. The boy breaks down and weeps. Michelle simply holds him, rocks him, tells him that Hannah's death was not his fault. The last scene follows the formality of the autopsy. With Michelle are Rosie, Ellen, and Peter, as well as Andrew and Louis, whose grief is also highlighted. Andrew to Michelle: "What you did for Michael, that was good. And it was not your fault either. You taught her well and she listened." As he gets into the car, Peter says to Andrew, "Andrew. Thank you." The cab pulls away and the episode ends. Tina Keeper won a well-deserved Gemini for this episode.

The first two episodes of the trilogy diverge significantly from the typical cop show/mystery television formula. To this point the mystery is about a missing girl, not about crime. Cops barely come into it. A deeper mystery to most viewers is Michelle's experience with Hannah's spirit. A human mystery lies behind Albert's refusal to be with Sarah during Elizabeth's birth. Finally, a basic rule of the genre is broken when a well-liked, quite young and attractive character dies through nobody's fault. Moreover, there are no lessons to be learned. Death and birth happen.

## THE TRILOGY (#3): "THE WEIGHT"

The third episode in the trilogy is the most demanding and the most complex emotionally. It becomes a portrait of grief, not a common subject in series television, and provides a deeper look both at the protagonist and at a web of relationships that fail and then succeed in reaching Michelle when, not if, she needs them. "The Weight" (an excellent title), written by Peter Lauterman, and directed by Alan Simmonds, is an episode that requires note-perfect dialogue, careful direction, and sensitive performances to reveal the complex subtext. Lauterman does an excellent job of writing strong dialogue for the actors to deliver. Most of the major characters, including recurring guest Tantoo Cardinal as Betty Moses, have to reach beyond the normal range of their characters to test the relationships they have established over several seasons.

"The Weight" begins with a shot of the community gathered at Hannah's grave. The sound of a drum and chant. Then a shot of Sarah rocking her baby inside Elsie's house, listening to the ceremony. (After Sarah's breakdown, there have been other times like this when she will not, cannot, go near a friend – in this case Michelle – because she cannot bear to be near such pain.) Natural sound. Elsie is the first to speak: "Sometimes our children get lost in the city, but Hannah was strong. Now she's back and her spirit will be with us always." Michelle looks on with her face closed.[12] When Lois, at the lunch after the funeral, says to Michelle, "I'm praying for Hannah. I know she's with Christ," Peter angrily warns her off. Throughout the series neither he nor Michelle are ever shown to be observant members of the church whose nuns and priests ran the residential schools.

As the episode progresses, Michelle refuses to deal with Hannah's things, go to a healing lodge with Betty, or agree to stay in Lynx River. Instead she requests a transfer to Yellowknife, a request that her mentor, Inspector Cormier, thinks is a mistake. The teenagers in Lynx River are also struggling with Hannah's death. William speaks roughly to Hannah's friend Wayne: "She went away because she wanted to. She croaked having a good time in the big city. Puppy, it's time to grow up." He does not get the last word. Wayne asks Rosie, then Rosemary, and finally Joe about why Hannah died. The adults don't do much better with his grief than they do with Michelle's, until he comes to Joe. Joe tells him, "She's just in another place," and then he gives the Slavey word for the place. (Note that the word and what it really entails is not spelled out for the non-Slavey audience.) "If she needs you, she'll come to you." Wayne asks, "What if I need her?" "She'll find you." Later Wayne asks Teevee and Gerry about where Hannah is. Gerry unloads his bleak world view on the boy, but Teevee tells Wayne that "if you're Dene you're in ___," also naming the place in Slavey. Later Teevee rounds on Gerry, "You tell what kids need to hear, not what you need to say." But grief takes many forms. Much later in this tightly structured episode, Teevee, talking to Bertha as he walks his baby daughter up and down, characterizes Hannah as one more failed Indian kid who tried to leave the reserve. In rhythm as he walks, he says, "Stupid Hannah. Stupid Hannah. Goes to the city, just another stupid Indian in the city. No one gets out of here alive." Bertha is furious: "Don't talk that way in front of Kyla!" and then asks him when he was ever really happy. Teevee, perhaps surprising the viewers, remembers that he had been really happy when he had "nailed that interview for Rec supervisor" – that is, he had been happy in a job he won through merit and then found he enjoyed. Bertha later asks Joey if he had ever been happy. He replies that he doesn't know.[13] Both conversations provide a context for Hannah's decision to go to Calgary to finish her studies.

Michelle, however, is the main focus. Throughout the episode, Michelle, atypically, is seen looking at television while Peter, Ellen, and Betty continually come in through her unlocked door and intrude, from her point of view, on her grief. But the audience also sees that she is fragile and that her withdrawal is dangerous. Peter expects the worst, harshly threatening William: "My sister is a strong woman. She's going through a bad time. If I find her with a bottle, I'll know where she got it." His solution to Michelle's grief is to propose that they go and fix up an uncle's cabin, but Michelle tells him that a few days in the bush is not going to do it. "I see Hannah everywhere, I hear her voice, I can't sleep – Hannah's dead." Betty tries shock treatment, telling her that she has seen Louis in Calgary and that he's a mess because he thinks Michelle is blaming him. No response. Like Peter, Betty assumes that Michelle is likely to return to the bottle, but she thinks she should go to a healing lodge, while Peter argues that she must heal "here with us, not with strangers." Both ideas suggest Dene values, that the community and the elders as teachers both have a role.

When Michelle, driven to anger and despair by Betty's abrasive ways and her attempts to persuade her to stay and face her grief, shouts at her, Betty, always probing, asks Michelle: "Why are you so angry with me?" Michelle, whose strong impulse is now to leave Lynx River, unconsciously defines her burdens in the series: "What'll they do if I'm not here. I'm not a mother anymore. My child is dead. I want to just be a cop. Find a guy maybe, whatever. If you love me, you'll let me go in peace … [Bitterly] Peter's bad enough. He comes here 10 times a day with his problems. His problems, not mine." Then she turns on Betty, accusing her of being jealous of Peter's relationship with her, of not having a life of her own; she refuses to be her "crippled daughter." She goes on: "I'm not your daughter or your friend. Find someone else. [Turning away tired out] There's a ton of food in the kitchen. [Lynx River has responded as most small communities do to tragedy with bread, meat, casseroles, and other food.] Help yourself." And she goes up the stairs. Betty had already dragged up ancient history (new to the viewer) about how Peter helped Michelle run away when she was trying to beat her alcoholism with Betty's help. Now she accuses Peter of again giving Michelle a way out, leaving Betty to pick up the pieces. Eventually the quarrel ends, Betty apologizes and, as she and Peter shake hands, she reminds him that "[Michelle] has more tricks up her sleeve than a raven." She also points out that he is still trying to take care of Michelle because he had not been able to in residential school. He flinches, visibly. Betty: "Quit beating up on yourself and let me do my work." It is self-evident that Betty and Peter both love Michelle and are in an unacknowledged contest about who can help her most; yet neither can really think of what to do.

In the first of two scenes set in Hannah's typically teenage and therefore quite touching bedroom, Betty, according to Dene custom, starts to dispose of Hannah's things, making Michelle very angry. When Michelle finally kicks Betty out of her house, she sleeps at Joe's. Note that neither Joe nor Elsie as elders has a role to play at this stage of Michelle's grief. It is her closest contemporaries who try intervene. Michelle to Sarah: "I'm sick of being used." Sarah says exactly the wrong thing: "Don't try to pretend to be strong. You're acting like me." Michelle coldly attacks her for making the comparison: "You had a little breakdown. I lost a child. You think it's the same? ... You're like every other white person who comes up here. You think you know something, but you don't. You think you know something about me, but you don't." She leans back, grimly satisfied, as a devastated Sarah leaves. Sarah goes to find Betty, who is getting ready to catch a plane, and pleads with her to stay. Betty, in an outburst of her own, says, "I take it day after day. It's her life not mine. Got lots of other work to do." Sarah, by acknowledging the barriers of cultural differences that exist between her and the rest of the community, including her friend, persuades her to try again: "You can't leave. Look, I'm white. It doesn't matter what she said. You have to try." Cultural and racial differences are never very far from the surface in *North of 60*. In the climactic sequence of scenes, Michelle apologizes, but Betty, barely acknowledging her, goes back into Hannah's room and resumes packing her things, ripping posters off the wall in the process. Michelle, outraged, tries to physically stop her and they end up struggling with one another – even the camera appears to be knocked around. Finally Betty, clinging to what she knows best as a counsellor of alcoholics as well as what she knows as a friend, almost screams at Michelle that she has to remember how she had to get rid of the old stuff to be sober. Michelle: "Get out!" Instead, Betty puts a bottle on the table and taunts her with it. Michelle sarcastically counters with "I've seen this show [i.e., tactic] before." Betty drives in on her, hoping to penetrate her defences by naming her worst fears: "You couldn't get along with your child. You drove her away to an unstable father ... it was your fault. You drove her away. You punish yourself." (A drumbeat and chant, rare in this series either as music or as sound effect, start on the sound track behind these words.) Michelle looks at the bottle and tears out of the house. Betty runs after her with the bottle, catching up with her by the river. Michelle shouts furiously, "Go to hell!" and takes off again. Betty finally stops her further along the river's edge and drives her words into Michelle's closed face: "You choose to live or die right here. What happened to Hannah was an accident. You were a good mom and she was a good kid. Here, now, or not at all." Shocking the viewer, Michelle grabs the bottle and takes huge gulps, then tries to force Betty to drink. When she fails, she runs off a third time. Long shot of Betty following her along the river's edge. Collapsed on a rock, Michelle finally sobs, "I let her go. I killed her." Betty: "She was having fun. She tripped and fell." Michelle: "I can't live without her. I don't have the strength." Betty, as she holds her firmly but gently: "Let the Creator hold you. Let the Creator hold you." It is a powerful and emotionally truthful sequence.

The next scene is at Hannah's grave. While Wayne looks again at his postcards from Hannah, Teevee unexpectedly finds the right words: "To tell you the truth, she wasn't my friend, but she was from here, one of us. She was doing good, getting really strong. You respect her memory ... you get strong like your mom and me. It's tough out there, man." The final scene is again by the river. Michelle burns Hannah's things in a bonfire as the rest, including Sarah this time, look on. When Wayne adds his postcards to the fire, Michelle puts her arm around him. The trilogy offers no easy answers, no simple meanings. It does offer new depths to the central characters. With this set of episodes, just over halfway through the series, the audience becomes more engaged with the characters, their past histories with one another, their unpredictable futures, and their considerable strengths and human weaknesses

Up to this point, the episodes have been linked by writer, theme, issues, or characters rather than chronologically. However, I will finish by looking at a cross-section of the series provided by three other very good episodes. The first, episode 12, "Sisters of Mercy," is drawn from the middle of the first season; the second, episode 47, "Life Is a Memory," is from the end of the third season; and the last, episode 90, "Borrowed Time," is the final episode of the last season.

## "SISTERS OF MERCY"

In an interview on CBC Television's *One on One*, on the AFN website, 21 May 2005, Phil Fontaine commented: "There is nothing more important ... between Canada and Aboriginal people than Residential Schools." Ten weeks later, the AFN website carried this story: "Assembly of First Nations National Chief Phil Fontaine announced today that he and the AFN are launching a class action lawsuit against the Government of Canada for the residential schools legacy. The claim, to be filed tomorrow, states that the residential schools policy and schools caused 'irreparable harm and damage' to First Nations' 'culture, language, way of life, family, community and social structures.'"[14] A settlement was finally reached, but little money has yet (2007) reached those survivors, some of whom have been expected to produce records long since lost by the churches and the state that had wrenched them from their communities.

Twelve weeks into the first season, after the basic characters had been established, "Sisters of Mercy"(an ironic title linked to Leonard Cohen's equally ironic inversions in his poem/song)[15] was the first episode in the series to tackle directly the emotionally charged territory of residential schools, laying vital groundwork for a major theme in the series. The episode was written by Rebecca Schechter, who won a Gemini, and directed by George Bloomfield. "Residential schools affected me personally," Tina Keeper said in an interview with Peter Gzowski on *Morningside*, 10 March 1997, since everyone of her parents' generation had been sent to residential school. Wilma Pelly (Elsie), who was also a survivor of residential schools, may have been additional resource for this episode.[16] In 1989 *Where the Spirit Lives* (touched on earlier), a controversial but widely seen two-hour CBC film (which was used in Ontario schools), had explored the world of residential schools in the 1930s.[17] Three years later *North of 60* brought the aftermath into the present, then kept on examining it until the last made-for-TV movie, *Distant Drumming* (2005). Without undercutting the basic argument that enforced enculturation had a deadly effect on children, parents, and their cultures, this episode makes the point that the schools also created opportunities for some students. Peter has some good memories. The bad ones surface later in the series. However, Michelle is the primary focus of this narrative. The plot centres on her encounter with an abusive nun from her residential school who visits the reserve.[18]

The second plot gives equal time to Eric's conflict with his rebellious young son, Andy, who has been sent to stay with his father because he has been expelled from school. (Part of the reason for this split in focus would be the need to keep John Oliver, the most obvious star of the first season, in the foreground for at least part of each episode.) Eric's problems with Andy loosely parallel Michelle's arguments with Hannah over what she writes for a contest to be judged by this visiting nun. Andy also conceals a secret – he shot out Sarah's window by accident. Teevee has impulsively taken the blame and then blackmails the younger, weaker white boy, demanding $500. But this narrative arc is troubling given the context. On the structural level, in the first narrative, Michelle had suffered severe and sustained abuse from Sister Simone, a part of her life she has kept secret until the nun arrives, while in the second, an alienated white child, uprooted from his home and feeling as if he has lost his father, comes to visit his dad and is threatened by a Dene teenager. The implied equation of his dilemma with Michelle's suffering may not be intentional, but it is insulting. To add to the problem, Andy, who has everything a kid could want materially, did shoot the forbidden gun, so his punishment of community service and an apology seems perfectly acceptable. Michelle was seven years old and entirely innocent when she was first hit by Sister Simone. The story of a father and son and of culture clash is competently told, but in juxtaposition to the other, more harrowing story, it feels at best like padding and at times like an insensitive sideshow. Here, as elsewhere, the writers for *North of 60* were faced with the formulaic demands of television series that create audience expectations of more than one plot line in an hour-long series. However, the other story or stories often seem to trivialize the weightier issues of the more demanding narrative and undercut its careful development. The danger in this particular case is that the white viewer might simply say, "See – 'they' can and will threaten and blackmail us too."

The more complicated storyline is superbly developed and has a memorable climax. It starts when Sister Simone (Diane Leblanc in a nuanced performance that earned her a Gemini nomination), now in quiet "civilian" clothes and with a friendly open demeanour, arrives to judge the Lynx River entries in an English-language essay contest. The essay topic is "Ancestors." The children are very excited, bickering about their chances of winning, and the parents welcome their new interest in writing. Peter, with a broad grin of surprise and delight when he catches sight of Sister Simone, welcomes his "all-time favourite teacher," who he says inspired him to be the best he could be. As a hint that she is never satisfied or perhaps merely that she continues to set high goals for him, she responds immediately that he should be a member in the Legislative Assembly (which he becomes in later seasons). She can't remember Michelle's name. When Michelle is introduced, Sister Simone dismisses her after saying, "A police officer of all things! So you have a child in school … well, now you know how difficult it is to raise children." Michelle's face turns to stone.

Michelle is at first unable to tell Peter or the other parents why she objects to Sister Simone as a judge – a reluctance that would ring true to many First Nations viewers,[19] so she fails to win over the other parents, who instead hear how good she was to Peter in his twice weekly English classes, even though Michelle protests that "she was *my* headmistress and she was in my face every single day. If you want to know about her talk to *me*."[20] It could be that the others want to forget their past and resist when she insists on reminding them of what it was like. Peter can't understand her, since he had had a very different experience with Sister Simone. She had taught him to write English well, and as far as he is concerned, she will not tell the kids what to write but will teach them how. Michelle: "This is different." Peter: "Come on, Michelle, that was twenty years ago and you were seven." But the key to her distress and anger is that, as she says to Peter, "I don't want her judging my kid" – unspoken are the words *the way the nuns continually judged all of us as Dene and found us little savages.* Eric perhaps speaks for too many south of 60 viewers when he tries to reassure Michelle by telling her that "[w]hatever she did, she can't hurt you any more," as if the damage can simply be set aside. The situation gets more tangled as Sister Simone takes Hannah under her wing, telling she is going to be a very good writer someday. To make it worse, Hannah, swinging delightedly in her mother's office chair at the detachment, points out that she has learned that "until the white man taught us" her people had no writing and no famous writers, so that, according to Sister Simone, she could be the first one.

Later, in a one-on-one session with Hannah, Sister Simone uses lots of praise and affectionate body language as she corrects Hannah's argument that (as Michelle had told her) traditional hunting had not changed for thousands of years. Sister Simone points out that the Dene had no iron, no knives, no scrapers, and so on, and lived in the stone age. Stroking Hannah's hair, but with no implications of sexual abuse, she continues: "You even got words from us." She tells her that there was no Slavey word for thank you, clearly implying that there is no concept of thanks in the culture. As Sister Simone continues, Michelle comes in to collect Hannah just in time to hear her say, "'[M]aasi' comes from the French." When Michelle forbids Hannah to work with the nun, Hannah accuses Michelle of ruining her chances in the contest. Michelle tells her firmly that 'maasi' sounds the same but does not come from the French word "merci."[21] Hannah protests, "She's a teacher. She knows history." Michelle fiercely: "From books! ... We know it from our grandparents and their grandparents. That's real history." Although Hannah claims that she has thrown away the essay she originally wrote, Michelle tells her to submit it or nothing at all.

Basil Johnston (Anishnabe), in "One Generation from Extinction" (1990),[22] is passionate about what happens when the languages are lost: "No longer will they think or feel Indian" (12). He goes on to say that not knowing the language meant that Indian legends like creation stories lost the subtle meanings that the narratives in the original languages had and that that helped people know how to live. He summarizes the attacks made on the languages – no good for abstract thought, difficult to say, useless for getting ahead – discusses the physical beatings and the verbal abuse, and then continues: "To instil respect for language, the old counselled youth 'don't talk too much' … [which] also meant 'Don't talk too often … don't talk too long, don't talk about those matters that you know nothing about' … So precious did the tribe regard language and speech that it held those who abused language and speech and truth in contempt and ridicule and withheld from them their trust and confidence" (12).

When Sister Simone, furious that Hannah has withdrawn from the contest, barges in at suppertime (Hannah is picking at her food) to confront Michelle, Michelle tells her bluntly that she won't let her daughter enter the contest "because what you made her write is garbage." Sister Simone launches into passionately indignant countercharges. Michelle's replies are contained, quiet, but forceful. Finally, when the two women give Hannah contradictory instructions, the girl runs from the room. Sister Simone's closing volley to Michelle: "You still have to turn everything into a fight. Even at your daughter's expense!" Then she walks out and slams the door. At this point, the dramatic conflict still looks like a battle of cultural narratives centred on a teacher who suited one child but not his sister. Peter, ever the diplomat, tries to explain Michelle's anger to Sister Simone. She seems to have functioned as an older and much-admired sister to him, someone he could be close to when he was a boy taken from his family and not allowed to see his real sister. Schechter has disarmed the average white member of her audience who is unaware of the issues raised by residential schools (more likely in the early 1990s) by providing rationalizations and layers of conflict, drawing the viewers further into the issue itself.

The climactic scene begins quietly with Michelle, seen in profile, looking at a dimly lit mask on her wall flanked by two candles. Peter comes in with Sister Simone. Hannah emerges from her room to listen. Peter: "Why did you do this to Hannah?" Michelle directly to Sister Simone: "You tell him, *you* tell him." "Tell him why you are so angry?" the sister asks, puzzled. She clearly doesn't remember – which to Michelle is much worse than lying about it. Michelle: "When she caught me braiding my hair, she took me into a closet and cut off all my hair. She slapped me until I was bleeding 'for the sin of vanity.'" Then, in a tightly controlled voice, looking Sister Simone in the eye: "Tell him about the bath of ice cubes." Reaction shot of Peter, appalled. The sister, with a small smile: "I honestly don't remember. I had hundreds of girls ... some just as difficult as you." Close-up on Michelle, still tightly controlled, close to tears but not giving in to them. In a strained voice, she replies: "Tell him how you herded us into the gym in the middle of the night. Tell him how you made me say 'my father is a drunk, my mother is a whore, God is the only one who loves me' [reaction shot of Hannah listening very intently] over and over in front of everyone." Sister Simone, quietly and with absolute conviction: "What did you want? To stay in the stone age? We had to break your connection with the past. I knew who you were and what you were ... I only wanted the best for you." As she begins to leave, she turns back and says, "When the time comes I can answer for it."[23] Michelle just looks at her.

As the door closes, the camera swings up to Peter's agonized face, but he does not meet her eyes. "Why didn't you talk to me about it. Why didn't you say something?" Michelle, not looking at him, says quietly, "You were always talking about Sister Simone. When I finally met her, I thought she was an angel." Peter flinches as Michelle says, with the barest of pauses, "and then she hit me." Peter, still in denial, says, "Nobody talked about that stuff happening at St Anne's, other places but not St Anne's." Michelle doesn't hear him. Lost in the memory, she says in an undertone, "My father is a drunk, my mother's a whore, my father's a drunk, my mother's a whore." Then she remembers that she had hidden from her mother when she had come to the school to visit because she was so ashamed of her, and the tears come. Peter gulps. Michelle goes to him, not he to her, and they embrace while Hannah watches.

In the coda we hear that Sister Simone has withdrawn "for personal reasons" as judge of the contest and that four essays will be going to the Deh Cho regional finals, including Hannah's and Wayne's. Michelle comes down the steps of the detachment to see Sister Simone leaving Lynx River, her bag in hand. As Hannah joins her mother, the camera follows the sister down the street. The dialogue is telling in the context of the time, 1992–93, as the complexity of the issue was dawning on the Canadian public. In 2007 the Canadian government had still not apologized for the harm done by residential schools. Hannah: "She's gone, Mom, isn't that what you wanted?" Michelle: "I wanted her to say she was sorry." They hug – but as the rest of the series demonstrates, one cathartic confrontation does not undo all the damage of those years. Having already established that Michelle had been an alcoholic for some years, the series launches one of its major themes with this episode – the ongoing aftermath of residential schools, one explanation for the epidemic of alcoholism among some First Nations people. But, of real importance, the series over its six years also showed how many adults have overcome and even used the residential school experience. The Dene cultural advisors on "Sisters of Mercy" were Nick Sibbeston, Eleanor Bran, and Leo Norwegian. Twelve years later Eleanor Bran was the cultural advisor on the fifth movie, *Distant Drumming*, which took up the issue again.

## "LIFE IS A MEMORY"

Episode 47, "Life Is a Memory," written by Rob Forsyth[24] and directed by Metis Gil Cardinal, was broadcast in the 1994 season. It was one of the best and most tightly written episodes in the series, focusing on Mohawk artist Ben Montour (August Schellenberg in a very strong performance) and the male prostitute Nevada (Adam Beach), who has taken refuge from the streets of Vancouver in Lynx River. The interlocking stories of Ben and Nevada are developed over several episodes. Ben has already been discussed above. Nevada is a "rent boy" (i.e., his body is for rent to make money for the rent). He had first met Teevee in Vancouver when Teevee had gone there in pursuit of a white student nurse, only to find she had a boyfriend. Nevada had called him "Snowman" and had helped him "make it" until Eric arrived to take him back home. Nevada is a survivor: "I'm still alive, man, that's what it's been all about since I was fourteen." Although HIV positive, he apparently does not use drugs (or alcohol). His disease comes from the sex trade. In 1994 AIDS was usually a death sentence, with no drug cocktails yet in common use. In Stacy Kaser's "Shelter," episode 45, Nevada tells Teevee about how a professor of native studies wrote a thesis on "Strong Cultural Links between the Navajo and the Dene" as cover for his trolling.[25] He had hooked Nevada (who is neither Navajo nor Dene) – a short, sharp jab at an academic's exploitation of his research to justify paying for sex with a young Indian man. Nevada tells the fascinated Teevee: "They like Indians cause their skin is so smooth. [He poses.] Let 'em see your ass. Let them think you're hungry. Look at these lips. [He gives a pucker and a sultry stare.]" He then calls Teevee a baby face tough guy because when he ran away to Vancouver, "your people just reached out and took you home." But in a later episode Nevada puts his deeply felt self-contempt into context, painting a vivid picture of his life before he fled to the streets. His drunken father, who beat him regularly, fell into the sea while hunting seals. When his young son pulled him out of the ocean, his father beat him "senseless" for not saving the seal. After that, Nevada ran away to survive by prostitution.

He has been staying with Willy at the airstrip, playing with the kids on the street like a big brother and learning things about life in the bush. Joey doesn't know what a rent boy is but asks, "Are you gay?" "Yeah." Nevada also hides from everyone but Willy the fact that he is sick with fever and is HIV positive. He has found that people are so ill-informed about AIDS, he has had to tell them there's no need to burn the sheets.[26] (Even though AIDS posters were prominent in the nursing station from the first episodes in 1992, it was nevertheless a time when denial compounded with ignorance on reserves was common.) However, this episode not only explores the issue on the factual level and through the characters' reactions, but also pushes through to a more intensely symbolic level where Ben's art becomes a metaphor for Nevada's life as well as for what happens to the people of Lynx River.

Nevada cuts his hand when he, Joey, and others go with Willy and Ben to help find material for Ben to work with – specifically, a huge old log driven ashore below the riverbank, water-scoured and weathered. Ben, rubbing it with his hand, senses within it a special sculpture waiting to be discovered. In the search, Nevada loses his balance, skidding down the bank and cutting his hand. Steadying himself on the grey wood, he leaves a handprint on it in blood. A close-up of the handprint is juxtaposed with one of a raven cawing. A reaction shot reveals that Nevada feels an unspoken affinity with Raven. But later, when he tells Joe with pride that he saw a raven and should have asked for his advice in "this place of healing," Joe replies, "You don't turn it on and off, you feel it when it goes, you feel it again ... How much time do you have?" Joe's implication is how much time does it take to learn how to get in touch with the spirit world, but also the audience knows that Nevada's time is short.

The fear of AIDS begins in Lynx River when Mary (Columpa Bob), the new nurse, checks out which children had played with Nevada while he had the deep open cut on his hand. The word about his AIDS quickly gets around. Rosie attacks him with rocks for playing with her kids. Teevee panics because Nevada had originally lived with them and helped with Kyla. Bertha, studying to be a nurse, straightens Teevee out, as does Sarah, who talks to others, but the panic spreads. Michelle is deeply concerned, reminding Peter that someone with AIDS in another town was run out of town, then tries to reassure herself and him: "We're not ignorant. We know about AIDS." Willy nurses Nevada and continues to give him shelter. When he and Nevada buy supplies, Gerry orders Nevada out of his store, the only real gathering place for the community. Then Gerry turns to Ben Montour, the artist-in-residence, with a smile. Ben says grimly, his voice overlapping a reaction shot of Gerry's smile fading, "I had a friend who was a dancer in Toronto who died of AIDS. [Then quietly, with authority] I kissed him goodbye. I wiped away his tears. So I suppose you don't want to sell me this chainsaw oil."[27] Gerry takes his money with no further words. The chainsaw is Ben's first tool in freeing the carving from the tree.

The consequences of Ben's casually dropping Lois as a lover are dealt with again in this episode. Montour is attacking the log with his chainsaw when Michelle enters and casually pours his bottle of booze into his cooler. Lynx River is still a dry town. They spar in a leisurely fashion. She wants him to leave Lois alone. Ben: "Good people change the world ... Go off and be good. You'll hear me cheer somewhere off in the rear." He starts the chainsaw, ending the conversation.

The narrative then juxtaposes Lois as the rejected victim of an outsider and Nevada as the outsider who is rejected. The sequence begins when Harris, furious and jealous, refuses to accept Lois back. Then there follows an unnecessary attempt at pathos, one of the very few false notes in this episode. We see Nevada alone in the empty, snow-trampled street at night, lights shining in all the windows. He shouts, "Won't anybody come out and play?" Cut to Lois, sitting beside a lamp as she prepares to slash her wrists. Teevee, having found her, carries her semi-conscious to the nursing station with Elsie following. Cut to Teevee dozing, Elsie sitting rigidly watching Lois, and Harris turned inward on himself. In the next scene, Nevada wakes up drenched with sweat and trembling violently. When Willy brings him water, Nevada asks, "Why aren't you scared?" Willy, very simply: "I took care of my wife when she was sick. She died, but we keep in touch." Willy has a set of values and a world view that Nevada longs for and cannot find.

Meanwhile, even the sensible Michelle is infected by the fear pervading the town, bringing the issue much closer to the viewers by prompting them to wonder how they might react when even this protagonist, who knows better, is needlessly afraid. She alienates Hannah when she asks her if Nevada has ever touched her "in a certain way." "Nope," says Hannah, but she goes on provocatively, "Maybe he had sex with Joey." With teenage bravado she says, "If he has AIDS, so what?" But later, when Hannah leads Nevada by the hand to a bush party, Joey repudiates him, the rest mutter about it being too crowded, and all of the boys piss on the fire to put it out – in this context, the most deliberate insult the adolescent male mind could think of. Back home, Hannah, ashamed of the fact that she too has betrayed him, explains to her mother: "I let go. He was crying. He didn't do anything. He just stood there." Michelle reassures her that the teenagers' rejection of Nevada is primarily the fault of the grown-ups, not the kids, and tries to comfort her. The younger viewer is on the hook along with the adults.

Next, Harris walks casually into Montour's place and kicks the sleeping artist in the gut. Michelle walks in at that point, having come to talk to Montour about Lois again, and throws Harris out. She tells Ben that Lois "sliced her wrists with a jackknife," and Montour replies sardonically, "Dull, no doubt." The raven caws in the distance. He asks reluctantly, "She's not dead?" "No." "Good." To Montour, Lois is what Janet Acoose calls an "easy squaw,"[28] a self-chosen victim. He reserves his rare sympathy for those he sees as real victims. Meanwhile, Peter and Albert are arguing about Xeroxes that Albert has assembled for a town meeting. Peter says they are full of "attitudes, prejudices," not facts. Ironically, when Peter is afraid the meeting will get out of hand, Albert mocks him with his own democratic values: "A community is a community. You can't pick and choose how it feels." That, too, describes the dilemma many small communities north and south of 60 faced when AIDS appeared.

Without regard for what is going on in the community, Ben focuses completely on his log, though it frustrates him. He gives it a push, then another, harder. "It's not talking to me," he says to Willy. To the log, with anger: "Talk to me!" and he begins attacking it with an axe, apparently at random. Finally he puts his hand where Nevada's bloody handprint stains the wood. He attacks the log again, but this time purposefully, with an adze. Nevada is watching. Montour almost shouts at Nevada: "Life is a memory, kid, not in the future, not happening now. Live the memory!"[29] He attacks the wood again for what seems like a long time (in television terms, that is). Michelle watches the shadows of the three of them, backlit behind the sheet of plastic that seals off a part of Willy's garage from the street, but she does not go in. Others from Lynx River join her. Ben exclaims, "There it is. Can you see it?" as he thrusts the adze to Nevada, who uses it with ferocity before collapsing on the floor exhausted. Ben's art does not capture the pain of the present or the clouded future. Instead, for Ben, to make a sculpture is to make in the present an immediate, concrete permanent memory of the past, for the future, a work of art that is open to interpretation by anyone who sees it at any time. Ironically, Ben has come to the Deh Cho, to a culture without a tradition of sculpture or mask-making. To live the memory is also to maintain a distance from fear. The Dene have their own ways of doing this when they must.

However, at the town meeting, Rosie stubbornly claims the right to be afraid if she wants to be. Others say that they are not anti-gay but that this is a problem in the south and that it should stay there, a common attitude on more remote reserves: "Not here, not in the North, not where my children are."[30] This scene is juxtaposed with one of Harris approaching Lois carefully, wordlessly, but finally with success. In the next scene Montour at last confronts Michelle, telling her that Lois has served her purpose, which was to put his "needs at rest, mind at rest, for the time it took ... She exists to be taken. She's one of *them*, a victim." Even in his bitter truth-telling he makes a joke about healing circles and born-again Indians, forcing a laugh out of Michelle, but he cannot conceal that he is unable to make any permanent connection with a woman. Over the river, Albert silences Sarah's protests about his role in the move to get rid of Nevada. As he points out, in this case he was speaking for his community. Albert: "The boy's sick. If the wolves take him, they do. He'll die anyhow. Protecting the weak endangers the strong." Consistently, over the years, this has been Albert's own creed. But it is not a teenager or someone from the adult community, or even Albert, who seeks out Nevada to tell him the community wants him to leave. It is Elsie.

When Nevada sees her approach on a bright wintry morning, he comes out of Willy's to meet her. She says gently but firmly, "I'm a tired old lady. Seen a lot of bad things. We have our own sickness." What that may be is unspecified, but the series has suggested several chronic hurts, including alcoholism, low self-esteem, and the absence of fathers and husbands who have deserted their families or must work far away. She places the responsibility of his care where she thinks it belongs: "You should go home to your own people." Throughout the series, to Elsie there is always "home" and it is always possible to go there. Unafraid, she lays her hand gently on his face, then turns and slowly walks away. Nevada has said nothing in the short scene. The camera tracks back into a long shot that catches Willy in the background. During yet another community meeting, Peter gets a phone call from Willy at the airstrip, saying, "Some rich guy in Edmonton has sent a chopper for Ben." A long ambivalent look passes between Peter and Albert, but whether Albert called in a favour, the viewer will never know. In a close-up of Nevada and Ben in the chopper over the sounds of the blades, Ben says, "Let it go, Nevada. Watch it and let it go. Life is a memory." The camera zooms in on Nevada's impassive face as the helicopter lifts. Perhaps some in the audience will realize that he has not said a word of dialogue since he attacked the log. Michelle watches the helicopter flying out over the church spire, not an accidental juxtaposition of his departure with the icon of a compassion that the community has failed to show. In the last scene, Joe and Willy, both elders in the community, enter Ben's now deserted workshop. First the partly open beak of Ben's sculpture appears in frame, and then the whole giant raven is revealed, with a carved red handprint folded over its head in the centre of its forehead, blessing it, resisting it, an inescapable metaphor for Nevada's presence and an enduring memory for Lynx River to live with.[31]

### "BORROWED TIME"

The closing episode of the series, 90, "Borrowed Time" (an ironic in-joke reference to the fact that they made the sixth season on "borrowed time," as well as to at least one of the narrative arcs that is completed), was written by Andrew Wreggitt and directed by Stacey Stewart Curtis.[32] The final episode of a long-running series often makes little sense to a new viewer, since it basically serves to tie up some loose ends. Unexpectedly, the final episode of *North of 60* has a climactic scene that lends a touch of Greek tragedy to the tale. What little comedy there is in the piece has to do with Andrew digging a hole to look for Gerry's broken water pipe. Lots of people kibitz, and each one remembers it being in a different place. But no one actually helps. As Andrew tells Charlie, if you ever get lost in the bush, dig a hole and everybody will find you so they can give you contradictory advice.

Dene values – as defined over six years by the actors, writers, producers, directors, editors, designers, composers, and crew and as understood by the audience as it got to know Lynx River – are at the centre of most of the narrative arcs in this episode. This is not immediately apparent as it begins. Michelle's newest partner, city-bred James Harper, uses his computer skills to find irrefutable proof that Albert has been illegally laundering money. Michelle, still suffering from a gunshot wound she thinks Albert ordered (the viewers know he did not) and therefore not technically on duty, finds that they finally have solid evidence they can use to arrest Albert, and she wants the satisfaction of this last confrontation. At the same time, Lynx River faces its most severe test as a community. The oil company in which Albert owns majority shares is willing to give each household $300,000 and a new house if the band will let it drill in the centre of the community, essentially destroying it. After all, as Albert points out, the Dene were traditionally nomads and had never lived in a town until recently. The whole territory, from Fort Liard to the Mackenzie

River, has always been theirs. Michelle is, of course, against the whole idea. But as Rosie points out to her, she and Peter have government salaries as well as "benefits up the wazoo" plus Peter's condo in Yellowknife. Rosie: "You never understood how bad it was for the rest of us." Rosie has a half share in the coffee shop, but her outburst is based on a long history of uncertainty and perhaps, for once, suggests that there are class distinctions even in Dene Lynx River. Michelle dismisses the company's offer as Albert's last attempt to destroy the town that the Kenidis so closely identify with. But the temptation for some in the town is very real. The ever practical Harris is for it but cannot vote. Lois is not heard from. Elsie is very much against the deal as one silent close-up shows. Sarah, unmarried though now very pregnant with Nathan's child, cannot vote. Sent by Elsie with Joe as a guide, Teevee is off on a quest into the bush as this discussion takes place.

The only improbable storyline of this complex narrative was included, I think, to give Gerry a choice as well. He has conveniently inherited half a million dollars and is tempted to leave Lynx River to find his dream home on Vancouver Island. Yet when Joe tells him that the others' decision to go or stay is none of his business, he bursts out: "Nine years and you never once made me feel part of this community!" Nevertheless, he is willing to sell his part of the business to his partner Rosie on very reasonable terms, which shows how much he has changed and how fond he is of her. One of the most credible moments in the episode resolves the long narrative arc of Gerry's unrequited love for Rosie. Looking at his old photographs with her, he shows her the uncle from whom he inherited and explains that he has lost touch with all of his family. Living in a world of extended families, she cannot imagine that and says so. Gerry had never loved anyone since he fell in love at seventeen with a Jewish girl. His uncle had forbidden him to marry her, and her parents also disapproved, taking her with them to Israel when they discovered that the young couple planned to elope. Now, despite the estrangement between them, his uncle has left him the money. Gerry tells Rosie that his heart "never burned like that again" – until he met her. She says nothing, they exchange a look, he leans over and gently, thoroughly, kisses her as she leans into the kiss. They part. She still says nothing, just looks at him with a small smile, which he returns. Then he thanks her for giving him that memory.

Another unresolved storyline involves Teevee, who is still estranged from Bertha and Kyla. Elsie has sent him to check out his father's old cabin, an errand disguising a purpose. Joe comes along to help him find it. When they spot a moose, Joe is in such pain with his bad knees he can't get into position to fire. Teevee shoots but only wounds the animal – this is where some southern viewers will get squeamish, but the series has never backed away from the result of a successful hunt or even the remains left by poachers. Joe angrily insists he follow it: "Didn't anyone ever teach you that!" Dene tradition does not permit a hunter to leave a wounded animal to suffer. Teevee reluctantly scrambles after it, and as he struggles to track it, keeps remembering Bertha's taunts after he had fled from his responsibility yet again. She had called him, bitterly, a "scared, gutless little punk!" Lashing out in a rage, he had decked her, repeating his dad's pattern of abusing his mother. Bertha (pregnant with his child, although he does not know it) had immediately left Lynx River without a word and without leaving an address. Now she has returned, taken the little cabin back from him, but has let him know she is not interested in any contact with him unless it concerns Kyla. He is clearly sorry for hitting her but cannot figure out how to approach her or say so. Family violence is a loaded subject among First Nations; the generations who were sent away to residential schools were often physically abused, were not parented for most or all of the year, and must now try to parent their own children. Breaking the chain of abuse is an ongoing struggle. As Teevee treks through the bush and wades in the river, the moment he hit her comes back to him repeatedly. At last he finds the moose and kills it. When we next see him, sitting by a small fire he has built, a little of the moose's blood smeared on his face, he cuts a small piece of meat from the animal and prays, "I pay the fire for bringing me my food, luck, blessings and health."[33]

Facing the fire, Teevee continues to pray in Slavey as he recalls in flashbacks loving moments with Bertha and then the blow. What he finds on the hunt is a way to tell Bertha how sorry he is and how much he cares for their children. With his first moose, which he will share with the community, he obeys what Blondin calls the "umbrella law; under it sit all other laws … Share what you have" (71). Thus in the last episode, Teevee finally becomes a man, which in turn helps him to become an adult, a father, and a partner. As Joan Ryan (1995) writes, "The kill of a young man's first big game was celebrated and feasted. Eventually when they left their fathers' tents for their own, or for those of their fathers-in-law, they eventually became 'the boss of themselves' and of 'their' women … Elders were cared for by the young with meat, fish, wood" (47–8). Martha Rabesca (Slavey) tells researchers that after a man's first kill the community held a big feast.[34] George Blondin's father (Blondin 1997) "would talk to the fire a long time, thanking the Creator for the food and asking for continued good life for his family and people" (59).

Just before the crucial meeting of the band, there is more discussion in the coffee shop about the oil company's (actually Albert's) offer. Peter, appearing in the episode for the first time, points out that they can scatter, go anywhere they want, including "Liard" (Fort Liard self-identifies as the real counterpart of Lynx River, a quick touch of self-reflexivity), because nothing will be holding them together. He also tells them they will no longer be a band. (The legal ins-and-outs of the land claim are unclear, and the brief point Michelle made earlier on, that the oil company could dig the well tangentially, seems forgotten. The needs of the drama are paramount here, not the politics). Appropriately, Michelle makes the final argument (recalling previous episodes) to Rosie: "Your father is here. Hannah is here. We've all buried our dead here. Who will remember our stories?" Enter Albert's white lawyer to urge them to go to the band meeting "that's going to make everyone rich." Just then Teevee comes in late, blood still on his face, and says, "I'm not going anywhere." He tells them he shot a moose and needs some help getting it into town. They all look at one another, a wordless understanding develops in a heartbeat, and they start to organize the help he needs. The lawyer, oblivious and a little condescending, tells them that he's "afraid this particular moose will have to wait." As they continue to ignore him, he asks, bewildered, "What about the meeting?" In the silence that follows, the camera looks at the face of each of the key *North of 60* characters, ending with Rosie as she says with a small grin, "We just had one." Harris simply shakes his head as everyone leaves to help skin the carcass, butcher the meat, clear the freezers. There is a long shot of Gerry's empty store and coffee shop from the lawyer's point of view. Then Peter, using the far exit, grins and closes the door. Here, as in many of the other compact scenes in this episode, there is no music to colour the emotions and underline what is happening. The producers and director trust the dialogue and the performers to make their own impact and the audience to respond without unnecessary prompting. The community's decision, well prepared for over six seasons, provides an open ending, encouraging the viewers to imagine the Lynx River band in the coming years.

Nevertheless, a few of the remaining narrative threads require some sort of resolution, specifically the ones involving Albert: Albert and Sarah; Albert and Michelle; Albert and Nathan; and Albert and Joe Gomba. It is eight months since Nathan shot Albert to defend the lives of Sarah and Elizabeth. Albert has come home an apparent winner because of his controlling shares in the oil company. However, as Sarah finds out through her medical connections, the bullet Albert still carries has created a painful and lethal infection. Because Albert had rheumatic fever as a child and now has a damaged heart, the wound is inoperable. Albert is dying. Sarah: "Albert, look at me please. [The shot is over his shoulder but the viewer sees him lift his head.] You knew all along you were going to die." His face is impassive. But when she urges him to go to a hospital, he laughs. "Maybe jail," he replies. No, he hasn't told Michelle about the infection, "and you don't tell her, either. You don't tell a soul! [With an ironic grin] It would be a breach of medical ethics." It is obvious he is in great pain and that he bears it stoically. The man's bleak courage wins sympathy from the audience, and his decision to continue on his own is consistent with the Albert the audience has come to know. Still, he appears to be bent on destroying the town. In their next (and last) scene together, out on the street where he is sitting resting, Sarah makes one final effort. She gives him their little daughter, Elizabeth, to hug. He greets the little girl with delight and snuggles her even as Sarah accuses him of taking one last shot from beyond the grave with his attempt to get the band to scatter. Yet, as she points out to him, two of his sons are in jail and one is half crazy with hatred and fear. She finishes sadly, "You loved me once and I loved you," to which he says nothing, still nuzzling his daughter. She turns away and goes down by the river to tell Nathan he is dying. Nathan says calmly: "So I killed him, after all. It just took him eight months to die." The next day Nathan is the one to bring Albert the news of the band's decision that "no one's leaving. They didn't want your money." Albert: "Who says? Peter?" "They all did." Then, with some dignity and to our surprise, Nathan continues, "I'm not sorry I shot you. I'd do it again to protect Elizabeth and Sarah." Albert, peaceably: "What's done is done." Nathan: "But I killed you. I'm sorry because you are my father." Albert: "You'll be a father soon. That's good. That's how it should be." Albert, looking at his own death, has perhaps changed enough to accept the fact that Sarah is carrying his son's child. Sarah also has new insight. She later tells Michelle that Albert has committed sins, not crimes, and that she "can't hate him any more."

A short sequence of scenes follows Albert's conversation with Nathan. Michelle, still not back on duty after being shot, asks Harper to let her talk to Albert before he arrests him. Sarah sits stunned at the nursing station, looking at Albert's will, which his lawyer has just handed her. Teevee brings a package of moose to Kyla and Bertha, and Bertha says laconically, "I heard." Unexpectedly, Teevee does not respond with bravado but with deprecation: "What a mess. Not exactly my thing." When he asks about this new man in the lives of the children she had talked about, specifically about what he is going to do to earn a living, she admits that she has no other man. She had invented another man to make Teevee understand that there is no going back to what they had before. Teevee: "I don't want to go back, not to that. [Pause] The problem is I love you, that just doesn't go away, ever." He turns to go and check on Kyla. Bertha, after a brief silent struggle, quietly, with some resignation: "You want some coffee?" and that is the last we see of them alone – another appropriately open ending in which the subtext rather than their words gets them over the hurdles into the start of something new.

Early in the episode Michelle, in uniform and looking both intent and pale, tells Harper a little more of the complicated history of Lynx River. Although Albert's grandfather, George Golo, was a very famous hunter, someone slept with his wife. When he found out, he tracked the man in the snow, caught up with him, and "cut off his head as he slept by the fire ... It's in his blood. It's not evil, not even a question in his mind. It's the way he is, like Wolverine" (the Latin name of the species wolverine is *Gulo gulo*).[35] Albert is in some ways a force of nature, something Michelle acknowledges for the first time even as she tries to set aside her burning sense of injustice because the RCMP can only jail him for tax evasion. The ongoing conflict with Albert has continued up to this last episode, yet the characters have changed. Thus, the long, long narrative arc demands a last confrontation between Michelle and Albert. Harper reluctantly gives her the arrest warrant to execute, despite the fact that she is still not on active duty, after she says, "I need to talk to him. [Pause] Please."

Michelle, out of uniform, wearing a blue pullover with her hair down, finds Albert at his cabin. He comes out onto his porch carrying his rifle, first standing erect, then quickly sitting down in the sunshine. Michelle: "We have a warrant for your arrest." Albert, in medium long shot: "Tax evasion, Michelle? You must be getting desperate." Michelle replies with what seems to be a non-sequitur (but is not): "I won't let you tear this town apart." Albert: "Then stop me." He gently mocks her because the government's "demand for tribute" is too late, but his laugh turns into a gasping cough. Then he continues: "I had nothin' to do with you being shot." To Albert this truth matters, but Michelle cannot hear it. As the camera starts to close in, Albert says, "I've done less than you think." Michelle, getting it all out, yet quietly: "You've murdered people. You've destroyed lives ..." "[S]o have you. You and your brother." She shakes her head in denial as he continues, also quietly but with direct eye contact: "People look at you, they think all they have to do is spruce up, get in line. But instead you get knocked down." The camera continues to close in on dialogue that south of

60 viewers would perhaps have rejected in the first season or two. Albert: "White people have been making war on us since the day they arrived. [Gesturing to himself] At least I fought back." Michelle: "And what have you got to show for it?" Reaction shot as he looks down with no expression as she continues: "Children who hate you, enemies everywhere, even among your own people ..." He is in tight close-up as his laugh cuts her off: "[A]nother time we'd have been on the same side." Michelle, with a certainty that the audience does not share, says quickly, "No, never." He winces and leans back: "I'm tired. Arrest me tomorrow when all my affairs are in order." She is going to refuse, takes a step towards him, then looks closely at him, a dawning realization on her face as a close-up of his face reveals pain he cannot conceal. In a subdued voice she says, "All right. Tomorrow ...," and turns away.

In the next scene Michelle asks Sarah, who is still sitting stunned in her office with Albert's will in her hand, how long he has. Sarah: "Not long." Michelle registers no surprise. Sarah then tells her that his will leaves the majority of his oil company shares to Elizabeth with 20 percent to Nathan. Sarah is the executor and Teevee is to have his place back on the board. As Sarah says, "He has given it back to the band through Elizabeth and Nathan." She knows Michelle had gone out to arrest him and asks her what he said. Michelle only shares one moment from that encounter with her: "He said he was tired."

From the start Albert has been a complicated character, and this last legacy to Lynx River, even though the community had passed his test by rejecting the temptation of money, does seem credible. He has confronted his death, held and played with his child, and heard words of truth, even of lost love from Sarah, as well as words of respect from his son. In some ways I am reminded both of Gloucester's murderous son, Edmund, and of King Lear – Edmund, who, mortally wounded, gasps: "Some good I mean to do / Despite of mine own nature," who tries to withdraw (too late) the writ that is on the life of Cordelia because he has discovered that "yet Edmund was beloved";[36] and Lear, the deeply flawed, destructive, stubborn, yet great patriarch who refuses to give in until his last breath.

Albert's last unresolved relationship is with Joe Gomba, the alpha-plus male to his powerful negative archetype. Years ago, in executing the unofficial part of a community punishment, Joe had deliberately and carefully wounded Albert and had then protected Sarah after she and Albert had parted. Albert retaliated by leaving Joe to die with a broken leg in the bush. Each man is the other's equal. They have two scenes together. Joe discovers in his camp, placed where he is sure to find it, a worn knife and

"Borrowed Time." A dying Albert talks to Michelle in their final encounter. *Alberta Filmworks, in association with the CBC, distributed by Alliance Atlantis.*

sheathe that he recognizes as Albert's. (The knife and sheathe will rise up out of the ground to reappear in *Dream Storm*.) He immediately goes to Albert's in response to the wordless summons. As Albert looks over some papers by lamplight, Joe walks into his cabin and without any preliminaries says, "This was your grandfather's." An attentive viewer may remember Michelle's earlier story about George Golo and may wonder if the man George killed was related to Joe. Albert, looking up and betraying little, says simply, with a touch of irony: "I left you out in the bush to die. I wouldn't rob a man of his revenge. [Small pause] I was thinking I might go hunting tomorrow. After the meeting." He gets up and turns away. Joe, not moving but in focus behind his shoulder, says slowly with just a little emphasis: "Why should I help you die? You should suffer like I did.

[Pause] Others too." Albert's face comes into focus, but he doesn't turn to look at Joe: "You're the only one I can ask." Joe, still out of focus, says, "I don't owe you any favours," and closes the door as he leaves.

The last scene in this narrative arc finishes Albert's story. A tragic protagonist in Shakespearean and Greek tragedy has to understand that he has made mistakes and must accept responsibility. Albert's legacy and his words to his son have suggested that this process is complete. What makes Oedipus, Antigone, Macbeth, or Lear tragic protagonists rather than victims is the degree to which they can still make choices or endure the fact that they can no longer choose and yet have the courage to understand the reasons why. Series television can create over the years a character who is so complex, so layered, that what happens to him or her can also have a certain scale and grandeur. Albert chooses to die secretly, in his own time (with Michelle's unspoken help), and at the hand of an enemy who is the only other person who understands the rules he lives by. Joe is also the best shot in Lynx River. In an earlier episode, when Joe entered Albert's cabin with a rifle only to discover that Albert was very ill, he agreed to give him the time he asked for. Perhaps the fact that Albert owes his life to Joe is Joe's best revenge. In any case, for reasons never articulated but perhaps having to do with his respect for Albert's courage, Joe again does as Albert asks. What both of them choose to do seems to come out of an older Dene tradition. Albert walks out into the bush with his rifle. Sound of birds and a raven over quiet, unobtrusive music. We see his profile as he stops when he hears a movement. A long shot of Joe standing half-screened behind some trees. Out of the corner of his eye, Albert sees him but keeps his back turned. He is not impassive. His body is braced, his face clenched, his eyes are closed. He hears the rifle being cocked. We glimpse Joe over his shoulder, aiming directly at him. Albert's face relaxes briefly as he says, very quietly, "Maasi"– thank you – to Joe and perhaps also to the spirit world of the Dene traditions that he has acknowledged since the beginning. We see him in a last close-up, jaw clenched, eyes shut. The sound of one shot. Blackout. One note of music continues as the camera refocuses on the trees. Sad but tranquil music continues as Joe walks out of the trees towards the camera, his face showing strain through his usual calm. He finds Sarah sitting on a rock by the river. He pauses, looks at her. She returns the look. Then he walks on. Her face shows great sadness as she senses that Albert is dead. Only one word has been spoken in the whole sequence, yet what has happened and why is absolutely clear.

As so often in *North of 60*, this episode turns the conventions of the crime show imperative – "Get the criminal"– upside down. Which side you are on changes for the characters and the audience. As Albert said, in an earlier time Peter and Michelle might have been his allies. But the episode cannot end with Albert's death, although the time borrowed in the title seems to refer directly to him. Instead, the farewell show leaves the ninety-episode saga with most of the characters faring well. The last sequence begins with Gerry on the verandah of his closed store showing Rosie pictures of west coast real estate, talking about costs, telling her that there is no rush to make a decision. Again the subtext is clear. Given the choice he now has, Gerry will probably stay. One by one, without much fuss, the people of Lynx River arrive at the coffee shop, and ignoring the closed sign, they go in – to put moose in the freezer, to buy macaroni. Peter, Sylvie, Teevee, and Elsie want something to eat. Andrew and Charlie remind Gerry he promised them burgers for trying to find his water pipe. Wryly Gerry and Rosie go in to "make some sandwiches," and we hear on the sound track country and western music that sounds like it might be sung in Slavey. As Michelle comes along, Harper runs to catch up with her, but when he asks what happened with Albert, she says only that Albert said little and that she'll tell him about it in the morning. It's clear she won't tell him most of it. As she sits on the steps, Peter comes out of the store and leans on the verandah railing, looking down at her. She says to him that Albert doesn't have much time and tells him about the will. Peter says quietly, showing no surprise, "That's good news" (the last part of what she said? or all of it?), then goes back into the store. Sarah, walking with Joe, meets her new lover, Martin, who gives her the hug she asks for as she holds back her tears. Joe goes in and Martin follows. Sarah, visibly pulling herself together, asks Michelle, "So what can you do with moose meat besides stew it?" Michelle grins: "You can fry it." She gets up as Sarah says, "I was thinking about Stroganoff" – a city thing of course. As they go up the steps together, Michelle asks, "What's Stroganoff?" Sarah, laughing as they go through the door: "I have no idea." Sound of laughter inside. The door shuts and the camera shows the audience a sign swinging in the window – SORRY WE ARE CLOSED. A piano plays a few phrases of the *North of 60* theme as the scene shifts to a long shot of the main street of Lynx River, its one street light shining at dusk.

*Discussions on three other episodes are posted at www.brocku.ca/hri/associates/ miller/outside_looking_in.pdf: "To Have and to Hold" (a revealing look at Harris through the preparations for his and Lois's wedding), "Peter and the Wolf" (the less successful cousin to "To Have and to Hold"), and "A Sparrow Falls" (a mixture of outhouse humour and the drama of the search for the person who shot Michelle).*

# FOURTEEN

# Exploring Issues and Themes in *North of 60*

Elsie (to Teevee): "[You're] looking like those people and acting like a stupid kid. You can't change the inside of your head in one day."

## OVERVIEW: DENE CULTURAL VALUES

Characters are the key elements that bring viewers back week after week in a series like *North of 60*. Motifs enrich the episodes and tie the narrative arcs together, but stories are the backbone of hour-long television series. What often characterizes CBC television drama is its docudrama flavour and texture, reflected in the casting, in the locations, sometimes in the shooting style, and above all in the topical issues that are foregrounded in the stories. *North of 60* was charged (unfairly, in my view) with being glum. The series does often have a dark tone, thanks in part to the personal dilemmas of the characters and to the cop-show elements in the series and in four of the movies, but also to the fact that the writers and producers increasingly explored the problems that are specific to the northern First Nations, as well as contemporary issues that concern the wider audience.

C. Roderick Wilson (2004) writes: "Leadership among the Northern Athapaskans was largely situational: people were listened to or followed not because they had power ... but because they had demonstrated an ability to lead in that particular activity" (154). The fur trade produced not only new goods like dogsleds but also new roles like "trading chiefs." Even the advent of guns and Christianity did not break the continuity with the past: "The ensuing way of life was remarkably stable for many groups for almost a century and a half" (154), a significant contrast with the experience of the Anishnabe of Northern Ontario, for example. "For much of the region, most adults over 50 have personal memory of what life was like before significant government-industrial presence. For some the 'traditional life' is still a present reality. Second, even for severely impacted groups, truly significant features of traditional life remain important" (155).

Jean-Guy A. Goulet (2004) begins with a list of the new institutions – church, store, school, RCMP detachment, nursing station – that now frame the experience of both young and old Dene people. The Dene he writes about are not the South Slavey but there are parallels. When the Dene moved into government housing, many kept their cabins in the bush, where some men still go for several months a year to hunt and trap. The older adults, even those who had been to residential schools, have animal helpers, but many in the younger generation do not take the time to seek such help. Yet healers who obtain power from visions still exist, and the people still gather roots, leaves, herbs, and animal parts, activities that depend not only on common knowledge but on the proper attitude and the giving of gifts to the plants and animals as thanks for their medicinal properties. The visits of the spirit of a dead person are related to grief, to the possibility of harm for the dreamer, and to reassurance that this is not the case – as in Hannah's visit to her mother before her body is found and in Albert's role as Michelle's guide in *Dream Storm*.

The book *In the Words of the Elders: Aboriginal Cultures in Transition* (Kulchyski, McCaskill, and Newhouse 1999) quotes an interview with George Blondin (Slavey/Dogrib from Rae Edzo, born 1922), a self-educated man who was in a residential school that had terrible food, no textbooks, and little curriculum. For four years he was told that his "language was from the devil." Late in life, for twenty years, he was deeply involved in Dene protests against the 1921 Treaty, the Indian Act, and similar causes. Then he wrote two books based on his grandfather's stories, *When the World Was New: Stories of the Sahtu* (1993) and *Yamoria the Lawmaker* (1997). He believes that "[a]nybody that becomes Elder, their responsibility is tell the story" (Blondin 1997, 386), not only to children daily, but also to parents to teach them how to bring the children up from babies with the values and ways of the grandfathers and grandmothers. Blondin discusses the many powers the Dene people have: medicine power from the animals; the ability to talk to the animals, fish, and birds; the prophet's ability to see events thousands of miles away and in the future. Overall, he emphasizes the importance of knowing and keeping Yamoria's laws. Sex is sacred and was not talked about in his day, and he says that there were no teenaged pregnancies then or single mothers: "parents and elders decided on who their children would marry" and people did not divorce (403).

*North of 60* reflects the changes that have taken place in Dene communities. Michelle is divorced, Peter gets a divorce, Leon has an affair, Teevee doesn't marry Bertha, AIDS comes to the community. When Ellen decides to have her baby in Lynx River against Sarah's wishes, Elsie gathers herbs and roots to help her, then presides over the breech baby, who turns at the last minute. Yet about babies who are miscarried or are born dead Elsie simply says, "It was not meant to be." In fact, later Ellen predicts that Sarah's baby "will be just another white on the town's doorstep" – yet another reversal of stereotype. However, when Rosemary asks Elsie for herbs to help her conceive, Elsie replies firmly, "It's not magic. It's things my mother taught me."

Blondin repeatedly says that young people are raising themselves today because they either receive no instruction as they grow up or pay no attention to their elders and grandparents. However, he says that young kids need to learn "not to be mouthy, not to hurt nobody, love each other and help each other and share everything that you got ... How do we transfer some of the culture, the good culture from the past?" he asks (Blondin 1997, 394–6). He thinks that the educational system divides the child in two. Goulet, like many others, emphasizes that the Dene way to learn is not by direct instruction but by observation and imitation, a method which he says is closely connected to "their value of autonomy." The Dene respect "people's ability to realize their goals on their own" (167). This approach is not simply a matter of non-interference but an ethical view that actively creates the circumstances "in which one can learn by oneself and for oneself what it is to live an autonomous life competently" (168). All this offers a perspective on Albert's contempt for Lynx River legislating itself into a dry town and his repeated refusal to take responsibility for others' behaviour. See also Albert's last words to Michelle, when he accuses her and Peter of trying "to impose straight lines on the people." This means of learning also makes the older people the natural role models and ensures that people will look out for one another without being asked. Traditional groups consult each other, mutually plan activities, and "stimulate each other with humour to co-operate with each other while avoiding conflict" (169). Violence, however, is traditionally viewed as an act committed by a person when his or her mind is gone, which makes the person not accountable. People deal with those who injure them by withdrawing or saying it was not intended, not by confronting them or laying a charge against them with the police. Brian Fletcher, for example, complains bitterly about the fact that the community will tell him nothing about who commits vandalism.[1]

Michael Asch (2004) outlines the history of Slavey pre-contact and contact periods, including the fact that "no later than 1960 the nuclear extended family ... became the primary self-sufficient unit" (186) and that the money that was generated in a cash economy in excess of survival needs was privately owned. For example, food was shared, radios were not (187). This may explain why Rosie is not interested in Peter's idea of a co-op store and finds instead a way of becoming Gerry's partner. When ancient family units are melded into one village, ancestral memories produce tensions that can remain unresolved. The Golos are ancient rivals of the Kenidis. In the final episode Rosie points out that the Kenidis do not understand the needs of the De'elas. Distinctions are also made between young men like Teevee, who work for wages, and "seemingly poor young men" like Joey, who learn the ways of the bush from Joe and bring those resources to Bertha and others (190).

OTHER DENE CULTURAL VALUES

One reason for the alcoholism in Lynx River is the clash of two cultures experienced by every adult and child in the community. The "two worlds" theme stressed in the early publicity for the series is threaded through almost every episode, casually, as in Elsie's remark to Bertha when she doesn't have thirty dollars (northern prices in the mid-1990s) for Huggies, "Use moss. It's better for the bum," or crucially, as in the band's attempt, when, thanks to the discovery of oil, the first-ever road from the outside was coming in, to set conditions to get jobs and royalties, rather than be irrevocably damaged by this change. Basically, the series shows how people take from, ignore, or adapt to the white southern culture that enters their lives through television, many of the foods in Gerry's store, school curricula, government bureaucracies, visitors from outside, and eventually an access road. But for people living in Lynx River, unlike the young adults living on the Kidiabanasee Rez, the fundamentals of Dene culture itself, not just memories of a culture, survive.

In the *North of 60* timeline, none of the adults would have read anything resembling the 1989 Dene Cultural Institute's book for children, *Dehcho: "Mom, we've been discovered!"*[2] when they were in school, but their children could have. The young reader learns the Dene names of all of the original communities and that Deh Cho is the name of the Mackenzie River and its territories. The book ends with the proposal that the original name be used for the river instead of "Mackenzie." Although Michelle's family story that Alexander Mackenzie gave her great-great-great grandmother a necklace, "We as a people do not perceive Alexander Mackenzie as a great person," says Joanne Barnaby, executive director of the Dene Cultural Institute in the introduction to *Dehcho*. It is noted in the book that

Mackenzie rarely mentioned the First Nations men and women who made his journey possible, but that white men's trade goods "made life a bit easier" (15). When in the last episode of the series the community decides not to move, Michelle makes the point that their dead are buried there. Willie MacDonald is quoted in *Dehcho*: "But wherever we go, we always see old signs from long ago. We know that long before us this country has been used … People are still using it. We belong to it, we belong to the land … That's where we're born and that's where we're going to die. There is no way we're going to leave it" (47).

Hugh Brody (1987) also makes this point about Dene culture to his non-Dene or Inuit readers:[3] "We must not mistake this for a journey through time: we are not contemplating here our own ancestry" (xiv), a fantasy that *North of 60* repeatedly deconstructs by using plots turning on Dene/white conflicts. As he points out, to outsiders the "ways of living and thinking [of northern peoples] is regarded as primitive, their wealth is characterized by poverty" (xv). It is unlikely that a viewer's first impression of Joe Gomba's self-chosen "primitive" living arrangements, including the ultimate stereotype of an open fire for cooking and logs for seats, will be the same as the way he or she sees Joe's cabin six years later. But most of the people of Lynx River live much as Brody describes life in the Deh Cho and the modern Arctic: "Every family lives with and makes use of industrial culture, yet depends on the resources of the land, on hunting and trapping" (xvi) – moose, caribou, and fish for basic food. Junk food and convenience food come from Gerry's but are expensive. The women make jam from the berries. Some of Lynx River's Dene may not be good hunters, but they know more than Frank on *The Rez*, who tried to thaw a frozen moose haunch with a blowtorch. Although Brody talks about "the skills and joys of eating moose" fresh, hung for longer periods of time, smoked, and so on (57), there are many jokes on *North of 60* about the monotony of a moose diet, right to the last few lines of dialogue in the last episode.

### JUSTICE, THE LAW, AND COMMUNITY

With a Dene protagonist who is an RCMP officer, *North of 60* puts the dominant culture's view of justice into focus. The producer/writers chose to create an isolated community where elders are still respected and the culture is still strong. When, in the first season of the series, Albert supplies booze to a man who then freezes to death, the community decides on an old punishment for Albert, from the days of scattered small bands hunting and trapping in the bush – banning. Albert tells Peter, "A banning is a terrible thing. Maybe you are too young to know." In effect, the banned person becomes invisible in the eyes of the community. The series shows a whole range of ways of dealing with crimes – from a sentencing circle resulting in a period of exile or banning, to short periods in jail on the reserve, to being sent outside to prison. In her book on traditional justice, *Doing Things the Right Way* (1995), Joan Ryan quotes Paul Haverman: "The policing of indigenous communities appears to fulfill a hybrid function of order maintenance and social service to a much greater degree than it does in other communities … [Unfortunately] since police define the problems, police solutions are found" (128). He concludes that this leads to larger aboriginal prison populations. Certainly the 1988 statistics (published four years before *North of 60* began) that Haverman provides, which are quoted by Ryan, confirm that the numbers of crimes committed per 100,000 people is much greater in the Northwest Territories than in the rest of Canada.

Although not centred on the Slavey Dene in *North of 60*, Ryan's detailed analysis of traditional justice has a bearing on the general uses and problems of sentencing circles. She outlines the old ways of doing things in a community with a strong language and cultural base, whose elders still know the "proper" ways of doing things. As she says, in the small mobile groups that characterized the way of life on the land, every member of the group was likely to know who had done what (26). Those who committed small transgressions were treated with ridicule. Those who were found guilty of more serious actions, like theft, were pressured by the community to replace the object with one of the same or higher value. Context determined what was theft, what was borrowing, what was justifiable need (57). Early in *North of 60*, there is a running joke about how Willy's axe keeps walking away. A young man like Teevee is expected to at least provide for his child and her mother, and his failures are one of the ongoing plot lines, as are his eventual successes. In the old days, "[i]f he refused, he was banished" (39). Serious offences like adultery, abandoning one's family, rape, or impregnating young unmarried women would involve a circle comprised of the entire community (33–4). A sentencing circle could only arrive at a conclusion by consensus – "Disorder and imbalance were dangerous for the group as well as individuals" (xxvii). Sentencing circles appear in both *The Rez* and *North of 60*, in the latter showing why and how the strategy was used, as well as its after-effects. The focus was on finding resolution for the victim, reconciling the person who had disrupted the social order with the victim and the group, and therefore restoring the group harmony so vital to survival in harsh conditions. The focus was on what had made the person behave in this way, not on the action itself (xxvii). Once the issue was resolved, it was over and not mentioned again. Ryan sees parallels with Anishnabe justice as described by Rupert Ross in *Dancing with a Ghost* (1992).[4]

### ALCOHOL

Alcohol abuse is a major issue in this series, reflecting situations on many reserves and in many other communities across the country. If it had been excluded, the series would have lost much of its claim to authenticity. On the other hand, the back story for Lynx River is that the community made the decision to go dry five years before the series opened. Despite the very real temptations offered by Albert's bootlegging, many people are staying sober. Not all – he continues to make money. In his painfully honest book *Crazy Water: Native Choices on Addiction and Recovery* (1993), Mohawk writer Brian Maracle sees addictions as a consequence of the "holocaust that has wreaked destruction" on his people and on the people from all over Canada he interviewed. In his introduction, he talks about the price paid by individuals and then about the price paid by his own people, "the Onkwehonwe of Great Turtle Island," who have had contact with settlers since the seventeenth century: "We have lost our languages, medicines and religions. We have lost out pride, dignity and confidence. We have lost our family values, social patterns and political structures. We have lost our stewardship over the land. We have lost control of our lives and our destiny. We have lost almost everything a race of people can lose" (9). Maracle blames both "Old Man Canada" and his own people, and sees hope only because there "are more sober native role models around these days." (13). He concludes his introduction by saying that his book stands for something: "It celebrates sobriety and it celebrates a revival of native culture and traditional spirituality" (15).

In *North of 60* the issues associated with alcoholism are complex. In the very first episode of the series, Eric has a severe bout of depression and won't get out of bed. Michelle's abrupt response is, "If I gave up that easy, I'd still be a drunk sleeping in the bush." Thus, from the top of the series she sets the tone for her own honesty and sense of self by deconstructing the stereotype of the helpless, drunken Indian. Early in the series, Rosie, who is much more voluble than Michelle, flatly refuses to marry Leon unless he stops drinking. They already have children and she has been sober for some time (as we learn later, they had nearly lost custody of their children when they were both drinking). In David Barlow's script for episode 13, "Freeze-out," one of Leon's drinking buddies freezes to death. Albert dismisses any accusation that he was responsible for supplying the booze, saying, "Ray was drunk for thirty years. That's not my fault ... he found it or made it or drank cough syrup." Over the course of several episodes, with a lot of difficulty, Leon stops drinking. He and Rosie then get married and take off on a motorcycle like a young couple, with the town rejoicing. However, in episode 31, "Harvest," by Stuart Margolin, some of the Lynx River Dene, including Rosie, get drunk when the tannery fails and all of the potential jobs are lost. But most of them do go back on the wagon. Over its six seasons the series shows a range of causes of alcoholism and also deals with coping strategies. Lois manages to avoid suicidal binges most of the time, and Rosie, through all kinds of pressures, stays sober for the rest of the series. Not everyone succeeds, which is why Michelle ends up adopting Susie Muskrat's son Charlie. Peter seems never to have been an alcoholic. He makes his own decisions about the matter clear when he says, in the context of Ellen's near breech delivery, that for the first time in five years (since the town went dry) he could use a drink. Albert mentions drinking beer in his youth but he no longer drinks. Michelle's years in residential school are named as the cause of her alcoholism, but clearly that experience is common to every soul in Lynx River of her generation.

When Peter is chief – and also (surprisingly) when Albert is chief – the town remains officially dry, and this is one of the reasons counsellor Betty Moses does not want the alcoholic rehab centre built in Lynx River. From her point of view, the centre would be too isolated and too free of temptation. Over the six seasons, some of the teens drink, do drugs, and sniff gasoline, partly out of boredom – another side effect of Lynx River's lack of jobs and remote location. Brenda Shore, the girl used by Albert to corrupt Fletcher, seems to be without family and does drugs as well as alcohol, although she does go to Edmonton to a detox centre for help eventually. In one of the best episodes, "You Can't Get There from Here" (episode 40), by Andrew Wreggitt, Charlie's mother, Susie Muskrat, a client at the rehab centre, manages to find a bottle to quell memories of her children who had died in a house fire while she was drunk and of her subsequent time in prison. Joey Smallboat's father does his best to stay away from drink, proudly using the money he saved to buy a snowmobile. Ben Montour, the visiting artist, on the other hand, believes that his art and his pain and his drinking are inextricably one, even when he makes a clown of himself, and he leaves Lynx River unchanged. Michelle has been a recovering alcoholic for ten years when the series starts. Her alcoholism colours her relations with Hannah. "I hated what she [her mother, a 'bush Indian'] was. I hated her in me. I drank and screwed around. That's why I'm so hard on [Hannah]." But Michelle is not driven back to the bottle by Hannah's death. Albert's sardonic comment about the rehab centre, "Indian pain is big business," could be seen as self-reflexive.

Lynx River is deliberately portrayed as a town that is struggling but is also healing, which may be why *North of 60* does not portray too much of the family devastation that alcoholism brings. No one beats his wife or kids; most kids don't starve, wander neglected, or get sick, although young Charlie Muskrat, a casualty of his mother's failure to stop drinking, has to find a home with Michelle. Interestingly, we rarely see Teevee having a drink, although for a while he makes money bootlegging for Albert. He has grown up with a mother whose sobriety is very fragile. Bertha, who is studying to be a nurse while trying to look after their baby, never touches a drop. As a teenager, Hannah chooses not to drink, even in the city, refusing to drink at a party the night she slipped into the river and drowned. The RCMP outsiders, Olssen and Fletcher, learn not to drink, even surreptitiously. Sarah does not drink and does not seem to be tempted by her ready access to drugs. Gerry takes an occasional drink and gets surly or maudlin. Harris sets out to get drunk, at least once, but doesn't seem to drink much otherwise. The irony of a rehab centre as another source of reliable employment is not lost on a community struggling to stay dry. Later, because of nepotism, it is moved to bigger settlement. The series shows the characters – from drunks to teetotallers – making a range of choices on the issue of alcohol, from abstention, to occasional use, to abuse. Alcoholism and the pain it causes comprise a major thread in *North of 60* – raising objections among some First Nations viewers – but what is important is that the series provides neither saints and martyrs nor helpless victims. And the long form of the series allows the issue to be thoroughly and honestly presented.

## LAND CLAIMS AND LAND USE

"It is no good to be scared of the land. We are from the land. We come from it. Why are we scared of ourselves ... We are the land."

Elizabeth Mackenzie, 4 April 1990[5]

Land claims and rights over resources raise fundamental questions not only of justice but also of cultural survival. Hugh Brody (1987) quotes Richard Nerysoo, a Kutchin Dene and former government leader in Fort Macpherson,

Michelle with her friend Betty Moses (Tantoo Cardinal), an alcohol and drug abuse counsellor whose work covers the Dene Cho. *Alberta Filmworks, in association with the CBC, distributed by Alliance Atlantis.*

speaking in 1977: "Being an Indian means ... saying the land is an old friend, an old friend your father knew, your grandfather knew, indeed your people have always known ... We see our land and much, much more than the white man sees it. To the Indian people our land really is our life" (9).[6] "According to Dene, Cree, and Naskapi theories of knowledge, success and happiness depend on the careful maintenance of good relations between people and all parts of the environment" (75). In the *North of 60* series and then in the movies, the issue of what kind of control the band can exert over its own territory (furs, oil and gas, diamonds, water diversion, lumber) is raised several times. In the sixth season, the producers introduced a road to Lynx River to open up new stories, but the decision also upped the ante when it came to the issue of keeping the Dene culture alive. The question of timing also comes up again and again. Is the band ready for change? Connected to the importance of communal decisions is the reiterated motif in *North of 60* that the time must be right before major decisions are taken. Ross (1992), in a section of his book called "The Notion That the Time Must Be Right" (38–40), points out that when people lived off the land, they had to know when the berries were ready to be picked, when the fish would appear, when pelts would be at their best. The time when everything was ready could not be rushed. Acting too soon could be fatal, but everyone had to be ready to tackle the hunting, fishing, or gathering. Mental, physical, and spiritual healing also occurs when the time is right, as the series demonstrates, but the series also makes it very clear that some wounds do not heal.[7]

## JOBS

Hydroelectric dams are just the latest issue in the region, as reflected in *Another Country*, the 2003 *North of 60* TV movie that explores what a dam built in the area to provide electricity for California will do, not only to the community of Lynx River, but also to the Lynx River itself and to the land. One of the major motifs in *North of 60* is jobs interlinked with land use. Oddly, there is little sense of this connection on *The Rez*, where jobs are also scarce. There is some sense of the land as life in *Spirit Bay* and even earlier in *The Beachcombers*. Jesse, a member of the Seahost band, is comfortable with a boat, with diving gear, with swimming. The sea is hundreds of miles away from the Deh Cho, but just as the sea provides so much for Jesse's band and the land and lake provide for the children of *Spirit Bay*, the Deh Cho once provided for almost every need. Kerry Abel (1993) emphasizes the usefulness of southern Canada's ignorance about the North, because it has meant that Ottawa did not made the decision to move the people of the Northwest Territories onto reserves. Abel also praises the Dene's adaptability and ability to make the best of their settlements so that their children could go to local schools, but she also notes that "they rejected those things that threatened their most important values" (265). Brody (1987) quotes one of his informants: "Our old people, when they talk about how the Dene ways should be kept by young people ... they are not looking back, they are looking forward. They are looking as far into the future as they possibly can" (9). He notes ironically, provocatively characterizing the stereotypes of northern peoples, that southerners are not looking at an empty land of pristine purity and "absolutely new opportunities" (15), inhabited by "savage, cunning Indians" who stand in their way and "smiling, innocent 'Eskimos'" who watch from the sidelines (19–21). Traditionally among the Dene, the family food supply depended on both men who hunted larger animals and women who harvested small mammals, birds, and fish. Winter was their friend, providing the best hunting and often fishing, and families scattered on the land. Summer was the time that their ancestors used to gather in small bands before the families dispersed for winter trapping and hunting.

Although their traditional land is immense, the Dene are not numerous by southern standards. The Dene population in total would fill a small city of twenty to thirty thousand people. Lynx River is an isolated community the size of a village. Joey chooses to learn traditional skills from Joe Gomba, but viewers see few young adult men working very often (or out on the land), which is also the reality in many small and isolated First Nations communities. The tannery depends on Italian money (topped up with a large chunk of Gerry's life savings), transient fashion trends, and the band's ability to resist the media blackmail of white anti-trappers, all of which illustrate both the necessity of and the perils of outside money. In the end, the tannery turns out to be a scam. Later Teevee, in partnership with Gerry, struggles to find reliable workers for his portable sawmill. However, the series merely touches on the problems inherent in a workforce that runs on "Indian time," and it does not present as a problem the men's need to take time off from employment to do the necessary hunting that feeds their extended family, both issues that can plague attempts to establish industries that would provide wage work in the North. Leon and others have to go many miles away to find work as carpenters or miners. Oil and gas exploration promises some jobs but not enough, and the band struggles to exert control over the company that controls the drilling. The issue of jobs also haunts the television movies. In the first movie, *In the Blue Ground*, the exploration for diamonds does not provide any local jobs. In *Trial by Fire*, an attempt to capitalize on tourism with a tourist lodge literally goes up in smoke. In *Dream Storm*, the issue is the gas company's right to lay a gas pipeline across traditional hunting grounds already despoiled by detritus from World War II (the last scene shows Teevee and Bertha putting some of that refuse in Teevee's truck). In *Another Country*, Teevee tries to get a better deal for the oil reserves on the band's traditional lands. In the last movie to date, *Distant Drumming*, the diversion of the Lynx River is an issue. Jobs and the uses of primary resources are intimately connected, the one providing serious temptation to accede to the outsiders who are exploiting the land, a dynamic familiar all over Canada.

What is not raised at any point in *North of 60* is the idea of full political nationhood for the Deh Cho region. Nor does the series address questions of status and non-status designations for individuals, although the Deh

Cho First Nations list of "member communities" identifies as Deh Cho peoples who may think of themselves today as more specifically Dene, Metis, status, or non-status.[8] A related issue to decision making about land use and ideas for potential jobs is the cultural expectation of consensus. In a later episode, "Bob," the bureaucrat who has been sent to close the treatment centre consults the board and asks, not for a vote, but for consensus – and gets it. In the last episode of the series, "Borrowed Time," after a long discussion in the coffee shop before the official band meeting, the members of the community reach a consensus. Despite a tempting offer from an oil company, they will not move away from Lynx River. The implication seems to be that if the band accepts the money and scatters, their title to the land will be extinguished – though the phrase itself is not used. True or not, the importance of the land to the community is made very clear in the last few scenes. Jobs are vital to the community's welfare but not at the expense of their way of life or their ties to the land.

POLITICS

Jobs can also depend on politics. "The personal is political" is, of course, an old feminist slogan, but it has always been true in the world of *realpolitik*, whether admitted or not. Nepotism and feuds between families are well-known hazards in large and small communities, all the more so in cultures where the family comes first. Who is family can determine who gets jobs, allocation of housing, schools, salaries. Complaints about nepotism in particular still appear in the pages of aboriginal newspapers and periodicals and in regular coverage of financial irregularities or of the distribution of scarce resources. In a community where everyone is related and ancient feuds persist, it is an even greater issue.[9] (The same issues appear in more comic mode in *The Rez*.) The normal *quid pro quo* that is intrinsic to all levels of political life to the present day is complicated by the intricate web of relationships, family, band, and nation that preceded the founding of the Northwest Territories. Tribal politics play themselves out in every season of *North of 60* and the flashpoint is often jobs. When Albert replaces Peter as chief (he has been chief before), Michelle's job is in danger. Albert muses about having a tribal police officer, at lower pay, with fewer qualifications, but in the end leaves her in place. Leon can't get a job working for the band, because, as he says, "I had to vote for Peter. He's my cousin. I never thought he'd lose." Eventually, when Albert blackmails Betty Moses – we never find out the details – into recommending that the rehab centre be housed in Lynx River, Leon is employed to build it but he has to use Albert's unskilled sons as assistants. When Joe and Joey find a bush fire, they report it, but not too soon, since fighting forest fires creates work – and also cleans the forest naturally. Initially, Albert wants to fire Harris as band manager because he worked for Peter, but Harris proves his worth as a schemer and keeps his job. It is always made clear that the Ministry of Indian Affairs both gives contracts and then takes them away, with little apparent warning and always with political overtones. When the issue of moving the treatment centre out of Lynx River arises, Rosie immediately suspects the reason is that the minister has three relatives on the governing board who live in the new location.[10]

Late in the fifth season, episode 73, "Suspicious Minds," brings to a climax the manoeuvring between Peter and Harry Dobbs, Peter and the band council, and Peter and Elsie (one of the council holdouts). The result is that future partnerships are to be established, but not yet – the elders are not ready. Like the partnership issue itself, the problems and values of the fictional Lynx River are negotiated day by day over several episodes, just as they have been negotiated over months and years with the communities and leaders in the real Deh Cho. In episode 86, "Heroes (For One Day)," when the oil company threatens to displace Joe and others who live on the edge of town with their rigs, Teevee summons native eco-activists (who are armed and media savvy) to a blockade of the proposed road that threatens to bring in uncontrolled change. He denounces the white managers and boards who take over resources from those who have lived there for thousands of years. But at the last moment, Teevee and his activist friends find out that the chief shareholder in the company is Albert – a nice plot twist. Harry Dobbs has been Albert Golo's agent all along.

Of course, for the majority of viewers, who are not aboriginal, one of the major subjects is the interface between the cultures, much of it played out on the economic front. When Ellen tells Sarah that her job has been eliminated so that the treatment centre can afford Andrew One Sky, a fully trained therapist, Sarah remarks bitterly, "I'm the wrong flavour. Vanilla's out. Strawberry's in." But the treatment centre will close unless they find the salary for One Sky (who is also good at grantsmanship, which is an invaluable skill in relations with government). That the closure would mean that Bertha who cooks and Ellen who is the administrator would lose their jobs does matter to Sarah. Like her, they have no reliable income. And she acknowledges that it is logical that they would want "a native with a degree ... not an ex-nurse with a few blown circuits." By the end of the series, the message is not that jobs are impossible to find but that finding jobs is very difficult. There will never be enough work in the small community for every adult, every young man and woman.

## MAN/WOMAN RELATIONSHIPS

The way in which the CBC publicity framed the series in its first season, as well as the remarks by Wayne Grigsby and Barbara Samuels reported in chapter 11, makes it clear that white/Dene relationships were the original focus of *North of 60*, a series that emphasized the collision of two worlds. There are four close white/Dene relationships in the series. With Michelle and David, the white archaeologist, in the second season, the love affair happens, it flourishes, he returns to his wife, and Michelle gets hurt. This is the stuff of thousands of TV dramas. Peter, though, does reverse another stereotype, that is, that all prejudice is white, when he expresses dismay that Michelle is attracted to someone white. The resolution of the Rosie/Gerry subplot is less predictable. Over the years, as he comes to recognize Rosie's skills as a business partner and even gets to know her kids, the gruff, self-centred Gerry falls in love with her. While Leo is working far from home with a girlfriend on the side, Gerry is almost a substitute parent for Wayne and the other children. Rosie's rejection is friendly but firm, leaving Gerry with some dignity, but alone. In the last episode, he shares his personal history with her, then kisses her for the first and clearly the last time. In that case, oddly, not much is made of the two different cultures, although there are a few references.

The issue of relationships between native women and white men, or native men and white women, has always been fraught, ever since the days of the captive narratives beginning in the seventeenth century and certainly in the eighteenth and nineteenth centuries when coureurs de bois, voyageurs, and then Hudson's Bay Company traders and factors married the "country wives" who were the mothers of their children, the Metis. Michael Hilger (1995) traces the theme of romances between the two peoples in cinema from the days of silent films to the present, providing an exhaustive checklist. However, it is worth noting that the concept that the Metis comprise a separate culture – one now granted rights in the Charter – is completely foreign to the United States. *North of 60* does not minimize the difficulties of such relationships. However, valid or not, the point of view prevailing in the series is that of the Dene community. The series seems to suggest that, on the whole, people in the two cultures, particularly women, should stick to their own. Harris and Lois Tenia are the only exceptions to the pattern. By mid-run of the series, Harris is sleeping with Lois, but both of them have unexorcized demons. They woo over a whole season, with the standard problems with step-kids and mother-in-law. But these problems are compounded by Lois's troubled past and

Harris's own insecurities and frailties; for example, he sabotages Teevee's application for training as band manager, fearing for his own job. Lois's masochistic desire to be hurt reaches a climax in her disastrous affair with Mohawk artist and womanizer Ben Montour. Harris is furious. At first Teevee likes Montour because he is "Indian," but when Montour abuses Lois emotionally, he comes to see that Harris is the first of Lois's men never to hit or abuse her. Michelle tells Harris that he is good for Lois. Harris and Lois both persevere, and their marriage brings that season to a traditional, mostly happy, climax. But when Albert forces Brenda to seduce Brian Fletcher, her success not only destroys Brian but also leads to her own suffering. On the other hand, the ambitious young white businesswoman with whom Teevee gets involved in Edmonton is a passing fling, with no one really hurt either way.

Not all Dene/Dene relationships work. Michelle is divorced. Peter's uncharacteristic, very brief affair with Sylvie, a Metis, ends abruptly when Ellen finds out. However, years after Sylvie is widowed and after his own marriage breaks down, he marries her. Bertha's problems with Teevee go on for six seasons. Sarah has a long and complicated relationship with Albert but ends up with Martin, who is white. Michelle ends up with Andrew. On the whole, the series pairs like with like.

## WOMEN IN *NORTH OF 60*

As a prelude to a discussion of the feminist issues raised by *North of 60*, it would be useful to look at the broadcasting context of the series during its conception and first years. The series began in 1992. An internal CBC document, "CBC Demographics from Social Trends on CBC Primetime Television 1977–1992: A Content Analysis Commissioned by the CBC,"[11] helps to situate *North of 60* in the context of CBC television of the late 1980s and early 1990s. I both quote it and summarize some of its sections here and in the endnotes.

According to the document, "The proportions of female and male characters in drama have remained stable over five studies of English CBC drama since 1981" (3). In the United States, the proportion of females has been lower. The figures are similar for co-productions and programs bought by the CBC. "The 1992 sample shows a large increase over previous years in the proportion of racial minority characters. Throughout the 1980s, approximately 7 percent of characters have been members of minority groups: in 1992 18 percent of characters were minorities" (3). Of course, this percentage would go up significantly when the CBC was

Teevee Tenia, Harris (Timothy Webber), and Lois Tenia (Willene Tootoosis) become a family. *Alberta Filmworks, in association with the CBC, distributed by Alliance Atlantis.*

broadcasting both *The Rez* and *North of 60*. "Age and gender are associated with power, in an interesting way. In occupations that are not associated with power or authority, age and gender are neatly balanced; there are very similar numbers of women and men, older and younger characters" (3). As one might expect, "[w]omen are more strongly associated than men with home and family roles. Men are more strongly associated with women in some occupational roles, and with physical violence" (4).[12]

As a series focused on several Dene women, *North of 60* is atypical on several levels. Its protagonist is an attractive woman in her twenties who wears no obvious makeup and is often swathed in a parka and her basic all-blue uniform or well-worn jeans. The series also presents a plump, feisty Rosie and a much older and highly respected, if conservative, Elsie. Moreover, this is an ensemble show with many subsidiary characters who take focus over a season – Lois, a middle-aged, beautiful mother; Mary, a strong and immensely competent nurse; Betty Moses, an intense rehab counsellor; Ellen and Sylvie, Peter's two wives; as well as a number of teenagers and children. The "de-feminizing" of Sarah, who begins as a blonde, lovely white nurse and becomes something of an outlaw – definitely a survivor in work shirts and jeans – adds to the atypical mix.

The report continues: "Gender is associated with power in a similar way [as compared to an age correlation, which gives power in the narratives primarily to thirty-five to sixty-four-year-olds]. Males outnumber females by a ratio of about 6:4 and males dominate the high prestige and high power occupational groups," especially in *North of 60*, where jobs other than counselling and trapping are resource based – mining and logging, and oil drilling – a man's world. "If women do appear in high prestige and power occupations, they usually hold a more junior rank" (35). In *North of 60*, except for Michelle as an RCMP constable who rises to corporal, women do not do a "man's job," although both Michelle and Rosie hunt for food for their families. Women do not do waged work in *Spirit Bay*, although Tafia's aunt is a well-regarded painter. On *The Beachcombers* Laurel, Jesse's wife, works in the bank. In *The Rez* things are a little more complicated because Silas is the storyteller/dreamer, while his girlfriend Sadie gets the job of assistant to the chief. Silas and Frank Fencepost both work part-time at the marina but never do find permanent work on the reserve. Eleanor runs the marina on the reserve, but Tanya, her daughter, is a server whose curves and choice of dress are intended to bring males into the bar.

"Drama programs typically provide more information on the marital status of female characters, rather than of male characters … more women, than men are given a romantic partner of the opposite sex." In other words, it was more acceptable in the 1980s and early 1990s for a man to be unattached than a woman. In *North of 60*, Michelle is a loner until the last two seasons, but most of the other women, of her age and younger, have relationships. "Fewer than 1% of characters have a romantic partner of the same sex" (41). Nevada is the only openly gay character on the show, and he is not allowed to stay, although AIDS, not homosexuality, is the apparent reason. As we see in *North of 60*, "women are more likely to have … friends [of their own sex] than men … Female characters support other characters, both female and male, with greater frequency than do male characters" (42). Women appear more often than men with members of their family, interacting with children under eighteen, performing child-care and household tasks. On *North of 60* women make crafts together and enjoy Scrabble nights. Men are rarely shown getting together on their own. When men are shown as caregivers, the child care tends to be part-time and they are often (not always) incompetent, although it is clear that Willy years ago had taken devoted care of his wife and so knew what to do with Nevada. One of the recurring motifs on *North of 60*, affecting a number of characters, is the absent father. When it comes to the loaded issue of physical violence, the report says, unsurprisingly, that "men are more likely to possess a weapon and to assault others," but it notes that while American programming favours female victims, on Canadian-made television, "women and men are equally likely to figure as victims of physical assault" (46). More females than males are blonde (young women on television are still overwhelmingly blonde), which makes *North of 60* and *The Rez*, with their predominantly black-haired women, quite different in this respect to viewers (though probably subconsciously). Overall the report throws into high relief the fact that both series did not follow many patterns displayed in television drama in the 1980s and early 1990s. Many of those patterns are still visible today.

Ryan (1995) discusses the traditional role of Dene women before the money economy intruded. Women married young, and marriages were usually arranged. A husband was allowed to beat his wife "if she did not do her work properly" (41), but would be chided by the leader if he was too abusive. Apparently the only acceptable reasons for couples to separate were if the husband committed adultery or was too abusive; in such cases, young children went with their mother. Yet Albert directly and indirectly attempts to get his daughter away from Sarah, despite the fact that traditionally men did not get involved in infant care. Joey becomes a surrogate father to Kyla because Teevee is irresponsible. Ryan says that some of women's work, such as making clothing, made hunting possible in all weathers. Other tasks traditionally performed by women – collecting wild food (116), caring for the camp and the children – were eventually devalued because they did not generate cash in the way fur trapping did. This "led to a change from the traditional economic sexual equality between men and women to male economic and social dominance" (60). In this series, except for Michelle, the women do the typically female jobs – teacher, storekeeper, cook, nurse, administrator – which is what is available in that environment.

When we turn to explore the specifically feminist issues raised in the *North of 60*, we see, first and most obviously, that the series is primarily about Michelle. The ensemble around her is very strong, but Tina Keeper as Michelle carries the show. Thus, since Michelle is a woman and a mother as well as a Dene cop, feminist issues are often foregrounded. That she is exemplary (though human) is spelled out several times, with all the pressures that being a very visible example entails. "I am a cop. That's what I do," she says more than once, but she also mothers the whole town, often feeling responsible for its failures, and she applies her own sense of justice in several instances.

Michelle can be both a cop and a mother to Hannah because there are people in the small community to pitch in. "It takes a village" like Lynx River. Nevertheless, Hannah's normal problems as a budding teenager are compounded by the fact that she is a cop's kid. Child-care issues are more clearly raised with Rosie, whose kids eat lunch in the coffee shop. She has real trouble with her young teenager Wayne when Leon is away for weeks at a time. But Rosie manages her children's problems, again with help from women friends and even, to his own surprise, from Gerry. This pattern is rooted in Dene tradition. Ryan (1995) says that in the old days, although women were not leaders, they were in charge of the camp when the men were away, in charge of the children, and in charge of their daughters for life. The family residence was originally matrilocal and multigenerational, as it is at Elsie's.

Nor is there any doubt that the ongoing conflict between Peter and Albert reflects an ancient impulse when the older alpha male and the up-coming contender for that role clash. The younger Peter challenges the older Albert, not only by seeking the role of chief, but also by pitting his communal vision against Albert's unbridled capitalism – or, to put it in more traditional terms, the good of the whole band (whose advice Peter sometimes seeks and sometimes ignores) against Albert's belief in the absolute responsibility of the individual. Their conflict is very different from the ongoing conflict between Michelle and Albert. Michelle helps Sarah when Albert deserts her, and she viscerally loathes Albert in his many guises because she deals every day with the ravages of his bootleg alcohol and the temptations he offers the younger men. Although it is not spelled out, the apparently long-standing rivalry between the Kenidis and the Golos that so exasperates Rosie and that plays itself out in many ways (including in the election of first one and then the other for chief) may be rooted in the old days when two such powerful families might have gone out on the land in winter and then in summer might have returned to one location to feast, play hand games, and introduce their young people to one another, usually in friendly fashion; but when the families were forced to settle in Lynx River to be near their children in school (this did not happen in many real Dene communities until the 1970s [Asch 1998, 359]), rivalries could erupt (Ryan 1995, 53).

Sarah is a nurse, not a doctor, partly because small communities like Lynx River cannot support a doctor. Like the male whites in the community, she is fleeing her past. She often embodies situations and conditions that women fear: she is videotaped while making love to Eric, goes crazy, gets pregnant, is deserted by Albert, endures threats and harassment from his sons, loses her job, has no roof of her own, goes home to a controlling relative, and finds she has no place any more in the culture she grew up in. She does tough it out, though not in a way that viewers can easily apply to their own lives. At times she is clearly disoriented and delusional, but she is not the standard mad woman of romance fiction or Hollywood horror films. She leaves her bleak room in Gerry's motel and wanders around until Albert takes her in. When the community disapproves, Joe rightly says that she wouldn't have gone to him "if we had looked out for her." (The stereotype of communal responsibility among First Nations takes a beating here, not for the first or last time.) Sarah learns to shoot the traditional way by watching Albert shoot. Albert even tells her he will teach her to build a travois. He accepts with few words what she has to say and why, gives her food, concern, and a bed separated from the rest of the cabin by a sheet. When eventually he comes to her in her bed, she welcomes him as gently and freely as he has helped her. Sarah says plainly to Eric (her ex-lover), "He doesn't need me to do things I don't want to do or make me into what he wants ... Albert is good for me." Eric finally asks her whether she will give up her room at the motel. She replies blandly (but the subtext is clearly ironic), "I'm sick. I can't make decisions. I leave that up to other 'good men.' You're a good man, you decide." From this point on, Sarah, though never assimilated into Lynx River, will belong in a way the government "nurse" could not, and she bears two children with Dene status. Eventually, she finds a more or less stable relationship with Martin, the foreman of an oil rig who is also at home in the North and who offers her some economic stability. Nevertheless, her children will be raised in part by Lynx River.

Sarah also breaks some of the more familiar television stereotypes. The fact that she wears camp shirts and no obvious makeup complicates the signification of available woman. Even though she is denied band housing (despite the fact that her children are half Dene), she refuses to live as a resident nurse in the apartment at the nursing station, because she cannot bear the routine or the responsibility implied. Yet she still functions as nurse when anyone is really sick. She is both stubborn and unrealistic about how tough things can be. For a while she subsists on Albert's irregular cheques and laughs about being a kept woman. Eventually, she tries to build a new house for her young children from a do-it-yourself kit, using the directions in the package. Martin is very negative about the project, to which she reacts as the feisty woman she has become: "You disappear for six weeks and you criticize my house?" Martin: "I just want my kids to have a real home." But they are not his kids, and she retorts,

"You know what? This doesn't involve you." Unfortunately, in feminist terms, the first movie – *In the Blue Ground* – is retrogressive. Sarah is kidnapped by a now quite mad Brian Fletcher, the ex-Mountie who was assumed to have committed suicide. The film presents too many scenes in the damsel-in-distress thriller mode, with heavy psycho-sexual/sado-masochistic overtones. Before being rescued, she is buried alive, a pretty obvious metaphor for the disposable woman, and there is a plot twist that belongs in the run-of-the-mill horror flick. It should not take a kidnapping for Martin to settle in and help build her house and for the community to pitch in.

Much earlier, "Birth Right," episode 8, by Jean Stawarz, presents the archetypal triad. Sarah is the maiden (in the sense that she has not given birth) who cannot help with a traditional birth; Ellen is the mother who gives birth; and Elsie is the wise crone/healer who has a brief crisis of confidence but then takes charge and delivers the baby safely. The men in the episode either fight or panic. As time goes on and Sarah's character moves to a more prominent position, she is not maiden but mother. Later, Teevee shows revulsion towards this archetype when Bertha nurses the baby in front of him. "You do it to turn me off your tits." Bertha, accurately, retorts, "You're stupid and selfish." She accuses him of not even knowing how to play with his own child or with the children in his job at the Rec Centre. In the end Bertha decides to go to back to high school, which means leaving the baby with Elsie and Lois, and moving from maiden and mother to healer in training. By episode 73, "Suspicious Minds" by Andrew Wreggitt, Bertha is studying to be a nurse and living with Teevee, who is a partner in a portable sawmill business. Even then he spends his money on a new jacket, not as they had agreed, on saving money for her course. Bertha: "You make the money, you think it's yours, I thought we were a family!"

If one looks again at the women through the lens of archetype, the characters fall into clear patterns. Elsie is Crone and Healer. Rosie is Friend, Advisor and Server, Mother and honourable Wife, but also, once, Daughter seeking revenge for the murder of her Hero/Father. Lois is ever-Daughter, ineffectual Mother, and, late in the series, Wife who becomes an initiate. Bertha begins as Maiden and becomes independent Mother and Healer/Adept. Although she has a job as an administrator, Ellen is mostly Wife and Mother. Seeking a new role and a new sense of self, she has to leave Lynx River to accomplish that. Sarah is Maiden/Whore/Mother/Healer/Holy Fool, with her limitations written large over the series. Michelle is Mother, sometimes to the whole community and often evoking another archetype, Athene the Judge. Interestingly, there is no sexual tension between Michelle and her RCMP partners after the first season (and then, with Eric, it was almost perfunctory). She is Comrade-in-Arms. For three crucial episodes she becomes the Mother/Avenger, Demeter seeking her lost child in the underbelly of Calgary squats, then Mourner. Eventually, for the first time in the series, she becomes Wife. Later, in *Dream Storm,* she undertakes a quest into the spirit world on behalf of her people, with Albert (not Virgil) as her guide. As Northrop Frye persuaded the critical world to acknowledge, archetypes like these give stories and characters an extra but often unconscious charge of emotional weight. They touch an audience at a visceral, often unconscious, level.

The series challenges other assumptions about women. In the powerful episode 60, "Traces and Tracks," written by Rob Forsyth and directed by Gil Cardinal, Michelle catches Albert's clever young punk, William, selling to two kids what turn out to be perfectly legal anti-nausea pills. In a typical scam, William has claimed they were an illegal drug. When she goes to handcuff him, he gives her a split lip and deep bruises that remain visible for the whole episode. Michelle retaliates, banging his head against a truck while cuffing him. In the cell, William taunts Michelle about Hannah (this is shortly after Hannah's accidental death) and finally provokes her into coldly, viciously beating him. She uses her baton on places where the bruises won't be visible, then leaves him cuffed unconscious on the floor. As Walter (one of the older Dene, who is guarding William because Fletcher is away) says ·wryly, "I guess he's scared to wake up." William, an often vicious henchman of Albert's, has Albert's gift of finding the weakness in everyone he encounters, and with a twist of wit at times, he can taunt people into submission or fury. This transgressive episode demonstrates that the female protagonist is just as capable as her male antagonists of brutalizing an opponent – but like any conscientious cop, she eventually regrets it.

Meanwhile, William lies there unconscious. The plane cannot pick him up for two days to take him to Yellowknife to be charged, and Michelle, hearing echoes of her own taunts about how he will be beaten by the cops and sodomized by other prisoners, tries to find out more about his background. He tells her that his mother was a prostitute and his father a drunkard "or the other way around" – classic macho (and Indian) stereotyping. She tells him that his father is a high-school teacher, his mother a nurse, and that he got a B in grade 11. At this point many viewers may identify with this problem, of kids from good homes going bad. Michelle, however, reframes the issue – "It's easier to fail, to be a drunk, go to prison, because that's what Indians are supposed to do" – leaving the viewer to wonder if William is indeed a case of socialized low self-esteem. *North of 60* will offer explanations of this kind for behaviour but seldom takes what happened to a person in the past as a reason for his or her not doing what needs to be done or choosing to behave ethically in the present. Teevee helps Michelle by reminding her that William was hitting the uniform, not Michelle. When William overhears that she thinks he's not so tough, he burns himself with cigarettes and later tries to brain himself on the cell door. He is clearly self-destructive. Eventually they come to an understanding of sorts – he has wet his pants, she gets him dry ones and a cigarette.[13] In the end she goes against the wishes of Rosie, Leon, Walter, and Joe. She does not press charges. Instead, she holds them in abeyance for six months, because, she says, William is not tough enough to take what will be dished out in Yellowknife – and because she identifies with his self-hatred for being Indian. Neither the men nor the women of the First Nations are immune to that condition.

### GUNS AND LYNX RIVER

Guns and Indians used to be inseparable in old Westerns. Historically, mounted Indian cavalry were deeply feared on the American western plains. But that history is not ours and not at all part of a Dene culture dependent on travelling on foot and with dogs. Guns have often represented a rural and urban divide. Most Canadians want handguns banned but the current laws compelling all citizens to register all guns, including rifles, make some farmers, hunters, and northerners very angry. Handguns, except for RCMP issue, are never seen in a Lynx River household, and even the RCMP constables often take a rifle rather than a handgun when dealing with an incident. *North of 60*, however, is full of Indians with guns – every family has a rifle. Most people of both sexes can use them and do, to hunt for food for their families. For some viewers with settler roots, life in Lynx River is not unlike their own past. Thus, southern urban viewers are shown a culture where weapons have been part of family life for thousands of years. In Canada's wilderness, every Mountie is not Sergeant Preston and it's far from clear at times just who are the good guys and who are the bad. What is clear in this series, as it was years ago in *Wojeck* (television's first crusading coroner, 1966–68), is that the characters, and sometimes the viewers in the dominant culture as well, are made responsible both for a wide range of problems and for whatever contingent solutions can be found, particularly when violence in any form occurs. In the community of Lynx River, violence happens very occasionally and only once anonymously. The audience is usually involved with the characters on both sides – the hunters and the hunted. Feuds are coloured by respect for the enemy, and past history is rewritten or remains unknowable.

In the earlier episode 20, "Hostage," by Rebecca Schechter, we see Michelle forced to shoot a dangerous armed man, André LeBret, with whom she had grown up. LeBret has just been cuckolded by her brother, Peter, which has fuelled his drunken murderous rage. To save lives, she kills him. Unlike a standard cop show, in this series the aftermath of this event goes on for weeks, in the loss to the tightly knit community, as well as in Michelle's own agonized second-guessing. In fact, the incident continues to cast a shadow through the next seasons. In the last season, we see a different kind of aftermath when Michelle herself is shot – the effect on her family, her own shattered strength, illness, pain – and also the effect on the city-bred constable Harper, who let her go into the situation alone because he was afraid of who might be behind a closed door. Later he obsessively seeks, finds, and captures her attacker, a cold-blooded middle-aged man named Terry Whitemud, who wears the spent bullet around his neck. Whitemud is clearly entranced by the novelty of a handgun and loves the feeling that possession of one gives him. Note, he is not an outsider. Michelle had stayed with his auntie and is shocked when his identity is revealed. What *North of 60* does is set these incidents within the context of a community made familiar to the audience over several years. The dramatic effects are complex.

## SPIRITUALITY

"White Christians 'worship' and 'pray'; Indians engage in 'ceremony' or 'ritual' and 'conjure.' Yet when the biased definitions are put aside, Indians and whites are doing essentially the same things: both are entertaining notions of the supernatural. Scientifically it can be said that ... both believe in the possibilities of 'an extraordinary power or influence seemingly from a supernatural force.'"

Emma Laroque (Plains Cree Metis, 1988)

"We don't have 'religion.' We are a spiritual people. Every once in a while we get together to make sure the stories are right" (201).

Mr Carlisle, a Tlingit dancer and sculptor, speaking to a tourist who had asked a direct (and inappropriate) question about his people's religion[14]

"Know that everything has a spirit and respect the power that lies in all things."

*Dene Kede Education: A Dene Perspective*, curriculum document[15]

"Partners and Other Strangers." Michelle takes her rifle away from her adopted son, Charlie (Simon Baker), who had been trying to avenge her. *Alberta Filmworks, in association with the CBC, distributed by Alliance Atlantis.*

First Nations spirituality and ceremony are subjects that require special care when discussed by outsiders looking in and especially when portrayed on television. During its run, *North of 60* had as many as six cultural advisors for a single episode. Every episode had consultants, not just about spirituality but also about all kinds of cultural details. This does not make the advisors responsible for the mistakes in the series, or for the writer's or director's use of dramatic licence, but the evidence drawn from the actors' performances is that the producers learned more as time went on and that, on the whole, they tried to be respectful of customs and beliefs. Even so,

Tina Keeper had to refuse to dance around a fire in one early episode. Much later, Michael Horse welcomed Gil Cardinal as a director because he didn't have to have things explained to him.

According to Hugh Brody (1987), "Men and women who had medicine powers were able to help out in time of severe illness and when game was scarce" (55). Such powers were acquired through dreaming and fasting in the bush, but specific skills were also passed down to qualified younger ones. People could misuse the powers and harm other people. Fights between those with medicine power were rare but not unknown. The Dene in Brody's study told him that people with medicine power were still active (55), but that, "[a]t this moment, neither Dogrib spiritual beliefs nor Catholic beliefs are being taught to young people in effective ways." Except for Christmas and Easter, there is little religious observance, and "fewer still are familiar with Dogrib Beliefs and rituals" (67). With no resident priest, this is also a problem in Lynx River.

The interview of Martha Rabesca (Slavey) reveals that she, like Elsie, managed to avoid residential school in the days when there were no settlements where she now lives (Kulchyski, McCaskill, and Newhouse 1999). She provides glimpses of beliefs touched on in *North of 60*: "On how the world came to be, they don't talk about it. They never did talk about it." She goes on to say that the stories she heard from "my Elders were that the Dene people turned themselves into different types of animal. They had the power to turn into a human being or into an animal" (364). She later says that there were shamans. "A long time ago they were really always praying because they had strong faith" in what she calls a higher power as well as God. "People hardly pray any more" (370). She knows about traditional medicines and curing ceremonies. Being a healer is a gift, she says. She and some of her family have this medicine power but they it keep secret (373).

Michelle, who cannot go home to Joe when she is searching for Hannah in Calgary, goes to see a Blackfoot medicine man. She has a respectful attitude towards him, brings tobacco, is made welcome, and is shown how to help herself. Hannah's spirit reappears in episode 64, "Tango," by Andrew Wreggitt, when Michelle is struggling with whether or not to adopt Charlie so soon after her daughter's death. As Michelle is walking home, Hannah appears, walking alongside her, and reassures her mother that taking Charlie into her home is fine. Sweat lodges appear twice – early in the series, when Eric, under Joe's direction, tries to understand the meaning of his vision of the spirit caribou, and in the movie *Dream Storm*, when Teevee seeks an explanation for the illness affecting the children. Viewers may have heard a little about sweat lodges, and in the series there is some intermingling of the practices of various First Nations. However, in a radio documentary (broadcast 5 August 2005) on Ojibway practices made by CBC Radio One's *First Voice* (a series that featured First Nations issues and peoples), the elders made it very clear that the sweat lodge was Ojibway; that it was one part of a series of practices; that it was very rarely used; and that the pan-Indian use of it was problematic because when others practised the rituals, they did so in isolation from the whole belief system of the Ojibway. They argued that eclectic use of practices from various First Nations weakened the individuality and efficacy of traditional ways. As the producers of *The Beachcombers* discovered in the 1980s, attempts to represent matters of First Nations spirituality can be problematic.[16]

According to Jean-Guy Goulet (1998), "Dreaming, sickness and death are 'journeys of the soul.' Dreaming sometimes brings the soul to the land of the ancestors" (142). What is learned there will be remembered. Sickness can mean the soul has left the body, and healers must struggle to bring it back. Through the visions of Michelle and Teevee, the viewers south of 60 of *Dream Storm* are helped to understand that Lynx River has lost its soul by not caring for the land, and so the children are sick. Crying for the dead impedes their progress to the other land, but of course the Dene do weep for their lost ones. Nevertheless, letting go is an important part of dealing with death. We see Rosie's young son dealing with Hannah's death in stages, and we see Michelle's longer, more painful grief, which requires the intervention of her friend Betty Moses and eventually time at a healing lodge with elders. Letting go also requires that the belongings of the newly dead person be burned. Beliefs in reincarnation vary considerably from group to group, which may be why they are not mentioned in the series (167). As for the complex relationship of "drum and rosary," the shortage of priests may mean that the syncretic or dual systems of belief will one day be formalized by practitioners who are not formally ordained priests (212). Father Smuts, the elderly travelling priest who ministers to Lynx River, accepts as real the experience Elsie has of the "star people." Two sets of beliefs practised side by side is not uncommon in the First Nations and Inuit worlds stretching from California to the Arctic.[17]

According to Brody, the shamans have "powers but not power ... expertise but not authority" (115), a contrast with Jesse's Coast Salish great-grandfather. Unlike Jesse, Teevee does not choose to go on a quest. Yet, when after much effort he kills his first moose, he finds some peace and balance in his prayers. Peter does not choose to search for the lost little boy, who turns out to be himself. Michelle and Teevee do not seek a dream storm. The special knowledge that they need seeks them, but then they follow with determination and courage. Their experiences also demonstrate the sense in the culture that "asking questions [is] for the most part, intrusive, unnecessary and counterproductive" (123). Harper finds this out when he asks Joe direct questions. Joe replies with silence or oblique answers. Eric, on the other hand, learns how to learn from Joe what Joe wants to teach him. Information imparted to Peter, Michelle, and Teevee is coded in what Brody calls "the metaphors of dreams and shamanism," but the "information" in these episodes is experienced very directly, with Peter wounded by the child and carrying that wound into his ordinary life, with Teevee and Michelle both experiencing the latter part of Michelle's vision and knowing that they shared it without speaking when they meet. Metaphors assert two contradictory things at once, and the contradiction, the paradox, gives them power. When the qualifying word "like" is eliminated, "a pebble is a star."[18] On stage a stick is both a fiddle and a gun *at the same time*. Television is a much more literal medium than theatre's "three boards, two actors, and a passion." But the worlds the characters experience are both the same as and yet completely different from the worlds of everyday Lynx River. The contradictions and paradoxes coexist.

George Blondin's *Yamoria the Lawmaker: Stories of the Dene* (1997) was published after the series was finished, but it is probable that the Dene consultants would have known the basic traditions and beliefs that are described in the book and perhaps others not recorded. Yamoria is a major teacher and healer who also wins battles with the giant animals who once ranged over the Denendah. Most important, he brought law to the people. There are many stories of battles, sickness, starvation, consultations with the leaders of the "Caribou" or the "Moose" so that they will offer themselves to the hunter. These stories are rarely alluded to in the series and are never told in full, which is appropriate, since they should be told only under very limited circumstances on particular occasions. Television is not one of them. People with medicine power are born with it, earn it, ask for it, or buy it, but they don't reveal the powers they have until they are needed, perhaps very late in their lives, and they never discuss them. Overusing one's powers can affect health and mental well-being, and the powers wane in old age, as happens to Elsie in *Dream Storm*.[19] The collection *Wolverine Myths and Legends* (Moore and Wheelock 1990) discusses prophets and "tea dances," where prophets shared their visions and answered certain questions common to many groups of Dene. Potlatches were held for the souls of people who died more than a year before (64). The great prophet Nogha told people to put tobacco on the fire and pray three times (75), but he also wanted them to use the rosary. It was said that he loved to laugh and to drum. Nogha was also called "Wolverine," an animal that is twice associated with Albert in the series.

In all First Nations cultures there are animals and birds that are special to the individual, the clan, the band, the nation. Martha Rabesca says, without elaboration, that "the wolverine is special" (265). She also says that the crow "has all negative characters but the people were grateful to it because it helped the people a lot, they learned from crow" (Kulchyski, McCaskill, and Newhouse 1999, 265). When Michelle tells David the archaeologist the story of Raven and Lynx River, she emphasizes that it can only be told "right here, where it happened." David says that it is a story he can tell his children. Michelle, perhaps reiterating obliquely the widely held belief that some stories can only be told by certain people at certain times replies, "Yeah but you have to bring them here to tell it." Blondin (1997) says that Raven power can help a shaman look into the future, know where the moose and caribou are and heal the sick (111). Raven is a motif of several episodes involving Nevada, the rent boy with AIDS from Vancouver who has come uninvited to Lynx River. Nevada thinks that ravens speak to him, to Joe's wry amusement. But the raven takes on a powerful meaning in Ben Montour's carving. It incorporates Nevada's bloody handprint – symbolizing both his AIDS and the community condemned to remember him.

As for Elsie's blend of Roman Catholicism and traditional practices, Brody (1987) writes that "several Dene groups quickly developed forms of syncretism ... and missionaries took advantage of shamanistic openness to new ideas, and insinuated their doctrines into existing belief systems" (207), as they made determined efforts "to undermine shamanistic ideas and influences" (209). Elsie, Joe, and Willy all have medicine power. (The tourist lodge burns down because of a crime – but also, according to Elsie, because Joe was not asked to bless it.) Elsie, however, does not have "love medicine." She has to try and bribe Teevee's outsider girlfriend to leave. Other practices appear without explanation or undue emphasis. When the dead hunter is reburied, when Eric dies, when Hannah dies, a feast is held with food offered to the spirits of the dead. Ideas about what happens after death come up in "The Weight" (see chapter 13), but no one explains the bonfire of Hannah's things, just as no one explains the gifts that go into the birchbark tubes that are put on the graves.

For the visiting Oblate[20] priest, the barrier that nearly derails the marriage of Lois to Harris is exactly the same as it is for Elsie when she and

Joe are trying to cure Lois of a dangerous illness – the fact that Harris does not believe in either the Catholic or the Dene form of spirituality. Even though Lois is a devout, ordained layperson in the Catholic Church, neither Elsie nor Joe can bring her out of her coma because, as Elsie reluctantly tells Harris, "What you want is good but in your heart you don't believe." In a finely tuned and moving performance by Timothy Webber, Harris storms out of the room muttering about them all being worse than the bloody Catholics he was brought up with. He then gets staggering drunk, thinks he sees Lois in the distance, and follows her into the church. "Bunch of phonies," he mumbles at the small statues and crucifix, "rivers of blood, mountains of bones, but why her? She's innocent … a bloody friggin' saint, she loves you! Me, not her, take me!" He passes out and wakes with the first verse of Psalm 23, "The Lord Is My Shepherd," on his lips, which he says aloud, at first in a stumbling fashion but increasingly with a sense of discovery. When he quietly returns to the house, he brushes Lois's long dark hair. The camera is placed behind the bed so that the viewer does not see her face – but she calls his name. She can speak again. When she had her stroke, she needed hospitals and doctors to save her life, but when she relapses, she also needs the prayers of Elsie and Joe and she needs Harris to believe in something outside himself. *North of 60* continues to suggest that the people are syncretic, able to reconcile both belief systems and live their lives. As Joe Couture says (Kulchyski, McCaskill, and Newhouse 1999), "'Elders … are resuming their traditional role and prominence, a manifest role variously expressed as teacher, counsellor, interpreter of history, expert on survival'" because "'we are all related and therefore we must be constantly aware of how our actions will affect others, whether they are plants, animals or people'" (xvi–xvii). In episode 87, "The Smell of Violets" by Tony Di Franco, Lois uses her choice of godfather to her new baby as a way to reach/help the now obviously ill Albert. Her choice may also reflect her need for the baby to have a Dene godfather – not Gerry (Ukrainian Orthodox he tells Father Smuts), who is hurt when he is not chosen. The dialogue and camera show both parents and godparents renouncing the works of evil and taking vows as the rite demands. Note that Father Smuts has no problem with the traditionalist Albert taking those vows.

Written into the series is both a marked ambivalence about traditional ways of seeing and thinking and a sense of deeply held beliefs. There is also humour rather than solemnity about some aspects of the culture, which grounds the way such details are presented, reflects a basic truth about most spiritual practice, and gently satirizes "wannabes," the tribe of outsiders who want to co-opt aboriginal culture with a few sweats and a smudge or two. For example, in episode 27, "Crossing the River" by Rob Forsyth, David the archaeologist tries to establish a land claim on a site Joe identifies as having spirits. When Joe asks David how he felt after camping on the site, he says, "Things happened there. I felt it." Joe, without a glimmer of a smile, replies, "You're lucky. All I felt was rock." Michelle's response to David's feeling that there are spirits on the site is more direct: "When white guys talk like that I worry. They try to find something to hang their hats on, something to help them be something they're not." Later, she asks Eric, the white Mountie, whether he has ever been up to the site, saying she has never felt what several others in the community have sensed. Joe has recognized that Eric has sensitivity in matters involving the spirit world. Such openness to white participation in spiritual practices, particularly when recorded by ethnographers, is not without controversy – on both sides.

Customs of one First Nation can baffle someone from another. After Hannah's death in episode 57, "Revolving Door" by Stacey Kaser, the elders at the healing lodge (never seen) have asked Michelle to hunt and kill a moose and then to tan the hide in the traditional way, using the moose's brains. Throughout the episode, Michelle is shown stretching the hide as she begins the work. Andrew One Sky, who is Arapaho, remarks that it's hard. She replies, "It's supposed to be." No other explanation is offered, and he is as puzzled as the audience. Eventually she gives it up, telling Inspector Cormier that she ruined the hide. But a combination of a friend's intervention, time, and the discipline prescribed by the elders does help her manage her grief. Spirituality does not always connote solemnity. Joe brings her the moose brains from his freezer in a plastic container, and Sarah later nearly mistakes them for butter.

Episode 66, "Bushman," written by Andrew Rai Berzins and directed by Gil Cardinal, was produced more than two-thirds of the way through the series. It tackles the archetype of a man-eating monster (who can be male or female, T'sonaqua, Windigo, or Polyphemus). Joan Ryan (1995) says that "[s]tories about the Bush Man kidnapping children in the bush taught children to stay near camp" (45). In this case, according to Joe, he is eight feet tall, his tracks end abruptly in the snow, he smells "something awful," like "beaver in the spring" or "rotten bait," and "he comes for you." Charlie is the first to sense him watching in the bush. Elsie smells him when out picking berries. Others, however, think he is a tale to scare kids. Joe finds a large smelly scat that isn't a bear's and bags it as evidence, but he says, "He's a lot of things. I don't go lookin'. Bushman shit is really evil." Thematically, this

To help with her grief, Michelle tans moosehide in the old way as the elders have taught her. Peter looks on. *Alberta Filmworks, in association with the CBC, distributed by Alliance Atlantis.*

creature is linked to Fletcher, whose seduction of a drunken teenaged Brenda leads to his ruin and a life as a vengeful madman/monster. In this episode, the Bushman does not literally capture and take anyone away, but he is a reality to the Dene in Lynx River.

*North of 60* does not plunge into the deep end on the subject of spirituality until the third television movie, *Dream Storm*. Robin Nelson's *TV Drama in Transition: Forms, Values and Cultural Changes* (1997) quotes Dennis Potter (as cited in Brandt 1982), one of Britain's most gifted television playwrights: "[The] best naturalist or realist drama ... breaks out of this cozy habit [of the generally received notion of 'reality'] by the vigour, clarity, originality and depth of its perceptions of a more comprehensive reality. The best non-naturalistic drama, in its very structure, disorientates the viewer smack in the middle of the orientation process which television perpetually uses ... It shows the frame in the picture when most television is showing the picture in the frame'" (27). The striking hybridity of naturalistic and non-naturalistic elements in *Dream Storm* is examined in a paper posted on Patty Winter's *North of 60* website, http://www.wintertime. com/OH/Nof60/mj-ds.html. See also http://www.wintertime.com/OH/Nof60/movies.html for more on the movie. In *Dream Storm*, Albert's character is given new dimensions and his relationship with Michelle changes, the spirituality of the Dene people is more deeply explored, and the responsibility of the people to take care of their land and their heritage is very effectively portrayed on several levels.

## WHAT IS MISSING FROM *NORTH OF 60*

As is evident, the series did introduce – and in some cases, explored in depth – issues specific to aboriginal communities. A few troubling subjects, however, were not touched upon. One was the question of status versus non-status Indians and the related problems of redress for women who lost their status when they married white men.[21] The original Indian Act reflected the Victorian values of its time, and thus, up until the enactment of Bill C-31 – "An Act to amend the Indian Act" – in 1985, aboriginal women who married white men lost their status but aboriginal men who married white women did not. With Bill C-31, the status of their children was also finally addressed. This created new problems about who remained an "Indian" through generations of intermarriage. Precise calculations of "blood quanta" using fractions of "Indianness" traced through ancestry became the norm. There were other issues. The influx onto reserves of women and children who had gained new rights as status Indians presented problems on already crowded land. In most cases, housing was in short supply – as *North of 60* demonstrates – and in some cases, housing was allocated by band chiefs to their relatives. The series certainly looks at band politics, but it does not include the troublesome question of governance where bands have both elected chiefs (insisted upon by the Department of Indian Affairs) and hereditary chiefs (important to the Haudenosaunee and others among the Six Nations in Ontario and to the Northwest Coast First Nations when negotiating treaty obligations, but not a vital political issue to the Dene). In fact, despite ironic references to the choking bureaucracy, the Indian Act gets off rather lightly. Peter, with his MBA and his good sense of the politics in Yellowknife and Ottawa, helps band members play the system for funds for training and for start-up capital. In the introduction to this volume, I looked at the issue of cultural appropriation with respect to intellectual property, traditional ceremonies, and stories, and more specifically with respect to various television series, made by the dominant culture, that focus on First Nations people. One would not expect these series to look at those issues self-reflexively. However, the more specific questions of intellectual property, the erosion of language (which continued, even after the closing of residential schools, with the introduction in the North of television from the South), and the losses of material culture might have been addressed in greater depth. Another missing element is the Metis. Sylvie LeBret appears in two early episodes and then disappears until much later in the series. There is very little mention of the Metis in the series, even though they too live in the Northwest Territories and are included on the Dene Cho website.

George Blondin (1997) wrote: "When you hit the drum, you are sounding the heartbeat of the people ... It opens up a channel to the Creator so our prayers are heard" (60). No one from outside the native cultures of North America can spend time with First Nations people without sensing the importance of the drum. It is true that in television drums are often used as a clichéd sound cue that says "Indian." A shot of drummers is commonplace in dramas, news, and documentaries about native and Metis people because drummers are so "colourful." Drums – groups of people who practise and play together – appear as protestors on the news, as healers in documentaries. There is not much drumming heard or even seen in *North of 60,* but the opening montage always includes a shot of Willy beating a hand drum. Joe tells Leon to make a drum to fight his alcohol addiction and uses one himself to pray by the river for Lois, but in none of the episodes does the drum play a central role. Not until the 2005 movie *Distant Drumming* does a drum take focus. Daniel De'ela remembers when, as a small boy at residential school, he stole out into the bush to play the small hand drum he had hidden there. His father had given him the drum before he'd had been taken away. He is broken-hearted when he loses this last link with home after a priest finds him, beats him, and smashes the drum.

Despite *North of 60's* emphasis on some contentious issues, there are no gay or lesbian relationships in the series. *The Rez,* where young people regularly have sex and enjoy it immensely (including its more ludicrous aspects), does not tackle that variant either. The story arc of Nevada is not about his homosexuality but about seduction, exploitation, and its aftermath. The tone is not judgmental. In fact, the younger males are curious about his experiences but his AIDS soon changes the picture. There are no other "two spirit" or "berdache" people, as they are sometimes called, in the series.[22]

Hand games, a major Dene activity, are also missing in *North of 60.* These are played with variations by many First Nations. Gambling, misdirection, songs, and stamina are all involved. The fact that there are no powwows, though, does reflect Dene tradition because Dene culture had no original ties to the powwow and giveaway customs of the Plains Indian (now pan-Indian). There is lots of communal bingo, less communal feasting. The healing lodge and its practices are mentioned but not shown. As for handwork and the arts, there are glimpses of how parkas and mitts are made and how beading is done (a wedding dress and some jackets are beautiful examples). The only sculpture that is featured is made by Mohawk Ben Montour.

## LIMITATIONS IN THE SERIES

By now it will be evident that there is much to admire in *North of 60*. Nevertheless, hour-long series shooting to deadlines on location are prone to "just do it and move on" moments. There are improbabilities in the plots; for example, five of the characters (not counting Eric's predecessor) have nervous breakdowns within four years: Eric, Sarah, Nathan, Lois, and Brian. This reinforces the stereotype that isolation in a small settlement in the North is not for the emotionally vulnerable, particularly the white outsider. Some themes are made overly explicit; over the years, for example, the dialogue repeats many variations on "once an outsider, always an outsider." Although obvious manipulation of suspense does not enhance the quality of a series, as argued in the concluding chapter of Miller 1987 (374–88), open ambivalent endings were very Canadian long before *The Sopranos* went suddenly to black. However, the cliff-hangers (there were only a few) seem contrived in the context of the ebb and flow of this program and the lives it portrayed. There are episodes where the foreboding music becomes wearisome, particularly when Fletcher is the focus, and sometimes the glowering confrontations and stubborn silences, as in episode 35, "Pulling Up Stakes," become far too repetitious. There are times when the connections between the various plot threads seem mechanical, for example, in episode 51, "At Home and Away," where the viewer endures continuous quarrelling between Sarah and Albert, Brian and Rosemary, Teevee and Bertha, and Gerry, Rosie, and Leon all in the same episode. There are also times when the subplots break into the rhythm of the developing main plot of the week without offering a complex counterpoint or a nuance that illuminates the major storyline. Commercials are a fact of life and viewers can often ignore the complete change in tone they introduce. Abrupt changes built into the dramatic structure can be more jarring.

In the next chapter, I note how critics speaking from the First Nations, as well as critics in mainstream publications, complain that *North of 60* is dour, the characters too serious, and the plot twists too agonizing, too often. The series did have some comedy in the first season, however, and later it lightened up again. Sarah's stint as holy fool/truth teller, Rosie's battles with Gerry, Elsie's oblique obstructionism, the occasionally wry one-liners of Joe and Harris, and particularly Andrew One Sky's relaxed persona leavened the dough. Nevertheless, there were times when the series focused on too many characters who rarely made a joke or saw the funny side of life. Fletcher as antagonist, Teevee with the sullen smoulder of youth, and even Michelle were rarely allowed to laugh. Even Harper, a latecomer to the series, was tensely over-anxious to prove himself as Michelle's partner. One does not have to understand all of the levels and connotations offered by many forms of aboriginal humour to know that all First Nations cultures, like almost all others, have a funny side. *The Rez*, which was contiguous with the last two seasons of *North of 60*, had problems of its own, but the basic premise of the show was how "the Rez," that is the community, can be viewed from a comic perspective by those who live there. It managed to do this, however, by ignoring or glossing over some very serious issues. In an ideal world there would be a dozen Canadian drama series on Canadian television and *The Rez* would have been given time to develop longer, more challenging story arcs while retaining its sense of humour. In the second season Silas mentions that people on the reserve watch *North of 60*. It would have been a treat to see a "cross-over," as is done occasionally in some American series. Silas and Sadie could have turned up in Lynx River for a visit, or Teevee could have met Sadie at an Assembly of First Nations (AFN) conference.

### CHALLENGING THE AUDIENCES

It seems to have puzzled John Haslett Cuff and one or two others who attacked the series with vigour over the years (see chapter 15) that audiences could form attachments to characters with all kinds of problems, especially those more specific to First Nations peoples. But that was to ignore the well-known preference among many Canadians for news, documentary, and docudrama.[23] Canadian television has explored these forms with success from the 1950s to the present, and viewers have continued to support them. Television drama and explorations of topical or long-standing issues have gone hand in hand since the 1960s. Examples are anthologies like *Festival* and *Q for Quest* through *Wojeck* in the late 1960s, *The Manipulators* and *Sidestreet* in the 1970s, the anthology *For the Record* in the 1970s and 1980s, and *Street Legal*, which ended in the 1990s. *North of 60* should be placed within that CBC tradition, but it also presents a fresh perspective. The people of Lynx River in the Northwest Territories have to be more self-sufficient on most counts than people in cities in the south. The responsibilities of the RCMP in remote communities are defined for Michelle and her partners by the community as well as by the book. There are no lawyers, no doctors, no stores but the general store, no banks or arenas. People are interdependent in very basic ways but also more self-reliant.

In an article in the *New York Times*, 24 April 2005,[24] provocatively titled "Watching TV Makes You Smarter" (excerpted from his book *Everything Bad Is Good for You: How Today's Popular Culture Is Actually Making You Smarter*, Steven Johnson writes about and even graphs the complexities of American television series since *Hill Street Blues* (for Canadians it was ten years earlier with *Wojeck*). Moving from one narrative thread to the other is demanding enough he says, but he argues that the popular HBO series *The Sopranos* "will often connect to three different threads at the same time, layering one plot atop another," and those threads will build on events from earlier episodes, even seasons. (Note that the series ran uncut on CTV but did not run on any of the major American networks.) Many, though by no means all, of the *North of 60* episodes achieve that layered effect. Johnson also praises the "mysteries" that appear in *West Wing* and other "quality" television shows – that is, details that are not explained, missing links, plot lines with no closure – all common elements in several Canadian television series for the past thirty years. In *North of 60*, these are imbedded in the details of the ways people live on the land, in ceremony, in the knowledge, values, and behaviour of Albert, Elsie, and Joe, in the increasing complexity of many of the characters. As we saw in the exploration of fandom, such richness encourages thoughtful commentary on fan sites. But unlike Tony, Carmella, and the rest of the *Sopranos* crew, this series depends on viewers fundamentally liking the leading characters and staying engaged with the others.[25] For the First Nations audience there is the added strength of recognizable characters in credible but interesting situations, characters who were Dene yet also represented a wider community of native and Metis people.

Viewers are still watching reruns ten years later. Audrey Flack, a self-identified eighty-three-year-old lady who lives alone, wrote me a letter in May 2002 after I had written on *North of 60* in one of my monthly television columns for *The St. Catharines Standard*. She was watching reruns weekly on Showcase (these continued through 2005) and loved the show so much that she felt she had to write to a complete stranger to say how much the series meant to her. She gave me permission to quote her letter. She told me that *North of 60* is the primary reason she pays for the second-tier cable. Her

Albert taunts Sarah, who is holding their little girl, Elizabeth (Shelby Crowchild), as Joe Gomba (Jimmy Herman) watches protectively. *Alberta Filmworks, in association with the* CBC, *distributed by Alliance Atlantis.*

favourite character is Elsie because she is wise and a grandmother, but she also likes Teevee, "the brat growing up and then trying so hard to be successful, and kind underneath"; Joe Gomba, "only speaking when it makes sense"; Peter, "so protective of his heritage"; Bertha, "and her baby, trying to study and better herself." She only wished she could see what happened after the series ended. When we spoke, I caught her up on the three television movies made to that date (repeated on APTN and Showcase in November 2006). I hope she saw the next two films. All of the movies have been repeated many times. She ended her letter to me this way: "For that hour, once a week, I'm lost in their show and it's Canadian."

By the 1990s, no hour-long series, even if made in the United States, could recoup the costs of the initial investment in the first run. Syndication (reruns) during their runs is what has kept *E.R., Law and Order,* and even the blockbuster franchise *C.S.I.* in production – with DVD collections now adding significant dollars. Movies, however, are another animal, even made-for-TV movies. They can be sold as movies for the cinema in other countries, they do not cost nearly as much as the sixteen or even thirteen episodes of an hour-long series, and being based on a popular series, they can perhaps guarantee a base audience to advertisers. Telefilm financed the first *North of 60* TV movie, *In the Blue Ground,* and found out that there was still an avid audience for *North of 60 Mysteries.* Four more have followed, and a sixth was financed to the scriptwriting stage but has not made it into production. Each one is different and of variable quality, but each extends at least one aspect, theme, issue, or character beyond where the series itself could go. The characters are now ten years older than they were in 1992. Yet for reasons unknown, the show's distributor, Alliance Atlantis, has not brought out the series or even the movies on video or DVD. A mildly popular Canadian teen soap, *Edgemont*,[26] is available on DVD, but *North of 60,* one of the best series made in Canada, is not. We make quality series in Canada – we just don't have enough confidence in their quality. The newspaper and magazine critics too often reflect that negative expectation, as will be evident in the next chapter. But some got it, and clearly over a million viewers understood and enjoyed the series for six seasons and the five television movies that followed.

# FIFTEEN

# Formal and Informal Responses to *North of 60*

Teevee asks his grandmother, Elsie, more than once, "What should I do?" Elsie often replies, "Think about it."

## LONG FORM: TELEVISION OVER MANY SEASONS

Some of the reasons for the success of *North of 60* and for the texture and nuance that it affords are to be found in a more general, very useful article on what Charles McGrath, a regular writer for the *New York Times*, calls "long-form television." In "The Triumph of the Prime Time Novel" (22 October 1995), written as *North of 60* entered the midway point, he argues that "TV drama is one of the few remaining art forms to continue the tradition of classic American realism ... the painstaking, almost literal examination of middle and working class lives, in the conviction that truth resides less in ideas than in details closely observed. More than many novels, TV tells us how we live now" (53). Changes of character and elaboration of theme, issue, or plot, "some great, some small, happen incrementally, over weeks of episodes – the way such things happen in life, and not the way they typically happen in movies, for example, or even in books ... [A long-form series] uses time the way the serial novel used to, incorporating the intervals between instalments and the tension between what we've learned and what we fear or hope ... Lesser characters can sometimes claim centre stage without necessarily taking on a new attribute [as Leon or Joey do]. They can do it, in fact, by simply becoming truer to their limited natures" (76). McGrath does not mention that in *North of 60*, as in some other long-form series, many of the secondary characters change substantially – it's one of the pleasures of *North of 60*. Nor does McGrath discuss the fact that the writers will add guests to episodes or to a set of episodes who enrich the stories and provide the variety necessary to series drama.

SCHOLARS THINK ABOUT *NORTH OF 60*

Unlike the other series discussed in this book, *North of 60* did attract some scholarly attention. There are to date three articles about the series. American scholar Diana George (1995), working with Susan Sanders, wrote about the first season; Linda Warley (1998) discussed the first three seasons; and Christopher Gittings (1998) considered the whole series a year after it ended. These accounts were followed by a non-academic article by Drew Hayden Taylor quoting aboriginal academics as well as others and a brief comment from Richard Wagamese, a novelist and journalist. George and Sanders contrasted the first season of *North of 60* with *Northern Exposure* and concluded that *North of 60* had already moved away from colonial discourse to create one of the potential "multi-ethnic/multicultural representations within the over-culture. To give one possibility for television, we turn to our neighbours to the north whose history with Indian people is not much better than our own but whose use of television is somewhat different. By the time the Canadian drama *North of 60* had completed its first season, it was already clear that Canada had managed to produce a program that repositions Indian people (in this case the Dene in the Northwest Territories) as contemporary Dene people whose lives are important, and whose communities have specific needs and raise specific issues" (448).[1] They note that the Dene of *North of 60* do not function, as do the somewhat generic Indian people of *Northern Exposure*, as background, set design, or character types. George concludes, "They do not just 'look Indian.' They are real people." After listing some of the issues covered, she points out that "the Dene are not romanticised on this program and neither are they degraded. The Anglo characters ... are not always right and they are not always wrong either" (448).

In "The Mountie and the Nurse: Cross-Cultural Relations in *North of 60*," Linda Warley presents the broadcast context of the early to mid-1990s in an odd way. She equates the continuing aboriginal characters in *Northern Exposure* and characters in series that include strangely pan–native Indian detail, such as *Star Trek* and *The X-Files* (173), with *The Rez* and *North of 60*, despite the fact that the protagonists and most of the other characters in the two Canadian series belong to specific branches of Anishnabe and Dene cultures. Both series have moments in which characters specifically say that an artifact or custom is not part of their tradition. Ron Grimes, an expert in native spirituality (primarily of the Southwest) with the Department of Religion and Culture, Wilfrid Laurier University, wrote this to me in an email of 12 December 1994, "I'm impressed with the series, its uncommonly good sense, its courage, and its lack of hype," and in another email, "I am waiting for the new season of N. of 60 to start. But I did notice the circumspection [about presenting Dene ceremony, which I had noted to him] quite a contrast to the last 3 sessions of *X-Files* where they have Navajos doing Blessingway to save an FBI agent!!"

In her article, Warley concentrates on Sarah but also discusses in some detail the relationship of Michelle and Sarah. She sees white characters as useful because they "make space" for white viewers (174), yet she notes that the series deals with issues that have "little if anything to do with white people." Her examples of such issues include feuds between families, intergenerational tensions and "the political wrangling of the band council." I would argue that analogies are easily identified in many neighbourhoods and small communities in many countries. She does point out that "the program ... depicts Native people as survivors, as competent human beings. And this in itself is appealing" (174). Referring to writer Thomas King, writer/story editor Jordan Wheeler, and director Gil Cardinal, she claims that this is the first time a program "creates the possibility for Native people to have at least some control over the images produced by that machine [the media industry]" (176). She then takes on the idea that authenticity is a "hegemonic concept that suggests a discourse of essentialism and suggests that identity categories such as 'Native' are homogeneous and unchanging ... The fact that characters speak in English and not in Slavey or another Dene language is already a distortion as Jordan Wheeler points out" (176–7). He did indeed do so, but Warley does not mention that the first season establishes that fluency in Slavey was beaten out of Michelle and many others at boarding school, that Elsie often uses Slavey when speaking to her family. Warley cannot know that in a later season the language competence of Sylvie LeBret is an issue when she applies for a teaching job. From a different perspective, Barbara Godard (1987) reports that at the Women and Words Conference, "[Beth] Cuthand emphasized the value of using the English language to communicate her tribal traditions to other Native Groups whose languages she cannot speak" (151).

Warley argues that "the program specifically avoids the issue of Native Sovereignty, thereby effacing the threat to Canadian unity that Native political subjectivity presents" (179). Land claims do arise repeatedly in later seasons and in the movies. Specific claims of sovereignty do not. The issues of self-government in all of its variations are (deliberately?) blurred. Warley does make a good point when she notes that the remoteness of Lynx River "reinscribes ... the stereotype of the Indian as close to nature living a simple life based on a subsistence economy and distanced from the urban waged economy"(179). Yet even in the first season, only Joe Gomba lives off the land – while eating Dare's chocolate chip cookies. Michelle, Rosie, Leon, Mary, Betty, Peter, Ellen, and even Teevee (who works at the Rec Centre, then as a miner, then as a part owner and operator of a sawmill) do waged work over the six seasons. From quite early in the series and running through all of the TV movies, the lack of jobs is an obsession with the band council.

Warley makes another good point when she argues that "one of the strengths of North of 60 is its careful treatment of the tensions created by the simultaneous and paradoxical integration and non-integration of white characters. Often it is a white character who is 'othered' in this additional text. Such a reversal of the conventional cinematic and television paradigms creates a subject position that is unfamiliar and uncomfortable for a white viewer" (180). White characters sometimes make the aboriginal "other" visible. More often as time goes on, it is the Dene characters who make the white characters visible as other. Yet as argued previously, the regular television viewer will soon identify with Michelle and Peter and their other friends, who drop in on viewers weekly, or in syndication daily, for a visit. Moreover, cultural differences form a major narrative thread but are seldom the focus of a primary plot. Thus, the viewer takes up multiple subject positions over six seasons. As is often the case, the regular viewer knows more about Albert, about Peter, about Michelle, and about Sarah than the characters ever know about each other and changes towards them as they change as characters.

Warley's article is primarily about Sarah. She writes: "Every relationship that Sarah has with native people in the community is, in some way, complicated by the historical fact of white settler colonialism. This is perhaps especially true of her relationships with women including Michelle." She does not have the advantage of viewing the much more nuanced relationship that develops later between Sarah and Michelle or between Sarah and Betty Moses, the hard-driving substance abuse counsellor who calls Sarah "Blondie," at first contemptuously and then with grudging admiration. Warley sees in the series a competition between Michelle and Sarah for Eric's attention, something I simply do not see. Michelle and Eric have one brief night together, more it seems because the town expects it than for their own enjoyment, and there is no follow-through. Sarah has an affair with Eric but ends it because she cannot make the commitment he wants. However, Warley is right when she says that "the [series'] treatment of the relationship between Sarah and

Michelle does not buy into the myths of universal sisterhood" (182). There are tensions and misunderstandings particularly when Michelle loses Hannah. The two women are given the last lines of dialogue in the series (see chapter 13), but even there the differences between them are as apparent as the depth of their friendship. Warley sees "unequal relations of power that result from settler colonialism" (182). But I see a series in which the native woman Michelle – as an RCMP officer, as a Kenidi, as a sister to the chief, as a strong woman connected to her community – is fundamentally in a position of power, one that the white woman Sarah will never be able to achieve. We do, however, agree that "the makers of North of 60 do not simplify the issues that shape the friendship between a particular white woman and a particular Dene woman [which] adds to its reality effect … They have to work at it" (183–4). She concludes that the series "offers a model of how individuals might work with one another in order to form both effective political alliances and deeply meaningful human relationships." And the rest of the series proved her right.

Christopher Gittings (1998), writing after the series had ended, is particularly interested in its portrayal of the RCMP:

> *North of 60* … challenges a hegemony of the white male Mountie figure with one of its lead characters, Michelle Kenidi, a female First Nations RCMP officer. Although the character of Michelle invites comparisons to anterior representations of the Mountie and Aboriginal women, it is not parody. Michelle becomes the site of a collision between … First Nations' culture and its "Other," the Canadian nation state that sought – through the agency of the North West Mounted Police, and later the RCMP – to extinguish Aboriginal title and cultural practices. The representation of Michelle as the ranking officer at Lynx River [only in the last two seasons] performs the political work of challenging the racist stereotypes of the white male Mountie as national icon, offering new co-ordinates for spectator identification with a re-imagined community … [Michelle] struggles to a position of power where she becomes the sign for a new transformed border that works toward equity between First Nations and the state. Michelle might, however, be read as an example of a successful assimilation of Native culture. Some might argue that, not dissimilar to *Rose Marie*,[2] Michelle's difference is absorbed when she becomes a cross-dressed member of the dominant group. Michelle is frequently conflicted by her double positioning as native/Mountie; however, it is our sense of aboriginal community that tempers her work as an officer of the national police force. (519)

This interpretation does not account for the potential for a structure like the RCMP to be subverted from within or the capacity of the viewer to accept paradox.

It is very difficult to see how Gittings can see a younger woman living in the Northwest Territories as "cross-dressed" because she wears pants, even the trousers of a uniform. Every other woman of her generation in the North wears pants, most southern Canadians of her generation wear pants, and by the mid-1990s, police uniforms were no longer routinely coded male. However, he does get the politics of one of the key dramatic conflicts right. There is no doubt that many episodes in the series turn on the conflict between Michelle's sense of Dene values and the expectations of her job, between her roles as mother and policewoman, compounded by her preconceptions as a Kenidi, a family that has had an ancient feud with the Golos, and her duty to be fair. The struggle between successful assimilation and Dene culture, however, is redefined in later seasons by her decision to stay in Lynx River. Her RCMP superiors (in an act of dramatic licence that names the exception Inspector Cormier is making for her in his dialogue) bend the rules to allow her to stay on, particularly, as Inspector Cormier suggests, if she marries Andrew. She does. In that crucial case, it takes both the dominant and marginalized culture to subvert the power structure, and compromises are made.

In a relevant though non-academic comment on the RCMP thread in the series, Liz Crompton writes in the *Globe and Mail*, 13 January 2000: "'*North of 60* obviously had some really good consultants, who know how policing is done in remote, northern communities' says Paul Gamble who was once an RCMP Sergeant stationed in Fort Simpson and now works for a private security firm. 'The majority of the things they are doing are pretty true to life.' Gamble ... says the show's producers had approached ... Mounties to ask for their perspective."

The most cogent critique of the series comes from Drew Hayden Taylor (Ojibway, Curve Lake First Nation), a columnist and playwright. The article, which looked at the first three seasons of *North of 60* was first published in the *Toronto Star* on 8 November 1995, but this discussion is based on the more accessible reprint called "North of Sixty, South of Accurate" (1996). Taylor's essay should be addressed in some detail, as he expresses not only his own views as an aboriginal writer who has worked for television and who even wrote an episode for the first season, but also the views of others, including those of First Nations academics. He begins by mentioning *North of 60*'s predecessor, *The Beachcombers*, with its "cast members of Native descent," which, as he says, paid very little attention over nineteen seasons to native issues (though more than he gives the show credit for), and also *Spirit Bay*, saying that both were "enjoyable but kind of light" and were made for children and families, not adults. He challenges the concept that the need to help the white audience identify with the series was the rationale for the early focus on Sarah and Eric. He also acknowledges that "gradually the focus of the show began to shift to the more interesting Native characters" (78). He names and praises the actors and the show for training native people in television jobs. Then he goes on to describe an apparent paradox: "Issues that were only statistics now have faces, voices and reasons. Perhaps this is also the show's biggest weakness – its preoccupation with and dedication to showing the negative aspects of Aboriginal life." Taylor had enjoyed the first episodes and identified his own adolescence with young Teevee's fixation with pop culture. However, eventually he developed "a growing concern that the show endorsed the perpetuation of Natives as victims." He quotes Alice Williams, who comes from Northern Ontario but lives in Taylor's home reserve, as saying that the show "confirms, affirms and promotes the dominant culture ideology about the Anishnawbe (Native people)" (79–80), a very serious charge against a program that claimed to be attempting to present an honest reflection of life in a Dene community.

An unnamed native academic told Taylor that he thought the white people in the show held all of the positions of power in the town – which is simply wrong. The second episode establishes that the band council has the right to fire Eric and is considering it until Michelle strongly defends him, even though, suffering from culture shock and depression, he curls up in bed and doesn't budge until she gives him a tongue-lashing. Harris serves at the band's pleasure, Gerry's store is on band-owned land, Sarah is replaced in season 3 by an aboriginal (presumably Dene) nurse. The limits placed by the Dene culture on the white RCMP corporals, who would ordinarily have authority in other jurisdictions when it comes to the law, are established in many episodes. The academic also argued that Albert "is only good enough to get a defective icon," meaning Sarah. The academic does not seem to have watched the episodes that show that Albert eventually found he couldn't control her, came to distrust her, and then refused to support her and her daughter. In fact, as we have seen, the entire narrative of Albert and Sarah's relationship becomes increasingly complex in the final three seasons of the series, after Taylor first wrote the piece.

Taylor also reports that Rodney Bobiwash, "director and agent provocateur" for the First Nations House at the University of Toronto,[3] often cites

*North of 60* in his lectures. Bobiwash thinks it perpetuates stereotypes of Indians as downtrodden and oppressed – "it provides a reverse sense of superiority" (80). (Taylor admits that the issues raised in the series are real and widespread.) Downtrodden? Oppressed? Michelle, a successful cop? Peter, an MBA? and Albert, a successful entrepreneur? Both Peter and Albert know more than Harris does about governance and finance. The elderly white priest has a huge parish and is rarely in one community for long. He has little visible influence with anyone but Lois. The schoolteachers are Dene or Metis. When the town boycotts his store/motel/restaurant, Gerry is forced to bring on Rosie as a partner. The band turns down jobs tied to manipulative oil, gas, and, later, hydro deals offered from outside, and the pace of "progress" is controlled by the elders and the band council. Michelle is promoted to corporal and eventually the viewers discover that Albert is the majority shareholder in Lynx River Resources.

Taylor's other charge is that the series lacks humour.[4] This criticism has become received doctrine about the show. Taylor writes: "What irks me and a lot of other Native people is the refusal by the Powers That Be (specifically the producers and story editors) to show the other side of Native life – the humour and good times. Throughout the horrific times, one of the things that has allowed us to face and overcome tragedies is our sense of humour" (81). His own plays, which address such issues as the threatened appropriation of Dreamer's Rock,[5] a focal point of Anishnabe spirituality, or the return of an adult adoptee to her family, are leavened with humour. (I wish he had commented in print on *The Rez*, which appeared two years later.) However, Taylor claims that a lack of humour was not due to the temperaments of the people involved but rather (according to his "Deep Quiver" source on set) to an unspoken CBC policy. This source told him that although Columpa Bob, who played Mary (the nurse who replaced Sarah for a season), insisted as an actress on smiling every time she was on-camera, she soon stopped. The source added that other cast members also wished to lighten up their roles a bit. Taylor reports that when writer and story editor Jordan Wheeler was asked at an aboriginal film festival about the lack of humour, he "responded, simply 'It's a drama. If you want comedy watch a sitcom'" (82). Taylor argues, and I agree, that this is not an adequate response. I could cite Shakespeare by the yard or several of Wheeler's own scripts for *The Rez* to illustrate that comedy, tragedy, irony, and romance can coexist within minutes of one another in a scene – even in television drama.[6]

Gary Farmer, a guest speaker at the "Aboriginal Experiences in the Media" day-long conference at Brock University (winter 2000), pointed out that "*North of 60* had no humour, yet that is the way we deal with 'it,'" and complained that the series "was conflict, after conflict, after conflict." Thomas King, who wrote sharp comedy into his episodes of *North of 60*, indirectly comments on the series in his comic detective novel *Dreadful Water Shows Up* (2002), published several years after the show ended. In dialogue between the old man Moses and the ex-detective Thumps Dreadful Water, Moses says: "'They cancelled *North of Sixty*. That was a regular thing.' [Thumps] 'That got cancelled a while back.' 'It was Okay.' Moses shifted in his chair. 'But those people up there at Lynx River didn't have much of a sense of humour.' 'It was a serious show.' 'Laughing and crying are good for you' said Moses, 'but being grim all the time will only make you sad'" (87). I must agree that given the culture the series portrayed there were definitely times when the series was too angst-ridden.

The description "glum" could certainly be applied to one long story arc. In the *Toronto Star* of 27 June 1999, Julie Stewart, who played Rosemary (Corporal Brian Fletcher's wife), was quoted by television columnist Jim Bawden: "'I practically cheered when Rosemary was written out [even though the role earned Stewart a Gemini nomination]. The character had become painful to play. There's only so much suffering that one can bear.'" It is true that her character was always alien to the town, made no friends, grew quickly tired of moose meat, made mistakes with the children at the Recreation Centre, had a miscarriage and then unsuccessful fertility treatments, learned that she could not have children of her own, failed in an attempt to adopt a child, and finally discovered that her husband had had intercourse with a teenager. She did befriend Hannah, but that put her at odds with Michelle. Making her the winner of the misery stakes was a mistake and her exit was a relief to the audience.

Richard Wagamese, in *Aboriginal Voices* (1995), strongly argues that "only we can tell our own stories accurately. Only we know the details that make us vibrant and unique … When was the last time we saw an Aboriginal person on television point with their lips? Stick out their tongue and say 'aaahh' at a joke? Use their hands like a parallel language when they talk?" I have no idea whether these details are specific to his Anishnabe culture or not, but they do not appear in *The Rez*. He certainly does not like some of the earlier series. "Who can forget the woodsy Joe Two Rivers from the *Forest Rangers*, the amiable Buckley Petawabano of *Rainbow Country* or the loyal Jessie [*sic*] Jim of *Beachcombers* fame? They live forever in infamy and cable syndication." He cites as "valiant efforts" "the short lived *Spirit Bay*" and some of the movies, like *Loyalties* and *Medicine River*, which "gave our people flesh and substance and the dignity that comes with it," but he has serious reservations about "the much bally-hooed *North of 60.*" (Since the article was published in January/February of 1996, he would likely have seen four seasons when he wrote it.) He continues: "Who among us has been to an aboriginal community so completely lacking in dogs and laughter for instance. Yet the non-aboriginal producers would have us believe that these are our lives played for real. That even in the far north every Aboriginal person speaks fluent CBC with the odd bit of dialect thrown in for colour." Elsie, Joe, Teevee, Albert, Lois, and even Michelle and Peter would be surprised to know that they speak fluent CBC. Their inflection, accent, idiom, pitch, pace, and in some cases vocabulary differ significantly not only from broadcast English but also from the apparently regionless accents of Toronto or Vancouver.

However, after Taylor and Wagamese had written their articles, viewers could see changes in tone in the last two seasons. The *Calgary Herald*, 22 April 1996, reported that before he took over as story editor from Jordan Wheeler (who went to *The Rez*), Andrew Wreggitt spent a week in February (a brief visit, but at least it was in winter) in the Northwest Territories. He called it "'a real eye opener. [The series] has been criticised for being too dour and black (in mood). We've heard that criticism and are going to address it.'" The last two seasons show a more relaxed Michelle enjoying life with Andrew One Sky, whose wry sense of humour lightens the episodes he appears in. There is also more humour in Rosie's deadpan remarks; Sarah makes more jokes with less of the outsider's refuge in sarcasm; Michelle's new partner, James Harper, takes himself much too seriously and is therefore a little comic in his earnestness; and there is some slapstick comedy around Gerry's affair with his lascivious loans officer. In episode 84, "Oil and Water," there is a lot of bathroom humour when the council – after hearing from Elsie that the roof a friend's outhouse blew off while she was in it – holds out for indoor plumbing for every house in return for a deal on oil reserves.

When I looked for humour "from the outside in" in a wide cross-section of the series, I found wry touches and even some fun in every season though not in every episode. Here are a few examples. Peter is on the phone trying to get government support for Sarah to work at the rehab centre as well as for her replacement as a nurse, who will be Dene, "Well, tell [the bureaucrats] she's your albino sister." Gerry runs a pool on when Ellen's baby will be born and another on what it will be named. Albert finds Sarah's idea of working animal hides to show she belongs "hard on the teeth," and he calls Lynx River "a bannock republic." Both visiting artist Ben Montour and activist/counsellor Betty Moses show a cutting wit in the episodes where they appear. Sarah, expecting Albert's baby, jokes about his mysterious disappearance from her life: "Send Albert for a quart of milk and look what happens." Even Michelle shows a rare bit of humour when she says loudly but crisply to a jealous and drunken Harris, who has tried to ram Ben Montour's motel room with a piece of heavy equipment: "You can shoot Ben Montour, but don't drink and drive in my town."

Taylor's own plays, rich with his brand of humour, provide his credentials for showing how comic truths can be achieved.[7] At the Brock University conference on "Aboriginal Experiences in the Media" in 2001, Taylor pointed out at that native humour can sometimes be of a vicious and very subtle kind, often teasing and self-deprecating, and argued that these characteristics form one of the few pan-Indian elements. But he also said that the humour of one community could be inappropriate in others and that humour differs from community to community. After reiterating that "not all of us are oppressed, depressed and suppressed," he showed his audience *Redskins, Tricksters and Puppy Stew,* a film he had directed for the NFB about First Nations comedy. The film included routines from Don Burnt Stick and a sequence on Thomas King in a studio rehearsal of his CBC radio series *The Dead Dog Café Comedy Hour.* The film and later Taylor's book *Me Funny* (2005) demonstrated a little of the wide diversity and the cultural specificity of First Nations humour. I do agree that not enough of this very wide range of humour found its way into *North of 60.*[8]

## NEWSPAPER AND MAGAZINE CRITICS

Among the professional critics in Canadian newspapers and magazines, one or two consistently disliked the show intensely, some praised it, others had varied reactions over the seasons. All were urban, all were white, and most were men. The critics writing in 1992 would have been responding in part to the publicity packages supplied by the CBC. As the seasons went on, they would more likely have reviewed the program in the context of its run, although it is clear that some saw very few episodes over the six years. Regrettably, a survey of the aboriginal publications uncovered only two reviews.

One of those who heartily disliked *North of 60* was John Haslett Cuff, television critic for the *Globe and Mail* during the 1990s, now a filmmaker. Ordinarily a good and balanced critic of television, he seems to have had a bug in his ear when it came to this show. He was unimpressed by the few episodes he saw in the beginning of the first season and remained largely hostile for the rest of the run. In his review titled "The Great Culturally Correct North" in the *Globe and Mail*, 3 December 1992, he began this way: "The new drama series North of 60 … represents the highest aspirations of Canada's national television policy and the sheer folly of gambling more than $9 million of taxpayers' money on something they may neither want nor need. North of 60 comes to air so freighted with politics and expectations that it seems irresponsible to simply review it as routinely as we might a similar mediocre effort from the purely market driven television factories to the south." Note that, from *Radisson* to *North of 60* and *Canada: A People's History*, the cost of drama programming has been a target for indignation in Parliament as well as in newspapers. Haslett Cuff continues:

> The show is probably the most culturally and regionally correct of any drama series made in this country … and while it predictably stars a macho, white male (John Oliver) as a cop and the requisite blond (Sarah Birkett) [which is the character's name, not the actor Tracey Cook's] as a nurse, most of the cast is either native, female or both. The other leads include a native woman (Tina Keeper) playing an RCMP officer, a handsome native actor (Tom Jackson) who portrays an activist band chief agitating for self-government and a hard working, recovering alcoholic native waitress (oops, should I have said "server"?) played by Tina Louise Bomberry. In other words a tale about a city slicker who is forced to confront his demons and change his ways amid the folksy ministrations of a rural, [*sic*] mostly Slavey, native population.

Haslett Cuff does say that "actually the native characters are the best thing in the first three hours of the series. They are naturally and skilfully played and possess a degree of mystery, a range of types and dimensions lacking in the two 'white' protagonists." But he argues that the CBC shouldn't take such risks and assumes that the show will never earn money in foreign sales. (The figures supplied in this book's chapter 11 prove him wrong, but such sales only occur when a series reaches the point where there are enough episodes for syndication, usually ninety to a hundred). Clearly, the idea that taxpayers' dollars should be invested in Canadian culture in the form of expensive television drama was not part of his universe, nor were the changes in the Broadcasting Act already cited. "The public network should not be producing shows that cost, as North of 60 does, $900,000 an hour, when they can't possibly earn that money back or hope to attract an audience of many millions, which U.S.

shows costing the same do ... Unlike its U.S. counterparts, the CBC is not making pilots or test marketing these expensive shows. All that's required, apparently, is a native Indian quotient, a geographically correct location, and producers who already have a track record of risking an enormous amount of taxpayers' money while enriching themselves (since 1977, Alliance has received more than 60 million from Telefilm Canada)." Haslett Cuff could not know then that over the next decade Alliance Atlantis would become the most successful independent maker and distributor in Canadian television history, creating millions of dollars in jobs, both in the industry and in the communities in which the company filmed – that is, until they gave up making Canadian television drama, becoming purely distributors, and finally sold the firm in 2007.

Haslett Cuff's colleague Stephen Godfrey, writing a month before ("Birth of a Nation," in the *Globe and Mail*, 21 November 1992), also seems concerned with the economics of television drama in the early 1990s, calling the series lucky to reach the air against the odds. Serious cutbacks in government subsidies to the CBC had begun in the mid-1980s. Godfrey writes: "From the start the CBC seemed like the perfect network for *North of 60*. The series seemed positively wreathed in maple leaves. It deals with a burnt out Mountie, posted to a small, isolated community in the NWT who finds his life changed by two women – a native constable and a white community nurse." He points out that the CBC makes sixteen episodes rather than the American norm of twenty-two to twenty-six because the National Hockey League finals make havoc of the spring schedule (and the May sweeps – both still a scheduling issue in 2007).[9] At that time, there was an agreement that in the Thursday 8–10 p.m. slot CBC-owned stations (but not CBC affiliates) would carry the series.[10] Godfrey continues his article by quoting CBC executive Nada Harcourt: "'There are certain issues that are just part of the temper of the times.'" (Note that, with the usual planning lead of at least a year and a half before shooting starts, the "times" when the series would have been under discussion and then commissioned [that is, 1990–91] would have been shaped by the dangerous, weeks-long confrontation at Oka in the summer of 1990 between traditional Mohawk clan mothers supported by "warriors" from the reserve and elsewhere and the Québec Sûreté, who called in the Canadian army.) Harcourt continues: "'[T]he relationship between natives and whites is one of [these issues]. We have been looking for a long time for a series that would deal intelligently with native characters and we felt that Wayne and Barbara would be able to deliver the quality we were after.'" It happened to be the right time at the CBC, and the show was intended for the right time slot. Harcourt elaborates: "'We look at the balance of our schedule and try to mix adult drama with family and comedy shows ... this was clearly in the adult-drama category.'" She also dismisses the inevitable inappropriate comparisons this way: "'*North of 60* is to *Northern Exposure* what *Black Robe* is to *Dances with Wolves*.'"

"An Inside Look at a People" by Chris Dafoe, 21 November 1992, was a third look at the first season of the series in the *Globe and Mail:* "Grigsby says that, in putting together the series, he and co-producer Barbara Samuels wanted to try something very different from their work on E.N.G. 'We wanted to get away from the jacked up environment of the news room and see if we could make television with lower key moments' says Grigsby of the decision to set the show in the north. 'We were inter- ested in the meeting of white European culture and aboriginal culture, but we wanted to do it in a way that wasn't so loaded. If we had set the show in Manitoba, for example, the relationship would have been much testier. Also, by setting it in the north we could portray a society in which ... semi-traditional life is possible.'" Both Samuels and Grigsby were familiar with the cultural conflicts endemic in Montreal and stressed in various interviews the drama intrinsic in two cultures rubbing up against one another. They also reiterated, along with the producers, that the series was an authentic reflection of the Dene culture, thanks to the help of their Dene advisors. On the questions of authenticity that have haunted the other series discussed in this book, Tina Keeper told Dafoe that "'they've done a great job in making the show realistic and they been very open to input ... There are so many stereotypes – both of romantic, Indian princess stereotypes and the negative ones – about us, that re- moves us from being human. I think the show really deals with those ste- reotypes very effectively. Michelle is a very realistic, well-rounded character – she's got scars and flaws and a past.'"

Patricia Hluchy in *Maclean's,* 7 December 1992, is not pleased with the first episode (apparently the only one the critics were able to preview): "Practically humour-proof," she complains. She finds Eric is even "more glum ... [W]ill viewers lose patience with such unremitting gloom? ... [He has] a ludicrously brief nervous breakdown ... [she has a point]. Too much hinges on the combative Eric, who is hard to like and often hard to be- lieve." However, Hluchy very much liked Michelle's character ("a resilient single mother") as well as Tina Keeper's performance. She could not antici- pate that Eric would go and that Michelle would be the real keeper.

"A Sense of Place, Culture Help Make *North of 60* Sing" is the headline in the *Ottawa Citizen,* 29 November 1992, for a column by Tony Atherton, one of the most consistent and thoughtful of the Canadian newspaper television critics. Unlike the other critics, who appear to have little memory of past television series, he sets the series, as he often does, in a broadcasting context:

> Prime-time fare, which used to include such modest but site specific drama as the Beachcombers and Spirit Bay, has made way for bigger budgets and a more uniformly urban look. That was what our producers thought they could sell to the new American cable markets, or what broadcasters thought would be the best bet to repatriate Canadian audiences who were raised on U.S. stuff. Frankly, we had become a little ashamed of our most distinct regions, thanks, in part, to Hollywood clichés about the Mounties and the tundra, and to a certain degree, to CBC family adventure stories, from the Forest Rangers and Caribou [*sic*] Country to the aforementioned Beachcombers. We came to associate the Canadian north with low-budgets or kitsch … Alliance Communications has, until now, concentrated on TV production skewed to action, from Night Heat to E.N.G (even though both series have a strong sense of character) … North of 60 … is really anti-action, the antithesis of [the wildly popular, late 1980s cop show] Miami Vice mayhem. Olssen's raid on the dry town's bootleggers for instance ends in wry anticlimax.

Bob Remington, also in the *Ottawa Citizen* (no date on the clipping in the CBC library), like Atherton, sets the series in the context of other television representations of native people, in this case, more predictably, of Tonto, the metonym of all things stereotypical in Indian Country. Then he goes on: "Jackson and Keeper are both Cree, not the Dene of the North whom they represent in the series. But both of them are veterans of battles to achieve native representation on TV." He quotes Tom Jackson: "'I've read cream of the crop scripts where the main character is Indian and I have been told, and this is a quotation 'I don't think we can take the chance on a native lead.'" Remington continues: "For urban Canadians, especially those in the south, TV finally has one valuable lesson: the dividing line that separates the Northwest Territories and the Yukon from the rest of Canada is purely geographic. The country doesn't end at the 60$^{th}$ parallel.'" Greg Quill in the *Toronto Star,* 18 December 18 1992, called *North of 60* "an out of the box hit" and supplied the ratings for the first two episodes (3 and 10 December), 1,265,000 and 1,037,000 respectively. A later CBC press release, 8 February 1993, says that audiences averaged close to 1 million. The reported numbers vary considerably, but by the end of the fifth season Miles Morriseau (1997), presumably quoting CBC or Nielsen figures directly, reports an average of 1.5 million.

D.B. Smith reviewed the series in the 3–16 January 1994 issue of *Windspeaker*, an aboriginal newspaper, after the series had been running for a year. He starts by describing the setting: "Except for the length of the airfield, the scenery resembles any number of tiny native communities north of the 60th parallel." When Smith asks Tom Jackson about how truthful to the North he thinks the show is, Jackson says, "'My belief, based on the feedback that I've gotten from people, particularly in the north ... is that the show is true ... Their lives are being exposed, and I say that in a friendly fashion. It was not a criticism, it was a compliment from the people that watch the show.'" After listing issues like chronic drinking or suicide – and here Samuels again claims for the series a different kind of authenticity than the merely visual , she tells him, "'We want [aboriginal] people to be able to see something of themselves that hadn't been shown on television before. We want people, who would never see that aspect of our aboriginal communities, to see it and realise there were different things going on ... That particular vision of the North – of a troubled community reshaping itself – has been criticised by some reviewers as too bleak for television audiences. But many northern natives say they see a lot of themselves and their communities in each episode.'" Smith writes: "Yet, [Samuels] also softens this statement, by saying, more modestly, that 'Teaching how to live or how things should be is not our intention here. It's just to explore what happens when you throw a bunch of characters together in a small town.'"

Meanwhile, at the beginning of the second season, John Haslett Cuff in the *Globe and Mail*, 28 October 1993, continues in a condescending way to express his dislike of the show: "While it is confidently produced in most respects, it is also facile and is so preoccupied with presenting its well scrubbed picture of life in the northern outpost that it lacks the grit and soul of authenticity" – that word again. Note also how the word "outpost" echoes his previous description of the series as "rural" (when presumably he meant "remote"), both words explicitly betraying Haslett Cuff's objection to the fact that the series never, ever acknowledges Toronto or even Ontario as the centre of Canada's universe. The nearest city to Lynx River is Yellowknife, home to the regional government, Vancouver is a glittering promise, Calgary is where Hannah went to high school, Edmonton is a centre of venture capital, and Ottawa is the distant battleground of bureaucrats, the source of procrastination, incomprehensible decisions, and funding. Throughout all six seasons (and the movies that followed) Toronto is invisible to the characters on *North of 60*. As for the adjective "well scrubbed," the people and most of the houses are clean.

Why does this surprise him? The settlement, however, is less than pristine. Even though there are too few houses and too many people, no one in Lynx River is shown as living nine or ten to a three-room house, a condition to be found on too many isolated northern reserves.[11] Nevertheless, housing is an issue right up to the last episode of the last season.

Haslett Cuff goes on to admit, "Yesterday morning, the first time I had looked at the show since its debut, I sat down and watched four complete episodes." He prefers the episode that turns on a hostage taking because it moves more quickly than the others and supplies him with a recognizable format, "the potential catharsis of watching a gun wielding miscreant shot by the police." Predictably, he praises *Northern Exposure,* which, also predictably (and erroneously), he calls *North of 60's* "U.S. cousin." As before, he sees the whole production as an exercise in the "intensely political game of government subsidised television production ... The series sacrifices the degree of realism and any sense of the genuine travails of remote northern life that viewers are familiar with from most media coverage." He seems to have taken the media's concentration on the deprivation of Davis Inlet and the chaos of Oka as the complete picture. He does remark, accurately enough, that "[e]pisode after episode and scene after scene end with conversations ending ... abruptly as someone slams the door or walks off in a huff into the woods ... Still a small community is analogous to a family, I suppose ... perhaps their real behaviour accurately reflects those dynamics. But it's irritating to watch ... [The producers] have to give us something more intellectually provocative or culturally insightful. Such insights have to go beyond sweet grass ceremonies [sweet grass ceremonies?? – there are none on *North of 60,* which is about the Dene] and aboriginals who worship [wrong again] animal spirits, especially to hold the attention of the average jaded viewer with 50 channels to flick through." Haslett Cuff seems to revel in subsuming every First Nation into one set of clichés.

However, to give him due credit, a year later, in his column of 20 December 1994 (the Christmas season, when there is little new television to watch or review), he did provide a selection of feedback on his negative criticism of *North of 60.* I quote verbatim:

From S.M., Cree Nation, Toronto: "All right, enough already. I have simply had enough of John Haslett Cuff's strange, misinformed and racist attitudes towards Native people. I've been keeping a file on Mr. Cuff and the pattern that has emerged is not pleasant. Mr. Cuff seems to want to bash Native people at every turn ... So when can I expect The Globe and Mail to hire an experienced native journalist to review and analyse

Native film, television and acting? ... I will continue to fill my bulging file with examples of your ethnocentric and completely nonsensical efforts at interpreting Native culture, art and life" ... From C.A.H., in Calgary: "It is clear that you have never made your home nor visited for any length of time the small communities that dot the vast area north of our 60th parallel ... I suggest you might be happier watching American produced 'real life' cop shows if that's what it takes to hold your attention. I think good Canadian television deserves better that your half page critique about a subject matter depicted on television that you clearly know very little about."

Wayne Roberts, a less-jaded critic, who lived closer to the Northwest Territories, writing for Edmonton's *Star Phoenix*, 7 October 1993, also saw the series differently: "As the [first] season unfolded and the actors became more comfortable in their characters, the series proved the CBC's faith was well placed. The affairs of the people of Lynx River became addictive for viewers ... The weakest characters in the program are the two white leads, Oliver and Cook. Their characters seem to be emotional children, unable to handle relationships." All of the white characters who remained on the show changed and grew over the next five years.

Unfortunately, Haslett Cuff's colleague John Doyle was clearly in his camp. In the *Broadcast Week* section of the *Globe and Mail*, 29 October 1994, Doyle did a feature article (headlined "Logger Heads") that depended on a running contrast of *North of 60* with Global's steamy night soap *Destiny Ridge*, presumably because both were set in the wilderness and also because *Destiny Ridge* featured one native actor, Raoul Trujillo, in a leading role: "Tree huggers and true believers in the inherent pain at the heart of the Canadian experience will head for Lynx River. Anyone who immediately associates the great outdoors with alfresco sex will be hot footing to the tiny town of Argent on Destiny Ridge ... [Eric] is gone and the show is an ensemble drama of stoic faces. The characters swap solemn insights into the beauty of nature [I do not recall a *North of 60* character ever directly commenting on the beauty of nature or even on a specific feature of the landscape, although the camera often does] and the dignity of native life. *Destiny Ridge* started last year as a co-production with German broadcasters [which] meant an emphasis on the thrills of outdoor adventures – park wardens rescuing tourists from raging rapids and scary bears getting too close to happy campers. The sensual element consisted of the camera lingering for a few seconds on [fading movie star] Elke Sommer ... It was tepid drama ... a theme-park version of the North." At least his summary of *Destiny Ridge* was accurate. Unlike its formulaic lovemaking, explosions of hormones on *North of 60* have consequences – both good and bad. Bertha and later Sarah, in overalls and bush shirts and carrying babies, do not at all resemble the blonde bombshell Sommer.

As well as not being sexy enough, the series was too serious for Doyle. He continues: "As well meant as *North of 60* clearly is, it also reeks of superior attitude ... The series tugs at the heart of white Canadian guilt. All the native elders are unbelievably wise [in actual fact they make serious mistakes] and the youths are good-hearted tearaways [some are, a few are brutal or duplicitous]. The result isn't art or entertainment – it's politically correct propaganda. Its redeeming merit is its visual elegance – the opening sequence of images in each episode ... is the weekly highlight. *Destiny Ridge* ... delivers the more honest pleasure of true escapism and great kitsch and Canadian TV badly needs a quota of kitsch to keep us in good humour." I think Doyle's occasional forays into the persona of an Irish lad (he left Ireland for graduate work at York University in 1980) may have got the better of him here. Three years later he expressed active dislike of *The Rez* (see chapter 9) for what he perceived as its overly serious tone. But I do agree with him about one thing. *North of 60* was never kitsch.

Christopher Hume seems to have watched the series with some care. In the *Starweek* section of the *Toronto Star*, 12 November 1994, he offers a more thoughtful comment on episode 37, "The Cure," broadcast in the third season: "The series does a delicate balancing act; how to depict the dreariness that drives so many young aboriginals to alcoholism and gas sniffing without collapsing into despair. It stays up by concentrating on characters and their personal struggles. Sometimes they win, sometimes they lose. In either case, the audience which at last count numbers a healthy 1.2 million seems to be watching."

By 1995, John Haslett Cuff was wavering between a little grudging admiration for the show and a continuing dislike of its basic themes, characters, and pace. He compares CTV's hit comedy/cop show *Due South* with *North of 60* in the *Globe and Mail*, 9 November: "Both shows have extremely loyal core audiences ... I know of a number of viewers who, having once lived in Canada's north, love to tune in to North of 60 every week. Although the two series are radically different in approach and sensibility, both seem to connect with audiences in a similar way, proving that Canadians do enjoy seeing themselves, or aspects of their lives and culture, reflected back on the television screen." He points out that *Due South* is clearly commercial while *North of 60* is "an unmistakably public broadcasting project ... *North of 60* is quintessentially Canadian, which means it is less glamorous and less flippant and more self consciously earnest albeit in an appealing way ... [It] is the inheritor of a long tradition (British in origin) of critical, naturalistic drama, in which the actors tend to look like 'real' often homely people." Like many other critics, Haslett Cuff is mistaken about the origins of the realistic television drama that the British independent channels imported from Canada along with some of our producer/directors in the late 1950s.[12]

But then he returns to home base: "The continuing drama derives from the petty, quotidian struggles of life in the isolated, inbred community of Lynx River ... This shows the biggest problem is a kind of emotional monotony in which all conflicts, however picayune, seemed to be given dramatic weight. This may well be an authentic representation of the peculiar dynamics of any claustrophobic and doomed social outpost [that word again], but it becomes tiresome." *Claustrophobic, doomed, outpost* – oh my! The series would indeed be tiresome if his description were accurate. Still, Haslett Cuff does try to balance the books in his column one-third of the way through the series' run, although he manages to mix up actresses Tina Keeper and Tina Louise Bomberry. With the show's emphasis on aboriginals, on a brother and sister, and on Hannah's death, he admits that "the program is groundbreaking in several important ways ... North of 60 is a specifically indigenous soap opera that succeeds on a cultural level because of its integrity, its fidelity to our reality, that is not otherwise represented on North American television, and for that alone it deserves applause."

Two years later, in the *Globe and Mail* of 9 January 1997, Haslett Cuff forgets his qualified praise and returns to the attack for the last time, also revealing who he thinks his audience is: "And any time the residents aren't sniffing gasoline ... or assaulting one another, there isn't much going on. Unless one is really fascinated by individual characters or their relationships, there's not much to keep a couch 'tater coming back for more every week." But programs based almost entirely on relationships are common (and popular) in television, from *The Honeymooners* to *Friends*. Ironically, in the same year that he left television reviewing for filmmaking, Haslett Cuff won a best writing award at the 2004 Geminis for *Crimes of the Heart*, a very personal confessional documentary about adultery. His blind spot with regard to this show may be attributable in part to his gender. Women viewers are generally more interested in narratives stressing character interplay than in narratives stressing action. That is why there are so many profiles and backgrounders in American Olympic coverage, for example. Later in his article, Haslett Cuff tries to restore a balance: "The refreshingly varied portrayal of aboriginal loss vividly contrasts with most urban Canadians' experience of that too long debased and undervalued culture of North America's first wave of migratory human inhabitants." However, again he pulls back and singles out the women characters for blame: "Entertainment wise, however, the series is more problematic. The central character, Michelle Kenidi … seems to don an aggrieved sense of centuries of oppression with her RCMP duds everyday and just looks generally [like] a miserable and unhappy woman." From these inaccurate generalizations, we might charitably conclude that he did not see very many episodes.

Given the stereotyping in some of the reviews by professional reviewers, it is fitting that a writer for an aboriginal newspaper should get the last word. In February 1996, five seasons into the run, John Copley, a reporter for the *Alberta Native News*, wrote: "It's the good old Canadian content there that really counts, eh? In particular it's the mystery of the people and their way of life, the down to earth situations they get themselves into … that keeps us … ready to watch the next episode each and every Thursday night." Copley talks about how realistic the continuing motif of red tape is and congratulates "a superb cast who gives the show that special identity, that feeling of 'it's ours' and it's better than the 'Hollywood hype' we're all used to."

### INFORMAL RESPONSES TO THE SERIES

Informal responses to a television series can come from websites, email, even casual conversations. Audience feedback for the first season, favourable of course given the context, is quoted in a CBC press release of 22 September 1993. From Nanaimo: "[T]hank you for giving us an intelligent and gentle humoured program." From Cape Breton: "Canadian writers had been trying to capture that … elusive spirit that is Canada. I think you found the secret." Someone from Quebec writes that the show is "[n]othing short of majestic." In Toronto someone writes: "Superior to much of what I see on TV."

Responses to an official website fall somewhere between the formal (though certainly not professional) and the informal. They often disappear when a series ends, or if the server continues to carry them, they sometimes have an unexpected half-life of years. The producers of *North of 60* took advantage of 1990s technology to put up interactive websites (I viewed, then printed, these), which have since disappeared from the web. They invited comment and questions from the audience, posting pictures of mailboxes for each character as well as one for questions to be considered at a "band council meeting." The producers claimed that they were influenced by this email feedback. Though it did not represent a scientific sample as a focus group would have, the mail instead came from people who had invested some time and interest in the series. The CBC *North of 60* website in the fifth season (also no longer up) provided this interesting comment from "Frank in Hamilton," who had yet another perspective: "I teach film, TV and popular culture in the Department of Film Studies at Queen's. I really like North of 60 for lots of reasons – its own high quality, its representations of Canadian issues and its representation of aboriginal issues." From the backgrounder page of the website for the last season (still extant),[13] the following praise for the show was posted:

[W]e are hooked and truly believe it is the best Canadian program on TV … sure beats the heck out of Melrose Place! Fabulous acting, great story, and truly real-life characters that allow you to get to know them.

I am so grateful to have a show that I cannot predict from beginning to end that also manages to be "real." I am not native and I am not from the north but I identify very strongly with the inhabitants of Lynx River. Your story lines are such that ordinary people can see themselves in those situations.

This is a rare production that, instead of finding a formula and playing it safe, has continued to go forward and take risks with the character and plot development. I care about the characters and admire that they are portrayed in their weaknesses as well as their strengths.

I was so desperate to see something of this show that I started watching it in French, and I couldn't understand a word of it.

The same website had a specific page headed "The Audience," which told the visitor that "[t]ime and time again fans relay how close they feel to Lynx River's stories, a fact that confounds some industry insiders. But the show's executive producer Peter Lauterman puts it quite simply: 'The audience has become part of the community,' he says. 'They identified with the townspeople and their problems and this became a critical factor in finding and maintaining their interest … They watch because the show is real, not phoney. Lynx River reflects small town values that many Canadians relate to' … He adds that the fact the show is about natives makes it more interesting, but it is not why [the majority] watch. 'The characters are under pressure, trying to make sense of their lives and this, more than anything, keeps our viewers tuned in.'"

When I was first thinking about this book and watching *North of 60* in 1993, I subscribed to NATIVE-L,[14] a list active from June 1991 to August 1997 that is still archived online. Nativenet lists broke up into various interest groups. These lists were initiated and lightly moderated by educator Gary Trujillo[15] and were part of the Nativenet lists NAT-LANG, NAT-EDU NAT-HLTH, and NAT-1492, which he maintained for some years. I also subscribed to NATCHAT,[16] archived from June 1994 to December 1996 online, and nn.nativecan, also moderated by Trujillo, which has not been archived separately but is included with NATCHAT online. nn.nativecan was chiefly an alternate source for current news on events in "Indian Country." NATCHAT included a broadly based list of people – First Nations (most self identified, e.g., Haudenosaunee, Kennai, et al.), Metis, white, and perhaps others. NATIVE-L and NATCHAT were participatory, lively, often very personal, and for me (like many others, self-identified by name, profession, nationality, and race) eye-openers. They went the way of many such early lists, as moderators burned out and more specialized groups formed and dissolved. Yet I still get odd bits of email from people I don't know who visit the archives. The lists introduced me to issues never raised in these series, including *North of 60*. There were debates about representations of First Peoples in the popular culture, including the use of "Indian" mascots, tomahawk chops, and offensive brand names. There were discussions about *Indian in the Cupboard* and, more passionately, Disney's *Pocahontas*; Ted Turner's television docudramas *Lakota Woman* and *The Broken Chain*; films like *Clearcut, Black Robe,* and *Dances with Wolves*; and books by Indian wannabes. The lists also included a survey on the legal status of Native American religions; lists of useful books and web addresses; discussions of pan-Indianism and Indians; various rules for powwows; accounts of experiences with anthropologists past and present (a topic that does appear on *North of 60*); an apparently complete translation of the "Iroquois" Great Law; information on the ongoing indigenous uprising in Chiapas, Mexico; various Aboriginal land claims in Australia; reports on the clear-cutting of old-growth forests and its impact on salmon runs (issues that appear briefly in *The Beachcombers*); and specifically feminist issues, such as whether a cultural revival or the preservation of complementary but equal system of customs and laws is oppressive. The lists discussed as well such issues as abortion, adoptions of First Nations babies and young children by white couples, and the existence and purposes of the American Indian Movement. It could be that the programs discussed persuaded some viewers to find out more – not only online, but also in libraries, out their front doors.

The anecdotal email that I report below was primarily sent and received during my membership on NATIVE-L and NATCHAT. Both the background of the respondents and their own thoughts about the series were mixed. Where I have permission, I quote the email responses directly. I was unable to trace every person who wrote, however, as many email addresses have changed in the intervening years; thus, a few unattributed responses are paraphrased and included.

I particularly value email I received during the actual run of *North of 60*. A linesman who worked in the city said he enjoyed the program because it carried him away each week up north to where his family was. Finding it both entertaining and moving, he mentioned that his friends discussed the show and asked questions about it. He said in response to a question that he was not sure that having native writers for the show made any difference. He also pointed out that the relationship of First Nations people to television can be complicated. For example, some elders do not like having their stories put in print or on tape because they feel it takes away from the experience of being there and sharing them first-hand. Yet they also acknowledge that tape and video (and now CDS and DVDS) ensure that stories survive. He talked about seeing programs about residential schools that shocked him but also helped him understand what his grandmother had gone through. When I mentioned the off-screen problems of a few of the actors in the series, which were widely reported during the run, he mentioned with some amusement that he knew people who confused the real-life actors with their characters.

Another correspondent, Edward A. "Ned" Bear, Wolastoqiyik First Nation, New Brunswick, watched the program often because of the native cast and content. He found it authentic, although he saw faults appearing now and then. Teevee really bothered him sometimes, perhaps because the character reminded him so much of someone with a similar attitude problem in his own community: "The way I criticise some of the faults in *North of 60* is by comparing what happens in the show to what actually happens or happened in my own reserve." In response to my remarks about problems with some of the multiple storylines (see chapter 13), he wrote: "I don't think that there are too many stories in one episode, since there is a lot happening in my own small community of approximately 600 people." When asked whether the frequent guests flying into Lynx River affected the show's credibility, he said that the outsiders add authenticity to the show. When I relayed Ojibway playwright Drew Hayden Taylor's complaint (reported anecdotally to me) that the producers felt his dialogue wasn't "Indian enough," he replied that, ironically, "some native communities [also] had only stereotypes left to hang on to." And then he corrected one of my misapprehensions, in this case about the silences (unusual in television series) that I had taken to be refusals to respond to comments or questions: "What you noticed as silence may actually be the response. It has been my experience that most native people, especially the older generation, respond with silence when the answer is apparent or obvious (or should be) to everyone present, particularly to the person asking." He continued: "Most native communities have an abundance of good humour. Mostly it is a quiet humour but it enriches the lives of many native people. Usually the jokes on the show are 'inside jokes' and you need to experience living in a native community for a length of time to get them. You are probably missing the jokes, since I believe they are directed toward other native people, which makes me like this show so much more." He concluded the exchange with: "There are many faults in a TV show, but I attribute these to the necessity to appeal to the greater viewing, non-native public and its survival as a prime-time show."

Another email correspondent, a librarian, said she was lucky to live in Detroit where the series was available on the CBC, because there was nothing like it on American television. A self-identified, middle-aged white woman who grew up in Montana, she had watched it faithfully in reruns and identified the characters with the natives she knew. She also liked the series because it showed situations everybody faces and yet did not provide predictable resolutions. Another correspondent, a woman employed at a university, saw the programs as interesting because they dealt in imaginative ways with topical issues and "iconic figures in the broader Canadian context, especially its revisiting of the Mountie and the Nurse." Over the years I have encountered many people who remember the series with affection, including several nurses and two Tlingit craftspeople, Mr Carlisle, who is also the leader of the North Wind Singers and Dancers, and Ms Jackson. Ms Jackson identified Lynx River with the community in which she had grown up, and she liked the fact that viewers were not shown sacred objects or the inside of a sweat lodge (a convention broken in *Dream Storm*).[17]

American and Canadian reactions were certainly varied. In 1999 a correspondent from North Carolina who was watching *North of 60* on an

American cable network reported that the first thing that grabbed his attention was the town. He had grown up in a town not much larger than Lynx River, at about the same "poverty level." In March of 2000, having left an email trail on the series in the places already mentioned, I had an email from Margaret Ivemey, who lives just below the border and had seen the CBC reruns of *North of 60* in the afternoons in 1999–2000 in a slot traditionally reserved for soap operas. Although *North of 60* moves much more rapidly than a soap and clearly has different production values, Ms Ivemey and, I would guess, many other viewers responded to it as to a superior soap opera. "This show is reality-based and it's a breath of fresh air to see a show that addresses everyday/life situations and meets them head on." Later, she wrote to me:

> What I really like about the series is that it … doesn't have silly story lines like U.S. soaps … The real-life problems faced by the characters, i.e. drugs/alcohol addictions, are handled in such a way that the characters have to face their problems – in real life this IS the biggie – and want to change. Much better than the "magic pill" type of approach of U.S. television daytime dramas. Also, I found the story lines involving the town's progress, i.e. the new road and drilling for gas, interesting in that various townspeople's opinions were expressed … some for and some against change and progress. Pretty much what went on at the Akwesasne reserve here with regard to building the casino. Heck, if that had been the story line in any U.S. daytime series they would probably have drawn straws or bartered their wives' affections. You can probably tell I don't have much respect for a lot of the programming here and the CBC was nuts in letting Michelle [*sic*] go out of production. What were they thinking???

Conversations in 1994 with Glenn Warren, a retired RCMP officer who served with the force for sixteen years in the Arctic,[18] with Sam Kingaunmiut, Glenn's partner, and with Page Burt, a naturalist, appear at www.brocku.ca/hri/associates/miller/outside_looking_in.pdf. Page and Glenn at that time lived in Bathurst Inlet, population 60 (counting the twenty-five tourists during July). Sam was a permanent resident of Bathurst Inlet.

Since no academic studies using focus groups have been done on the series, any speculation about conversations among its viewers after an episode would be just that – speculation. The large number of people who viewed *North of 60* on a regular basis suggests that the series had a broad appeal. Unfortunately, two of the academic critics did not see the full series. The third concentrated on Michelle as a female RCMP officer who both broke popular culture stereotypes and, in his opinion, invoked them. Alice Williams, Rodney Bobiwash, and another First Nations academic, unnamed by Drew Hayden Taylor, found that the series reinforced negative stereotypes, and all three actively disliked the series. So did Richard Wagamese. A few newspaper and periodical critics agreed. Yet other reporters and critics – white as well as First Nations writers (including John Copley and Miles Morriseau) – enjoyed the show. Anecdotal email and conversations provide some of the reasons why. The fan base (see chapter 10) points to a broad cross-section of people who truly loved *North of 60* and who responded to the opportunity to discuss it online with like-minded people. Ten years after the first run ended, they are still at it. The series and the five movies are rerun on APTN and Showcase and are syndicated around the world. Even with its limitations, *North of 60* does strike a chord as no other series in Canada has been able to do, both in the neglected demographic of First Nations viewers as well as in a broader spectrum of Canadian viewers. With the much shorter overlapping series *The Rez*, the series has informed both rural and urban audiences south of 60 about many aspects of non-urban aboriginal life. Its concentration on issues, problems, and strengths specific to some of the South Slavey Dene, as well as on issues, problems, and strengths that viewers south of 60 may share, is key to that ongoing impact. As the only successful prime-time series for adults featuring First Nations characters, *North of 60* is a treasure that deserves to be in reruns (as indeed it is), but the masters should also be copied onto DVD so that viewers could enjoy the series when and where they wish and perhaps see additional features as is common with most DVD series. Legitimate study copies of the programs as broadcast, including whatever commercials appeared in the first run or rerun, have been recorded on tape and DVD, but are scattered in private collections, if they exist at all; these are the only backups to the official copies deposited in the National Archives of Canada and are available for scholarly use through an informal network of people working on Canadian television.

In any recording format, *North of 60* is a keeper. Moreover, as quality Canadian content, at least in syndication, it will survive across many platforms. The bright side is that, at least in syndication, *North of 60* will be around for many years to come.

# CONCLUSION

# Others Will Continue to Explore

At Expo 67, our celebration of Canada's centennial year, we represented ourselves to the world architecturally as an inverted pyramid (109 feet tall with nine floors of exhibits) called Katimavik. Jeffrey Stanton says the name was an "Eskimo word for 'gathering place.'" His site has a wonderful picture of this structure. He recalls, as I do that there were sculptures on the four sloping sides open to the sky.[1] I also remember, as he does, that one represented a Haida transformation mask that opened to reveal its interior face. Perhaps the last sentence of H.V. Nelles's *A Little History of Canada* (2004) recalls that sculpture: "But just as surely as in the past, history is tugging at the strings and the Transformation Mask is opening yet again" (257).[2] Forty years later, on 9 April 2007, transformation was visible at a very different commemoration, the rededication of the newly refurbished Vimy Memorial (broadcast live by the CBC and CTV) on the occasion of the ninetieth anniversary of the Battle of Vimy Ridge. In front of Queen Elizabeth, the prime ministers of Canada and France, and thousands of students and veterans, a woman chaplain carrying an eagle feather said a blessing in Cree. Susan Aglukark (Inuit) sang with a choir. Most moving of all, Sierra Noble (Manitoba Metis)[3] played the Metis warrior's lament on her fiddle, standing alone, silhouetted against the sky next to the huge female figure that represents Canada mourning for her dead.

The television representation of First Nations peoples has been transformed over an even longer span. A commercial that appeared on 17 October 1956, when *Radisson* was being made, marks the distance travelled.[4] It was presented during a live drama titled *Black of Moon*, which was commissioned by Canada Savings Bonds (the implication being the Canadian government's blessing of this CBC production) and portrayed a remarkably racist version of Big Bear's role in the 1885 Metis uprising, reflecting the attitude of many people at the time. The commercial, backed by soothing orchestral music, shows the handsome, deep-voiced announcer Joel Aldred, wearing evening dress, standing against luxurious flocked wallpaper, the coat of arms of Canada displayed above his head. He is cradling in his arms an old-fashioned rifle as he reflects what many viewers saw as change: "There was a time when a house wife might have to stand on guard all night behind a flour sack propped in a window. But now your window looks out on grass that has never heard the soundless tread of an Indian moccasin and, if you have one of these [rifles], it is likely above your mantel. Times have certainly changed." Houses are no longer "roofed with sod and protected by shooting" but instead are "built and protected by savings."[5] He then discusses how to save a thousand dollars for the down payment on land from which the Indian is assumed to have vanished. More than the price of housing has changed in the last fifty years. So have many viewers. They know that within the outer masks of the many different First Nations, the peoples are still undergoing significant transformations that television across the spectrum – news, documentaries, sports, drama series – must try to reflect.

I suggest in this book that since its inception in 1952, CBC television has rarely been far out in front of the general audience in the way it represents "Indians," while the private networks, apart from running two children's programs in the 1980s and a few other shows very recently, have scarcely been in the parade. In chapter 1, I quote the 1991 Broadcasting Act,[6] which recognizes that the broadcasting system as a whole has an obligation to reflect not just the multicultural nature of the country but also its First Peoples. In section 3, subsection (o), of the act, the CBC, specifically, is told to provide "programming that reflects the aboriginal cultures of Canada ... as resources become available for that purpose." There is no way to know whether that Broadcasting Act was a deciding factor in the CBC's decision that same year to devote scarce resources to *North of 60*, a series for adults about an isolated band of Dene in the Northwest Territories. Regrettably, the subsection continues with a phrase that excuses both the government and the network – "as resources become available." This could be read as a reason why no other drama series like *North of 60* and *The Rez* (both ended in 1997) were made in the next decade. Despite parliamentary task forces, committees, and reports, despite CBC internal reviews for the Canadian Radio-television and Telecommunications Commission (CRTC), and research prepared and reports written for the CRTC, every federal government since the mid-1980s has devalued the CBC and the job it has done while insisting on a mandate that has not realistically reflected the dollars those governments have actually given the network. The funding of *North of 60* that was cobbled together for the sixth season is a good example of that growing gap – one that, despite changes in Telefilm and government policy, persists today, a decade later.

We could only know what effect, if any, these programs (made by people from the outside) have had on general public perceptions of First Nations peoples had there been independent scholarly audience research, focus groups, and longitudinal studies over the last fifty years, research that never happened.[7] However, there is one very widely held assumption (one vital to getting sponsors to top up the CBC's governmental funding), and it is that every program affects its audience, even if the effect is to send the viewer to the channel changer. Public and private efforts at censorship and the self-censorship of television itself demonstrate this widespread belief. Most of the people I have talked to in the industry hope and believe that the programs they make affect viewers. I cannot demonstrate irrefutably that the series discussed in this book, particularly the handful of long- running ones, *Forest Rangers, The Beachcombers,* and *North of 60,* and perhaps the short-lived pioneering 1980s series *Spirit Bay,* with its all-aboriginal cast, educated and informed their audiences and entertained them as well. But the anecdotal postings on fan sites for some of the shows, cited earlier, suggest that they did. The programs may also have reinforced the perceptions of those viewers who were more informed and had more progressive attitudes. In all cases, for good or ill, by engaging the imagination through drama rather than through news or documentary, television was able to work powerfully on its audience and their attitudes to First Nations peoples. The "Boomer" portion of the television audience may have had childhood encounters with Joe Two Rivers in *Forest Rangers,* Pete in *Adventures in Rainbow Country,* Jesse and Sara in *The Beachcombers,* or even Rabbit, Eldon, and Tafia in *Spirit Bay* – then later turned with adult enjoyment to *North of 60* while their older teenaged children watched *The Rez.* For some viewers, each of these programs would be part of the experience of the next, each one reflecting changing times, changing ways of life.

CHANGE/NO CHANGE

I began thinking about this book just before the summer of 1990 and the confrontations of warriors, clan mothers, children, and old people with the Québec Sûreté and the Canadian army at Oka/Kanesatake. I end it when there is no resolution in sight to the occupation by the members of the Six Nations Reserve of land in Caledonia originally given to them in 1784.[8] In some ways the view from the outside – and perhaps for many aboriginal people from the inside – has not changed at all. Land claims; joblessness on reserves; corruption; the erosion of languages; a too often dysfunctional and bloated bureaucracy in the Indian affairs ministry, with its tangle of laws and regulations; higher than average instances of alcoholism, drug use, and family violence; controversies about status and non-status Indians – some or all of these problems continue to plague First Peoples in the North, on reserves, and in the cities. But there have also been marked changes: education down to the band level focused on the specific traditions of each nation; national recognition of aboriginal achievements in politics, the arts, medicine, and law (broadcast on different networks and APTN); progress (very recently) in the settlement of the claims of residential school victims; the rising voices of women locally and nationally; the sustained attempt to make a new deal with the federal government; new income from newly discovered natural resources and, after battles that went on for years, some influence on when, where, and how these resources are extracted; better and more focused health care in some places; recognition of the voices of youth; better relations between the old and the young; increased use of new technologies to preserve old traditions; rediscovered forms of justice; and new forms of self-government.

Very few of these long-standing issues found their way into the programming of the 1950s and 1960s, and only in a limited way into that of the 1970s and 1980s. *The Beachcombers*, for example, did not dwell on these problems, partly because it was a half-hour show with a largely comic perspective intended for family viewing. As a show for children, *Spirit Bay* was also limited in the issues it raised, although like *The Beachcombers* it showed fully functioning, loving adults who were connected to their traditions and available to the children in the community. In the 1990s a different kind of comedy, *The Rez*, took sideways glances at all kinds of problems – absent fathers, lack of jobs for young people, the erosion of culture, band politics, drugs. But unlike the books and the film that preceded it, the series had a light tone. Its characters were more rounded and interconnected within functioning families. On this rez the young people tended to win when racism appeared, whether it showed up in "made in Taiwan" figures on sale at the marina or in the remarks of a construction boss or a Toronto film crew. Adult viewers, however, had to wait until the early 1990s for a program that consistently presented adult struggles, failures, and achievements. Repeatedly, *North of 60* provided the back story for some of the characters' ongoing problems, yet most of the adult characters in the series took responsibility for dealing with them. The movies then brought the characters and their community into the twenty-first century.

The slapstick and gentle irony of *The Beachcombers*, the often oblique gentle humour of *Spirit Bay*, and the more spirited ironies and wisecracks of *The Rez* would have leavened *North of 60* and made it even more representative of First Nations ways of coping and simply enjoying life. Even so, within its limitations *North of 60* provided some memorable television. Taken together, these series – in stories played out on television screens across the country – reflect how attitudes to First Nations changed over the years from 1957 to 1997.

## A FEW QUESTIONS REVISITED

Chapter 1 posed a few specific questions about the ways "Indians" have been presented in television series. One question was whether they have consistently been presented as victims. Victims do appear in these series, but they are not a prevailing character type. Women struggle – and often prevail. Men are represented by a wide range of characters, very few of them victims. Some teens are, as Elsie would say, lost to drugs, alcohol, the city streets. Others flourish. The old are sometimes ignored, sometimes out of touch, but usually honoured. The mix of children, younger adults, the middle-aged, and the old in series from the 1970s onward reflect the demographic of the audience "outside." Another question was whether the dominant culture has persisted in seeing the native people as mysterious and often hostile antagonists. This is not the case in the series set in contemporary times, nor in the earliest series, *The Forest Rangers*. Among the historical series, *Radisson* represents the Iroquois as hostile. Historically this was true, as they were an independent and powerful force in the French/Indian/English wars as well as middlemen in the fur trade. But other nations were also sources of furs. Although utterly strange to Radisson in the beginning, they were masters of the skills he needed to survive.

In the series of the late 1950s – *Hawkeye, Hudson's Bay*, and *Radisson* (as well as *The Forest Rangers* a few years later) – no First Nations actors actually played the Indians, which meant that there were no aboriginals acting as unpaid consultants on the sets as there were for later series. At that time, the articles, novels, plays, pageants, poems, and histories about Indians were almost entirely written by Europeans and white North

Americans. Eloquent voices like Basil Johnston's for the Anishnabe were not yet in print. In the 1950s there was much less scholarship to serve as sources for actors, writers, and designers – though the CBC proudly claimed to have done a lot of research for *Radisson*. Finally, at that time and for several generations before, most schoolbooks, storybooks, and then films and radio reinforced stereotypes of the noble savage/Indian princess/squaw/firewater-addled Indian. Although stereotypes can still be found in reruns of relatively recent television series such as *X-Files*, *Star Trek Voyager, Stargate,* and even sitcoms, there is no longer any excuse for making these errors. Now there are dozens of books and articles written both from without and from within many of the different cultures of First Nations that makers of TV series can use and viewers can read. Documentaries made by First Nations filmmakers are shown on several specialty channels as well as on APTN.

A third question is whether Indians have been portrayed as sources of some unknowable, magical, but natural wisdom? Yes, in both the 1950s historical series and the two later ones, *Matt and Jenny on the Wilderness Trail* and *The Campbells*. Sometimes such references are romanticized. At other times First Nations knowledge of plants and dreams is presented as lifesaving and quite real. Regrettably, *Matt and Jenny's* usual source of wilderness wisdom is Kit, the mid-nineteenth-century version of a coureur de bois. In the later series, as a doctor trained in Scotland, Dr Campbell usually knows best. But the CBC shows of the same period, like *The Beachcombers* and *Spirit Bay,* present this wisdom and other spiritual practices in context, usually with attempts to be accurate and culturally specific (disputed in some cases by the actors) but nevertheless not as generic "Indian medicine." *Spirit Bay* is clear and specific about the abilities and responsibilities of elders and treats the power of dreams respectfully. Unfortunately, Mad Etta in *The Rez* is often, not always, presented as some sort of comic witch/psychic rather than as a healer and repository of tradition. *North of 60* presents a very complex, increasingly subtle view of Dene belief systems and of the roles of the keepers of traditions and the practitioners of the old ways. Elsie, Willie, and Joe, as well as Michelle and Peter and later Teevee, are in contact with the dead. The show slyly mocks outsiders like David, the white archaeologist, and Nevada, Teevee's Coast Salish city-bred friend, who both seek native spirituality in the bush. The complicated relationship between the traditional ways and the church's teachings are presented primarily through Lois, a devout Catholic, and Elsie, whose syncretic beliefs and practices are usually effective in healing physical and spiritual illnesses.

## ETHNOGRAPHY, GENDER, GENRE

Issues of ethnography, gender, verbal and gestural language differences, raised in chapter 2, are further explored in this chapter in an analysis of themes and episodes in the series as well as their context. How the series was shaped by both the context and the processes involved in making television is also examined. All of these elements contribute to high-quality long-form television as well as to the performance of identities. With the rise of the second wave of feminism in the 1970s, expectations about characters and issues changed. Questions of authenticity, which are often linked to questions about cultural appropriation, arise in every series in this book, but with different outcomes, depending in part on the period and film/television context and also on the genre, the audience targeted, and the skills of the makers of the programs. These questions become more overtly political as time passes. European viewers, drawn by the wilderness settings and the idea of exotic Indians, discovered instead programs that deconstructed their romanticized northern wilderness with jet boats, satellite dishes, and stores selling Coke and potato chips. Not every Indian was a competent hunter; expertise in dealing with Ottawa bureaucracy was equally useful. Ideas about what the North is have changed for Canadian viewers as well. Clichés of snow, ice, trees, and wolves (and lots of adventures) have given way to the riches in lumber and fish of the Northwest Coast. Oil, gas, and diamond exploration also intrude, with their attendant opportunities and problems, on "the True North." These series eventually came to reflect and even amplify these transformations.

The expectations of fans have always been shaped by the durable genres – sitcoms, cop shows, soaps, family adventure – and these series both fulfilled and sometimes inflected those expectations into programs that were distinctively different from their American progenitors. Since the earliest days of live Canadian television drama, Canadian viewers have tolerated, even preferred, in their own television drama open endings, ambiguities, a refusal to present oversimplifications or a quick fix for a long-standing social problem. Viewers like these have opened a space for some of the programs discussed in this study.

## CULTURAL APPROPRIATION

The serious and vexed issues of cultural appropriation arise in most chapters of this book without clear resolution. When the CBC makes a movie about residential schools, such as the 1980s film *Where the Spirit Lives,* which is still in circulation, and when residential schools are a major theme in *North of 60*, does this fill the economic and cultural space that should be occupied by First Nations makers telling their own individual and collective stories about that experience and its aftermath? For mainstream television, the answer is – yes, it does. Wrenching documentaries made by First Nations filmmakers and discussions about the subject have been broadcast on Newsworld and on the educational and specialty channels, as well as on APTN, but on the major networks, except for news items, there has been very little of this nature in the last ten years.

On the other hand, theories of cultural appropriation strictly applied would mean that only the Haudenosaunee and others from the Six Nations could write the story of Oka, not a Metis like Gil Cardinal, who did write and direct the miniseries *Indian Summer: The Oka Crisis* (2006) for the CBC. The Haudenosaunee's formal participation would presumably have made the drama more authentic than it was. Even so, like every program discussed in this book, *Indian Summer* was essentially made from the outside looking in because the production was controlled by the producers at Ciné Télé Action, who were white, and that fact imposes a basic limitation on its authenticity. I do note, however, that it was presented in the CBC online program guide as "Gil Cardinal's *Indian Summer.*"[9] The CBC's putting Cardinal's name above the title represents progress. Although aboriginal writers supplied storylines for some episodes of *Spirit River* and a few wrote scripts for *North of 60*, it is not possible for an outsider to extrapolate from the episodes in question to say what either *Spirit Bay* or *North of 60* would have looked like had they been made by, respectively, Anishnabe or Dene people. But aboriginal and Metis story editors, writers, directors, and actors, together with the aboriginal communities that served as locations, have helped Canadian television series come closer to their subjects. Moreover, *North of 60* had Dene consultants for every episode, every movie, which is progress. Over the years, thousands of viewers became acquainted with and absorbed accurate details about aboriginal lives and cultures even though some might have seemed irrelevant or puzzling. There is also anecdotal evidence that some First Nations viewers learned to accept the level of compromise made necessary by the format of series television and the economics of making television in a small market. In *Adventures in Rainbow Country*, *The Beachcombers*, *Spirit Bay*, *The Rez*, and *North of 60*, they could recognize themselves playing themselves, even if imperfectly.

At the other end of the spectrum, it would have been inconceivable in the 1950s to imagine a television drama where an aboriginal actor simply played an ordinary role, not an "Indian." It was hard enough to fir.d an Indian who was cast as an Indian. But in 2004 Lorne Cardinal (*North of 60's* Daniel De'ela) was cast as police chief Davis in the quite successful CTV sitcom *Corner Gas*, with no particular reference to his origins.[10] It is clear that Cardinal is from a First Nation, not only because of his appearance but also because some of the viewers might remember his previous roles – but his being an aboriginal is rarely if ever referred to as a plot point. In another example, Graham Greene appears simply as the narrator of the crime reality series *Exhibit A*, not as an Indian. Although he seldom gets to play a full-blood Oneida, he did play Shylock at Stratford in 2007. These examples point to a day that has not yet arrived, particularly for First Nations women, when aboriginal actors can appear regularly in stage and television roles that are not about being aboriginal.

The last word goes to Lorna Roth. In *Something New in the Air* (2005), she asserts that the media have the potential to "transform [Fourth World] consciousness from that of powerless objectified beings to subject-agents who can publicly act and speak in the language of their choice on the basis of their own cultural histories, knowledge and capacities. Media play a critical role in documenting and publicly asserting their ownership rights to these things" (227). She also points to both the problems and opportunities in Canada: "First Peoples' producers operate on the assumption that their programming and production values are complex, multilayered and sometimes unpredictable because their cross-cultural perspectives can be so at odds with those of their audiences. There is no simplistic audience theory embedded in their programming: it is assumed that the sender and the receiver will not necessarily be, quite literally, on the same wavelength." She points out that the "emphasis on social interchange and interactivity" of some of that programming "blatantly contradicts the work of Jean Baudrillard who argues that the media, in their very essence forbid such a direct response" (223).

## CULTURES CLASH, MAKE BRIDGES, INTERSECT

What about the representation of the forms of culture clash that developed as settlements and then residential schools, the Indian Act, resource extraction, and finally the media spread throughout Indian country? Unlike the late 1950s series set in the seventeenth, eighteenth, and nineteenth centuries, which occasionally pitted individual white settlers or the army against the First Nations who farmed and hunted on their lands, *Matt and Jenny on the Wilderness Trail* (1981) and *The Campbells* (1986–89), set in the

1830s to 1850s, showed in a minor way the impact of encroaching settlements on aboriginal neighbours. Contemporary series like *The Forest Rangers* and *Adventures in Rainbow Country* were set far enough north that there were no direct clashes. Moreover, the cast of characters in both were overwhelmingly white. Indians, though, are the sources of dramatic culture clashes in these contemporary series, even when they are not the major focus. Often they provide plots for adventure stories. Joe Two Rivers, Pete Gawa, and Jesse also do their share of rescuing less-skilled white children and adults who got into trouble.

The nineteen-year run for *The Beachcombers* meant that a whole generation of children grew up with it. Nick Adonidas usually assumes that everything is fine, and he is sometimes brought up short by his own ignorance or obliviousness. Not only was Jesse Jim a marked contrast to Nick, he introduced viewers in the early 1970s to elements of Coast Salish culture few would have ever known. He was also a role model for teens both within and outside of aboriginal cultures. In the last few seasons, *The Beachcombers* lost some of its coherence and appeal, but this does not diminish the accomplishment of a series that saw a young Coast Salish man grow into mature adulthood, succeed at a demanding job, marry and raise a family. The producers did struggle with how to depict Jesse's traditions as well as those of Laurel's Nootka heritage. They did not always get it right. But the producers and directors usually tried to make it honest.

Tanya, the white waitress and the daughter of the marina owner in *The Rez*, thinks that by ignoring the Anishnabe cultural differences while enjoying dating or making friends with the young people on the Rez, she can make those differences go away. They don't. In the second season the writers began the promising storyline of her increasingly complicated relationship with Charlie, the chief's son, but then the series ended. Before it did, Frank drifts, Sadie tries to make the reserve a better place, Lucy is drawn to the city to make a singing career. Only Silas, as narrator/short story writer, builds bridges to the outside world. In *North of 60*, conflicts between white culture and Dene customs are a major recurring theme. Some are resolved, some are not. Sarah and Harris both form sexual relationships with Dene members of the Lynx River band. In both cases, babies are produced, enrolled as band members, and loved. Although Harris and Lois face some serious problems, after conflict and hurt on both sides, they make their way past their differences – not all of them cultural – to a good marriage. Sarah is looked after by and eventually has a relationship with Albert, the complex antagonist of the series. However, their personalities clash and the cultural differences between them are too great, making a long-term relationship impossible. Sarah also learns that her friendships with Michelle, Elsie, and Rosie have limits that are rooted in their different cultural perspectives. In *North of 60*, Harris, Sarah, and even Gerry create bridges between the cultures, yet they articulate their inside/outside status, even in the last episode of the series.

Related to the issue of culture clash is this question: Did the makers of these series concentrate on the idea of what was needed for the different cultures to coexist? Or did they assume that this goal had been achieved? In the series from the 1960s onward, the adult characters and the communities depicted take responsibility for their own lives and circumstances, although *The Rez*, unlike *Spirit Bay*, showed a community with more economic constraints, fewer traditions, and less-distinct cultural practices than the others. But the series also showed the conflicts that a First Nations person experiences within the dominant culture, on or off the reserve. *Spirit Bay* showed its young audience some of the roots of conflict: ancestral bones being confiscated, a parent opposing a contest that could take his daughter south, a museum eager to buy a medicine bundle with no questions asked. In each of these cases the conflict is resolved. In *The Rez* and *North of 60*, the adult characters are more likely to live with the contradictions.

The bridging elements for the young viewers of *Spirit Bay* included subjects such as fitting in with new friends, having fun, making your way in the wider world, valuing your heritage, respecting the wisdom of parents and elders. In *The Rez*, which was intended primarily for older youth, the shared elements included a mentally and physically challenged brother, a small community where everyone knows what is going on but where there are no jobs, and, repeatedly, the inevitable problems between girlfriends and boyfriends. *North of 60* also used the narrative strategy of familiar situations – job loss, courtship, adultery, family conflicts, community politics – as well as white characters – Harris, Gerry, Sarah, and Michelle's partners, Eric and Brian – to make the series more intelligible to a broad audience.

## LONG-FORM TELEVISION REVISITED

Series television is by definition uneven in quality. The number of shows in a season that must be produced, performed, and shot in a compressed space of time, then edited under pressure, is a significant factor in whether there will be adequate episodes, decent episodes, inevitably a few clinkers, and, in a quality series, some that stand out. Commitment to a television series on the part of the viewers means that they can discover a very culturally specific world, such as that of the South Slavey Dene in the Deh Cho, over a period of time. Yet most of these series, even those with children in mind, were made for the CBC's broad audience. They had to offer characters with whom that audience could identify and situations that found an echo in ordinary lives The long-form allows viewers to explore the similarities between life in Gibson's or Lynx River or on "the Rez" and life in other small Canadian towns and villages, while the unbridgeable differences between Dene, Coast Salish, or Anishnabe traditional ways and their contemporary ways of life in the outside world create real interest in diverse audiences. Because *North of 60* had ninety episodes, it has special value. Over six seasons the long narrative arcs could show significant changes in the characters as well as introduce serious issues. The series gave viewers complex subtext and presented the long-term effects of characters' decisions on the lives of everyone in Lynx River. Six seasons gave secondary characters like Rosie De'ela and Joe Gomba the chance to take focus in some episodes and become more rounded characters. Others, like Teevee Tenia and Bertha Kizha, had the opportunity to literally grow up both as actors and as characters. Antagonist Albert Golo also became a fully rounded, complex character. Band chief Peter Kenidi grew and changed, came and went and came again to Lynx River as his duties as an MLA allowed. By the end of season 2, Michelle Kenidi had become the undisputed protagonist of the series, showing unexpected depths, vulnerabilities, and strengths as she dealt with the death of her daughter, found a new love, and was tested by both friends and adversaries.

Long-form television gives the viewers the opportunity to take an in-depth look, over time, at a complete television world. If the producers stay involved, the writers will return to the series repeatedly, as will good directors. Continuity, a resonance back and forth between episodes, enriches the drama for those who watch over several seasons. But above all, the viewers connect to the characters, and thus to the actors who bring them to life. That these characters appear on the screen in the corner of the living room every week (or every day in some reruns) creates for many viewers a real interplay of identification; they will try to unsnarl or anticipate the plot twists and will constantly evaluate whether the plot or character development is credible. Measured over the years, long-form television is the television form that is most effective in opening up the masks to the faces within the masks.

Television movies of the week are a different breed. In the *North of 60* movies as well as the series, generic elements of soaps and cop shows, with occasional elements of psychological thrillers, police procedurals, and even (too rarely) slapstick and other more subtle forms of humour, have been inflected to serve the needs of the particular subject. The movies must be self-sufficient enough to make sense to new viewers, particularly in the many countries abroad where they were broadcast. However, they must also satisfy viewers who want to know what happened after the last episode, "Borrowed Time," was broadcast. The fans on the *North of 60* list tend to prefer the three movies set in Lynx River – *In the Blue Ground* (1999), *Dream Storm* (2001), and *Distant Drumming* (2005) – over *Trial by Fire* (2000), set for the most part in Yellowknife, and *Another Country* (2003), set in Calgary. They particularly look for the return of familiar characters. What they find in all of the movies is that lives continue and economic conditions improve. However, even though the format demands that the mysteries in each movie be solved, as in the preceding series, other problems remain unresolved.

I hope that the readers are now equipped to assess for themselves the conclusions suggested in earlier chapters: (*a*) that the same basic obstacles to understanding between the dominant and the aboriginal cultures and the same basic problems bedevilling remote aboriginal communities and aboriginals in cities have constantly reappeared over nearly fifty years; (*b*) that the CBC has made some balanced, occasionally proactive television series about some of the First Nations peoples, which helped viewers to better understand First Nations issues as well as the diversity of their responses; (*c*) that series drama, particularly *The Beachcombers* and *North of 60*, with their long story arcs, revisited problems, showed new perspectives on various themes, provided back stories for characters, and showed why and how characters like Nick, Sarah, and Harris – and by analogy the viewer outside – could change in their understanding over time; (*d*) that there are odd omissions (e.g., there have been very few dramas about Inuit across the years, which may be a function of distance/weather/costs); (*e*) equally important, that the 1950s and early 1960s representation of the generic Indian has given way to a more accurate reflection of a small part of the diversity of the First Nations in Canada.

## 2007 AND BEYOND ...

This book is about fifty years of mainstream broadcasting that, in the case of the CBC, was not primarily dependent on satellite or cable delivery to cover most of the country. After a ten-year hiatus on network television since *North of 60* stopped production, viewers need adult hour-long *television drama* about First Nations, as well as about the as yet largely invisible

Metis and Inuit peoples. There should be resources for such work, not only for regional or specialty channels but also (and especially) for prime-time series on the CBC, the network owned by the citizens of this country. There should also be opportunities for those who are "inside" to make drama for the CBC that looks out and tells the rest of us what they, as individuals and perhaps by analogy as peoples, see happening in our rapidly changing country, what they feel about their place in it, and, most of all, what the rest of us "outside" need to learn to see. When that time comes, one crucial part of the CBC's mandate will be fulfilled.

Few things in television are predictable. After thinking about television drama for many years and learning a little about how it is conceived, made, publicized, and received in the media, I know one thing – making television drama that people want to watch really is a "black art." There may be scholars who will approach from different perspectives the programs discussed in this study. Scholars from new generations will explore the technology and production process as it evolves. Some will discuss programming that will come from "inside," made entirely by First Nations people primarily for themselves but sometimes for the audience "outside." There may be makers of television drama from the outside who take up Jeanette Armstrong's challenge quoted at the end of chapter 1 (p. 32): "Imagine interpreting for us your own people's thinking towards us, instead of interpreting for us our thinking, our lives and our stories." Both scholars and other viewers may eventually enjoy television drama made by partnerships of writers, producers, and directors from both the inside and the outside that builds bridges between the two worlds. That is my hope.

# Notes

CHAPTER ONE

1 In an interview by Jason Silverman, "Uncommon Visions: The Films of Loretta Todd" (2002), 380. See also www.collectionscanada.ca/women/002026-717-e.html, accessed 26 August 2006.

2 She also talks about how she grew into the freedom to use her own personal voice instead of always speaking for her people, an issue for many First Nations and Metis artists.

3 Ernest J. Dick, who went on to become the CBC archivist, prepared the *Guide to CBC Sources at the Public Archives 1936–1986* (1987). This is an invaluable descriptive guide to the holdings of CBC programs up to 1986. No later guides appear to have been published.

4 *Turn Up the Contrast: CBC Television Drama since 1952* (hereafter Miller 1987). I completed my second book on the subject in 1996, *Rewind and Search: Makers and Decision Makers of Canadian Television Drama* (hereafter Miller 1996).

5 Female and middle-aged also describes the primary demographic of much of the CBC's drama specials and anthologies according to CBC audience research. That would not be true of *The Rez*, *The Beachcombers*, or *Spirit Bay*. *North of 60* seems to have attracted a mixed audience of all ages according to both the ASCRT and the AERTC at the Learned Societies Congress in Vancouver.

5 Female and middle-aged also describes the primary demographic of much of the CBC's drama specials and anthologies according to CBC audience research. That would not be true of *The Rez*, *The Beachcombers*, or *Spirit Bay*. *North of 60* seems to have attracted a mixed audience of all ages and both sexes, including viewers in "Indian Country."

6 Forty of the tapes and transcripts of the interviews are deposited at the Library and National Archives. They will all be accessible to anyone interested in 2010. The edited versions are in Miller 1996.

7 Canada lags far behind other nations in placing "fair use" for classrooms and scholarship into its copyright law, even for materials made for the publicly owned CBC or that use Telefilm (i.e., taxpayers') money. The cultural cost is high.

8 Such as the anthology *Cariboo Country* intended for adults in the 1960s, from which came *Festival's The Education of Phyllistine*, and *How to Break a Quarterhorse, Contrast*, chapter 3, 69–90.

9 Among them, on audiences, Miller, *Rewind and Search* (1996, 234–5, 255–63, 270–85, 297–301, 397–8, 468–9, 481–3). In the same volume, see also chapter 9 on "Policy" and chapter 10 on "Ethos"; for an overview of technologies on the cusp of major changes, see chapter 5, "Other Roles behind the Camera" and *passim*.

10 http://laws.justice.gc.ca/en/B-9.01/-39 ELIZABETH II, 1991 11 c Broad-casting Act reads:

(i) serve to safeguard, enrich and strengthen the cultural, political, social and economic fabric of Canada,

(ii) encourage the development of Canadian expression by providing a wide range of programming that reflects Canadian attitudes, opinions, ideas, values and artistic creativity, by displaying Canadian talent in entertainment programming and by offering information and analysis concerning Canada and other countries from a Canadian point of view,

(iii) through its programming and the employment opportunities arising out of its operations, serve the needs and interests, and reflect the circumstances and aspirations, of Canadian men, women and children, including equal rights, the linguistic duality and multicultural and multiracial nature of Canadian society and the special place of aboriginal peoples within that society, and

(iv) be readily adaptable to scientific and technological change.

11 Copied verbatim from a tape of the program, as is all the dialogue quoted in this book.

12 Jacquelyn Kilpatrick, *Celluloid Indians: Native Americans and Film* (1999), xv–xvii, 176–7.

13 Rennard Strickland's "Coyote Goes Hollywood," in *Native People's Magazine* (1997), begins with this anecdote about a John Ford epic: "The cameras stop. The Navajo actors dismount and take off their Sioux war bonnets. One of the film crew says to the Indians, 'That was wonderful. You did it just right.' An Indian actor replies, 'Yeah, we did it just like we saw it in the movies.'" www.nativepeoples.com/np_features/np_articles/1997_fall_article/coyote_hollywood_cont.html, no longer online.

14 www.aLibrary and Archives of Canada.on.ca/Documents/leonard%20george%20bio%202%20_2_.pdf, accessed 25 August 2006.

15 Chief Dan George co-starred in the film *Little Big Man* after a decade of playing Ol' Antoine on *Cariboo Country*. He is also remembered as David Joe in George Ryga's seminal play *The Ecstasy of Rita Joe* in 1967, and he appears in the print "Siwash Rock" by Roy Vickers (Vickers 1990).

16 See Goldie 1989 for chapters on sexuality and violence. See also Francis 1992 and interviews with playwrights in Lutz 1991. "Sucking Kumaras" by Gary Boire (1990) is a trenchant critique of Goldie's book.

17 Mojica 1991, 3. See also Schier, Sheard, and Wachtel, *Language in Her Eye* (1990).

18 See Acoose 1995.

19 See his overview in "Phantom Indians" (1992), 42–5.

20 www.lsoft.com/scripts/wl.exe?SL1=NATCHAT&H=LISTSERV.TAMU.EDU, accessed 27 August 2006. I belonged to the list for several years in the 1990s.

21 In the catalogue for *Land Spirit Power: First Nations at the National Art Gallery of Canada* (1992).

22 Later published in his collection *Funny You Don't Look Like One* (1996), 54–5.

23 Renée Legris, professor of literature at the Université du Québec à Montréal, in private conversation. For another discussion of this complex question of a people and a nation, see also Allor, Juteau, and Shepherd 2000. The political and general obfuscation around the word nation became clear in November 2006 when a huge all-party majority that included the separatist Bloc Québécois in the House of Commons passed a motion affirming that "Quebecois are a nation within a united Canada."

24 http://www.qesn.meq.gouv.qc.ca/mpages/toc.htm, accessed 14 November 2005, a supplement to the history of Quebec taught in Quebec schools prepared by the Quebec Board of Black Educators and other partners.

25 Valaskakis co-curated the 2000 exhibition *Indian Princesses and Cowgirls: Stereotypes from the Frontier*. Her nation is identified in a report in *Windspeaker*, November 1999. She has also had a distinguished academic career at Concordia and the Université à Montréal and received a National Aboriginal Achievement Award in 2002.

26 She begins with this "borrowed story" and the useful reminder that many stories in First Nations' cultures belong to a specific person or group and are told for particular purposes to a specific audience. A blind wolf is given two eyes, one by a mouse and one by a buffalo so that "the wolf can see the full range of the world in which he lives. And so the wolf continues on his journey, now able to see with both his mouse eye and his buffalo eye, sight which reveals the simultaneity of past and present, individual and collective, Indian and non-Indian" (287). This issue concentrates on First Nations' problems and achievements in mass communications.

27 In Todd 1990, 24–33. See also Lenore Keeshig-Tobias, "Stop Stealing Native Stories," *Globe and Mail*, 26 January 1990; and Jeanette Armstrong, *Looking at the Words of Our People* (1993).

28 See also Dionne Brand's "Whose Gaze and Who Speaks for Whom" (1998), 109–39. Like bell hooks (see chapter 2), she challenges the images and expectations that surround her as a writer and activist, as a woman, a lesbian, and an African Canadian.

29 Needless to say her story ends differently from the white man's stories about the white man and the "'the Native Indian' (God how I hate that word 'Indian') ... [Y]ou could call him a trickster, you know. He's like that, clever. But he's not smart." In her ending, the white man is caught in a hole he can never get out of – his women see to that – and all of the children are taught "the real history, before 1492 and since. Those stories will guide them for the next 500 years. Tell them to do as the Trickster (I mean white man) has done" (McMaster and Martin 1992, 108).

30 "Cultural Appropriation and Aboriginal Literature," in the classroom edition of *Windspeaker*, www.ammsa.com/classroom/CLASS3appropriation.html, visited 25 May 2007. There is no date on this document or on the home page, which has not been updated since 2001, but internal evidence suggests it is August 2001 classroom edition posted online.

31 See also John Bentley Mays's review of the exhibition when it came to the Royal Ontario Museum, "Face to Face with Racism," *Globe and Mail*, 19 December 1992.

32 In his preface to *Contemporary Challenges* (1991), Lutz writes a sensitive and very clearly thought-out outline of the dilemma of a non-native scholar analysing materials written by native writers. In *Aboriginal Voices*, May/June 1999, Beth Brant (Mohawk) writes: "There is no doubt that we see the universe through a different set of values and beliefs. It is impossible for non-Natives to feel the sorts of emotions that are called upon when Indigenous peoples speak about their ancestors, about earth, about the symbiosis that exists between human and animal" (54).

33 Brian D. Johnson, "Tribal Tribulations," *Maclean's*, 19 February 1990, 53.

34 Richard Ouzounian, *Toronto Star*, 5 October 2006.

35 Sid Adilman, "Writer Urges CBC to Let Natives Tell Their Own Stories," *Toronto Star*, 20 November 1993. See also www.cbc.radio-canada.ca/annualreports/1996-1997/pdf/E2prgrm2.pdf, accessed 27 August 2006.

36 See interview with Sydney Newman in Miller 1996, 16–17, 49–50. Thanks to the CBC, Canada's radio culture has been distinctive since the 1940s and remains so.

37 Miller 1987, 189–354, and McRoberts 1995, 182–201.

38 See Doxtator 1992, *passim.*

39 www.beavers.westlancashirescouts.org.uk/Program%20Ideas/indians.htm, and http://cheesecakeandfriends.com/Troop1440/songs/Indians.htm, still online 4 January 2007. The home page has the words to the song on the first page under the general title "Indians."

40 See the interview with John Kennedy, head of TV drama in the 1980s, in chapter 11 of Miller 1987.

41 Miller 1987, 100.

42 Ibid., 68–90.

43 "Langscape" is McGregor's term (43). She goes on to argue that what distinguishes the Indian is "Acceptance" – a one-word sentence that she elaborates by arguing that such a stance is what "we must, imitating him, learn to adopt." She concludes that Canadian literature's treatment of Indians is different from American literature's (220–3).

44 The anthology *Cariboo Country,* George Ryga's "Indian" on *Q for Quest,* and the prize-winning "Death of a Nobody" in the 1960s; *Dreamspeaker, A Thousand Moons,* and *Homecoming* in the early to mid-1970s.

45 The group refers to Gayatri Chakravorty Spivak, "Subaltern Studies: Deconstruction Historiography," in *Selected Subaltern Studies,* ed. Ranajit Guah and Spivak (New York, 1988), 3–32.

46 www.ayn.ca/ViewNews.aspx?id=348, accessed 25 May 2007, has a list of thirteen such programs that were showcased on APTN in January 2005.

47 Shelley Niro's satire *Honey Moccasin,* made in 1994 for the Smithsonian, is a take on various television genres as if played by and broadcast by native TV. Drew Hayden Taylor's *Redskins, Tricksters and Puppy Stew* is a National Film Board (NFB) production; there is no equivalent agency in the United States. Other examples are Sherman Alexie's script for Chris Eyre's film *Smoke Signals;* Eyre's next film *Skins;* Alexie's *The Business of Fancy Dancing;* and Gloria Cranmer Webster's *A Strict Law Bids Us Dance.*

48 From a visit to Alert Bay on a school day, I saw that some white children in Alert Bay choose to attend the school and that boys as well as girls make button blankets. No tradition is completely static.

49 Reported in Wheeler 1991, 11. Wheeler went on to be story editor on *North of 60* and to write scripts for both *North of 60* and *The Rez.*

50 Ibid., 10.

51 His paper, "One Thing about Television and 10 Things about Canadian TV," is quoted with permission.

52 See also Doyle's *A Great Feast of Light: Growing Up Irish in the Television Age,* (2005) which argues that television opened up Irish life to the modern world in the 50s and 60s in a way no other medium could.

53 According to the Friars' *The Only Good Indian … The Hollywood Gospel* (1972),
May (1842–1912) finally came to North America when he was sixty-six. They
also point out that none of his works had been translated into English to that
date (10). Perhaps this was because the dime novels as well as the more
respectable novels of James Oliver Curwood and dozens of others had already
filled that gap. The Friars' lively book casts a wide net over such forms of
popular culture as the Wild West Show and has plenty of illustrations.

54 Cf. *Globe and Mail*, 3 May 2001: "'About 95 percent of the German market is
looking for an aboriginal experience,' said Debbie Parent, executive director of
the Yukon First Nations Tourism Association, 'but their ideas of First Nations
and what they actually see is quite different. They are expecting to be greeted
by someone in a headdress and on horseback.'" Alberta's government seemed
to agree. An article by Jessica Leeder in the *National Post*, 6 June 2002, begins,
"Critics of an Alberta government proposal asking native bands to build
aboriginal theme parks for tourists wanting to camp out in teepees, eat moose
meat and watch staged Indian pow-wow say the parks run the risk of
becoming a circus filled with stereotypes." The spokesman for the minister of
aboriginal affairs and northern development had promised jobs and a
showcase for culture and had suggested that there could be "[h]oney moon
packages, private teepees, opportunities to sleep under the northern lights or a
chance to visit any aboriginal community in the province." Walter Janvier,
chief of Chipewyan Prairies First Nation outside Fort McMurray, replied that
First Nations in Alberta have their own plans for increasing tourism, which
they intend to implement without trivializing native culture. "'We're not
going to put on a headdress, do a dance,'" he said.

55 See also chapter 10. In *If Only I Were an Indian*, a 1995 co-production with the
NFB with funding from Vision and TVO, there is a complex interaction of issues regarding cultural appropriation. A Canadian anthropologist who
speaks the Czech language takes as a subject for research a devoted group of
young Czechoslovakians (as they were then), who were influenced by Karl
May and Ernest Seton and who have tried to recreate for themselves, at least
for a little while in the summer, the life of the Plains First Nations, using as
much research as they can find. The complexities arise from the perspectives
of three middle-aged Cree guests. One in particular finds it very strange indeed to find tipis, a couple of ponies, most people in loincloths or buckskin
dresses and skirts, paint and jewellery, sitting in a circle offering pipe smoke
to the Creator. But by the end of the film the elders are impressed with the
Czechs' dedication and knowledge. They turn out not to be wannabes but
serious people. An elder comments that they cannot get the beat right for
dancing, so he has a huge problem dancing with them – he says that drum

beating and dancing are hard to learn from books. Ironically, he concludes that it would be good to send young Cree to the encampment to recover some lost skills and to see the dedication of people who are willing to live as the Plains peoples did 150 years ago.

56 See Boyce Richardson's *People of Terra Nullius: Betrayal and Rebirth in Aboriginal Canada* (1993).

57 See Gary Granzberg and Jack Steinbring, eds., *Television and the Canadian Indian: Impact and Meaning among Algonkians of Central Canada* (1980), a monograph on how two communities perceived television and its genres and how they used it in the late 1970s. Also very helpful are "Southern Exposure: Portrayals of the North," the first chapter of Valerie Alia's *Un/Covering the North: News, Media and Aboriginal People* (1999), 13–35; and Lorna Roth's *Something New in the Air* (2005), 223–7.

58 See the chapters "Directing" and "Producing" in Miller 1996.

## CHAPTER 2

1 www.quotegarden.com/columbus-day.html, accessed 25 May 2007.

2 See Karim 1993. http://info.wlu.ca/~wwwpress/jrls/cjc/BackIssues/18.2/karim.html, accessed 15 November 2005, no longer online.

3 See also Kathleen M. Sands, "Narrative Resistance: Native American Collaborative Autobiography," *Studies in American Indian Literatures Series* (1998). http://oncampus.richmond.edu/faculty/ASAIL/SAIL2/101.html, accessed 15 May 2007.

4 http://arcticcircle.uconn.edu/Museum/Anthropology/NorthernReview/cruikshank.html, accessed 25 May 2007.

5 See also the introduction to Mark Janovich and James Lyons, eds, *Quality Popular Television: Cult TV, the Industry and Fans* (2003), which critiques British quality TV for being directed at "white, affluent, urban, middle-classes" (3).

6 Johnston is a 2004 National Aboriginal Achievement Awards winner. See also his own retellings of the stories in *The Manitous: The Supernatural World of the Ojibway* (1995) and Rob McKinley's article "Aboriginal Language – When It's Gone That's It. No More Indians," with interviews of several elders, including Basil Johnston, *Windspeaker,* no date given, at www.ammsa.com/classroom/CLASS4language.html, accessed 25 May 2007.

7 Tom Barrett, *Vancouver Sun,* 29 March 1993.

8 See also Clifford's pictorial representation of the art-culture system, subtitled "A Machine for Making Authenticity" (Clifford 1988, 224), and his example of the "beaded 'fancies'" (hanging birds, mirror frames) made by Matilda Hill, a Tuscarora, in a traditional form of trade that is said to go back to 1812. Matilda

Hill is not simply making "tourist curios," but rather what she and her family have made for 190 years (249) – which raises apposite feminist questions about "art" defined as what men make and "crafts and curios" defined as what women make.

9 See actor and playwright Floyd Favel's (1993, 8–11) very personal take on performing in English when his mother tongue is one of the First Nations languages.

10 Judith Butler, *Bodies That Matter: On the Discursive Limits of Sex* (New York: Routledge, 1993).

11 Who can leave before a series is hopelessly compromised is specific to each show. In *North of 60* the original creator and writers left and directors have come and gone. But various combinations of producers who worked on the early seasons, a stable of returning writers, and Tina Keeper as Michelle Kenidi have anchored the series through six seasons and five movies.

12 In an interview on 30 August 2004.

13 In *White Women, Race Matters: The Social Construction of Whiteness* (Minneapolis: University of Minnesota Press, 1993).

14 Page 7 of the executive summary: //www.cab-acr.ca/english/ culturaldiversity/report.shtm, accessed 14 November 2005, no longer online. The executive summary is written by Richard Cavanaugh, former vice-president of CAB and project manager of the team that prepared the report. It includes a complete bibliography, fifteen case studies of best practices in non-broadcasting corporations and multinationals, as well as ABC, NBC, BBC, and Channel 4 et al., interviews, and focus groups.

15 www12.statcan.ca/english/census01/Products/Analytic/companion/abor/ groups1.cfm.

16 In Murray et al. 2000.

17 The cover of this journal features three stylized Plains Indians robed in bright red in front of a tipi – perhaps not what Legris or I would have chosen for an issue of a journal in which we both wrote on problematic representations of the First Nations.

18 "What Makes an Aboriginal an Aboriginal?" *Windspeaker*, January, 2003.

19 Note that only Indians who look "right" play Indians in Paris Disneyworld's Wild West shows, which present warriors attacking stage coaches and a stampeding buffalo or two – from off-air notes made on a documentary produced by Sarah Richards, CBC radio's *The Current*, 25 April 2004.

20 King also points out that native writers tend to avoid setting their work in the nineteenth century and that they are influenced by contemporary oral history and storytelling, by a strong sense of community (signified in his choice of title for the anthology), and that some writers take the decision to incorporate

traditional figures and details of specific cultures. Penny Petrone (1990), in *Native Literature in Canada: From the Oral Tradition to the Present,* points out that for many indigenous cultures, eloquence and the power of oratory were highly valued. This survey of native literature identifies up-and-comers like Daniel David Moses, Drew Hayden Taylor, Thomas King, and Jordan Wheeler, all of whom wrote episodes or provided story treatments for at least one of the series discussed in this book. According to Petrone, Drew Hayden Taylor wrote scripts for *The Beachcombers* and *Street Legal,* as well as (later) one for *North of 60* (179). See also Michelle Pagni Stewart, "Can This Be Cinderella If There Is No glass Slipper? Native American 'Fairy Tales," at http://oncampus.richmond.edu/faculty/ASAIL/SAIL2/121.html, accessed 14 November 2005.

21 For another perspective, see also the conclusions drawn in Joan Ryan, *Doing Things the Right Way: Dene Traditional Justice at Lac La Martre, NWT* (1995). The relationship between First Nations traditional justice and the laws of Canada has been a complex one for generations.

22 Quoted in David Hogarth, "Public Service Broadcasting as a Modern Project: A Case Study of Early Public-Affairs Television in Canada," *Canadian Journal of Communication* 26, no. 3 (2001), at www.cjc-online.ca/viewarticle.php? id=656&layout=html, accessed 25 May 2007.

23 The chapter in *Woman's Ways of Knowing* titled "Family Life and the Politics of Talk" remains particularly apposite to *North of 60* and *The Rez.* Gilligan won the Distinguished Publication Award of the Association of Women in Psychology in 1987.

24 See chapter 8 of that volume, "Identity in Feminist Television Criticism," 114–25.

25 See also www.indigenouspeople.net/stories1.htm, accessed 25 May 2007. Even in the "Nation's Capital," or perhaps especially there, the texts on display also record a problem of nomenclature. In a display that stresses the diversity of aboriginal people from "reserves, and … hamlets, towns and cities across Canada," the text states that "[i]t has been hard to find an acceptable common name because we are, in fact, hundreds of distinct peoples. Each of these people has its own name, language, ancestral lands and culture."

26 Jesse J. Cornplanter (Seneca), in his *Legends of the Longhouse Told to Sah-Nee-Wah, the White Sister* (1998), often comments on the fact that his version of a story differs from versions told by others.

27 The book includes East Coast fishing peoples, the longhouse cultures of the eastern woodland, the sweat lodge cultures of the Canadian Shield, the sun dance cultures of the Prairies, the potlatch cultures of the Pacific Coast, the hand-drum cultures of the western sub-Arctic, the Inuit of the Arctic, and

the connections of all of these to "the individual, the family, the clan, the nation" (xix–xx).

28 See Jefferson Faye (Polar Inuit), "Ethical Publication of Inuit Stories" (2001), 159–70.

29 See the controversies about the authenticity of Robert Bringhurst's *A Story Sharp as a Knife: The Classical Mythtellers and Their World* (1999), in which he translates into English stories of the Haida but also contextualizes them in relation to the relationships between the anthropologist and the speakers. See also Freda Ahenakew and H.C. Wolfart's (eds and trans.) less controversial "intimate conversations" in *Kohkiminawak Otacimowiniwawa: Our Grandmother's Lives as Told in Their Own Words* (1992) – eighteen stories from the North that are about being caught between two worlds but are full of laughter, recorded originally in Woods Cree and Plains Cree (28), presented in Cree syllabics and transliterations as well as in English; Harry Robinson (Okanagan), *Nature Power: In the Spirit of an Okanagan Storyteller* (1992); and Darwin Hanna and Mamie Henry, eds, *Our Tellings: Interior Salish Stories of the Nlha7kapmx People* (1996), "based on [the transcribers] personal relationships with both the elders and their families" (186). On the other hand, the traditional stories and songs in Alan R. Velie, ed., *American Indian Literature,* rev. ed. (1991), are translations by white anthropologists, followed by poems, stories, and extracts from novels by Indians selected according to "literary quality" and "judged as serious literature" (9).

30 "The Legitimation of Beliefs in a Hunter-Gatherer Society: Bear Lake Athapaskan Knowledge and Authority," *American Ethnologist,* 1992: 483–500; and "Political Resistance in a Contemporary Hunter-Gatherer Society: More about Bear Lake Athapaskan Knowledge and Authority," *American Ethnologist,*1994: 335–52.

31 See his chapter "The Emerging Native View of History and Culture" (77–88).

32 This point of view was prefigured in the last scene of Salutin's extraordinarily successful play *Les Canadiens* (1977), where, after the Parti Québécois victory, members of the team face the transition from being political icons to just being a hockey team that people still care about. Salutin is the token left-wing columnist for the *Globe and Mail,* and he was a member of the *This Magazine Is about Schools* editorial collective (1973–94) and is still a contributing editor. In recent years the cover of *This* has carried the subtitle "Because Everything Is Political."

CHAPTER THREE

1 Rob Shields, "True North: Inuit Art and the Canadian Imagination," in *Places on the Margin* (London: Routledge, 2001). In Hulan 2002, Leanne Stuart

Pupchek points out that "Inuit imagery has become a synecdoche, symbolic part for the whole, of Canadian identity" (191). As well as embodying survival, "[t]he perceived purity, essentialness and innocence that gold-seekers found in the Inuit work issued from the little they knew about the people of the North" (198–9).

2 For a largely accurate account of that memorable time, see Erno Rossi's *White Death: Blizzard of '77* (St Catharines: Seventy-Seven Publishing, 1978).

3 Yet this collection of plays originating from northern communities is far more bleak than *North of 60*. The writers confront suicide and despair, the neglect of elders, and the loss of culture very directly, sometimes with humour, more often with anguish. Their teaching/sharing function is sometimes obvious.

4 In her chapter "Bridges-over-the-Air: Aboriginal Television as Cross-Cultural Bridge," Roth also documents the tensions felt by one of APTN's predecessors, NNBY (Northern Native Broadcasting, Yukon), in the attempt to present the cultures of the territory without compromise and make programs that would interest a broader audience. *Neda'a,* a general magazine program about the North, was presented on CBC Newsworld. In her chapter "APTN," Roth discusses both the "cutting-edge cultural information" found on *Contact,* the APTN review of the news in "Indian Country" and the North, and the fact that discussion on the phone-in part of the show can be taken over by someone who wants to chat for a long time, in this case about "two-spirited people."

5 John C. Mohawk (1994), professor of native studies, State University of New York at Buffalo, sounds a cautionary word in his short piece "Impact of Television on Native Communities," *Runner.* As he says, at first anyone new to television watches everything, then they settle on action-adventure series, drama, and soap operas, watching "less and less educational television" (44). Certainly in Lynx River, the television at Rosie's or Elsie's is usually tuned to soaps or cop shows. Mohawk says, "Statistically, Native viewers tend to watch soap operas and not the drum dances – television is an ever present intruder, teacher, hypnotist, game player, and at times trickster, who never goes to sleep." Also in Mohawk 1994, see the article by Alan Lawrence (senior producer at Wawatay and a contributor to TVNC Sioux Lookout, Ontario), "Electronic Drum: A Day in the Life of Northern Native Television Station," 17–19; and the article by Gil Cardinal, "Producer's Dilemma: Producing *Our Home and Native Land*," 24–5. Cardinal, one of the directors on *North of 60*, discusses two versions of his film *Our Home and Native Land,* the original at eighty-six minutes and the one cut for Global to forty-eight to fit the commercial breaks permitted in an hour-long format. "Explore North" provides a useful short summary of broadcasting in the North at a general site called www.explorenorth.com/library/weekly/more/bl-milestones.htm, accessed 26 October 2007.

6 www.easterndoor.com/VOL.8/8-33.htm, visited in 2002, no longer online.

7 See also Fil Fraser who in 1994 had done a survey of the literature and also some of the programs broadcast during the early years of *North of 60* for *The Canadian Journal of Communications* "The participation of Aboriginal and Other Cultural Minorities in Cultural Development." He points out that "the audiences of First Nations peoples, like other ethnocultural communities transcend borders ... Canadians have both national and cultural citizenship," 480.

8 For more localized strategies, see Charles Fairfield, "Below the Hamelin Line: CKRZ and Aboriginal Cultural Survival" (1998), a look at a Six Nations and New Credit community radio station that struggles to maintain professional standards without sacrificing its cultural identity, reinforcement of local languages (a divisive issue), cultural traditions, and the flow of communication between various affiliations (163).

9 According to Paul Barnsley, *Windspeaker*, August 2005.

10 www.crtc.gc.ca/eng/publications/reports/drama/drama2.htm, accessed 28 May 2007.

CHAPTER FOUR

1 An overview of similar activities can be found in Hayes 1999 (131–46), where it is made clear that pageants and other dramatic entertainments were used to retune the story of the German settlers in Kitchener (once Berlin) to accommodate the anti-German sentiments during and after the world wars. The tradition ended in 1952, when "Waterloo County's founding myth was confirmed" (146) in a "dramatic outdoor spectacle" attended by six hundred people.

2 These words appear on a brass plaque on a cairn in Durham as well as in E.L. Marsh, *A History of the County of Grey* (1931), 181. In the latter, contemporary readers will find, perhaps to their surprise, five chapters on pre-contact and colonial history that acknowledge that the treaties were unfair and that the explorers and settlers were dependent on the Huron, then the Ojibway and Pottawotamies, for their safety and survival.

3 The two Gracchi were metonyms for probity and reform in Ancient Rome.

4 Huge burial mounds, possibly representing serpents and other figures, had been discovered at Rice Lake and Rainy River. www.adamsheritage.com/pre/ preont1.htm, accessed 3 October 2005, has information on influences on local First Nations by the sophisticated Adena/Hopewell culture, which built the huge mounds and places of worship in Ohio and points south. www.shakerwssg.org/ fort_ancient_hopewell_native_ame.htm, visited May 2002, no longer posted.

5 Is this so very different from the rather homemade-looking floats in the parade down the Mall in London for the Queen's Jubilee on 4 June 2002?

A million flag-waving people sang "Land of Hope and Glory" to end that spectacle as well.

6  Some of them were very odd; for example, the young girls who danced as Indian mound builders carried potato mashers, wore green cheesecloth dresses, and had balloons attached to their wrists. A bagpiper, a fiddler, a bugler, the Durham band, and a small orchestra of three accompanied the performance.

7  *The Only Good Indian ... The Hollywood Gospel,* by R.E. Friar and N.A. Friar (1972), has a short section on American pageants and plays (31–6). The authors even trace the origins of "How!" and "Ugh!" to an 1878 novel (47).

8  1 April 2000, at Brock University's first Aboriginal Media Day.

9  *The Fifth Book of Reading Lessons* was "entered" in 1867 by "Reverend Egerton Ryerson, LL.D., Chief Superintendent of Education for Ontario, in the Office of the Registrar of the Province of Canada." The book discusses science, geography, history, industry, and all kinds of other things thought useful at the time.

10  Connor enjoyed a good reputation for many years because of his blend of appealing characters, his use of history and romance, and his moral reflections on the action. Here is a sample of the dialogue: "'Well, you see, Little Thunder is one of the Blood Tribe and rather swift with his knife at times, I confess. Besides, his family has suffered at the hands of the whiskey runners. He is a chief ... You may imagine he is somewhat touchy on the point of whiskey traders'" (335–6). Connor is still remembered by tourists and local people in Glengarry Township in eastern Ontario. James Oliver Curwood, an American who spent time in the north of Canada, was another early twentieth-century writer whose novels, such as *The Black Hunter* (1926) about a man who joins the Iroquois enemies of the French, seemed very romantic to a teenager in the 1950s. A list of movies made from his novels can be found at www.shianet. org/community/tour/joc.html#books, accessed October 2005.

11  This reprint, accompanied by line drawings, was clearly sparked by the centennial celebrations – see the unsigned foreword. It covers stories from Bruce and Grey Counties. Indians appear in many places, not just in the chapters "The Indian Camp" and "The Pow Wow," in which many Indians as well as settlers are named. The "Pow Wow" chapter is a very odd mixture of detailed observations of a dignified ceremony, racist language, and stereotypes of the worst kind.

12  The site that provided this information was last revised in 1999, http://pw1. netcom.com/~drmike99/BobbRevis.html, and was still posted on 28 May 2007. According to this site, the book is the thirteenth in the series. It was completely rewritten and reissued in 1966, well after *Radisson* was aired.

13　See also *Little Indians* by Mabel Guinnip LaRue (1930, the fifth reprint 1932), in which "baby Indian," "one winter and four moons old," is fed wild rice and meat soup, plays with a wolf skin, and becomes the young boy Red Bird. The book is an odd mixture of fact and fiction. It is an effort to teach children something about Indians, but these are Indians who have both Plains war bonnets and Woodland canoes, as well as raccoons and bear cubs as pets. It does not reinforce some of the more egregious stereotypes, but as a reader for younger children (grade 2 or 3?), it certainly oversimplifies. It was, perhaps, better than some.

14　For some reason Longfellow is never named. He is simply "the poet" in the retelling, yet many of his lines are used. His 1855 *The Song of Hiawatha* was familiar to generations of readers.

15　Copyright 1939, just before World War II, but not published until 1943. Readers like these were also given as regular gifts to children during the war, when books were in short supply.

16　In 1994, the summer after her death at age eighty-two, Jean Harding, a dancer in the 1927 pageant, was honoured by a "Washing of Tears" ceremony at Wikwemekong Unceded Indian Reservation, held for the Ontario Historical Society. In her teaching and in her retirement, she had lived to see and helped to bring about many changes.

17　No place of publication is given. From the introduction (dated 1940) and a list of contributors at the back, headed by the lieutenant governor of British Columbia, I infer that "the Committee formed to promote the Revival and Development of their latent gifts among the Native Tribes of British Columbia" published the story. In 2003 the Vancouver Art Gallery included art from the Inkameep Day School in an exhibition: www.goodminds.com, *Nk'Mip Chronicles: Art from the Inkameep Day School.*

18　Although the language belongs to the 1940s, the tradition of specific local gifts comes from the cycle plays of the Middle Ages (see *The Second Shepherd's Play*, a favourite of dramatic literature anthologies) and is found again in the English translation of Brebeuf's "Huron Carol."

19　The award was established 1947. A medal is presented annually to the author of the best children's book published in Canada. The author must be a citizen or resident of Canada. www.ucalgary.ca/~dkbrown/cla.html, accessed 28 May 2007.

20　www.nlc-bnc.ca/3/6/t6-703-e.html#top, accessed 28 May 2007.

21　This is the revised edition by E.L. Marsh (1927).

22　"In early 1886, books of passes were issued to Indian agents, and subsequently First Nations people could not leave their reserve unless they had a pass signed by the Indian agent and describing when they could leave, where they could go, and when they had to return. The pass system, however, was never passed into legislation and as a result was never legal – although it was enforced well into the 1940s" (Canadian Plains Research Center, *The Encyclopedia of Saskatchewan* [Regina: University of Regina, 2006] http://esask.uregina.ca/entry/indian_policy_and_the_early_reserve_period.html). The encyclopedia appears to have been published only online.

23  Authorized by the minister of education for the public schools of Ontario (1928, reprinted eleven times up to 1938). This text would probably have been used through the war but was perhaps replaced after 1945.

24  See also a book – bought at a private school garage sale in 2003 – that is organized in units for teachers. It had been in the school's library and features an Indian stalking buffalo with a bow and arrow. The short chapter "Life in America before the White Man Came" has a heading "Why Had the Indians Not Become Civilized?" (4), under which we find mention of Mexico's great cities, astronomy, etc. However, the chapter concludes: "Yet their worship proves they were not truly civilized for their priests sacrificed thousands of human beings a year and ate their flesh" (5). A little later one of the characters asks the young student, "[W]hat would we have done if foreigners had tried to drive us from the land of our fathers?" (7) and goes on to list all the contributions in food and technology provided by the "early North Americans" (8) – a remarkably mixed set of messages to teach children.

25  Hogan was then an associate professor of English at the University of Guelph. His text is a paperback, full of black and white close-ups of the poets and songwriters cited, as well as of rainy city streets and "teach-ins." Joni Mitchell and Gordon Lightfoot can be seen among the psychedelic orange and pink images on the front cover.

## CHAPTER FIVE

1  *The Queen's University Directory of Television Series 1952–1982* (hereafter *Queen's*), a descriptive catalogue by Blaine Allen and his researchers, is an invaluable online research tool. Hosted by Queen's University Film Department, it is located at www.film.queensu.ca/CBC/R.html. I quote here and elsewhere with permission.

2  www.geocities.com/TelevisionCity/Stage/2950/index.html, accessed 30 October 2007. The webmaster, Des Martin, who lives in the United Kingdom, asks for comments. In a private email to me, 10 May 2005, he cautions that the Radisson site is still in a very unsatisfactory state, with episodes potentially in the wrong order and some synopses missing. He also tells me that he remembers the series being shown circa 1959–60 and that the station, not realizing that it was a serial, "aired the episodes in random order."

3 See also Jennifer S.H. Brown and C. Roderick Wilson, "The Northern Algonquians: A Regional Overview" (2003), which provides a map that shows that the peoples in the south and the near north are Algonquin, Huron, Iroquois, Odawa, and Ojibway, and to the farther north, Cree.

4 My copy is unbound. I have it thanks to Professor Ted Jojola (Pueblo), who rescued many unbound copies.

5 Alex McNeil, *Total Television* (1980), n.p. (grid for 1956–57).

6 Boyce Hart and Alan Keeling of the West Midlands provided some information, and John King did synopses of episodes 1–14; all three are together an excellent example of the informal web of contacts who supply information to many fan sites – see also chapter 10. After sharing information with Des Martin, he has given me a credit on the site as well: www. angelfire.com/retro/cta/Can/RadissonTomahawk.htm, accessed 28 May 2007. I have Martin's permission to use the information he has posted. Where I could cross-check, I found it to be remarkably accurate. I have not checked the American sources. The site has been very useful for research on chapters 5 and 6.

7 An example of his writing is his one paragraph on *The Beachcombers*, which lists the main characters. Unfortunately, Jesse Jim, Nick's Coast Salish partner, becomes Jessie. He quotes two sources on the origin of Robert Clothier's character, Relic (the antagonist of the series), but does not discuss the character of Nick Adonidas, the protagonist. The plots are summed up in one sentence: "As in many families, there are quarrels, usually centred on Relic" (121). Rainsberry left the CBC in 1966. Older readers may affectionately remember his decision to find a home on the CBC for *Uncle Chichimus* and *The Friendly Giant*. His first chapter outlines the policy, the inadequate funding, and the work of the people in charge of children's television from the 1950s to the mid-1980s. His account also includes information about children's programming that Radio-Canada produced. Although not error free, it is a valuable source of information from a decision maker on children's programming.

8 From the *Queen's* entry on the Plouffes: "Lemelin's Plouffe family first appeared on English language television almost a year after their premiere on French stations, and the broadcasts marked a rare example of accord between French and English language services and recognition of Quebec culture in English Canada. Lemelin wrote a French and, with the aid of Bill Stewart from the Montreal office of the Canadian Press, an English version of the script each week, and the cast and crew prepared for two live broadcasts, a French reading on Wednesday nights and an English performance on Fridays (Thursdays for the first eight weeks)." See www.film.queensu.ca/CBC/Per.html, accessed 30 October 2007.

9  TV Westerns broadcast in 1957 included *Have Gun Will Travel* at 9:30 and *Gunsmoke* at 10:00 on Saturday night – adult prime time and in the 1950s a night when most of the potential audience watched television. Not all of the Westerns then or later were great successes, but *Gunsmoke* and the more family-oriented *Bonanza* both ran into the early 1970s (McNeil 1980).

10  Ibid. See his entry on Walt Disney – the book is alphabetically organized.

11  www.geocities.com/toppsgreen/04Cap.html, accessed 28 May 2007.

12  Again starring Fess Parker, but this time with a native character as his sidekick (although played by the very successful actor and singer Ed Ames), "Mingo, a college-educated Cherokee." See McNeil's (1980) entry on Daniel Boone. Two years after Fess Parker's *Daniel Boone* ended (26 March 1972), the more upmarket audience of PBS saw an eight-part series based on Fennimore Cooper's *The Last of the Mohicans* (www.pbs.org/wgbh/masterpiece/archive/10/10.html, accessed 1 November 2007, now available on DVD). But this series was made by the BBC (www.shoppbs.org/sm-pbs-masterpiece-theatre-the-last-of-the-mohicans-2pk-dvd--pi-2647099.html, accessed 1 November 2007), although the BBC site says both that the BBC made it and that its country of origin is the United States. Most other sites on Google say that *The Last of the Mohicans* was made by the BBC, including this one: www.scotlandthemovie.com/movies/fmohicans.html, accessed 1 November 2007, which points out that the series was filmed in Scotland. A PBS-BBC co-production would have been filmed in the United States. Not in Halliwell 1982.

13  Barbara Moon, *Maclean's*, 19 January 1957.

14  "[A]n English woman raised in Paris" according to the *Star Weekly* (Toronto), 20 October 1956. She does not appear in Rainsberry's book, but the *Star*'s weekend magazine and Moon in *Maclean's* above give her full credit for the idea.

15  Contrast the importance given Radisson as an early explorer with his absence in *Pirates and Pathfinders* (1954), the grade 5 history textbook by M. Hamilton used in the 1950s in Ontario, with eight reprints into 1962 and perhaps beyond. This textbook, which looks at exploration around the world, does not mention Radisson at all. North American Indians, who, of course, guided the explorers, are mentioned twice.

16  See Miller 2000, 51–74.

17  www.imdb.com/name/nm0524058/, accessed 11 January 2007. Lucarotti was clearly an imaginative writer. Since the scripts have disappeared, I cannot comment directly, but I note that few people mention the dialogue.

18  Gauvreau, a painter, was one of those who signed the *Refus Global*, the famous manifesto by intellectuals and artists in Quebec in 1948. He continued to paint but joined the youth section of the SRC and later did teleromans, including *D'Iberville*, according to the *Archivist /L'archiviste*, no. 118 (1999): 48.

19 *Montreal Gazette,* 25 August 1956.

20 Rutherford 1990, 375–6. Rutherford provides very useful details about the programming across the spectrum at that time.

21 Without those 8 mm kinescopes, terrible though their quality was, much of the early heritage of Canadian television would be lost. In fact, some of "kines" arrived at the National Archives/CBC collection from Flin Flon, where an unknown person had the sense not to throw them out (the fate of many early kines shipped around the country) but had put them away in a broom closet or some other out-of-the-way space. There was no cross-country transmission then, so kines were sent overland. I know this because I worked with the cans of film and saw the labels. I also found a stack of kines used as a doorstop in Vancouver in the mid-1980s. In 1979, when I saw some of the original kines, they were stored in a warehouse in Etobicoke. The Library and Archives of Canada now holds whatever programming has survived, which is catalogued and shelved in appropriate storage conditions.

22 Godin had appeared at the Stratford Festival as Montjoy, the French herald in *Henry V* in 1956, another attempt to present the two cultures, this time in one theatre. The production, which included Gratien Gélinas, was memorable even to a fourteen-year-old. However, no further attempts were made at Stratford to cast both anglophone and francophone actors under one roof, in one play – with one very successful exception in 1991, Michel Tremblay's *Les Belles Soeurs.*

23 *Star Weekly,* 20 October 1956.

24 www.imdb.com/title/tt0159220/, accessed 28 May 2007.

25 Miller 1987, 307–8. Rodriguez was a versatile performer indeed, with a rich voice and a strong presence.

26 The book does not include any miniseries or drama specials.

27 Robert Stacey writes in the *Canadian Encyclopedia,* second edition (1988), that "Jefferys is one of the most frequently reproduced of Canadian illustrators and is best known for his 'visual reconstructions' of Canadian history." Stacey's article is accompanied by an illustration by Jefferys with this caption: "Radisson meeting Indians in a winter camp during his thrilling exploits."

28 *Weekend* 6, no. 42 (1956).

29 The CBC *Times* of 3 February 1957 gave a cast list for the speaking parts for the first six episodes, which included seven roles for First Nations actors. In 1990 the producers of *Divided Loyalties* were still making excuses for casting a white actor in the role of Joseph Brant, the protagonist of their CTV film. This time they simply "couldn't find an appropriate actor." That there was a lot of controversy about the decision in the newspapers and periodical press at the time could be construed as progress.

30 The online *Canadian Dictionary of Biography,* www.biographi.ca, tentatively suggests that Radisson was born in Avignon, and a CBC pamphlet (mentioned later) states that he was born in St Malo. Despite writing his own journals, he remains an elusive figure in so many ways.

31 Laurendeau, a nationalist but not a separatist, would later co-chair Prime Minister Lester Pearson's Royal Commission on Bilingualism and Biculturalism.

32 Miller 1987, 384–7.

33 CBC press release, 21 January 1957.

34 No one in the 1950s, even actors (except Yul Brynner), shaved his head, but Godin's long hair also made him conspicuous on the streets of Montreal in 1957. There were other glitches, including the contrail of a plane overhead, which had not been caught by the "continuity girl" or the editors.

35 Lucarotti's citizenship remained an issue. The *Telegram,* 5 September 1956, and various other papers made a point of Lucarotti being an Englishman. Nationalism did not confine itself to creating new "national" heroes.

36 Much to the amusement, Moon (1957) says, of the NFB, which was often contemptuous of the CBC's efforts to film anything at all. The exact figure was announced by Revenue Minister John McCann and reported in the *Globe and Mail* two years later, on 14 March 1959. To put the sum in perspective, fifty years later, an hour-long episode of a historical series shot on location would be inexpensive at $1.5 million per episode. That is why so few are made.

37 McNeil (1980) dismisses *Tomahawk* in two lines: "… 1957. Produced in Canada, this little-known western starred Jacques Godet [*sic*] as Pierre Radisson and Rene Caron as Médard [Americans had trouble with Des Groseilliers's full name, so used his first name only], a pair of scouts [not fur traders and explorers, making three mistakes in two lines]." Nevertheless, McNeil's programming grids are accurate and helpful.

38 Ron Poulton, *Telegram,* 6 September 1956. Poulton also reports that, when building a cottage near Bracebridge, Ontario, Lucarotti blasted a rifle out of the ground dated 1651. Radisson was in the area in 1653.

39 A survey was also commissioned for the francophone version of *Radisson.* A few of its findings are reported in the English research report.

40 See Eamon 1994 for a history of CBC audience research methodology.

41 Yet the report says that the children also felt that they were learning things from television that helped their studies. They made frequent mention of *Disneyland,* but *Radisson* ran a close second. Apparently, CBC TV news was mentioned frequently in grades 7 and 8.

42 Posted on IMDb: www.imdb.com/title/tt0159220/, from Dundee. I have his emailed permission to quote his remarks.

43 In the 1980s one more attempt was made to shoot a series in both French and English so that CBC and SRC viewers could share the same television experience at the same time. The drama series *He Shoots, He Scores/Il lance, il compte!* should have been foolproof, since it was about a hockey team's tribulations on ice and off. Quebec loved it. The rest of Canada didn't watch in sufficient numbers to keep it going. Nevertheless, *Canada: A People's History*, shot in both languages, seems to have beaten the hex – and in the most contentious realm of all, our often mutually incomprehensible versions of our shared history.

44 *Ottawa Citizen*, 2000 (n.d.).

45 *Riel* was not quite the triumph he remembers, as my ongoing research on historical representations of *Riel* reveals.

46 Ibid.

47 Address to the ASCRT / AERTC at the Learned Societies Congress in Vancouver, 1990.

### CHAPTER SIX

1 Posted on the web when I quoted this but which has now disappeared. The print document will still exist at the CRTC archives and in other collections of governmental publications in libraries.

2 www.angelfire.com/retro/cta/Can/Hawkeye1957.htm, updated January 2006, visited 28 May 2007.

3 www.angelfire.com/retro/cta/Can/HudsonsBay.htm, updated July 2002, visited 28 May 2007.

4 Sandy Sunderland, who has a long memory and is familiar to me from NATIVE-L, posted a comment on the nativecelebs website, http://nativecelebs.com/film9.htm, accessed 28 May 2007, about the visible lack of research by the writers. As she tells it, "An old Hawkeye episode shows Chingachgook … standing at a site of numerous Plains style 'burial' platforms. (How's that for an oxymoron?) The Delaware/Mohican peoples interred their dead. They would place them on platforms or in trees only for a short time while the ground might be frozen." I would add to her comment that the idea that a "gang of desperadoes" would make raids "wearing special masks" so that they would be mistaken for Indians is also well off the mark, since masks, as opposed to face paint, were never used in warfare by eastern First Nations but rather in very specific ceremonial practices.

5 www.imdb.com/title/tt0163940/maindetails, accessed 10 October 2005. Not to be confused with the 1940 movie *Hudson's Bay* as the *New York Times* movie guide does, though it then calls the television series an" unjustly neglected

Canadian filmed 1958 adventure series (1959)": http://movies2.
nytimes.com/gst/movies/filmography.html?p_id=52160&mod=bio, accessed
28 May 2007.

6  www.imdb.com/name/nmo864869/bio, accessed 4 October 2005.

7  www.film.queensu.ca/CBC/Hob.html, visited 15 November 2005.

8  www.findarticles.com/p/articles/mi_moJSF/is_20_7/ai_30555234, accessed
27 February 2007.

9  Just to illustrate how tentative these guesses must be, Alan Crowfoot does not
appear again as an actor here or elsewhere in the databases, but Alan Crofoot,
a white actor and singer, can be found on the *Canadian Encyclopedia* site:
www.thecanadianencyclopedia.com/index.cfm?PgNm=TCE&Params=
U1ARTU0000849/, accessed 4 October 2005.

10  www.imdb.com/name/nmo199325/. See also www.findarticles.com/p/
articles/mi_moJSF/is_20_7/ai_30555234/, accessed 15 November 2005.

11  Sandy Stewart, *Here's Looking at Us: A Personal History of Television in Canada*
(1986). This book must be approached with caution regarding some facts and
omissions, but it does provide an invaluable picture gallery of early CBC
television; see chapter 18, 215–32. He identifies Michael Zenon, who played
the Metis Joe Two Rivers in *The Forest Rangers,* as "the Indian" – a mistake
others make as well (245).

12  www.angelfire.com/retro/cta/Can/ForestRangers.htm, visited 27 February
2007. Being dubbed in French widened the international market for the show.

13  Much later, on a nostalgic revisit to the program on *Fresh Air,* CBC radio's
weekend early-morning program, Susan Conway lamented that Kathy (the
only girl ranger on later episodes) was always having to be rescued, always a
little behind the boys.

14  www.imavision.com/en/eStore%2CwciCatalogue%2CType-P%2CID-
3074%2CLoadCat-1.html, accessed 27 February 2007.

15  www.angelfire.com/retro/cta/Can/ForestRangers.htm, accessed 27 February
2007.

16  Clayton Self's fan site also includes pictures of the ruins of the set and of a
reunion in June 2004: www.geocities.com/forestrangers1965/
ShingWaukclear.jpg, accessed 27 February 2007.

17  Compiled by www.angelfire.com/retro/cta/Can/ForestRangers.htm,
accessed 27 February 2007. The information has been "verified on film" by
Rina Fox, Classic TV Archive – Canadian Children's Adventure Series, which
should make it reliable.

18  www.ecclectica.ca/issues/2003/2/sawchuk.asp, accessed 28 May 2007.

19  www.imdb.com/title/tt0057750/usercomments, accessed 28 May 2007.

20  www.culttv.net/index.php?cm_id=131&cm_type=article, accessed 28 May 2007.

21 Unnumbered second-page introduction with the quote at the top from "Isn't It Ironic" by Alanis Morissette to set the tone.

22 Halliwell (1982) is his usual dismissive self in his remarks: "Stories of a group of junior rangers in the Canadian Northwoods. Flabbily shot outdoor adventure for kids." He is equally caustic on *Adventures in Rainbow Country*: "A 14-year-old boy has fun growing up near Lake Huron. Unexceptional and rather boring, open-air series for youngsters and indulgent adults." Outdoor family adventure series were clearly not his cup of tea, although he did find *The Beachcombers* "a moderately pleasant open-air series for young people." His description of that show was odd, however: "Children help a middle-aged man who prefers to live a rugged existence on the beaches north of Vancouver."

23 www.angelfire.com/tv2/rainbowcountry, accessed 27 February 2007.

24 Their definition of the "Great Outdoor Adventure Show" was a modified version of that in Miller 1987, which they acknowledged as a general source.

25 www.pulpanddagger.com/movies/a.html is the site of the highly personal "The Great Canadian Guide to the Movies & tv," which says that *Adventures in Rainbow Country* was "[c]reated by William Davidson, who wrote a novel spin-off in 1975 called Return to Rainbow Country." Last visited 16 May 2005. www.imdb.com/ title/tt0063861/trivia says that a feature film of that title was planned and never made, which William Davidson confirms on the Classic tv Archive site.

26 Rainsberry (1988) also mentions *Shadow Puppets* in that period, a seven-part children's series done by access, then Alberta's educational network, "based on the oral traditions of the Cree and Blackfoot Indians … narrated in … English, French and Cree. The puppets were crafted from sketches made by a native artists" (135).

27 The dates given for the series are puzzling, with a season in 1971 – September to March. That would mean 1970 – 71 and another in 1975. The economics of television makes this latter impossible, as does the fact that the children would have perceptibly grown up. I suspect the April to September 1975 date is an unidentified repeat. www.imdb.com/name/nm0735471/#guest-appearances, visited 16 May 2005.

28 www.angelfire.com/retro/cta/Can/RainbowCountry.htm, accessed October 2005, and www.angelfire.com/tv2/rainbowcountry, by Clay Self, accessed 15 November 2005.

29 He went on to perform in two nfb films, then disappeared from the record as an actor. But he co-founded a radio station in Mistissini (www.crtc.gc.ca/eng/ transcripts/2001/tt1113.htm, accessed 12 October 2005). In 2004 he was working on fibre optics for the region with Cree Telecom (www.rtscanada.com/srticle.pdf).

30 www.angelfire.com/retro/cta/Can/RainbowCountry.htm, accessed 12 October 2005.

31  www.imdb.com/title/tt0063861/usercomments, accessed 12 October 2005, gives a running list of episodes and includes praise from a German fan who, as an adult, travelled to White Fish Falls to revisit the scene.

32  Redbird's art can be seen on *We Are Metis: A Metis View of the Development of a Canadian Native People*, www.othermetis.net/WAM/WAM.html, accessed 12 October 2005. The site points to the "other" Metis with conscious irony, meaning those who did not come from the West. He wrote a master's thesis about the issue that was published in 1980.

33  See also Worker's Health and Safety Centre, www.whsc.on.ca/eyesonlives.html, accessed 15 May 2005: "Dreamer's Rock, a most sacred place on Manitoulin Island, where people of all walks come to visit, each seeking direction in their lives. In the native tradition this seeking is called a vision quest. Not so long ago, Dreamer's Rock was desecrated by young people, who may not have been aware of its significance. Local natives reclaimed the spot – cleansing it and blessing it – much like we must reclaim our earth for future generations." According to the Classic TV Archive site, the episode was "based on a true story."

34  http://collections.ic.gc.ca/cape_croker/ccheifs.htm, accessed October 12 2005, is an "evolutionary historical tour which lists the chiefs from 1863."

35  www.liberationchildren.org/billboard/nadjiwon, accessed 12 October 2005, has a section on Nadjiwon's life. He was chief "for 14 years … Throughout his life [he] fought to preserve his people's culture and heritage." A World War II veteran, he was also a well-known woodcarver.

36  Clips from that time were on http://archives.cbc.ca/IDD-1-71-99/conflict_war/oka.

37  http://translate.google.com/translate?hl=en&sl=fr&u=http://generikz.free.fr/paroles/M/matt_et_jenny.html&prev=/search%3Fq%3DMatt%2Band%2BJenny%26hl%3Den, visited December 2004 but no longer there.

38  www.angelfire.com/retro/cta/Can/MattAndJenny.htm, accessed 15 November 2005.

39  www.geocities.com/duncan_regehr/official/tv/mattandjenny.html, last visited 15 May 2005.

40  http://fans80s.dynalias.com/fans80s/series-tv_42.html was a site devoted to 1980s fans where interesting comments, a few of them more politicized than one might find on a North American site, could be found. No longer – it is gone. A little more information can be found at www.emissions.ca/emission/043-9611-284359,sur_la_route_de_l'amitie_(matt_et_jenny)/?Emission=043-9611-284359/, accessed 15 November 2005.

41  www.imdb.com/title/tt0078654/, accessed 11 October 2005. The production date, 1979, is a mistake.

42 The site http://croque-vacances.chez.tiscali.fr/matt.htm, visited 5 March
   2005, is now gone.

43 Yesno had done a brilliant job as the protagonist in "The Last Man in the
   World" on *Wojeck* thirteen years before.

44 www.imdb.com/name/nm0030516/, accessed 16 May 2005.

45 www.tv.com/campbells/show/3300/summary.html, accessed 17 October 2005.

46 http://hometown.aol.com/cjangle/thecampbells.html, accessed 16 May
   2005, now gone.

47 www.tvarchive.ca/database/16467/campbells%2c_the/details, accessed
   5 June 2007.

48 www-2.cs.cmu.edu/Unofficial/Canadiana/tv/exports/Exports.latest. The site is
   hosted by Carnegie Mellon. It looks as though it might include part of a thesis by a
   graduate student named Stuart M. Clamen (Canadian TV Exports List Version: 1.7.
   Last updated: Monday, Dec 18 04:11:36 EST 1995, accessed 30 October 2007). That
   this material remains on the site suggests that the information in the thesis is correct.

49 Jameson wrote *Winter Studies and Summer Rambles in Canada* (first published
   in 1838).

50 By chance, I had an opportunity to talk to Cedric Smith (12 June 2005), who
   played Captain Sims and wrote a few scripts. He remembers that there was
   money from a Christian broadcasting service in the show and consequently
   some censorship of the plot lines. There is no written record of this, but the Family Channel, which was owned by televangelist Pat Robertson at that time,
   broadcast the series at the same time as CTV, which suggests that it was an important market. This may well explain any self-censorship. Smith remembers,
   for example, having to reshoot a scene in which he took his ten- or eleven-year-
   old daughter on his knee. As he recalls, few episodes featured Indians. He says
   that when the producers wanted his character to be defined as someone who
   hated Indians, he successfully fought off the suggestion by pointing out that it
   had already been established that Captain Sims had fought at the Battle of
   Queenston Heights, where Brock's Indian allies played a key role.

51 Two American sites provide viewing opportunities. Volume 3 (four episodes)
   of *Hawkeye* is apparently available on DVD at www.cduniverse.com/
   productinfo.asp?pid=6965529, and second-hand individual tapes of twenty of
   the twenty-six episodes of *Hudson's Bay* are available at www.fesfilms.com/
   TV.html. Both were located too late to be viewed for this study.

CHAPTER SEVEN

1 For an update, see Miller, "Beachcombers," in *The Encyclopedia of Television*, 2nd ed.
  (2004). The first edition is online at www.museum.tv/archives/etv/index.html.

2 http://avtrust.ca/masterworks/2004/en_television_3.htm, accessed 17 June 2007.

3 www.avtrust.ca/mw/mw.php?display&en&70/ has a clip from the show.

4 www.thebeachcombers.ca/intro.htm, accessed 30 October 2007. There is no live site for the first movie, but my printout of the CBC site emphasizes in its brief plot summary the romantic triangle.

5 From a clip in a retrospective broadcast, 17 November 2002.

6 See Miller 1987, 106–7.

7 The website www.tvarchive.ca has been constructed by Patrick Allec, who, by the time this book is published, will have completed the almost-complete episode guide already posted. *The Beachcombers* site contains useful information, such as major cast members and the dates they entered and left the series.

8 In a CBC press release of 7 December 1966 on Paul St Pierre's *How to Break a Quarterhorse* (a drama special for *Festival* derived from the *Cariboo Country* anthology), the perceptive critic Pat Pearce of the *Montreal Star* is quoted: "What a joy it must have been for writer Paul St. Pierre and producer Philip Keatley to come on Chief Dan George [playing Ol' Antoine]. This old man needs only look at a camera for us to feel the winds of a nation's life. He can hold us with every stubborn move, every slow word … for there is humour here too." Subsequently Chief Dan George became known for his role as Old Lodge Skins in the Hollywood film *Little Big Man*. He was also a leader of his people, a singer and entertainer, as well as a logger and a man who spoke out on behalf of all First Nations during the celebrations for Canada's centennial year, 1967. Loretta Todd made a documentary film about his life, *Today Is a Good Day: Remembering Chief Dan George* (1999).

9 See Miller 1987, 106, on "Steelhead," 16 October 1977.

10 Years later Jesse's stepson Tommy finds that he has a special relationship with a spirit animal, a bear. In "Keep the Pride," the bear becomes his special friend/ guide when he faces his fears with the help of his grandfather and saves two boys who have been bullying him. Finally, in "The Gift," a tribute to actor George Clutesi, who had played Tommy's grandfather, Jesse, Laurel, and Tommy in particular struggle with Tommy's grandfather's sudden death. The synopsis does not explain how they come to terms with this death, but Joe David's listing as a "shaman" suggests the representation of a largely private ritual.

11 Here, as in similar instances in the drama special *Where the Spirit Lives* and later in *Spirit Bay*, it is presumably not appropriate to have a child perform or even be actively included in such a ritual in real life, in this case because a soul catcher was a sacred object that belonged only to shamans. Shamans were respected and feared in the Northwest culture. They endured many ordeals to gain the knowledge that distinguished them as shamans. Their regalia was not

shown at potlatches. Their ceremonies were often secret or held only with those persons they sought to help.

12 See Drew Hayden Taylor's very funny version of *A Christmas Carol* in *Education Is Our Right*, one of two plays published in his *Toronto at Dreamer's Rock/Education Is Our Right* (1990). Education Past tries to educate the politician Cadieux about the effect that television shows like *Bonanza* and *The Lone Ranger* had on him (90ff.).

13 As a consultant to the CBC in a legal matter, I was sent forty of the first scripts to analyse, including the first pilot (never broadcast), as well as the tapes for those scripts and the pilot.

14 The car appears again in episode 188, "Leadfoot."

15 Octavio Paz, *Claude Levi Strauss: An Introduction* (1970), 36.

16 But I offer here this unverifiable but fascinating glimpse into how it was at the height of the series' success. Bill Brioux, in the *Toronto Sun*, 3 May 2002, writes: "At its peak, around three million Canadians a week tuned in. The series even had a fan in Conan O'Brien, who, before he became a late night host, traveled to B.C. with a buddy in search of cast member Pat Johns." http://jam.canoe. ca/Television/TV_Shows/B/The_Beachcombers/2004/08/12/579878.html, accessed 2 March 2007. See also Tony Atherton's article in the *Ottawa Citizen*, 27 November 2002, at www.brucegreenwood.com/mov-tv/beach/beach-arts.htm.

17 "From the U.K to the Middle East to Australia," *Queen's University Directory* of CBC series from 1952 to 1982, at www.film.queensu.ca/CBC/Index.html. See also my short article for the first edition of *The Encyclopedia of Television*, now posted online at www.museum.tv/archives/etv/B/htmlB/beachcombers/beachcombers.htm. Thirty-six episodes were dubbed into French, but no more are indicated. Perhaps the series did not catch on with a francophone audience. Jesse is written out of the series in episode 52, which has an open-ended storyline that allows him to come back in episode 70. Pat Johns felt he needed a break.

18 See www-2.cs.cmu.edu/Unofficial/Canadiana/tv/exports/Exports.latest, hosted by Carnegie Mellon, accessed 29 May 2007.

19 Quotations are, as usual, from notes made off-air.

20 The episode ends with Nick and Relic looking at the sunset and talking. After the credits, as a last image, a note from the producers appears on the screen thanking the people of Gibson's Landing, the Sunshine Coast, and "the millions who for a generation have watched the show."

### CHAPTER EIGHT

1 *Ojibway Heritage* (1990), 3. See also Rupert Ross, *Dancing with a Ghost: Exploring Indian Reality* (1992), 126ff. and 166ff.

2 Exact dates are thanks to John Corcelli of Corcelli-Research.

3 See Michele Byers, *Growing Up Degrassi: Television, Identity and Youth Cultures* (2005), for all thing *Degrassi*. Writing an introduction to that book in 2004 sparked several of the questions raised in this section on children's television. There are dozens of websites for both "Degrassi Classic" and the new series, successfully revived after a ten-year gap and widely sold abroad. Degrassi DVDs are sold, and graphic novels now appear in bookstores.

4 Norval Morrisseau: "b. 1931, Sandy Point Reserve, Ontario, First Nations Affiliation: Ojibwa. A member of the Royal Canadian Academy of Arts since 1970, Norval Morrisseau was the celebrated founder of the Woodland School, which revitalized Anishnaube iconography, traditionally incised on rocks and Midewiwin birchbark scrolls." http://collections.ic.gc.ca/artists/ morriseau_norval.html, accessed 31 October 2007.

5 From a Cornell University website: "Since 1973, Doxtater has written, directed and/or produced 20 documentaries that have appeared on public television in the United States and Canada, some of which have received awards and nominations from the Sundance Festival, Native American Film Festival, Gemini Awards and the Dreamspeakers Festival. He has written children's television drama for the Spirit Bay and Beachcombers network series. A Turtle Clan Mohawk." www.news.cornell.edu/releases/March99/Native.writers. lgk.html, accessed 29 May 2007.

6 According to York University, where Moses was a writer in residence, he "is a registered Delaware Indian from the Six Nations lands on the Grand River in southern Ontario. He holds an honours BA from York University and an MFA in creative writing from the University of British Columbia. He is a regular visitor to university classes [including Dramatic Arts at Brock] of English, Drama, and Native Studies as an artist in residence. His plays include 'Coyote City,' 'Big Buck City,' 'Almighty Voice and His Wife' and 'The Indian Medicine Shows.'" www.edu.yorku.ca/~WIER/ddm.html, now gone. Moses has written several books of poetry.

7 The "Sisters of Mercy" episode in the first season of *North of 60* replays some of the elements of this episode with a far darker emphasis and more detail. See chapter 13.

8 http://northernblue.ca/ablog/categories/29-OjibwaNishnawbe-Aski was a site with all kinds of information when I visited it on 14 October 2005; it is now gone. Anishnabe seems to be the other name for Nishnawbe, both of them referring to Ojibway, which is what many people still call themselves. www.firstnationsseeker.ca/NishnawbeAski.html is a collection of portals for individual Cree-Ojibway-Nishnawbe-Aski nations. The map shows their territory to be well north of the Great Lakes. Accessed 29 May 2007.

9 Graham Greene won the Earle Grey Award on 13 December 2004 for "an outstanding body of work." www.geminiawards.ca/gemini19/special-seg.cfm, now gone.

10 In fact, the producers on *The Beachcombers* did consult with native people, just as, earlier, in *Cariboo Country*, Keatley and writer Paul St Pierre had used stories from the Shushwap First Nations as well as from the ranchers who lived in the Cariboo, and had learned from their reactions to the resulting episodes.

11 See a short account of the debate about cultural appropriation between Keeshig-Tobias and the Leckies in Miller 2001, 71–84.

12 See also Greer's "Native Americans Still Battling Stereotyping," *Broadcast Weekly*, 21 April 1990, at www.angelfire.com/ny3/buckstop/greggarticles/gregg7.html, accessed 29 May 2007. This article discusses attempts that were made in two period Western series on American television to be more historically accurate, and castigates the CTV/France co-production *Bordertown*, a series set in a very grubby border town in the 1880s, because it "romanticizes native people as monosyllabic helpless victims" in season 1, 1989–90, as indeed it did. The producer claimed that the second season had "stronger, more authentic stories," which may have included the one that surprised me by acknowledging the grievances of the Metis.

13 *Take One*, summer 2000, at www.findarticles.com/p/articles/mi_moJSF/is_28_9/ai_30574609/, accessed 16 November 2007.

14 This series apparently began broadcasting while Rainsberry was writing the end of his book on children's television (1988), which has a delightful picture of some of the children in *Spirit Bay* playing broomball on page 131.

15 The Media Awareness Network, a Canadian not-for-profit centre for media literacy in the schools and media and Internet education, points out on www.media-awareness.ca/english/issues/stereotyping/aboriginal_people/aboriginal_portrayals.cfm (last visited 29 May 2007) that "[i]n the 1980s and 1990s, the Canadian Broadcasting Corporation (CBC) made a real effort to improve the portrayals of Aboriginal people in its television dramas. *Spirit Bay, The Beachcombers, North of 60* and *The Rez* used Native actors to portray their own people, living real lives and earning believable livelihoods in identifiable parts of the country. *The Beachcombers* and *North of 60* drew substantial audiences among Natives and non-Natives alike … Television in the United States has been slower to respond to criticism. Indigenous faces are still almost entirely absent from the small screen, except in the news or in documentaries. There have been a few efforts to change the situation, however. In the late 1990s, the American Indian Registry for the Performing Arts in Los Angeles published a directory of Native American performing arts professionals. And in 2001, after acknowledging that 'Native Americans are virtually invisible on TV,' CBS and

NBC held talent showcases in major cities across North America to strengthen their databases of Aboriginal performers."

CHAPTER NINE

1 Organized by the seasons over a year, *Back on the Rez* is an absorbing account of Maracle's life as he makes the return to the reserve and of the lives of his extended family and friends who have never left.

2 The rather arch headline is "Reservations about Riverdale." See www.eye.net/eye/issue/issue_09.18.97/film/reel18.html, accessed 18 October 2005.

3 My copy is an Oberon Press reissue (no city or town indicated, just Canada), with a still from the movie of Ryan Black and Adam Beach on the back cover. The back cover also tells the reader that "Kinsella refuses to take a tragic (he would call it sentimental) view of Indian life. His view is unrepentantly comic and his stories are extremely funny. Not that he laughs at the expense of Indians. On the contrary, it is the white man and his civilization that are seen to be absurd ... a classic of its kind, chaste[?], infectious, irresistible."

4 See a short account of the debate between Keeshig-Tobias and the Leckies about cultural appropriation in Miller, "Where the Spirit Lives: An Influential and Contentious Television Drama about Residential Schools" (2001), 71–84.

5 By Brian D. Johnson, with Diane Turbide and Pamela Young.

6 The article concludes: "[N]ow as both native and non-native artists lay claim to North America's aboriginal legacy, new treaties will have to be forged on the frontier of the imagination."

7 "Waiting for Kinsella," 70–1. See also Taylor's article on cultural appropriation titled "What Colour Is a Rose?" Both essays are in *Funny You Don't Look Like One: Observations from a Blue-Eyed Ojibway* (1996).

8 A staff writer, in the classroom edition of *Windspeaker*, at www.ammsa.com/classroom/CLASS3appropriation.html, accessed 1 November 2007. There is no date on this, but internal evidence suggests that it is the August 2001 classroom edition posted online.

9 The omitted portion of the quote is a proofreading error that makes no sense.

10 *Dance Me Outside* won McDonald the best director award at the American Indian Film Festival in San Francisco in 1995.

11 The *Alberta Native News* (no writer credited), March 1995, found the film "refreshing, entertaining ... a must see." This reviewer does not make any other analytical comment but quotes director Bruce McDonald: "'[the film is about] growin' up, the power of women and the healing circle of community." (It has been reported several times that Tomson Highway was asked to write

the screenplay for the film but his script was turned down. Bronwyn Drainie mentioned this in a profile on Highway in the *Globe and Mail*, 17 October 1998.) Don McKellar and John Frizzell wrote the screenplay with McDonald, who was one of the executive producers of the series. Frizzell produced *The Rez*. Google reveals that there is also a version called *Dance Me Outside: The Illustrated Screenplay*, adapted to the page by Nick Craine from the screenplay by Bruce McDonald, Don McKellar, and John Frizzell, based on the book by W.P. Kinsella (Cambridge ON: Black Eye Productions, 1994); see www.filmreferencelibrary.ca/index.asp?navid=95/, visited 4 June 2007, and www.graphicclassics.com/pgs/rosebudx.htm, visited 4 June 2007.

12 *Dance Me Outside* has been rebroadcast on Showcase, on Moviepix, and on APTN, which also rebroadcast *The Rez* from January to June 2002. *The Rez* was back in reruns on APTN in March 2007.

13 Sisters Jennifer Podemski and Tamara Podemski share Salteaux/Ojibway and Israeli heritage. In the *Jerusalem Report*, 17 July 2002, Tamara says that her first love is music and dance, that she is married to Darrell Dennis (Shuswap), and that she calls herself "a survivor on both sides of her family": "From my experience, half-breeds usually choose one culture over the other. It's a simpler alternative than doing the balancing act, which I have chosen" (43). Jennifer, a producer, writer, and performer of material with a strongly aboriginal focus (such as *Moccasin Flats*), seems to have tipped towards that part of her heritage. An article titled "About the 2001 Cancom Ross Charles Awards Recipients" describes Jennifer this way: "Jennifer Podemski (Saulteaux/Israeli) made her first television appearance on Wonderstruck at age 12. Jennifer has appeared opposite Sonya Smits in The Diviners, as well as in Dance Me Outside, The Rez, and Don't Think Twice … Since its inception, [Big Soul, the company she cofounded,] has produced an award winning Aboriginal youth role model series for television entitled, The Seventh Generation, which is hosted by Jennifer. This article was at www.banffcentre.ab.ca/aboriginal_arts/programs/2001/ ross_charles_bckgd.htm, accessed 10 April 2002, no longer there.

14 www3.sympatico.ca/amaurice/frame2.html, accessed 4 June 2007. "Shirley Cheechoo first gained international attention … with her play, 'Path With No Moccasins.' In it, Shirley gives a very personal account of her struggle to maintain her identity and a connection to her Cree upbringing and heritage while enduring the human rights abuses of the residential school system. While often very moving, the story is also infused with a wonderful sense of humour … A woman of boundless energy and many talents, Shirley is a founder of the respected theatre group De-Ba-Jeh-Mu-Jig, where actors such as Gary Farmer and Grahame Green were part of the company. She has

received many honours and awards over the years, including 'The Eagle Spirit Award' from the American Indian Film Institute and an Honorary Doctorate of Letters from Laurentian University in Sudbury, Ontario."

15 "Mojica is Kuna [Panamanian] and Rappahoannock [Renapoak Widokodadiwin Powhatan Confederation, currently in Virginia] on her mother's side," according to the site www.nativecelebs.com/profiles/goddard2.htm, accessed 4 June 2007. She was a past artistic director of Native Earth Theatre.

16 Extended families appear in many novels and poems written by aboriginal writers. Eden Robinson, Lee Maracle, Maria Campbell, Brian Maracle, and Drew Hayden Taylor are a few of the First Nations writers living in Canada who talk about the complex family connections on and off the reserve.

17 Tomson Highway on Nanabush: "Essentially a comic, clownish sort of character, he teaches us about the nature and meaning of existence on the planet earth." Tomson Highway, *The Rez Sisters* {Saskatoon: Fifth House Publishers, 1988), xii.

18 Currently, dozens of websites across the country are put up by reserves offering "native" experiences.

19 *Walrus* 1, no. 1 (September 2003): 75–81. See also Ben Sherman (Oglala Lakota), "Native People and Culture: Prized Assets of Indian Country Tourism," and other related articles in *Native Peoples: Arts and Lifeways,* special issue, March/April 2002.

20 http://news.degrassi.ca/article.php?a_id=509. There is no detailed episode guide for this series currently on the web. *Growing Up Degrassi* has a partial episode guide that sends the reader to Kathryn Ellis, *Degrassi: Generations* (Toronto: Fenn Publishing/Madison Press, 2005), for a complete guide. Michele Byers, ed., *Growing Up Degrassi: Television, Identity and Youth Cultures* (2005), for which I wrote the introduction, is an accessible but scholarly anthology on both "editions" of the series.

21 www.playbackmag.com/articles/magazine/19950619/4434.html, accessed 20 October 2005, no longer there.

22 www.playbackmag.com/articles/magazine/19960212/5030.html, accessed 20 October 2005, no longer there.

23 www.tvtome.com/tvtome/servlet/ShowMainServlet/showid-5344/Northwood, visited 4 June 2007. *Madison* focused on the students of "Madison High." In the first season, a selection of characters appear in an anthology format, but the series reverted to the more customary show for teens, creating recurring characters the teen viewers could identify with. Still, looking for a series to attract teenagers, the CBC tried a "six-pack" of episodes for *Straight Up* (1996–97), which featured high school students. In an interesting and then

uncommon experiment, the series used one story arc over the whole length of its slightly longer second season. *Straight Up* also overlapped *The Rez* and, like it, was not renewed for a third season: www.tv.com/madison/show/1876/summary.html&full_summary=1, accessed 4 June 2007. In work now underway, Michele Byers will trace the influence of *Degrassi Classic* on two contemporary series in which urban First Nations people finally appear on a regular basis, *renegadepress.com* and *Moccasin Flats*.

24 The award was dated 5 October 1998: http://cbc.radio-canada.ca/htmen/pdf_rtf/fall98.pdf, no longer posted.

25 www.telefilm.gc.ca/en/prod/tv96/25.htm, visited in May 2002, no longer there.

26 Adilman attributes the fact that the CBC permitted "colourful language" (for 1996 – there were still no "F---" words in the dialogue) on the show to a more relaxed management.

27 Kinsella's dialogue is halting and ungrammatical, but a book, unlike a human voice cannot be monotone in dialogue; monotone in that context means monotonous, which for all its faults, the book is not.

28 Jim Bawden in the *Starweek*, October 11, 1997, reported that, according to producer Brian Dennis, Bruce McDonald had reviewed the scripts for the new season and Norman Jewison's expertise in the editing suite was proving to be most valuable.

29 Alanis Obamsawin, a distinguished filmmaker of documentaries at the National Film Board starting in 1971, was presumably, the exception to this comment: www.collectionscanada.ca/women/002026-709-e.html, accessed 4 June 2007.

30 www.banffcentre.ca/media_room/Media_Releases/Arts_Ab_Arts/2001/010501_cancom_ross_charles_award.asp– aboriginal arts program" that appears to have been written by Wheeler. "Program Director Jordan Wheeler (Cree/ Irish) was born to a Cree mother (Bernelda) who was a CBC journalist and an Irish father (Peter). Following family through protests, Powwows, media scrums, and the urban Native experience, Wheeler became a journalist and later published short stories using those early experiences as fodder. To support his writing, Wheeler worked on the technical side of a string of independent productions, from CBC anthology dramas to in-house corporate training videos. Starting in 1989, he combined his two occupations by co-writing Welcome Home Hero, a half-hour film starring Tom Jackson and Rene Highway. In 1992, Wheeler became writer and story editor with CBC's North of 60. After four years and sixty-four episodes, nine of which he wrote, he moved on to other projects such as, The Rez, Big Bear, Black Harbour, The Adventures of Shirley Holmes, and The Longhouse Tales ... "

31 Some additional quotes from First Nations actors in her piece: unattributed – "I think the show's trying to get across the fact that humor exists. And it's really

not all that different from anyone else's"; Ryan Black, who plays Silas Crow –
"There is definitely a lack of humour in all shows about native people, because
we laugh at everything"; aboriginal actress Pamela Matthews – "I find native
people have the greatest sense of humour in the world. They never really quite
get to that in the show, but that's a choice they made"; and Tom Jackson, star of
*North of 60* – "That show (*North of 60*) is very popular with the native community. But for them, it's true, if there's a singular aspect missing, it's the sense of
humor." Talking to Jim Bawden (*Starweek*, 11 October 1997), Tamara Podemski
(Lucy) reminded readers that every reserve is different and that staying or leaving is a decision every kid on the rez has to make. www.canoe.ca/Television-
ShowsR/rez.html, accessed April 2002, no longer there.

32 Fall 1998, www.cbc.radio-canada.ca/docs/equity/pdf/ee-news04e.pdf,
accessed 20 October 2005, no longer there.

33 Cf. 126ff. for *Spirit Bay* and 166ff. for *The Rez*.

34 In one chapter this ex-pat from Missouri talks about working on a newspaper
in Sioux Lookout and then for a radio station in its infancy, and then about
travelling with a company of aboriginal actors, including Graham Greene, as
their playwright. Her successor in the company was Tomson Highway. Near
the end of the book, there is a very moving account of a feast for the dead on
the first anniversary of the death of an elder and friend (282–4).

35 Information on Lawrence Paul Yuxweluptun and his essay from *Land Spirit
Power* is to be found on www.lawrencepaulyuxweluptun.com, accessed
4 June 2007.

CHAPTER TEN

1 www.angelfire.com/retro/cta/Can/_Canada.htm, accessed 1 November
2007.

2 www.tvarchive.ca. The entry is dated 8 November 2005, but the full details are
still being added (26 May 2007). Like many fan sites this one has valuable
information but does contain errors and is still being updated and corrected.

3 http://avtrust.ca/masterworks/2004/en_television_3.htm, accessed 5 June 2007.

4 www.leg.bc.ca/hansard/37th3rd/h20515p.htm, 5 June 2007. But note this bit
of self-reflexivity on the site www.gasworks.org.uk/shows/beach, accessed
17 November 2005, now gone. An exhibition of work by Geoffrey Farmer,
Brian Jungen (who is identified as aboriginal), and Myfanwy MacLeod was
called *The Beachcombers* and appeared at the Gasworks in London, UK, June–
11 August 2002: "This group of artists are beachcombers of popular culture,
taking inspiration both in subject matter and form from the regional and
global culture that surrounds them. The work is hybrid – they share a

humorous attitude and a lightness of touch which distinguishes them from an older generation of Vancouver artists."

5 www.angelfire.com/retro/cta/Can/_Canada.htm, accessed 7 June 2007.

6 www.culttv.net/index.php?cm_id=131&cm_type=article, accessed 5 June 2007.

7 www.angelfire.com/retro/cta/Can/MattAndJenny.htm, accessed 5 June 2007.

8 www.tv.com/the-campbells/show/3300/summary.html, accessed 5 June 2007; and http://hometown.aol.com/cjangle/thecampbells.html, "its companion page," visited 16 May 2005, but like many fan sites gone by November 2005.

9 www.wintertime.com/OH/nof60.html, accessed 5 June 2007. Patty Winter has obtained full copyright clearance for all of the materials on her site. Not all fan sites are so meticulous.

10 http://tv.groups.yahoo.com/group/Northof60/messages, 13,984 messages on 5 June 2007.

11 Note also that Hills provides valuable caveats about academic fan ethnography in his chapter "Between 'Knowledge' and 'Justification'" (65–89).

12 Robert B, one of the fans on the *North of 60* list, reported on 22 August 2006 that a CD of the music for *North of 60* sold for $255 US on eBay that day.

13 audiovisioncanada is the company that somehow obtained rights to the film. See www.audiovisioncanada.com/ACCFMX/stores/2/_P697.cfm, accessed 3 April 2007.

14 http://tv.groups.yahoo.com/group/Northof60/files.

15 Compare the CBC generic www.cbc.ca/northof60 and the layered and imaginative "official" website www.northof60.net/distant_drumming/index.htm of the CBC and Alberta Filmworks, both still on line as of 12 March 2007. The German one-page *North of 60* site "Die Mounties von Lynx River" – www.kotat.homepage.t-online.de/northof60.htm, accessed 12 March 2007 – has a list of the thirty-two episodes that were shown on a pay channel in Germany and all five movies. It also has links to the official website, Patty Winter's website, and to websites of Tom Jackson and Graham Greene.

16 www.geocities.com/forestrangers1965 and the archives. Comments from fans who found the site are at www.geocities.com/forestrangers1965/archive1.html, accessed 12 March 2007.

17 www.angelfire.com/tv2/rainbowcountry/, accessed 12 March 2007.

18 http://tv.groups.yahoo.com/group/northof60_fans. It had twelve messages in February 2001 when it was founded, none for the rest of the year, and then one in 2004, one in 2005, twelve in 2006, and sixteen to April 2007. It claims to have thirty-nine members. Some lists work. Some struggle. Many disappear.

19 What TRIO stands for is never spelled out on the home page of its website and there appears to be only one page. www.triotv.com/, accessed 1 November 2007.

20 For years, some fans have created and shared pornographic variations on television shows. The rise of Youtube in the mid-2000s has opened new paths.

21 In all but *The Beachcombers* the leading actors, aboriginal and other, were not well known to television viewers. The only well-known aboriginal actor who performed regularly in any of these series was Tom Jackson. He had already appeared in several movies of the week before *North of 60* and had a separate career as a singer. Some who were more familiar appeared as guests – August Schellenberg, Graham Greene, and Tantoo Cardinal.

22 www.wintertime.com/OH/Nof60/Slavey/slavey.html.

23 On 23 December 2001, in a completely unscientific poll done on the list, there were 51 (or 72.86%) self-identified females and 19 (or 27.14%) males. By age group, out of 68 who responded 2.94% were under 21; 14.71% were 21–30 (the demographic with disposable income); 33.82% were 31–40 (i.e., 47% of the audience were in the age group also favoured by advertisers at that time); 30.88% were 40–50 (baby boomers); and 11.76% were 51–60. Only 5.88% were over 60, but that number may have been skewed by generational differences in the use of computers.

24 www.retro-media.de/wl/links.pl?s=7769&nc=1&p=0&mode, accessed 5 June 2007, says that thirty-nine episodes were broadcast; and www.kabeleins.de/serienlexikon/ergebnis.php?action=exact&id=3427&searchstring=M, indicates that there were more. The latter no longer lists the series.

25 Atherton's article is headlined "How Bruno the Greek Rewrote TV, The Beachcombers broke Toronto's grip on TV drama and lay [*sic*] the foundation for a TV and film industry in B.C." He writes: "It was also blessed by a relatively low profile. It was not costly to make and the network did not think of it as a flagship show. It was easy to sell abroad (eventually seen in more than 40 countries), and proved to be an amazing training ground." www.brucegreenwood.com/mov-tv/beach/beach-arts.htm, accessed 5 June 2007.

26 Quoted in Edles 2002.

27 Ibid.

28 In the last chapter of this exhaustive review of the literature, Douglas outlines a set of questions unanswered, gaps in the research, and future directions that could be of future interest to Canadian scholars.

29 For an account of sitcoms and soaps to the mid-1980s, see chapters 2, 3, and 4 in Miller 1987 and more recently the overview of Canadian broadcasting in English in *Encyclopedia of Television*, 2nd ed. (2004), 424–34, as well as articles on other specific programs by Canadian scholars.

### CHAPTER ELEVEN

1 http://tv.groups.yahoo.com/group/Northof6o/messages.
2 www.cancom.net/~dehchofn/dehchofn.htm. Deh Cho is the name of the
  region used in the series. The people in Lynx River are South Slavey and the
  village of Fort Liard or Acho Dene Koe sees itself as its real life counterpart.
  www.fortliard.com, accessed 13 March 2007.
3 Already they use many different methods of story telling to make drama for
  an adult audience. I have found that watching an unmoving camera on an
  elder who recalls earlier days, even in translation, can be riveting.
4 www.telefilm.gc.ca/en/prod/tv/tv98/145.htm, accessed 29 April 2002, no
  longer online. For an outline of this and other technological shifts to the mid-
  1990s, see chapter 6 of Miller 1996.
5 Since the early 1990s, the CBC has been forced by budget cuts and CRTC policy
  to give up all in-house drama series productions.
6 See Patty Winter's FAQ on her *North of 60* website, quoted with permission:
  www.wintertime.com/OH/Nof6o/nof6ofaq.html.
7 But a CBC financial year has been April 1 to March 31. In 1990, the brilliant CBC
  drama special *Sanity Clause* was made for the Christmas season but shown on
  April Fools Day because it could then be charged to the next fiscal year. Fortunately in the closing credits, Santa Claus is dancing with the Easter Bunny.
8 www.nof6o.com/backgrounder.html, visited 22 November 1996, but no
  longer online; the hard copy is not in CBC library files.
9 www.films.qc.ca/doublage/aunord6oe.html, accessed 21 October 2005, supplies
  a full cast list of the originals and the actors who dubbed them as well as a list of
  the directors of the dubs. (Although not all anglophone Canadian series appear
  to have been dubbed, the site also lists many other series.) It has been suggested
  to me that Quebecers might see the series through their different history and thus
  perhaps identify the Lynx River community with the Northern Quebec Cree.
10 See Miller 1996, *passim*, for several different accounts of the process for
   sitcoms, legal shows, and other series.
11 See "Out of the Darkness," *Aboriginal Voices* 22 (1997). Morriseau reports that
   Keeper credits Jordan Wheeler, who had already been asked to write for the
   show, with telling her about the role. At that time, she was finishing her BA
   and had almost no acting experience. Learning on the job is not necessarily the
   worst way to work on television – look at Chief Dan George.
12 Jane Brown, in "Tom Jackson: Helping Others in Need Is Actor's Life Work,"
   *Saskatchewan Sage*, 1998, writes: "The son of a Cree mother and an English father,
   Jackson was born on the One Arrow reserve near Batoche and raised in Winnipeg.
   He struck out his own at an early age and after dropping out of school before age
   15, he voluntarily lived life in the city's back streets until he was 22." He went on

to have a successful career as an actor and singer, both before the series and after it ended, and established his own film production studio. He is an officer of the Order of Canada with many honorary degrees, and after the suicide of Mervin Good Eagle, who played Joey, he initiated the Dreamcatcher Tour of 170 reserves over eight years, bringing "workshops, music and overall messages of empowerment to communities suffering the loss of young lives to suicide." www.tomali.com/main/tomJackson/bio.shtml, accessed 6 June 2007.

13 The website for season 6 – www.northof60.net/pages/ series_cast_gordon.html, accessed 13 March 2007 – provides the following information: "Tootoosis [Cree/Stoney] describes Albert as 'an Indian who exploits Indians. He doesn't realize that he's the negative energy that's going against a positive energy.' Tootoosis adds [very perceptively] that, 'Albert is a very sharp, intelligent man who hasn't yet discovered who he is, or perhaps, just doesn't want to know.' In addition to his more than 25 years experience as a performer, Gordon Tootoosis was a real-life band chief as well as vice-president of the Federation of Saskatchewan Indian Nations. He manages to fit television, film, stage and dance performances into his busy schedule." He also starred in the miniseries *Big Bear* in the title role and had many other major roles. http://us.imdb.com/name/nm0867588, accessed 6 June 2007.

Tootoosis "was raised with a strong Cree belief system and a knowledge of the Cree language, art and world view. At an early age, he became a cowboy and is a champion Calf Roper and Team Roper. He is also an accomplished Native dancer. He toured with the Plains Intertribal Dance Troupe in the 60s and 70s across Canada, Europe and South America." www.northernstars.ca/actorsstu/tootoosis _gordon.html, accessed 6 June 2007. I also note that he was awarded the Order of Canada in October 2005 and delivered a monologue by Floyd Favel in the Senate Chamber during the installation of Governor General Michaelle Jean in 2006.

14 See www.northof60.net/pages/series_cast_dakota.html, accessed 6 June 2007. House is identified as an urban Indian who grew up in an inner-city neighbourhood in Edmonton (earning a black belt in Hapkido) at www.saymag.com/dakotahouse/bio.html (accessed 13 July 2005; now gone), which may well have contributed to the edge he gave the role of Teevee. He starred as Dudley George in *One Dead Indian* (2005).

15 "[A native of] St. Catharines, Ontario, Cook was a successful model appearing on numerous covers of fashion magazines including Chatelaine, Toronto Life and Canadian Living … Cook was nominated in 1995 and 1996 for a Gemini Award for Best Performance by an Actress in a Continuing Leading Dramatic Role for her work on North of 60." www.northof60.net/pages/ series_cast_tracey.html, accessed 13 July 2005.

16 Oliver (also known as John Bean) has many film and television credits listed on http://us.imdb.com/Name?Bean,+Gerry, accessed 2 May 2005. In an

interview conducted by Montreal journalist Hélèna Katz in March 2001, he
remembered a few things about *North of 60*, but from his point of view it was
ten years ago and he had not remain connected to the series as the other cast
members had. The interview is posted on www.wintertime.com/OH/Nof60/
Interviews/john.html.

17  "He has performed in and directed dozens and dozens of professional plays,
particularly with the Great Canadian Theatre Company where he acted in several plays by George Walker [whose dark and savagely funny visions would
be good preparation for Brian Fletcher's spiral downwards, especially his stint
as Fletcher/mad trapper/vengeful nemesis in the movie *Into the Blue Ground*].
He has acted for most major theatre companies across the country."
www.northof60.net/pages/ITBG_cast_robert.html, accessed 2 May 2002.

18  Harper is Huron and Miskika. "In 1985, he started a five-year stint of
international travel as a dancer with Les Ballets Jazz de Montréal.
Following an extensive leg injury, he returned cautiously to acting."
www.northof60.net/pages/series_cast_peter.html, accessed 6 June 2007.

19  "In 1991 [Morriseau] created the Coyote Collective, a group of First Nations producers, directors, technicians and writers from across Canada who are dedicated
to advancing First Nations Issues through broadcast television. Her documentaries have won critical acclaim ... [including] in 1996 a best Public Service Awarded
for her documentary Echoes of the Sister." www.northernstars.ca/
actorsmno/morriseau_renae.html, accessed 13 March 2007.

20  Kinistino was a band counsellor on the Ochapawase reserve and appeared
in plays by Tomson Highway and George Ryga (www.sakewewak.org/
storytellers/2002.html, accessed 13 July 2005, no longer online) and is an
actor/singer/performance artist, director, and grass dancer, performing with
the collective Dancing Sky Theatre, which is based in rural Saskatchewan and
toured for the Centennial celebrations in 2005 (www.dancingskytheatre.com/
All%20My%20Bio.html, accessed 13 July 2005, no longer online).

21  Bomberry has done work ranging from a benefit performance of Eve Ensler's *The
Vagina Monologues* (www.urbannation.com/v-day.html, accessed 14 July 2005, no
longer online) to a full-time job (as of 2004) working with developmentally challenged adults for the Six Nations of the Grand River Territory (www.winter-
time.com/OH/Nof60/Interviews/tinalouise2.html, accessed 6 June 2007).

22  A competitive powwow dancer in women's traditional buckskin and with no
real background in acting before the series, Pelly has taken occasional roles
since. www.wintertime.com/OH/Nof60/Interviews/wilma2.html, accessed 6
June 2007.

23  "Herman's father was a trapper, a useful background for the character.
Herman worked in the Native Counselling Services of Alberta for several

years before becoming an actor, another useful experience to bring to this role." He is also politically active with issues involving Treaty 6 nations. Online information now gone, but see www.dreamspeakers.org/2006/walk.htm, accessed 1 November 2007.

24 www.nativecelebs.com/profiles/north_of_60_2.htm, accessed 13 March 2007. Obey is now making videos and films.

25 www.nativecelebs.com/profiles/north_of_60_2.htm, accessed 13 March 2007. Horse continues to act but is also a master jeweller and ledger artist.

26 Arcand's background, like Dakota House's, was as a teenager living in tough circumstances in Edmonton. http://nathaniel-arcand.iwarp.com/html/page2.htm, accessed 13 March 2007, not recently updated.

27 Mykytiuk had an important role in the 1977 collective play *Paper Wheat* (which toured all over the country) and won a Gemini for episode 43, "Refugees" (www.wintertime.com/OH/Nof60/Interviews/lubo.html, accessed 6 June 2007). He appears in all of the *North of 60* films and continues to pursue a strong acting career in a wide variety of roles in radio, theatre, television, and film.

28 Webber's acting career continues to flourish in theatre, radio, television, and film. www.northernstars.ca/actorsvz/webber_timothy.html, accessed 13 March 2007.

29 The website www.spiderandi.com/nadb/Television/Drama/North_of_60.htm (accessed 2 May 2002, now gone) lists for the series the following aboriginal guest actors: Apesanahkwat as Senator Jack Harper; Jesse Ed Azure as Herbert Golo; Lawrence Bayne as John Wolf; Terry Big Charles as Mike Thunderchild; Ryan Black as Lawrence Poor Man; Buffalo Child as André LeBret; Ben Cardinal as Gabe Coulee; Lorne Cardinal as Daniel De'ela; Marty Chief Calf as Terry Whitemud; Curtis Nelson Chief as Justin Small Boat; Byron Chief-Moon as Louis Claybank; Cam Courchene as Wayne De'ela; Glen Gould as Alvin Bran; Graham Greene as Rico Nez; Amanda McLeod as Chrissy; Morningstar Mercredi as Sandra Farrel; Carmen Moore as Janine Carr; Allan Little Moustache as George Small Boat; and Danny Rabbit as Walter Golo. There is no information about the sources used on this site or about who put it up, but when cross-checked with Patty Winter's character list on her *North of 60* site (www.wintertime.com/OH/Nof60/nof60cast.txt, accessed 6 June 2007), it appears to be accurate.

30 That is, scheduled one night a week rather than daily in the afternoons. Many of the shows featuring doctors and lawyers (*Grey's Anatomy, Boston Legal*) have strong elements of soaps in them.

31 Tootoosis provides a different point of view in his interview with John Lagimodiere, "Gordon Tootoosis – Leading the Way," *Eagle Feather News*, April 1999, www.sicc.sk.ca/faces/mtootgo.htm, visited 2002, now gone:

Q: "I saw you at the National Aboriginal Achievement Awards and you didn't have a moment of peace. How do you deal with the crowds?"
A: "It is very difficult. I have to spend time alone and prepare for it like I do for work. It needs a lot of energy and focus and I can't think about myself for that time. Some people are jerks. Two fellows came up to me in the airport in Montreal and spoke French to me. When I didn't respond, they got ignorant. They saw North of 60 with French dubbed in so they assumed I was bilingual. Finally, a bilingual guy came and cleared up the situation, but people expect you to take time for them."

32 Keeper herself became very confident and more comfortable with her fame. She certainly looked like she was having fun in a publicity shot for the Geminis in 1997 that showed her in a glamorous sheathe and velvet jacket, wearing a Mountie hat and leaning on her co-host Paul Gross, the Mountie from *Due South*, under the headline "In case the Geminis get out of hand we called in the Mounties."

33 The conference on another politically charged subject, English Canada without Quebec, was held in May 1994, a time when it looked like Canada could lose the 1995 Quebec referendum. Only invited participants attended. They discussed draft papers that had already been circulated among them. The rewritten papers became *Beyond Quebec: Taking Stock of Canada*, edited by Kenneth McRoberts (1995). Relevant to this book are the chapters by Alfred Young Man, "Native Arts in Canada: The State, Academia and the Cultural Establishment," 218–48; and by Frances Abele, "Various Matters of Nationhood: Aboriginal Peoples and 'Canada outside Quebec,'" 297–312.

34 www.nof60.com/backgrounder.html, visited 22 November 1996, no longer on the web.

35 One of the many problems of the standard ratings systems is that they do not count viewers who time-shift using videotape or DVD. These systems also stop at the border. The television signals do not.

36 Patty Winter reports that "North of 60's six seasons garnered nearly 50 Gemini nominations and five awards. The follow-up movies have also received several Gemini nominations." For example, Gemini nominees for the 1995 season, according to *Playback* ("Special Report: Gemini Nominees," 12 February 1996), include Tom Jackson for continuing male leading dramatic role, Tina Keeper for continuing female lead, Tantoo Cardinal and August Schellenberg for best performances in guest roles, the five producers, composer Tim McCauley, and Dakota House and Lubomir Mykytiuk for actors in supporting roles. www.playbackmag.com/articles/magazine/19960212/5034.html, accessed October 2005, no longer there.

37 Morriseau makes a nice point when he says that her "full, throaty laugh signifies that the actress is at a place that Michelle hopes to reach ... two sides

of the mirror, connected but untouchable" (22). "Lauterman said she has 'it' star quality. 'Of course it doesn't hurt that she is a beautiful woman, tall, slim and with great cheekbones'" (24). In my opinion, and fortunately for the dramatic needs of the series, that beauty often disappears behind shapeless clothes, tightly confined hair, and a guarded expression. In the early seasons, when Michelle relaxes into a smile, it is a revelation.

38 On Bravo, co-produced with APTN, and directed by Susan Cardinal. Stacy Da Silva and Nathaniel Arcand both said that the show helped them become actors.

CHAPTER TWELVE

1 The details of the jobs to be done in television drama, from the major techni-cians to the head of TV drama up to the end of the run, are given in Miller 1996, chaps 1–6. The basic responsibilities are the same for independent pro-ductions with CBC input.

2 These lists are extrapolated from Patty Winter's website (www.wintertime.com/OH/Nof60/nof60guide.txt), with permission, with my observations (asterisks signify responsibility for more than one episode).

The writers for each season were as follows:

Season 1 (1992–93): Creators and producers Wayne Grigsby and Barbara Samuels; Rebecca Schechter;* Charles Lazer; David Barlow,* story editor; David Young; Jean Stawarz; Michael Mercer; Jordan Wheeler,* also a story editor; Drew Hayden Taylor; and Peter Lauterman,* who became a producer as well.

Season 2 (1993–94): New writers were Andrew Wreggitt;* Conni Massing; Rob Forsyth;* Arthur Samuels (who wrote the pilot for *King of Kensington*); Hart Hanson,* also a story editor; Thomas King; and Stuart Margolin.

Season 3 (1994–95): The only new writer was Stacy Kaser.*

Season 4 (1995–96): This season was written almost exclusively by previous writers, except for Andrew Rai Berzins.

Season 5 (1996–97): Katherine Schlemmer was added.

Season 6 (fall 1997, as previously explained, an add-on): New writers were Tony di Franco, who wrote two; and Cheryl Foggo, Drew Birch, and Tim Southam, who wrote one each.

Directors included Stuart Margolin,* Anne Wheeler, George Bloomfield, Stacey Stewart Curtis,* Eleanore Lindo,* Randy Bradshaw, Tom W. Peacocke,* Gerard Ciccoritti, Joseph Scanlan, Sturla Gunnarsson, Bruce Pittman, Richard Lewis,* Gil Cardinal* (the only First Nations or Metis director, he arrived in season 3 and directed several episodes), Brad Turner,* Joanna McIntyre, Alan

Simmonds,* Ken Jubenvill,* Jeff Woolnough,* Jeremy Podeswa, Scott Summersgill,* and David Warry-Smith.

3 Cole (2002) quotes Tom Jackson as saying that the series was often shot in the dead of winter and at high elevations: "What you got out of people under those conditions was something beyond professionalism" (227).

4 http://nativecelebs.com/film9.htm, accessed 7 June 2007.

5 One could also point to Gibson's Landing, Spirit Bay, and the Kidiabanassee Rez for other examples.

6 A medevac (medical evacuation) involves flying a sick person out by helicopter in a medical emergency – if a helicopter is available and the weather cooperates.

7 Miggs Morris, in *Return to the Drum* (2000), says that for women in particular craft-making is declining because there is little money in it and the younger women do not want to learn the techniques (187).

8 It is not always evident who the key person in an ensemble show will be or even if there is one. *M*A*S*H* required Hawkeye. *All in the Family* did not succeed without Edith. However, *Law and Order* changed protagonists several times, as did *E.R.* It is not necessarily planned who the pivotal figure will be, but the issue is part of the show's chemistry, which develops over some years.

9 Perhaps Canadians find *Dudley Do Right* and *Due South* funny in a different way from viewers abroad because they know something about the real RCMP. *Due South* picks up on the paradoxes. Frazer seldom takes his gun out of his holster while trying "to be helpful" to the Chicago police. In the very different context of the Mayerthorpe tragedy, where four young officers were gunned down, during the background interviews, a retired twenty-seven-year RCMP veteran confirmed that they seldom draw their guns.

10 From notes made during a rerun, broadcast 25 December 1998.

11 Yellowknife, Denendeh, NWT: Dene Nation. This is a book of photographs by René Fumoleau celebrating the fifteenth anniversary of the Indian Brotherhood. www.antiqbook.com/boox/grn/029038.shtml, accessed 2 November 2007.

12 Elijah Harper stopped the Meech Lake Constitutional Accord in its tracks in the Manitoba legislature in 1990, a few years before this episode, because the accord did not acknowledge First Nations among Canada's founding nations.

13 Ovide Mercredi was at that time grand chief of the Assembly of First Nations.

14 Since the CRTC hearings in 1973, which I attended, people in the North have worried about the impact of satellite television, satellite transmissions, which brought the CBC to the North then, and more recently satellite reception of hundreds of channels. It is not just portrayals of southern Canada that shape the views of those who live there, it is the tide of images from New York and Los Angeles that flood the satellites and meld with images

of the rest of Canada. We cannot go back, but the implications were clear more than thirty years ago.

15  www.cherryamespage.com, accessed 7 June 2007.The twenty-seven Cherry Ames books, which had a wide international audience among young teenaged girls, went out of print in 1978, but Harlequin romances and other nurse books listed on the site have filled the gap. Four Cherry Ames books are back in print.

16  Morris (2000) talks about how it is still difficult to train enough teachers to fill the need and then to recruit Dene teachers for the small isolated communities of the North (192). Given the eight languages, materials have to come from the community as well as from Yellowknife. After spending years back down south Morris returned in 1995 to a hugely changed environment, she found that there was now much more culturally specific material but that the dropout rate was still much too high (193). Parents do not spend enough time with their children. Often, says Jimmy Tutcho, instead of teaching by showing or "teaching our values with stories … [they] either just yell at them or give in to their wants" (195), behaviour not apparent on *North of 60*.

17  Ibid. In Morris's view, the prophets, holy men, and preachers like Naedzo and the Oblate missionaries got along quite well, from the 1950s to the 1970s (219, cf. Cruikshank 1997). Elsie and the Oblate father also get along. Morris cites Charlie Neyelle, who is a lay reader and preacher in the Catholic church in Deline (there is no permanent priest now) and highly regarded throughout the Denendeh for spiritual healing and his songs. *Ik'o*, or medicine power, is also still highly regarded, but it is not practised openly for healing or for success in hunting (220).

18  Ibid. "Ehtsi" means grandmother (41).

19  Mykytiuk won a Gemini for episode 49, "Refugees," a somewhat comic episode about Gerry's attempts to live in a trailer owned by the band. Patty Winter's website has a complete list of the forty-eight Gemini nominations and the five wins for the series. www.wintertime.com/OH/Nof60/ nof60awards.html.

CHAPTER THIRTEEN

1  Bridget Bardot's cleavage on the icefields of Newfoundland may have also helped the cause in the early 1970s. In the North more humane traps were proposed and eventually accepted, but the billboards and magazine ads against wearing fur continue. In March 2007 people from the North in traditional fur clothing confronted EU delegates in Brussels, asking why seal products were to be banned when no one addressed the conditions on France's veal farms.

2 After all, the industry started with the enduring fashion of furs for the wealthy, followed by beaver felt hats in the 1700s. Beaver became very scarce in some provinces. When buffalo robes were used for sleighs and coats, and buffalo bones for fertilizer, the buffalo was nearly hunted to extinction. For good or ill, the fact is that the fur trade changed the history of North America for all who first lived here.

3 Gerald R. McMaster (1995): "I have argued for a view of contemporary (Native) artists as not just carriers but innovators of culture, living 'betwixt and between' several cultures and communities" (87).

4 Ibid., 80–1. It is a place of heteroglossia, of displacement and disruption, where writers (and painters) can be "smugglers, *coyotes* or tricksters" (82).

5 www.whetung.com/chee.html, visited 27 March 2007.

6 The famous Ojibway artist went through a period where he was living on the streets and trading paintings and drawings for money or liquor. There are allusions to his work in *Spirit Bay*; see chapter 8.

7 The CBC's *The National*, on 21 April 2005, showed a short documentary about Cree being taught at the elementary school level off-reserve. As a Cree speaker said, "[L]anguage is the cornerstone of the culture."

8 Ironically, history records that Mackenzie (1764–1820) never acknowledged, in his journals, the help he received from First Nations people. Note that Metis historian Olive Dickason (1992) scarcely mentions him except to point out that he followed Amerindian trading routes from the Peace River to the Pacific. Her story of this period recounts how the various First Nations expanded the fur trade. It may be going too far to detect dramatic irony in Michelle's version of historical events, but this first edition of Dickason was available for researchers in seasons 2–6. See also the version of the history of Fort Liard that is given on the Fort Liard website: www.fortliard.com/history.htm, accessed 12 July 2005.

9 Blondin 1997, x.

10 Tina Keeper, exhausted, had asked for some relief from being the centre of most episodes. This episode is one where she was given a break.

11 The whole interview can be found at www.wintertime.com/OH/Nof60/ Interviews/andrew.html, quoted with permission.

12 Tina Keeper is quoted in Morriseau 1997: "'The story just sent me reeling. I was a mess. I remember filming a scene by the gravesite and the stage direction is 'Michelle's face is emotionless.' I thought that's easy, no lines, just stare into space but I am standing beside this phony grave in a phony graveyard and I'm thinking 'this really happens, people really lose their children, and then it just goes on and on' and it can take you to some really dark places. I'm not the kind of actor that can get away from that'" (25).

13 Too often on this show, life imitates art. The issue of suicide among teenagers is briefly raised in this episode. Rosemary talks to Brian about three people who hanged themselves in Hay River, one of them an assistant at her daycare centre. Mervin Good Eagle, who played Joey Smallboat, later committed suicide. The *North of 60* home page for that season, which was live when I made notes, carried a tribute to his natural dancing and athletic skills and told fans that his family and colleagues prepared one last meal for him in the cafeteria on set. "They passed an eagle feather from hand to hand, telling stories about the actor who always grinned and yet felt too sad to carry on. Dakota House and the first assistant director, put on hip waders and carried the plate of food through the creek that was filmed so often during Mr. Good Eagle's five years as Joey. They walked up the hill on the other side and buried the plate near a tree. And as Native drums beat out a searing rhythm, they all prayed for the spirit of the man whose pain never showed on his face." Note that the viewer had to be interested enough to find the web page to learn this. Thus, the viewer likely had to be a fan, part of the *North of 60* family, in order to find out about and to share, even at second hand, in this ritual.

14 AFN national chief Phil Fontaine, a survivor of sexual abuse in residential school, is quoted as follows: "Other residential schools class actions have been certified or are making their way through the courts, but the AFN class provides for a more comprehensive process, as it deals with loss of language and culture and not only specific acts of physical or sexual abuse, and also includes truth and reconciliation mechanisms and other collective remedies that will benefit all First Nations … The Accord [which set up the process 'to resolve the legacy of the schools' and was signed with the federal government on 30 May 2005] has provided a political vehicle to move forward, but a legal vehicle is required to finalize the process with the AFN in a central and representative role, which this action now provides." He also pledged to work with the mediator Mr Justice Frank Iacobucci. The media had set the stage in April 2005, when they reported that the millions in the fund set aside for swift resolution of claims by residential school survivors has been spent on the bureaucracy and lawyers, with very little going to the survivors (www.afn.ca/article.asp?id=1632, dated 3 August 2005, visited 27 March 2007). The impact of residential schools was a thread that ran through the 2007 Fourteenth Annual Aboriginal Achievement Awards, 31 March 2007.

15 The first line of the song is "They are not departed or gone." Rebecca Schechter was the story editor for the series at that time, with the very experienced producer/writer David Barlow serving as executive story editor that first year. Jordan Wheeler, who started as associate story editor, eventually took over as story editor.

16 Pelly attended Lebret Residential School in Saskatchewan. She speaks to schoolchildren, and when they ask her why she left school in grade 10 at the age of sixteen, she says, "If you went to the school I went to, you wouldn't finish school either!" However, two of her daughters did finish (from an interview at www.wintertime.com/OH/Nof60/Interviews/wilma3.html). Mr Carlisle, a Tlingit sculptor and dancer, talked to me about growing up in a residential school "without any language, without any art," the latter something that had not occurred to me. The Northwest Coast First Nations are some of the finest artists in the world, whose cultures included carvings of everyday objects such as bowls, fishhooks, decorated woven hats and baskets, painted and carved house poles. Growing up without those representations of the natural and supernatural world that permeates those cultures would be like losing a language of thought and feeling. He also told me that when the native language is taught in school without it being spoken at home, "the air takes it" (August 2004, quoted with permission).

17 See Miller 2001 and Miller, "Haunting Public Discourse" (forthcoming).

18 See Pauline Dempsey's "Recollections of Life at a Residential School," *Windspeaker*, May 1995; and Elizabeth Furniss, *Victims of Benevolence* (1995). Furniss says in her introduction that the point of view is hers, not the Cariboo Tribal Council's, but that the research was initially undertaken at the council's request, with its help, and was reported to the council and the book written for its readers.

19 See Brian Maracle's *Crazy Water* (1993), in which he quotes "Christine" (Nisga'a): "'It seems like there's more and more people in our family willing to look at the awful things that happened in our family: residential school, child abuse, sexual abuse, all that stuff. I know that for me, personal recovery has brought these things out into the open … my brothers and I actually sit and talk and have a decent conversation.

   "'Now I am very proud to be native and I am even *more proud* to be a native woman … I don't *tell* people I'm proud to be a native woman, I *act* the way I think a proud native woman should act'" (263). Hers is one of many voices in this wrenchingly honest, yet hopeful book.

20 See Devon Babin, "Help from Above: How Aboriginal Leaders Can Promote Healing in Native Communities," *This Magazine*, May/June 2005, 8, in which leaders in Nunavut talk about how native leaders must talk about sexual and other abuse in residential schools instead of avoiding the issue.

21 The NWT Dene website www.cancom.net/~dehchofn/ confirmed this in an email to me when I inquired about the source of the word.

22 See also Basil Johnston, *Indian School Days* (1988); J.R. Miller, *Shingwauk's Vision* (1996); and Johnston's "Owen Glendower, Hotspur and Canadian

Indian Policy" (1991), 323–52; Furniss 1995; Tomson Highway, *The Kiss of the Fur Queen* (Toronto: Doubleday Canada, 1998); and Cheryl Patten "Programs on Residential Schools Elicit Strong Viewer Response," *Windspeaker*, March 2001. The "Residential Schools: Moving beyond Survival" programs were made by Newsworld, APTN, and VISION and were shown within an eight-day period.

23 This is some years before the churches and the parishes were sued, long before the government acknowledged that there was a problem to be addressed, and well before some of the churches apologized. The last federally run residential school closed in Saskatchewan in 1996. A backgrounder from Indian and Northern Affairs Canada appears at www.ainc-inac.gc.ca/gs/schl_e.html, accessed 7 June 2007.

24 Rob Forsyth won a Gemini for episode 70, "The Watchers," which I did not find the equal to this one.

25 These cultural links have existed from pre-contact times, when the ancestral group split into two.

26 I will share with the reader a touch of synchronicity. The *National Post* reported on 18 March 2002, the day I began working on this section, that Canada's first AIDS patient was identified "20 years ago this month." There were over 12,000 aids-attributed deaths in Canada to that date.

27 Perhaps a reference to René Highway's untimely death of AIDS. Like his brother Tomson Highway, he was a survivor of residential school and a very gifted dancer, who played Nanabush in the original production of *The Rez Sisters*.

28 Acoose 1995, 29.

29 Gerald R. McMaster (1995, 74–90) talks about the liminality of the artist, the border zone between urban and rez tradition and innovation, between social norms and their critique, which artists inhabit.

30 In the late 1990s *Windspeaker* carried a regular column by a man with AIDS who wrote about his attempt to educate First Nations all over the country, the ignorance he met, and the support he received.

31 See the section "Homosexuality, the 'Other,' and Being Indian," in an online 2002 interview called "Hold Me Closer, Fancy Dancer: A Conversation with Sherman Alexie" by Aileo Weinmann, at www.filmcritic.com/misc/emporium.nsf/0/1adbe1e88680513188256c340015b7b9?OpenDocument, accessed 27 March 2007.

32 It was shown before Christmas, on 18 December 1997, a time when viewing numbers sag as the audience turns to other holiday activities.

33 *Dene Kede Education: A Dene Perspective*, curriculum document: "Fire is a living force which has declared that all men will live and survive with it till the end of time. To show our respect to the gift of life, we pay the fire." www.ece.

gov.nt.ca/Divisions/kindergarten_g12/curriculum/Dene%20Kede%20
Curriculum%20Document/Spiritual/Fire.htm, accessed 7 June 2007.

34 Kulchyski, McCaskill, and Newhouse 1999, 368.

35 Attentive viewers might remember that Nathan, when he was huddled in terror on the top of the cabin to which he had been banished, saw Albert as wolverine about to attack. Albert climbs onto the roof even as his son aims his rifle at him, takes the weapon away from him quite gently, and brings him into town. Whittaker's (1991) description of a wolverine points out that the animal is rarely found south of 60, is solitary, uses terrain that can be a thousand square miles, is sparsely distributed, and is a glutton that will eat anything and can drive a cougar or bear from its kill. In Griffiths and Campbell's play *The Book of Jessica* (1989), Wolverine is the last spirit animal that the white character, Jessica, can incorporate into her life, embodying the pure spirit of survival in its most basic and ruthless form.

36 *King Lear* (conflated text) 5.3.238.

### CHAPTER FOURTEEN

1 Goulet records the split among the Dene on the question of whether or not there should be a pipeline. In 1991 the Sahtu, Dogrib, and Gwich'in made separate deals, and in 1993 they declared they were no longer Dene (171). The Deh Cho, who include the fictional Lynx River band, were the outstanding holdouts of the 1990s (www.cancom.net/~dehchofn/member.htm, visited 25 October 2005, no longer online). In the series *Hay River*, (Fort) Providence and (Fort) Simpson are referred to by their English names.

2 The book (Holmes 1989) has a full map of Dene communities, beautiful photographs, and gently ironic and funny pen-and-ink illustrations by Gloria Miller (such as the one on page 15 that shows a Dene offering a trader "July 1789 specials on canoe repair." Captions are in English and various Dene languages.

3 Brody states in a footnote that Athapaskans have borrowed the phrase *marsai* from the French *merci* for thank you (153). When contacted, the people at the Deh Cho website replied that the word has always been Dene.

4 Ross also discusses band elections as places where family rivalries play themselves out (156).

5 The curriculum document titled *Dene Kede Education: A Dene Perspective* amplifies the point in the section under the heading "Primary Objective": "The students should experience the Living Force in its concrete and powerful form so that they can come to understand and accept the force. If the students are involved in the rituals which acknowledge the Living Force, they will

come to see the land, water and air differently. They will become more connected to the land and have a stronger commitment to it. They will come to respect the land and to protect it from pollution. The experiences for the Living Force unit should be integrated into the activities which take place on the land in other thematic units." www.ece.gov.nt.ca/Divisions/kindergarten _g12/curriculum/Dene%20Kede%20Curriculum%20Document/Spiritual/ Living_Force.htm, accessed 20 November 2005.

6 Also quoted in Morton 2003.

7 Ed Struzik, "Changing Courses," *Canadian Geographic* (special edition, "The New N.W.T") 122, no. 5 (September/October 2002). This edition includes wonderful photographs of the Deh Cho and includes a timeline. Struzik reports that the Fort Liard band (the total population of the village is 546), which is self-identified with Lynx River, "has assets that include an airline and helicopter company, part ownership in a drilling operation ... does seismic cutting, builds roads, feeds up to 1,500 workers in the oil and gas explorations camps, supplies fuel and rents out equipment" (51), all of which are varied sources of employment and income that Peter Kenidi might have only dreamed about ten years earlier. Struzik also reports his conversations with the elders still living on the land, who see the medicines of their people and even the ways of the Dene disappearing.

8 www.cancom.net/~dehchofn/dehchofn.htm, visited 21 November 2005, posted since 2002, no longer there. But see www.dehchofirstnations.com/ home.htm, accessed 3 April 2007, the home page of the Deh Cho First Nations, which begins: "Strong, proud, happy people through self-government and sustainable economic development while maintaining the integrity of the land and Dene/Metis Traditions."

9 See Asch 1988 for glimpses of the world of Elsie and Joe in the early days of people being brought in off the land to settlements around a school. This was a community where Euro-Canadians lived separately, where the drum dance was used in an attempt to re-establish harmony among the disparate families, where knowledge about all the skills needed in the bush for survival came mostly from observation and practice, not from verbal teachings, where dog teams were still vital, where food was communal (28), and where people who had only met for special occasions when they lived on the land now lived side by side, creating many new tensions (35).

10 The *National Post*, which is no champion of the political aspirations and demands of many First Nations, is the unlikely source of another picture of Dene life and issues in the last ten years and confirms some of the detail on *North of 60*. In its Business supplement, January 2002, Mark Anderson's article (which

was sensationally headlined "Brinkmanship and Betrayal") provided a detailed portrait of the Deh Cho. The article includes, among those people described, a tiny traditionalist band that lives from hunting, trapping, and fishing as well as from other gifts from the land, a band that lets the prospectors and problems from southern Canada into their town and their lives, and a progressive/ conservative band that tries to balance the values of the ancient culture with the needs of the present and the hopes (and fears) for the future, with questions and debates analogous to those in the series and the movies.

11 Done by Erin Research, George Spears, and Kasia Seydegart. The report was made available to me thanks to Monique Coupal, director of equitable portrayal in programming, CBC, with permission to quote it.

12 "Even with this turnover [of drama series and specials], there is a remarkable degree of stability in the social reality portrayed in the three years [since 1989]" (27). Looking strictly at the numbers of women who appeared onscreen, the study gives the percentages as follows with punctuation added for clarity: "Percentage of women portrayed from 7 p.m. to 11 p.m. in 1981 – 37 %, in 1983 – 42%, in 1987 – 39%, in 1989 – 40%; and from 7 p.m. to 12 midnight [note the extra hour] in 1992 – 39%." CTV's figures for 1984 are reported as 35% and for 1988, 34%. "The overrepresentation of males occurs almost entirely in the 35–64 ... categories. The representation of women peaks at the ages 25–34" (30).

13 Some of the key moments in the episode, the most violent ones, do not have music, making it far more intense and intimate. In a few of the more emotional scenes, however, music can be heard.

14 30 July 2004. Quoted with permission.

15 www.ece.gov.nt.ca/Divisions/kindergarten_g12/curriculum/Dene%20Kede %20Curriculum%20Document/ Spiritual/Spiritual_Power.htm, accessed 3 April 2007. Dene students from kindergarten to grade 4 are expected to learn this in the schools where the curriculum is adopted.

16 It should be remembered that it was forbidden to portray Jesus Christ in the theatre of the nineteenth and early twentieth centuries. As late as the films of the early 1950s, such as *The Robe* and *Ben Hur,* Christ either appeared off-camera or was shown from the back. Dorothy L. Sayers created a scandal in Britain when she emphasized the humanity of Jesus in *The Man Born to Be King* (1943), one of a series of radio plays written for the BBC in the early 1940s.

17 See also Clifford 1988, 319.

18 James Reaney, *Colours in the Dark* (Vancouver: Talonbooks, 1969), 54ff. It is much easier to show the rich transformations and potential interrelationships of objects and verbal metaphors in the live theatre than it is in a medium like television. But sometimes television comes close.

19 One can be "born to be poor" (13), i.e., to have no medicine power. Mind control is also one of the attributes of the medicine people. Why is there less medicine power now? Blondin concludes: "The Creator saw the Dene no longer needed medicine and so it was taken away" (28).

20 See Susan Cardinal's documentary film *God's Explorers*, for a look at the Oblate history in NWT Dene territory, (broadcast on the History Channel, January 3 2002). In an interview before the film she said that when she asked about the residential school system one of them cried silently "as he talked about how the missionaries sacrificed themselves to help the native peoples, building schools and farms ... Over the next few years I would start to see how the Oblates changed the Dene but to be sure, how the Dene also changed them." See also http://www3.telus.net/public/kisa1/godsexplorers/interviews.htm #The%20Producers April 3, 2007. Senator Sibbeston, one of the consultants on *North of 60* from the start, said in the documentary about his experience of residential schools that "a lot of people have died. I'm still not totally healthy."

21 www.parl.gc.ca/information/library/PRBpubs/bp410-e.htm, accessed 13 June 2007.

22 www.asu.edu/clas/history/h-amindian/bibs/gay.html (accessed 3 April 2007) provides a concise bibliography of sources on the subject.

23 See Hogarth 2002. Hogarth sees docudrama as one part of a spectrum of documentary and discusses at some length the privileged position of documentary in our national discourse. I would trace Canadians' preference for including topical issues and attributing responsibility to the community further back, to the wildly popular *Wojeck* (1967–69), one of the first filmed series for adults made by the CBC. See also in Miller 1987 the early preference in Canadian television for docudrama as well as docudrama-flavoured series.

24 www.nytimes.com/2005/04/24/magazine/24TV.html, accessed 25 April 2004, no longer available. The article stirred up a lot of comment in the blogosphere and elsewhere, as a Google search revealed a few days later. See also Malcolm Gladwell's interesting response to the book in the *New Yorker*, 16 May 2005, at www.newyorker.com/critics/books/articles/050516crbo_books, visited 21 November 2005.

25 See also Alan McKee's article "What Is Television For?" (2003).

26 www.edgemont.tv, visited 3 April 2007. Commercial availability will determine what Canadian programming scholars will analyse (if they haven't been taping off-air study copies for twenty years) – not a good way to select material for study. The National Archives can provide samples from its holdings, but it does not have the resources that would allow it to give access to researchers of whole series or even whole seasons.

CHAPTER FIFTEEN

1 On the other hand, they find the character of Marilyn on *Northern Exposure* a generalized stoic Indian.

2 The 1930s film in which Jeannette MacDonald, who plays Rose Marie, the daughter of a local trapper, warbled to Nelson Eddy's Mountie while "Indians" in front of a set composed of totem poles and tipis danced on a giant drum in the unintentionally (?) funny number called "Totem Tom Tom."

3 From a memorial/biography written in 2002, "Wacoquaakmik, Anishinabe, Bear Clan" at www.ncct.on.ca/historyproject/htmlpages/rodney.html, still there 5 April 2007.

4 The executive producers and originators of *North of 60*, Barbara Samuels and Wayne Grigsby, went on from *North of 60*, while it was still in production, to do a fraught series called *Black Harbour*, which people on the East Coast also found rather gloomy. And yet the team had worked on *E.N.G.*, a series set in a TV newsroom that often had sardonic and sometimes slapstick humour.

5 Carlisle, a Tlingit sculptor and dancer, told me that when he saw *Toronto at Dreamer's Rock* twenty years earlier, it changed his life by giving him hope (interview 30 July 2004, quoted with permission).

6 Michael Valpy, a respected social affairs columnist for the *Globe and Mail* obviously agreed with Drew Hayden Taylor. Under a headline "Must Our Serious TV Dramas Be Freakishly Glum?" (19 December 1995), he lumps together *Street Legal* (which focuses on topical issues as well as offering steamy sex), *Side Effects* (a series about the doctors and clients at a walk-in clinic), and *North of 60* as "nicely acted, visually familiar entertainments, but not credible reflections of Canadian life … It must strike you as odd, as it strikes me, that in a country whose primary mythology is peace, order and good government our heavy-hitting television drama is fixated on mayhem, deviance and what … Globe arts writer Liam Lacey, in a conversation yesterday, termed 'the freakishly glum.' I don't understand how these television dramas pull us together as Canadians, mirror the social environment in which we live [he ignores, for example, *Street Legal*'s story arc about First Nations land claims and timber rights in Northern Ontario], enlighten us as to the workings of our institutions or our prevailing mythologies or in any way save us from increasingly being tourists in our own culture." Negative myths from the 1960s about Canadian television, from its early production values to its tone and subject matter, still persist.

7 See *Education Is Our Right* in *Toronto at Dreamer's Rock/Education Is Our Right* (1990); *Someday* (1993); *Only Drunks and Children Tell the Truth* (1998); *The Baby Blues* (1999), *Alternatives* (2000), *The Buz'gem Blues* (2002), *400 Kilometres* (2005),

*In a World Created by a Drunken God* (2006), and Taylor's webpage www. drewhaydentaylor.com/index.html, accessed 17 June 2007.

8 Agnes Grant (1995), writing about the theatre, not television, comments: "Native people cannot be portrayed accurately without humour and laughter. Native humour is hearty and spontaneous and is often directed at misfortune turned into a joke" (112). She objects to the characterization of all native humour as dark and concludes that "[n]on-natives need to see these plays in the company of native audiences in order to understand and appreciate the humour" (113). The question raised by programs like APTN's *Buffalo Tracks* is whether too much culturally specific humour works for mainstream television. Yet for several years Thomas King's sharp humour on *Dead Dog Café* and later on *Dead Dog in the City* (2005–06) was enjoyed by the cross-section of Canadians (and some Americans) who listened to CBC morning radio. It offered a wide range of humour.

9 The "sweeps" happen four times a year – November, February, May, and July. Nielsen ratings for these periods set the advertising rates for the next quarter.

10 This was also the slot reserved for the arts. Beginning in the 1950s, the CBC had a place in the schedule reserved for ballet, opera, theatre, jazz, or contemporary dance. In April 2007 this slot – which allowed viewers who do not live in big cities to discover or enjoy even a short season of such work – disappeared.

11 And in the last two weeks of October 2005, as attested in headlines across the country, undrinkable and dangerous water forced an evacuation of Kashechewan (population 1,900). The story resonated all over Ontario, which had had its own unconscionable and unnecessary water crisis in Walkerton. That one had been addressed as soon as the citizens fell ill. Kashechewan's problems persisted and were well known to the province and the federal government for years.

12 Even in the later 1960s when *Wojeck* was exported to British television, some reviewers found John Vernon not handsome enough for a male lead.

13 www.northof60.net/pages/series_backgrounder.html, 5 April 2007.

14 www.native-net.org/archive/nl/, 5 April 2007.

15 NativeWeb began its existence in May of 1994 as an outgrowth of Trujillo's NA-TIVENET listserv, which "began as one of the first global listservs on the Internet." The whole history of these lists up to 2002 (when it was posted to that site) is available at www.nativeweb.org/info/paper.php, accessed 12 November 2007.

16 www.native-net.org/archive/nc/, 5 April 2007.

17 30 July 2004, quoted with permission.

18 www.bathurstinletlodge.com/02_history.htm (accessed 17 June 2007) gives its history. The emphasis for visitors is on education. I took notes on those conversations within a few hours – and have permission to use them.

CONCLUSION

1 www.westland.net/expo67/map-docs/canada.htm accessed 12 November 2007. I remember the sculptures as made of various metals.

2 A professor of Canadian history, Nelles wears his considerable learning lightly in this book. Some of his conclusions are also worth noting in the context. He points out that "[n]ative resistance and insistence upon their rights" has prevailed over assimilationist policies. Nelles writes: "Justice for Native Peoples, based on land claims, human rights, and a broader interpretation of treaties, reposed one of Canada's long-standing questions in a new and compelling form. How could indigenous peoples fully share in Canadian prosperity and a citizenship [note that Canadian citizenship is in itself contentious among some First Nations] while maintaining a separate, self-determining identity?"

3 See www.backtothesugarcamp.com/N.htm for her background. It is worth noting progress in more than one area. The chaplain was female.

4 Fortunately, the kinescopes in the National Archives include commercials made in some of the broadcasts. In those days, some broadcasts did not have sponsors. See Miller 1987, *passim*.

5 This is copied word for word from a repeated viewing of the kine.

6 38–39 ELIZABETH II Chapter 11 (www.crtc.gc.ca/eng/LEGAL/BROAD.HTM, 9 April 2007).

7 The history of the CBC's internal and commissioned audience research is to be found in Eamon 1994.

8 Little progress has been made, despite the fact that changes to expedite the settlement of the dozens of land claims across Canada were promised in the fall of 2007. The Six Nations' claims are based on land grants to Joseph Brant and the Six Nations allies of the British loyalists who lost everything in the American Revolution.

9 www3.cbc.ca/sections/newitem_redux.asp?ID=4367, accessed 13 November 2007.

10 Lorne Cardinal has also hosted APTN's variety/comedy program *Buffalo Tracks* and has a recurring role in *renegadepress.com*.

# Bibliography

Abel, Kerry. *Drum Songs: Glimpses of Dene History.* Montreal and Kingston: McGill-Queen's University Press, 1993.

Abelman, Robert. *Reaching a Critical Mass: A Critical Analysis of Television Entertainment.* Mahwah, NJ: Laurence Erlbaum Associates Publishers, 1998.

Alia, Valerie. *Un/covering the North: News, Media and Aboriginal People.* Vancouver: University of British Columbia Press, 1999.

Allen, Robert C. *Speaking of Soap Opera.* Chapel Hill: University of North Carolina Press, 1985.

Allor, Martin, Daniel Juteau, and John Shepherd. "Contingencies of Culture: The Space of Culture in Canada and Québec." *Australian Key Centre for Cultural and Media Policy* 6, no. 1 (2000), www.gu.edu.au/centre/cmp/6_1_03.html.

Ames, Michael. *Cannibal Tours and Glass Boxes: The Anthropology of Museums.* Vancouver: University of British Columbia Press, 1992.

Anderson, Steve. "History TV and Popular Memory." In *Television Histories: Shaping Collective Memory in the Media Age,* edited by Gary R. Edgerton and Peter C. Rollins. Lexington: University Press of Kentucky, 2001.

Ang, Ien, "Melodramatic Identifications: Television Fiction and Women's Fantasy." In *Feminist Television Criticism: A Reader,* edited by Charlotte Brunsdon, Julie Acci, and Lynn Spiegel. Oxford, UK: Clarendon Press, 1997.

Angus, Ian. *A Border Within: National Identity, Cultural Plurality, and Wilderness.* Montreal and Kingston: McGill-Queen's University Press, 1997.

Asch, Michael. "Kinship and the Drum Dance in a Northern Dene Community." In *The Circumpolar Research Series.* N.p.: Boreal Institute for Northern Studies and Academic Printing and Publishing, 1988.

– with Robert Wishart. "The Slavey Indians: The Relevance of Ethnohistory to Development." In *Native Peoples: The Canadian Experience,* edited by R. Bruce Morrison and C. Roderick Wilson. 3rd ed. Don Mills, ON: Oxford University Press, 2004.

Atwood, Margaret. *The Journals of Susanna Moodie.* Toronto: Oxford University Press, 1970.

– *Survival: A Thematic Guide to Canadian Literature.* Toronto: Anansi, 1972.

– "A Double-Bladed Knife: Subversive Laughter in Two Stories by Thomas King." In *Native Writers and Canadian Writing,* edited by W.H New. Special issue of *Canadian Literature.* Vancouver: University of British Columbia Press, 1990.

– "If you can't say anything nice, don't say anything at all." In *Dropped Threads: What We Aren't Told,* edited by Carol Shields and Marjorie Anderson. Toronto: Vintage Canada, 2001.

Baltruschat, Doris. "Television and Canada's Women's Aboriginal Communities: Seeking Opportunities through Traditional Storytelling and Digital Technologies." *Canadian Journal of Communication* 29 (2004).

Banarjee, Subhabrata Bobby, and Goldie Osuri. "Whiting Out Aboriginality in Making News and Making History." *Media, Culture and Society* 22 (2002).

Beard, Wm, and Jerry White, eds. *North of Everything: English-Canadian Cinema.* Edmonton: University of Alberta Press, 2002.

Belenky, Mary Field, Blythe McVicker Clinchy, Nancy Rule Goldberger, and Jill Mattuck Tarule, eds. *Women's Ways of Knowing: The Development of Self, Mind and Voice.* New York: Basic Books, 1986.

Bhabi, Homi K. "Cultures In-between." In *Questions of Cultural Identity,* edited by Stuart Hall and Paul Du Gay. London: Sage Publications, 1996.

Blackman, Margaret B. *During My Time: Florence Edenshaw Davidson, a Haida Woman.* Vancouver: Douglas & McIntyre, 1982.

Boire, Gary, "Sucking Kumaras." In *Native Writers and Canadian Writing,* edited by W.H. New. Special issue of *Canadian Literature.* Vancouver: University of British Columbia Press, 1990.

Brand, Dionne. "Whose Gaze and Who Speaks for Whom." In *BrEad OuT of STone: Reflections on Sex, Recognitions, Race, Dreaming and Politics.* N.p: Vintage Canada, 1998.

Brandt, George, ed. *British Television Drama.* Cambridge: Cambridge University Press, 1982.

Bringhurst, Robert. *A Story Sharp as a Knife: The Classical Mythtellers and Their World.* Vancouver: Douglas & McIntyre, 1999.

Brodsky, Anne Trueblood, ed. *Stones, Bones and Skin: Ritual and Shamanic Art.* 30th anniversary issue of *artscanada,* nos 184, 185, 186, 187 (December 1973/January 1974).

Brody, Hugh. *The Living Arctic: Hunters and Trappers of the Canadian North.* Vancouver: Douglas & McIntyre, 1987.

Brown, Jennifer H., and Robert Brightman, eds. *"The Orders of the Dreamed"; George Nelson on Cree and Northern Ojibwa Religion and Myth, 1823.* Manitoba Studies in Native History series 3. Winnipeg: University of Manitoba Press, 1988.

Brown, Jennifer S.H., and C.R. Wilson. "The Northern Algonquians: A Regional Overview." In *Canada's Changing North*, edited by William C. Wonders. Rev. ed. Montreal and Kingston: McGill-Queen's University Press, 2003.

Brown, W.M. *The Queen's Bush: A Tale of the Early Days of Bruce County*. London: John Bale Sons and Danielson, 1932. Reprint, Owen Sound: Richardson, Bond and Wright, 1967.

Brunsdon, Charlotte. "Identity in Feminist Television Criticism." In *Feminist Television Criticism: A Reader*. Oxford, UK: Clarendon Press, 1997.

Brunsdon, Charlotte, Julie D'Acci, and Lynn Spiegel, eds. *Feminist Television Criticism: A Reader*. Oxford Television Studies series, edited by John Caughie and Charlotte Brunsdon. Oxford, UK: Clarendon Press, 1997.

Byers, Michele, ed. *Growing Up Degrassi: Television, Identity and Youth Cultures*. Toronto: Sumach Press, 2005.

*Camera Obscura*, nos 20 and 21 (May and September 1989–90). Bloomington: Indiana University Press: 1990.

Canada, House of Commons Standing Committee on Canadian Heritage. *Our Cultural Sovereignty: The Second Century of Canadian Broadcasting*. Ottawa: Communication Canada, June 2003, http://cmte.parl.gc.ca/cmte/committeepublication.aspx?sourceid=37522.

Carter, Elsie Hobart. *Christmas Candles: Plays for Boys and Girls*. New York: Henry Holt and Company, 1915.

Caughie, John. *Television Drama: Realism, Modernism and British Culture*. Oxford Television series, edited by John Caughie and Charlotte Brunsdon. Oxford: Oxford University Press, 2000.

"CBC Demographics from Social Trends on CBC Primetime Television 1977–1992: A Content Analysis Commissioned by the CBC." Erin Research, George Spears and Kasia Seydegart. Internal CBC document, 1992.

Chafe, J.W. *Canada: Your Country*. Toronto: Ryerson Press, 1950.

Chicago Cultural Studies Group. "Critical Multiculturalism." *Cultural Inquiry* 18 (spring 1992).

Clark, Catharine Anthony. *The Sun Horse*. Toronto: Macmillan Company of Canada, 1952.

– *The Golden Pine Cone*. Illustrated by Claire Bice. Toronto: Macmillan Company of Canada, 1950. A new edition by Harbour Publishing appeared in 1994.

Clifford, James. *The Predicament of Culture: Twentieth-Century Ethnography, Literature and Art*. Cambridge, MA: Harvard University Press, 1988.

Cole, Stephen. *Here's Looking at Us*. Toronto: McClelland & Stewart, 2002.

Connor, Ralph. *Glengarry Schooldays: Early Days in Glengarry*. Toronto: Westminster Co., 1902.

- *Corporal Cameron of the North West Mounted Police*: *A Tale of the Macleod Trail*. Toronto: Westminster Co., 1912.

Cooper, Amy Jo. *Dream Quest*: *Stories from Spirit Bay*. Willowdale, ON: Annick Press, 1987.

Cornell, George L. "The Imposition of Western Definitions of Literature on Indian Oral Traditions." In *The Native in Literature*, edited by Thomas King, Cheryl Calver, and Helen Hoy. Downsview: ECW Press, 1987.

Cruikshank, Julie. *The Social Life of Stories*: *Narrative and Knowledge in the Yukon Territory*. Vancouver: University of British Columbia Press, 1998.

Day, Richard J.F. *Multiculturalism and the History of Canadian Diversity*. Toronto: University of Toronto Press, 2000.

Demay, Joel, "Culture and Media Use in Saskatchewan's Indian Country." *Canadian Journal of Communication* 16, nos 3 and 4 (1991).

De Rosa, Maria. "Studio One: Of Storytellers and Stories." In *North of Everything*: *English-Canadian Cinema*, edited by Wm. Beard and Jerry White. Edmonton: University of Alberta Press, 2002.

Dick, Ernest J. *Guide to CBC Sources at the Public Archives 1936–1986*. Ottawa: Minister of Supply and Services, 1987.

Douglas, William. *Television Families: Is Something Wrong in Suburbia?* Lea's Communication series. Mahwah, NJ: Lawrence Erlbaum Associates Publishers, 2003.

Dymond, Greg, and Geoff Pevere. *Mondo Canuck*. Toronto: Prentice-Hall Canada, 1996.

Eamon, Ross. *Channels of Influence*: *CBC Audience Research and the Canadian Public*. Toronto: University of Toronto Press, 1994.

Edles, Laura. *Cultural Sociology in Practice*. Malden, MA: Blackwell Publishers, 2002.

Ellis, Scott. "Phantom Indians: Some Observations on Recent Cinema." *Border-Crossings*, fall 1992.

Fairfield, Charles. "Below the Hamelin Line: CKRZ and Aboriginal Cultural Survival." *Canadian Journal of Communications* 23 (1998).

Fee, Margery. "Romantic Nationalism and the Image of Native People in Contemporary English-Canadian Literature." In *The Native in Literature*, edited by Thomas King, Cheryl Calver, and Helen Hoy. Downsview, ON: ECW Press, 1987.

Feldman, Seth. Foreword to *North of Everything: English-Canadian Cinema*, edited by Wm Beard and Jerry White. Edmonton: University of Alberta Press, 2002.

*The Fifth Book of Reading Lessons*. "Entered" (1867) by "Reverend Egerton Ryerson, LL.D, Chief Superintendent of Education for Ontario, in the Office of the Registrar of the Province of Canada." Canadian Series of School Books. Toronto: James Campbell and Son, 1868.

Fiske, John. *Television Culture*. London: Methuen, 1987.

– "The Cultural Economy of Fandom." In *The Adoring Audience: Fan Culture and Popular Media*, edited by Lisa A. Lewis. London: Routledge, 1992.

– "Technostruggles." In *Media Matters: Everyday Culture and Political Change*. Minneapolis: University of Minnesota Press, 1994.

Francis, Daniel. *Imaginary Indians: Image of the Indian in Canadian Culture*. Vancouver: Arsenal Pulp Press, 1992.

Fraser, Fil. "The Participation of Aboriginal and Other Cultural Minorities in Cultural Development." *Canadian Journal of Communication* 19 (1994).

Friar, Ralph E., and Natasha A. Friar, *The Only Good Indian ... The Hollywood Gospel*. New York: Drama Book Specialists, 1972.

Frideres, Jim. *Native Peoples in Canada: Contemporary Conflicts*. 3rd ed. Scarborough, ON: Prentice-Hall Canada, 1988.

– "Native Canadian Deviance and the Social Control of Race." In *Social Control in Canada: A Reader of the Social Construction of Deviance*, edited by Bernard Schissel and Linda Mahood. Toronto: Oxford University Press, 1996.

Frye, Northrop. *The Bush Garden: Essays in the Canadian Imagination*. Toronto: Anansi, 1971.

Furniss, Elizabeth. *Victims of Benevolence: The Dark Legacy of the Williams Lake Residential School*. Copyright by the Cariboo Tribal Council. Vancouver: Arsenal Pulp Press, 1995.

*A Garden of Stories for Grade Two*. No editor. Toronto: Copp Clarke, 1943.

Garland, Aileen. *Canada Then and Now*. Toronto: Macmillan of Canada, 1954. Reprinted with revisions in 1955.

George, Diana, with Susan Sanders. "Reconstructing Tonto: Cultural Formations and American Indians in 1990s Television Fiction." *Cultural Studies* 9, no. 3 (1995).

Gittings, Christopher. "Imaging Canada: The Singing Mountie and *Other* Commodification of Nation." *Canadian Journal of Communication* 23, no. 4 (1998).

Godard, Barbara. "Listening for the Silence: Native Women's Traditional Narratives." In *The Native in Literature*, edited by Thomas King, Cheryl Calver, and Helen Hoy. Downsview, ON: ECW Press, 1987.

– "The Politics of Representation: Some Native Canadian Women Writers." In *Native Writers and Canadian Writing*, edited by W.H. New. Special issue of *Canadian Literature*. Vancouver: University of British Columbia Press, 1990.

Goldie, Terry. *Fear and Temptation: The Image of the Indigene in Canadian, Australian and New Zealand Literature*. Montreal and Kingston: McGill-Queen's University Press, 1989.

Goldie, Terry, and Daniel David Moses, eds. *An Anthology of Canadian Native Literature in English*. Toronto: Oxford University Press, 1992.

Goulet, Jean-Guy A. *Ways of Knowing: Experience, Knowledge and Power among the Dene Tha*. Vancouver: University of British Columbia Press 1998.

– "The Dene Tha of Chateh: Continuities and Transformations." In *Native Peoples: The Canadian Experience,* edited by R. Bruce Morrison and C. Roderick Wilson. 3rd ed. Don Mills, ON: Oxford University Press, 2004.

Grace, Sherrill. *Canada and the Idea of North.* Montreal and Kingston: McGill-Queen's University Press, 2001.

Grace, Sherrill, Eve D'aeth, and Lisa Chalykoff, eds. *Staging the North: Twelve Canadian Plays.* Toronto: Playwrights Canada Press, 1999.

Grant, Agnes. "Native Drama: A Celebration of Native Culture." In *Contemporary Issues in Canadian Drama,* edited by Per Brask. Winnipeg: Blizzard Publishing, 1995.

Granzberg, Gary, and Jack Steinbring, eds. *Television and the Canadian Indian: Impact and Meaning among Algonkians.* Winnipeg: University of Winnipeg, 1980.

Gray, Herman. "The Endless Slide of Difference: Critical Television Studies, Television and the Question of Race." *Critical Studies of Mass Communications* 10, no. 2 (1993).

Grossberg, Lawrence. "The Affective Sensibility of Fandom." In *The Adoring Audience: Fan Culture and Popular Media,* edited by Lisa A. Lewis. London: Routledge, 1992.

Hall, Stuart. *New Reflections on the Revolution of Our Times.* London: Verso, 1990.

Hall, Stuart, and Paul Du Gay, eds. *Questions of Cultural Identity.* London: Sage Publications, 1996.

Halliwell, Leslie, with Philip Purser. *Halliwell's Television Companion.* 2nd ed. London: Grenada, 1982.

Hamelin, Louis-Edmond. "An Attempt to Regionalize the Canadian North." In *Canada's Changing North,* edited by William C. Wonders. Rev. ed. Montreal and Kingston: McGill-Queen's University Press, 2003.

Hamilton, Marjorie W. *Pirates and Pathfinders.* Toronto: Irwin and Company, 1954; eight reprints to 1962.

Haycock, Ronald. *The Image of the Indian: The Canadian Indian as a Subject and a Concept in a Sampling of the Popular National Magazines Read in Canada 1900–1970.* Waterloo, ON: Wilfrid Laurier University Press, 1970.

Hayes, Geoffrey. "From Berlin to the Trek of the Conestoga." *Ontario History* 91, no. 2 (autumn 1999).

Hilger, Michael. *From Savage to Nobleman: Images of Native Americans in Film.* Lanham, MD, and London: Scarecrow Press, 1995.

Hills, Matt. *Fan Cultures.* Sussex Studies in Culture and Communication series, edited by Jane Cowan. London: Routledge, 2002.

*A History of the Town of Durham: 1842–1994.* Composed by the Durham Historical Committee. Owen Sound, ON: Stan Brown Printers, 1994.

Hogan, Homer, ed., with Dorothy Hogan. *Listen! Songs and Poems of Canada.* Methuen Canadian Literature series. Toronto: Methuen, 1972.

Hogarth, David. "Public Service Broadcasting as a Modern Project: A Case Study of Early Public-Affairs Television in Canada." *Canadian Journal of Communications* 26, no. 3 (2001).

– *Documentary Television in Canada: From National Public Service to Global Marketplace.* Montreal and Kingston: McGill-Queen's University Press, 2002.

Holmes, Doug, ed. *Dehcho: "Mom, we've been discovered!"* Yellowknife, NWT: Dene Cultural Institute, 1989.

hooks, bell. *Yearning: Race, Gender and Cultural Politics.* Toronto: Between the Lines, 1990.

– *Feminist Theory: From Margin to Center.* 2nd ed. South End Press Classics. Cambridge, MA: South End Press, 2000.

Hope, Laura Lee. *The Bobbsey Twins in the Great West.* New York: Grosset and Dunlap, 1920.

Hulan, Renée. *Northern Experience and the Myths of Canadian Culture.* Rev. ed. Montreal and Kingston: McGill-Queen's University Press, 2002.

Janovich, Mark, and James Lyons, eds. *Quality Popular Television: Cult TV, the Industry and Fans.* London: BFI Publishing, 2003.

Jiles, Paulette. *North Spirit: Travels among the Cree and the Ojibway Nations and Their Star Maps.* Toronto: Doubleday Canada, 1995.

Jonaitis, Aldona, ed. *Chiefly Feasts: The Enduring Kwakiutl Potlatch.* Seattle: American Museum of Natural History and University of Washington Press, 1991.

Joyrich, Lynne. *Re-Viewing Reception: Television, Gender and Postmodern Culture.* Theories of Contemporary Culture series, vol. 18, edited by Kathleen Woodward. Bloomington: Indiana University Press, 1996.

Kalant, Amelia. *National Identity and the Conflict at Oka: Native Belonging and Myths of Postcolonial Nationhood in Canada.* London: Routledge, 2004.

Karim, Karim H. "Constructions, Deconstructions, and Reconstructions: Competing Canadian Discourses on Ethnocultural Terminology." *Canadian Journal of Communications* 18 (1993).

Keifl, Barry. *International TV Programming and Audience Trends, 1996–2001.* Commissioned by the CRTC, May 2003, www.crtc.gc.ca/eng/publications/reports/drama/drama3.htm.

Kentner, Peter. *TV North: everything you wanted to know about canadian television* [*sic*]. With notes by Martin Levin. Vancouver and Toronto: Whitecap Books, 2001.

Kilpatrick, Jaquelyn. *Celluloid Indians: Native Americans and Film.* Lincoln: University of Nebraska Press, 1999.

Kinsella, Warren. *Dance Me Outside.* 1977. Reprint, n.p.: Oberon, n.d.

– *Shoeless Joe.* New York: Ballantine Books, 1982.

– *The Moccasin Telegraph and Other Stories.* Markham ON: Penguin, 1988.

Krotz, Larry. *Indian Country: Inside Another Canada* (with a section written after Oka). Toronto: McClelland & Stewart, 1992.

*Land Spirit Power: First Nations at the National Art Gallery of Canada.* With essays by Diana Nemiroff, Charlotte Townsend-Gault, and Robert Houle. Ottawa: National Art Gallery of Canada, 1992.

LaRue, Mabel Guinnip. *Little Indians.* Illustrated by Maud and Miska Petersham. New York: Macmillan Company, 1932.

Legris, Renée. "O indio Americano no teleteatro e na telenovela do Quebec (1952–2000)." Translated by Humberto Luis de Oliviera. *Canadart VIII Revista do Nucleo de Estudos Canadenses* 8 (2000).

Lippard, Lucy R., ed. *Partial Recall: With Essays on Photographs on Native North Americans.* New York: New Press, 1992.

Longfellow, Henry Wadsworth. *Hiawatha.* Illustrated by Robert Smith, abridged for the use of schools. Boston: Educational Publishing Company, 1899.

Lutz, Herman. *Contemporary Challenges: Conversations with Canadian Native Authors.* Saskatoon: Fifth House Publishers, 1991.

McGregor, Gaile. *The Wacousta Syndrome: Explorations in the Canadian Langscape.* Toronto: University of Toronto Press, 1985.

McKee, Alan. "What Is Television For?" In *Quality Television: Cult TV, the Industry and Fans,* edited by Mark Janovich and James Lyons. London: British Film Institute, 2003.

Mackey, Eva. *The House of Difference: Cultural Politics and National Identity in Canada.* London: Routledge, 1999.

Macnair, Peter, Robert Joseph, and Bruce Grenville, eds. *Down from the Shimmering Sky: Masks of the Northwest Coast.* Vancouver: Douglas & McIntyre and Vancouver Art Gallery, 1998.

McNeil, Alex. *Total Television: Comprehensive Guide to Programming from 1948–1980.* Markham, ON: Penguin Books, 1980.

McQueen, Trina. *Dramatic Choices: A Report on Canadian English-Language Drama.* Commissioned by the CRTC and Telefilm, May 2003. www.crtc.gc.ca/eng/publications/reports/drama/drama2.htm.

McRoberts, Kenneth, ed. *Beyond Quebec: Taking Stock of Canada.* Montreal and Kingston: McGill-Queen's University Press, 1995.

Marsh, E.L. *The Story of Canada.* Rev. ed. Toronto: Thomas Nelson and Sons, 1927.

– *A History of the County of Grey.* Published with the authority of the Grey County Council. Owen Sound, ON: Fleming Publishing Co., 1931.

Mepham, John. "Ethics of Quality in Television." In *The Question of Quality,* edited by Geoff Mulgan. London: British Film Institute, 1990.

Miller, J.R. *Skyscrapers Hide the Heavens: A History of Indian-White Relations in Canada.* Rev. ed. Toronto: University of Toronto Press, 1989.

– ed. *Sweet Promises: A Reader on Indian-White Relations in Canada.* Toronto: University of Toronto Press, 1991.

– *Shingwauk's Vision: A History of Native Residential Schools.* Toronto: University of Toronto Press, 1996.

Miller, M.J. "Three Self-reflexive Masks." *Theatre Research International* 7, no. 1 (winter 1981/82).

– *Turn Up the Contrast: CBC Television Drama Since 1952.* Vancouver: University of British Columbia Press and CBC, 1987.

– "Breaking the Formula: Street Legal and L.A. Law as Characteristic Examples of Contrasting Canadian and American Television Series." In *The Beaver Bites Back,* edited by David H. Flaherty and Frank E. Manning. Montreal and Kingston: McGill-Queen's University Press, 1993.

– "Mirrors in the Robing Room: Reflections of Lawyers and the Law in Canadian Television Drama." *Canadian Journal of Law and Society* 10, no. 2 (fall 1995).

– "Will English Language Television Remain Distinctive? Probably." In *Beyond Quebec: Taking Stock of Canada,* edited by Kenneth McRoberts. Montreal and Kingston: McGill-Queen's University Press, 1995.

– *Rewind and Search: Makers and Decision Makers of Canadian Television Drama.* Montreal and Kingston: McGill-Queen's University Press, 1996.

– "Shehaweh through Anglophone Eyes." *Canadart VIII Revista do Nucleo de Estudos Canadenses* 8 (2000).

– "Where the Spirit Lives: An Influential and Contentious Television Drama about Residential Schools." *American Journal of Canadian Studies* 31, nos 1 and 2 (spring/summer 2001).

– "Canadian Television Programming." In *Encyclopedia of Television,* edited by Horace Newcomb. 2nd ed. Chicago: Fitzroy and Dearborn, 2004.

– Introduction to *Growing Up Degrassi: Television, Identity and Youth Cultures,* edited by Michele Byers. Toronto: Sumach Press, 2005.

– "Haunting Public Discourse: The Representation of Residential Schools in CBC Television Drama." In *Television between Reality and Fiction: The Canadian Case,* edited by Zoe Druick and Patsy Kotsopoulos. Waterloo, ON: Wilfrid Laurier University Press, forthcoming.

Modleski, Tanya. "The Search for Tomorrow in Today's Soap Operas." *Film Quarterly* 33 (fall 1979).

Money, Mary Alice. "Native Americans in Popular Culture." In *American Indian Studies: An Interdisciplinary Approach to Contemporary Issues,* edited by Dane Morrison. New York: Peter Lang, 1997.

Monkman, Leslie. *A Native Heritage: Images of the Indian in English-Canadian Literature.* Toronto: University of Toronto Press, 1981.

Monroe, E. Price. *Television, the Public Sphere and National Identity.* Oxford, UK: Clarendon Press, 1995.

Moon, Barbara. "How They're Making a Hero of Pierre Radisson." *Maclean's,* 19 January 1957.

Morris, Miggs Wynne. *Return to the Drum: Teaching among the Dene in Canada's North*. Edmonton: NeWest Press, 2000.

Morrison, Dana, ed. *American Indian Studies: An Interdisciplinary Approach to Contemporary Issues*. New York: Peter Lang, 1997.

Morrison, R. Bruce, and C. Roderick Wilson, eds. *Native Peoples: The Canadian Experience*. 1986. Reprint, Toronto: McClelland & Stewart, 1993.

Morton, W.L. "The North in Canadian History."In *Canada's Changing North*, edited by William C. Wonders. Montreal and Kingston: McGill-Queen's University Press, 2003.

Murray, Catherine, Roger De la Garde, and Claude Martin, eds. "Star Wars: Canadian TV Drama." Centre for Policy Research on Science and Technology, School of Communication, Simon Fraser University, 2000. www.sfu.ca/cmns/faculty/murray_c/ assets/EuroCanadianFiction.pdf, accessed 25 May 2007.

Nabokov, Peter, ed. *Native American Testimony: A Chronicle of Indian-White Relations from Prophecy to the Present 1492–1992*. Foreword by Vine Deloria. New York: Viking Penguin, 1991.

Nelles, H.V. *A Little History of Canada*. Toronto: Oxford University Press, 2004.

Nelson, Robin. *TV Drama in Transition: Forms, Values and Cultural Changes*. London: Macmillan Press, 1997.

New, W.H., ed. *Native Writers and Canadian Writing*. Special issue of *Canadian Literature*. Vancouver: University of British Columbia Press, 1990.

Newcomb, Horace. *TV: The Most Popular Art*. Garden City, NY: Anchor Books, 1974.

Norris Nicholson, Heather. "At the Centre of It All Are the Children: Aboriginal Childhoods and the National Film Board." *London Journal of Canadian Studies* 17 (2001/02). www.bbk.ac.uk/cgi-bin/htsearch, accessed 25 May 2007.

– ed. Introduction to Part 1 of *Screening Culture: Constructing Image and Identity*. Landham, MD: Lexington Books, Rowman and Littlefield Publishing Group, 2003.

Paz, Octavio. *Claude Levi Strauss: An Introduction*. Translated by J.S. Bernstein and M. Bernstein. Ithaca, NY: Cornell University Press, 1970.

Peters, Evelyn J. "Subversive Spaces: First Nations Women and the City." *Environment and Planning: Society and Space* 16 (1998).

Petrone, Penny. *Native Literature in Canada: From the Oral Tradition to the Present*. Toronto: Oxford University Press, 1990.

Pratley, Gerald. *A Century of Canadian Cinema: Gerald Pratley's Feature Film Guide, 1900 to the Present*. Toronto: Lynx Images, 2003.

Rainsberry, Fred. "Program Policy for Children's Television in the Eighties: An Address to a National Policy Conference." A response to a UNESCO report on the child film audience, presented by the Faculty of Education, Simon Fraser University, 31 March 1982. Xerox sent to author by Dr Rainsberry, then professor emeritus of the Ontario Institute for Studies in Education.

- *A History of Children's Television in English Canada 1952–1986*. Metuchen, NJ: Scarecrow Press, 1988.

Ray, Arthur J. "Searching for Settlement." In *I have Lived Here Since the World Began: An Illustrated History of Canada's Native People*. Toronto: Key Porter Books, 1996.

Richardson, Boyce. *People of Terra Nullius: Betrayal and Rebirth in Aboriginal Canada*. Vancouver: Douglas & McIntyre, 1993.

Rogers, Edward S., and Donald B. Smith, eds. *Aboriginal Ontario: Historical Perspectives on the First Nations*. Ontario Historical Studies series for the Government of Ontario. Toronto: Dundurn Press, 1994.

Ross, Rupert. *Dancing with a Ghost: Exploring Indian Reality*. Foreword by Basil H. Johnston. Markham, ON: Octopus Publishing Group, 1992.

Roth, Lorna. "First People's Television Canada's North: A Case Study of the Aboriginal Peoples Television Network." In *Mediascapes: New Patterns in Canadian Communication*, edited by Paul Atallah and Leslie Regan Shade. Scarborough, ON: Nelson Thomson, 2002.

- *Something New in the Air: The Story of First Peoples Television Broadcasting in Canada*. McGill-Queen's Native and Northern series. Montreal and Kingston: McGill-Queen's University Press, 2005.

Rutherford, Paul. *Primetime Canada: When Television Was Young, 1952–1967*. Toronto: University of Toronto Press, 1990.

Ryan, Allan J. *The Trickster Shift: Humour and Irony in Contemporary Native Art*. Vancouver: University of British Columbia Press, 1999.

Ryan, Joan. *Doing Things the Right Way: Dene Traditional Justice at Lac La Martre, NWT*. With research partners Lac La Martre Band Council, Dene Cultural Institute, and Arctic Institute of North America. Calgary: University of Calgary Press and Arctic Institute of North America, 1995.

Salutin, Rick. "Because *Not* Everything Is Political." *This Magazine* 40, no. 3 (2006).

Sands, Kathleen M. "Narrative Resistance: Native American Collaborative Autobiography." *Studies in American Indian Literatures*, 2nd ser., 10, no. 1 (1998).

Sayers, Dorothy. *The Man Born to Be King*. London: Victor Gollancz, 1943.

Schier, Libby, Sarah Sheard, and Eleanor Wachtel, eds. *Language in Her Eye: Views on Writing and Gender by Canadian Women Writing in English*. Toronto: Coach House Press, 1990.

Schmalz, Peter S. *The Ojibwa of Southern Ontario*. Toronto: University of Toronto Press, 1991.

Scott, J. Karen, ed., with Joan E. Kieser. *Northern Nurses: True Nursing Adventures from Canada's North*. 2nd ed. Oakville, ON: Kokum, 2002.

Shakespeare, William. *King Lear* (conflated text). In *The Norton Shakespeare* (based on Oxford edition). General editor, Stephen Greenblatt. Edited by Stephen Greenblatt, Walter Cohen, Jean E. Howard, and Katharine Eisaman Maus. New York and London: W.W. Norton and Co., 1997.

Shohat, Ella, and Robert Stam. *Unthinking Eurocentrism: Multiculturalism and the Media*. London: Routledge 1994.

Silverman, Jason. "Uncommon Visions: The Films of Loretta Todd." *North of Everything: English-Canadian Cinema since 1980*, edited by William Beard and Jerry White. Edmonton: University of Alberta Press, 2002.

Stewart, Michelle Pagni. "Can This Be Cinderella If There Is No glass Slipper? Native American 'Fairy' Tales." *Studies in American Indian Literatures*, Children's Literature series no. 2, vol. 12, no. 1 (spring 2000).

Stewart, Sandy. *Here's Looking at Us: A Personal History of Television in Canada*. Montreal and Toronto: CBC Enterprises, 1986.

*Tale of the Nativity as told by the Indian children of Inkameep, British Columbia* [to Anthony Walsh]. N.p.: n.p., 1940. Probably published by "The Committee formed to promote the Revival and Development of their latent gifts among the Native Tribes of British Columbia."

Thorburn, David. "Television as an Aesthetic Medium." In *Media Myths and Narratives: Television and the Press*, edited by James W. Carey. Newbury Park, CA: Sage Publications, 1988.

Townsend-Gault, Charlotte. "First Nations Culture: Who Knows What?" *Canadian Journal of Communication* 23 (1998).

Trinh, T. Minh-ha. *Woman, Native, Other: Writing Postcoloniality and Feminism*. Bloomington: Indiana University Press, 1989.

Van de Berg, Leah R., and Laurence A. Wenner, eds. *Television Criticism: Approaches and Applications*. New York: Longman, 1991.

Velie, Alan R., ed. *American Indian Literature*. Rev. ed. Norman: University of Oklahoma Press, 1991.

Walcott, Rinaldo. "Lament for a Nation: The Racial The OH! Canada Project.'" *Fuse Magazine* 18, no. 4.

Wallace, W. Stewart. *A First Book of Canadian History*. Toronto: Macmillan Company of Canada, 1928. Reprinted eleven times to 1938.

Warkentin, Germaine. "Discovering Radisson: A Renaissance Adventurer between Two Worlds." In *Reading Beyond Words: Contexts for Native History*, edited by Jennifer S.H. Brown and Elizabeth Vibert. Orchard Park, NY: Broadview Press, 1996.

Warley, Linda. "The Mountie and the Nurse: Cross-Cultural Relations in *North of 60*." In *Painting Maple: Essays on Race, Gender and the Construction of Canada*, edited by Veronica Strong-Boag, Sherrill Grace, Avigail Eisenberg, and Joan Anderson. Vancouver: University of British Columbia Press, 1998.

Whittaker, John O. *The Audubon Society Field Guide to North American Mammals*. Text consultant Robert Elman; illustrations by Carol Nehrig. New York: Alfred A. Knopf, 1991.

Williams, Carol Traynor. *"It's Time for My Story"*: *Soap Opera Sources, Structure and Response*. Media and Society series. General editor, J. Fred MacDonald. Westport, CT, and London: Praeger, 1992.

Williams, Raymond. *Drama in a Dramatised Society: An Inaugural Lecture*. Cambridge, UK: Cambridge University Press, 1975.

Wilson, C. Roderick. "The Northern Athapaskans: A Regional Overview." In *Native Peoples: The Canadian Experience*, edited by R. Bruce Morrison and C. Roderick Wilson. 3rd ed. Don Mills, ON: Oxford University Press, 2004.

Wonders, William C., ed. *Canada's Changing North*. Montreal and Kingston: McGill-Queen's University Press, 2003.

*Voices – First Nations, Metis, and Inuit*
*(Academic and Other) – from the "Inside"*

Abele, Francis. "Various Matters of Nationhood: Aboriginal Peoples and 'Canada outside Quebec.'" In *Beyond Quebec: Taking Stock of Canada*, edited by Kenneth McRoberts. Montreal and Kingston: McGill-Queen's University Press, 1995.

Acoose, Janet (Misko-Kisikawihkwe). *Iskwewak – kah'ki yaw ni wahkomakanak: Neither Indian Princesses nor Easy Squaws*. Toronto: Women's Press, 1995.

Adams, Howard. *Prison of Grass: Canada from a Native Point of View*. Rev. ed. Saskatoon: Fifth House, 1989.

Ahenakew, Freda, and Wolfart H.C., eds and trans. *Kohkominawak Otacimowiniwawa: Our Grandmothers' Lives as Told in Their Own Words*. Saskatoon: Fifth House, 1992.

Allen, Paula Gunn, ed. *Spider Woman's Granddaughters: Traditional Tales and Contemporary Writing by Native American Women*. Boston: Beacon Press, 1989.

Armstrong, Jeanette, comp. *Looking at the Words of Our People: First Nations Analysis of Literature*. Penticton, BC: Theytus Books, 1993.

Asu, Harry, with Joy Inglis. *Assu of Cape Mudge: Recollections of a Coastal Indian Chief*. Vancouver: University of British Columbia Press, 1989.

Baker, Marie Annharte. "Carte Blanche" section. *Canadian Theatre Review* 68 (fall 1991).

Bellfy, Phil, ed. *Aboriginal Peoples*. Special issue of *American Review of Canadian Studies* 31, nos 1 and 2 (spring and summer 2001).

Bird, Madeline, with Agnes Sutherland. *Living Kindness: The Dream of My Life*. Northern Heritage series: People and Places. Edited by C. Outcrop Stephens. Yellowknife, NWT: 1991.

Blondin, George. *Yamoria the Lawmaker: Stories of the Dene*. Edmonton: NeWest Press, 1997.

Brant, Beth (Degonwadonti), ed. *A Gathering of Spirit: A Collection by North American Indian Women*. 3rd ed. Toronto: Women's Press, 1988.

– *Writing as Witness: Essay and Talk.* Toronto: Women's Press, 1994.

Cardinal, Tantoo, Tomson Highway, Basil Johnston, Thomas King, Brian Maracle, Lee Maracle, Jovette Marchessault, Rachel A. Qitsualik, and Drew Hayden Taylor. *Our Story: Aboriginal Voices of Canada's Past.* Preface by Rudyard Griffiths; foreword by Adrienne Clarkson. N.p.: Dominion Institute and Doubleday Canada, 2004.

Churchill, Ward. *Fantasies of the Master Race: Literature, Cinema and Colonisation of the American Indians.* Edited by M. Annette Jaimes. Munroe, ME: Common Courage Press, 1992.

Cook, Philip, and William White/Xelimuxw. "Traditional Knowledge and Children's Rights." In *Aboriginal Peoples,* edited by Phil Bellfy. Special issue of *American Review of Canadian Studies* 31, nos 1 and 2 (spring and summer 2001).

Cornplanter, Jesse J. *Legends of the Longhouse Told to Sah-Nee-Wah, the White Sister.* 1938; reprint, Ohsweken, ON: Iroqrafts, 1998.

Deer, Kenneth. "The Aboriginal Peoples Television Network: Pro and Contra." *Eastern Door,* 17 September 1999.

Deloria, Philip J. *Playing Indian.* Yale University History series. Chelsea, MI: Yale University, 1998.

Deloria, Vine. *Red Earth, White Lies: Native Americans and the Myth of Scientific Fact.* New York and Toronto: Scribner, 1995.

Dickason, Olive. *Canada's First Nations: A History of Founding People from Earliest Times.* Toronto: McClelland & Stewart, 1992.

Doxtator, Deborah. *Fluffs and Feathers: An Exhibit on the Symbols of Indianness.* Brantford, ON: Woodland Cultural Centre, 1992.

Favel, Floyd. "The Theatre of Orphans: Native Language on Stage." *Canadian Theatre Review,* no. 75 (1993).

Faye, Jefferson. "Ethical Publication of Inuit Stories." *American Journal of Canadian Studies* 31, nos 1 and 2 (2001).

George, Leonard, "Native Spirituality, Past, Present and Future." In *Celebration of Our Survival: The First Nations of British Columbia,* edited by Doreen Jensen and Cheryl Brooks. Vancouver: University of British Columbia Press, 1991.

Goodleaf, Donna. *Entering the War Zone: A Mohawk Perspective on Resisting Invasions.* Penticton, BC: Theytus, 1995.

Griffiths, Linda, and Maria Campbell. *The Book of Jessica: A Theatrical Transformation.* Toronto: Coach House Press, 1989.

Hanna, Darwin, and Mamie Henry, eds. *Our Tellings: Interior Salish Stories of the Nlha7kapmx People.* Vancouver: University of British Columbia Press, 1996.

Johnston, Basil. *Indian School Days.* Toronto: Key Porter Books, 1988.

– *Ojibway Heritage: The Ceremonies, Rituals, Songs, Dances, Prayers and Legends of the Ojibway.* 1973. Reprint, Toronto: McClelland & Stewart, 1990.

- "One Generation from Extinction." In *Native Writers and Canadian Writing*, edited by W.H. New. Special issue of *Canadian Literature*. Vancouver: University of British Columbia Press, 1990.
- *The Manitous: The Supernatural World of the Ojibway*. Toronto: Key Porter Books, 1995.

Jojola, Ted. "Absurd Reality: Hollywood Goes to the Indian." In *Hollywood's Indian: The Portrayal of Native Americans in Film*, edited by Peter C. Rollins and John E. O'Connor. Lexington: University Press of Kentucky, 1998.

Joseph, Robert. "Behind the Mask." In *Down from the Shimmering Sky: Masks of the Northwest Coast*, edited by Peter Macnair, Robert Joseph, and Bruce Grenville. Vancouver: Douglas & McIntyre and Vancouver Art Gallery, 1998.

Kalafatic, Carol. "Keepers of the Power: Story as Covenant in the Films of Loretta Todd, Shelley Niro and Christine Welsh." In *Gendering the Nation: Canadian Women's Cinema*, edited by Kay Armatage, Kass Banning, Brenda Longfellow, and Janine Marchesseault. Toronto: University of Toronto Press, 1999.

King, Thomas. *All My Relations: An Anthology of Contemporary Canadian Native Fiction*. Toronto: McClelland & Stewart, 1990.

King, Thomas, Cheryl Calver, and Helen Hoy, eds. *The Native in Literature*. Downsview, ON: ECW Press, 1987.

Knockwood, Isabelle, with Gyllian Thomas. *Out of the Depths: The Experience of Mi'kmaw Children at the Indian Residential School at Shubenacadie, Nova Scotia*. Lockport, NS: Roseway Publishing, 1992.

Kulchyski, Peter, Don McCaskill, and David Newhouse, eds. *In the Words of the Elders: Aboriginal Cultures in Transition*. Toronto: University of Toronto Press, 1999.

Laroque, Emma. Preface to *Writing the Circle: Native Women of Western Canada*, compiled and edited by Jeanne Perreault and Sylvia Vance. Edmonton: NeWest, 1990.

Maracle, Brian. *Crazy Water: Native Voices on Addiction and Recovery*. Toronto: Penguin Books, 1993.
- *Back on the Rez: Finding the Way Home*. Toronto: Viking, 1996.
- "One More Whining Indian Tilting at Windmills." In *Clash of Identities: Essays on Media, Manipulation and Politics of the Self*, edited by James Littleton. CBC publication. Toronto: Prentice Hall, 1996.

McMaster, Gerald R. "Borderzones: The 'Injun-unity' of Aesthetic Tricks." In *First Peoples: Cultures, Policies, Politics*, edited by Tony Bennett and Valda Blundell. Special issue of *Cultural Studies* 9, no. 1 (1995).
- ed. *Reservation X: The Power of Place in Aboriginal Contemporary Art*. Fredericton and Hull: Goose Lane Editions and Canadian Museum of Civilization, 1998.

McMaster, Gerald, and Lee-Ann Martin, eds. *Indigena: Contemporary Native Perspectives*. Vancouver: Douglas & McIntyre, 1992.

Maskegon-Iskwew, Ahasiw. "Native Love: Subverting the Boundaries of the Heart." *Fuse Magazine* 18, no. 4 (summer 1996).

Mihesuah, Devon A., ed. *Natives and Academics: Researching and Writing about American Indians.* Lincoln: University of Nebraska Press, 1998.

Mohawk, John C. "Impact of Television on Native Communities." *Runner,* spring 1994.

Moore, Patrick, and Anglea Wheelock, eds. *Wolverine Myths and Legends: Dene Traditions from Northern Alberta.* Compiled by the Dene Wodih Society and illustrated by Dia Thurston. Edmonton: University of Alberta Press, 1990.

Morriseau, Miles. "Out of the Darkness." *Aboriginal Voices* 4, no. 1 (January/February/March 1997): 20–5.

Robinson, Harry. *Write It on Your Heart: The Epic World of an Okanagan Story Teller.* Compiled and edited by Wendy Wickwire. Vancouver: Theytus/Talonbooks, 1989.

– *Nature Power: In the Spirit of an Okanagan Storyteller.* Compiled and edited by Wendy Wickwire. Vancouver: Douglas & McIntyre, 1992.

Strickland, Rennard. "Coyote Goes Hollywood." *Native People's Magazine,* fall 1997.

Taylor, Drew Hayden. *Toronto at Dreamer's Rock/Education Is Our Right.* Calgary: Fifth House Publishers, 1990.

– "North of Sixty, South of Accurate," "Waiting for Kinsella," "An Indian by Any Other Name," and "What Colour Is a Rose?" In *Funny You Don't Look Like One: Observations from a Blue-Eyed Ojibway.* Penticton, BC: Theytus Books, 1996.

– ed. and comp. *Me Funny.* Vancouver: Douglas & McIntyre, 2005.

Todd. Loretta, "Notes on Appropriation/L'Appropriation." Translated by Jean-Luc Voboda. *Parallélogramme* 16, no. 1 (June 1990).

Trout, Lawana, ed. *Native American Literature: An Anthology.* Lincolnwood, IL: NTC Publishing Group, 1999.

Valaskakis, Gail Guthrie. "Communication, Culture, and Technology: Satellites and Northern Native Broadcasting in Canada." In *Ethnic Minority Media: An International Perspective,* edited by Stephen Harold Riggins. Communication and Human Values series. General editors, Robert A. White and Michael Traber. Newbury Park, CA: Sage Publications, 1992.

– guest ed. Introduction to *Canadian Journal of Communications* 18, no. 3 (1993).

– "Dance Me Inside: Pow Wow and Being Indian." *Fuse,* summer 1993.

Vickers, Roy Henry. *The Elders Are Watching.* Text by Dave Bouchard; images by Roy Henry Vickers. Vancouver: Eagle Dancer Enterprises and Raincoast Books, 1990.

Wagamese, Richard. "The Final Word" section. *Aboriginal Voices* 3, no. 1 (1996): 50.

Wheeler, Jordan. "Our Own Stories: A Revolution in Aboriginal Theatre." *Canadian Theatre Review* 66 (spring 1991).

– "Lynx River Has Trout: An Inside Look at CBC's Popular TV Series *North of 60."* *Runner* 1, no. 2 (1994).

Young Man, Alfred. "Native Arts in Canada: The State, Academia and the Cultural Establishment." In *Beyond Quebec: Taking Stock of Canada*, edited by Kenneth McRoberts. Montreal and Kingston: McGill-Queen's University Press, 1995.

# Index

*Note: Fictional characters are alphabetized by first name.*